FIFTH EDITION

Learning PHP, MySQL & JavaScript

With jQuery, CSS & HTML5

Robin Nixon

Beijing · Boston · Farnham · Sebastopol · Tokyo

Learning PHP, MySQL & JavaScript

by Robin Nixon

Copyright © 2018 Robin Nixon. All rights reserved.

Printed in the United States of America.

Published by O'Reilly Media, Inc., 1005 Gravenstein Highway North, Sebastopol, CA 95472.

O'Reilly books may be purchased for educational, business, or sales promotional use. Online editions are also available for most titles (*http://oreilly.com/safari*). For more information, contact our corporate/institutional sales department: 800-998-9938 or *corporate@oreilly.com*.

Editor: Andy Oram	**Indexer:** Judy McConville
Production Editor: Melanie Yarbrough	**Interior Designer:** David Futato
Copyeditor: Rachel Head	**Cover Designer:** Karen Montgomery
Proofreader: Rachel Monaghan	**Illustrator:** Rebecca Demarest

July 2009:	First Edition
August 2012:	Second Edition
June 2014:	Third Edition
December 2014:	Fourth Edition
May 2018:	Fifth Edition

Revision History for the Fifth Edition

2018-05-08:	First Release
2018-07-27:	Second Release

See *http://oreilly.com/catalog/errata.csp?isbn=9781491978917* for release details.

The O'Reilly logo is a registered trademark of O'Reilly Media, Inc. *Learning PHP, MySQL & JavaScript*, the cover image, and related trade dress are trademarks of O'Reilly Media, Inc.

978-1-491-97891-7

[LSCH]

For Julie

Table of Contents

Preface

The combination of PHP and MySQL is the most convenient approach to dynamic, database-driven web design, holding its own in the face of challenges from integrated frameworks—such as Ruby on Rails—that are harder to learn. Due to its open source roots (unlike the competing Microsoft .NET Framework), it is free to implement and is therefore an extremely popular option for web development.

Any would-be developer on a Unix/Linux or even a Windows/Apache platform will need to master these technologies. And, combined with the partner technologies of JavaScript, jQuery, CSS, and HTML5, you will be able to create websites of the caliber of industry standards like Facebook, Twitter, and Gmail.

Audience

This book is for people who wish to learn how to create effective and dynamic websites. This may include webmasters or graphic designers who are already creating static websites but wish to take their skills to the next level, as well as high school and college students, recent graduates, and self-taught individuals.

In fact, anyone ready to learn the fundamentals behind responsive web design will obtain a thorough grounding in the core technologies of PHP, MySQL, JavaScript, CSS, and HTML5, and you'll learn the basics of the jQuery and jQuery Mobile libraries, too.

Assumptions This Book Makes

This book assumes that you have a basic understanding of HTML and can at least put together a simple, static website, but does not assume that you have any prior knowledge of PHP, MySQL, JavaScript, CSS, or HTML5—although if you do, your progress through the book will be even quicker.

Organization of This Book

The chapters in this book are written in a specific order, first introducing all of the core technologies it covers and then walking you through their installation on a web development server so that you will be ready to work through the examples.

In the first section, you will gain a grounding in the PHP programming language, covering the basics of syntax, arrays, functions, and object-oriented programming.

Then, with PHP under your belt, you will move on to an introduction to the MySQL database system, where you will learn everything from how MySQL databases are structured to how to generate complex queries.

After that, you will learn how you can combine PHP and MySQL to start creating your own dynamic web pages by integrating forms and other HTML features. You will then get down to the nitty-gritty practical aspects of PHP and MySQL development by learning a variety of useful functions and how to manage cookies and sessions, as well as how to maintain a high level of security.

In the next few chapters, you will gain a thorough grounding in JavaScript, from simple functions and event handling to accessing the Document Object Model, in-browser validation, and error handling. You'll also get a comprehensive primer on using the popular jQuery library for JavaScript.

With an understanding of all three of these core technologies, you will then learn how to make behind-the-scenes Ajax calls and turn your websites into highly dynamic environments.

Next, you'll spend two chapters learning all about using CSS to style and lay out your web pages, before discovering how the jQuery libraries can make your development job a great deal easier. You'll then move on to the final section on the interactive features built into HTML5, including geolocation, audio, video, and the canvas. After this, you'll put together everything you've learned in a complete set of programs that together constitute a fully functional social networking website.

Along the way, you'll find plenty of advice on good programming practices and tips that can help you find and solve hard-to-detect programming errors. There are also plenty of links to websites containing further details on the topics covered.

Supporting Books

Once you have learned to develop using PHP, MySQL, JavaScript, CSS, and HTML5, you will be ready to take your skills to the next level using the following O'Reilly reference books:

- *Dynamic HTML: The Definitive Reference* by Danny Goodman

- *PHP in a Nutshell* by Paul Hudson
- *MySQL in a Nutshell* by Russell Dyer
- *JavaScript: The Definitive Guide* by David Flanagan
- *CSS: The Definitive Guide* by Eric A. Meyer and Estelle Weyl
- *HTML5: The Missing Manual* by Matthew MacDonald

Conventions Used in This Book

The following typographical conventions are used in this book:

Plain text
> Indicates menu titles, options, and buttons.

Italic
> Indicates new terms, URLs, email addresses, filenames, file extensions, path-names, directories, and Unix utilities. Also used for database, table, and column names.

`Constant width`
> Indicates commands and command-line options, variables and other code elements, HTML tags, and the contents of files.

`Constant width bold`
> Shows program output and is used to highlight sections of code that are discussed in the text.

`Constant width italic`
> Shows text that should be replaced with user-supplied values.

 This element signifies a tip, suggestion, or general note.

 This element indicates a warning or caution.

Using Code Examples

Supplemental material (code examples, exercises, etc.) is available for download at *http://lpmj.net*.

This book is here to help you get your job done. In general, if example code is offered with this book, you may use it in your programs and documentation. You do not need to contact us for permission unless you're reproducing a significant portion of the code. For example, writing a program that uses several chunks of code from this book does not require permission. Selling or distributing a CD-ROM of examples from O'Reilly books does require permission. Answering a question by citing this book and quoting example code does not require permission. Incorporating a significant amount of example code from this book into your product's documentation does require permission.

We appreciate, but do not require, attribution. An attribution usually includes the title, author, publisher, and ISBN. For example: *"Learning PHP, MySQL & JavaScript* by Robin Nixon (O'Reilly). Copyright 2018 Robin Nixon, 978-1-491-97891-7."

If you feel your use of code examples falls outside fair use or the permission given above, feel free to contact us at *permissions@oreilly.com*.

O'Reilly Safari

 Safari (formerly Safari Books Online) is a membership-based training and reference platform for enterprise, government, educators, and individuals.

Members have access to thousands of books, training videos, Learning Paths, interactive tutorials, and curated playlists from over 250 publishers, including O'Reilly Media, Harvard Business Review, Prentice Hall Professional, Addison-Wesley Professional, Microsoft Press, Sams, Que, Peachpit Press, Adobe, Focal Press, Cisco Press, John Wiley & Sons, Syngress, Morgan Kaufmann, IBM Redbooks, Packt, Adobe Press, FT Press, Apress, Manning, New Riders, McGraw-Hill, Jones & Bartlett, and Course Technology, among others.

For more information, please visit *http://oreilly.com/safari*.

How to Contact Us

Please address comments and questions concerning this book to the publisher:

O'Reilly Media, Inc.
1005 Gravenstein Highway North

Sebastopol, CA 95472
(800) 998-9938 (in the United States or Canada)
(707) 829-0515 (international or local)
(707) 829-0104 (fax)

We have a web page for this book, where we list errata, examples, and any additional information. You can access this page at *http://bit.ly/lpmjch_5e*.

To comment or ask technical questions about this book, send email to *bookquestions@oreilly.com*.

For more information about our books, courses, conferences, and news, see our website at *http://www.oreilly.com*.

Find us on Facebook: *http://facebook.com/oreilly*

Follow us on Twitter: *http://twitter.com/oreillymedia*

Watch us on YouTube: *http://www.youtube.com/oreillymedia*

Acknowledgments

I would like to once again thank my editor, Andy Oram, and everyone who worked so hard on this book, including Jon Reid, Michal Špaček, and John Craig for their comprehensive technical reviews, Melanie Yarbrough for overseeing production, Rachel Head for copy editing, Rachel Monaghan for proofreading, Rebecca Demarest for illustrations, Judy McConville for creating the index, Karen Montgomery for the original sugar glider front cover design, Randy Comer for the latest book cover, and everyone else too numerous to name who submitted errata and offered suggestions for this new edition.

CHAPTER 1

Introduction to Dynamic Web Content

The World Wide Web is a constantly evolving network that has already traveled far beyond its conception in the early 1990s, when it was created to solve a specific problem. State-of-the-art experiments at CERN (the European Laboratory for Particle Physics, now best known as the operator of the Large Hadron Collider) were producing incredible amounts of data—so much that the data was proving unwieldy to distribute to the participating scientists, who were spread out across the world.

At this time, the internet was already in place, connecting several hundred thousand computers, so Tim Berners-Lee (a CERN fellow) devised a method of navigating between them using a hyperlinking framework, which came to be known as Hypertext Transfer Protocol, or HTTP. He also created a markup language called Hypertext Markup Language, or HTML. To bring these together, he wrote the first web browser and web server.

Today we take these tools for granted, but back then, the concept was revolutionary. The most connectivity so far experienced by at-home modem users was dialing up and connecting to a bulletin board that was hosted by a single computer, where you could communicate and swap data only with other users of that service. Consequently, you needed to be a member of many bulletin board systems in order to effectively communicate electronically with your colleagues and friends.

But Berners-Lee changed all that in one fell swoop, and by the mid-1990s, there were three major graphical web browsers competing for the attention of 5 million users. It soon became obvious, though, that something was missing. Yes, pages of text and graphics with hyperlinks to take you to other pages was a brilliant concept, but the results didn't reflect the instantaneous potential of computers and the internet to meet the particular needs of each user with dynamically changing content. Using the web was a very dry and plain experience, even if we did now have scrolling text and animated GIFs!

Shopping carts, search engines, and social networks have clearly altered how we use the web. In this chapter, we'll take a brief look at the various components that make up the web, and the software that helps make using it a rich and dynamic experience.

 It is necessary to start using some acronyms more or less right away. I have tried to clearly explain them before proceeding, but don't worry too much about what they stand for or what these names mean, because the details will become clear as you read on.

HTTP and HTML: Berners-Lee's Basics

HTTP is a communication standard governing the requests and responses that are sent between the browser running on the end user's computer and the web server. The server's job is to accept a request from the client and attempt to reply to it in a meaningful way, usually by serving up a requested web page—that's why the term *server* is used. The natural counterpart to a server is a *client*, so that term is applied both to the web browser and the computer on which it's running.

Between the client and the server there can be several other devices, such as routers, proxies, gateways, and so on. They serve different roles in ensuring that the requests and responses are correctly transferred between the client and server. Typically, they use the internet to send this information. Some of these in-between devices can also help speed up the internet by storing pages or information locally in what is called a *cache*, and then serving this content up to clients directly from the cache rather than fetching it all the way from the source server.

A web server can usually handle multiple simultaneous connections, and when not communicating with a client, it spends its time listening for an incoming connection. When one arrives, the server sends back a response to confirm its receipt.

The Request/Response Procedure

At its most basic level, the request/response process consists of a web browser asking the web server to send it a web page and the server sending back the page. The browser then takes care of displaying the page (see Figure 1-1).

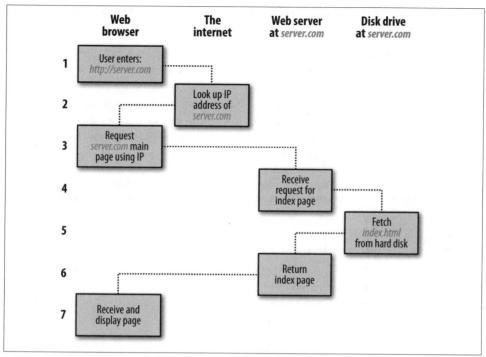

Figure 1-1. The basic client/server request/response sequence

The steps in the request and response sequence are as follows:

1. You enter *http://server.com* into your browser's address bar.
2. Your browser looks up the Internet Protocol (IP) address for *server.com*.
3. Your browser issues a request for the home page at *server.com*.
4. The request crosses the internet and arrives at the *server.com* web server.
5. The web server, having received the request, looks for the web page on its disk.
6. The web server retrieves the page and returns it to the browser.
7. Your browser displays the web page.

For an average web page, this process also takes place once for each object within the page: a graphic, an embedded video or Flash file, and even a CSS template.

In step 2, notice that the browser looks up the IP address of *server.com*. Every machine attached to the internet has an IP address—your computer included—but we generally access web servers by name, such as *google.com*. As you probably know, the browser consults an additional internet service called the Domain Name Service

(DNS) to find the server's associated IP address and then uses it to communicate with the computer.

For dynamic web pages, the procedure is a little more involved, because it may bring both PHP and MySQL into the mix. For instance, you may click on a picture of a raincoat. Then PHP will put together a request using the standard database language, SQL—many of whose commands you will learn in this book—and send the request to the MySQL server. The MySQL server will return information about the raincoat you selected, and the PHP code will wrap it all up in some HTML, which the server will send to your browser (see Figure 1-2).

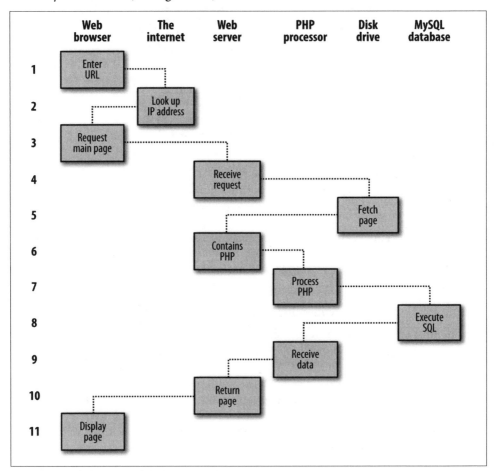

Figure 1-2. A dynamic client/server request/response sequence

The steps are as follows:

1. You enter *http://server.com* into your browser's address bar.

2. Your browser looks up the IP address for *server.com*.

3. Your browser issues a request to that address for the web server's home page.

4. The request crosses the internet and arrives at the *server.com* web server.

5. The web server, having received the request, fetches the home page from its hard disk.

6. With the home page now in memory, the web server notices that it is a file incorporating PHP scripting and passes the page to the PHP interpreter.

7. The PHP interpreter executes the PHP code.

8. Some of the PHP contains SQL statements, which the PHP interpreter now passes to the MySQL database engine.

9. The MySQL database returns the results of the statements to the PHP interpreter.

10. The PHP interpreter returns the results of the executed PHP code, along with the results from the MySQL database, to the web server.

11. The web server returns the page to the requesting client, which displays it.

Although it's helpful to be aware of this process so that you know how the three elements work together, in practice you don't really need to concern yourself with these details, because they all happen automatically.

The HTML pages returned to the browser in each example may well contain JavaScript, which will be interpreted locally by the client, and which could initiate another request—the same way embedded objects such as images would.

The Benefits of PHP, MySQL, JavaScript, CSS, and HTML5

At the start of this chapter, I introduced the world of Web 1.0, but it wasn't long before the rush was on to create Web 1.1, with the development of such browser enhancements as Java, JavaScript, JScript (Microsoft's slight variant of JavaScript), and ActiveX. On the server side, progress was being made on the Common Gateway Interface (CGI) using scripting languages such as Perl (an alternative to the PHP language) and *server-side scripting*—inserting the contents of one file (or the output of running a local program) into another one dynamically.

Once the dust had settled, three main technologies stood head and shoulders above the others. Although Perl was still a popular scripting language with a strong following, PHP's simplicity and built-in links to the MySQL database program had earned it more than double the number of users. And JavaScript, which had become an essential part of the equation for dynamically manipulating Cascading Style Sheets (CSS) and HTML, now took on the even more muscular task of handling the client side of the asynchronous communication (exchanging data between a client and server after a web page has loaded). Using asynchronous communication, web pages perform data handling and send requests to web servers in the background—without the web user being aware that this is going on.

No doubt the symbiotic nature of PHP and MySQL helped propel them both forward, but what attracted developers to them in the first place? The simple answer has to be the ease with which you can use them to quickly create dynamic elements on websites. MySQL is a fast and powerful yet easy-to-use database system that offers just about anything a website would need in order to find and serve up data to browsers. When PHP allies with MySQL to store and retrieve this data, you have the fundamental parts required for the development of social networking sites and the beginnings of Web 2.0.

And when you bring JavaScript and CSS into the mix too, you have a recipe for building highly dynamic and interactive websites—especially as there is now a wide range of sophisticated frameworks of JavaScript functions you can call on to really speed up web development, such as the well-known jQuery, which is now probably the most common way programmers access asynchronous communication features.

MariaDB: The MySQL Clone

After Oracle purchased Sun Microsystems (the owners of MySQL), the community became wary that MySQL might not remain fully open source, so MariaDB was forked from it to keep it free under the GNU GPL. Development of MariaDB is led by some of the original developers of MySQL and it retains exceedingly close compatibility with MySQL. Therefore, you may well encounter MariaDB on some servers in place of MySQL—but not to worry, everything in this book works equally well on both MySQL and MariaDB, which is based on the same code base as MySQL Server 5.5. To all intents and purposes you can swap one with the other and notice no difference.

Anyway, as it turns out, many of the initial fears appear to have been allayed as MySQL remains open source, with Oracle simply charging for support and for editions that provide additional features such as geo-replication and automatic scaling. However, unlike MariaDB, MySQL is no longer community driven, so knowing that MariaDB will always be there if ever needed will keep many developers sleeping at night, and probably ensures that MySQL itself will remain open source.

Using PHP

With PHP, it's a simple matter to embed dynamic activity in web pages. When you give pages the *.php* extension, they have instant access to the scripting language. From a developer's point of view, all you have to do is write code such as the following:

```php
<?php
  echo " Today is " . date("l") . ". ";
?>
```

```
Here's the latest news.
```

The opening <?php tells the web server to allow the PHP program to interpret all the following code up to the ?> tag. Outside of this construct, everything is sent to the client as direct HTML. So, the text Here's the latest news. is simply output to the browser; within the PHP tags, the built-in date function displays the current day of the week according to the server's system time.

The final output of the two parts looks like this:

```
Today is Wednesday. Here's the latest news.
```

PHP is a flexible language, and some people prefer to place the PHP construct directly next to PHP code, like this:

```
Today is <?php echo date("l"); ?>. Here's the latest news.
```

There are even more ways of formatting and outputting information, which I'll explain in the chapters on PHP. The point is that with PHP, web developers have a scripting language that, although not as fast as compiling your code in C or a similar language, is incredibly speedy and also integrates seamlessly with HTML markup.

 If you intend to enter the PHP examples in this book into a program editor to work along with me, you must remember to add <?php in front and ?> after them to ensure that the PHP interpreter processes them. To facilitate this, you may wish to prepare a file called *example.php* with those tags in place.

Using PHP, you have unlimited control over your web server. Whether you need to modify HTML on the fly, process a credit card, add user details to a database, or fetch information from a third-party website, you can do it all from within the same PHP files in which the HTML itself resides.

Using MySQL

Of course, there's not a lot of point to being able to change HTML output dynamically unless you also have a means to track the information users provide to your website as they use it. In the early days of the web, many sites used "flat" text files to store data such as usernames and passwords. But this approach could cause problems if the file wasn't correctly locked against corruption from multiple simultaneous accesses. Also, a flat file can get only so big before it becomes unwieldy to manage—not to mention the difficulty of trying to merge files and perform complex searches in any kind of reasonable time.

That's where relational databases with structured querying become essential. And MySQL, being free to use and installed on vast numbers of internet web servers, rises superbly to the occasion. It is a robust and exceptionally fast database management system that uses English-like commands.

The highest level of MySQL structure is a database, within which you can have one or more tables that contain your data. For example, let's suppose you are working on a table called users, within which you have created columns for surname, firstname, and email, and you now wish to add another user. One command that you might use to do this is as follows:

```
INSERT INTO users VALUES('Smith', 'John', 'jsmith@mysite.com');
```

You will previously have issued other commands to create the database and table and to set up all the correct fields, but the SQL INSERT command here shows how simple it can be to add new data to a database. SQL is a language designed in the early 1970s that is reminiscent of one of the oldest programming languages, COBOL. It is well suited, however, to database queries, which is why it is still in use after all this time.

It's equally easy to look up data. Let's assume that you have an email address for a user and need to look up that person's name. To do this, you could issue a MySQL query such as the following:

```
SELECT surname,firstname FROM users WHERE email='jsmith@mysite.com';
```

MySQL will then return Smith, John and any other pairs of names that may be associated with that email address in the database.

As you'd expect, there's quite a bit more that you can do with MySQL than just simple INSERT and SELECT commands. For example, you can combine related data sets to bring related pieces of information together, ask for results in a variety of orders, make partial matches when you know only part of the string that you are searching for, return only the *n*th result, and a lot more.

Using PHP, you can make all these calls directly to MySQL without having to directly access the MySQL command-line interface yourself. This means you can save the results in arrays for processing and perform multiple lookups, each dependent on the results returned from earlier ones, to drill down to the item of data you need.

For even more power, as you'll see later, there are additional functions built right into MySQL that you can call up to efficiently run common operations within MySQL, rather than creating them out of multiple PHP calls to MySQL.

Using JavaScript

The oldest of the three core technologies discussed in this book, JavaScript, was created to enable scripting access to all the elements of an HTML document. In other words, it provides a means for dynamic user interaction such as checking email address validity in input forms and displaying prompts such as "Did you really mean that?" (although it cannot be relied upon for security, which should always be performed on the web server).

Combined with CSS (see the following section), JavaScript is the power behind dynamic web pages that change in front of your eyes rather than when a new page is returned by the server.

However, JavaScript can also be tricky to use, due to some major differences in the ways different browser designers have chosen to implement it. This mainly came about when some manufacturers tried to put additional functionality into their browsers at the expense of compatibility with their rivals.

Thankfully, the developers have mostly now come to their senses and have realized the need for full compatibility with one another, so it is less necessary these days to have to optimize your code for different browsers. However, there remain millions of users using legacy browsers, and this will likely be the case for a good many years to come. Luckily, there are solutions for the incompatibility problems, and later in this book we'll look at libraries and techniques that enable you to safely ignore these differences.

For now, let's take a look at how to use basic JavaScript, accepted by all browsers:

```
<script type="text/javascript">
  document.write("Today is " + Date() );
</script>
```

This code snippet tells the web browser to interpret everything within the `<script>` tags as JavaScript, which the browser does by writing the text `Today is` to the current document, along with the date, using the JavaScript function `Date`. The result will look something like this:

`Today is Sun Jan 01 2017 01:23:45`

 Unless you need to specify an exact version of JavaScript, you can normally omit the `type="text/javascript"` and just use `<script>` to start the interpretation of the JavaScript.

As previously mentioned, JavaScript was originally developed to offer dynamic control over the various elements within an HTML document, and that is still its main use. But more and more, JavaScript is being used for *asynchronous communication*, the process of accessing the web server in the background.

Asynchronous communication is what allows web pages to begin to resemble standalone programs, because they don't have to be reloaded in their entirety to display new content. Instead, an asynchronous call can pull in and update a single element on a web page, such as changing your photograph on a social networking site or replacing a button that you click with the answer to a question. This subject is fully covered in Chapter 17.

Then, in Chapter 21, we take a good look at the jQuery framework, which you can use to save reinventing the wheel when you need fast, cross-browser code to manipulate your web pages. Of course, there are other frameworks available too, but jQuery is by far the most popular. Due to continuous maintenance, it is extremely reliable, and it's a major tool in the utility kit of many seasoned web developers.

Using CSS

CSS is the crucial companion to HTML, ensuring that the HTML text and embedded images are laid out consistently and in a manner appropriate for the user's screen. With the emergence of the CSS3 standard in recent years, CSS now offers a level of dynamic interactivity previously supported only by JavaScript. For example, not only can you style any HTML element to change its dimensions, colors, borders, spacing, and so on, but now you can also add animated transitions and transformations to your web pages, using only a few lines of CSS.

Using CSS can be as simple as inserting a few rules between `<style>` and `</style>` tags in the head of a web page, like this:

```
<style>
  p {
    text-align:justify;
    font-family:Helvetica;
  }
</style>
```

These rules change the default text alignment of the `<p>` tag so that paragraphs contained in it are fully justified and use the Helvetica font.

As you'll learn in Chapter 18, there are many different ways you can lay out CSS rules, and you can also include them directly within tags or save a set of rules to an external file to be loaded in separately. This flexibility not only lets you style your HTML precisely, but can also (for example) provide built-in hover functionality to animate objects as the mouse passes over them. You will also learn how to access all of an element's CSS properties from JavaScript as well as HTML.

And Then There's HTML5

As useful as all these additions to the web standards became, they were not enough for ever more ambitious developers. For example, there was still no simple way to manipulate graphics in a web browser without resorting to plug-ins such as Flash. And the same went for inserting audio and video into web pages. Plus, several annoying inconsistencies had crept into HTML during its evolution.

So, to clear all this up and take the internet beyond Web 2.0 and into its next iteration, a new standard for HTML was created to address all these shortcomings: *HTML5*. Its development began as long ago as 2004, when the first draft was drawn up by the Mozilla Foundation and Opera Software (developers of two popular web browsers), but it wasn't until the start of 2013 that the final draft was submitted to the World Wide Web Consortium (W3C), the international governing body for web standards.

It has taken a few years for HTML5 to develop, but now we are at a very solid and stable version 5.1 (since 2016). It's a never-ending cycle of development, though, and more functionality is sure to be built into it over time. Some of the best features in HTML5 for handling and displaying media include the `<audio>`, `<video>`, and `<canvas>` elements, which add sound, video, and advanced graphics. Everything you need to know about these and all other aspects of HTML5 is covered in detail starting in Chapter 23.

 One of the little things I like about the HTML5 specification is that XHTML syntax is no longer required for self-closing elements. In the past, you could display a line break using the `<br>` element. Then, to ensure future compatibility with XHTML (the planned replacement for HTML that never happened), this was changed to `<br />`, in which a closing / character was added (since all elements were expected to include a closing tag featuring this character). But now things have gone full circle, and you can use either version of these types of elements. So, for the sake of brevity and fewer keystrokes, in this book I have reverted to the former style of `<br>`, `<hr>`, and so on.

The Apache Web Server

In addition to PHP, MySQL, JavaScript, CSS, and HTML5, there's a sixth hero in the dynamic web: the web server. In the case of this book, that means the Apache web server. We've discussed a little of what a web server does during the HTTP server/client exchange, but it does much more behind the scenes.

For example, Apache doesn't serve up just HTML files—it handles a wide range of files, from images and Flash files to MP3 audio files, RSS (Really Simple Syndication) feeds, and so on. And these objects don't have to be static files such as GIF images. They can all be generated by programs such as PHP scripts. That's right: PHP can even create images and other files for you, either on the fly or in advance to serve up later.

To do this, you normally have modules either precompiled into Apache or PHP or called up at runtime. One such module is the GD (Graphics Draw) library, which PHP uses to create and handle graphics.

Apache also supports a huge range of modules of its own. In addition to the PHP module, the most important for your purposes as a web programmer are the modules that handle security. Other examples are the Rewrite module, which enables the web server to handle a range of URL types and rewrite them to its own internal requirements, and the Proxy module, which you can use to serve up often-requested pages from a cache to ease the load on the server.

Later in the book, you'll see how to use some of these modules to enhance the features provided by the three core technologies.

Handling Mobile Devices

We are now firmly in a world of interconnected mobile computing devices, and the concept of developing websites solely for desktop computers has become rather dated. Instead, developers now aim to develop responsive websites and web apps that tailor themselves to the environment in which they find themselves running.

So, new in this edition, I show how you can easily create these types of products using just the technologies detailed in this book, along with the powerful jQuery Mobile library of responsive JavaScript functions. With it, you'll be able to focus on the content and usability of your websites and web apps, knowing that how they display will be automatically optimized for a range of different computing devices—one less thing for you to worry about.

To demonstrate how to make full use of its power, the final chapter of this book creates a simple social networking example website, using jQuery Mobile to make it fully responsive and ensure it displays well on anything from a small mobile phone screen to a tablet or a desktop computer.

About Open Source

The technologies in this book are open source: anyone is allowed to read and change the code. Whether or not this status is the reason these technologies are so popular has often been debated, but PHP, MySQL, and Apache *are* the three most commonly used tools in their categories. What can be said definitively, though, is that their being open source means they have been developed in the community by teams of programmers writing the features they themselves want and need, with the original code available for all to see and change. Bugs can be found quickly and security breaches can be prevented before they happen.

There's another benefit: all these programs are free to use. There's no worrying about having to purchase additional licenses if you have to scale up your website and add more servers, and you don't need to check the budget before deciding whether to upgrade to the latest versions of these products.

Bringing It All Together

The real beauty of PHP, MySQL, JavaScript (sometimes aided by jQuery or other frameworks), CSS, and HTML5 is the wonderful way in which they all work together to produce dynamic web content: PHP handles all the main work on the web server, MySQL manages all the data, and the combination of CSS and JavaScript looks after web page presentation. JavaScript can also talk with your PHP code on the web server whenever it needs to update something (either on the server or on the web page). And with the powerful new features in HTML5, such as the canvas, audio and video, and geolocation, you can make your web pages highly dynamic, interactive, and multimedia-packed.

Without using program code, let's summarize the contents of this chapter by looking at the process of combining some of these technologies into an everyday asynchronous communication feature that many websites use: checking whether a desired username already exists on the site when a user is signing up for a new account. A good example of this can be seen with Gmail (see Figure 1-3).

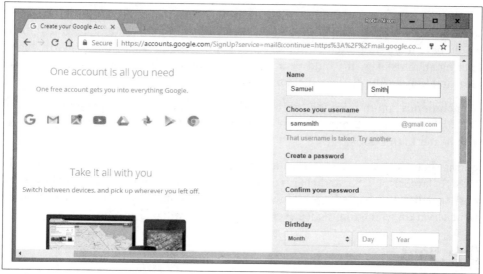

Figure 1-3. Gmail uses asynchronous communication to check the availability of usernames

The steps involved in this asynchronous process will be similar to the following:

1. The server outputs the HTML to create the web form, which asks for the necessary details, such as username, first name, last name, and email address.

2. At the same time, the server attaches some JavaScript to the HTML to monitor the username input box and check for two things: whether some text has been typed into it, and whether the input has been deselected because the user has clicked on another input box.

3. Once the text has been entered and the field deselected, in the background the JavaScript code passes the username that was entered back to a PHP script on the web server and awaits a response.

4. The web server looks up the username and replies back to the JavaScript regarding whether that name has already been taken.

5. The JavaScript then places an indication next to the username input box to show whether the name is available to the user—perhaps a green checkmark or a red cross graphic, along with some text.

6. If the username is not available and the user still submits the form, the JavaScript interrupts the submission and reemphasizes (perhaps with a larger graphic and/or an alert box) that the user needs to choose another username.

7. Optionally, an improved version of this process could even look at the username requested by the user and suggest an alternative that is currently available.

All of this takes place quietly in the background and makes for a comfortable and seamless user experience. Without asynchronous communication, the entire form would have to be submitted to the server, which would then send back HTML, highlighting any mistakes. It would be a workable solution, but nowhere near as tidy or pleasurable as on-the-fly form field processing.

Asynchronous communication can be used for a lot more than simple input verification and processing, though; we'll explore many additional things that you can do with it later in this book.

In this chapter, you have read a good introduction to the core technologies of PHP, MySQL, JavaScript, CSS, and HTML5 (as well as Apache), and have learned how they work together. In Chapter 2, we'll look at how you can install your own web development server on which to practice everything that you will be learning.

Questions

1. What four components (at the minimum) are needed to create a fully dynamic web page?

2. What does *HTML* stand for?

3. Why does the name *MySQL* contain the letters *SQL*?

4. PHP and JavaScript are both programming languages that generate dynamic results for web pages. What is their main difference, and why would you use both of them?

5. What does *CSS* stand for?

6. List three major new elements introduced in HTML5.

7. If you encounter a bug (which is rare) in one of the open source tools, how do you think you could get it fixed?

8. Why is a framework such as jQuery Mobile so important for developing modern websites and web apps?

See "Chapter 1 Answers" on page 713 in Appendix A for the answers to these questions.

CHAPTER 2

Setting Up a Development Server

If you wish to develop internet applications but don't have your own development server, you will have to upload every modification you make to a server somewhere else on the web before you can test it.

Even on a fast broadband connection, this can still represent a significant slowdown in development time. On a local computer, however, testing can be as easy as saving an update (usually just a matter of clicking once on an icon) and then hitting the Refresh button in your browser.

Another advantage of a development server is that you don't have to worry about embarrassing errors or security problems while you're writing and testing, whereas you need to be aware of what people may see or do with your application when it's on a public website. It's best to iron everything out while you're still on a home or small office system, presumably protected by firewalls and other safeguards.

Once you have your own development server, you'll wonder how you ever managed without one, and it's easy to set one up. Just follow the steps in the following sections, using the appropriate instructions for a PC, a Mac, or a Linux system.

In this chapter, we cover just the server side of the web experience, as described in Chapter 1. But to test the results of your work—particularly when we start using JavaScript, CSS, and HTML5 later in this book—you should ideally have an instance of every major web browser running on some system convenient to you. Whenever possible, the list of browsers should include at least Microsoft Edge, Mozilla Firefox, Opera, Safari, and Google Chrome. If you plan to ensure that your sites look good on mobile devices too, you should try to arrange access to a wide range of iOS and Android devices.

What Is a WAMP, MAMP, or LAMP?

WAMP, MAMP, and LAMP are abbreviations for "Windows, Apache, MySQL, and PHP," "Mac, Apache, MySQL, and PHP," and "Linux, Apache, MySQL, and PHP." These abbreviations each describe a fully functioning setup used for developing dynamic internet web pages.

WAMPs, MAMPs, and LAMPs come in the form of packages that bind the bundled programs together so that you don't have to install and set them up separately. This means you can simply download and install a single program and follow a few easy prompts to get your web development server up and running fast, with minimal hassle.

During installation, several default settings are created for you. The security configurations of such an installation will not be as tight as on a production web server, because it is optimized for local use. For these reasons, you should never install such a setup as a production server.

However, for developing and testing websites and applications, one of these installations should be entirely sufficient.

If you choose not to go the WAMP/MAMP/LAMP route for building your own development system, you should know that downloading and integrating the various parts yourself can be very time-consuming and may require a lot of research in order to configure everything fully. But if you already have all the components installed and integrated with one another, they should work with the examples in this book.

Installing AMPPS on Windows

There are several available WAMP servers, each offering slightly different configurations. Of the various open source and free options, one of the best is AMPPS. You can download it by clicking the button on the website's home page (*http://ampps.com*), shown in Figure 2-1.

I recommend that you always download the latest stable release (as I write this, it's 3.8, which is about 128 MB in size). The various Windows, macOS, and Linux installers are listed on the download page.

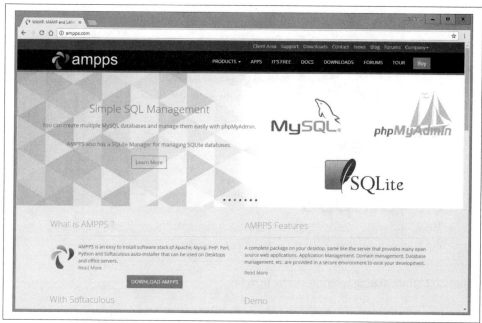

Figure 2-1. The AMPPS website

 During the lifetime of this edition, some of the screens and options shown in the following walk-through may change. If so, just use your common sense to proceed in as similar a manner as possible to the sequence of actions described.

Once you've downloaded the installer, run it to bring up the window shown in Figure 2-2. Before arriving at that window, though, if you use an antivirus program or have User Account Control activated on Windows, you may first be shown one or more advisory notices, and will have to click Yes and/or OK to continue with the installation.

Click Next, after which you must accept the agreement. Click Next once again, and then once more to move past the information screen. You will now need to confirm the installation location. This will probably be suggested as something like the following, depending on the letter of your main hard drive, but you can change this if you wish:

```
C:\Program Files (x86)\Ampps
```

Figure 2-2. The opening window of the installer

Once you have decided where to install AMPPS, click Next, choose a Start menu folder name, and click Next again. You can choose which icons you wish to install, as shown in Figure 2-3. On the screen that follows, click the Install button to start the process.

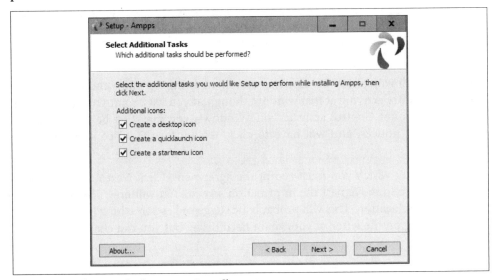

Figure 2-3. Choose which icons to install

Installation will take a few minutes, after which you should see the completion screen in Figure 2-4, and you can click Finish.

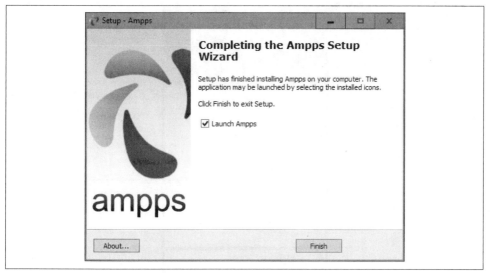

Figure 2-4. AMPPS is now installed

The final thing you must do is install C++ Redistributable Visual Studio, if you haven't already. Visual Studio is an environment in which you'll be doing development work. A window will pop up to prompt you, as shown in Figure 2-5. Click Yes to start the installation or No if you are certain you already have it.

Figure 2-5. Install C++ Redistributable Visual Studio if you don't already have it

If you choose to go ahead and install, you will have to agree to the terms and conditions in the pop-up window that appears, and then click Install. Installation of this should be fairly fast. Click Close to finish.

Once AMPPS is installed, the control window shown in Figure 2-6 should appear at the bottom right of your desktop. You can also call up this window using the AMPPS application shortcut in the Start menu or on the desktop, if you allowed these icons to be created.

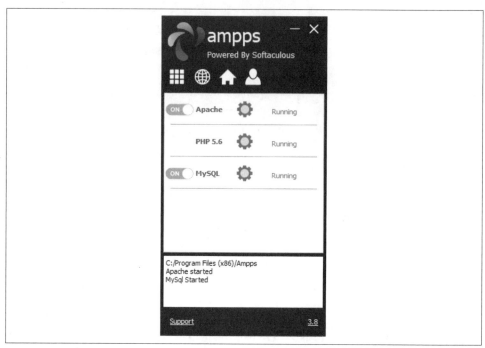

Figure 2-6. The AMPPS control window

Before proceeding, I recommend you acquaint yourself with the AMPPS documentation (*http://ampps.com/wiki*). Once you have digested this, should you still have an issue, there's a Support link at the bottom of the control window that will take you to the AMPPS website, where you can open up a trouble ticket.

 You may notice that the default version of PHP in AMPPS is 5.6. In other sections of this book I detail some of the more important changes in PHP 7. If you wish to try them out for yourself, click the Options button (nine white boxes in a square) within the AMPPS control window, and then select Change PHP Version, whereupon a new menu will appear from which you can choose a version between 5.6 and 7.1.

Testing the Installation

The first thing to do at this point is verify that everything is working correctly. To do this, enter either of the following two URLs into the address bar of your browser:

```
localhost
127.0.0.1
```

This will call up an introductory screen, where you will have the opportunity to secure AMPPS by giving it a password (see Figure 2-7). I recommend you don't check the box and just click the Submit button to proceed without setting a password.

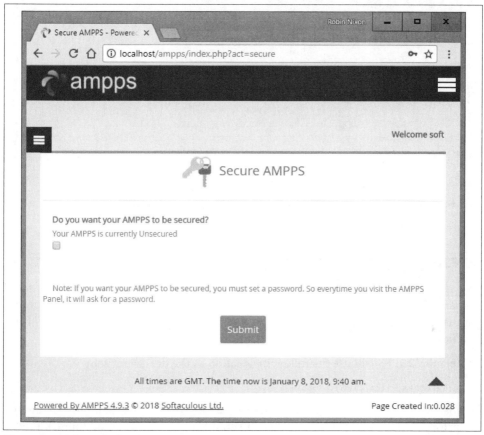

Figure 2-7. The initial security setup screen

Once this has been done you will be taken to the main control page at *localhost/ampps/* (from now on I will assume you are accessing AMPPS through *localhost* rather than *127.0.0.1*). From here you can configure and control all aspects of the AMPPS stack, so make a note of this for future reference, or perhaps set a bookmark in your browser.

Next, type the following to view the document root (described in the following section) of your new Apache web server:

```
localhost
```

This time, rather than seeing the initial screen about setting up security, you should see something similar to Figure 2-8.

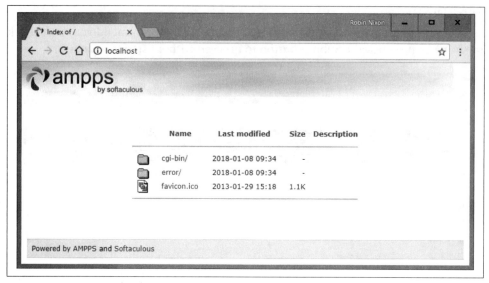

Figure 2-8. Viewing the document root

Accessing the Document Root (Windows)

The *document root* is the directory that contains the main web documents for a domain. This directory is the one that the server uses when a basic URL without a path is typed into a browser, such as *http://yahoo.com* or, for your local server, *http://localhost*.

By default AMPPS will use the following location as the document root:

```
C:\Program Files (x86)\Ampps\www
```

To ensure that you have everything correctly configured, you should now create the obligatory "Hello World" file. So, create a small HTML file along the following lines using Windows Notepad or any other program or text editor, but not a rich word processor such as Microsoft Word (unless you save as plain text):

```
<!DOCTYPE html>
<html lang="en">
  <head>
    <title>A quick test</title>
  </head>
  <body>
    Hello World!
  </body>
</html>
```

Once you have typed this, save the file into the document root directory, using the filename *test.html*. If you are using Notepad, make sure that the value in the "Save as type" box is changed from "Text Documents (*.txt)" to "All Files (*.*)".

You can now call this page up in your browser by entering the following URL in its address bar (see Figure 2-9):

```
localhost/test.html
```

Figure 2-9. Your first web page

 Remember that serving a web page from the document root (or a subfolder) is different from loading one into a web browser from your computer's filesystem. The former will ensure access to PHP, MySQL, and all the features of a web server, while the latter will simply load the file into the browser, which will do its best to display it but will be unable to process any PHP or other server instructions. So, you should generally run examples using the *localhost* preface from your browser's address bar, unless you are certain that the file doesn't rely on web server functionality.

Alternative WAMPs

When software is updated, it sometimes works differently from how you expect, and bugs can even be introduced. So, if you encounter difficulties that you cannot resolve in AMPPS, you may prefer to choose one of the other solutions available on the web.

You will still be able to make use of all the examples in this book, but you'll have to follow the instructions supplied with each WAMP, which may not be as easy to follow as the preceding guide.

Here's a selection of some of the best, in my opinion:

- EasyPHP (*http://easyphp.org*)
- XAMPP (*http://apachefriends.org*)
- WAMPServer (*http://wampserver.com/en*)
- Glossword WAMP (*http://glossword.biz/glosswordwamp*)

Updates to AMPPS

Over the life of this edition of the book, it is very likely that the developers of AMPPS will make improvements to the software, and therefore the installation screens and method of use may evolve over time, as may versions of Apache, PHP, or MySQL. So, please don't assume something is wrong if the screens and operation look different. The AMPPS developers take every care to ensure it is easy to use, so just follow any prompts given, and refer to the documentation on the website (*http://ampps.com*).

Installing AMPPS on macOS

AMPPS is also available on macOS, and you can download it from the website (*http://apachefriends.org*), as shown previously in Figure 2-1 (as I write, the current version is 3.8 and its size is around 270 MB).

If your browser doesn't open it automatically once it has downloaded, double-click the *.dmg* file, and then drag the *AMPPS* folder over to your *Applications* folder (see Figure 2-10).

Figure 2-10. Drag the AMPPS folder to Applications

Now open your *Applications* folder in the usual manner, and double-click the AMPPS program. If your security settings prevent the file being opened, hold down the

Control key and click the icon once. A new window will pop up asking if you are sure you wish to open it. Click Open to do so. When the app starts you may have to enter your macOS password to proceed.

Once AMPPS is up and running, a control window similar to the one shown in Figure 2-6 will appear at the bottom left of your desktop.

 You may notice that the default version of PHP in AMPPS is 5.6. In other sections of this book I detail some of the more important changes in PHP 7. If you wish to try them out for yourself, click the Options button (nine white boxes in a square) within the AMPPS control window, and then select Change PHP Version, whereupon a new menu will appear in which you can choose a version between 5.6 and 7.1.

Accessing the Document Root (macOS)

By default, AMPPS will use the following location as the document root:

```
/Applications/Ampps/www
```

To ensure that you have everything correctly configured, you should now create the obligatory "Hello World" file. So, create a small HTML file along the following lines using the TextEdit program or any other program or text editor, but not a rich word processor such as Microsoft Word (unless you save as plain text):

```
<html>
  <head>
    <title>A quick test</title>
  </head>
  <body>
    Hello World!
  </body>
</html>
```

Once you have typed this, save the file into the document root directory using the filename *test.html*.

You can now call this page up in your browser by entering the following URL in its address bar (to see a similar result to Figure 2-9):

```
localhost/test.html
```

Remember that serving a web page from the document root (or a subfolder) is different from loading one into a web browser from your computer's filesystem. The former will ensure access to PHP, MySQL, and all the features of a web server, while the latter will simply load the file into the browser, which will do its best to display it but will be unable to process any PHP or other server instructions. So, you should generally run examples using the *localhost* preface from your browser's address bar, unless you are certain that the file doesn't rely on web server functionality.

Installing a LAMP on Linux

This book is aimed mostly at PC and Mac users, but its contents will work equally well on a Linux computer. However, there are dozens of popular flavors of Linux, and each of them may require installing a LAMP in a slightly different way, so I can't cover them all in this book.

That said, many Linux versions come preinstalled with a web server and MySQL, and the chances are that you may already be all set to go. To find out, try entering the following into a browser and see whether you get a default document root web page:

```
localhost
```

If this works, you probably have the Apache server installed and may well have MySQL up and running too; check with your system administrator to be sure.

If you don't yet have a web server installed, however, there's a version of AMPPS available that you can download from the website (*http://apachefriends.org*).

Installation is similar to the sequence shown in the preceding section. If you need further assistance on using the software, please refer to the documentation (*http://ampps.com/wiki*).

Working Remotely

If you have access to a web server already configured with PHP and MySQL, you can always use that for your web development. But unless you have a high-speed connection, it is not always your best option. Developing locally allows you to test modifications with little or no upload delay.

Accessing MySQL remotely may not be easy either. You should use the secure SSH protocol to log into your server to manually create databases and set permissions from the command line. Your web hosting company will advise you on how best to do this and provide you with any password it has set for your MySQL access (as well as, of course, for getting into the server in the first place). Unless you have no choice,

I recommend you do not use the insecure Telnet protocol to remotely log into any server.

Logging In

I recommend that, at minimum, Windows users should install a program such as PuTTY (*http://putty.org*), for Telnet and SSH access (remember that SSH is much more secure than Telnet).

On a Mac, you already have SSH available. Just select the *Applications* folder, followed by *Utilities*, and then launch Terminal. In the Terminal window, log in to a server using SSH as follows:

```
ssh mylogin@server.com
```

where *server.com* is the name of the server you wish to log into and *mylogin* is the username you will log in under. You will then be prompted for the correct password for that username and, if you enter it correctly, you will be logged in.

Using FTP

To transfer files to and from your web server, you will need an FTP program. If you go searching the web for a good one, you'll find so many that it could take you quite a while to come across one with all the right features for you.

My preferred FTP program is the open source FileZilla (*http://filezilla-project.org*), for Windows, Linux, and macOS 10.5 or newer (see Figure 2-11). Full instructions on how to use FileZilla are available on the wiki (*http://wiki.filezilla-project.org*).

Figure 2-11. FileZilla is a full-featured FTP program

Of course, if you already have an FTP program, all the better—stick with what you know.

Using a Program Editor

Although a plain-text editor works for editing HTML, PHP, and JavaScript, there have been some tremendous improvements in dedicated program editors, which now incorporate very handy features such as colored syntax highlighting. Today's program editors are smart and can show you where you have syntax errors before you even run a program. Once you've used a modern editor, you'll wonder how you ever managed without one.

There are a number of good programs available, but I have settled on Editra (see Figure 2-12), because it's free and available on macOS, Windows, and Linux/Unix, and it suits the way I program. You can download a copy by visiting Editra's website (*http://editra.org*) and selecting the Download link at the top of the page, where you can also find a link to the documentation. Everyone has different programming styles and preferences, though, so if you don't get on with it, there are plenty more program editors available to choose from—or you may wish to go directly for an integrated development environment (IDE), as described in the following section.

```
1753    $contents = @file_get_contents($page);
1754    if (!$contents) return FALSE;
1755
1756    $checksum = md5($contents);
1757
1758    if (file_exists($datafile))
1759    {
1760        $rawfile = file_get_contents($datafile);
1761        $data    = explode("\n", rtrim($rawfile));
1762        $left    = array_map("PU_F1", $data);
1763        $right   = array_map("PU_F2", $data);
1764        $exists  = -1;
1765
1766        for ($j = 0 ; $j < count($left) ; ++$j)
1767        {
1768            if ($left[$j] == $page)
1769            {
1770                $exists = $j;
1771                if ($right[$j] == $checksum) return 0;
1772            }
1773        }
```

Figure 2-12. Program editors (like Editra, pictured here) are superior to plain-text editors

As you can see from Figure 2-12, Editra highlights the syntax appropriately, using colors to help clarify what's going on. What's more, you can place the cursor next to brackets or braces, and Editra will highlight the matching ones so that you can check whether you have too many or too few. In fact, Editra does a lot more in addition, which you will discover and enjoy as you use it.

Again, if you have a different preferred program editor, use that; it's always a good idea to use programs you're already familiar with.

Using an IDE

As good as dedicated program editors can be for your programming productivity, their utility pales into insignificance when compared to integrated development environments, which offer many additional features such as in-editor debugging and program testing, as well as function descriptions and much more.

Figure 2-13 shows the popular phpDesigner IDE with a PHP program loaded into the main frame, and the righthand Code Explorer listing the various classes, functions, and variables that it uses.

Figure 2-13. When you're using an IDE such as phpDesigner, PHP development becomes much quicker and easier

When developing with an IDE, you can set breakpoints and then run all (or portions) of your code, which will stop at the breakpoints and provide you with information about the program's current state.

As an aid to learning programming, the examples in this book can be entered into an IDE and run there and then, without the need to call up your web browser. There are several IDEs available for different platforms, most of which are commercial, but there are some free ones too. Table 2-1 lists some of the most popular PHP IDEs, along with their download URLs.

Table 2-1. A selection of PHP IDEs

IDE	Download URL	Cost	Win	Mac	Lin
Eclipse PDT	*http://eclipse.org/pdt/downloads/*	Free	✓	✓	✓
Komodo IDE	*http://activestate.com/Products/komodo_ide*	$295	✓	✓	✓
NetBeans	*http://www.netbeans.org*	Free	✓	✓	✓
phpDesigner	*http://mpsoftware.dk*	$39	✓		
PHPeclipse	*https://sourceforge.net/projects/phpeclipse/*	Free	✓	✓	✓
PhpED	*http://nusphere.com*	$99	✓		✓
PHPEdit	*https://phpedit.en.softonic.com*	$117	✓		

Choosing an IDE can be a very personal thing, so if you intend to use one, I advise you to download a couple or more to try them out first; they all either have trial versions or are free to use, so it won't cost you anything.

You should take the time to install a program editor or IDE you are comfortable with now; you'll then be ready to try out the examples in the coming chapters.

Armed with these tools, you are now ready to move on to Chapter 3, where we'll start exploring PHP in further depth and find out how to get HTML and PHP to work together, as well as how the PHP language itself is structured. But before moving on, I suggest you test your new knowledge with the following questions.

Questions

1. What is the difference between a WAMP, a MAMP, and a LAMP?
2. What do the IP address 127.0.0.1 and the URL *http://localhost* have in common?
3. What is the purpose of an FTP program?
4. Name the main disadvantage of working on a remote web server.
5. Why is it better to use a program editor instead of a plain-text editor?

See "Chapter 2 Answers" on page 714 in Appendix A for the answers to these questions.

CHAPTER 3

Introduction to PHP

In Chapter 1, I explained that PHP is the language that you use to make the server generate dynamic output—output that is potentially different each time a browser requests a page. In this chapter, you'll start learning this simple but powerful language; it will be the topic of the following chapters up through Chapter 7.

I encourage you to develop your PHP code using one of the IDEs listed in Chapter 2. It will help you catch typos and speed up learning tremendously in comparison to a less feature-rich editor.

Many of these development environments will let you run the PHP code and see the output discussed in this chapter. I'll also show you how to embed the PHP in an HTML file so that you can see what the output looks like in a web page (the way your users will ultimately see it). But that step, as thrilling as it may be at first, isn't really important at this stage.

In production, your web pages will be a combination of PHP, HTML, JavaScript, and some MySQL statements laid out using CSS. Furthermore, each page can lead to other pages to provide users with ways to click through links and fill out forms. We can avoid all that complexity while learning each language, though. Focus for now on just writing PHP code and making sure that you get the output you expect—or at least that you understand the output you actually get!

Incorporating PHP Within HTML

By default, PHP documents end with the extension *.php*. When a web server encounters this extension in a requested file, it automatically passes it to the PHP processor. Of course, web servers are highly configurable, and some web developers choose to force files ending with *.htm* or *.html* to also get parsed by the PHP processor, usually because they want to hide their use of PHP.

Your PHP program is responsible for passing back a clean file suitable for display in a web browser. At its very simplest, a PHP document will output only HTML. To prove this, you can take any normal HTML document and save it as a PHP document (for example, saving *index.html* as *index.php*), and it will display identically to the original.

To trigger the PHP commands, you need to learn a new tag. Here is the first part:

```
<?php
```

The first thing you may notice is that the tag has not been closed. This is because entire sections of PHP can be placed inside this tag, and they finish only when the closing part is encountered, which looks like this:

```
?>
```

A small PHP "Hello World" program might look like Example 3-1.

Example 3-1. Invoking PHP

```
<?php
  echo "Hello world";
?>
```

Use of this tag can be quite flexible. Some programmers open the tag at the start of a document and close it right at the end, outputting any HTML directly from PHP commands. Others, however, choose to insert only the smallest possible fragments of PHP within these tags wherever dynamic scripting is required, leaving the rest of the document in standard HTML.

The latter type of programmer generally argues that their style of coding results in faster code, while the former says that the speed increase is so minimal that it doesn't justify the additional complexity of dropping in and out of PHP many times in a single document.

As you learn more, you will surely discover your preferred style of PHP development, but for the sake of making the examples in this book easier to follow, I have adopted the approach of keeping the number of transfers between PHP and HTML to a minimum—generally only once or twice in a document.

By the way, there is a slight variation to the PHP syntax. If you browse the internet for PHP examples, you may also encounter code where the opening and closing syntax looks like this:

```
<?
  echo "Hello world";
?>
```

Although it's not as obvious that the PHP parser is being called, this is a valid, alternative syntax that also usually works. But I discourage its use, as it is incompatible with XML and is now deprecated (meaning that it is no longer recommended and support could be removed in future versions).

 If you have only PHP code in a file, you may omit the closing ?>. This can be a good practice, as it will ensure that you have no excess whitespace leaking from your PHP files (especially important when you're writing object-oriented code).

This Book's Examples

To save you the time it would take to type them all in, all the examples from this book have been archived onto the companion website (*http://lpmj.net*). You can download the archive to your computer by clicking the 5th Edition Examples link in the heading section (see Figure 3-1).

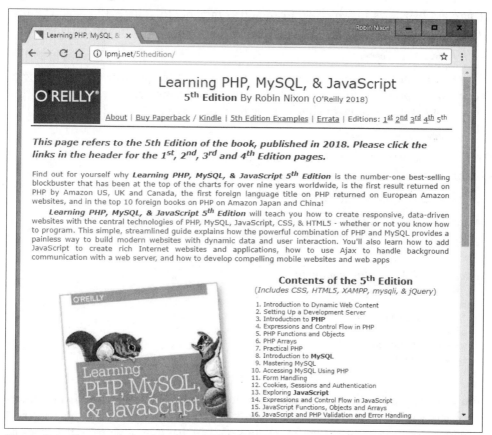

Figure 3-1. Chapter examples are available for download on the book's website (http:// lpmj.net/)

In addition to listing all the examples by chapter and example number (such as *example3-1.php*), the provided archive also contains an additional directory called *named_examples* in which you'll find all the examples I suggest you save using a specific filename (such as the upcoming Example 3-4, which should be saved as *test1.php*).

The Structure of PHP

We're going to cover quite a lot of ground in this section. It's not too difficult, but I recommend that you work your way through it carefully, as it sets the foundation for everything else in this book. As always, there are some useful questions at the end of the chapter that you can use to test how much you've learned.

Using Comments

There are two ways in which you can add comments to your PHP code. The first turns a single line into a comment by preceding it with a pair of forward slashes:

```
// This is a comment
```

This version of the comment feature is a great way to temporarily remove a line of code from a program that is giving you errors. For example, you could use such a comment to hide a debugging line of code until you need it, like this:

```
// echo "X equals $x";
```

You can also use this type of comment directly after a line of code to describe its action, like this:

```
$x += 10; // Increment $x by 10
```

When you need multiple-line comments, there's a second type of comment, which looks like Example 3-2.

Example 3-2. A multiline comment

```
<?php
/* This is a section
   of multiline comments
   which will not be
   interpreted */
?>
```

You can use the /* and */ pairs of characters to open and close comments almost anywhere you like inside your code. Most, if not all, programmers use this construct to temporarily comment out entire sections of code that do not work or that, for one reason or another, they do not wish to be interpreted.

A common error is to use /* and */ to comment out a large section of code that already contains a commented-out section that uses those characters. You can't nest comments this way; the PHP interpreter won't know where a comment ends and will display an error message. However, if you use a program editor or IDE with syntax highlighting, this type of error is easier to spot.

Basic Syntax

PHP is quite a simple language with roots in C and Perl, yet it looks more like Java. It is also very flexible, but there are a few rules that you need to learn about its syntax and structure.

Semicolons

You may have noticed in the previous examples that the PHP commands ended with a semicolon, like this:

```
$x += 10;
```

Probably the most common cause of errors you will encounter with PHP is forgetting this semicolon. This causes PHP to treat multiple statements like one statement, which it is unable to understand, prompting it to produce a `Parse error` message.

The $ symbol

The $ symbol has come to be used in many different ways by different programming languages. For example, in the BASIC language, it was used to terminate variable names to denote them as strings.

In PHP, however, you must place a $ in front of *all* variables. This is required to make the PHP parser faster, as it instantly knows whenever it comes across a variable. Whether your variables are numbers, strings, or arrays, they should all look something like those in Example 3-3.

Example 3-3. Three different types of variable assignment

```
<?php
  $mycounter = 1;
  $mystring  = "Hello";
  $myarray   = array("One", "Two", "Three");
?>
```

And really that's pretty much all the syntax that you have to remember. Unlike languages such as Python, which are very strict about how you indent and lay out your code, PHP leaves you completely free to use (or not use) all the indenting and spacing you like. In fact, sensible use of whitespace is generally encouraged (along with comprehensive commenting) to help you understand your code when you come back to it. It also helps other programmers when they have to maintain your code.

Variables

There's a simple metaphor that will help you understand what PHP variables are all about. Just think of them as little (or big) matchboxes! That's right—matchboxes that you've painted over and written names on.

String variables

Imagine you have a matchbox on which you have written the word *username*. You then write *Fred Smith* on a piece of paper and place it into the box (see Figure 3-2). Well, that's the same process as assigning a string value to a variable, like this:

```
$username = "Fred Smith";
```

Figure 3-2. You can think of variables as matchboxes containing items

The quotation marks indicate that "Fred Smith" is a *string* of characters. You must enclose each string in either quotation marks or apostrophes (single quotes), although there is a subtle difference between the two types of quote, which is explained later. When you want to see what's in the box, you open it, take the piece of paper out, and read it. In PHP, doing so looks like this (which displays the contents of the variable to screen):

```
echo $username;
```

Or you can assign it to another variable (photocopy the paper and place the copy in another matchbox), like this:

```
$current_user = $username;
```

If you are keen to start trying out PHP for yourself, you could enter the examples in this chapter into an IDE (as recommended at the end of Chapter 2) to see instant results, or you could enter the code in Example 3-4 into a program editor and save it to your server's document root directory (also discussed in Chapter 2) as *test1.php*.

Example 3-4. Your first PHP program

```php
<?php // test1.php
  $username = "Fred Smith";
  echo $username;
  echo "<br>";
  $current_user = $username;
  echo $current_user;
?>
```

Now you can call it up by entering the following into your browser's address bar:

```
http://localhost/test1.php
```

 In the unlikely event that during the installation of your web server (as detailed in Chapter 2) you changed the port assigned to the server to anything other than 80, then you must place that port number within the URL in this and all other examples in this book. So, for example, if you changed the port to 8080, the preceding URL would become this:

```
http://localhost:8080/test1.php
```

I won't mention this again, so just remember to use the port number (if required) when trying examples or writing your own code.

The result of running this code should be two occurrences of the name *Fred Smith*, the first of which is the result of the echo $username command and the second of the echo $current_user command.

Numeric variables

Variables don't have to contain just strings—they can contain numbers too. If we return to the matchbox analogy, to store the number 17 in the variable $count, the equivalent would be placing, say, 17 beads in a matchbox on which you have written the word *count*:

```
$count = 17;
```

You could also use a floating-point number (containing a decimal point). The syntax is the same:

```
$count = 17.5;
```

To see the contents of the matchbox, you would simply open it and count the beads. In PHP, you would assign the value of $count to another variable or perhaps just echo it to the web browser.

Arrays

So what are arrays? Well, you can think of them as several matchboxes glued together. For example, let's say we want to store the player names for a five-person soccer team in an array called $team. To do this, we could glue five matchboxes side by side and write down the names of all the players on separate pieces of paper, placing one in each matchbox.

Across the top of the whole matchbox assembly we would write the word *team* (see Figure 3-3). The equivalent of this in PHP would be the following:

```
$team = array('Bill', 'Mary', 'Mike', 'Chris', 'Anne');
```

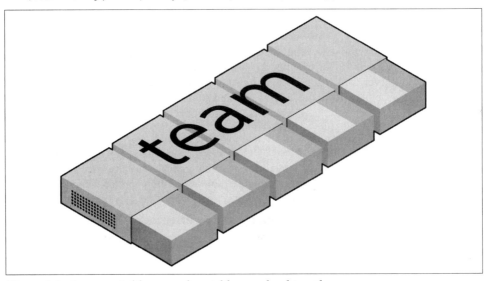

Figure 3-3. An array is like several matchboxes glued together

This syntax is more complicated than the other examples you've seen so far. The array-building code consists of the following construct:

```
array();
```

with five strings inside. Each string is enclosed in apostrophes, and strings must be separated with commas.

If we then wanted to know who player 4 is, we could use this command:

```
echo $team[3]; // Displays the name Chris
```

The reason the previous statement has the number 3, not 4, is because the first element of a PHP array is actually the zeroth element, so the player numbers will therefore be 0 through 4.

Two-dimensional arrays

There's a lot more you can do with arrays. For example, instead of being single-dimensional lines of matchboxes, they can be two-dimensional matrixes or can even have more dimensions.

As an example of a two-dimensional array, let's say we want to keep track of a game of tic-tac-toe, which requires a data structure of nine cells arranged in a 3 × 3 square. To represent this with matchboxes, imagine nine of them glued to each other in a matrix of three rows by three columns (see Figure 3-4).

Figure 3-4. A multidimensional array simulated with matchboxes

You can now place a piece of paper with either an *x* or an *o* on it in the correct match-box for each move played. To do this in PHP code, you have to set up an array containing three more arrays, as in Example 3-5, in which the array is set up with a game already in progress.

Example 3-5. Defining a two-dimensional array

```php
<?php
  $oxo = array(array('x', ' ', 'o'),
               array('o', 'o', 'x'),
               array('x', 'o', ' '));
?>
```

Once again, we've moved up a step in complexity, but it's easy to understand if you grasp the basic array syntax. There are three `array()` constructs nested inside the outer `array()` construct. We've filled each row with an array consisting of just one character: an *x*, an *o*, or a blank space. (We use a blank space so that all the cells will be the same width when they are displayed.)

To then return the third element in the second row of this array, you would use the following PHP command, which will display an x:

```
echo $oxo[1][2];
```

Remember that array indexes (pointers at elements within an array) start from zero, not one, so the [1] in the previous command refers to the second of the three arrays, and the [2] references the third position within that array. This command will return the contents of the matchbox three along and two down.

As mentioned, we can support arrays with even more dimensions by simply creating more arrays within arrays. However, we will not be covering arrays of more than two dimensions in this book.

And don't worry if you're still having difficulty coming to grips with using arrays, as the subject is explained in detail in Chapter 6.

Variable-naming rules

When creating PHP variables, you must follow these four rules:

- Variable names, after the dollar sign, must start with a letter of the alphabet or the _ (underscore) character.
- Variable names can contain only the characters a-z, A-Z, 0-9, and _ (underscore).
- Variable names may not contain spaces. If a variable name must comprise more than one word, a good idea is to separate the words with the _ (underscore) character (e.g., $user_name).
- Variable names are case-sensitive. The variable $High_Score is not the same as the variable $high_score.

To allow extended ASCII characters that include accents, PHP also supports the bytes from 127 through 255 in variable names. But unless your code will be maintained only by programmers who are used to those characters, it's probably best to avoid them, because programmers using English keyboards will have difficulty accessing them.

Operators

Operators let you specify mathematical operations to perform, such as addition, subtraction, multiplication, and division. But several other types of operators exist too, such as the string, comparison, and logical operators. Math in PHP looks a lot like plain arithmetic—for instance, the following statement outputs 8:

```
echo 6 + 2;
```

Before moving on to learn what PHP can do for you, take a moment to learn about the various operators it provides.

Arithmetic operators

Arithmetic operators do what you would expect—they are used to perform mathematics. You can use them for the main four operations (add, subtract, multiply, and divide) as well as to find a modulus (the remainder after a division) and to increment or decrement a value (see Table 3-1).

Table 3-1. Arithmetic operators

Operator	Description	Example
+	Addition	$j + 1
-	Subtraction	$j - 6
*	Multiplication	$j * 11
/	Division	$j / 4
%	Modulus (the remainder after a division is performed)	$j % 9
++	Increment	++$j
--	Decrement	--$j
**	Exponentiation (or power)	$j**2

Assignment operators

These operators assign values to variables. They start with the very simple = and move on to +=, -=, and so on (see Table 3-2). The operator += adds the value on the right side to the variable on the left, instead of totally replacing the value on the left. Thus, if $count starts with the value 5, the statement:

```
$count += 1;
```

sets $count to 6, just like the more familiar assignment statement:

```
$count = $count + 1;
```

Table 3-2. Assignment operators

Operator	Example	Equivalent to
=	$j = 15	$j = 15
+=	$j += 5	$j = $j + 5
-=	$j -= 3	$j = $j - 3
*=	$j *= 8	$j = $j * 8
/=	$j /= 16	$j = $j / 16
.=	$j .= $k	$j = $j . $k
%=	$j %= 4	$j = $j % 4

Comparison operators

Comparison operators are generally used inside a construct such as an `if` statement in which you need to compare two items. For example, you may wish to know whether a variable you have been incrementing has reached a specific value, or whether another variable is less than a set value, and so on (see Table 3-3).

Table 3-3. Comparison operators

Operator	Description	Example
==	Is *equal* to	$j == 4
!=	Is *not equal* to	$j != 21
>	Is *greater than*	$j > 3
<	Is *less than*	$j < 100
>=	Is *greater than or equal to*	$j >= 15
<=	Is *less than or equal to*	$j <= 8
<>	Is *not equal to* to	$j <> 23
===	Is *identical to* to	$j === "987"
!==	Is *not identical to* to	$j !== "1.2e3"

Note the difference between = and ==. The first is an assignment operator, and the second is a comparison operator. Even advanced programmers can sometimes mix up the two when coding hurriedly, so be careful.

Logical operators

If you haven't used them before, logical operators may at first seem a little daunting. But just think of them the way you would use logic in English. For example, you might say to yourself, "If the time is later than 12 p.m. and earlier than 2 p.m., have lunch." In PHP, the code for this might look something like the following (using military time):

```
if ($hour > 12 && $hour < 14) dolunch();
```

Here we have moved the set of instructions for actually going to lunch into a function that we will have to create later called dolunch.

As the previous example shows, you generally use a logical operator to combine the results of two of the comparison operators shown in the previous section. A logical operator can also be input to another logical operator: "If the time is later than 12 p.m. and earlier than 2 p.m., or if the smell of a roast is permeating the hallway and there are plates on the table." As a rule, if something has a TRUE or FALSE value, it can be input to a logical operator. A logical operator takes two true or false inputs and produces a true or false result.

Table 3-4 shows the logical operators.

Table 3-4. Logical operators

Operator	Description	Example
&&	*And*	`$j == 3 && $k == 2`
and	Low-precedence *and*	`$j == 3 and $k == 2`
||	*Or*	`$j < 5 || $j > 10`
or	Low-precedence *or*	`$j < 5 or $j > 10`
!	*Not*	`! ($j == $k)`
xor	*Exclusive or*	`$j xor $k`

Note that && is usually interchangeable with and; the same is true for || and or. However, because and and or have a lower precedence you should avoid using them except when they are the only option, as in the following statement, which *must* use the or operator (|| cannot be used to force a second statement to execute if the first fails):

```
$html = file_get_contents($site) or die("Cannot download from $site");
```

The most unusual of these operators is xor, which stands for *exclusive or* and returns a TRUE value if either value is TRUE, but a FALSE value if both inputs are TRUE or both inputs are FALSE. To understand this, imagine that you want to concoct your own cleaner for household items. Ammonia makes a good cleaner, and so does bleach, so you want your cleaner to have one of these. But the cleaner must not have both, because the combination is hazardous. In PHP, you could represent this as follows:

```
$ingredient = $ammonia xor $bleach;
```

In this example, if either $ammonia or $bleach is TRUE, $ingredient will also be set to TRUE. But if both are TRUE or both are FALSE, $ingredient will be set to FALSE.

Variable Assignment

The syntax to assign a value to a variable is always *variable = value*. Or, to reassign the value to another variable, it is *other_variable = variable*.

There are also a couple of other assignment operators that you will find useful. For example, we've already seen this:

```
$x += 10;
```

which tells the PHP parser to add the value on the right (in this instance, the value 10) to the variable $x. Likewise, we could subtract as follows:

```
$y -= 10;
```

Variable incrementing and decrementing

Adding or subtracting 1 is such a common operation that PHP provides special operators for it. You can use one of the following in place of the += and -= operators:

```
++$x;
--$y;
```

In conjunction with a test (an if statement), you could use the following code:

```
if (++$x == 10) echo $x;
```

This tells PHP to *first* increment the value of $x and then to test whether it has the value 10 and, if it does, to output its value. But you can also require PHP to increment (or, as in the following example, decrement) a variable *after* it has tested the value, like this:

```
if ($y-- == 0) echo $y;
```

which gives a subtly different result. Suppose $y starts out as 0 before the statement is executed. The comparison will return a TRUE result, but $y will be set to –1 after the comparison is made. So what will the echo statement display: 0 or –1? Try to guess, and then try out the statement in a PHP processor to confirm. Because this combination of statements is confusing, it should be taken as just an educational example and not as a guide to good programming style.

In short, a variable is incremented or decremented before the test if the operator is placed before the variable, whereas the variable is incremented or decremented after the test if the operator is placed after the variable.

By the way, the correct answer to the previous question is that the echo statement will display the result –1, because $y was decremented right after it was accessed in the if statement, and before the echo statement.

String concatenation

Concatenation is a somewhat arcane term for putting something after another thing. So, string concatenation uses the period (.) to append one string of characters to another. The simplest way to do this is as follows:

```
echo "You have " . $msgs . " messages.";
```

Assuming that the variable $msgs is set to the value 5, the output from this line of code will be the following:

You have 5 messages.

Just as you can add a value to a numeric variable with the += operator, you can append one string to another using .=, like this:

```
$bulletin .= $newsflash;
```

In this case, if $bulletin contains a news bulletin and $newsflash has a news flash, the command appends the news flash to the news bulletin so that $bulletin now comprises both strings of text.

String types

PHP supports two types of strings that are denoted by the type of quotation mark that you use. If you wish to assign a literal string, preserving the exact contents, you should use single quotation marks (apostrophes), like this:

```
$info = 'Preface variables with a $ like this: $variable';
```

In this case, every character within the single-quoted string is assigned to $info. If you had used double quotes, PHP would have attempted to evaluate $variable as a variable.

On the other hand, when you want to include the value of a variable inside a string, you do so by using double-quoted strings:

```
echo "This week $count people have viewed your profile";
```

As you will realize, this syntax also offers a simpler option to concatenation in which you don't need to use a period, or close and reopen quotes, to append one string to another. This is called *variable substitution*, and some programmers use it extensively whereas others don't use it at all.

Escaping characters

Sometimes a string needs to contain characters with special meanings that might be interpreted incorrectly. For example, the following line of code will not work, because the second quotation mark encountered in the word *spelling's* will tell the PHP parser that the string's end has been reached. Consequently, the rest of the line will be rejected as an error:

```
$text = 'My spelling's atroshus'; // Erroneous syntax
```

To correct this, you can add a backslash directly before the offending quotation mark to tell PHP to treat the character literally and not to interpret it:

```
$text = 'My spelling\'s still atroshus';
```

And you can perform this trick in almost all situations in which PHP would otherwise return an error by trying to interpret a character. For example, the following double-quoted string will be correctly assigned:

```
$text = "She wrote upon it, \"Return to sender\".";
```

Additionally, you can use escape characters to insert various special characters into strings, such as tabs, newlines, and carriage returns. These are represented, as you might guess, by \t, \n, and \r. Here is an example using tabs to lay out a heading—it is included here merely to illustrate escapes, because in web pages there are always better ways to do layout:

```
$heading = "Date\tName\tPayment";
```

These special backslash-preceded characters work only in double-quoted strings. In single-quoted strings, the preceding string would be displayed with the ugly \t sequences instead of tabs. Within single-quoted strings, only the escaped apostrophe (\') and escaped backslash itself (\\) are recognized as escaped characters.

Multiple-Line Commands

There are times when you need to output quite a lot of text from PHP, and using several echo (or print) statements would be time-consuming and messy. To overcome this, PHP offers two conveniences. The first is just to put multiple lines between quotes, as in Example 3-6. Variables can also be assigned, as in Example 3-7.

Example 3-6. A multiline string echo statement

```php
<?php
  $author = "Steve Ballmer";

  echo "Developers, developers, developers, developers, developers,
  developers, developers, developers, developers!

  - $author.";
?>
```

Example 3-7. A multiline string assignment

```php
<?php
  $author = "Bill Gates";
```

```
  $text = "Measuring programming progress by lines of code is like
  Measuring aircraft building progress by weight.

  - $author.";
?>
```

PHP also offers a multiline sequence using the <<< operator—commonly referred to as a *here-document* or *heredoc*—as a way of specifying a string literal, preserving the line breaks and other whitespace (including indentation) in the text. Its use can be seen in Example 3-8.

Example 3-8. Alternative multiline echo statement

```
<?php
  $author = "Brian W. Kernighan";

  echo <<<_END
  Debugging is twice as hard as writing the code in the first place.
  Therefore, if you write the code as cleverly as possible, you are,
  by definition, not smart enough to debug it.

  - $author.
_END;
?>
```

This code tells PHP to output everything between the two _END tags as if it were a double-quoted string (except that quotes in a heredoc do not need to be escaped). This means it's possible, for example, for a developer to write entire sections of HTML directly into PHP code and then just replace specific dynamic parts with PHP variables.

It is important to remember that the closing _END; *must* appear right at the start of a new line and it must be the *only* thing on that line—not even a comment is allowed to be added after it (nor even a single space). Once you have closed a multiline block, you are free to use the same tag name again.

 Remember: using the <<<_END..._END; heredoc construct, you don't have to add \n linefeed characters to send a linefeed—just press Return and start a new line. Also, unlike in either a double-quote- or single-quote-delimited string, you are free to use all the single and double quotes you like within a heredoc, without escaping them by preceding them with a backslash (\).

Example 3-9 shows how to use the same syntax to assign multiple lines to a variable.

Example 3-9. A multiline string variable assignment

```php
<?php
  $author = "Scott Adams";

  $out = <<<_END
  Normal people believe that if it ain't broke, don't fix it.
  Engineers believe that if it ain't broke, it doesn't have enough
  features yet.

    - $author.
_END;
echo $out;
?>
```

The variable $out will then be populated with the contents between the two tags. If you were appending, rather than assigning, you could also have used .= in place of = to append the string to $out.

Be careful not to place a semicolon directly after the first occurrence of _END, as that would terminate the multiline block before it had even started and cause a Parse error message. The only place for the semicolon is after the terminating _END tag, although it is safe to use semicolons within the block as normal text characters.

By the way, the _END tag is simply one I chose for these examples because it is unlikely to be used anywhere else in PHP code and is therefore unique. You can use any tag you like, such as _SECTION1 or _OUTPUT and so on. Also, to help differentiate tags such as this from variables or functions, the general practice is to preface them with an underscore, but you don't have to use one if you choose not to.

Laying out text over multiple lines is usually just a convenience to make your PHP code easier to read, because once it is displayed in a web page, HTML formatting rules take over and whitespace is suppressed (but $author in our example will still be replaced with the variable's value).

So, for example, if you load these multiline output examples into a browser, they will *not* display over several lines, because all browsers treat newlines just like spaces. However, if you use the browser's View Source feature, you will find that the newlines are correctly placed, and that PHP preserved the line breaks.

Variable Typing

PHP is a very loosely typed language. This means that variables do not have to be declared before they are used, and that PHP always converts variables to the type required by their context when they are accessed.

For example, you can create a multiple-digit number and extract the *n*th digit from it simply by assuming it to be a string. In Example 3-10, the numbers 12345 and 67890 are multiplied together, returning a result of 838102050, which is then placed in the variable $number.

Example 3-10. Automatic conversion from a number to a string

```php
<?php
  $number = 12345 * 67890;
  echo substr($number, 3, 1);
?>
```

At the point of the assignment, $number is a numeric variable. But on the second line, a call is placed to the PHP function substr, which asks for one character to be returned from $number, starting at the fourth position (remember that PHP offsets start from zero). To do this, PHP turns $number into a nine-character string, so that substr can access it and return the character, which in this case is 1.

The same goes for turning a string into a number, and so on. In Example 3-11, the variable $pi is set to a string value, which is then automatically turned into a floating-point number in the third line by the equation for calculating a circle's area, which outputs the value 78.5398175.

Example 3-11. Automatically converting a string to a number

```php
<?php
  $pi     = "3.1415927";
  $radius = 5;
  echo $pi * ($radius * $radius);
?>
```

In practice, what this all means is that you don't have to worry too much about your variable types. Just assign them values that make sense to you, and PHP will convert them if necessary. Then, when you want to retrieve values, just ask for them—for example, with an echo statement.

Constants

Constants are similar to variables, holding information to be accessed later, except that they are what they sound like—constant. In other words, once you have defined one, its value is set for the remainder of the program and cannot be altered.

One example of a use for a constant is to hold the location of your server root (the folder with the main files of your website). You would define such a constant like this:

```php
define("ROOT_LOCATION", "/usr/local/www/");
```

Then, to read the contents of the variable, you just refer to it like a regular variable (but it isn't preceded by a dollar sign):

```
$directory = ROOT_LOCATION;
```

Now, whenever you need to run your PHP code on a different server with a different folder configuration, you have only a single line of code to change.

 The main two things you have to remember about constants are that they must *not* be prefaced with a $ (unlike regular variables), and that you can define them only using the define function.

It is generally considered a good practice to use only uppercase letters for constant variable names, especially if other people will also read your code.

Predefined Constants

PHP comes ready-made with dozens of predefined constants that you won't generally use as a beginner. However, there are a few—known as the *magic constants*—that you will find useful. The names of the magic constants always have two underscores at the beginning and two at the end, so that you won't accidentally try to name one of your own constants with a name that is already taken. They are detailed in Table 3-5. The concepts referred to in the table will be introduced in future chapters.

Table 3-5. PHP's magic constants

Magic constant	Description
__LINE__	The current line number of the file.
__FILE__	The full path and filename of the file. If used inside an include, the name of the included file is returned. Some operating systems allow aliases for directories, called *symbolic links*; in __FILE__ these are always changed to the actual directories.
__DIR__	The directory of the file. (Added in PHP 5.3.0.) If used inside an include, the directory of the included file is returned. This is equivalent to *dirname(*__FILE__*)*. This directory name does not have a trailing slash unless it is the root directory.
__FUNCTION__	The function name. (Added in PHP 4.3.0.) As of PHP 5, returns the function name as it was declared (case-sensitive). In PHP 4, its value is always lowercase.
__CLASS__	The class name. (Added in PHP 4.3.0.) As of PHP 5, returns the class name as it was declared (case-sensitive). In PHP 4, its value is always lowercased.
__METHOD__	The class method name. (Added in PHP 5.0.0.) The method name is returned as it was declared (case-sensitive).
__NAMESPACE__	The name of the current namespace. (Added in PHP 5.3.0.) This constant is defined at compile time (case-sensitive).

One handy use of these variables is for debugging, when you need to insert a line of code to see whether the program flow reaches it:

```
echo "This is line " . __LINE__ . " of file " . __FILE__;
```

This prints the current program line in the current file (including the path) to the web browser.

The Difference Between the echo and print Commands

So far, you have seen the echo command used in a number of different ways to output text from the server to your browser. In some cases, a string literal has been output. In others, strings have first been concatenated or variables have been evaluated. I've also shown output spread over multiple lines.

But there is an alternative to echo that you can use: print. The two commands are quite similar, but print is a function-like construct that takes a single parameter and has a return value (which is always 1), whereas echo is purely a PHP language construct. Since both commands are constructs, neither requires parentheses.

By and large, the echo command usually will be a tad faster than print, because it doesn't set a return value. On the other hand, because it isn't implemented like a function, echo cannot be used as part of a more complex expression, whereas print can. Here's an example to output whether the value of a variable is TRUE or FALSE using print—something you could not perform in the same manner with echo, because it would display a Parse error message:

```
$b ? print "TRUE" : print "FALSE";
```

The question mark is simply a way of interrogating whether variable $b is TRUE or FALSE. Whichever command is on the left of the following colon is executed if $b is TRUE, whereas the command to the right of the colon is executed if $b is FALSE.

Generally, though, the examples in this book use echo, and I recommend that you do so as well until you reach such a point in your PHP development that you discover the need for using print.

Functions

Functions separate sections of code that perform a particular task. For example, maybe you often need to look up a date and return it in a certain format. That would be a good example to turn into a function. The code doing it might be only three lines long, but if you have to paste it into your program a dozen times, you're making your program unnecessarily large and complex if you don't use a function. And if you decide to change the date format later, putting it in a function means having to change it in only one place.

Placing code into a function not only shortens your program and makes it more readable, but also adds extra functionality (pun intended), because functions can be passed parameters to make them perform differently. They can also return values to the calling code.

To create a function, declare it in the manner shown in Example 3-12.

Example 3-12. A simple function declaration

```php
<?php
  function longdate($timestamp)
  {
    return date("l F jS Y", $timestamp);
  }
?>
```

This function returns a date in the format *Sunday May 2nd 2021*. Any number of parameters can be passed between the initial parentheses; we have chosen to accept just one. The curly braces enclose all the code that is executed when you later call the function. Note that the first letter within the date function call in this example is a lowercase letter L, not to be confused with the number 1.

To output today's date using this function, place the following call in your code:

```php
echo longdate(time());
```

If you need to print out the date 17 days ago, you now just have to issue the following call:

```php
echo longdate(time() - 17 * 24 * 60 * 60);
```

which passes to longdate the current time less the number of seconds since 17 days ago (17 days × 24 hours × 60 minutes × 60 seconds).

Functions can also accept multiple parameters and return multiple results, using techniques that I'll introduce over the following chapters.

Variable Scope

If you have a very long program, it's quite possible that you could start to run out of good variable names, but with PHP you can decide the *scope* of a variable. In other words, you can, for example, tell it that you want the variable $temp to be used only inside a particular function and to forget it was ever used when the function returns. In fact, this is the default scope for PHP variables.

Alternatively, you could inform PHP that a variable is global in scope and thus can be accessed by every other part of your program.

Local variables

Local variables are variables that are created within, and can be accessed only by, a function. They are generally temporary variables that are used to store partially processed results prior to the function's return.

One set of local variables is the list of arguments to a function. In the previous section, we defined a function that accepted a parameter named $timestamp. This is meaningful only in the body of the function; you can't get or set its value outside the function.

For another example of a local variable, take another look at the longdate function, which is modified slightly in Example 3-13.

Example 3-13. An expanded version of the longdate function

```php
<?php
  function longdate($timestamp)
  {
    $temp = date("l F jS Y", $timestamp);
    return "The date is $temp";
  }
?>
```

Here we have assigned the value returned by the date function to the temporary variable $temp, which is then inserted into the string returned by the function. As soon as the function returns, the $temp variable and its contents disappear, as if they had never been used at all.

Now, to see the effects of variable scope, let's look at some similar code in Example 3-14. Here $temp has been created *before* we call the longdate function.

Example 3-14. This attempt to access $temp in function longdate will fail

```php
<?php
  $temp = "The date is ";
  echo longdate(time());

  function longdate($timestamp)
  {
    return $temp . date("l F jS Y", $timestamp);
  }
?>
```

However, because $temp was neither created within the longdate function nor passed to it as a parameter, longdate cannot access it. Therefore, this code snippet outputs only the date, not the preceding text. In fact, depending on how PHP is configured, it may first display the error message Notice: Undefined variable: temp, something you don't want your users to see.

The reason for this is that, by default, variables created within a function are local to that function, and variables created outside of any functions can be accessed only by nonfunction code.

Some ways to repair Example 3-14 appear in Examples 3-15 and 3-16.

Example 3-15. Rewriting to refer to $temp within its local scope fixes the problem

```php
<?php
  $temp = "The date is ";
  echo $temp . longdate(time());

  function longdate($timestamp)
  {
    return date("l F jS Y", $timestamp);
  }
?>
```

Example 3-15 moves the reference to $temp out of the function. The reference appears in the same scope where the variable was defined.

Example 3-16. An alternative solution: passing $temp as an argument

```php
<?php
  $temp = "The date is ";
  echo longdate($temp, time());

  function longdate($text, $timestamp)
  {
    return $text . date("l F jS Y", $timestamp);
  }
?>
```

The solution in Example 3-16 passes $temp to the longdate function as an extra argument. longdate reads it into a temporary variable that it creates called $text and outputs the desired result.

 Forgetting the scope of a variable is a common programming error, so remembering how variable scope works will help you debug some quite obscure problems. Suffice it to say that unless you have declared a variable otherwise, its scope is limited to being local: either to the current function, or to the code outside of any functions, depending on whether it was first created or accessed inside or outside a function.

Global variables

There are cases when you need a variable to have *global* scope, because you want all your code to be able to access it. Also, some data may be large and complex, and you don't want to keep passing it as arguments to functions.

To access variables from global scope, add the keyword `global`. Let's assume that you have a way of logging your users into your website and want all your code to know whether it is interacting with a logged-in user or a guest. One way to do this is to use the `global` keyword before a variable such as `$is_logged_in`:

```
global $is_logged_in;
```

Now your login function simply has to set that variable to 1 upon a successful login attempt, or 0 upon failure. Because the scope of the variable is set to global, every line of code in your program can access it.

You should use variables given global access with caution, though. I recommend that you create them only when you absolutely cannot find another way of achieving the result you desire. In general, programs that are broken into small parts and segregated data are less buggy and easier to maintain. If you have a thousand-line program (and some day you will) in which you discover that a global variable has the wrong value at some point, how long will it take you to find the code that set it incorrectly?

Also, if you have too many variables with global scope, you run the risk of using one of those names again locally, or at least thinking you have used it locally, when in fact it has already been declared as global. All manner of strange bugs can arise from such situations.

 Sometimes I adopt the convention of making all variable names that require global access uppercase (just as it's recommended that constants should be uppercase) so that I can see at a glance the scope of a variable.

Static variables

In the section "Local variables" on page 57, I mentioned that the value of a local variable is wiped out when the function ends. If a function runs many times, it starts with a fresh copy of the variable and the previous setting has no effect.

Here's an interesting case. What if you have a local variable inside a function that you don't want any other parts of your code to have access to, but you would also like to keep its value for the next time the function is called? Why? Perhaps because you want a counter to track how many times a function is called. The solution is to declare a *static* variable, as shown in Example 3-17.

Example 3-17. A function using a static variable

```php
<?php
  function test()
  {
    static $count = 0;
    echo $count;
    $count++;
  }
?>
```

Here, the very first line of the function `test` creates a static variable called `$count` and initializes it to a value of `0`. The next line outputs the variable's value; the final one increments it.

The next time the function is called, because `$count` has already been declared, the first line of the function is skipped. Then the previously incremented value of `$count` is displayed before the variable is again incremented.

If you plan to use static variables, you should note that you cannot assign the result of an expression in their definitions. They can be initialized only with predetermined values (see Example 3-18).

Example 3-18. Allowed and disallowed static variable declarations

```php
<?php
  static $int = 0;          // Allowed
  static $int = 1+2;        // Disallowed (will produce a parse error)
  static $int = sqrt(144);  // Disallowed
?>
```

Superglobal variables

Starting with PHP 4.1.0, several predefined variables are available. These are known as *superglobal variables*, which means that they are provided by the PHP environment but are global within the program, accessible absolutely everywhere.

These superglobals contain lots of useful information about the currently running program and its environment (see Table 3-6). They are structured as associative arrays, a topic discussed in Chapter 6.

Table 3-6. PHP's superglobal variables

Superglobal name	Contents
$GLOBALS	All variables that are currently defined in the global scope of the script. The variable names are the keys of the array.
$_SERVER	Information such as headers, paths, and locations of scripts. The entries in this array are created by the web server, and there is no guarantee that every web server will provide any or all of these.

Superglobal name	Contents
$_GET	Variables passed to the current script via the HTTP GET method.
$_POST	Variables passed to the current script via the HTTP POST method.
$_FILES	Items uploaded to the current script via the HTTP POST method.
$_COOKIE	Variables passed to the current script via HTTP cookies.
$_SESSION	Session variables available to the current script.
$_REQUEST	Contents of information passed from the browser; by default, $_GET, $_POST, and $_COOKIE.
$_ENV	Variables passed to the current script via the environment method.

All of the superglobals (except for $GLOBALS) are named with a single initial underscore and only capital letters; therefore, you should avoid naming your own variables in this manner to avoid potential confusion.

To illustrate how you use them, let's look at a common example. Among the many nuggets of information supplied by superglobal variables is the URL of the page that referred the user to the current web page. This referring page information can be accessed like this:

```
$came_from = $_SERVER['HTTP_REFERER'];
```

It's that simple. Oh, and if the user came straight to your web page, such as by typing its URL directly into a browser, $came_from will be set to an empty string.

Superglobals and security

A word of caution is in order before you start using superglobal variables, because they are often used by hackers trying to find exploits to break into your website. What they do is load up $_POST, $_GET, or other superglobals with malicious code, such as Unix or MySQL commands that can damage or display sensitive data if you naïvely access them.

Therefore, you should always sanitize superglobals before using them. One way to do this is via the PHP htmlentities function. It converts all characters into HTML entities. For example, less-than and greater-than characters (< and >) are transformed into the strings < and > so that they are rendered harmless, as are all quotes and backslashes, and so on.

Therefore, a much better way to access $_SERVER (and other superglobals) is:

```
$came_from = htmlentities($_SERVER['HTTP_REFERER']);
```

 Using the htmlentities function for sanitization is an important practice in any circumstance where user or other third-party data is being processed for output, not just with superglobals.

This chapter has provided you with a solid introduction to using PHP. In Chapter 4, you'll start using what you've learned to build expressions and control program flow—in other words, do some actual programming.

But before moving on, I recommend that you test yourself with some (if not all) of the following questions to ensure that you have fully digested the contents of this chapter.

Questions

1. What tag is used to invoke PHP to start interpreting program code? And what is the short form of the tag?
2. What are the two types of comment tags?
3. Which character must be placed at the end of every PHP statement?
4. Which symbol is used to preface all PHP variables?
5. What can a variable store?
6. What is the difference between $variable = 1 and $variable == 1?
7. Why do you suppose that an underscore is allowed in variable names ($current_user), whereas hyphens are not ($current-user)?
8. Are variable names case-sensitive?
9. Can you use spaces in variable names?
10. How do you convert one variable type to another (say, a string to a number)?
11. What is the difference between ++$j and $j++?
12. Are the operators && and and interchangeable?
13. How can you create a multiline echo or assignment?
14. Can you redefine a constant?
15. How do you escape a quotation mark?
16. What is the difference between the echo and print commands?
17. What is the purpose of functions?
18. How can you make a variable accessible to all parts of a PHP program?
19. If you generate data within a function, what are a couple of ways to convey the data to the rest of the program?
20. What is the result of combining a string with a number?

See "Chapter 3 Answers" on page 714 in Appendix A for the answers to these questions.

CHAPTER 4

Expressions and Control Flow in PHP

The previous chapter introduced several topics in passing that this chapter covers more fully, such as making choices (branching) and creating complex expressions. In the previous chapter, I wanted to focus on the most basic syntax and operations in PHP, but I couldn't avoid touching on more advanced topics. Now I can fill in the background that you need to use these powerful PHP features properly.

In this chapter, you will get a thorough grounding in how PHP programming works in practice and how to control the flow of the program.

Expressions

Let's start with the most fundamental part of any programming language: *expressions*.

An expression is a combination of values, variables, operators, and functions that results in a value. It's familiar to anyone who has taken high-school algebra. Here's an example:

$$y = 3 \ (|2x| + 4)$$

Which in PHP would be:

```
$y = 3 * (abs(2 * $x) + 4);
```

The value returned (y in this mathematical statement, or y in the PHP) can be a number, a string, or a *Boolean value* (named after George Boole, a 19th-century English mathematician and philosopher). By now, you should be familiar with the first two value types, but I'll explain the third.

TRUE or FALSE?

A basic Boolean value can be either TRUE or FALSE. For example, the expression 20 > 9 (20 is greater than 9) is TRUE, and the expression 5 == 6 (5 is equal to 6) is FALSE. (You can combine such operations using other classic Boolean operators such as AND, OR, and XOR, which are covered later in this chapter.)

 Note that I am using uppercase letters for the names TRUE and FALSE. This is because they are predefined constants in PHP. You can use the lowercase versions if you prefer, as they are also predefined. In fact, the lowercase versions are more stable, because PHP does not allow you to redefine them; the uppercase ones may be redefined, which is something you should bear in mind if you import third-party code.

PHP doesn't actually print the predefined constants if you ask it to do so as in Example 4-1. For each line, the example prints out a letter followed by a colon and a predefined constant. PHP arbitrarily assigns a numerical value of 1 to TRUE, so 1 is displayed after a: when the example runs. Even more mysteriously, because b: evaluates to FALSE, it does not show any value. In PHP the constant FALSE is defined as NULL, another predefined constant that denotes nothing.

Example 4-1. Outputting the values of TRUE and FALSE

```php
<?php // test2.php
  echo "a: [" . TRUE  . "]<br>";
  echo "b: [" . FALSE . "]<br>";
?>
```

The <br> tags are there to create line breaks and thus separate the output into two lines in HTML. Here is the output:

```
a: [1]
b: []
```

Turning to Boolean expressions, Example 4-2 shows some simple expressions: the two I mentioned earlier, plus a couple more.

Example 4-2. Four simple Boolean expressions

```php
<?php
  echo "a: [" . (20 > 9) . "]<br>";
  echo "b: [" . (5 == 6) . "]<br>";
  echo "c: [" . (1 == 0) . "]<br>";
  echo "d: [" . (1 == 1) . "]<br>";
?>
```

The output from this code is:

```
a: [1]
b: []
c: []
d: [1]
```

By the way, in some languages FALSE may be defined as 0 or even -1, so it's worth checking on its definition in each language you use. Luckily, Boolean expressions are usually buried in other code, so you don't normally have to worry about what TRUE and FALSE look like internally. In fact, even those names rarely appear in code.

Literals and Variables

These are the most basic elements of programming, and the building blocks of expressions. A *literal* simply means something that evaluates to itself, such as the number 73 or the string "Hello". A variable, which we've already seen has a name beginning with a dollar sign, evaluates to the value that has been assigned to it. The simplest expression is just a single literal or variable, because both return a value.

Example 4-3 shows three literals and two variables, all of which return values, albeit of different types.

Example 4-3. Literals and variables

```php
<?php
  $myname = "Brian";
  $myage  = 37;

  echo "a: " . 73      . "<br>"; // Numeric literal
  echo "b: " . "Hello" . "<br>"; // String literal
  echo "c: " . FALSE   . "<br>"; // Constant literal
  echo "d: " . $myname . "<br>"; // String variable
  echo "e: " . $myage  . "<br>"; // Numeric variable
?>
```

And, as you'd expect, you see a return value from all of these with the exception of c:, which evaluates to FALSE, returning nothing in the following output:

```
a: 73
b: Hello
c:
d: Brian
e: 37
```

In conjunction with operators, it's possible to create more complex expressions that evaluate to useful results.

Programmers combine expressions with other language constructs, such as the assignment operators we saw earlier, to form *statements*. Example 4-4 shows two statements. The first assigns the result of the expression 366 - $day_number to the variable $days_to_new_year, and the second outputs a friendly message only if the expression $days_to_new_year < 30 evaluates to TRUE.

Example 4-4. An expression and a statement

```
<?php
  $days_to_new_year = 366 - $day_number; // Expression

  if ($days_to_new_year < 30)
  {
    echo "Not long now till new year";  // Statement
  }
?>
```

Operators

PHP offers a lot of powerful operators of different types—arithmetic, string, logical, assignment, comparison, and more (see Table 4-1).

Table 4-1. PHP operator types

Operator	Description	Example
Arithmetic	Basic mathematics	$a + $b
Array	Array union	$a + $b
Assignment	Assign values	$a = $b + 23
Bitwise	Manipulate bits within bytes	12 ^ 9
Comparison	Compare two values	$a < $b
Execution	Execute contents of backticks	`ls -al`
Increment/decrement	Add or subtract 1	$a++
Logical	Boolean	$a and $b
String	Concatenation	$a . $b

Each operator takes a different number of operands:

- *Unary* operators, such as incrementing ($a++) or negation (!$a), take a single operand.
- *Binary* operators, which represent the bulk of PHP operators (including addition, subtraction, multiplication, and division), take two operands.

- The one *ternary* operator, which takes the form `expr ? x : y`, requires three operands. It's a terse, single-line `if` statement that returns x if m `expr` is TRUE and y if `expr` is FALSE.

Operator Precedence

If all operators had the same precedence, they would be processed in the order in which they are encountered. In fact, many operators do have the same precedence. Take a look at Example 4-5.

Example 4-5. Three equivalent expressions

```
1 + 2 + 3 - 4 + 5
2 - 4 + 5 + 3 + 1
5 + 2 - 4 + 1 + 3
```

Here you will see that although the numbers (and their preceding operators) have been moved around, the result of each expression is the value 7, because the plus and minus operators have the same precedence. We can try the same thing with multiplication and division (see Example 4-6).

Example 4-6. Three expressions that are also equivalent

```
1 * 2 * 3 / 4 * 5
2 / 4 * 5 * 3 * 1
5 * 2 / 4 * 1 * 3
```

Here the resulting value is always 7.5. But things change when we mix operators with *different* precedences in an expression, as in Example 4-7.

Example 4-7. Three expressions using operators of mixed precedence

```
1 + 2 * 3 - 4 * 5
2 - 4 * 5 * 3 + 1
5 + 2 - 4 + 1 * 3
```

If there were no operator precedence, these three expressions would evaluate to 25, –29, and 12, respectively. But because multiplication and division take precedence over addition and subtraction, the expressions are evaluated as if there were parentheses around these parts of the expressions, just like mathematical notation (see Example 4-8).

Example 4-8. Three expressions showing implied parentheses

```
1 + (2 * 3) - (4 * 5)
2 - (4 * 5 * 3) + 1
5 + 2 - 4 + (1 * 3)
```

PHP evaluates the subexpressions within parentheses first to derive the semi-completed expressions in Example 4-9.

Example 4-9. After evaluating the subexpressions in parentheses

```
1 + (6) - (20)
2 - (60) + 1
5 + 2 - 4 + (3)
```

The final results of these expressions are –13, –57, and 6, respectively (quite different from the results of 25, –29, and 12 that we would have seen had there been no operator precedence).

Of course, you can override the default operator precedence by inserting your own parentheses and forcing whatever order you want (see Example 4-10).

Example 4-10. Forcing left-to-right evaluation

```
((1 + 2) * 3 - 4) * 5
(2 - 4) * 5 * 3 + 1
(5 + 2 - 4 + 1) * 3
```

With parentheses correctly inserted, we now see the values 25, –29, and 12, respectively.

Table 4-2 lists PHP's operators in order of precedence from high to low.

Table 4-2. The precedence of PHP operators (high to low)

Operator(s)	Type
( )	Parentheses
++ --	Increment/decrement
!	Logical
* / %	Arithmetic
+ - .	Arithmetic and string
<< >>	Bitwise
< <= > >= <>	Comparison
== != === !==	Comparison
&	Bitwise (and references)
^	Bitwise

Operator(s)	Type
|	Bitwise
&&	Logical
||	Logical
? :	Ternary
= += -= *= /= .= %= &= != ^= <<= >>=	Assignment
and	Logical
xor	Logical
or	Logical

The order in this table is not arbitrary, but carefully designed so that the most common and intuitive precedences are the ones you can get without parentheses. For instance, you can separate two comparisons with an and or or and get what you'd expect.

Associativity

We've been looking at processing expressions from left to right, except where operator precedence is in effect. But some operators require processing from right to left, and this direction of processing is called the operator's *associativity*. For some operators, there is no associativity.

Associativity (as detailed in Table 4-3) becomes important in cases in which you do not explicitly force precedence, so you need to be aware of the default actions of operators.

Table 4-3. Operator associativity

Operator	Description	Associativity
< <= >= == != === !== <>	Comparison	None
!	Logical NOT	Right
~	Bitwise NOT	Right
++ --	Increment and decrement	Right
(int)	Cast to an integer	Right
(double) (float) (real)	Cast to a floating-point number	Right
(string)	Cast to a string	Right
(array)	Cast to an array	Right
(object)	Cast to an object	Right
@	Inhibit error reporting	Right
= += -= *= /=	Assignment	Right
.= %= &= |= ^= <<= >>=	Assignment	Right
+	Addition and unary plus	Left
-	Subtraction and negation	Left

Operator	Description	Associativity
*	Multiplication	Left
/	Division	Left
%	Modulus	Left
.	String concatenation	Left
<< >> & ^ |	Bitwise	Left
?:	Ternary	Left
|| && and or xor	Logical	Left
,	Separator	Left

For example, let's take a look at the assignment operator in Example 4-11, where three variables are all set to the value 0.

Example 4-11. A multiple-assignment statement

```php
<?php
  $level = $score = $time = 0;
?>
```

This multiple assignment is possible only if the rightmost part of the expression is evaluated first, and then processing continues in a right-to-left direction.

 As a newcomer to PHP, you should avoid the potential pitfalls of operator associativity by always nesting your subexpressions within parentheses to force the order of evaluation. This will also help other programmers who may have to maintain your code to understand what is happening.

Relational Operators

Relational operators answer questions such as "Does this variable have a value of zero?" and "Which variable has a greater value?" These operators test two operands and return a Boolean result of either TRUE or FALSE. There are three types of relational operators: *equality*, *comparison*, and *logical*.

Equality

As we've already seen a few times in this chapter, the equality operator is == (two equals signs). It is important not to confuse it with the = (single equals sign) assignment operator. In Example 4-12, the first statement assigns a value and the second tests it for equality.

Example 4-12. Assigning a value and testing for equality

```php
<?php
  $month = "March";

  if ($month == "March") echo "It's springtime";
?>
```

As you see, by returning either TRUE or FALSE, the equality operator enables you to test for conditions using, for example, an if statement. But that's not the whole story, because PHP is a loosely typed language. If the two operands of an equality expression are of different types, PHP will convert them to whatever type makes the best sense to it. A rarely used *identity* operator, which consists of three equals signs in a row, can be used to compare items without doing conversion.

For example, any strings composed entirely of numbers will be converted to numbers whenever compared with a number. In Example 4-13, $a and $b are two different strings, and we would therefore expect neither of the if statements to output a result.

Example 4-13. The equality and identity operators

```php
<?php
  $a = "1000";
  $b = "+1000";

  if ($a == $b)  echo "1";
  if ($a === $b) echo "2";
?>
```

However, if you run the example, you will see that it outputs the number 1, which means that the first if statement evaluated to TRUE. This is because both strings were first converted to numbers, and 1000 is the same numerical value as +1000. In contrast, the second if statement uses the identity operator, so it compares $a and $b as strings, sees that they are different, and thus doesn't output anything.

As with forcing operator precedence, whenever you have any doubt about how PHP will convert operand types, you can use the identity operator to turn this behavior off.

In the same way that you can use the equality operator to test for operands being equal, you can test for them *not* being equal using !=, the inequality operator. Take a look at Example 4-14, which is a rewrite of Example 4-13, in which the equality and identity operators have been replaced with their inverses.

Example 4-14. The inequality and not-identical operators

```php
<?php
  $a = "1000";
  $b = "+1000";

  if ($a != $b)  echo "1";
  if ($a !== $b) echo "2";
?>
```

And, as you might expect, the first if statement does not output the number 1, because the code is asking whether $a and $b are *not* equal to each other numerically.

Instead, this code outputs the number 2, because the second if statement is asking whether $a and $b are *not* identical to each other in their actual string type, and the answer is TRUE; they are not the same.

Comparison operators

Using comparison operators, you can test for more than just equality and inequality. PHP also gives you > (is greater than), < (is less than), >= (is greater than or equal to), and <= (is less than or equal to) to play with. Example 4-15 shows these in use.

Example 4-15. The four comparison operators

```php
<?php
  $a = 2; $b = 3;

  if ($a > $b)  echo "$a is greater than $b<br>";
  if ($a < $b)  echo "$a is less than $b<br>";
  if ($a >= $b) echo "$a is greater than or equal to $b<br>";
  if ($a <= $b) echo "$a is less than or equal to $b<br>";
?>
```

In this example, where $a is 2 and $b is 3, the following is output:

```
2 is less than 3
2 is less than or equal to 3
```

Try this example yourself, altering the values of $a and $b, to see the results. Try setting them to the same value and see what happens.

Logical operators

Logical operators produce true or false results, and therefore are also known as *Boolean operators*. There are four of them (see Table 4-4).

Table 4-4. The logical operators

Logical operator	Description
AND	TRUE if both operands are TRUE
OR	TRUE if either operand is TRUE
XOR	TRUE if one of the two operands is TRUE
! (NOT)	TRUE if the operand is FALSE, or FALSE if the operand is TRUE

You can see these operators used in Example 4-16. Note that the ! symbol is required by PHP in place of NOT. Furthermore, the operators can be lower- or uppercase.

Example 4-16. The logical operators in use

```php
<?php
  $a = 1; $b = 0;

  echo ($a AND $b) . "<br>";
  echo ($a or $b)  . "<br>";
  echo ($a XOR $b) . "<br>";
  echo !$a          . "<br>";
?>
```

Line by line, this example outputs nothing, 1, 1, and nothing, meaning that only the second and third echo statements evaluate as TRUE. (Remember that NULL—or nothing—represents a value of FALSE.) This is because the AND statement requires both operands to be TRUE if it is going to return a value of TRUE, while the fourth statement performs a NOT on the value of $a, turning it from TRUE (a value of 1) to FALSE. If you wish to experiment with this, try out the code, giving $a and $b varying values of 1 and 0.

When coding, remember that AND and OR have lower precedence than the other versions of the operators, && and ||.

The OR operator can cause unintentional problems in if statements, because the second operand will not be evaluated if the first is evaluated as TRUE. In Example 4-17, the function getnext will never be called if $finished has a value of 1.

Example 4-17. A statement using the OR operator

```php
<?php
  if ($finished == 1 OR getnext() == 1) exit;
?>
```

If you need `getnext` to be called at each `if` statement, you could rewrite the code as has been done in Example 4-18.

Example 4-18. The if...OR statement modified to ensure calling of getnext

```php
<?php
  $gn = getnext();

  if ($finished == 1 OR $gn == 1) exit;
?>
```

In this case, the code executes the `getnext` function and stores the value returned in `$gn` before executing the `if` statement.

 Another solution is to switch the two clauses to make sure that `getnext` is executed, as it will then appear first in the expression.

Table 4-5 shows all the possible variations of using the logical operators. You should also note that `!TRUE` equals `FALSE`, and `!FALSE` equals `TRUE`.

Table 4-5. All possible PHP logical expressions

Inputs		Operators and results		
a	b	AND	OR	XOR
TRUE	TRUE	TRUE	TRUE	FALSE
TRUE	FALSE	FALSE	TRUE	TRUE
FALSE	TRUE	FALSE	TRUE	TRUE
FALSE	FALSE	FALSE	FALSE	FALSE

Conditionals

Conditionals alter program flow. They enable you to ask questions about certain things and respond to the answers you get in different ways. Conditionals are central to creating dynamic web pages—the goal of using PHP in the first place—because they make it easy to render different output each time a page is viewed.

I'll present three basic conditionals in this section: the `if` statement, the `switch` statement, and the `?` operator. In addition, looping conditionals (which we'll get to shortly) execute code over and over until a condition is met.

The if Statement

One way of thinking about program flow is to imagine it as a single-lane highway that you are driving along. It's pretty much a straight line, but now and then you encounter various signs telling you where to go.

In the case of an if statement, you could imagine coming across a detour sign that you have to follow if a certain condition is TRUE. If so, you drive off and follow the detour until you return to the main road and then continue on your way in your original direction. Or, if the condition isn't TRUE, you ignore the detour and carry on driving (see Figure 4-1).

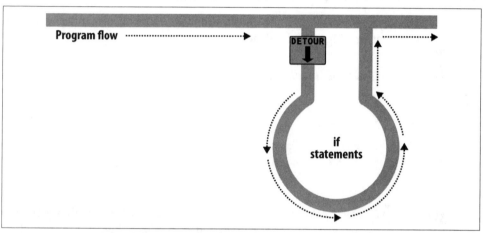

Figure 4-1. Program flow is like a single-lane highway

The contents of the if condition can be any valid PHP expression, including tests for equality, comparison expressions, tests for 0 and NULL, and even functions (either built-in functions or ones that you write).

The actions to take when an if condition is TRUE are generally placed inside curly braces ({ }). You can ignore the braces if you have only a single statement to execute, but if you always use curly braces, you'll avoid having to hunt down difficult-to-trace bugs, such as when you add an extra line to a condition and it doesn't get evaluated due to the lack of braces.

A notorious security vulnerability known as the "goto fail" bug haunted the Secure Sockets Layer (SSL) code in Apple's products for many years because a programmer had forgotten the curly braces around an if statement, causing a function to sometimes report a successful connection when that may not actually have always been the case. This allowed a malicious attacker to get a secure certificate to be accepted when it should have been rejected. If in doubt, place braces around your if statements.

Note that for brevity and clarity, however, many of the examples in this book ignore this suggestion and omit the braces for single statements.

In Example 4-19, imagine that it is the end of the month and all your bills have been paid, so you are performing some bank account maintenance.

Example 4-19. An if statement with curly braces

```php
<?php
  if ($bank_balance < 100)
  {
    $money        = 1000;
    $bank_balance += $money;
  }
?>
```

In this example, you are checking your balance to see whether it is less than $100 (or whatever your currency is). If so, you pay yourself $1,000 and then add it to the balance. (If only making money were that simple!)

If the bank balance is $100 or greater, the conditional statements are ignored and program flow skips to the next line (not shown).

In this book, opening curly braces generally start on a new line. Some people like to place the first curly brace to the right of the conditional expression; others start a new line with it. Either of these is fine, because PHP allows you to set out your whitespace characters (spaces, newlines, and tabs) any way you choose. However, you will find your code easier to read and debug if you indent each level of conditionals with a tab.

The else Statement

Sometimes when a conditional is not TRUE, you may not want to continue on to the main program code immediately but might wish to do something else instead. This is where the else statement comes in. With it, you can set up a second detour on your highway, as in Figure 4-2.

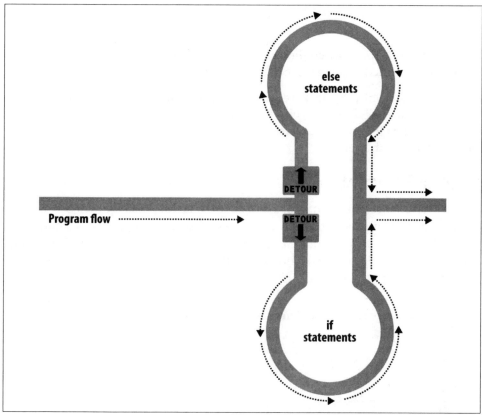

Figure 4-2. The highway now has an if detour and an else detour

With an `if...else` statement, the first conditional statement is executed if the condition is `TRUE`. But if it's `FALSE`, the second one is executed. One of the two choices *must* be executed. Under no circumstance can both (or neither) be executed. Example 4-20 shows the use of the `if...else` structure.

Example 4-20. An if...else statement with curly braces

```php
<?php
  if ($bank_balance < 100)
  {
    $money        = 1000;
    $bank_balance += $money;
  }
  else
  {
    $savings      += 50;
    $bank_balance -= 50;
```

```
    }
?>
```

In this example, if you've ascertained that you have $100 or more in the bank the `else` statement is executed, placing some of this money into your savings account.

As with `if` statements, if your `else` has only one conditional statement, you can opt to leave out the curly braces. (Curly braces are always recommended, though. First, they make the code easier to understand. Second, they let you easily add more statements to the branch later.)

The elseif Statement

There are also times when you want a number of different possibilities to occur, based upon a sequence of conditions. You can achieve this using the `elseif` statement. As you might imagine, it is like an `else` statement, except that you place a further conditional expression prior to the conditional code. In Example 4-21, you can see a complete `if...elseif...else` construct.

Example 4-21. An if...elseif...else statement with curly braces

```php
<?php
  if ($bank_balance < 100)
  {
    $money        = 1000;
    $bank_balance += $money;
  }
  elseif ($bank_balance > 200)
  {
    $savings      += 100;
    $bank_balance -= 100;
  }
  else
  {
    $savings      += 50;
    $bank_balance -= 50;
  }
?>
```

In the example, an `elseif` statement has been inserted between the `if` and `else` statements. It checks whether your bank balance exceeds $200 and, if so, decides that you can afford to save $100 of it this month.

Although I'm starting to stretch the metaphor a bit too far, you can imagine this as a multiway set of detours (see Figure 4-3).

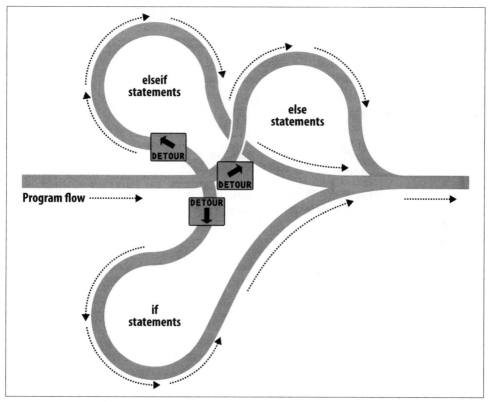

Figure 4-3. The highway with if, elseif, and else detours

 An `else` statement closes either an `if...else` or an `if...elseif...else` statement. You can leave out a final `else` if it is not required, but you cannot have one before an `elseif`; neither can you have an `elseif` before an `if` statement.

You may have as many `elseif` statements as you like. But as the number of `elseif` statements increases, you would probably be better advised to consider a `switch` statement if it fits your needs. We'll look at that next.

The switch Statement

The `switch` statement is useful where one variable, or the result of an expression, can have multiple values, each of which should trigger a different activity.

For example, consider a PHP-driven menu system that passes a single string to the main menu code according to what the user requests. Let's say the options are Home,

About, News, Login, and Links, and we set the variable $page to one of these, according to the user's input.

If we write the code for this using if...elseif...else, it might look like Example 4-22.

Example 4-22. A multiple-line if...elseif...else statement

```php
<?php
  if     ($page == "Home")  echo "You selected Home";
  elseif ($page == "About") echo "You selected About";
  elseif ($page == "News")  echo "You selected News";
  elseif ($page == "Login") echo "You selected Login";
  elseif ($page == "Links") echo "You selected Links";
  else                      echo "Unrecognized selection";
?>
```

If we use a switch statement, the code might look like Example 4-23.

Example 4-23. A switch statement

```php
<?php
  switch ($page)
  {
    case "Home":
        echo "You selected Home";
        break;
    case "About":
        echo "You selected About";
        break;
    case "News":
        echo "You selected News";
        break;
    case "Login":
        echo "You selected Login";
        break;
    case "Links":
        echo "You selected Links";
        break;
  }
?>
```

As you can see, $page is mentioned only once at the start of the switch statement. Thereafter, the case command checks for matches. When one occurs, the matching conditional statement is executed. Of course, in a real program you would have code here to display or jump to a page, rather than simply telling the user what was selected.

With `switch` statements, you do not use curly braces inside `case` commands. Instead, they commence with a colon and end with the `break` statement. The entire list of cases in the `switch` statement is enclosed in a set of curly braces, though.

Breaking out

If you wish to break out of the `switch` statement because a condition has been fulfilled, use the `break` command. This command tells PHP to exit the `switch` and jump to the following statement.

If you were to leave out the `break` commands in Example 4-23 and the case of Home evaluated to be TRUE, all five cases would then be executed. Or, if `$page` had the value News, all the `case` commands from then on would execute. This is deliberate and allows for some advanced programming, but generally you should always remember to issue a `break` command every time a set of `case` conditionals has finished executing. In fact, leaving out the `break` statement is a common error.

Default action

A typical requirement in `switch` statements is to fall back on a default action if none of the `case` conditions are met. For example, in the case of the menu code in Example 4-23, you could add the code in Example 4-24 immediately before the final curly brace.

Example 4-24. A default statement to add to Example 4-23

```
default:
    echo "Unrecognized selection";
    break;
```

This replicates the effect of the `else` statement in Example 4-22.

Although a `break` command is not required here because the default is the final substatement and program flow will automatically continue to the closing curly brace, should you decide to place the `default` statement higher up, it would definitely need a `break` command to prevent program flow from dropping into the following statements. Generally, the safest practice is to always include the `break` command.

Alternative syntax

If you prefer, you may replace the first curly brace in a `switch` statement with a single colon and the final curly brace with an `endswitch` command, as in Example 4-25. However, this approach is not commonly used and is mentioned here only in case you encounter it in third-party code.

Example 4-25. Alternate switch statement syntax

```php
<?php
  switch ($page):
    case "Home":
        echo "You selected Home";
        break;

    // etc

    case "Links":
        echo "You selected Links";
        break;
  endswitch;
?>
```

The ? Operator

One way of avoiding the verbosity of if and else statements is to use the more compact ternary operator, ?, which is unusual in that it takes three operands rather than the typical two.

We briefly came across this in Chapter 3 in the discussion about the difference between the print and echo statements as an example of an operator type that works well with print but not echo.

The ? operator is passed an expression that it must evaluate, along with two statements to execute: one for when the expression evaluates to TRUE, the other for when it is FALSE. Example 4-26 shows code we might use for writing a warning about the fuel level of a car to its digital dashboard.

Example 4-26. Using the ? operator

```php
<?php
  echo $fuel <= 1 ? "Fill tank now" : "There's enough fuel";
?>
```

In this statement, if there is one gallon or less of fuel (in other words, $fuel is set to 1 or less), the string Fill tank now is returned to the preceding echo statement. Otherwise, the string There's enough fuel is returned. You can also assign the value returned in a ? statement to a variable (see Example 4-27).

Example 4-27. Assigning a ? conditional result to a variable

```php
<?php
  $enough = $fuel <= 1 ? FALSE : TRUE;
?>
```

Here, $enough will be assigned the value TRUE only when there is more than a gallon of fuel; otherwise, it is assigned the value FALSE.

If you find the ? operator confusing, you are free to stick to if statements, but you should be familiar with the operator because you'll see it in other people's code. It can be hard to read, because it often mixes multiple occurrences of the same variable. For instance, code such as the following is quite popular:

```
$saved = $saved >= $new ? $saved : $new;
```

If you take it apart carefully, you can figure out what this code does:

```
$saved =                // Set the value of $saved to...
        $saved >= $new  // Check $saved against $new
    ?                   // Yes, comparison is true...
        $saved          // ... so assign the current value of $saved
    :                   // No, comparison is false...
        $new;           // ... so assign the value of $new
```

It's a concise way to keep track of the largest value that you've seen as a program progresses. You save the largest value in $saved and compare it to $new each time you get a new value. Programmers familiar with the ? operator find it more convenient than if statements for such short comparisons. When not used for writing compact code, it is typically used to make some decision inline, such as when you are testing whether a variable is set before passing it to a function.

Looping

One of the great things about computers is that they can repeat calculating tasks quickly and tirelessly. Often you may want a program to repeat the same sequence of code again and again until something happens, such as a user inputting a value or reaching a natural end. PHP's loop structures provide the perfect way to do this.

To picture how this works, look at Figure 4-4. It is much the same as the highway metaphor used to illustrate if statements, except the detour also has a loop section that—once a vehicle has entered it—can be exited only under the right program conditions.

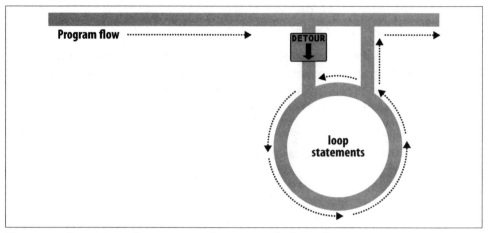

Figure 4-4. Imagining a loop as part of a program highway layout

while Loops

Let's turn the digital car dashboard in Example 4-26 into a loop that continuously checks the fuel level as you drive, using a `while` loop (Example 4-28).

Example 4-28. A while loop

```php
<?php
  $fuel = 10;

  while ($fuel > 1)
  {
    // Keep driving...
    echo "There's enough fuel";
  }
?>
```

Actually, you might prefer to keep a green light lit rather than output text, but the point is that whatever positive indication you wish to make about the level of fuel is placed inside the `while` loop. By the way, if you try this example for yourself, note that it will keep printing the string until you click the Stop button in your browser.

> As with `if` statements, you will notice that curly braces are required to hold the statements inside the `while` statements, unless there's only one.

For another example of a `while` loop that displays the 12 times table, see Example 4-29.

Example 4-29. A while loop to print the 12 times table

```php
<?php
  $count = 1;

  while ($count <= 12)
  {
    echo "$count times 12 is " . $count * 12 . "<br>";
    ++$count;
  }
?>
```

Here the variable $count is initialized to a value of 1, and then a while loop starts with the comparative expression $count <= 12. This loop will continue executing until the variable is greater than 12. The output from this code is as follows:

```
1 times 12 is 12
2 times 12 is 24
3 times 12 is 36
and so on...
```

Inside the loop, a string is printed along with the value of $count multiplied by 12. For neatness, this is followed with a <br> tag to force a new line. Then $count is incremented, ready for the final curly brace that tells PHP to return to the start of the loop.

At this point, $count is again tested to see whether it is greater than 12. It isn't, but it now has the value 2, and after another 11 times around the loop, it will have the value 13. When that happens, the code within the while loop is skipped and execution passes to the code following the loop, which, in this case, is the end of the program.

If the ++$count statement (which could equally have been $count++) had not been there, this loop would be like the first one in this section. It would never end, and only the result of 1 * 12 would be printed over and over.

But there is a much neater way this loop can be written, which I think you will like. Take a look at Example 4-30.

Example 4-30. A shortened version of Example 4-29

```php
<?php
  $count = 0;

  while (++$count <= 12)
    echo "$count times 12 is " . $count * 12 . "<br>";
?>
```

In this example, it was possible to move the ++$count statement from the statements inside the while loop into the conditional expression of the loop. What now happens is that PHP encounters the variable $count at the start of each iteration of the loop and, noticing that it is prefaced with the increment operator, first increments the variable and only then compares it to the value 12. You can therefore see that $count now has to be initialized to 0, not 1, because it is incremented as soon as the loop is entered. If you keep the initialization at 1, only results between 2 and 12 will be output.

do...while Loops

A slight variation to the while loop is the do...while loop, used when you want a block of code to be executed at least once and made conditional only after that. Example 4-31 shows a modified version of the code for the 12 times table that uses such a loop.

Example 4-31. A do...while loop for printing the 12 times table

```php
<?php
  $count = 1;
  do
    echo "$count times 12 is " . $count * 12 . "<br>";
  while (++$count <= 12);
?>
```

Notice how we are back to initializing $count to 1 (rather than 0) because of the loop's echo statement being executed before we have an opportunity to increment the variable. Other than that, though, the code looks pretty similar.

Of course, if you have more than a single statement inside a do...while loop, remember to use curly braces, as in Example 4-32.

Example 4-32. Expanding Example 4-31 to use curly braces

```php
<?php
  $count = 1;

  do {
    echo "$count times 12 is " . $count * 12;
    echo "<br>";
  } while (++$count <= 12);
?>
```

for Loops

The final kind of loop statement, the for loop, is also the most powerful, as it combines the abilities to set up variables as you enter the loop, test for conditions while iterating loops, and modify variables after each iteration.

Example 4-33 shows how to write the multiplication table program with a `for` loop.

Example 4-33. Outputting the 12 times table from a for loop

```php
<?php
  for ($count = 1 ; $count <= 12 ; ++$count)
    echo "$count times 12 is " . $count * 12 . "<br>";
?>
```

See how the code has been reduced to a single `for` statement containing a single conditional statement? Here's what is going on. Each `for` statement takes three parameters:

- An initialization expression
- A condition expression
- A modification expression

These are separated by semicolons like this: `for (expr1 ; expr2 ; expr3)`. At the start of the first iteration of the loop, the initialization expression is executed. In the case of the times table code, `$count` is initialized to the value 1. Then, each time around the loop, the condition expression (in this case, `$count <= 12`) is tested, and the loop is entered only if the condition is TRUE. Finally, at the end of each iteration, the modification expression is executed. In the case of the times table code, the variable `$count` is incremented.

All this structure neatly removes any requirement to place the controls for a loop within its body, freeing it up just for the statements you want the loop to perform.

Remember to use curly braces with a `for` loop if it will contain more than one statement, as in Example 4-34.

Example 4-34. The for loop from Example 4-33 with added curly braces

```php
<?php
  for ($count = 1 ; $count <= 12 ; ++$count)
  {
    echo "$count times 12 is " . $count * 12;
    echo "<br>";
  }
?>
```

Let's compare when to use `for` and `while` loops. The `for` loop is explicitly designed around a single value that changes on a regular basis. Usually you have a value that increments, as when you are passed a list of user choices and want to process each choice in turn. But you can transform the variable any way you like. A more complex form of the `for` statement even lets you perform multiple operations in each of the three parameters:

```php
for ($i = 1, $j = 1 ; $i + $j < 10 ; $i++ , $j++)
{
  // ...
}
```

That's complicated and not recommended for first-time users, though. The key is to distinguish commas from semicolons. The three parameters must be separated by semicolons. Within each parameter, multiple statements can be separated by commas. Thus, in the previous example, the first and third parameters each contain two statements:

```php
$i = 1, $j = 1  // Initialize $i and $j
$i + $j < 10    // Terminating condition
$i++ , $j++     // Modify $i and $j at the end of each iteration
```

The main thing to take from this example is that you must separate the three parameter sections with semicolons, not commas (which should be used only to separate statements within a parameter section).

So, when is a `while` statement more appropriate than a `for` statement? When your condition doesn't depend on a simple, regular change to a variable. For instance, if you want to check for some special input or error and end the loop when it occurs, use a `while` statement.

Breaking Out of a Loop

Just as you saw how to break out of a `switch` statement, you can also break out of a `for` loop (or any loop) using the same `break` command. This step can be necessary when, for example, one of your statements returns an error and the loop cannot continue executing safely.

One case in which this might occur is when writing a file returns an error, possibly because the disk is full (see Example 4-35).

Example 4-35. Writing a file using a for loop with error trapping

```php
<?php
  $fp = fopen("text.txt", 'wb');

  for ($j = 0 ; $j < 100 ; ++$j)
  {
    $written = fwrite($fp, "data");

    if ($written == FALSE) break;
  }
```

```
  fclose($fp);
?>
```

This is the most complicated piece of code that you have seen so far, but you're ready for it. We'll look into the file-handling commands in a Chapter 7, but for now all you need to know is that the first line opens the file *text.txt* for writing in binary mode, and then returns a pointer to the file in the variable $fp, which is used later to refer to the open file.

The loop then iterates 100 times (from 0 to 99), writing the string data to the file. After each write, the variable $written is assigned a value by the fwrite function representing the number of characters correctly written. But if there is an error, the fwrite function assigns the value FALSE.

The behavior of fwrite makes it easy for the code to check the variable $written to see whether it is set to FALSE and, if so, to break out of the loop to the following statement that closes the file.

If you are looking to improve the code, you can simplify the line:

```
    if ($written == FALSE) break;
```

using the NOT operator, like this:

```
    if (!$written) break;
```

In fact, the pair of inner loop statements can be shortened to a single statement:

```
    if (!fwrite($fp, "data")) break;
```

In other words, you can eliminate the $written variable, because it existed only to check the value returned from fwrite. You can instead test the return value directly.

The break command is even more powerful than you might think, because if you have code nested more than one layer deep that you need to break out of, you can follow the break command with a number to indicate how many levels to break out of:

```
    break 2;
```

The continue Statement

The continue statement is a little like a break statement, except that it instructs PHP to stop processing the current iteration of the loop and move right to its next iteration. So, instead of breaking out of the whole loop, PHP exits only the current iteration.

This approach can be useful in cases where you know there is no point continuing execution within the current loop and you want to save processor cycles or prevent an error from occurring by moving right along to the next iteration of the loop. In

Example 4-36, a `continue` statement is used to prevent a division-by-zero error from being issued when the variable `$j` has a value of 0.

Example 4-36. Trapping division-by-zero errors using continue

```php
<?php
  $j = 10;

  while ($j > -10)
  {
    $j--;

    if ($j == 0) continue;

    echo (10 / $j) . "<br>";
  }
?>
```

For all values of `$j` between 10 and –10, with the exception of 0, the result of calculating 10 divided by `$j` is displayed. But for the case of `$j` being 0, the `continue` statement is issued and execution skips immediately to the next iteration of the loop.

Implicit and Explicit Casting

PHP is a loosely typed language that allows you to declare a variable and its type simply by using it. It also automatically converts values from one type to another whenever required. This is called *implicit casting*.

However, at times PHP's implicit casting may not be what you want. In Example 4-37, note that the inputs to the division are integers. By default, PHP converts the output to floating point so it can give the most precise value—4.66 recurring.

Example 4-37. This expression returns a floating-point number

```php
<?php
  $a = 56;
  $b = 12;
  $c = $a / $b;

  echo $c;
?>
```

But what if we had wanted `$c` to be an integer instead? There are various ways we could achieve this, one of which is to force the result of `$a / $b` to be cast to an integer value using the integer cast type (`int`), like this:

```php
$c = (int) ($a / $b);
```

This is called *explicit* casting. Note that in order to ensure that the value of the entire expression is cast to an integer, we place the expression within parentheses. Otherwise, only the variable $a would have been cast to an integer—a pointless exercise, as the division by $b would still have returned a floating-point number.

You can explicitly cast variables and literals to the types shown in Table 4-6.

Table 4-6. PHP's cast types

Cast type	Description
(int) (integer)	Cast to an integer by dropping the decimal portion.
(bool) (boolean)	Cast to a Boolean.
(float) (double) (real)	Cast to a floating-point number.
(string)	Cast to a string.
(array)	Cast to an array.
(object)	Cast to an object.

> You can usually avoid having to use a cast by calling one of PHP's built-in functions. For example, to obtain an integer value, you could use the intval function. As with some other sections in this book, this section is here mainly to help you understand third-party code that you may encounter.

PHP Dynamic Linking

Because PHP is a programming language, and the output from it can be completely different for each user, it's possible for an entire website to run from a single PHP web page. Each time the user clicks on something, the details can be sent back to the same web page, which decides what to do next according to the various cookies and/or other session details it may have stored.

But although it is possible to build an entire website this way, it's not recommended, because your source code will grow and grow and start to become unwieldy, as it has to account for every possible action a user could take.

Instead, it's much more sensible to split your website development into different parts. For example, one distinct process is signing up for a website, along with all the checking this entails to validate an email address, determine whether a username is already taken, and so on.

A second module might be one that logs users in before handing them off to the main part of your website. Then you might have a messaging module with the facility for users to leave comments, a module containing links and useful information, another to allow uploading of images, and more.

As long as you have created a way to track your user through your website by means of cookies or session variables (both of which we'll look at more closely in later chapters), you can split up your website into sensible sections of PHP code, each one self-contained, and therefore treat yourself to a much easier future, developing each new feature and maintaining old ones. If you have a team, different people can work on different modules, so that each programmer needs to learn just one part of the program thoroughly.

Dynamic Linking in Action

One of the more popular PHP-driven applications on the web today is the blogging platform WordPress (see Figure 4-5). As a blogger or a blog reader, you might not realize it, but every major section has been given its own main PHP file, and a whole raft of generic, shared functions have been placed in separate files that are included by the main PHP pages as necessary.

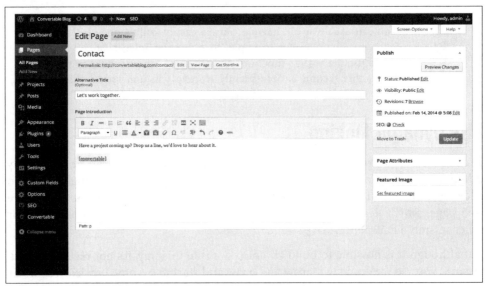

Figure 4-5. The WordPress blogging platform's dashboard

The whole platform is held together with behind-the-scenes session tracking, so that you hardly know when you are transitioning from one subsection to another. Therefore, a web developer who wants to tweak WordPress can easily find the particular file they need, modify it, and test and debug it without messing around with unconnected parts of the program. Next time you use WordPress, keep an eye on your browser's address bar, particularly if you are managing a blog, and you'll notice some of the different PHP files that it uses.

This chapter has covered quite a lot of ground, and by now you should be able to put together your own small PHP programs. But before you do, and before proceeding with the following chapter on functions and objects, you may wish to test your new knowledge by answering the following questions.

Questions

1. What actual underlying values are represented by TRUE and FALSE?

2. What are the simplest two forms of expressions?

3. What is the difference between unary, binary, and ternary operators?

4. What is the best way to force your own operator precedence?

5. What is meant by *operator associativity*?

6. When would you use the === (identity) operator?

7. Name the three conditional statement types.

8. What command can you use to skip the current iteration of a loop and move on to the next one?

9. Why is a for loop more powerful than a while loop?

10. How do if and while statements interpret conditional expressions of different data types?

See "Chapter 4 Answers" on page 716 in Appendix A for the answers to these questions.

CHAPTER 5

PHP Functions and Objects

The basic requirements of any programming language include somewhere to store data, a means of directing program flow, and a few bits and pieces such as expression evaluation, file management, and text output. PHP has all these, plus tools like `else` and `elseif` to make life easier. But even with all these in your toolkit, programming can be clumsy and tedious, especially if you have to rewrite portions of very similar code each time you need them.

That's where functions and objects come in. As you might guess, a *function* is a set of statements that performs a particular function and—optionally—returns a value. You can pull out a section of code that you have used more than once, place it into a function, and call the function by name when you want the code.

Functions have many advantages over contiguous, inline code. For example, they:

- Involve less typing
- Reduce syntax and other programming errors
- Decrease the loading time of program files
- Decrease execution time, because each function is compiled only once, no matter how often you call it
- Accept arguments and can therefore be used for general as well as specific cases

Objects take this concept a step further. An *object* incorporates one or more functions, and the data they use, into a single structure called a *class*.

In this chapter, you'll learn all about using functions, from defining and calling them to passing arguments back and forth. With that knowledge under your belt, you'll start creating functions and using them in your own objects (where they will be referred to as *methods*).

It is now highly unusual (and definitely not recommended) to use any version of PHP lower than 5.4. Therefore, this chapter assumes that this release is the bare minimum version you will be working with. Generally I would recommend version 5.6, or the new version 7.0 or 7.1 (there is no version 6). You can select any of these from the AMPPS control panel, as described in Chapter 2.

PHP Functions

PHP comes with hundreds of ready-made, built-in functions, making it a very rich language. To use a function, call it by name. For example, you can see the date function in action here:

```
echo date("l"); // Displays the day of the week
```

The parentheses tell PHP that you're referring to a function. Otherwise, it thinks you're referring to a constant.

Functions can take any number of arguments, including zero. For example, phpinfo, as shown next, displays lots of information about the current installation of PHP and requires no argument. The result of calling this function can be seen in Figure 5-1.

```
phpinfo();
```

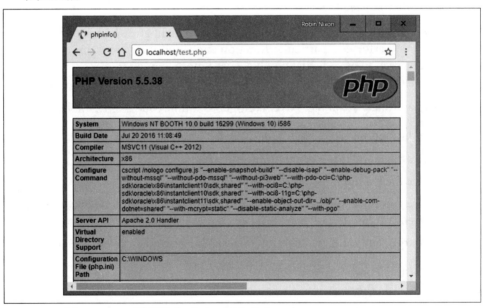

Figure 5-1. The output of PHP's built-in phpinfo function

The phpinfo function is extremely useful for obtaining information about your current PHP installation, but that information could also be very useful to potential hackers. Therefore, never leave a call to this function in any web-ready code.

Some of the built-in functions that use one or more arguments appear in Example 5-1.

Example 5-1. Three string functions

```php
<?php
  echo strrev(" .dlrow olleH"); // Reverse string
  echo str_repeat("Hip ", 2);   // Repeat string
  echo strtoupper("hooray!");    // String to uppercase
?>
```

This example uses three string functions to output the following text:

Hello world. Hip Hip HOORAY!

As you can see, the strrev function reversed the order of characters in the string, str_repeat repeated the string "Hip " twice (as required by the second argument), and strtoupper converted "hooray!" to uppercase.

Defining a Function

The general syntax for a function is as follows:

```
function function_name([parameter [, ...]])
{
  // Statements
}
```

The first line of the syntax indicates the following:

- A definition starts with the word function.
- A name follows, which must start with a letter or underscore, followed by any number of letters, numbers, or underscores.
- The parentheses are required.
- One or more parameters, separated by commas, are optional (as indicated by the square brackets).

Function names are case-insensitive, so all of the following strings can refer to the print function: PRINT, Print, and PrInT.

The opening curly brace starts the statements that will execute when you call the function; a matching curly brace must close it. These statements may include one or more `return` statements, which force the function to cease execution and return to the calling code. If a value is attached to the `return` statement, the calling code can retrieve it, as we'll see next.

Returning a Value

Let's take a look at a simple function to convert a person's full name to lowercase and then capitalize the first letter of each part of the name.

We've already seen an example of PHP's built-in `strtoupper` function in Example 5-1. For our current function, we'll use its counterpart, `strtolower`:

```
$lowered = strtolower("aNY # of Letters and Punctuation you WANT");

echo $lowered;
```

The output of this experiment is as follows:

any # of letters and punctuation you want

We don't want names all lowercase, though; we want the first letter of each part of the name capitalized. (We're not going to deal with subtle cases such as Mary-Ann or Jo-En-Lai for this example.) Luckily, PHP also provides a `ucfirst` function that sets the first character of a string to uppercase:

```
$ucfixed = ucfirst("any # of letters and punctuation you want");

echo $ucfixed;
```

The output is as follows:

Any # of letters and punctuation you want

Now we can do our first bit of program design: to get a word with its initial letter capitalized, we call `strtolower` on the string first, and then `ucfirst`. The way to do this is to nest a call to `strtolower` within `ucfirst`. Let's see why, because it's important to understand the order in which code is evaluated.

Say you make a simple call to the `print` function:

```
print(5-8);
```

The expression 5-8 is evaluated first, and the output is –3. (As you saw in the previous chapter, PHP converts the result to a string in order to display it.) If the expression contains a function, that function is evaluated first as well:

```
print(abs(5-8));
```

PHP is doing several things in executing that short statement:

1. Evaluate 5-8 to produce –3.

2. Use the abs function to turn –3 into 3.

3. Convert the result to a string and output it using the print function.

It all works because PHP evaluates each element from the inside out. The same procedure is in operation when we call the following:

```
ucfirst(strtolower("aNY # of Letters and Punctuation you WANT"))
```

PHP passes our string to strtolower and then to ucfirst, producing (as we've already seen when we played with the functions separately):

Any # of letters and punctuation you want

Now let's define a function (shown in Example 5-2) that takes three names and makes each one lowercase, with an initial capital letter.

Example 5-2. Cleaning up a full name

```php
<?php
  echo fix_names("WILLIAM", "henry", "gatES");

  function fix_names($n1, $n2, $n3)
  {
    $n1 = ucfirst(strtolower($n1));
    $n2 = ucfirst(strtolower($n2));
    $n3 = ucfirst(strtolower($n3));

    return $n1 . " " . $n2 . " " . $n3;
  }
?>
```

You may well find yourself writing this type of code, because users often leave their Caps Lock key on, accidentally insert capital letters in the wrong places, and even forget capitals altogether. The output from this example is shown here:

William Henry Gates

Returning an Array

We just saw a function returning a single value. There are also ways of getting multiple values from a function.

The first method is to return them within an array. As you saw in Chapter 3, an array is like a bunch of variables stuck together in a row. Example 5-3 shows how you can use an array to return function values.

Example 5-3. Returning multiple values in an array

```php
<?php
  $names = fix_names("WILLIAM", "henry", "gatES");
  echo $names[0] . " " . $names[1] . " " . $names[2];

  function fix_names($n1, $n2, $n3)
  {
    $n1 = ucfirst(strtolower($n1));
    $n2 = ucfirst(strtolower($n2));
    $n3 = ucfirst(strtolower($n3));

    return array($n1, $n2, $n3);
  }
?>
```

This method has the benefit of keeping all three names separate, rather than concatenating them into a single string, so you can refer to any user simply by first or last name without having to extract either name from the returned string.

Passing Arguments by Reference

In PHP versions prior to 5.3, you used to be able to preface a variable with the & symbol at the time of calling a function (for example, `increment(&$myvar);`) to tell the parser to pass a reference to the variable, not the variable's value. This granted a function access to the variable (allowing different values to be written back to it).

> Call-time pass-by-reference was deprecated in PHP 5.3 and removed in PHP 5.4. You should therefore not use this feature other than on legacy websites, and even there you are recommended to rewrite code that passes by reference, because it will halt with a fatal error on newer versions of PHP.

However, *within* a function definition, you may continue to access arguments by reference. This concept can be hard to get your head around, so let's go back to the matchbox metaphor from Chapter 3.

Imagine that, instead of taking a piece of paper out of a matchbox, reading it, copying what's on it onto another piece of paper, putting the original back, and passing the copy to a function (phew!), you could simply attach a piece of thread to the original piece of paper and pass one end of it to the function (see Figure 5-2).

Figure 5-2. Imagining a reference as a thread attached to a variable

Now the function can follow the thread to find the data to be accessed. This avoids all the overhead of creating a copy of the variable just for the function's use. What's more, the function can now modify the variable's value.

This means you can rewrite Example 5-3 to pass references to all the parameters, and then the function can modify these directly (see Example 5-4).

Example 5-4. Passing values to a function by reference

```php
<?php
  $a1 = "WILLIAM";
  $a2 = "henry";
  $a3 = "gatES";

  echo $a1 . " " . $a2 . " " . $a3 . "<br>";
  fix_names($a1, $a2, $a3);
  echo $a1 . " " . $a2 . " " . $a3;

  function fix_names(&$n1, &$n2, &$n3)
  {
    $n1 = ucfirst(strtolower($n1));
    $n2 = ucfirst(strtolower($n2));
    $n3 = ucfirst(strtolower($n3));
  }
?>
```

Rather than passing strings directly to the function, you first assign them to variables and print them out to see their "before" values. Then you call the function as before, but within the function definition you place a & symbol in front of each parameter to be passed by reference.

Now the variables $n1, $n2, and $n3 are attached to "threads" that lead to the values of $a1, $a2, and $a3. In other words, there is one group of values, but two sets of variable names are allowed to access them.

Therefore, the function fix_names only has to assign new values to $n1, $n2, and $n3 to update the values of $a1, $a2, and $a3. The output from this code is:

```
WILLIAM henry gatES
William Henry Gates
```

As you see, both of the echo statements use only the values of $a1, $a2, and $a3.

Returning Global Variables

The better way to give a function access to an externally created variable is by declaring it to have global access from within the function. The global keyword followed by the variable name gives every part of your code full access to it (see Example 5-5).

Example 5-5. Returning values in global variables

```php
<?php
  $a1 = "WILLIAM";
  $a2 = "henry";
  $a3 = "gatES";

  echo $a1 . " " . $a2 . " " . $a3 . "<br>";
  fix_names();
  echo $a1 . " " . $a2 . " " . $a3;

  function fix_names()
  {
    global $a1; $a1 = ucfirst(strtolower($a1));
    global $a2; $a2 = ucfirst(strtolower($a2));
    global $a3; $a3 = ucfirst(strtolower($a3));
  }
?>
```

Now you don't have to pass parameters to the function, and it doesn't have to accept them. Once declared, these variables retain global access and are available to the rest of your program, including its functions.

Recap of Variable Scope

A quick reminder of what you know from Chapter 3:

- *Local variables* are accessible just from the part of your code where you define them. If they're outside of a function, they can be accessed by all code outside of functions, classes, and so on. If a variable is inside a function, only that function can access the variable, and its value is lost when the function returns.

- *Global variables* are accessible from all parts of your code.

- *Static variables* are accessible only within the function that declared them but retain their value over multiple calls.

Including and Requiring Files

As you progress in your use of PHP programming, you are likely to start building a library of functions that you think you will need again. You'll also probably start using libraries created by other programmers.

There's no need to copy and paste these functions into your code. You can save them in separate files and use commands to pull them in. There are two commands to perform this action: `include` and `require`.

The include Statement

Using `include`, you can tell PHP to fetch a particular file and load all its contents. It's as if you pasted the included file into the current file at the insertion point. Example 5-6 shows how you would include a file called *library.php*.

Example 5-6. Including a PHP file

```php
<?php
  include "library.php";

  // Your code goes here
?>
```

Using include_once

Each time you issue the `include` directive, it includes the requested file again, even if you've already inserted it. For instance, suppose that *library.php* contains a lot of useful functions, so you include it in your file, but you also include another library that includes *library.php*. Through nesting, you've inadvertently included *library.php* twice. This will produce error messages, because you're trying to define the same constant or function multiple times. So, you should use `include_once` instead (see Example 5-7).

Example 5-7. Including a PHP file only once

```php
<?php
  include_once "library.php";

  // Your code goes here
?>
```

Then, any further attempts to include the same file (with include or include_once) will be ignored. To determine whether the requested file has already been executed, the absolute file path is matched after all relative paths are resolved and the file is found in your include path.

 In general, it's probably best to stick with include_once and ignore the basic include statement. That way, you will never have the problem of files being included multiple times.

Using require and require_once

A potential problem with include and include_once is that PHP will only *attempt* to include the requested file. Program execution continues even if the file is not found.

When it is absolutely essential to include a file, require it. For the same reasons I gave for using include_once, I recommend that you generally stick with require_once whenever you need to require a file (see Example 5-8).

Example 5-8. Requiring a PHP file only once

```php
<?php
  require_once "library.php";

  // Your code goes here
?>
```

PHP Version Compatibility

PHP is in an ongoing process of development, and there are multiple versions. If you need to check whether a particular function is available to your code, you can use the function_exists function, which checks all predefined and user-created functions.

Example 5-9 checks for array_combine, a function specific to PHP version 5.

Example 5-9. Checking for a function's existence

```php
<?php
  if (function_exists("array_combine"))
  {
    echo "Function exists";
  }
  else
  {
    echo "Function does not exist - better write our own";
  }
?>
```

Using code such as this, you can take advantage of features in newer versions of PHP and yet still have your code run on earlier versions, as long as you replicate any features that are missing. Your functions may be slower than the built-in ones, but at least your code will be much more portable.

You can also use the `phpversion` function to determine which version of PHP your code is running on. The returned result will be similar to the following, depending on the version:

    `5.5.38`

PHP Objects

In much the same way that functions represent a huge increase in programming power over the early days of computing, where sometimes the best program navigation available was a very basic `GOTO` or `GOSUB` statement, *object-oriented programming* (OOP) takes the use of functions to a whole new level.

Once you get the hang of condensing reusable bits of code into functions, it's not that great a leap to consider bundling the functions and their data into objects.

Let's take a social networking site that has many parts. One handles all user functions —that is, code to enable new users to sign up and existing users to modify their details. In standard PHP, you might create a few functions to handle this and embed some calls to the MySQL database to keep track of all the users.

Imagine how much easier it would be to create an object to represent the current user. To do this, you could create a class, perhaps called `User`, that would contain all the code required for handling users and all the variables needed for manipulating the data within the class. Then, whenever you need to manipulate a user's data, you could simply create a new object with the `User` class.

You could treat this new object as if it were the actual user. For example, you could pass the object a name, password, and email address; ask it whether such a user already exists; and, if not, have it create a new user with those attributes. You could even have an instant messaging object, or one for managing whether two users are friends.

Terminology

When creating a program to use objects, you need to design a composite of data and code called a *class*. Each new object based on this class is called an *instance* (or *occurrence*) of that class.

The data associated with an object is called its *properties*; the functions it uses are called *methods*. In defining a class, you supply the names of its properties and the code for its methods. See Figure 5-3 for a jukebox metaphor for an object. Think of the CDs that it holds in the carousel as its properties; the method of playing them is to press buttons on the front panel. There is also a slot for inserting coins (the method used to activate the object), and the laser disc reader (the method used to retrieve the music, or properties, from the CDs).

Figure 5-3. A jukebox: a great example of a self-contained object

When you're creating objects, it is best to use *encapsulation*, or writing a class in such a way that only its methods can be used to manipulate its properties. In other words, you deny outside code direct access to its data. The methods you supply are known as the object's *interface*.

This approach makes debugging easy: you have to fix faulty code only within a class. Additionally, when you want to upgrade a program, if you have used proper encapsulation and maintained the same interface, you can simply develop new replacement classes, debug them fully, and then swap them in for the old ones. If they don't work, you can swap the old ones back in to immediately fix the problem before further debugging the new classes.

Once you have created a class, you may find that you need another class that is similar to it but not quite the same. The quick and easy thing to do is to define a new class using *inheritance*. When you do this, your new class has all the properties of the one it has inherited from. The original class is now called the *superclass*, and the new one is the *subclass* (or *derived* class).

In our jukebox example, if you invent a new jukebox that can play a video along with the music, you can inherit all the properties and methods from the original jukebox superclass and add some new properties (videos) and new methods (a movie player).

An excellent benefit of this system is that if you improve the speed or any other aspect of the superclass, its subclasses will receive the same benefit.

Declaring a Class

Before you can use an object, you must define a class with the `class` keyword. Class definitions contain the class name (which is case-sensitive), its properties, and its methods. Example 5-10 defines the class `User` with two properties, which are `$name` and `$password` (indicated by the `public` keyword—see "Property and Method Scope" on page 114). It also creates a new instance (called `$object`) of this class.

Example 5-10. Declaring a class and examining an object

```php
<?php
  $object = new User;
  print_r($object);

  class User
  {
    public $name, $password;

    function save_user()
    {
      echo "Save User code goes here";
    }
  }
?>
```

Here I have also used an invaluable function called `print_r`. It asks PHP to display information about a variable in human-readable form. (The `_r` stands for *human-readable*.) In the case of the new object `$object`, it displays the following:

```
User Object
(
  [name]      =>
  [password] =>
)
```

However, a browser compresses all the whitespace, so the output in a browser is slightly harder to read:

```
User Object ( [name] => [password] => )
```

In any case, the output says that `$object` is a user-defined object that has the properties `name` and `password`.

Creating an Object

To create an object with a specified class, use the `new` keyword, like this: `$object = new Class`. Here are a couple of ways in which we could do this:

```php
$object = new User;
$temp   = new User('name', 'password');
```

On the first line, we simply assign an object to the `User` class. In the second, we pass parameters to the call.

A class may require or prohibit arguments; it may also allow arguments without explicitly requiring them.

Accessing Objects

Let's add a few lines to Example 5-10 and check the results. Example 5-11 extends the previous code by setting object properties and calling a method.

Example 5-11. Creating and interacting with an object

```php
<?php
  $object = new User;
  print_r($object); echo "<br>";

  $object->name     = "Joe";
  $object->password = "mypass";
  print_r($object); echo "<br>";

  $object->save_user();

  class User
```

```
    {
      public $name, $password;

      function save_user()
      {
        echo "Save User code goes here";
      }
    }
?>
```

As you can see, the syntax for accessing an object's property is $object->property. Likewise, you call a method like this: $object->method().

You should note that the example property and method do not have $ signs in front of them. If you were to preface them with $ signs, the code would not work, as it would try to reference the value inside a variable. For example, the expression $object->$property would attempt to look up the value assigned to a variable named $property (let's say that value is the string brown) and then attempt to reference the property $object->brown. If $property is undefined, an attempt to reference $object->NULL would occur and cause an error.

When looked at using a browser's View Source facility, the output from Example 5-11 is as follows:

```
User Object
(
  [name]     =>
  [password] =>
)
User Object
(
  [name]     => Joe
  [password] => mypass
)
Save User code goes here
```

Again, print_r shows its utility by providing the contents of $object before and after property assignment. From now on, I'll omit print_r statements, but if you are working along with this book on your development server, you can put some in to see exactly what is happening.

You can also see that the code in the method save_user was executed via the call to that method. It printed the string reminding us to create some code.

 You can place functions and class definitions anywhere in your code, before or after statements that use them. Generally, though, it is considered good practice to place them toward the end of a file.

Cloning Objects

Once you have created an object, it is passed by reference when you pass it as a parameter. In the matchbox metaphor, this is like keeping several threads attached to an object stored in a matchbox, so that you can follow any attached thread to access it.

In other words, making object assignments does not copy objects in their entirety. You'll see how this works in Example 5-12, where we define a very simple User class with no methods and only the property name.

Example 5-12. Copying an object?

```php
<?php
  $object1       = new User();
  $object1->name = "Alice";
  $object2       = $object1;
  $object2->name = "Amy";

  echo "object1 name = " . $object1->name . "<br>";
  echo "object2 name = " . $object2->name;

  class User
  {
    public $name;
  }
?>
```

Here, we first create the object $object1 and assign the value Alice to the name property. Then we create $object2, assigning it the value of $object1, and assign the value Amy just to the name property of $object2—or so we might think. But this code outputs the following:

```
object1 name = Amy
object2 name = Amy
```

What has happened? Both $object1 and $object2 refer to the *same* object, so changing the name property of $object2 to Amy also sets that property for $object1.

To avoid this confusion, you can use the clone operator, which creates a new instance of the class and copies the property values from the original instance to the new instance. Example 5-13 illustrates this usage.

Example 5-13. Cloning an object

```php
<?php
  $object1       = new User();
  $object1->name = "Alice";
```

```
$object2       = clone $object1;
$object2->name = "Amy";

echo "object1 name = " . $object1->name . "<br>";
echo "object2 name = " . $object2->name;

class User
{
  public $name;
}
?>
```

Voilà! The output from this code is what we initially wanted:

```
object1 name = Alice
object2 name = Amy
```

Constructors

When creating a new object, you can pass a list of arguments to the class being called. These are passed to a special method within the class, called the *constructor*, which initializes various properties.

To do this you use the function name __construct (that is, construct preceded by two underscore characters), as in Example 5-14.

Example 5-14. Creating a constructor method

```
<?php
  class User
  {
    function __construct($param1, $param2)
    {
      // Constructor statements go here
      public $username = "Guest";
    }
  }
?>
```

Destructors

You also have the ability to create *destructor* methods. This ability is useful when code has made the last reference to an object or when a script reaches the end. Example 5-15 shows how to create a destructor method. The destructor can do clean-up such as releasing a connection to a database or some other resource that you reserved within the class. Because you reserved the resource within the class, you have to release it here, or it will stick around indefinitely. Many system-wide problems are caused by programs reserving resources and forgetting to release them.

Example 5-15. Creating a destructor method

```php
<?php
  class User
  {
    function __destruct()
    {
      // Destructor code goes here
    }
  }
?>
```

Writing Methods

As you have seen, declaring a method is similar to declaring a function, but there are a few differences. For example, method names beginning with a double underscore (__) are reserved, and you should not create any of this form.

You also have access to a special variable called $this, which can be used to access the current object's properties. To see how it works, take a look at Example 5-16, which contains a different method from the User class definition called get_password.

Example 5-16. Using the variable $this in a method

```php
<?php
  class User
  {
    public $name, $password;

    function get_password()
    {
      return $this->password;
    }
  }
?>
```

get_password uses the $this variable to access the current object and then return the value of that object's password property. Note how the preceding $ of the property $password is omitted when we use the -> operator. Leaving the $ in place is a typical error you may run into, particularly when you first use this feature.

Here's how you would use the class defined in Example 5-16:

```php
$object          = new User;
$object->password = "secret";

echo $object->get_password();
```

This code prints the password secret.

Declaring Properties

It is not necessary to explicitly declare properties within classes, as they can be implicitly defined when first used. To illustrate this, in Example 5-17 the class `User` has no properties and no methods but is legal code.

Example 5-17. Defining a property implicitly

```php
<?php
  $object1        = new User();
  $object1->name = "Alice";

  echo $object1->name;

  class User {}
?>
```

This code correctly outputs the string `Alice` without a problem, because PHP implicitly declares the property `$object1->name` for you. But this kind of programming can lead to bugs that are infuriatingly difficult to discover, because `name` was declared from outside the class.

To help yourself and anyone else who will maintain your code, I advise that you get into the habit of always declaring your properties explicitly within classes. You'll be glad you did.

Also, when you declare a property within a class, you may assign a default value to it. The value you use must be a constant and not the result of a function or expression. Example 5-18 shows a few valid and invalid assignments.

Example 5-18. Valid and invalid property declarations

```php
<?php
  class Test
  {
    public $name  = "Paul Smith"; // Valid
    public $age   = 42;           // Valid
    public $time  = time();       // Invalid - calls a function
    public $score = $level * 2;   // Invalid - uses an expression
  }
?>
```

Declaring Constants

In the same way that you can create a global constant with the `define` function, you can define constants inside classes. The generally accepted practice is to use uppercase letters to make them stand out, as in Example 5-19.

Example 5-19. Defining constants within a class

```php
<?php
  Translate::lookup();

  class Translate
  {
    const ENGLISH = 0;
    const SPANISH = 1;
    const FRENCH  = 2;
    const GERMAN  = 3;
    // ...

    static function lookup()
    {
      echo self::SPANISH;
    }
  }
?>
```

You can reference constants directly, using the `self` keyword and double colon operator. Note that this code calls the class directly, using the double colon operator at line 1, without creating an instance of it first. As you would expect, the value printed when you run this code is 1.

Remember that once you define a constant, you can't change it.

Property and Method Scope

PHP provides three keywords for controlling the scope of properties and methods (*members*):

public

> Public members can be referenced anywhere, including by other classes and instances of the object. This is the default when variables are declared with the `var` or `public` keywords, or when a variable is implicitly declared the first time it is used. The keywords `var` and `public` are interchangeable because, although deprecated, `var` is retained for compatibility with previous versions of PHP. Methods are assumed to be `public` by default.

protected

> These members can be referenced only by the object's class methods and those of any subclasses.

private

> These members can be referenced only by methods within the same class—not by subclasses.

Here's how to decide which you need to use:

- Use public when outside code *should* access this member and extending classes *should* also inherit it.

- Use protected when outside code *should not* access this member but extending classes *should* inherit it.

- Use private when outside code *should not* access this member and extending classes also *should not* inherit it.

Example 5-20 illustrates the use of these keywords.

Example 5-20. Changing property and method scope

```php
<?php
  class Example
  {
    var $name   = "Michael"; // Same as public but deprecated
    public $age = 23;        // Public property
    protected $usercount;    // Protected property

    private function admin() // Private method
    {
      // Admin code goes here
    }
  }
?>
```

Static Methods

You can define a method as static, which means that it is called on a class, not on an object. A static method has no access to any object properties and is created and accessed as in Example 5-21.

Example 5-21. Creating and accessing a static method

```php
<?php
  User::pwd_string();

  class User
  {
    static function pwd_string()
    {
      echo "Please enter your password";
    }
  }
?>
```

Note how we call the class itself, along with the static method, using a double colon (also known as the *scope resolution* operator), not ->. Static functions are useful for performing actions relating to the class itself, but not to specific instances of the class. You can see another example of a static method in Example 5-19.

 If you try to access $this->property, or other object properties from within a static function, you will receive an error message.

Static Properties

Most data and methods apply to instances of a class. For example, in a User class, you want to do such things as set a particular user's password or check when the user has been registered. These facts and operations apply separately to each user and therefore use instance-specific properties and methods.

But occasionally you'll want to maintain data about a whole class. For instance, to report how many users are registered, you will store a variable that applies to the whole User class. PHP provides static properties and methods for such data.

As shown briefly in Example 5-21, declaring members of a class static makes them accessible without an instantiation of the class. A property declared static cannot be directly accessed within an instance of a class, but a static method can.

Example 5-22 defines a class called Test with a static property and a public method.

Example 5-22. Defining a class with a static property

```php
<?php
  $temp = new Test();

  echo "Test A: " . Test::$static_property . "<br>";
  echo "Test B: " . $temp->get_sp()        . "<br>";
  echo "Test C: " . $temp->static_property . "<br>";

  class Test
  {
    static $static_property = "I'm static";

    function get_sp()
    {
      return self::$static_property;
    }
  }
?>
```

When you run this code, it returns the following output:

```
Test A: I'm static
Test B: I'm static

Notice: Undefined property: Test::$static_property
Test C:
```

This example shows that the property $static_property could be directly referenced from the class itself via the double colon operator in Test A. Also, Test B could obtain its value by calling the get_sp method of the object $temp, created from class Test. But Test C failed, because the static property $static_property was not accessible to the object $temp.

Note how the method get_sp accesses $static_property using the keyword self. This is how a static property or constant can be directly accessed within a class.

Inheritance

Once you have written a class, you can derive subclasses from it. This can save lots of painstaking code rewriting: you can take a class similar to the one you need to write, extend it to a subclass, and just modify the parts that are different. You achieve this using the extends keyword.

In Example 5-23, the class Subscriber is declared a subclass of User by means of the extends keyword.

Example 5-23. Inheriting and extending a class

```php
<?php
  $object           = new Subscriber;
  $object->name     = "Fred";
  $object->password = "pword";
  $object->phone    = "012 345 6789";
  $object->email    = "fred@bloggs.com";
  $object->display();

  class User
  {
    public $name, $password;

    function save_user()
    {
      echo "Save User code goes here";
    }
  }

  class Subscriber extends User
  {
```

```
      public $phone, $email;

      function display()
      {
        echo "Name:  " . $this->name     . "<br>";
        echo "Pass:  " . $this->password . "<br>";
        echo "Phone: " . $this->phone    . "<br>";
        echo "Email: " . $this->email;
      }
  }
?>
```

The original User class has two properties, $name and $password, and a method to save the current user to the database. Subscriber extends this class by adding an additional two properties, $phone and $email, and includes a method of displaying the properties of the current object using the variable $this, which refers to the current values of the object being accessed. The output from this code is as follows:

```
Name:  Fred
Pass:  pword
Phone: 012 345 6789
Email: fred@bloggs.com
```

The parent keyword

If you write a method in a subclass with the same name as one in its parent class, its statements will override those of the parent class. Sometimes this is not the behavior you want, and you need to access the parent's method. To do this, you can use the parent operator, as in Example 5-24.

Example 5-24. Overriding a method and using the parent operator

```
<?php
  $object = new Son;
  $object->test();
  $object->test2();

  class Dad
  {
    function test()
    {
      echo "[Class Dad] I am your Father<br>";
    }
  }

  class Son extends Dad
  {
    function test()
    {
      echo "[Class Son] I am Luke<br>";
```

```
    }

    function test2()
    {
      parent::test();
    }
  }
?>
```

This code creates a class called Dad and a subclass called Son that inherits its properties and methods, and then overrides the method test. Therefore, when line 2 calls the method test, the new method is executed. The only way to execute the overridden test method in the Dad class is to use the parent operator, as shown in function test2 of class Son. The code outputs the following:

```
[Class Son] I am Luke
[Class Dad] I am your Father
```

If you wish to ensure that your code calls a method from the current class, you can use the self keyword, like this:

```
self::method();
```

Subclass constructors

When you extend a class and declare your own constructor, you should be aware that PHP will not automatically call the constructor method of the parent class. If you want to be certain that all initialization code is executed, subclasses should always call the parent constructors, as in Example 5-25.

Example 5-25. Calling the parent class constructor

```
<?php
  $object = new Tiger();

  echo "Tigers have...<br>";
  echo "Fur: " . $object->fur . "<br>";
  echo "Stripes: " . $object->stripes;

  class Wildcat
  {
    public $fur; // Wildcats have fur

    function __construct()
    {
      $this->fur = "TRUE";
    }
  }

  class Tiger extends Wildcat
```

```
  {
    public $stripes; // Tigers have stripes

    function __construct()
    {
      parent::__construct(); // Call parent constructor first
      $this->stripes = "TRUE";
    }
  }
?>
```

This example takes advantage of inheritance in the typical manner. The Wildcat class has created the property $fur, which we'd like to reuse, so we create the Tiger class to inherit $fur and additionally create another property, $stripes. To verify that both constructors have been called, the program outputs the following:

```
Tigers have...
Fur: TRUE
Stripes: TRUE
```

Final methods

When you wish to prevent a subclass from overriding a superclass method, you can use the final keyword. Example 5-26 shows how.

Example 5-26. Creating a final method

```
<?php
  class User
  {
    final function copyright()
    {
      echo "This class was written by Joe Smith";
    }
  }
?>
```

Once you have digested the contents of this chapter, you should have a strong feel for what PHP can do for you. You should be able to use functions with ease and, if you wish, write object-oriented code. In Chapter 6, we'll finish off our initial exploration of PHP by looking at the workings of PHP arrays.

Questions

1. What is the main benefit of using a function?

2. How many values can a function return?

3. What is the difference between accessing a variable by name and by reference?

---

4. What is the meaning of *scope* in PHP?

5. How can you incorporate one PHP file within another?

6. How is an object different from a function?

7. How do you create a new object in PHP?

8. What syntax would you use to create a subclass from an existing one?

9. How can you cause an object to be initialized when you create it?

10. Why is it a good idea to explicitly declare properties within a class?

See "Chapter 5 Answers" on page 716 in Appendix A for the answers to these questions.

CHAPTER 6

PHP Arrays

In Chapter 3, I gave a very brief introduction to PHP's arrays—just enough for a little taste of their power. In this chapter, I'll show you many more things that you can do with arrays, some of which—if you have ever used a strongly typed language such as C—may surprise you with their elegance and simplicity.

Arrays are an example of what has made PHP so popular. Not only do they remove the tedium of writing code to deal with complicated data structures, but they also provide numerous ways to access data while remaining amazingly fast.

Basic Access

We've already looked at arrays as if they were clusters of matchboxes glued together. Another way to think of an array is like a string of beads, with the beads representing variables that can be numbers, strings, or even other arrays. They are like bead strings because each element has its own location and (with the exception of the first and last ones) each has other elements on either side.

Some arrays are referenced by numeric indexes; others allow alphanumeric identifiers. Built-in functions let you sort them, add or remove sections, and walk through them to handle each item through a special kind of loop. And by placing one or more arrays inside another, you can create arrays of two, three, or any number of dimensions.

Numerically Indexed Arrays

Let's assume that you've been tasked with creating a simple website for a local office supply company and you're currently working on the section devoted to paper. One way to manage the various items of stock in this category would be to place them in a numeric array. You can see the simplest way of doing so in Example 6-1.

Example 6-1. Adding items to an array

```php
<?php
  $paper[] = "Copier";
  $paper[] = "Inkjet";
  $paper[] = "Laser";
  $paper[] = "Photo";

  print_r($paper);
?>
```

In this example, each time you assign a value to the array $paper, the first empty location within that array is used to store the value, and a pointer internal to PHP is incremented to point to the next free location, ready for future insertions. The familiar print_r function (which prints out the contents of a variable, array, or object) is used to verify that the array has been correctly populated. It prints out the following:

```
Array
(
   [0] => Copier
   [1] => Inkjet
   [2] => Laser
   [3] => Photo
)
```

The previous code could also have been written as shown in Example 6-2, where the exact location of each item within the array is specified. But, as you can see, that approach requires extra typing and makes your code harder to maintain if you want to insert supplies into or remove them from the array. So, unless you wish to specify a different order, it's usually better to simply let PHP handle the actual location numbers.

Example 6-2. Adding items to an array using explicit locations

```php
<?php
  $paper[0] = "Copier";
  $paper[1] = "Inkjet";
  $paper[2] = "Laser";
  $paper[3] = "Photo";

  print_r($paper);
?>
```

The output from these examples is identical, but you are not likely to use print_r in a developed website, so Example 6-3 shows how you might print out the various types of paper the website offers using a for loop.

Example 6-3. Adding items to an array and retrieving them

```php
<?php
  $paper[] = "Copier";
  $paper[] = "Inkjet";
  $paper[] = "Laser";
  $paper[] = "Photo";

  for ($j = 0 ; $j < 4 ; ++$j)
    echo "$j: $paper[$j]<br>";
?>
```

This example prints out the following:

```
0: Copier
1: Inkjet
2: Laser
3: Photo
```

So far, you've seen a couple of ways in which you can add items to an array and one way of referencing them. PHP offers many more, which I'll get to shortly. But first, we'll look at another type of array.

Associative Arrays

Keeping track of array elements by index works just fine, but can require extra work in terms of remembering which number refers to which product. It can also make code hard for other programmers to follow.

This is where associative arrays come into their own. Using them, you can reference the items in an array by name rather than by number. Example 6-4 expands on the previous code by giving each element in the array an identifying name and a longer, more explanatory string value.

Example 6-4. Adding items to an associative array and retrieving them

```php
<?php
  $paper['copier'] = "Copier & Multipurpose";
  $paper['inkjet'] = "Inkjet Printer";
  $paper['laser']  = "Laser Printer";
  $paper['photo']  = "Photographic Paper";

  echo $paper['laser'];
?>
```

In place of a number (which doesn't convey any useful information, aside from the position of the item in the array), each item now has a unique name that you can use to reference it elsewhere, as with the echo statement—which simply prints out Laser

Printer. The names (copier, inkjet, and so on) are called *indexes* or *keys*, and the items assigned to them (such as Laser Printer) are called *values*.

This very powerful feature of PHP is often used when you are extracting information from XML and HTML. For example, an HTML parser such as those used by a search engine could place all the elements of a web page into an associative array whose names reflect the page's structure:

```
$html['title'] = "My web page";
$html['body']  = "... body of web page ...";
```

The program would also probably break down all the links found within a page into another array, and all the headings and subheadings into another. When you use associative rather than numeric arrays, the code to refer to all of these items is easy to write and debug.

Assignment Using the array Keyword

So far, you've seen how to assign values to arrays by just adding new items one at a time. Whether you specify keys, specify numeric identifiers, or let PHP assign numeric identifiers implicitly, this is a long-winded approach. A more compact and faster assignment method uses the array keyword. Example 6-5 shows both a numeric and an associative array assigned using this method.

Example 6-5. Adding items to an array using the array keyword

```php
<?php
  $p1 = array("Copier", "Inkjet", "Laser", "Photo");

  echo "p1 element: " . $p1[2] . "<br>";

  $p2 = array('copier' => "Copier & Multipurpose",
              'inkjet' => "Inkjet Printer",
              'laser'  => "Laser Printer",
              'photo'  => "Photographic Paper");

  echo "p2 element: " . $p2['inkjet'] . "<br>";
?>
```

The first half of this snippet assigns the old, shortened product descriptions to the array $p1. There are four items, so they will occupy slots 0 through 3. Therefore, the echo statement prints out the following:

    p1 element: Laser

The second half assigns associative identifiers and accompanying longer product descriptions to the array $p2 using the format *key* => *value*. The use of => is similar to the regular = assignment operator, except that you are assigning a value to an *index* and not to a *variable*. The index is then inextricably linked with that value, unless it is assigned a new value. The echo command therefore prints out this:

```
p2 element: Inkjet Printer
```

You can verify that $p1 and $p2 are different types of array, because both of the following commands, when appended to the code, will cause an Undefined index or Undefined offset error, as the array identifier for each is incorrect:

```
echo $p1['inkjet']; // Undefined index
echo $p2[3];        // Undefined offset
```

The foreach...as Loop

The creators of PHP have gone to great lengths to make the language easy to use. So, not content with the loop structures already provided, they added another one especially for arrays: the foreach...as loop. Using it, you can step through all the items in an array, one at a time, and do something with them.

The process starts with the first item and ends with the last one, so you don't even have to know how many items there are in an array. Example 6-6 shows how foreach...as can be used to rewrite Example 6-3.

Example 6-6. Walking through a numeric array using foreach...as

```
<?php
  $paper = array("Copier", "Inkjet", "Laser", "Photo");
  $j = 0;

  foreach($paper as $item)
  {
    echo "$j: $item<br>";
    ++$j;
  }
?>
```

When PHP encounters a foreach statement, it takes the first item of the array and places it in the variable following the as keyword; and each time control flow returns to the foreach, the next array element is placed in the as keyword. In this case, the variable $item is set to each of the four values in turn in the array $paper. Once all values have been used, execution of the loop ends. The output from this code is exactly the same as in Example 6-3.

Now let's see how foreach works with an associative array by taking a look at Example 6-7, which is a rewrite of the second half of Example 6-5.

Example 6-7. Walking through an associative array using foreach...as

```php
<?php
  $paper = array('copier' => "Copier & Multipurpose",
                 'inkjet' => "Inkjet Printer",
                 'laser'  => "Laser Printer",
                 'photo'  => "Photographic Paper");

  foreach($paper as $item => $description)
    echo "$item: $description<br>";
?>
```

Remember that associative arrays do not require numeric indexes, so the variable $j is not used in this example. Instead, each item of the array $paper is fed into the key/value pair of variables $item and $description, from which they are printed out. The displayed result of this code is as follows:

```
copier: Copier & Multipurpose
inkjet: Inkjet Printer
laser: Laser Printer
photo: Photographic Paper
```

As list function an alternative syntax to foreach...as, you can use the list function in conjunction with the each function, as in Example 6-8.

Example 6-8. Walking through an associative array using each and list

```php
<?php
  $paper = array('copier' => "Copier & Multipurpose",
                 'inkjet' => "Inkjet Printer",
                 'laser'  => "Laser Printer",
                 'photo'  => "Photographic Paper");

  while (list($item, $description) = each($paper))
    echo "$item: $description<br>";
?>
```

In this example, a while loop is set up and will continue looping until each returns a value of FALSE. The each function acts like foreach: it returns an array containing a key/value pair from the array $paper and then moves its built-in pointer to the next pair in that array. When there are no more pairs to return, each returns FALSE.

The list function takes an array as its argument (in this case, the key/value pair returned by the function each) and then assigns the values of the array to the variables listed within parentheses.

You can see how list works a little more clearly in Example 6-9, where an array is created out of the two strings Alice and Bob and then passed to the list function, which assigns those strings as values to the variables $a and $b.

Example 6-9. Using the list function

```php
<?php
  list($a, $b) = array('Alice', 'Bob');
  echo "a=$a b=$b";
?>
```

The output from this code is as follows:

a=Alice b=Bob

So, you can take your pick when walking through arrays. Use `foreach...as` to create a loop that extracts values to the variable following the `as`, or use the `each` function and create your own looping system.

Multidimensional Arrays

A simple design feature in PHP's array syntax makes it possible to create arrays of more than one dimension. In fact, they can be as many dimensions as you like (although it's a rare application that goes further than three).

That feature is the ability to include an entire array as a part of another one, and to be able to keep doing so, just like the old rhyme: "Big fleas have little fleas upon their backs to bite 'em. Little fleas have lesser fleas, add flea, ad infinitum."

Let's look at how this works by taking the associative array in the previous example and extending it; see Example 6-10.

Example 6-10. Creating a multidimensional associative array

```php
<?php
  $products = array(

    'paper' => array(

      'copier' => "Copier & Multipurpose",
      'inkjet' => "Inkjet Printer",
      'laser'  => "Laser Printer",
      'photo'  => "Photographic Paper"),

    'pens' => array(

      'ball'   => "Ball Point",
      'hilite' => "Highlighters",
      'marker' => "Markers"),

    'misc' => array(

      'tape'  => "Sticky Tape",
      'glue'  => "Adhesives",
```

```
        'clips'  => "Paperclips"
      )
  );

  echo "<pre>";

  foreach($products as $section => $items)
    foreach($items as $key => $value)
      echo "$section:\t$key\t($value)<br>";

  echo "</pre>";
?>
```

To make things clearer now that the code is starting to grow, I've renamed some of the elements. For example, because the previous array $paper is now just a subsection of a larger array, the main array is now called $products. Within this array, there are three items—paper, pens, and misc—each of which contains another array with key/value pairs.

If necessary, these subarrays could have contained even further arrays. For example, under ball there might be many different types and colors of ballpoint pens available in the online store. But for now, I've restricted the code to a depth of just two.

Once the array data has been assigned, I use a pair of nested foreach...as loops to print out the various values. The outer loop extracts the main sections from the top level of the array, and the inner loop extracts the key/value pairs for the categories within each section.

As long as you remember that each level of the array works the same way (it's a key/value pair), you can easily write code to access any element at any level.

The echo statement makes use of the PHP escape character \t, which outputs a tab. Although tabs are not normally significant to the web browser, I let them be used for layout by using the <pre>...</pre> tags, which tell the web browser to format the text as preformatted and monospaced, and *not* to ignore whitespace characters such as tabs and line feeds. The output from this code looks like the following:

```
paper:  copier  (Copier & Multipurpose)
paper:  inkjet  (Inkjet Printer)
paper:  laser   (Laser Printer)
paper:  photo   (Photographic Paper)
pens:   ball    (Ball Point)
pens:   hilite  (Highlighters)
pens:   marker  (Markers)
misc:   tape    (Sticky Tape)
misc:   glue    (Adhesives)
misc:   clips   (Paperclips)
```

You can directly access a particular element of the array by using square brackets:

```
echo $products['misc']['glue'];
```

This outputs the value Adhesives.

You can also create numeric multidimensional arrays that are accessed directly by indexes rather than by alphanumeric identifiers. Example 6-11 creates the board for a chess game with the pieces in their starting positions.

Example 6-11. Creating a multidimensional numeric array

```php
<?php
  $chessboard = array(
    array('r', 'n', 'b', 'q', 'k', 'b', 'n', 'r'),
    array('p', 'p', 'p', 'p', 'p', 'p', 'p', 'p'),
    array(' ', ' ', ' ', ' ', ' ', ' ', ' ', ' '),
    array(' ', ' ', ' ', ' ', ' ', ' ', ' ', ' '),
    array(' ', ' ', ' ', ' ', ' ', ' ', ' ', ' '),
    array(' ', ' ', ' ', ' ', ' ', ' ', ' ', ' '),
    array('P', 'P', 'P', 'P', 'P', 'P', 'P', 'P'),
    array('R', 'N', 'B', 'Q', 'K', 'B', 'N', 'R')
  );

  echo "<pre>";

  foreach($chessboard as $row)
  {
    foreach ($row as $piece)
      echo "$piece ";

    echo "<br>";
  }

  echo "</pre>";
?>
```

In this example, the lowercase letters represent black pieces, and the uppercase white. The key is r = rook, n = knight, b = bishop, k = king, q = queen, and p = pawn. Again, a pair of nested foreach...as loops walks through the array and displays its contents. The outer loop processes each row into the variable $row, which itself is an array, because the $chessboard array uses a subarray for each row. This loop has two statements within it, so curly braces enclose them.

The inner loop then processes each square in a row, outputting the character ($piece) stored in it, followed by a space (to square up the printout). This loop has a single statement, so curly braces are not required to enclose it. The <pre> and </pre> tags ensure that the output displays correctly, like this:

```
r n b q k b n r
p p p p p p p p
```

```
P P P P P P P
R N B Q K B N R
```

You can also directly access any element within this array by using square brackets:

```
echo $chessboard[7][3];
```

This statement outputs the uppercase letter Q, the eighth element down and the fourth along (remember that array indexes start at 0, not 1).

Using Array Functions

You've already seen the list and each functions, but PHP comes with numerous other functions for handling arrays. You can find the full list in the documentation (*http://tinyurl.com/arraysinphp*). However, some of these functions are so fundamental that it's worth taking the time to look at them here.

is_array

Arrays and variables share the same namespace. This means that you cannot have a string variable called $fred and an array also called $fred. If you're in doubt and your code needs to check whether a variable is an array, you can use the is_array function, like this:

```
echo (is_array($fred)) ? "Is an array" : "Is not an array";
```

Note that if $fred has not yet been assigned a value, an Undefined variable message will be generated.

count

Although the each function and foreach...as loop structure are excellent ways to walk through an array's contents, sometimes you need to know exactly how many elements there are in your array, particularly if you will be referencing them directly. To count all the elements in the top level of an array, use a command such as this:

```
echo count($fred);
```

Should you wish to know how many elements there are altogether in a multidimensional array, you can use a statement such as the following:

```
echo count($fred, 1);
```

The second parameter is optional and sets the mode to use. It should be either 0 to limit counting to only the top level, or 1 to force recursive counting of all subarray elements too.

sort

Sorting is so common that PHP provides a built-in function for it. In its simplest form, you would use it like this:

```
sort($fred);
```

Unlike some other functions, `sort` will act directly on the supplied array rather than returning a new array of sorted elements. It returns TRUE on success and FALSE on error and also supports a few flags—the main two that you might wish to use force items to be sorted either numerically or as strings, like this:

```
sort($fred, SORT_NUMERIC);
sort($fred, SORT_STRING);
```

You can also sort an array in reverse order using the `rsort` function, like this:

```
rsort($fred, SORT_NUMERIC);
rsort($fred, SORT_STRING);
```

shuffle

There may be times when you need the elements of an array to be put in random order, such as when you're creating a game of playing cards:

```
shuffle($cards);
```

Like `sort`, `shuffle` acts directly on the supplied array and returns TRUE on success or FALSE on error.

explode

explode is a very useful function with which you can take a string containing several items separated by a single character (or string of characters) and then place each of these items into an array. One handy example is to split up a sentence into an array containing all its words, as in Example 6-12.

Example 6-12. Exploding a string into an array using spaces

```
<?php
  $temp = explode(' ', "This is a sentence with seven words");
  print_r($temp);
?>
```

This example prints out the following (on a single line when viewed in a browser):

```
Array
(
  [0] => This
  [1] => is
```

```
      [2] => a
      [3] => sentence
      [4] => with
      [5] => seven
      [6] => words
  )
```

The first parameter, the delimiter, need not be a space or even a single character. Example 6-13 shows a slight variation.

Example 6-13. Exploding a string delimited with *** into an array

```php
<?php
  $temp = explode('***', "A***sentence***with***asterisks");
  print_r($temp);
?>
```

The code in Example 6-13 prints out the following:

```
  Array
  (
    [0] => A
    [1] => sentence
    [2] => with
    [3] => asterisks
  )
```

extract

Sometimes it can be convenient to turn the key/value pairs from an array into PHP variables. One such time might be when you are processing the $_GET or $_POST variables sent to a PHP script by a form.

When a form is submitted over the web, the web server unpacks the variables into a global array for the PHP script. If the variables were sent using the GET method, they will be placed in an associative array called $_GET; if they were sent using POST, they will be placed in an associative array called $_POST.

You could, of course, walk through such associative arrays in the manner shown in the examples so far. However, sometimes you just want to store the values sent into variables for later use. In this case, you can have PHP do the job automatically:

```php
extract($_GET);
```

So, if the query string parameter q is sent to a PHP script along with the associated value Hi there, a new variable called $q will be created and assigned that value.

Be careful with this approach, though, because if any extracted variables conflict with ones that you have already defined, your existing values will be overwritten. To avoid this possibility, you can use one of the many additional parameters available to this function, like this:

```
extract($_GET, EXTR_PREFIX_ALL, 'fromget');
```

In this case, all the new variables will begin with the given prefix string followed by an underscore, so $q will become $fromget_q. I strongly recommend that you use this version of the function when handling the $_GET and $_POST arrays, or any other array whose keys could be controlled by the user, because malicious users could submit keys chosen deliberately to overwrite commonly used variable names and compromise your website.

compact

At times you may want to use compact, the inverse of extract, to create an array from variables and their values. Example 6-14 shows how you might use this function.

Example 6-14. Using the compact function

```php
<?php
  $fname        = "Doctor";
  $sname        = "Who";
  $planet       = "Gallifrey";
  $system       = "Gridlock";
  $constellation = "Kasterborous";

  $contact = compact('fname', 'sname', 'planet', 'system', 'constellation');

  print_r($contact);
?>
```

The result of running Example 6-14 is as follows:

```
Array
(
  [fname] => Doctor
  [sname] => Who
  [planet] => Gallifrey
  [system] => Gridlock
  [constellation] => Kasterborous
)
```

Note how compact requires the variable names to be supplied in quotes, not preceded by a $ symbol. This is because compact is looking for a list of variable names, not their values.

Another use of this function is for debugging, when you wish to quickly view several variables and their values, as in Example 6-15.

Example 6-15. Using compact to help with debugging

```php
<?php
  $j       = 23;
  $temp    = "Hello";
  $address = "1 Old Street";
  $age     = 61;

  print_r(compact(explode(' ', 'j temp address age')));
?>
```

This works by using the `explode` function to extract all the words from the string into an array, which is then passed to the `compact` function, which in turn returns an array to `print_r`, which finally shows its contents.

If you copy and paste the `print_r` line of code, you only need to alter the variables named there for a quick printout of a group of variables' values. In this example, the output is shown here:

```
Array
(
  [j] => 23
  [temp] => Hello
  [address] => 1 Old Street
  [age] => 61
)
```

reset

When the `foreach...as` construct or the `each` function walks through an array, it keeps an internal PHP pointer that makes a note of which element of the array it should return next. If your code ever needs to return to the start of an array, you can issue `reset`, which also returns the value of that element. Examples of how to use this function are as follows:

```php
reset($fred);        // Throw away return value
$item = reset($fred); // Keep first element of the array in $item
```

end

As with `reset`, you can move PHP's internal array pointer to the final element in an array using the `end` function, which also returns the value of the element, and can be used as in these examples:

```php
end($fred);
$item = end($fred);
```

This chapter concludes your basic introduction to PHP, and you should now be able to write quite complex programs using the skills you have learned. In the next chapter, we'll look at using PHP for common, practical tasks.

Questions

1. What is the difference between a numeric and an associative array?
2. What is the main benefit of the `array` keyword?
3. What is the difference between `foreach` and `each`?
4. How can you create a multidimensional array?
5. How can you determine the number of elements in an array?
6. What is the purpose of the `explode` function?
7. How can you set PHP's internal pointer into an array back to the first element of the array?

See "Chapter 6 Answers" on page 717 in Appendix A for the answers to these questions.

CHAPTER 7

Practical PHP

The previous chapters went over the elements of the PHP language. This chapter builds on your new programming skills to teach you how to perform some common but important practical tasks. You will learn the best ways to handle strings in order to achieve clear and concise code that displays in web browsers exactly how you want it to, including advanced date and time management. You'll also find out how to create and otherwise modify files, including those uploaded by users.

Using printf

You've already seen the `print` and `echo` functions, which simply output text to the browser. But a much more powerful function, `printf`, controls the format of the output by letting you put special formatting characters in a string. For each formatting character, `printf` expects you to pass an argument that it will display using that format. For instance, the following example uses the `%d` conversion specifier to display the value 3 in decimal:

```
printf("There are %d items in your basket", 3);
```

If you replace the `%d` with `%b`, the value 3 will be displayed in binary (11). Table 7-1 shows the conversion specifiers supported.

Table 7-1. The printf conversion specifiers

Specifier	Conversion action on argument arg	Example (for an arg of 123)
%	Display a % character (no arg required)	%
b	Display arg as a binary integer	1111011
c	Display ASCII character for arg	{
d	Display arg as a signed decimal integer	123
e	Display arg using scientific notation	1.23000e+2

Specifier	Conversion action on argument arg	Example (for an arg of 123)
f	Display arg as floating point	123.000000
o	Display arg as an octal integer	173
s	Display arg as a string	123
u	Display arg as an unsigned decimal	123
x	Display arg in lowercase hexadecimal	7b
X	Display arg in uppercase hexadecimal	7B

You can have as many specifiers as you like in a `printf` function, as long as you pass a matching number of arguments and as long as each specifier is prefaced by a `%` symbol. Therefore, the following code is valid, and will output "My name is Simon. I'm 33 years old, which is 21 in hexadecimal":

```
printf("My name is %s. I'm %d years old, which is %X in hexadecimal",
    'Simon', 33, 33);
```

If you leave out any arguments, you will receive a parse error informing you that a right bracket,), was unexpectedly encountered.

A more practical example of `printf` sets colors in HTML using decimal values. For example, suppose you know you want a color that has a triplet value of 65 red, 127 green, and 245 blue, but don't want to convert this to hexadecimal yourself. Here's an easy solution:

```
printf("<span style='color:#%X%X%X'>Hello</span>", 65, 127, 245);
```

Check the format of the color specification between the apostrophes (`''`) carefully. First comes the pound, or hash, sign (#) expected by the color specification. Then come three `%X` format specifiers, one for each of your numbers. The resulting output from this command is as follows:

```
<span style='color:#417FF5'>Hello</span>
```

Usually, you'll find it convenient to use variables or expressions as arguments to `printf`. For instance, if you stored values for your colors in the three variables $r, $g, and $b, you could create a darker color with this:

```
printf("<span style='color:#%X%X%X'>Hello</span>", $r-20, $g-20, $b-20);
```

Precision Setting

Not only can you specify a conversion type, but you can also set the precision of the displayed result. For example, amounts of currency are usually displayed with only two digits of precision. However, after a calculation, a value may have a greater precision than this, such as 123.42 / 12, which results in 10.285. To ensure that such values are correctly stored internally, but displayed with only two digits of precision, you can insert the string ".2" between the `%` symbol and the conversion specifier:

```php
printf("The result is: $%.2f", 123.42 / 12);
```

The output from this command is as follows:

The result is $10.29

But you actually have even more control than that, because you can also specify whether to pad output with either zeros or spaces by prefacing the specifier with certain values. Example 7-1 shows four possible combinations.

Example 7-1. Precision setting

```php
<?php
  echo "<pre>"; // Enables viewing of the spaces

  // Pad to 15 spaces
  printf("The result is $%15f\n", 123.42 / 12);

  // Pad to 15 spaces, fill with zeros
  printf("The result is $%015f\n", 123.42 / 12);

  // Pad to 15 spaces, 2 decimal places precision
  printf("The result is $%15.2f\n", 123.42 / 12);

  // Pad to 15 spaces, 2 decimal places precision, fill with zeros
  printf("The result is $%015.2f\n", 123.42 / 12);

  // Pad to 15 spaces, 2 decimal places precision, fill with # symbol
  printf("The result is $%'#15.2f\n", 123.42 / 12);
?>
```

The output from this example looks like this:

```
The result is $      10.285000
The result is $00000010.285000
The result is $         10.29
The result is $000000000010.29
The result is $##########10.29
```

The way it works is simple if you go from right to left (see Table 7-2). Notice that:

- The rightmost character is the conversion specifier: in this case, f for floating point.

- Just before the conversion specifier, if there is a period and a number together, then the precision of the output is specified as the value of the number.

- Regardless of whether there's a precision specifier, if there is a number, then that represents the number of characters to which the output should be padded. In the previous example, this is 15 characters. If the output is already equal to or greater than the padding length, then this argument is ignored.

- The leftmost parameter allowed after the % symbol is a 0, which is ignored unless a padding value has been set, in which case the output is padded with zeros instead of spaces. If a pad character other than zero or a space is required, you can use any one of your choice as long as you preface it with a single quotation mark, like this: '#.
- On the left is the % symbol, which starts the conversion.

Table 7-2. Conversion specifier components

Start conversion	Pad character	Number of pad characters	Display precision	Conversion specifier	Example
%		15		f	10.285000
%	0	15	.2	f	000000000010.29
%	'#	15	.4	f	########10.2850

String Padding

You can also pad strings to required lengths (as you can with numbers), select different padding characters, and even choose between left and right justification. Example 7-2 shows various examples.

Example 7-2. String padding

```php
<?php
  echo "<pre>"; // Enables viewing of the spaces

  $h = 'Rasmus';

  printf("[%s]\n",        $h); // Standard string output
  printf("[%12s]\n",      $h); // Right justify with spaces to width 12
  printf("[%-12s]\n",     $h); // Left justify with spaces
  printf("[%012s]\n",     $h); // Pad with zeros
  printf("[%'#12s]\n\n",  $h); // Use the custom padding character '#'

  $d = 'Rasmus Lerdorf';       // The original creator of PHP

  printf("[%12.8s]\n",    $d); // Right justify, cutoff of 8 characters
  printf("[%-12.12s]\n",  $d); // Left justify, cutoff of 12 characters
  printf("[%-'@12.10s]\n", $d); // Left justify, pad with '@', cutoff 10 chars
?>
```

Note how for purposes of layout in a web page, I've used the <pre> HTML tag to preserve all the spaces and the \n newline character after each of the lines to be displayed. The output from this example is as follows:

```
[Rasmus]
[       Rasmus]
[Rasmus       ]
[000000Rasmus]
[######Rasmus]

[     Rasmus L]
[Rasmus Lerdo]
[Rasmus Ler@@]
```

When you specify a padding value, strings of a length equal to or greater than that value will be ignored, *unless* a cutoff value is given that shortens the strings back to less than the padding value.

Table 7-3 shows the components available to string conversion specifiers.

Table 7-3. String conversion specifier components

Start conversion	Left/right justify	Padding character	Number of pad characters	Cutoff	Conversion specifier	Example (using "Rasmus")
%					s	[Rasmus]
%	-		10		s	[Rasmus]
%		'#	8	.4	s	[####Rasm]

Using sprintf

Often, you don't want to output the result of a conversion but need it to use elsewhere in your code. This is where the `sprintf` function comes in. With it, you can send the output to another variable rather than to the browser.

You might use it to make a conversion, as in the following example, which returns the hexadecimal string value for the RGB color group 65, 127, 245 in `$hexstring`:

```
$hexstring = sprintf("%X%X%X", 65, 127, 245);
```

Or you may wish to store output ready to display later on:

```
$out = sprintf("The result is: $%.2f", 123.42 / 12);
echo $out;
```

Date and Time Functions

To keep track of the date and time, PHP uses standard Unix timestamps, which are simply the number of seconds since the start of January 1, 1970. To determine the current timestamp, you can use the `time` function:

```
echo time();
```

Because the value is stored as seconds, to obtain the timestamp for this time next week, you would use the following, which adds 7 days × 24 hours × 60 minutes × 60 seconds to the returned value:

```
echo time() + 7 * 24 * 60 * 60;
```

If you wish to create a timestamp for a given date, you can use the mktime function. Its output is the timestamp 946684800 for the first second of the first minute of the first hour of the first day of the year 2000:

```
echo mktime(0, 0, 0, 1, 1, 2000);
```

The parameters to pass are, in order from left to right:

- The number of the hour (0–23)
- The number of the minute (0–59)
- The number of seconds (0–59)
- The number of the month (1–12)
- The number of the day (1–31)
- The year (1970–2038, or 1901–2038 with PHP 5.1.0+ on 32-bit signed systems)

You may ask why you are limited to the years 1970 through 2038. Well, it's because the original developers of Unix chose the start of the year 1970 as the base date that no programmer should need to go before!

Luckily, as of version 5.1.0, PHP supports systems using a signed 32-bit integer for the timestamp, and dates from 1901 to 2038 are allowed on them. However, that introduces a problem even worse than the original one, because the Unix designers also decided that nobody would still be using Unix after about 70 years or so and therefore believed they could get away with storing the timestamp as a 32-bit value—which will run out on January 19, 2038!

This will create what has come to be known as the Y2K38 bug (much like the millennium bug, which was caused by storing years as two-digit values, and which also had to be fixed). PHP introduced the DateTime class in version 5.2 to overcome this issue, but it will work only on 64-bit architecture, which most computers will be these days (but do check before you use it).

To display the date, use the date function, which supports a plethora of formatting options enabling you to display the date any way you wish. The format is as follows:

```
date($format, $timestamp);
```

The parameter $format should be a string containing formatting specifiers as detailed in Table 7-4, and $timestamp should be a Unix timestamp. For the complete list of specifiers, please see the documentation (*http://php.net/manual/en/function.date.php*). The following command will output the current date and time in the format "Thursday July 6th, 2017 - 1:38pm":

```
echo date("l F jS, Y - g:ia", time());
```

Table 7-4. The major date function format specifiers

Format	Description	Returned value
Day specifiers		
d	Day of month, two digits, with leading zeros	01 to 31
D	Day of the week, three letters	Mon to Sun
j	Day of month, no leading zeros	1 to 31
l	Day of week, full names	Sunday to Saturday
N	Day of week, numeric, Monday to Sunday	1 to 7
S	Suffix for day of month (useful with specifier j)	st, nd, rd, or th
w	Day of week, numeric, Sunday to Saturday	0 to 6
z	Day of year	0 to 365
Week specifier		
W	Week number of year	01 to 52
Month specifiers		
F	Month name	January to December
m	Month number with leading zeros	01 to 12
M	Month name, three letters	Jan to Dec
n	Month number, no leading zeros	1 to 12
t	Number of days in given month	28 to 31
Year specifiers		
L	Leap year	1 = Yes, 0 = No
y	Year, 2 digits	00 to 99
Y	Year, 4 digits	0000 to 9999
Time specifiers		
a	Before or after midday, lowercase	am or pm
A	Before or after midday, uppercase	AM or PM
g	Hour of day, 12-hour format, no leading zeros	1 to 12
G	Hour of day, 24-hour format, no leading zeros	0 to 23
h	Hour of day, 12-hour format, with leading zeros	01 to 12
H	Hour of day, 24-hour format, with leading zeros	00 to 23
i	Minutes, with leading zeros	00 to 59
s	Seconds, with leading zeros	00 to 59

Date Constants

There are a number of useful constants that you can use with the `date` command to return the date in specific formats. For example, `date(DATE_RSS)` returns the current date and time in the valid format for an RSS feed. Some of the more commonly used constants are as follows:

DATE_ATOM
> This is the format for Atom feeds. The PHP format is `"Y-m-d\TH:i:sP"` and example output is `"2022-10-22T12:00:00+00:00"`.

DATE_COOKIE
> This is the format for cookies set from a web server or JavaScript. The PHP format is `"l, d-M-y H:i:s T"` and example output is `"Wednesday, 26-Oct-22 12:00:00 UTC"`.

DATE_RSS
> This is the format for RSS feeds. The PHP format is `"D, d M Y H:i:s O"` and example output is `"Wed, 26 Oct 2022 12:00:00 UTC"`.

DATE_W3C
> This is the format for the World Wide Web Consortium. The PHP format is `"Y-m-d\TH:i:sP"` and example output is `"2022-10-26T12:00:00+00:00"`.

The complete list can be found in the documentation (*http://php.net/manual/en/ class.datetime.php*).

Using checkdate

You've seen how to display a valid date in a variety of formats. But how can you check whether a user has submitted a valid date to your program? The answer is to pass the month, day, and year to the `checkdate` function, which returns a value of TRUE if the date is valid, or FALSE if it is not.

For example, if September 31 of any year is input, it will always be an invalid date. Example 7-3 shows code that you could use for this. As it stands, it will find the given date invalid.

Example 7-3. Checking for the validity of a date

```php
<?php
  $month = 9;    // September (only has 30 days)
  $day   = 31;   // 31st
  $year  = 2022; // 2022

  if (checkdate($month, $day, $year)) echo "Date is valid";
```

```
    else echo "Date is invalid";
?>
```

File Handling

Powerful as it is, MySQL is not the only (or necessarily the best) way to store all data on a web server. Sometimes it can be quicker and more convenient to directly access files on the hard disk. Cases in which you might need to do this are when modifying images such as uploaded user avatars, or with log files that you wish to process.

First, though, a note about file naming: if you are writing code that may be used on various PHP installations, there is no way of knowing whether these systems are case-sensitive. For example, Windows and macOS filenames are not case-sensitive, but Linux and Unix ones are. Therefore, you should always assume that the system is case-sensitive and stick to a convention such as all-lowercase filenames.

Checking Whether a File Exists

To determine whether a file already exists, you can use the file_exists function, which returns either TRUE or FALSE and is used like this:

```
    if (file_exists("testfile.txt")) echo "File exists";
```

Creating a File

At this point, *testfile.txt* doesn't exist, so let's create it and write a few lines to it. Type Example 7-4 and save it as *testfile.php*.

Example 7-4. Creating a simple text file

```
<?php // testfile.php
  $fh = fopen("testfile.txt", 'w') or die("Failed to create file");

  $text = <<<_END
Line 1
Line 2
Line 3
_END;

  fwrite($fh, $text) or die("Could not write to file");
  fclose($fh);
  echo "File 'testfile.txt' written successfully";
?>
```

Should a program call the die function, the open file will be automatically closed as part of terminating the program.

When you run this in a browser, all being well, you will receive the message File 'testfile.txt' written successfully. If you receive an error message, your hard disk may be full or, more likely, you may not have permission to create or write to the file, in which case you should modify the attributes of the destination folder according to your operating system. Otherwise, the file *testfile.txt* should now be residing in the same folder in which you saved the *testfile.php* program. Try opening the file in a text or program editor—the contents will look like this:

```
Line 1
Line 2
Line 3
```

This simple example shows the sequence that all file handling takes:

1. Always start by opening the file. You do this through a call to fopen.

2. Then you can call other functions; here we write to the file (fwrite), but you can also read from an existing file (fread or fgets) and do other things.

3. Finish by closing the file (fclose). Although the program does this for you when it ends, you should clean up by closing the file when you're finished.

Every open file requires a file resource so that PHP can access and manage it. The preceding example sets the variable $fh (which I chose to stand for *file handle*) to the value returned by the fopen function. Thereafter, each file-handling function that accesses the opened file, such as fwrite or fclose, must be passed $fh as a parameter to identify the file being accessed. Don't worry about the content of the $fh variable; it's a number PHP uses to refer to internal information about the file—you just pass the variable to other functions.

Upon failure, FALSE will be returned by fopen. The previous example shows a simple way to capture and respond to the failure: it calls the die function to end the program and give the user an error message. A web application would never abort in this crude way (you would create a web page with an error message instead), but this is fine for our testing purposes.

Notice the second parameter to the fopen call. It is simply the character w, which tells the function to open the file for writing. The function creates the file if it doesn't already exist. Be careful when playing around with these functions: if the file already exists, the w mode parameter causes the fopen call to delete the old contents (even if you don't write anything new!).

There are several different mode parameters that can be used here, as detailed in Table 7-5. The modes that include a + symbol are further explained in the section "Updating Files" on page 151.

Table 7-5. *The supported fopen modes*

Mode	Action	Description
'r'	Read from file's beginning	Open for reading only; place the file pointer at the beginning of the file. Return FALSE if the file doesn't already exist.
'r+'	Read from file's beginning and allow writing	Open for reading and writing; place the file pointer at the beginning of the file. Return FALSE if the file doesn't already exist.
'w'	Write from file's beginning and truncate file	Open for writing only; place the file pointer at the beginning of the file and truncate the file to zero length. If the file doesn't exist, attempt to create it.
'w+'	Write from file's beginning, truncate file, and allow reading	Open for reading and writing; place the file pointer at the beginning of the file and truncate the file to zero length. If the file doesn't exist, attempt to create it.
'a'	Append to file's end	Open for writing only; place the file pointer at the end of the file. If the file doesn't exist, attempt to create it.
'a+'	Append to file's end and allow reading	Open for reading and writing; place the file pointer at the end of the file. If the file doesn't exist, attempt to create it.

Reading from Files

The easiest way to read from a text file is to grab a whole line through `fgets` (think of the final s as standing for *string*), as in Example 7-5.

Example 7-5. Reading a file with fgets

```php
<?php
  $fh = fopen("testfile.txt", 'r') or
    die("File does not exist or you lack permission to open it");

  $line = fgets($fh);
  fclose($fh);
  echo $line;
?>
```

If you created the file as shown in Example 7-4, you'll get the first line:

```
Line 1
```

You can retrieve multiple lines or portions of lines through the `fread` function, as in Example 7-6.

Example 7-6. Reading a file with fread

```php
<?php
  $fh = fopen("testfile.txt", 'r') or
    die("File does not exist or you lack permission to open it");

  $text = fread($fh, 3);
  fclose($fh);
```

```
    echo $text;
?>
```

I've requested three characters in the fread call, so the program displays this:

```
    Lin
```

The fread function is commonly used with binary data. If you use it on text data that spans more than one line, remember to count newline characters.

Copying Files

Let's try out the PHP copy function to create a clone of *testfile.txt*. Type Example 7-7, save it as *copyfile.php*, and then call up the program in your browser.

Example 7-7. Copying a file

```
<?php // copyfile.php
  copy('testfile.txt', 'testfile2.txt') or die("Could not copy file");
  echo "File successfully copied to 'testfile2.txt'";
?>
```

If you check your folder again, you'll see that you now have the new file *testfile2.txt* in it. By the way, if you don't want your programs to exit on a failed copy attempt, you could try the alternate syntax in Example 7-8. This uses the ! (NOT) operator as a quick and easy shorthand. Placed in front of an expression, it applies the NOT operator to it, so the equivalent statement here in English would begin "If not able to copy..."

Example 7-8. Alternate syntax for copying a file

```
<?php // copyfile2.php
  if (!copy('testfile.txt', 'testfile2.txt')) echo "Could not copy file";
  else echo "File successfully copied to 'testfile2.txt'";
?>
```

Moving a File

To move a file, rename it with the rename function, as in Example 7-9.

Example 7-9. Moving a file

```
<?php // movefile.php
  if (!rename('testfile2.txt', 'testfile2.new'))
    echo "Could not rename file";
  else echo "File successfully renamed to 'testfile2.new'";
?>
```

You can use the `rename` function on directories, too. To avoid any warning messages if the original file doesn't exist, you can call the `file_exists` function first to check.

Deleting a File

Deleting a file is just a matter of using the `unlink` function to remove it from the filesystem, as in Example 7-10.

Example 7-10. Deleting a file

```
<?php // deletefile.php
  if (!unlink('testfile2.new')) echo "Could not delete file";
  else echo "File 'testfile2.new' successfully deleted";
?>
```

> Whenever you access files on your hard disk directly, you must also always ensure that it is impossible for your filesystem to be compromised. For example, if you are deleting a file based on user input, you must make absolutely certain it is a file that can be safely deleted and that the user is allowed to delete it.

As with moving a file, a warning message will be displayed if the file doesn't exist, which you can avoid by using `file_exists` to first check for its existence before calling `unlink`.

Updating Files

Often, you will want to add more data to a saved file, which you can do in many ways. You can use one of the append write modes (see Table 7-5), or you can simply open a file for reading and writing with one of the other modes that supports writing, and move the file pointer to the correct place within the file that you wish to write to or read from.

The *file pointer* is the position within a file at which the next file access will take place, whether it's a read or a write. It is not the same as the *file handle* (as stored in the variable `$fh` in Example 7-4), which contains details about the file being accessed.

You can see this in action by typing Example 7-11 and saving it as *update.php*. Then call it up in your browser.

Example 7-11. Updating a file

```
<?php // update.php
  $fh   = fopen("testfile.txt", 'r+') or die("Failed to open file");
  $text = fgets($fh);
```

```
    fseek($fh, 0, SEEK_END);
    fwrite($fh, "$text") or die("Could not write to file");
    fclose($fh);

    echo "File 'testfile.txt' successfully updated";
?>
```

This program opens *testfile.txt* for both reading and writing by setting the mode with
'r+', which puts the file pointer right at the start. It then uses the fgets function to
read in a single line from the file (up to the first line feed). After that, the fseek function is called to move the file pointer right to the file end, at which point the line of
text that was extracted from the start of the file (stored in $text) is then appended to
the file's end and the file is closed. The resulting file now looks like this:

```
    Line 1
    Line 2
    Line 3
    Line 1
```

The first line has successfully been copied and then appended to the file's end.

As used here, in addition to the $fh file handle, the fseek function was passed two
other parameters, 0 and SEEK_END. SEEK_END tells the function to move the file
pointer to the end of the file, and 0 tells it how many positions it should then be
moved backward from that point. In the case of Example 7-11, a value of 0 is used
because the pointer is required to remain at the file's end.

There are two other seek options available to the fseek function: SEEK_SET and
SEEK_CUR. The SEEK_SET option tells the function to set the file pointer to the exact
position given by the preceding parameter. Thus, the following example moves the
file pointer to position 18:

```
    fseek($fh, 18, SEEK_SET);
```

SEEK_CUR sets the file pointer to the current position *plus* the value of the given offset.
Therefore, if the file pointer is currently at position 18, the following call will move it
to position 23:

```
    fseek($fh, 5, SEEK_CUR);
```

Although this is not recommended unless you have very specific reasons for it, it is
even possible to use text files such as this (but with fixed line lengths) as simple flat
file databases. Your program can then use fseek to move back and forth within such
a file to retrieve, update, and add new records. You can also delete records by over-
writing them with zero characters, and so on.

Locking Files for Multiple Accesses

Web programs are often called by many users at the same time. If more than one person tries to write to a file simultaneously, it can become corrupted. And if one person writes to it while another is reading from it, the file is all right, but the person reading it can get odd results. To handle simultaneous users, you must use the file-locking flock function. This function queues up all other requests to access a file until your program releases the lock. So, whenever your programs use write access on files that may be accessed concurrently by multiple users, you should also add file locking to them, as in Example 7-12, which is an updated version of Example 7-11.

Example 7-12. Updating a file with file locking

```php
<?php
  $fh   = fopen("testfile.txt", 'r+') or die("Failed to open file");
  $text = fgets($fh);

  if (flock($fh, LOCK_EX))
  {
    fseek($fh, 0, SEEK_END);
    fwrite($fh, "$text") or die("Could not write to file");
    flock($fh, LOCK_UN);
  }

  fclose($fh);
  echo "File 'testfile.txt' successfully updated";
?>
```

There is a trick to file locking to preserve the best possible response time for your website visitors: perform it directly before a change you make to a file, and then unlock it immediately afterward. Having a file locked for any longer than this will slow down your application unnecessarily. This is why the calls to flock in Example 7-12 are directly before and after the fwrite call.

The first call to flock sets an exclusive file lock on the file referred to by $fh using the LOCK_EX parameter:

```php
flock($fh, LOCK_EX);
```

From this point onward, no other processes can write to (or even read from) the file until you release the lock by using the LOCK_UN parameter, like this:

```php
flock($fh, LOCK_UN);
```

As soon as the lock is released, other processes are again allowed access to the file. This is one reason why you should reseek to the point you wish to access in a file each time you need to read or write data—another process could have changed the file since the last access.

However, did you notice that the call to request an exclusive lock is nested as part of an `if` statement? This is because `flock` is not supported on all systems; thus, it is wise to check whether you successfully secured a lock, just in case one could not be obtained.

Something else you must consider is that `flock` is what is known as an *advisory* lock. This means that it locks out only other processes that call the function. If you have any code that goes right in and modifies files without implementing `flock` file locking, it will always override the locking and could wreak havoc on your files.

By the way, implementing file locking and then accidentally leaving it out in one section of code can lead to an extremely hard-to-locate bug.

 `flock` will not work on NFS and many other networked filesystems. Also, when using a multithreaded server like ISAPI, you may not be able to rely on `flock` to protect files against other PHP scripts running in parallel threads of the same server instance. Additionally, `flock` is not supported on any system using the old FAT filesystem, such as older versions of Windows.

If in doubt, you can try making a quick lock on a test file at the start of a program to see whether you can obtain a lock on the file. Don't forget to unlock it (and maybe delete it if not needed) after checking.

Also remember that any call to the `die` function automatically unlocks a lock and closes the file as part of ending the program.

Reading an Entire File

A handy function for reading in an entire file without having to use file handles is `file_get_contents`. It's very easy to use, as you can see in Example 7-13.

Example 7-13. Using file_get_contents

```php
<?php
  echo "<pre>";  // Enables display of line feeds
  echo file_get_contents("testfile.txt");
  echo "</pre>"; // Terminates <pre> tag
?>
```

But the function is actually a lot more useful than that, because you can also use it to fetch a file from a server across the internet, as in Example 7-14, which requests the HTML from the O'Reilly home page, and then displays it as if the user had surfed to the page itself. The result will be similar to Figure 7-1.

Example 7-14. Grabbing the O'Reilly home page

```php
<?php
  echo file_get_contents("http://oreilly.com");
?>
```

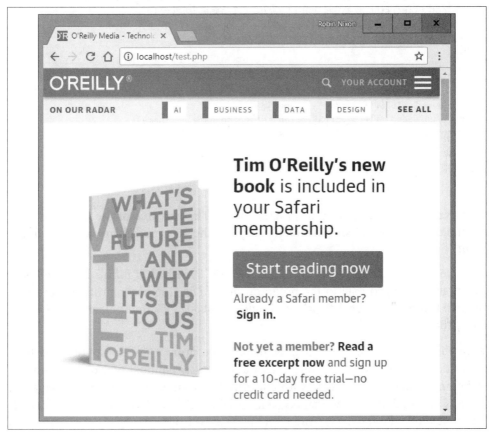

Figure 7-1. The O'Reilly home page grabbed with file_get_contents

Uploading Files

Uploading files to a web server is a subject that seems daunting to many people, but it actually couldn't be much easier. All you need to do to upload a file from a form is choose a special type of encoding called multipart/form-data, and your browser will handle the rest. To see how this works, type the program in Example 7-15 and save it as *upload.php*. When you run it, you'll see a form in your browser that lets you upload a file of your choice.

Example 7-15. Image uploader upload.php

```php
<?php // upload.php
  echo <<<_END
    <html><head><title>PHP Form Upload</title></head><body>
    <form method='post' action='upload.php' enctype='multipart/form-data'>
    Select File: <input type='file' name='filename' size='10'>
    <input type='submit' value='Upload'>
    </form>
_END;

  if ($_FILES)
  {
    $name = $_FILES['filename']['name'];
    move_uploaded_file($_FILES['filename']['tmp_name'], $name);
    echo "Uploaded image '$name'<br><img src='$name'>";
  }

  echo "</body></html>";
?>
```

Let's examine this program a section at a time. The first line of the multiline echo statement starts an HTML document, displays the title, and then starts the document's body.

Next we come to the form, which selects the POST method of form submission, sets the target for posted data to the program *upload.php* (the program itself), and tells the web browser that the data posted should be encoded via the content type of multi part/form-data.

With the form set up, the next lines display the prompt Select File: and then request two inputs. The first request is for a file; it uses an input type of file, a name of filename, and an input field with a width of 10 characters. The second requested input is just a submit button that is given the label Upload (which replaces the default button text of Submit Query). And then the form is closed.

This short program shows a common technique in web programming in which a single program is called twice: once when the user first visits a page, and again when the user presses the submit button.

The PHP code to receive the uploaded data is fairly simple, because all uploaded files are placed into the associative system array $_FILES. Therefore, a quick check to see whether $_FILES contains anything is sufficient to determine whether the user has uploaded a file. This is done with the statement if ($_FILES).

The first time the user visits the page, before uploading a file, $_FILES is empty, so the program skips this block of code. When the user uploads a file, the program runs again and discovers an element in the $_FILES array.

Once the program realizes that a file was uploaded, the actual name, as read from the uploading computer, is retrieved and placed into the variable $name. Now all that's necessary is to move the uploaded file from the temporary location in which PHP stored it to a more permanent one. We do this using the move_uploaded_file function, passing it the original name of the file, with which it is saved to the current directory.

Finally, the uploaded image is displayed within an IMG tag, and the result should look like Figure 7-2.

 If you run this program and receive a warning message such as Permission denied for the move_uploaded_file function call, then you may not have the correct permissions set for the folder in which the program is running.

Figure 7-2. Uploading an image as form data

Using $_FILES

Five things are stored in the $_FILES array when a file is uploaded, as shown in Table 7-6 (where *file* is the file upload field name supplied by the submitting form).

Table 7-6. The contents of the $_FILES array

Array element	Contents
$_FILES['*file*']['*name*']	The name of the uploaded file (e.g., *smiley.jpg*)
$_FILES['*file*']['*type*']	The content type of the file (e.g., *image/jpeg*)
$_FILES['*file*']['*size*']	The file's size in bytes
$_FILES['*file*']['*tmp_name*']	The name of the temporary file stored on the server
$_FILES['*file*']['*error*']	The error code resulting from the file upload

Content types used to be known as *MIME* (Multipurpose Internet Mail Extension) types, but because their use later expanded to the whole internet, now they are often called *internet media types*. Table 7-7 shows some of the more frequently used types that turn up in $_FILES['*file*']['*type*'].

Table 7-7. Some common internet media content types

application/pdf	image/gif	multipart/form-data	text/xml
application/zip	image/jpeg	text/css	video/mpeg
audio/mpeg	image/png	text/html	video/mp4
audio/x-wav	image/tiff	text/plain	video/quicktime

Validation

I hope it now goes without saying (although I'll do so anyway) that form data validation is of the utmost importance, due to the possibility of users attempting to hack into your server.

In addition to maliciously formed input data, some of the things you also have to check are whether a file was actually received and, if so, whether the right type of data was sent.

Taking all these things into account, Example 7-16, *upload2.php*, is a more secure rewrite of *upload.php*.

Example 7-16. A more secure version of upload.php

```php
<?php // upload2.php
  echo <<<_END
    <html><head><title>PHP Form Upload</title></head><body>
    <form method='post' action='upload2.php' enctype='multipart/form-data'>
    Select a JPG, GIF, PNG or TIF File:
    <input type='file' name='filename' size='10'>
    <input type='submit' value='Upload'></form>
_END;

  if ($_FILES)
```

```
  {
    $name = $_FILES['filename']['name'];

    switch($_FILES['filename']['type'])
    {
      case 'image/jpeg': $ext = 'jpg'; break;
      case 'image/gif':  $ext = 'gif'; break;
      case 'image/png':  $ext = 'png'; break;
      case 'image/tiff': $ext = 'tif'; break;
      default:           $ext = '';    break;
    }
    if ($ext)
    {
      $n = "image.$ext";
      move_uploaded_file($_FILES['filename']['tmp_name'], $n);
      echo "Uploaded image '$name' as '$n':<br>";
      echo "<img src='$n'>";
    }
    else echo "'$name' is not an accepted image file";
  }
  else echo "No image has been uploaded";

  echo "</body></html>";
?>
```

The non-HTML section of code has been expanded from the half-dozen lines of Example 7-15 to more than 20 lines, starting at if ($_FILES).

As with the previous version, this if line checks whether any data was actually posted, but there is now a matching else near the bottom of the program that echoes a message to the screen when nothing has been uploaded.

Within the if statement, the variable $name is assigned the value of the filename as retrieved from the uploading computer (just as before), but this time we won't rely on the user having sent us valid data. Instead, a switch statement checks the uploaded content type against the four types of image this program supports. If a match is made, the variable $ext is set to the three-letter file extension for that type. Should no match be found, the file uploaded was not of an accepted type and the variable $ext is set to the empty string "".

The next section of code then checks the variable $ext to see whether it contains a string and, if so, creates a new filename called $n with the base name *image* and the extension stored in $ext. This means that the program has full control over the name of the file to be created, as it can be only one of *image.jpg*, *image.gif*, *image.png*, or *image.tif*.

Safe in the knowledge that the program has not been compromised, the rest of the PHP code is much the same as in the previous version. It moves the uploaded temporary image to its new location and then displays it, while also displaying the old and new image names.

 Don't worry about having to delete the temporary file that PHP creates during the upload process, because if the file has not been moved or renamed, it will be automatically removed when the program exits.

After the `if` statement, there is a matching `else`, which is executed only if an unsupported image type was uploaded (in which case it displays an appropriate error message).

When you write your own file-uploading routines, I strongly advise you to use a similar approach and have prechosen names and locations for uploaded files. That way, no attempts to add pathnames and other malicious data to the variables you use can get through. If this means that more than one user could end up having a file uploaded with the same name, you could prefix such files with their user's usernames, or save them to individually created folders for each user.

But if you must use a supplied filename, you should sanitize it by allowing only alphanumeric characters and the period, which you can do with the following command, using a regular expression (see Chapter 17) to perform a search and replace on `$name`:

```
$name = preg_replace("/[^A-Za-z0-9.]/", "", $name);
```

This leaves only the characters A–Z, a–z, 0–9, and periods in the string `$name`, and strips out everything else.

Even better, to ensure that your program will work on all systems, regardless of whether they are case-sensitive or case-insensitive, you should probably use the following command instead, which changes all uppercase characters to lowercase at the same time:

```
$name = strtolower(ereg_replace("[^A-Za-z0-9.]", "", $name));
```

 Sometimes you may encounter the media type of `image/pjpeg`, which indicates a progressive JPEG, but you can safely add this to your code as an alias of `image/jpeg`, like this:

```
case 'image/pjpeg':
case 'image/jpeg': $ext = 'jpg'; break;
```

System Calls

Sometimes PHP will not have the function you need to perform a certain action, but the operating system it is running on may. In such cases, you can use the exec system call to do the job.

For example, to quickly view the contents of the current directory, you can use a program such as Example 7-17. If you are on a Windows system, it will run as is using the Windows dir command. On Linux, Unix, or macOS, comment out or remove the first line and uncomment the second to use the ls system command. You may wish to type this program, save it as *exec.php*, and call it up in your browser.

Example 7-17. Executing a system command

```php
<?php // exec.php
  $cmd = "dir";    // Windows
  // $cmd = "ls"; // Linux, Unix & Mac

  exec(escapeshellcmd($cmd), $output, $status);

  if ($status) echo "Exec command failed";
  else
  {
    echo "<pre>";
    foreach($output as $line) echo htmlspecialchars("$line\n");
    echo "</pre>";
  }
?>
```

The htmlspecialchars function is called to turn any special characters returned by the system into ones that HTML can understand and properly display, neatening the output. Depending on the system you are using, the result of running this program will look something like this (from a Windows dir command):

```
Volume in drive C is Hard Disk
 Volume Serial Number is DC63-0E29

 Directory of C:\Program Files (x86)\Ampps\www

11/04/2018  11:58    <DIR>          .
11/04/2018  11:58    <DIR>          ..
28/01/2018  16:45    <DIR>          5th_edition_examples
08/01/2018  10:34    <DIR>          cgi-bin
08/01/2018  10:34    <DIR>          error
29/01/2018  16:18             1,150 favicon.ico
              1 File(s)         1,150 bytes
              5 Dir(s)  1,611,387,486,208 bytes free
```

exec takes three arguments:

- The command itself (in the previous case, $cmd)
- An array in which the system will put the output from the command (in the previous case, $output)
- A variable to contain the returned status of the call (which, in the previous case, is $status)

If you wish, you can omit the $output and $status parameters, but you will not know the output created by the call or even whether it completed successfully.

You should also note the use of the escapeshellcmd function. It is a good habit to always use this when issuing an exec call, because it sanitizes the command string, preventing the execution of arbitrary commands, should you supply user input to the call.

 The system call functions are typically disabled on shared web hosts, as they pose a security risk. You should always try to solve your problems within PHP if you can, and go to the system directly only if it is really necessary. Also, going to the system is relatively slow, and you need to code two implementations if your application is expected to run on both Windows and Linux/Unix systems.

XHTML or HTML5?

Because XHTML documents need to be well formed, you can parse them using standard XML parsers—unlike HTML, which requires a lenient HTML-specific parser (which, thankfully, most popular web browsers are). For this reason, XHTML never really caught on, and when the time came to devise a new standard, the World Wide Web Consortium chose to support HTML5 rather than the newer XHTML2 standard.

HTML5 has some of the features of both HTML4 and XHTML, but is much simpler to use and less strict to validate—and, happily, there is now just a single document type you need to place at the head of an HTML5 document (instead of the variety of strict, transitional, and frameset types previously required):

```
<!DOCTYPE html>
```

Just the simple word html is sufficient to tell the browser that your web page is designed for HTML5 and, because all the latest versions of the most popular browsers have been supporting most of the HTML5 specification since 2011 or so, this document type is generally the only one you need, unless you choose to cater to older browsers.

For all intents and purposes, when writing HTML documents, web developers can safely ignore the old XHTML document types and syntax (such as using <br /> instead of the simpler <br> tag). But if you find yourself having to cater to a very old browser or an unusual application that relies on XHTML, then you can get more information on how to do that at *http://xhtml.com*.

Questions

1. Which `printf` conversion specifier would you use to display a floating-point number?

2. What `printf` statement could be used to take the input string `"Happy Birthday"` and output the string `"**Happy"`?

3. To send the output from `printf` to a variable instead of to a browser, what alternative function would you use?

4. How would you create a Unix timestamp for 7:11 a.m. on May 2, 2016?

5. Which file access mode would you use with `fopen` to open a file in write and read mode, with the file truncated and the file pointer at the start?

6. What is the PHP command for deleting the file *file.txt*?

7. Which PHP function is used to read in an entire file in one go, even from across the web?

8. Which PHP superglobal variable holds the details on uploaded files?

9. Which PHP function enables the running of system commands?

10. Which of the following tag styles is preferred in HTML5: `<hr>` or `<hr />`?

See "Chapter 7 Answers" on page 718 in Appendix A for the answers to these questions.

CHAPTER 8

Introduction to MySQL

With well over 10 million installations, MySQL is probably the most popular database management system for web servers. Developed in the mid-1990s, it's now a mature technology that powers many of today's most-visited internet destinations.

One reason for its success must be that, like PHP, it's free to use. But it's also extremely powerful and exceptionally fast—it can run on even the most basic of hardware, and it hardly puts a dent in system resources.

MySQL is also highly scalable, which means that it can grow with your website (the latest benchmarks are kept up to date online (*http://mysql.com/why-mysql/bench marks*)).

MySQL Basics

A *database* is a structured collection of records or data stored in a computer system and organized in such a way that it can be quickly searched and information can be rapidly retrieved.

The *SQL* in MySQL stands for *Structured Query Language*. This language is loosely based on English and also used in other databases such as Oracle and Microsoft SQL Server. It is designed to allow simple requests from a database via commands such as:

```
SELECT title FROM publications WHERE author = 'Charles Dickens';
```

A MySQL database contains one or more *tables*, each of which contains *records* or *rows*. Within these rows are various *columns* or *fields* that contain the data itself. Table 8-1 shows the contents of an example database of five publications detailing the author, title, type, and year of publication.

Table 8-1. Example of a simple database

Author	Title	Type	Year
Mark Twain	The Adventures of Tom Sawyer	Fiction	1876
Jane Austen	Pride and Prejudice	Fiction	1811
Charles Darwin	The Origin of Species	Non-fiction	1856
Charles Dickens	The Old Curiosity Shop	Fiction	1841
William Shakespeare	Romeo and Juliet	Play	1594

Each row in the table is the same as a row in a MySQL table, a column in the table corresponds to a column in MySQL, and each element within a row is the same as a MySQL field.

To uniquely identify this database, I'll refer to it as the *publications* database in the examples that follow. And, as you will have observed, all these publications are considered to be classics of literature, so I'll call the table within the database that holds the details *classics*.

Summary of Database Terms

The main terms you need to acquaint yourself with for now are as follows:

Database
    The overall container for a collection of MySQL data

Table
    A subcontainer within a database that stores the actual data

Row
    A single record within a table, which may contain several fields

Column
    The name of a field within a row

I should note that I'm not trying to reproduce the precise terminology used in academic literature about relational databases, but just to provide simple, everyday terms to help you quickly grasp basic concepts and get started with a database.

Accessing MySQL via the Command Line

There are three main ways you can interact with MySQL: using a command line, via a web interface such as phpMyAdmin, and through a programming language like PHP. We'll start doing the third of these in Chapter 10, but for now, let's look at the first two.

Starting the Command-Line Interface

The following sections describe relevant instructions for Windows, macOS, and Linux.

Windows users

If you installed AMPPS (as explained in Chapter 2) in the usual way, you will be able to access the MySQL executable from the following directory:

```
C:\Program Files (x86)\Ampps\mysql\bin
```

 If you installed AMPPS in any other place, you will need to use that directory instead.

By default, the initial MySQL user is *root*, and it will have a default password of *mysql*. So, to enter MySQL's command-line interface, select Start→Run, enter CMD into the Run box, and press Return. This will call up a Windows command prompt. From there, enter the following (making any appropriate changes as just discussed):

```
cd C:\"Program Files (x86)\Ampps\mysql\bin"
mysql -u root -pmysql
```

The first command changes to the MySQL directory, and the second tells MySQL to log you in as user *root*, with the password *mysql*. You will now be logged into MySQL and can start entering commands.

To be sure everything is working as it should be, enter the following—the results should be similar to Figure 8-1:

```
SHOW databases;
```

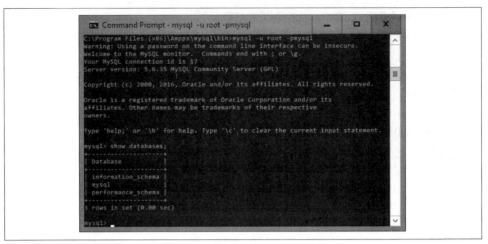

Figure 8-1. Accessing MySQL from a Windows command prompt

You are now ready to move on to the next section, "Using the Command-Line Interface" on page 171.

macOS users

To proceed with this chapter, you should have installed AMPPS as detailed in Chapter 2. You should also have the web server running and the MySQL server started.

To enter the MySQL command-line interface, start the Terminal program (which should be available in Finder→Utilities). Then call up the MySQL program, which will have been installed in the directory */Applications/ampps/mysql/bin.*

By default, the initial MySQL user is *root*, and it will have a password of *mysql*. So, to start the program, type the following:

```
/Applications/ampps/mysql/bin/mysql -u root -pmysql
```

This command tells MySQL to log you in as user *root* using the password *mysql*. To verify that all is well, type the following (Figure 8-2 should be the result):

```
SHOW databases;
```

```
● ○ ○                    mysql.client — 85×24
iMac:bin mysql —u root
Welcome to the MySQL monitor.  Commands end with ; or \g.
Your MySQL connection id is 2
Server version: 5.1.54 MySQL Community Server (GPL)

Copyright (c) 2000, 2010, Oracle and/or its affiliates. All rights reserved.
This software comes with ABSOLUTELY NO WARRANTY. This is free software,
and you are welcome to modify and redistribute it under the GPL v2 license

Type 'help;' or '\h' for help. Type '\c' to clear the current input statement.

mysql> show databases;
+--------------------+
| Database           |
+--------------------+
| information_schema |
| mysql              |
| test               |
+--------------------+
3 rows in set (0.00 sec)

mysql>
```

Figure 8-2. Accessing MySQL from the macOS Terminal program

If you receive an error such as Can't connect to local MySQL server through socket, you will need to first start the MySQL server as described in Chapter 2.

You should now be ready to move on to the next section, "Using the Command-Line Interface" on page 171.

Linux users

On a system running a Unix-like operating system such as Linux, you will almost certainly already have PHP and MySQL installed and running, and you will be able to enter the examples in the next section (if not, you can follow the procedure outlined in Chapter 2 to install AMPPS). First, you should type the following to log into your MySQL system:

```
mysql -u root -p
```

This tells MySQL to log you in as the user *root* and to request your password. If you have a password, enter it; otherwise, just press Return.

Once you are logged in, type the following to test the program—you should see something like Figure 8-3 in response:

```
SHOW databases;
```

```
You may also use sysinstall(8) to re-enter the installation and
configuration utility.  Edit /etc/motd to change this login announcement.

robnix# mysql -u root -p
Enter password:
Welcome to the MySQL monitor.  Commands end with ; or \g.
Your MySQL connection id is 4377812
Server version: mysql-server-5.0.51a

Type 'help;' or '\h' for help. Type '\c' to clear the buffer.

mysql> show databases;
+--------------------+
| Database           |
+--------------------+
| information_schema |
| mysql              |
| test               |
+--------------------+
3 rows in set (0.02 sec)

mysql>
```

Figure 8-3. Accessing MySQL using Linux

If this procedure fails at any point, please refer to Chapter 2 to ensure that you have MySQL properly installed. Otherwise, you should now be ready to move on to the next section, "Using the Command-Line Interface" on page 171.

MySQL on a remote server

If you are accessing MySQL on a remote server, it will probably be a Linux/FreeBSD/ Unix type of box, and you should connect to it via the secure SSH protocol (avoid using the insecure Telnet protocol at all costs). Once in there, you might find that things are a little different, depending on how the system administrator has set the server up—especially if it's a shared hosting server. Therefore, you need to ensure that you have been given access to MySQL and that you have your username and password. Armed with these, you can then type the following, where *username* is the name supplied:

```
mysql -u username -p
```

Enter your password when prompted. You can then try the following command, which should result in something like Figure 8-3:

```
SHOW databases;
```

There may be other databases already created, and the *test* database may not be there.

Bear in mind also that system administrators have ultimate control over everything and that you can encounter some unexpected setups. For example, you may find that you are required to preface all database names that you create with a unique identifying string to ensure that your names do not conflict with those of databases created by other users.

Therefore, if you have any problems, talk with your system administrator, who will get you sorted out. Just let the sysadmin know that you need a username and password. You should also ask for the ability to create new databases or, at a minimum, to have at least one database created for you ready to use. You can then create all the tables you require within that database.

Using the Command-Line Interface

From here on out, it makes no difference whether you are using Windows, macOS, or Linux to access MySQL directly, as all the commands used (and errors you may receive) are identical.

The semicolon

Let's start with the basics. Did you notice the semicolon (;) at the end of the SHOW databases; command that you typed? The semicolon is used by MySQL to separate or end commands. If you forget to enter it, MySQL will issue a prompt and wait for you to do so. The required semicolon was made part of the syntax to let you enter multiple-line commands, which can be convenient because some commands get quite long. It also allows you to issue more than one command at a time by placing a semicolon after each one. The interpreter gets them all in a batch when you press the Enter (or Return) key and executes them in order.

> It's very common to receive a MySQL prompt instead of the results of your command; it means that you forgot the final semicolon. Just enter the semicolon and press the Enter key, and you'll get what you want.

There are six different prompts that MySQL may present you with (see Table 8-2), so you will always know where you are during a multiline input.

Table 8-2. MySQL's six command prompts

MySQL prompt	Meaning
mysql>	Ready and waiting for a command
->	Waiting for the next line of a command
'>	Waiting for the next line of a string started with a single quote
">	Waiting for the next line of a string started with a double quote
`>	Waiting for the next line of a string started with a backtick
/*>	Waiting for the next line of a comment started with /*

Canceling a command

If you are partway through entering a command and decide you don't wish to execute it after all, whatever you do, *don't press Ctrl-C!* That will close the program. Instead, you can enter \c and press Return. Example 8-1 shows how to use the command.

Example 8-1. Canceling a line of input

```
meaningless gibberish to mysql \c
```

When you type that line, MySQL will ignore everything you typed and issue a new prompt. Without the \c, it would have displayed an error message. Be careful, though: if you have opened a string or comment, close it first before using the \c or MySQL will think the \c is just part of the string. Example 8-2 shows the right way to do this.

Example 8-2. Canceling input from inside a string

```
this is "meaningless gibberish to mysql" \c
```

Also note that using \c after a semicolon will not cancel the preceding command, as it is then a new statement.

MySQL Commands

You've already seen the SHOW command, which lists tables, databases, and many other items. The commands you'll use most often are listed in Table 8-3.

Table 8-3. Common MySQL commands

Command	Action
ALTER	Alter a database or table
BACKUP	Back up a table
\c	Cancel input
CREATE	Create a database
DELETE	Delete a row from a table
DESCRIBE	Describe a table's columns
DROP	Delete a database or table
EXIT (Ctrl-C)	Exit
GRANT	Change user privileges
HELP (\h, \?)	Display help
INSERT	Insert data
LOCK	Lock table(s)
QUIT (\q)	Same as EXIT

Command	Action
RENAME	Rename a table
SHOW	List details about an object
SOURCE	Execute a file
STATUS (\s)	Display the current status
TRUNCATE	Empty a table
UNLOCK	Unlock table(s)
UPDATE	Update an existing record
USE	Use a database

I'll cover most of these as we proceed, but first, you need to remember a couple of points about MySQL commands:

- SQL commands and keywords are case-insensitive. CREATE, create, and CrEaTe all mean the same thing. However, for the sake of clarity, you may prefer to use uppercase.

- Table names are case-sensitive on Linux and macOS, but case-insensitive on Windows. So, for the sake of portability, you should always choose a case and stick to it. The recommended style is to use lowercase for table names.

Creating a database

If you are working on a remote server and have only a single user account and access to a single database that was created for you, move on to the section "Creating a table" on page 175. Otherwise, get the ball rolling by issuing the following command to create a new database called *publications*:

```
CREATE DATABASE publications;
```

A successful command will return a message that doesn't mean much yet—Query OK, 1 row affected (0.00 sec)—but will make sense soon. Now that you've created the database, you want to work with it, so issue the following command:

```
USE publications;
```

You should now see the message Database changed and will then be set to proceed with the following examples.

Creating users

Now that you've seen how easy it is to use MySQL and created your first database, it's time to look at how you create users, as you probably won't want to grant your PHP scripts root access to MySQL—it could cause a real headache should you get hacked.

To create a user, issue the GRANT command, which takes the following form (don't type this in; it's not an actual working command):

```
GRANT PRIVILEGES ON database.object TO 'username'@'hostname'
  IDENTIFIED BY 'password';
```

This should all look pretty straightforward, with the possible exception of the `database.object` part, which refers to the database itself and the objects it contains, such as tables (see Table 8-4).

Table 8-4. Example parameters for the GRANT command

Arguments	Meaning
.	All databases and all their objects
database.*	Only the database called *database* and all its objects
database.object	Only the database called *database* and its object called *object*

So, let's create a user who can access just the new *publications* database and all its objects, by entering the following (replacing the username *jim* and also the password *mypasswd* with ones of your choosing):

```
GRANT ALL ON publications.* TO 'jim'@'localhost'
  IDENTIFIED BY 'mypasswd';
```

What this does is allow the user *jim@localhost* full access to the *publications* database using the password *mypasswd*. You can test whether this step has worked by entering quit to exit and then rerunning MySQL the way you did before, but instead of entering -u root -p, type -u jim -p, or whatever username you created. See Table 8-5 for the correct command for your operating system. Modify it as necessary if the *mysql* client program is installed in a different directory on your system.

Table 8-5. Starting MySQL and logging in as jim@localhost

OS	Example command
Windows	C:\"Program Files (x86)\Ampps\mysql\bin\mysql" -u jim -p
macOS	/Applications/ampps/mysql/bin/mysql -u jim -p
Linux	mysql -u jim -p

All you have to do now is enter your password when prompted and you will be logged in. If you prefer, you can place your password immediately following the -p (without any spaces) to avoid having to enter it when prompted, but this is considered poor practice because if other people are logged into your system, there may be ways for them to look at the command you entered and find out your password.

You can grant only privileges that you already have, and you must also have the privilege to issue GRANT commands. There are a whole range of privileges you can choose to grant if you are not granting all privileges. For further details on the GRANT command and the REVOKE command, which can remove privileges once granted, see the documentation (*http://tinyurl.com/mysqlgrant*). Also be aware that if you create a new user but do not specify an IDENTIFIED BY clause, the user will have no password, a situation that is very insecure and should be avoided.

Creating a table

At this point, you should now be logged into MySQL with ALL privileges granted for the database *publications* (or a database that was created for you), so you're ready to create your first table. Make sure the correct database is in use by typing the following (replacing publications with the name of your database if it is different):

```
USE publications;
```

Now enter the command in Example 8-3 one line at a time.

Example 8-3. Creating a table called classics

```
CREATE TABLE classics (
  author VARCHAR(128),
  title VARCHAR(128),
  type VARCHAR(16),
  year CHAR(4)) ENGINE InnoDB;
```

The final two words in this command require a little explanation. MySQL can process queries in many different ways internally, and these different ways are supported by different *engines*. From version 5.6 onwards *InnoDB* is the default storage engine for MySQL, and we use it here because it supports FULLTEXT searches. So long as you have a relatively up-to-date version of MySQL, you can omit the ENGINE InnoDB section of the command when creating a table, but I have kept it in for now to emphasize that this is the engine being used.

If you are running a version of MySQL prior to 5.6, the InnoDB engine will not support FULLTEXT indexes, so you will have to replace InnoDB in the command with MyISAM to indicate that you want to use that engine (see "Creating a FULLTEXT index" on page 192).

InnoDB is generally more efficient and the recommended option. If you installed the AMPPS stack as detailed in Chapter 2, you should have at least version 5.6.35 of MySQL.

You could also issue the previous command on a single line, like this:

```
CREATE TABLE classics (author VARCHAR(128), title
VARCHAR(128), type VARCHAR(16), year CHAR(4)) ENGINE
InnoDB;
```

But MySQL commands can be long and complicated, so I recommend using the format shown in Example 8-3 until you are comfortable with longer ones.

MySQL should then issue the response `Query OK, 0 rows affected`, along with how long it took to execute the command. If you see an error message instead, check your syntax carefully. Every parenthesis and comma counts, and typing errors are easy to make.

To check whether your new table has been created, type the following:

```
DESCRIBE classics;
```

All being well, you will see the sequence of commands and responses shown in Example 8-4, where you should particularly note the table format displayed.

Example 8-4. A MySQL session: creating and checking a new table

```
mysql> USE publications;
Database changed
mysql> CREATE TABLE classics (
    ->   author VARCHAR(128),
    ->   title VARCHAR(128),
    ->   type VARCHAR(16),
    ->   year CHAR(4)) ENGINE InnoDB;
Query OK, 0 rows affected (0.03 sec)

mysql> DESCRIBE classics;
+--------+--------------+------+-----+---------+-------+
| Field  | Type         | Null | Key | Default | Extra |
+--------+--------------+------+-----+---------+-------+
| author | varchar(128) | YES  |     | NULL    |       |
| title  | varchar(128) | YES  |     | NULL    |       |
| type   | varchar(16)  | YES  |     | NULL    |       |
| year   | char(4)      | YES  |     | NULL    |       |
+--------+--------------+------+-----+---------+-------+
4 rows in set (0.00 sec)
```

The DESCRIBE command is an invaluable debugging aid when you need to ensure that you have correctly created a MySQL table. You can also use it to remind yourself about a table's field or column names and the types of data in each one. Let's look at each of the headings in detail:

Field
> The name of each field or column within a table

Type
> The type of data being stored in the field

Null
> Whether the field is allowed to contain a value of NULL

Key
> What type of key, if any, has been applied (*keys* or *indexes* in MySQL are quick ways to look up and search for data)

Default
> The default value that will be assigned to the field if no value is specified when a new row is created

Extra
> Additional information, such as whether a field is set to auto-increment

Data Types

In Example 8-3, you may have noticed that three of the table's fields were given the data type of VARCHAR, and one was given the type CHAR. The term VARCHAR stands for *VARiable length CHARacter string*, and the command takes a numeric value that tells MySQL the maximum length allowed for a string stored in this field.

Both CHAR and VARCHAR accept text strings and impose a limit on the size of the field. The difference is that every string in a CHAR field has the specified size. If you put in a smaller string, it is padded with spaces. A VARCHAR field does not pad the text; it lets the size of the field vary to fit the text that is inserted. But VARCHAR requires a small amount of overhead to keep track of the size of each value. So, CHAR is slightly more efficient if the sizes are similar in all records, whereas VARCHAR is more efficient if sizes can vary a lot and get large. In addition, the overhead causes access to VARCHAR data to be slightly slower than to CHAR data.

Another feature of character and text columns, important for today's global web reach, is *character sets*. These assign particular binary values to particular characters. The character set you use for English is obviously different from the one you'd use for Russian. You can assign the character set to a character or text column when you create it.

VARCHAR is useful in our example, because it can accommodate author names and titles of different lengths, while helping MySQL plan the size of the database and perform lookups and searches more easily. Just be aware that if you ever attempt to assign a string value longer than the length allowed, it will be truncated to the maximum length declared in the table definition.

The year field, however, has predictable values, so instead of VARCHAR we use the more efficient CHAR(4) data type. The parameter of 4 allows for 4 bytes of data, supporting all years from –999 to 9999; a byte comprises 8 bits and can have the values 00000000 through 11111111, which are 0 to 255 in decimal.

You could, of course, just store two-digit values for the year, but if your data is going to still be needed in the following century, or may otherwise wrap around, it will have to be sanitized first—think of the "millennium bug" that would have caused dates beginning on January 1, 2000, to be treated as 1900 on many of the world's biggest computer installations.

 I didn't use the YEAR data type in the *classics* table because it supports only the years 0000 and 1901 through 2155. This is because MySQL stores the year in a single byte for reasons of efficiency, but it means that only 256 years are available, and the publication years of the titles in the *classics* table are well before 1901.

The CHAR data type

Table 8-6 lists the CHAR data types. Both types offer a parameter that sets the maximum (or exact) length of the string allowed in the field. As the table shows, each type has a built-in maximum number of bytes it can occupy.

Table 8-6. MySQL's CHAR data types

Data type	Bytes used	Examples
CHAR(*n*)	Exactly *n* (<= 255)	CHAR(5) *"Hello" uses 5 bytes*
		CHAR(57) *"Goodbye" uses 57 bytes*
VARCHAR(*n*)	Up to *n* (<= 65535)	VARCHAR(7) *"Hello" uses 5 bytes*
		VARCHAR(100) *"Goodbye" uses 7 bytes*

The BINARY data type

The BINARY data types (see Table 8-7) store strings of bytes that do not have an associated character set. For example, you might use the BINARY data type to store a GIF image.

Table 8-7. MySQL's BINARY data types

Data type	Bytes used	Examples
BINARY(*n*)	Exactly *n* (<= 255)	As CHAR but contains binary data
VARBINARY(*n*)	Up to *n* (<= 65535)	As VARCHAR but contains binary data

The TEXT data types

Character data can also be stored in one of the set of TEXT fields. The differences between these fields and VARCHAR fields are small:

- Prior to version 5.0.3, MySQL would remove leading and trailing spaces from VARCHAR fields.
- TEXT fields cannot have default values.
- MySQL indexes only the first *n* characters of a TEXT column (you specify *n* when you create the index).

What this means is that VARCHAR is the better and faster data type to use if you need to search the entire contents of a field. If you will never search more than a certain number of leading characters in a field, you should probably use a TEXT data type (see Table 8-8).

Table 8-8. MySQL's TEXT data types

Data type	Bytes used	Attributes
TINYTEXT(*n*)	Up to *n* (<= 255)	Treated as a string with a character set
TEXT(*n*)	Up to *n* (<= 65535)	Treated as a string with a character set
MEDIUMTEXT(*n*)	Up to *n* (<= 1.67e+7)	Treated as a string with a character set
LONGTEXT(*n*)	Up to *n* (<= 4.29e+9)	Treated as a string with a character set

The data types that have smaller maximums are also more efficient; therefore, you should use the one with the smallest maximum that you know is enough for any string you will be storing in the field.

The BLOB data types

The term BLOB stands for *Binar Large OBject*, and therefore, as you would think, the BLOB data type is most useful for binary data in excess of 65,536 bytes in size. The main other difference between the BLOB and BINARY data types is that BLOBs cannot have default values. The BLOB data types are listed in Table 8-9.

Table 8-9. MySQL's BLOB data types

Data type	Bytes used	Attributes
TINYBLOB(*n*)	Up to *n* (<= 255)	Treated as binary data—no character set
BLOB(*n*)	Up to *n* (<= 65535)	Treated as binary data—no character set
MEDIUMBLOB(*n*)	Up to *n* (<= 1.67e+7)	Treated as binary data—no character set
LONGBLOB(*n*)	Up to *n* (<= 4.29e+9)	Treated as binary data—no character set

Numeric data types

MySQL supports various numeric data types, from a single byte up to double-precision floating-point numbers. Although the most memory that a numeric field can use up is 8 bytes, you are well advised to choose the smallest data type that will adequately handle the largest value you expect. This will help keep your databases small and quickly accessible.

Table 8-10 lists the numeric data types supported by MySQL and the ranges of values they can contain. In case you are not acquainted with the terms, a *signed number* is one with a possible range from a minus value, through 0, to a positive one; and an *unsigned number* has a value ranging from 0 to a positive one. They can both hold the same number of values; just picture a signed number as being shifted halfway to the left so that half its values are negative and half are positive. Note that floating-point values (of any precision) may only be signed.

Table 8-10. MySQL's numeric data types

Data type	Bytes used	Minimum value		Maximum value	
		Signed	Unsigned	Signed	Unsigned
TINYINT	1	-128	0	127	255
SMALLINT	2	-32768	0	32767	65535
MEDIUMINT	3	-8.38e+6	0	8.38e+6	1.67e+7
INT / INTEGER	4	-2.15e+9	0	2.15e+9	4.29e+9
BIGINT	8	-9.22e+18	0	9.22e+18	1.84e+19
FLOAT	4	-3.40e+38	*n/a*	3.4e+38	*n/a*
DOUBLE / REAL	8	-1.80e+308	*n/a*	1.80e+308	*n/a*

To specify whether a data type is unsigned, use the UNSIGNED qualifier. The following example creates a table called *tablename* with a field in it called *fieldname* of the data type UNSIGNED INTEGER:

```
CREATE TABLE tablename (fieldname INT UNSIGNED);
```

When creating a numeric field, you can also pass an optional number as a parameter, like this:

```
CREATE TABLE tablename (fieldname INT(4));
```

But you must remember that, unlike with the BINARY and CHAR data types, this parameter does not indicate the number of bytes of storage to use. It may seem counterintuitive, but what the number actually represents is the display width of the data in the field when it is retrieved. It is commonly used with the ZEROFILL qualifier, like this:

```
CREATE TABLE tablename (fieldname INT(4) ZEROFILL);
```

What this does is cause any numbers with a width of less than four characters to be padded with one or more zeros, sufficient to make the display width of the field four characters long. When a field is already of the specified width or greater, no padding takes place.

DATE and TIME types

The main remaining data types supported by MySQL relate to the date and time and can be seen in Table 8-11.

Table 8-11. MySQL's DATE and TIME data types

Data type	Time/date format
DATETIME	'0000-00-00 00:00:00'
DATE	'0000-00-00'
TIMESTAMP	'0000-00-00 00:00:00'
TIME	'00:00:00'
YEAR	0000 (Only years 0000 and 1901–2155)

The DATETIME and TIMESTAMP data types display the same way. The main difference is that TIMESTAMP has a very narrow range (from the years 1970 through 2037), whereas DATETIME will hold just about any date you're likely to specify, unless you're interested in ancient history or science fiction.

TIMESTAMP is useful, however, because you can let MySQL set the value for you. If you don't specify the value when adding a row, the current time is automatically inserted. You can also have MySQL update a TIMESTAMP column each time you change a row.

The AUTO_INCREMENT attribute

Sometimes you need to ensure that every row in your database is guaranteed to be unique. You could do this in your program by carefully checking the data you enter and making sure that there is at least one value that differs in any two rows, but this approach is error-prone and works only in certain circumstances. In the *classics* table, for instance, an author may appear multiple times. Likewise, the year of publication will also be frequently duplicated, and so on. It would be hard to guarantee that you have no duplicate rows.

The general solution is to use an extra column just for this purpose. In a while, we'll look at using a publication's ISBN (International Standard Book Number), but first I'd like to introduce the AUTO_INCREMENT data type.

As its name implies, a column given this data type will set the value of its contents to that of the column entry in the previously inserted row, plus 1. Example 8-5 shows how to add a new column called *id* to the table *classics* with auto-incrementing.

Example 8-5. Adding the auto-incrementing column id

```
ALTER TABLE classics ADD id INT UNSIGNED NOT NULL AUTO_INCREMENT KEY;
```

This is your introduction to the `ALTER` command, which is very similar to `CREATE`. `ALTER` operates on an existing table and can add, change, or delete columns. Our example adds a column named *id* with the following characteristics:

`INT UNSIGNED`
Makes the column take an integer large enough for us to store more than 4 billion records in the table.

`NOT NULL`
Ensures that every column has a value. Many programmers use `NULL` in a field to indicate that it doesn't have any value. But that would allow duplicates, which would violate the whole reason for this column's existence, so we disallow `NULL` values.

`AUTO_INCREMENT`
Causes MySQL to set a unique value for this column in every row, as described earlier. We don't really have control over the value that this column will take in each row, but we don't care: all we care about is that we are guaranteed a unique value.

`KEY`
An auto-increment column is useful as a key, because you will tend to search for rows based on this column. This will be explained in the section "Indexes" on page 187.

Each entry in the column *id* will now have a unique number, with the first starting at 1 and the others counting upward from there. And whenever a new row is inserted, its *id* column will automatically be given the next number in the sequence.

Rather than applying the column retroactively, you could have included it by issuing the `CREATE` command in a slightly different format. In that case, the command in Example 8-3 would be replaced with Example 8-6. Check the final line in particular.

Example 8-6. Adding the auto-incrementing id column at table creation

```
CREATE TABLE classics (
 author VARCHAR(128),
 title VARCHAR(128),
 type VARCHAR(16),
 year CHAR(4),
 id INT UNSIGNED NOT NULL AUTO_INCREMENT KEY) ENGINE InnoDB;
```

If you wish to check whether the column has been added, use the following command to view the table's columns and data types:

```
DESCRIBE classics;
```

Now that we've finished with it, the *id* column is no longer needed, so if you created it using Example 8-5, you should now remove the column using the command in Example 8-7.

Example 8-7. Removing the id column

```
ALTER TABLE classics DROP id;
```

Adding data to a table

To add data to a table, use the INSERT command. Let's see this in action by populating the table *classics* with the data from Table 8-1, using one form of the INSERT command repeatedly (Example 8-8).

Example 8-8. Populating the classics table

```
INSERT INTO classics(author, title, type, year)
 VALUES('Mark Twain','The Adventures of Tom Sawyer','Fiction','1876');
INSERT INTO classics(author, title, type, year)
 VALUES('Jane Austen','Pride and Prejudice','Fiction','1811');
INSERT INTO classics(author, title, type, year)
 VALUES('Charles Darwin','The Origin of Species','Non-Fiction','1856');
INSERT INTO classics(author, title, type, year)
 VALUES('Charles Dickens','The Old Curiosity Shop','Fiction','1841');
INSERT INTO classics(author, title, type, year)
 VALUES('William Shakespeare','Romeo and Juliet','Play','1594');
```

After every second line, you should see a Query OK message. Once all lines have been entered, type the following command, which will display the table's contents. The result should look like Figure 8-4:

```
SELECT * FROM classics;
```

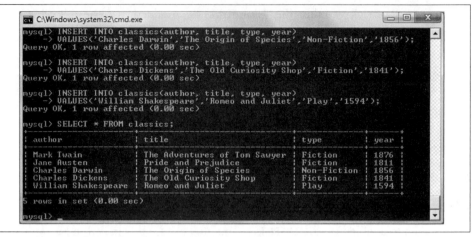

Figure 8-4. Populating the classics table and viewing its contents

Don't worry about the SELECT command for now—we'll come to it in the section "Querying a MySQL Database" on page 193. Suffice it to say that, as typed, it will display all the data you just entered.

Let's go back and look at how we used the INSERT command. The first part, INSERT INTO classics, tells MySQL where to insert the following data. Then, within parentheses, the four column names are listed—*author*, *title*, *type*, and *year*—all separated by commas. This tells MySQL that these are the fields into which the data is to be inserted.

The second line of each INSERT command contains the keyword VALUES followed by four strings within parentheses, separated by commas. This supplies MySQL with the four values to be inserted into the four columns previously specified. (As always, my choice of where to break the lines was arbitrary.)

Each item of data will be inserted into the corresponding column, in a one-to-one correspondence. If you accidentally listed the columns in a different order from the data, the data would go into the wrong columns. Also, the number of columns must match the number of data items. (There are safer ways of using INSERT, which we'll see soon.)

Renaming a table

Renaming a table, like any other change to the structure or meta-information about a table, is achieved via the ALTER command. So, for example, to change the name of the table *classics* to *pre1900*, you would use the following command:

```
ALTER TABLE classics RENAME pre1900;
```

If you tried that command, you should revert the table name by entering the following, so that later examples in this chapter will work as printed:

```
ALTER TABLE pre1900 RENAME classics;
```

Changing the data type of a column

Changing a column's data type also makes use of the ALTER command, this time in conjunction with the MODIFY keyword. To change the data type of the column *year* from CHAR(4) to SMALLINT (which requires only 2 bytes of storage and so will save disk space), enter the following:

```
ALTER TABLE classics MODIFY year SMALLINT;
```

When you do this, if the conversion of data type makes sense to MySQL, it will automatically change the data while keeping the meaning. In this case, it will change each string to a comparable integer, so long as the string is recognizable as referring to an integer.

Adding a new column

Let's suppose that you have created a table and populated it with plenty of data, only to discover you need an additional column. Not to worry. Here's how to add the new column *pages*, which will be used to store the number of pages in a publication:

```
ALTER TABLE classics ADD pages SMALLINT UNSIGNED;
```

This adds the new column with the name *pages* using the UNSIGNED SMALLINT data type, sufficient to hold a value of up to 65,535—hopefully that's more than enough for any book ever published!

And, if you ask MySQL to describe the updated table by using the DESCRIBE command, as follows, you will see the change has been made (see Figure 8-5):

```
DESCRIBE classics;
```

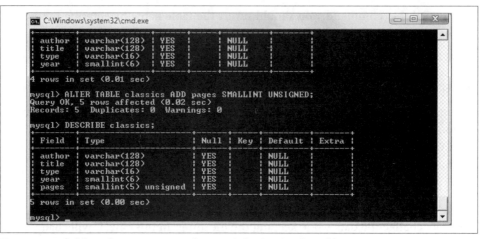

Figure 8-5. Adding the new pages column and viewing the table

Renaming a column

Looking again at Figure 8-5, you may decide that having a column named *type* is confusing, because that is the name used by MySQL to identify data types. Again, no problem—let's change its name to *category*, like this:

```
ALTER TABLE classics CHANGE type category VARCHAR(16);
```

Note the addition of VARCHAR(16) on the end of this command. That's because the CHANGE keyword requires the data type to be specified, even if you don't intend to change it, and VARCHAR(16) was the data type specified when that column was initially created as *type*.

Removing a column

Actually, upon reflection, you might decide that the page count column *pages* isn't actually all that useful for this particular database, so here's how to remove that column by using the DROP keyword:

```
ALTER TABLE classics DROP pages;
```

 Remember that DROP is irreversible. You should always use it with caution, because you could inadvertently delete entire tables (and even databases) with it if you are not careful!

Deleting a table

Deleting a table is very easy indeed. But, because I don't want you to have to reenter all the data for the *classics* table, let's quickly create a new table, verify its existence, and then delete it. You can do this by typing the commands in Example 8-9. The result of these four commands should look like Figure 8-6.

Example 8-9. Creating, viewing, and deleting a table

```
CREATE TABLE disposable(trash INT);
DESCRIBE disposable;
DROP TABLE disposable;
SHOW tables;
```

Figure 8-6. Creating, viewing, and deleting a table

Indexes

As things stand, the table *classics* works and can be searched without problem by MySQL—until it grows to more than a couple of hundred rows. At that point, database accesses will get slower and slower with every new row added, because MySQL has to search through every row whenever a query is issued. This is like searching through every book in a library whenever you need to look something up.

Of course, you don't have to search libraries that way, because they have either a card index system or, most likely, a database of their own. And the same goes for MySQL, because at the expense of a slight overhead in memory and disk space, you can create a "card index" for a table that MySQL will use to conduct lightning-fast searches.

Creating an Index

The way to achieve fast searches is to add an *index*, either when creating a table or at any time afterward. But the decision is not so simple. For example, there are different index types, such as a regular INDEX, a PRIMARY KEY, or a FULLTEXT index. Also, you must decide which columns require an index, a judgment that requires you to predict whether you will be searching any of the data in each column. Indexes can get more complicated too, because you can combine multiple columns in one index. And even when you've decided that, you still have the option of reducing index size by limiting the amount of each column to be indexed.

If we imagine the searches that may be made on the *classics* table, it becomes apparent that all of the columns may need to be searched. However, if the *pages* column created in the section "Adding a new column" on page 185 had not been deleted, it would probably not have needed an index, as most people would be unlikely to search for books by the number of pages they have. Anyway, go ahead and add an index to each of the columns, using the commands in Example 8-10.

Example 8-10. Adding indexes to the classics table

```
ALTER TABLE classics ADD INDEX(author(20));
ALTER TABLE classics ADD INDEX(title(20));
ALTER TABLE classics ADD INDEX(category(4));
ALTER TABLE classics ADD INDEX(year);
DESCRIBE classics;
```

The first two commands create indexes on the *author* and *title* columns, limiting each index to only the first 20 characters. For instance, when MySQL indexes the following title:

```
The Adventures of Tom Sawyer
```

It will actually store in the index only the first 20 characters:

```
The Adventures of To
```

This is done to minimize the size of the index, and to optimize database access speed. I chose 20 because it's likely to be sufficient to ensure uniqueness for most strings in these columns. If MySQL finds two indexes with the same contents, it will have to waste time going to the table itself and checking the column that was indexed to find out which rows really matched.

With the *category* column, currently only the first character is required to identify a string as unique (F for Fiction, N for Non-fiction, and P for Play), but I chose an index of four characters to allow for future categories that may share the first three characters. You can also reindex this column later, when you have a more complete set of categories. And finally, I set no limit to the *year* column's index, because it has a clearly defined length of four characters.

The results of issuing these commands (and a DESCRIBE command to confirm that they worked) can be seen in Figure 8-7, which shows the key MUL for each column. This key means that multiple occurrences of a value may occur within that column, which is exactly what we want, as authors may appear many times, the same book title could be used by multiple authors, and so on.

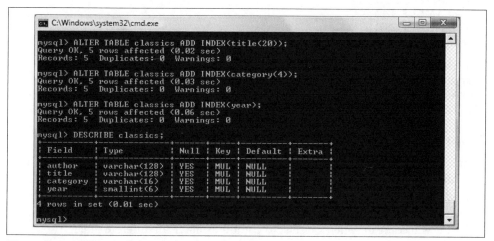

Figure 8-7. Adding indexes to the classics table

Using CREATE INDEX

An alternative to using `ALTER TABLE` to add an index is to use the `CREATE INDEX` command. They are equivalent, except that `CREATE INDEX` cannot be used for creating a `PRIMARY KEY` (see the section "Primary keys" on page 190). The format of this command is shown in the second line of Example 8-11.

Example 8-11. These two commands are equivalent

```
ALTER TABLE classics ADD INDEX(author(20));
CREATE INDEX author ON classics (author(20));
```

Adding indexes when creating tables

You don't have to wait until after creating a table to add indexes. In fact, doing so can be time-consuming, as adding an index to a large table can take a very long time. Therefore, let's look at a command that creates the table *classics* with indexes already in place.

Example 8-12 is a reworking of Example 8-3 in which the indexes are created at the same time as the table. Note that to incorporate the modifications made in this chapter, this version uses the new column name *category* instead of *type* and sets the data type of *year* to `SMALLINT` instead of `CHAR(4)`. If you want to try it out without first deleting your current *classics* table, change the word *classics* in line 1 to something else like *classics1*, and then drop *classics1* after you have finished with it.

Example 8-12. Creating the table classics with indexes

```
CREATE TABLE classics (
  author VARCHAR(128),
  title VARCHAR(128),
  category VARCHAR(16),
  year SMALLINT,
  INDEX(author(20)),
  INDEX(title(20)),
  INDEX(category(4)),
  INDEX(year)) ENGINE InnoDB;
```

Primary keys

So far, you've created the table *classics* and ensured that MySQL can search it quickly by adding indexes, but there's still something missing. All the publications in the table can be searched, but there is no single unique key for each publication to enable instant accessing of a row. The importance of having a key with a unique value for each row will come up when we start to combine data from different tables.

The section "The AUTO_INCREMENT attribute" on page 181 briefly introduced the idea of a primary key when creating the auto-incrementing column *id*, which could have been used as a primary key for this table. However, I wanted to reserve that task for a more appropriate column: the internationally recognized ISBN.

So let's go ahead and create a new column for this key. Now, bearing in mind that ISBNs are 13 characters long, you might think that the following command would do the job:

```
ALTER TABLE classics ADD isbn CHAR(13) PRIMARY KEY;
```

But it doesn't. If you try it, you'll get the error Duplicate entry for key 1. The reason is that the table is already populated with some data and this command is trying to add a column with the value NULL to each row, which is not allowed, as all values must be unique in any column having a primary key index. However, if there were no data already in the table, this command would work just fine, as would adding the primary key index upon table creation.

In our current situation, we have to be a bit sneaky and create the new column without an index, populate it with data, and then add the index retrospectively using the commands in Example 8-13. Luckily, each of the years is unique in the current set of data, so we can use the *year* column to identify each row for updating. Note that this example uses the UPDATE command and WHERE keyword, which are explained in more detail in the section "Querying a MySQL Database" on page 193.

Example 8-13. Populating the isbn column with data and using a primary key

```
ALTER TABLE classics ADD isbn CHAR(13);
UPDATE classics SET isbn='9781598184891' WHERE year='1876';
UPDATE classics SET isbn='9780582506206' WHERE year='1811';
UPDATE classics SET isbn='9780517123201' WHERE year='1856';
UPDATE classics SET isbn='9780099533474' WHERE year='1841';
UPDATE classics SET isbn='9780192814968' WHERE year='1594';
ALTER TABLE classics ADD PRIMARY KEY(isbn);
DESCRIBE classics;
```

Once you have typed these commands, the results should look like Figure 8-8. Note that the keywords PRIMARY KEY replace the keyword INDEX in the ALTER TABLE syntax (compare Examples 8-10 and 8-13).

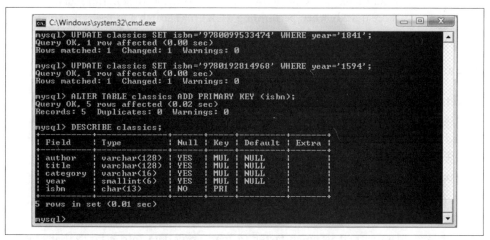

Figure 8-8. Retrospectively adding a primary key to the classics table

To have created a primary key when the table *classics* was created, you could have used the commands in Example 8-14. Again, rename *classics* in line 1 to something else if you wish to try this example, and then delete the test table afterward.

Example 8-14. Creating the table classics with a primary key

```
CREATE TABLE classics (
 author VARCHAR(128),
 title VARCHAR(128),
 category VARCHAR(16),
 year SMALLINT,
 isbn CHAR(13),
 INDEX(author(20)),
 INDEX(title(20)),
 INDEX(category(4)),
```

```
INDEX(year),
PRIMARY KEY (isbn)) ENGINE InnoDB;
```

Creating a FULLTEXT index

Unlike a regular index, MySQL's FULLTEXT allows super-fast searches of entire columns of text. It stores every word in every data string in a special index that you can search using "natural language," in a similar manner to using a search engine.

 It's not strictly true that MySQL stores *all* the words in a FULLTEXT index, because it has a built-in list of more than 500 words that it chooses to ignore because they are so common that they aren't very helpful for searching anyway—so-called *stopwords*. This list includes *the*, *as*, *is*, *of*, and so on. The list helps MySQL run much more quickly when performing a FULLTEXT search and keeps database sizes down. Appendix C contains the full list of stopwords.

Here are some things that you should know about FULLTEXT indexes:

- Since MySQL 5.6, InnoDB tables can use FULLTEXT indexes, but prior to that FULLTEXT indexes could be used only with MyISAM tables. If you need to convert a table to MyISAM, you can usually use the MySQL command ALTER TABLE tablename ENGINE = MyISAM;.

- FULLTEXT indexes can be created for CHAR, VARCHAR, and TEXT columns only.

- A FULLTEXT index definition can be given in the CREATE TABLE statement when a table is created, or added later using ALTER TABLE (or CREATE INDEX).

- For large data sets, it is *much* faster to load your data into a table that has no FULLTEXT index and then create the index than to load data into a table that has an existing FULLTEXT index.

To create a FULLTEXT index, apply it to one or more records as in Example 8-15, which adds a FULLTEXT index to the pair of columns *author* and *title* in the *classics* table (this index is in addition to the ones already created and does not affect them).

Example 8-15. Adding a FULLTEXT index to the table classics

```
ALTER TABLE classics ADD FULLTEXT(author,title);
```

You can now perform FULLTEXT searches across this pair of columns. This feature could really come into its own if you could now add the entire text of these publications to the database (particularly as they're out of copyright protection) and they would be fully searchable. See the section "MATCH...AGAINST" on page 198 for a description of searches using FULLTEXT.

If you find that MySQL is running slower than you think it should be when accessing your database, the problem is usually related to your indexes. Either you don't have an index where you need one, or the indexes are not optimally designed. Tweaking a table's indexes will often solve such a problem. Performance is beyond the scope of this book, but in Chapter 9 I'll give you a few tips so you know what to look for.

Querying a MySQL Database

So far, we've created a MySQL database and tables, populated them with data, and added indexes to make them fast to search. Now it's time to look at how these searches are performed, and the various commands and qualifiers available.

SELECT

As you saw in Figure 8-4, the SELECT command is used to extract data from a table. In that section, I used its simplest form to select all data and display it—something you will never want to do on anything but the smallest tables, because all the data will scroll by at an unreadable pace. Alternatively, on Unix/Linux computers, you can tell MySQL to page output a screen at a time by issuing the command:

```
pager less;
```

This pipes output to the less program. To restore standard output and turn paging off, you can issue this command:

```
nopager;
```

Let's now examine SELECT in more detail. The basic syntax is:

```
SELECT something FROM tablename;
```

The *something* can be an * (asterisk) as you saw before, which means *every column*, or you can choose to select only certain columns. For instance, Example 8-16 shows how to select just the *author* and *title* and just the *title* and *isbn*. The result of typing these commands can be seen in Figure 8-9.

Example 8-16. Two different SELECT statements

```
SELECT author,title FROM classics;
SELECT title,isbn FROM classics;
```

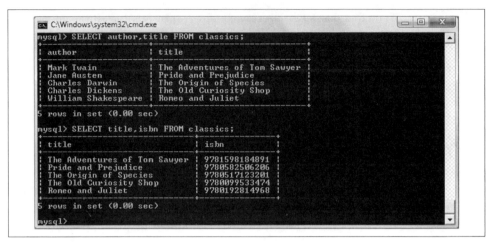

Figure 8-9. The output from two different SELECT statements

SELECT COUNT

Another replacement for the *something* parameter is COUNT, which can be used in many ways. In Example 8-17, it displays the number of rows in the table by passing * as a parameter, which means *all rows*. As you'd expect, the result returned is 5, as there are five publications in the table.

Example 8-17. Counting rows

```
SELECT COUNT(*) FROM classics;
```

SELECT DISTINCT

The DISTINCT qualifier (and its synonym DISTINCTROW) allows you to weed out multiple entries when they contain the same data. For instance, suppose that you want a list of all authors in the table. If you select just the *author* column from a table containing multiple books by the same author, you'll normally see a long list with the same author names over and over. But by adding the DISTINCT keyword, you can show each author just once. So, let's test that out by adding another row that repeats one of our existing authors (Example 8-18).

Example 8-18. Duplicating data

```
INSERT INTO classics(author, title, category, year, isbn)
 VALUES('Charles Dickens','Little Dorrit','Fiction','1857', '9780141439969');
```

Now that Charles Dickens appears twice in the table, we can compare the results of using SELECT with and without the DISTINCT qualifier. Example 8-19 and Figure 8-10

---

show that the simple SELECT lists Dickens twice, and the command with the DISTINCT qualifier shows him only once.

Example 8-19. With and without the DISTINCT qualifier

```
SELECT author FROM classics;
SELECT DISTINCT author FROM classics;
```

Figure 8-10. Selecting data with and without DISTINCT

DELETE

When you need to remove a row from a table, use the DELETE command. Its syntax is similar to the SELECT command and allows you to narrow down the exact row or rows to delete using qualifiers such as WHERE and LIMIT.

Now that you've seen the effects of the DISTINCT qualifier, if you typed Example 8-18, you should remove *Little Dorrit* by entering the commands in Example 8-20.

Example 8-20. Removing the new entry

```
DELETE FROM classics WHERE title='Little Dorrit';
```

This example issues a DELETE command for all rows whose *title* column contains the string Little Dorrit.

The WHERE keyword is very powerful, and important to enter correctly; an error could lead a command to the wrong rows (or have no effect in cases where nothing matches the WHERE clause). So now we'll spend some time on that clause, which is the heart and soul of SQL.

WHERE

The WHERE keyword enables you to narrow down queries by returning only those where a certain expression is true. Example 8-20 returns only the rows where the column exactly matches the string Little Dorrit, using the equality operator =. Example 8-21 shows a couple more examples of using WHERE with =.

Example 8-21. Using the WHERE keyword

```
SELECT author,title FROM classics WHERE author="Mark Twain";
SELECT author,title FROM classics WHERE isbn="9781598184891";
```

Given our current table, the two commands in Example 8-21 display the same results. But we could easily add more books by Mark Twain, in which case the first line would display all the titles he wrote and the second line would continue (because we know the ISBN is unique) to display The Adventures of Tom Sawyer. In other words, searches using a unique key are more predictable, and you'll see further evidence later of the value of unique and primary keys.

You can also do pattern matching for your searches using the LIKE qualifier, which allows searches on parts of strings. This qualifier should be used with a % character before or after some text. When placed before a keyword, % means *anything before*. After a keyword, it means *anything after*. Example 8-22 performs three different queries, one for the start of a string, one for the end, and one for anywhere in a string.

Example 8-22. Using the LIKE qualifier

```
SELECT author,title FROM classics WHERE author LIKE "Charles%";
SELECT author,title FROM classics WHERE title LIKE "%Species";
SELECT author,title FROM classics WHERE title LIKE "%and%";
```

You can see the results of these commands in Figure 8-11. The first command outputs the publications by both Charles Darwin and Charles Dickens because the LIKE qualifier was set to return anything matching the string Charles followed by any other text. Then just The Origin of Species is returned, because it's the only row whose column ends with the string Species. Last, both Pride and Prejudice and Romeo and Juliet are returned, because they both matched the string and anywhere in the column. The % will also match if there is nothing in the position it occupies; in other words, it can match an empty string.

Figure 8-11. Using WHERE with the LIKE qualifier

LIMIT

The LIMIT qualifier enables you to choose how many rows to return in a query, and where in the table to start returning them. When passed a single parameter, it tells MySQL to start at the beginning of the results and just return the number of rows given in that parameter. If you pass it two parameters, the first indicates the offset from the start of the results where MySQL should start the display, and the second indicates how many to return. You can think of the first parameter as saying, "Skip this number of results at the start."

Example 8-23 includes three commands. The first returns the first three rows from the table. The second returns two rows starting at position 1 (skipping the first row). The last command returns a single row starting at position 3 (skipping the first three rows). Figure 8-12 shows the results of issuing these three commands.

Example 8-23. Limiting the number of results returned

```
SELECT author,title FROM classics LIMIT 3;
SELECT author,title FROM classics LIMIT 1,2;
SELECT author,title FROM classics LIMIT 3,1;
```

> Be careful with the LIMIT keyword, because offsets start at 0, but the number of rows to return starts at 1. So, LIMIT 1,3 means return *three* rows starting from the *second* row. You could look at the first argument as stating how many rows to skip, so that in English the instruction would be "Return 3 rows, skipping the first 1."

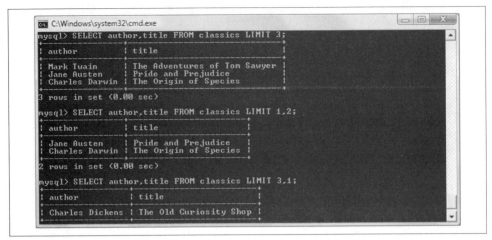

Figure 8-12. Restricting the rows returned with LIMIT

MATCH...AGAINST

The MATCH...AGAINST construct can be used on columns that have been given a FULL
TEXT index (see the section "Creating a FULLTEXT index" on page 192). With it, you
can make natural-language searches as you would in an internet search engine.
Unlike the use of WHERE...= or WHERE...LIKE, MATCH...AGAINST lets you enter multiple words in a search query and checks them against all words in the FULLTEXT columns. FULLTEXT indexes are case-insensitive, so it makes no difference what case is
used in your queries.

Assuming that you have added a FULLTEXT index to the *author* and *title* columns,
enter the three queries shown in Example 8-24. The first asks for any rows that contain the word *and* to be returned. Because *and* is a stopword, MySQL will ignore it
and the query will always produce an empty set—no matter what is stored in the columns. The second query asks for any rows that contain both of the words *curiosity*
and *shop* anywhere in them, in any order, to be returned. And the last query applies
the same kind of search for the words *tom* and *sawyer*. Figure 8-13 shows the results
of these queries.

Example 8-24. Using MATCH...AGAINST on FULLTEXT indexes

```
SELECT author,title FROM classics
 WHERE MATCH(author,title) AGAINST('and');
SELECT author,title FROM classics
 WHERE MATCH(author,title) AGAINST('curiosity shop');
SELECT author,title FROM classics
 WHERE MATCH(author,title) AGAINST('tom sawyer');
```

Figure 8-13. Using MATCH...AGAINST on FULLTEXT indexes

MATCH...AGAINST in Boolean mode

If you wish to give your `MATCH...AGAINST` queries even more power, use *Boolean mode*. This changes the effect of the standard `FULLTEXT` query so that it searches for any combination of search words, instead of requiring all search words to be in the text. The presence of a single word in a column causes the search to return the row.

Boolean mode also allows you to preface search words with a + or - sign to indicate whether they must be included or excluded. If normal Boolean mode says, "Any of these words will do," a plus sign means, "This word must be present; otherwise, don't return the row." A minus sign means, "This word must not be present; its presence disqualifies the row from being returned."

Example 8-25 illustrates Boolean mode through two queries. The first asks for all rows containing the word *charles* and not the word *species* to be returned. The second uses double quotes to request that all rows containing the exact phrase *origin of* be returned. Figure 8-14 shows the results of these queries.

Example 8-25. Using MATCH...AGAINST in Boolean mode

```
SELECT author,title FROM classics
 WHERE MATCH(author,title)
 AGAINST('+charles -species' IN BOOLEAN MODE);
SELECT author,title FROM classics
 WHERE MATCH(author,title)
 AGAINST('"origin of"' IN BOOLEAN MODE);
```

Figure 8-14. Using MATCH...AGAINST in Boolean mode

As you would expect, the first request returns only The Old Curiosity Shop by Charles Dickens; any rows containing the word *species* have been excluded, so Charles Darwin's publication is ignored.

> There is something of interest to note in the second query: the stopword *of* is part of the search string, but it is still used by the search because the double quotation marks override stopwords.

UPDATE...SET

This construct allows you to update the contents of a field. If you wish to change the contents of one or more fields, you need to first narrow in on just the field or fields to be changed, in much the same way you use the SELECT command. Example 8-26 shows the use of UPDATE...SET in two different ways. You can see the results in Figure 8-15.

Example 8-26. Using UPDATE...SET

```
UPDATE classics SET author='Mark Twain (Samuel Langhorne Clemens)'
 WHERE author='Mark Twain';
UPDATE classics SET category='Classic Fiction'
 WHERE category='Fiction';
```

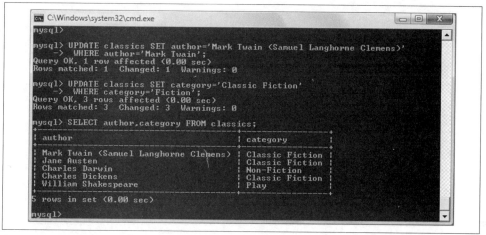

Figure 8-15. Updating columns in the classics table

In the first query, Mark Twain's real name of Samuel Langhorne Clemens was appended to his pen name in parentheses, which affected only one row. The second query, however, affected three rows, because it changed all occurrences of the word *Fiction* in the *category* column to the term *Classic Fiction*.

When performing an update, you can also make use of the qualifiers you have already seen, such as LIMIT, and the following ORDER BY and GROUP BY keywords.

ORDER BY

ORDER BY sorts returned results by one or more columns in ascending or descending order. Example 8-27 shows two such queries, the results of which can be seen in Figure 8-16.

Example 8-27. Using ORDER BY

```
SELECT author,title FROM classics ORDER BY author;
SELECT author,title FROM classics ORDER BY title DESC;
```

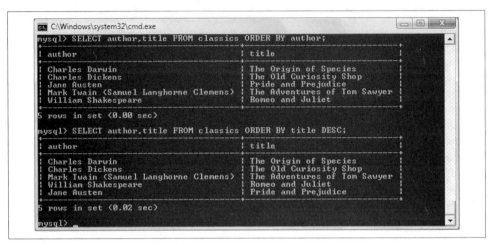

Figure 8-16. Sorting the results of requests

As you can see, the first query returns the publications by *author* in ascending alphabetical order (the default), and the second returns them by *title* in descending order.

If you wanted to sort all the rows by *author* and then by descending *year* of publication (to view the most recent first), you would issue the following query:

```
SELECT author,title,year FROM classics ORDER BY author,year DESC;
```

This shows that each ascending and descending qualifier applies to a single column. The DESC keyword applies only to the preceding column, *year*. Because you allow *author* to use the default sort order, it is sorted in ascending order. You could also have explicitly specified ascending order for that column, with the same results:

```
SELECT author,title,year FROM classics ORDER BY author ASC,year DESC;
```

GROUP BY

In a similar fashion to ORDER BY, you can group results returned from queries using GROUP BY, which is good for retrieving information about a group of data. For example, if you want to know how many publications there are of each category in the *classics* table, you can issue the following query:

```
SELECT category,COUNT(author) FROM classics GROUP BY category;
```

which returns the following output:

```
+----------------+----------------+
| category       | COUNT(author)  |
+----------------+----------------+
| Classic Fiction |              3 |
| Non-Fiction    |              1 |
| Play           |              1 |
+----------------+----------------+
3 rows in set (0.00 sec)
```

Joining Tables Together

It is quite normal to maintain multiple tables within a database, each holding a different type of information. For example, consider the case of a *customers* table that needs to be able to be cross-referenced with publications purchased from the *classics* table. Enter the commands in Example 8-28 to create this new table and populate it with three customers and their purchases. Figure 8-17 shows the result.

Example 8-28. Creating and populating the customers table

```
CREATE TABLE customers (
 name VARCHAR(128),
 isbn VARCHAR(13),
 PRIMARY KEY (isbn)) ENGINE InnoDB;
INSERT INTO customers(name,isbn)
 VALUES('Joe Bloggs','9780099533474');
INSERT INTO customers(name,isbn)
 VALUES('Mary Smith','9780582506206');
INSERT INTO customers(name,isbn)
 VALUES('Jack Wilson','9780517123201');
SELECT * FROM customers;
```

Figure 8-17. Creating the customers table

There's also a shortcut for inserting multiple rows of data, as in Example 8-28, in which you can replace the three separate INSERT INTO queries with a single one listing the data to be inserted, separated by commas, like this:

```
INSERT INTO customers(name,isbn) VALUES
 ('Joe Bloggs','9780099533474'),
 ('Mary Smith','9780582506206'),
 ('Jack Wilson','9780517123201');
```

Of course, in a proper table containing customers' details there would also be addresses, phone numbers, email addresses, and so on, but they aren't necessary for this explanation. While creating the new table, you should have noticed that it has something in common with the *classics* table: a column called *isbn*. Because it has the same meaning in both tables (an ISBN refers to a book, and always the same book), we can use this column to tie the two tables together into a single query, as in Example 8-29.

Example 8-29. Joining two tables into a single SELECT

```
SELECT name,author,title FROM customers,classics
 WHERE customers.isbn=classics.isbn;
```

The result of this operation is the following:

```
+-------------+-----------------+------------------------+
| name        | author          | title                  |
+-------------+-----------------+------------------------+
| Joe Bloggs  | Charles Dickens | The Old Curiosity Shop |
| Mary Smith  | Jane Austen     | Pride and Prejudice    |
| Jack Wilson | Charles Darwin  | The Origin of Species  |
+-------------+-----------------+------------------------+
3 rows in set (0.00 sec)
```

See how this query has neatly linked the tables together to show the publications purchased from the *classics* table by the people in the *customers* table?

NATURAL JOIN

Using NATURAL JOIN, you can save yourself some typing and make queries a little clearer. This kind of join takes two tables and automatically joins columns that have the same name. So, to achieve the same results as from Example 8-29, you would enter the following:

```
SELECT name,author,title FROM customers NATURAL JOIN classics;
```

JOIN...ON

If you wish to specify the column on which to join two tables, use the `JOIN...ON` construct, as follows, to achieve results identical to those of Example 8-29:

```
SELECT name,author,title FROM customers
  JOIN classics ON customers.isbn=classics.isbn;
```

Using AS

You can also save yourself some typing and improve query readability by creating aliases using the AS keyword. Simply follow a table name with AS and the alias to use. The following code, therefore, is also identical in action to Example 8-29:

```
SELECT name,author,title from
  customers AS cust, classics AS class WHERE cust.isbn=class.isbn;
```

The result of this operation is the following:

```
+-------------+-----------------+-----------------------+
| name        | author          | title                 |
+-------------+-----------------+-----------------------+
| Joe Bloggs  | Charles Dickens | The Old Curiosity Shop |
| Mary Smith  | Jane Austen     | Pride and Prejudice   |
| Jack Wilson | Charles Darwin  | The Origin of Species |
+-------------+-----------------+-----------------------+
3 rows in set (0.00 sec)
```

You can also use AS to rename a column (whether or not joining tables), like this:

```
SELECT name AS customer FROM customers ORDER BY customer;
```

Which results in the following output:

```
+-------------+
| customer    |
+-------------+
| Jack Wilson |
| Joe Bloggs  |
| Mary Smith  |
+-------------+
3 rows in set (0.00 sec)
```

Aliases can be particularly useful when you have long queries that reference the same table names many times.

Using Logical Operators

You can also use the logical operators AND, OR, and NOT in your MySQL WHERE queries to further narrow down your selections. Example 8-30 shows one instance of each, but you can mix and match them in any way you need.

Example 8-30. Using logical operators

```
SELECT author,title FROM classics WHERE
 author LIKE "Charles%" AND author LIKE "%Darwin";
SELECT author,title FROM classics WHERE
 author LIKE "%Mark Twain%" OR author LIKE "%Samuel Langhorne Clemens%";
SELECT author,title FROM classics WHERE
 author LIKE "Charles%" AND author NOT LIKE "%Darwin";
```

I've chosen the first query because Charles Darwin might be listed in some rows by his full name, Charles Robert Darwin. The query returns any publications for which the *author* column starts with *Charles* and ends with *Darwin*. The second query searches for publications written using either Mark Twain's pen name or his real name, Samuel Langhorne Clemens. The third query returns publications written by authors with the first name Charles but not the surname Darwin.

MySQL Functions

You might wonder why anyone would want to use MySQL functions when PHP comes with a whole bunch of powerful functions of its own. The answer is very simple: the MySQL functions work on the data right there in the database. If you were to use PHP, you would first have to extract raw data from MySQL, manipulate it, and then perform the database query you wanted.

Having functions built into MySQL substantially reduces the time needed for performing complex queries, as well as their complexity. You can learn more about all the available string (*http://tinyurl.com/mysqlstrings*) and date/time (*http://tinyurl.com/mysqldates*) functions from the documentation. However, to get you started, Appendix D describes a subset of the most useful functions.

Accessing MySQL via phpMyAdmin

Although to use MySQL you have to learn these main commands and how they work, once you understand them, it can be much quicker and simpler to use a program such as *phpMyAdmin* to manage your databases and tables.

To do this, assuming you have installed AMPPS as described in Chapter 2, type the following to open up the program (see Figure 8-18):

```
http://localhost/phpmyadmin
```

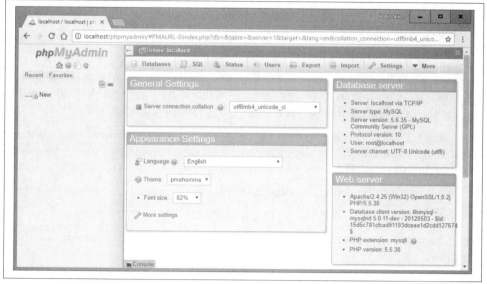

Figure 8-18. The phpMyAdmin main screen

In the lefthand pane of the main phpMyAdmin screen, you can click to select any tables you wish to work with (although none will be available until created). You can also click New to create a new database.

From here, you can perform all the main operations, such as creating new databases, adding tables, creating indexes, and much more. To find out more about phpMyAdmin, consult the documentation (*https://docs.phpmyadmin.net*).

If you worked with me through the examples in this chapter, congratulations—it has been quite a long journey. You've come all the way from learning how to create a MySQL database, through issuing complex queries that combine multiple tables, to using Boolean operators and leveraging MySQL's various qualifiers.

In the next chapter, we'll start looking at how to approach efficient database design, advanced SQL techniques, and MySQL functions and transactions.

Questions

1. What is the purpose of the semicolon in MySQL queries?

2. Which command would you use to view the available databases or tables?

3. How would you create a new MySQL user on the local host called *newuser* with a password of *newpass* and with access to everything in the database *newdatabase*?

4. How can you view the structure of a table?

5. What is the purpose of a MySQL index?

6. What benefit does a FULLTEXT index provide?

7. What is a stopword?

8. Both SELECT DISTINCT and GROUP BY cause the display to show only one output row for each value in a column, even if multiple rows contain that value. What are the main differences between SELECT DISTINCT and GROUP BY?

9. Using the SELECT...WHERE construct, how would you return only rows containing the word *Langhorne* somewhere in the *author* column of the *classics* table used in this chapter?

10. What needs to be defined in two tables to make it possible for you to join them together?

See "Chapter 8 Answers" on page 719 in Appendix A for the answers to these questions.

CHAPTER 9

Mastering MySQL

Chapter 8 provided you with a good grounding in the practice of using relational databases with the Structured Query Language. You've learned about creating databases and the tables they comprise, as well as inserting, looking up, changing, and deleting data.

With that knowledge under your belt, we now need to look at how to design databases for maximum speed and efficiency. For example, how do you decide what data to place in which table? Well, over the years, a number of guidelines have been developed that—if you follow them—ensure that your databases will be efficient and capable of growing as you feed them more and more data.

Database Design

It's very important that you design a database correctly before you start to create it; otherwise, you are almost certainly going to have to go back and change it by splitting up some tables, merging others, and moving various columns about in order to achieve sensible relationships that MySQL can easily use.

Sitting down with a sheet of paper and a pencil and writing down a selection of the queries that you think you and your users are likely to ask is an excellent starting point. In the case of an online bookstore's database, some of your questions could be:

- How many authors, books, and customers are in the database?
- Which author wrote a certain book?
- Which books were written by a certain author?
- What is the most expensive book?
- What is the best-selling book?

- Which books have not sold this year?
- Which books did a certain customer buy?
- Which books have been purchased along with the same other books?

Of course, there are many more queries that you could make on such a database, but even this small sample will begin to give you insights into how to lay out your tables. For example, books and ISBNs can probably be combined into one table, because they are closely linked (we'll examine some of the subtleties later). In contrast, books and customers should be in separate tables, because their connection is very loose. A customer can buy any book, and even multiple copies of a book, yet a book can be bought by many customers and be ignored by still more potential customers.

When you plan to do a lot of searches on something, it can often benefit by having its own table. And when couplings between things are loose, it's best to put them in separate tables.

Taking into account those simple rules of thumb, we can guess we'll need at least three tables to accommodate all these queries:

Authors

> There will be lots of searches for authors, many of whom have collaborated on titles, and many of whom will be featured in collections. Listing all the information about each author together, linked to that author, will produce optimal results for searches—hence an *Authors* table.

Books

> Many books appear in different editions. Sometimes they change publisher and sometimes they have the same titles as other, unrelated books. So, the links between books and authors are complicated enough to call for a separate table.

Customers

> It's even more clear why customers should get their own table, as they are free to purchase any book by any author.

Primary Keys: The Keys to Relational Databases

Using the power of relational databases, we can define information for each author, book, and customer in just one place. Obviously, what interests us is the links between them—such as who wrote each book and who purchased it—but we can store that information just by making links between the three tables. I'll show you the basic principles, and then it just takes practice for it to feel natural.

The magic involves giving every author a unique identifier. We'll do the same for every book and for every customer. We saw the means of doing that in the previous chapter: the *primary key*. For a book, it makes sense to use the ISBN, although you then have to deal with multiple editions that have different ISBNs. For authors and customers, you can just assign arbitrary keys, which the AUTO_INCREMENT feature that you saw in the last chapter makes easy.

In short, every table will be designed around some object that you're likely to search for a lot—an author, book, or customer, in this case—and that object will have a primary key. Don't choose a key that could possibly have the same value for different objects. The ISBN is a rare case for which an industry has provided a primary key that you can rely on to be unique for each product. Most of the time, you'll create an arbitrary key for this purpose, using AUTO_INCREMENT.

Normalization

The process of separating your data into tables and creating primary keys is called *normalization*. Its main goal is to make sure each piece of information appears in the database only once. Duplicating data is inefficient, because it makes databases larger than they need to be and therefore slows access. More importantly, the presence of duplicates creates a strong risk that you'll update only one row of duplicated data, creating inconsistencies in a database and potentially causing serious errors.

For example, if you list the titles of books in the *Authors* table as well as the *Books* table, and you have to correct a typographic error in a title, you'll have to search through both tables and make sure you make the same change every place the title is listed. It's better to keep the title in one place and use the ISBN in other places.

But in the process of splitting a database into multiple tables, it's important not to go too far and create more tables than is necessary, which would also lead to inefficient design and slower access.

Luckily, E. F. Codd, the inventor of the relational model, analyzed the concept of normalization and split it into three separate schemas called *First*, *Second*, and *Third Normal Form*. If you modify a database to satisfy each of these forms in order, you will ensure that your database is optimally balanced for fast access and minimum memory and disk space usage.

To see how the normalization process works, let's start with the rather monstrous database in Table 9-1, which shows a single table containing all of the author names, book titles, and (fictional) customer details. You could consider it a first attempt at a table intended to keep track of which customers have ordered books. Obviously this is an inefficient design, because data is duplicated all over the place (duplications are highlighted), but it represents a starting point.

Table 9-1. A highly inefficient design for a database table

Author 1	Author 2	Title	ISBN	Price	Customer name	Customer address	Purchase date
David Sklar	*Adam Trachtenberg*	*PHP Cookbook*	*0596101015*	*44.99*	Emma Brown	1565 Rainbow Road, Los Angeles, CA 90014	Mar 03 2009
Danny Goodman		Dynamic HTML	0596527403	59.99	**Darren Ryder**	**4758 Emily Drive, Richmond, VA 23219**	**Dec 19 2008**
Hugh E. Williams	David Lane	PHP and MySQL	0596005436	44.95	Earl B. Thurston	862 Gregory Lane, Frankfort, KY 40601	Jun 22 2009
David Sklar	*Adam Trachtenberg*	*PHP Cookbook*	*0596101015*	*44.99*	**Darren Ryder**	**4758 Emily Drive, Richmond, VA 23219**	**Dec 19 2008**
Rasmus Lerdorf	Kevin Tatroe & Peter MacIntyre	Programming PHP	0596006815	39.99	David Miller	3647 Cedar Lane, Waltham, MA 02154	Jan 16 2009

In the following three sections, we will examine this database design, and you'll see how we can improve it by removing the various duplicate entries and splitting the single table into multiple tables, each containing one type of data.

First Normal Form

For a database to satisfy the *First Normal Form*, it must fulfill three requirements:

- There should be no repeating columns containing the same kind of data.
- All columns should contain a single value.
- There should be a primary key to uniquely identify each row.

Looking at these requirements in order, you should notice straightaway that both the *Author 1* and *Author 2* columns constitute repeating data types. So we already have a target column for pulling into a separate table, as the repeated *Author* columns violate Rule 1.

Second, there are three authors listed for the final book, *Programming PHP*. I've handled that by making Kevin Tatroe and Peter MacIntyre share the *Author 2* column, which violates Rule 2—yet another reason to transfer the *Author* details to a separate table.

However, Rule 3 is satisfied, because the primary key of ISBN has already been created.

Table 9-2 shows the result of removing the *Author* columns from Table 9-1. Already it looks a lot less cluttered, although there remain duplications that are highlighted.

Table 9-2. The result of stripping the Author columns from Table 9-1

Title	ISBN	Price	Customer name	Customer address	Purchase date
PHP Cookbook	*0596101015*	*44.99*	Emma Brown	1565 Rainbow Road, Los Angeles, CA 90014	Mar 03 2009
Dynamic HTML	0596527403	59.99	**Darren Ryder**	**4758 Emily Drive, Richmond, VA 23219**	**Dec 19 2008**
PHP and MySQL	0596005436	44.95	Earl B. Thurston	862 Gregory Lane, Frankfort, KY 40601	Jun 22 2009
PHP Cookbook	*0596101015*	*44.99*	**Darren Ryder**	**4758 Emily Drive, Richmond, VA 23219**	**Dec 19 2008**
Programming PHP	0596006815	39.99	David Miller	3647 Cedar Lane, Waltham, MA 02154	Jan 16 2009

The new *Authors* table shown in Table 9-3 is small and simple. It just lists the ISBN of a title along with an author. If a title has more than one author, additional authors get their own rows. At first, you may feel ill at ease with this table, because you can't tell which author wrote which book. But don't worry: MySQL can quickly tell you. All you have to do is tell it which book you want information for, and MySQL will use its ISBN to search the *Authors* table in a matter of milliseconds.

Table 9-3. The new Authors table

ISBN	Author
0596101015	David Sklar
0596101015	Adam Trachtenberg
0596527403	Danny Goodman
0596005436	Hugh E. Williams
0596005436	David Lane
0596006815	Rasmus Lerdorf
0596006815	Kevin Tatroe
0596006815	Peter MacIntyre

As I mentioned earlier, the ISBN will be the primary key for the *Books* table, when we get around to creating that table. I mention that here in order to emphasize that the ISBN is not, however, the primary key for the *Authors* table. In the real world, the *Authors* table would deserve a primary key, too, so that each author would have a key to uniquely identify them.

So, in the *Authors* table, *ISBN* is just a column that—for the purposes of speeding up searches—we'll probably make a key, but not the primary key. In fact, it *cannot* be the primary key in this table, because it's not unique: the same ISBN appears multiple times whenever two or more authors have collaborated on a book.

Because we'll use it to link authors to books in another table, this column is called a *foreign* key.

Keys (also called *indexes*) have several purposes in MySQL. The fundamental reason for defining a key is to make searches faster. You've seen examples in Chapter 8 in which keys are used in WHERE clauses for searching. But a key can also be useful to uniquely identify an item. Thus, a unique key is often used as a primary key in one table, and as a foreign key to link rows in that table to rows in another table.

Second Normal Form

The First Normal Form deals with duplicate data (or redundancy) across multiple columns. The *Second Normal Form* is all about redundancy across multiple rows. To achieve Second Normal Form, your tables must already be in First Normal Form. Once this has been done, you achieve Second Normal Form by identifying columns whose data repeats in different places and then removing them to their own tables.

So, let's look again at Table 9-2. Notice how Darren Ryder bought two books and therefore his details are duplicated. This tells us that the *Customer* columns need to be pulled into their own table. Table 9-4 shows the result of removing the *Customer* columns from Table 9-2.

Table 9-4. The new Titles table

ISBN	Title	Price
0596101015	PHP Cookbook	44.99
0596527403	Dynamic HTML	59.99
0596005436	PHP and MySQL	44.95
0596006815	Programming PHP	39.99

As you can see, all that's left in Table 9-4 are the *ISBN*, *Title*, and *Price* columns for four unique books, so this now constitutes an efficient and self-contained table that satisfies the requirements of both the First and Second Normal Forms. Along the way, we've managed to reduce the information to data closely related to book titles. This table could also include years of publication, page counts, numbers of reprints, and so on, as these details are also closely related. The only rule is that we can't put in any column that could have multiple values for a single book, because then we'd have to list the same book in multiple rows and would thus violate Second Normal Form. Restoring an *Author* column, for instance, would violate this normalization.

However, looking at the extracted *Customer* columns, now in Table 9-5, we can see that there's still more normalization work to do, because Darren Ryder's details are still duplicated. And it could also be argued that First Normal Form Rule 2 (all columns should contain a single value) has not been properly complied with, because the addresses really need to be broken into separate columns for *Address*, *City*, *State*, and *Zip*.

Table 9-5. The customer details from Table 9-2

ISBN	Customer name	Customer address	Purchase date
0596101015	Emma Brown	1565 Rainbow Road, Los Angeles, CA 90014	Mar 03 2009
0596527403	Darren Ryder	4758 Emily Drive, Richmond, VA 23219	Dec 19 2008
0596005436	Earl B. Thurston	862 Gregory Lane, Frankfort, KY 40601	Jun 22 2009
0596101015	Darren Ryder	4758 Emily Drive, Richmond, VA 23219	Dec 19 2008
0596006815	David Miller	3647 Cedar Lane, Waltham, MA 02154	Jan 16 2009

What we have to do is split this table further to ensure that each customer's details are entered only once. Because the ISBN is not and cannot be used as a primary key to identify customers (or authors), a new key must be created.

Table 9-6 is the result of normalizing the *Customers* table into both First and Second Normal Forms. Each customer now has a unique customer number called *CustNo* that is the table's primary key, and that will most likely have been created via `AUTO_INCREMENT`. All the parts of customer addresses have also been separated into distinct columns to make them easily searchable and updateable.

Table 9-6. The new Customers table

CustNo	Name	Address	City	State	Zip
1	Emma Brown	1565 Rainbow Road	Los Angeles	CA	90014
2	Darren Ryder	4758 Emily Drive	Richmond	VA	23219
3	Earl B. Thurston	862 Gregory Lane	Frankfort	KY	40601
4	David Miller	3647 Cedar Lane	Waltham	MA	02154

At the same time, in order to normalize Table 9-6, we had to remove the information on customer purchases, because otherwise, there would be multiple instances of customer details for each book purchased. Instead, the purchase data is now placed in a new table called *Purchases* (see Table 9-7).

Table 9-7. The new Purchases table

CustNo	ISBN	Date
1	0596101015	Mar 03 2009
2	0596527403	Dec 19 2008
2	0596101015	Dec 19 2008
3	0596005436	Jun 22 2009
4	0596006815	Jan 16 2009

Here the *CustNo* column from Table 9-6 is reused as a key to tie the *Customers* and *Purchases* tables together. Because the *ISBN* column is also repeated here, this table can be linked with the *Authors* and *Titles* tables, too.

The *CustNo* column may be a useful key in the *Purchases* table, but it's not a primary key. A single customer can buy multiple books (and even multiple copies of one book), so the *CustNo* column is not a primary key. In fact, the *Purchases* table has no primary key. That's all right, because we don't expect to need to keep track of unique purchases. If one customer buys two copies of the same book on the same day, we'll just allow two rows with the same information. For easy searching, we can define both *CustNo* and *ISBN* as keys—just not as primary keys.

 There are now four tables, one more than the three we had initially assumed would be needed. We arrived at this decision through the normalization process, by methodically following the First and Second Normal Form rules, which made it plain that a fourth table called *Purchases* would also be required.

The tables we now have are *Authors* (Table 9-3), *Titles* (Table 9-4), *Customers* (Table 9-6), and *Purchases* (Table 9-7), and we can link each table to any other using either the *CustNo* or the *ISBN* key.

For example, to see which books Darren Ryder has purchased, you can look him up in Table 9-6, the *Customers* table, where you will see his *CustNo* is 2. Armed with this number, you can now go to Table 9-7, the *Purchases* table; looking at the *ISBN* column here, you will see that he purchased titles 0596527403 and 0596101015 on December 19, 2008. This looks like a lot of trouble for a human, but it's not so hard for MySQL.

To determine what these titles were, you can then refer to Table 9-4, the *Titles* table, and see that the books he bought were *Dynamic HTML* and *PHP Cookbook*. Should you wish to know the authors of these books, you could also use the ISBNs you just looked up on Table 9-3, the *Authors* table, and you would see that ISBN 0596527403, *Dynamic HTML*, was written by Danny Goodman, and that ISBN 0596101015, *PHP Cookbook*, was written by David Sklar and Adam Trachtenberg.

Third Normal Form

Once you have a database that complies with both the First and Second Normal Forms, it is in pretty good shape and you might not have to modify it any further. However, if you wish to be very strict with your database, you can ensure that it adheres to the *Third Normal Form*, which requires that data that is *not* directly dependent on the primary key but *is* dependent on another value in the table should also be moved into separate tables, according to the dependence.

For example, in Table 9-6, the *Customers* table, it could be argued that the *State*, *City*, and *Zip* keys are not directly related to each customer, because many other people will have the same details in their addresses, too. However, they are directly related to each other, in that the *Address* relies on the *City*, and the *City* relies on the *State*.

Therefore, to satisfy Third Normal Form for Table 9-6, you would need to split it into Tables 9–8 through 9–11.

Table 9-8. Third Normal Form Customers table

CustNo	Name	Address	Zip
1	Emma Brown	1565 Rainbow Road	90014
2	Darren Ryder	4758 Emily Drive	23219
3	Earl B. Thurston	862 Gregory Lane	40601
4	David Miller	3647 Cedar Lane	02154

Table 9-9. Third Normal Form Zip codes table

Zip	CityID
90014	1234
23219	5678
40601	4321
02154	8765

Table 9-10. Third Normal Form Cities table

CityID	Name	StateID
1234	Los Angeles	5
5678	Richmond	46
4321	Frankfort	17
8765	Waltham	21

Table 9-11. Third Normal Form States table

StateID	Name	Abbreviation
5	California	CA
46	Virginia	VA
17	Kentucky	KY
21	Massachusetts	MA

So, how would you use this set of four tables instead of the single Table 9-6? Well, you would look up the *Zip code* in Table 9-8, and then find the matching *CityID* in Table 9-9. Given this information, you could look up the city *Name* in Table 9-10 and then also find the *StateID*, which you could use in Table 9-11 to look up the state's *Name*.

Although using the Third Normal Form in this way may seem like overkill, it can have advantages. For example, take a look at Table 9-11, where it has been possible to include both a state's name and its two-letter abbreviation. It could also contain population details and other demographics, if you desired.

 Table 9-10 could also contain even more localized demographics that could be useful to you and/or your customers. By splitting up these pieces of data, you can make it easier to maintain your database in the future, should it be necessary to add columns.

Deciding whether to use the Third Normal Form can be tricky. Your evaluation should rest on what data you may need to add at a later date. If you are absolutely certain that the name and address of a customer is all that you will ever require, you probably will want to leave out this final normalization stage.

On the other hand, suppose you are writing a database for a large organization such as the US Postal Service. What would you do if a city were to be renamed? With a table such as Table 9-6, you would need to perform a global search-and-replace on every instance of that city. But if you have your database set up according to the Third Normal Form, you would have to change only a single entry in Table 9-10 for the change to be reflected throughout the entire database.

Therefore, I suggest that you ask yourself two questions to help you decide whether to perform a Third Normal Form normalization on any table:

- Is it likely that many new columns will need to be added to this table?
- Could any of this table's fields require a global update at any point?

If either of the answers is yes, you should probably consider performing this final stage of normalization.

When Not to Use Normalization

Now that you know all about normalization, I'm going to tell you why you should throw these rules out of the window on high-traffic sites. That's right—you should never fully normalize your tables on sites that will cause MySQL to thrash.

Normalization requires spreading data across multiple tables, and this means making multiple calls to MySQL for each query. On a very popular site, if you have normalized tables, your database access will slow down considerably once you get above a few dozen concurrent users, because they will be creating hundreds of database accesses between them. In fact, I would go so far as to say you should *denormalize* any commonly looked-up data as much as you can.

You see, if you have data duplicated across your tables, you can substantially reduce the number of additional requests that need to be made, because most of the data you want is available in each table. This means that you can simply add an extra column to a query and that field will be available for all matching results.

Of course, you have to deal with the downsides previously mentioned, such as using up large amounts of disk space, and ensuring that you update every single duplicate copy of the data when it needs modifying.

Multiple updates can be computerized, though. MySQL provides a feature called *triggers* that make automatic changes to the database in response to changes you make. (Triggers are, however, beyond the scope of this book.) Another way to propagate redundant data is to set up a PHP program to run regularly and keep all copies in sync. The program reads changes from a "master" table and updates all the others. (You'll see how to access MySQL from PHP in the next chapter.)

However, until you are very experienced with MySQL, I recommend that you fully normalize all your tables (at least to First and Second Normal Form), as this will instill the habit and put you in good stead. Only when you actually start to see MySQL logjams should you consider looking at denormalization.

Relationships

MySQL is called a *relational* database management system because its tables store not only data but the *relationships* among the data. There are three categories of relationships.

One-to-One

A *one-to-one relationship* is like a (traditional) marriage: each item has a relationship to only one item of the other type. This is surprisingly rare. For instance, an author can write multiple books, a book can have multiple authors, and even an address can be associated with multiple customers. Perhaps the best example in this chapter so far of a one-to-one relationship is the relationship between the name of a state and its two-character abbreviation.

However, for the sake of argument, let's assume that there can always be only one customer at any address. In such a case, the Customers–Addresses relationship in Figure 9-1 is a one-to-one relationship: only one customer lives at each address, and each address can have only one customer.

Table 9-8a (Customers)		Table 9-8b (Addresses)	
CustNo	Name	Address	Zip
1	Emma Brown ·····················1565 Rainbow Road		90014
2	Darren Ryder ·····················4758 Emily Drive		23219
3	Earl B. Thurston ·····················862 Gregory Lane		40601
4	David Miller·····················3647 Cedar Lane		02154

Figure 9-1. The Customers table, Table 9-8, split into two tables

Usually, when two items have a one-to-one relationship, you just include them as columns in the same table. There are two reasons for splitting them into separate tables:

- You want to be prepared in case the relationship changes later and is no longer one-to-one.
- The table has a lot of columns, and you think that performance or maintenance would be improved by splitting it.

Of course, when you build your own databases in the real world, you will have to create one-to-many Customer–Address relationships (*one* address, *many* customers).

One-to-Many

One-to-many (or many-to-one) relationships occur when one row in one table is linked to many rows in another table. You have already seen how Table 9-8 would take on a one-to-many relationship if multiple customers were allowed at the same address, which is why it would have to be split up if that were the case.

So, looking at Table 9-8a within Figure 9-1, you can see that it shares a one-to-many relationship with Table 9-7 because there is only one of each customer in Table 9-8a. However Table 9-7, the *Purchases* table, can (and does) contain more than one purchase from a given customer. Therefore, *one* customer has a relationship with *many* purchases.

You can see these two tables alongside each other in Figure 9-2, where the dashed lines joining rows in each table start from a single row in the lefthand table but can connect to more than one row in the righthand table. This one-to-many relationship is also the preferred scheme to use when describing a many-to-one relationship, in which case you would normally swap the left and right tables to view them as a one-to-many relationship.

Table 9-8a (Customers)			Table 9-7. (Purchases)		
CustNo	Name		CustNo	ISBN	Date
1	Emma Brown ···················· 1			0596101015	Mar 03 2009
2	Darren Ryder ·············· 2			0596527403	Dec 19 2008
	(etc...) ·············· 2			0596101015	Dec 19 2008
3	Earl B. Thurston ················ 3			0596005436	Jun 22 2009
4	David Miller················ 4			0596006815	Jan 16 2009

Figure 9-2. Illustrating the relationship between two tables

To represent a one-to-many relationship in a relational database, create a table for the "many" and a table for the "one." The table for the "many" must contain a column that lists the primary key from the "one" table. Thus, the *Purchases* table will contain a column that lists the primary key of the customer.

Many-to-Many

In a *many-to-many relationship*, many rows in one table are linked to many rows in another table. To create this relationship, add a third table containing the same key column from each of the other tables. This third table contains nothing else, as its sole purpose is to link up the other tables.

Table 9-12 is just such a table. It was extracted from Table 9-7, the *Purchases* table, but omits the purchase date information. It contains a copy of the ISBN of every title sold, along with the customer number of each purchaser.

Table 9-12. An intermediary table

Cust No	ISBN
1	0596101015
2	0596527403
2	0596101015
3	0596005436
4	0596006815

With this intermediary table in place, you can traverse all the information in the database through a series of relations. You can take an address as a starting point and find out the authors of any books purchased by the customer living at that address.

For example, let's suppose that you want to find out about purchases in the 23219 zip code. Look that zip code up in Table 9-8b, and you'll find that customer number 2 has bought at least one item from the database. At this point, you can use Table 9-8a to find out that customer's name, or use the new intermediary Table 9-12 to see the book(s) purchased.

From here, you will find that two titles were purchased and can follow them back to Table 9-4 to find the titles and prices of these books, or to Table 9-3 to see who the authors were.

If it seems to you that this is really combining multiple one-to-many relationships, then you are absolutely correct. To illustrate, Figure 9-3 brings three tables together.

Columns from Table 9-8 (Customers)		Intermediary Table 9-12 (Customer/ISBN)		Columns from Table 9-4 (Titles)	
Zip	**CustNo**	**CustNo**	**ISBN**	**ISBN**	**Title**
90014	1 ············· 1		0596101015 ·············	0596101015	PHP Cookbook
23219	2 ············· 2		0596101015 ·······┘	(etc...)	
(etc...)	┆······ 2		0596527403 ············	0596527403	Dynamic HTML
40601	3 ············· 3		0596005436 ············	0596005436	PHP and MySQL
02154	4 ············· 4		0596006815 ············	0596006815	Programming PHP

Figure 9-3. Creating a many-to-many relationship via a third table

Follow any zip code in the lefthand table to the associated customer IDs. From there, you can link to the middle table, which joins the left and right tables by linking customer IDs and ISBNs. Now all you have to do is follow an ISBN over to the righthand table to see which book it relates to.

You can also use the intermediary table to work your way backward from book titles to zip codes. The *Titles* table can tell you the ISBN, which you can use in the middle table to find the ID numbers of customers who bought the book, and finally you can use the *Customers* table to match the customer ID numbers to the customers' zip codes.

Databases and Anonymity

An interesting aspect of using relations is that you can accumulate a lot of information about some item—such as a customer—without actually knowing who that customer is. Note that in the previous example we went from customers' zip codes to customers' purchases, and back again, without finding out the name of a customer. Databases can be used to track people, but they can also be used to help preserve people's privacy while still finding useful information.

Transactions

In some applications, it is vitally important that a sequence of queries runs in the correct order and that every single query successfully completes. For example, suppose that you are creating a sequence of queries to transfer funds from one bank account to another. You would not want either of the following events to occur:

- You add the funds to the second account, but when you try to subtract them from the first account, the update fails, and now both accounts have the funds.
- You subtract the funds from the first bank account, but the update request to add them to the second account fails, and the funds have disappeared into thin air.

As you can see, not only is the order of queries important in this type of transaction, but it is also vital that all parts of the transaction complete successfully. But how can you ensure this happens, because surely after a query has occurred, it cannot be undone? Do you have to keep track of all parts of a transaction and then undo them all one at a time if any one fails? The answer is absolutely not, because MySQL comes with powerful transaction-handling features to cover just these types of eventualities.

In addition, transactions allow concurrent access to a database by many users or programs at the same time. MySQL handles this seamlessly by ensuring that all transactions are queued and that users or programs take their turns and don't tread on each other's toes.

Transaction Storage Engines

To be able to use MySQL's transaction facility, you have to be using MySQL's InnoDB storage engine (which is the default from version 5.5 onward). If you are not sure which version of MySQL your code will be running on, rather than assuming InnoDB is the default engine you can force its use when creating a table, as follows.

Create a table of bank accounts by typing the commands in Example 9-1. (Remember that to do this, you will need access to the MySQL command line, and must also have already selected a suitable database in which to create this table.)

Example 9-1. Creating a transaction-ready table

```
CREATE TABLE accounts (
 number INT, balance FLOAT, PRIMARY KEY(number)
 ) ENGINE InnoDB;
DESCRIBE accounts;
```

The final line of this example displays the contents of the new table so you can ensure that it was correctly created. The output from it should look like this:

```
+---------+---------+------+-----+---------+-------+
| Field   | Type    | Null | Key | Default | Extra |
+---------+---------+------+-----+---------+-------+
| number  | int(11) | NO   | PRI | 0       |       |
| balance | float   | YES  |     | NULL    |       |
+---------+---------+------+-----+---------+-------+
2 rows in set (0.00 sec)
```

Now let's create two rows within the table so that you can practice using transactions. Type the commands in Example 9-2.

Example 9-2. Populating the accounts table

```
INSERT INTO accounts(number, balance) VALUES(12345, 1025.50);
INSERT INTO accounts(number, balance) VALUES(67890, 140.00);
SELECT * FROM accounts;
```

The third line displays the contents of the table to confirm that the rows were correctly inserted. The output should look like this:

```
+--------+---------+
| number | balance |
+--------+---------+
|  12345 |  1025.5 |
|  67890 |     140 |
+--------+---------+
2 rows in set (0.00 sec)
```

With this table created and prepopulated, you are ready to start using transactions.

Using BEGIN

Transactions in MySQL start with either a BEGIN or a START TRANSACTION statement. Type the commands in Example 9-3 to send a transaction to MySQL.

Example 9-3. A MySQL transaction

```
BEGIN;
UPDATE accounts SET balance=balance+25.11 WHERE number=12345;
COMMIT;
SELECT * FROM accounts;
```

The result of this transaction is displayed by the final line, and should look like this:

```
+--------+---------+
| number | balance |
+--------+---------+
|  12345 | 1050.61 |
|  67890 |     140 |
+--------+---------+
2 rows in set (0.00 sec)
```

As you can see, the balance of account number 12345 was increased by 25.11 and is now 1050.61. You may also have noticed the COMMIT command in Example 9-3, which is explained next.

Using COMMIT

When you are satisfied that a series of queries in a transaction has successfully completed, issue a COMMIT command to commit all the changes to the database. Until it receives a COMMIT, MySQL considers all the changes you make to be merely temporary. This feature gives you the opportunity to cancel a transaction by not sending a COMMIT but issuing a ROLLBACK command instead.

Using ROLLBACK

Using the ROLLBACK command, you can tell MySQL to forget all the queries made since the start of a transaction and to cancel the transaction. See this in action by entering the funds transfer transaction in Example 9-4.

Example 9-4. A funds transfer transaction

```
BEGIN;
UPDATE accounts SET balance=balance-250 WHERE number=12345;
UPDATE accounts SET balance=balance+250 WHERE number=67890;
SELECT * FROM accounts;
```

Once you have entered these lines, you should see the following result:

```
+--------+---------+
| number | balance |
+--------+---------+
|  12345 |  800.61 |
|  67890 |     390 |
+--------+---------+
2 rows in set (0.00 sec)
```

The first bank account now has a value that is 250 less than before, and the second has been incremented by 250; you have transferred a value of 250 between them. But let's assume that something went wrong and you wish to undo this transaction. All you have to do is issue the commands in Example 9-5.

Example 9-5. Canceling a transaction using ROLLBACK

```
ROLLBACK;
SELECT * FROM accounts;
```

You should now see the following output, showing that the two accounts have had their previous balances restored, due to the entire transaction being cancelled via the ROLLBACK command:

```
+--------+---------+
| number | balance |
+--------+---------+
|  12345 | 1050.61 |
|  67890 |     140 |
+--------+---------+
2 rows in set (0.00 sec)
```

Using EXPLAIN

MySQL comes with a powerful tool for investigating how the queries you issue to it are interpreted. Using EXPLAIN, you can get a snapshot of any query to find out whether you could issue it in a better or more efficient way. Example 9-6 shows how to use it with the *accounts* table you created earlier.

Example 9-6. Using the EXPLAIN command

```
EXPLAIN SELECT * FROM accounts WHERE number='12345';
```

The results of this EXPLAIN command should look like the following:

```
+--+-----------+--------+-----+-------------+-------+-------+-----+----+-----+
|id|select_type|table   |type |possible_keys|key    |key_len|ref  |rows|Extra|
+--+-----------+--------+-----+-------------+-------+-------+-----+----+-----+
| 1|SIMPLE     |accounts|const|PRIMARY      |PRIMARY|4      |const|  1|     |
+--+-----------+--------+-----+-------------+-------+-------+-----+----+-----+
1 row in set (0.00 sec)
```

The information that MySQL is giving you here is as follows:

select_type
: The selection type is SIMPLE. If you were joining tables together, this would show the join type.

table
: The current table being queried is accounts.

type
: The query type is const. From the least efficient to the most efficient type, the possible values can be ALL, index, range, ref, eq_ref, const, system, and NULL.

possible_keys
: There is a possible PRIMARY key, which means that accessing should be fast.

---

key

The key actually used is PRIMARY. This is good.

key_len

The key length is 4. This is the number of bytes of the index that MySQL will use.

ref

The ref column displays which columns or constants are used with the key. In this case, a constant key is being used.

rows

The number of rows that need to be searched by this query is 1. This is good.

Whenever you have a query that seems to be taking longer than you think it should to execute, try using EXPLAIN to see where you can optimize it. You will discover which keys (if any) are being used, their lengths, and so on, and will be able to adjust your query or the design of your table(s) accordingly.

When you have finished experimenting with the temporary *accounts* table, you may wish to remove it by entering the following command:

```
DROP TABLE accounts;
```

Backing Up and Restoring

Whatever kind of data you are storing in your database, it must have some value to you, even if it's only the cost of the time required for reentering it should the hard disk fail. Therefore, it's important that you keep backups to protect your investment. Also, there will be times when you have to migrate your database over to a new server; the best way to do this is usually to back it up first. It is also important that you test your backups from time to time to ensure that they are valid and will work if they need to be used.

Thankfully, backing up and restoring MySQL data is easy with the mysqldump command.

Using mysqldump

With mysqldump, you can dump a database or collection of databases into one or more files containing all the instructions necessary to re-create all your tables and repopulate them with your data. This command can also generate files in *CSV* (comma-separated values) and other delimited text formats, or even in XML format. Its main drawback is that you must make sure that no one writes to a table while you're backing it up. There are various ways to do this, but the easiest is to shut down

the MySQL server before running mysqldump and start up the server again after mysql
dump finishes.

Alternatively, you can lock the tables you are backing up before running mysqldump.
To lock tables for reading (as we want to read the data), from the MySQL command
line issue this command:

```
LOCK TABLES tablename1 READ, tablename2 READ ...
```

Then, to release the lock(s), enter the following:

```
UNLOCK TABLES;
```

By default, the output from mysqldump is simply printed out, but you can capture it in
a file through the > redirect symbol.

The basic format of the mysqldump command is shown here:

```
mysqldump -u user -ppassword database
```

However, before you can dump the contents of a database, you must make sure that
mysqldump is in your path, or else specify its location as part of your command.
Table 9-13 shows the likely locations of the program for the different installations and
operating systems covered in Chapter 2. If you have a different installation, it may be
in a slightly different location.

Table 9-13. Likely locations of mysqldump for different installations

Operating system and program	Likely folder location
Windows AMPPS	C:\Program Files (x86)\Ampps\mysql\bin
macOS AMPPS	/Applications/ampps/mysql/bin
Linux AMPPS	/Applications/ampps/mysql/bin

So, to dump the contents of the *publications* database that you created in Chapter 8 to
the screen, first exit MySQL and then enter the command in Example 9-7 (specifying
the full path to mysqldump if necessary).

Example 9-7. Dumping the publications database to screen

```
mysqldump -u user -ppassword publications
```

Make sure that you replace *user* and *password* with the correct details for your
installation of MySQL. If there is no password set for the user, you can omit that part
of the command, but the -u *user* part is mandatory unless you have root access
without a password and are executing as root (not recommended). The result of issuing this command will look something like Figure 9-4.

Figure 9-4. Dumping the publications database to the screen

Creating a Backup File

Now that you have `mysqldump` working, and have verified it outputs correctly to the screen, you can send the backup data directly to a file using the > redirect symbol. Assuming that you wish to call the backup file *publications.sql*, type the command in Example 9-8 (remembering to replace *user* and *password* with the correct details).

Example 9-8. Dumping the publications database to a file

```
mysqldump -u user -p password publications > publications.sql
```

> The command in Example 9-8 stores the backup file into the current directory. If you need it to be saved elsewhere, you should insert a file path before the filename. You must also ensure that the directory you are backing up to has the right permissions set to allow the file to be written.

If you echo the backup file to screen or load it into a text editor, you will see that it comprises sequences of SQL commands such as the following:

```
DROP TABLE IF EXISTS 'classics';
CREATE TABLE 'classics' (
  'author' varchar(128) default NULL,
  'title' varchar(128) default NULL,
  'category' varchar(16) default NULL,
  'year' smallint(6) default NULL,
  'isbn' char(13) NOT NULL default '',
  PRIMARY KEY ('isbn'),
  KEY 'author' ('author'(20)),
```

```
    KEY 'title' ('title'(20)),
    KEY 'category' ('category'(4)),
    KEY 'year' ('year'),
    FULLTEXT KEY 'author_2' ('author','title')
) ENGINE=InnoDB DEFAULT CHARSET=latin1;
```

This is smart code that can be used to restore a database from a backup, even if it currently exists; it will first drop any tables that need to be re-created, thus avoiding potential MySQL errors.

Backing up a single table

To back up only a single table from a database (such as the *classics* table from the *publications* database), you should first lock the table from within the MySQL command line, by issuing a command such as the following:

```
LOCK TABLES publications.classics READ;
```

This ensures that MySQL remains running for read purposes, but writes cannot be made. Then, while keeping the MySQL command line open, use another terminal window to issue the following command from the operating system command line:

```
mysqldump -u user -ppassword publications classics > classics.sql
```

You must now release the table lock by entering the following command from the MySQL command line in the first terminal window, which unlocks all tables that have been locked during the current session:

```
UNLOCK TABLES;
```

Backing up all tables

If you want to back up all your MySQL databases at once (including the system databases such as *mysql*), you can use a command such as the one in Example 9-9, which would enable you to restore an entire MySQL database installation. Remember to use locking where required.

Example 9-9. Dumping all the MySQL databases to file

```
mysqldump -u user -ppassword --all-databases > all_databases.sql
```

 Of course, there's a lot more than just a few lines of SQL code in backed-up database files. I recommend that you take a few minutes to examine a couple in order to familiarize yourself with the types of commands that appear in backup files and how they work.

Restoring from a Backup File

To perform a restore from a file, call the *mysql* executable, passing it the file to restore from using the < symbol. So, to recover an entire database that you dumped using the --all-databases option, use a command such as that in Example 9-10.

Example 9-10. Restoring an entire set of databases

```
mysql -u user -ppassword < all_databases.sql
```

To restore a single database, use the -D option followed by the name of the database, as in Example 9-11, where the *publications* database is being restored from the backup made in Example 9-8.

Example 9-11. Restoring the publications database

```
mysql -u user -ppassword -D publications < publications.sql
```

To restore a single table to a database, use a command such as that in Example 9-12, where just the *classics* table is being restored to the *publications* database.

Example 9-12. Restoring the classics table to the publications database

```
mysql -u user -ppassword -D publications < classics.sql
```

Dumping Data in CSV Format

As previously mentioned, the mysqldump program is very flexible and supports various types of output, such as the CSV format, which you might use to import data into a spreadsheet, among other purposes. Example 9-13 shows how you can dump the data from the *classics* and *customers* tables in the *publications* database to the files *classics.txt* and *customers.txt* in the folder *c:/temp*. On macOS or Linux systems, you should modify the destination path to an existing folder.

Example 9-13. Dumping data to CSV-format files

```
mysqldump -u user -ppassword --no-create-info --tab=c:/temp
  --fields-terminated-by=',' publications
```

This command is quite long and is shown here wrapped over two lines, but you must type it all as a single line. The result is the following:

```
Mark Twain (Samuel Langhorne Clemens)','The Adventures of Tom Sawyer',
 'Classic Fiction','1876','9781598184891
Jane Austen','Pride and Prejudice','Classic Fiction','1811','9780582506206
Charles Darwin','The Origin of Species','Non-Fiction','1856','9780517123201
```

```
Charles Dickens','The Old Curiosity Shop','Classic Fiction','1841','9780099533474
William Shakespeare','Romeo and Juliet','Play','1594','9780192814968

Mary Smith','9780582506206
Jack Wilson','9780517123201
```

Planning Your Backups

The golden rule to backing up is to do so as often as you find practical. The more valuable the data, the more often you should back it up, and the more copies you should make. If your database gets updated at least once a day, you should really back it up on a daily basis. If, on the other hand, it is not updated very often, you could probably get by with less frequent backups.

 You should consider making multiple backups and storing them in different locations. If you have several servers, it is a simple matter to copy your backups between them. You would also be well advised to make physical backups on removable hard disks, thumb drives, CDs or DVDs, and so on, and to keep these in separate locations—preferably somewhere like a fireproof safe.

It's important to test restoring a database once in a while, too, to make sure your backups are done correctly. You also want to be familiar with restoring a database because you may have to do so when you are stressed and in a hurry, such as after a power failure that takes down the website. You can restore a database to a private server and run a few SQL commands to make sure the data is as you think it should be.

Once you've digested the contents of this chapter, you will be proficient in using both PHP and MySQL; the next chapter will show you how to bring these two technologies together.

Questions

1. What does the word *relationship* mean in reference to a relational database?

2. What is the term for the process of removing duplicate data and optimizing tables?

3. What are the three rules of the First Normal Form?

4. How can you make a table satisfy the Second Normal Form?

5. What do you put in a column to tie together two tables that contain items having a one-to-many relationship?

6. How can you create a database with a many-to-many relationship?

7. What commands initiate and end a MySQL transaction?

8. What feature does MySQL provide to enable you to examine how a query will work in detail?

9. What command would you use to back up the database *publications* to a file called *publications.sql*?

See "Chapter 9 Answers" on page 719 in Appendix A for the answers to these questions.

CHAPTER 10

Accessing MySQL Using PHP

If you worked through the previous chapters, you're proficient in using both MySQL and PHP. In this chapter, you will learn how to integrate the two by using PHP's built-in functions to access MySQL.

Querying a MySQL Database with PHP

The reason for using PHP as an interface to MySQL is to format the results of SQL queries in a form visible in a web page. As long as you can log into your MySQL installation using your username and password, you can also do so from PHP.

However, instead of using MySQL's command line to enter instructions and view output, you will create query strings that are passed to MySQL. When MySQL returns its response, it will come as a data structure that PHP can recognize instead of the formatted output you see when you work on the command line. Further PHP commands can retrieve the data and format it for the web page.

The Process

The process of using MySQL with PHP is as follows:

1. Connect to MySQL and select the database to use.
2. Prepare a query string.
3. Perform the query.
4. Retrieve the results and output them to a web page.
5. Repeat steps 2 to 4 until all desired data has been retrieved.
6. Disconnect from MySQL.

We'll work through these steps in turn, but first it's important to set up your login details in a secure manner so people snooping around on your system have trouble getting access to your database.

Creating a Login File

Most websites developed with PHP contain multiple program files that will require access to MySQL and will thus need the login and password details. Therefore, it's sensible to create a single file to store these and then include that file wherever it's needed. Example 10-1 shows such a file, which I've called *login.php*.

Example 10-1. The login.php file

```php
<?php // login.php
  $hn = 'localhost';
  $db = 'publications';
  $un = 'username';
  $pw = 'password';
?>
```

Type the example, replacing *username* and *password* with the values you use for your MySQL database, and save it to the document root directory you set up in Chapter 2. We'll be making use of the file shortly.

The hostname localhost should work as long as you're using a MySQL database on your local system, and the database publications should work if you're typing the examples I've used so far.

The enclosing <?php and ?> tags are especially important for the *login.php* file in Example 10-1, because they mean that the lines between can be interpreted *only* as PHP code. If you were to leave them out and someone were to call up the file directly from your website, it would display as text and reveal your secrets. But, with the tags in place, all that person will see is a blank page. The file will correctly include your other PHP files.

The $hn variable will tell PHP which computer to use when connecting to a database. This is required because you can access MySQL databases on any computer connected to your PHP installation, and that potentially includes any host anywhere on the web. However, the examples in this chapter will be working on the local server. So, in place of specifying a domain such as mysql.myserver.com, you can just use the word localhost (or the IP address 127.0.0.1).

The database we'll be using, $db, is the one called *publications* that we created in Chapter 8 (if you're using a different database—one provided by your server administrator—you'll have to modify *login.php* accordingly).

Another benefit of keeping these login details in a single place is that you can change your password as frequently as you like and there will be only one file to update when you do, no matter how many PHP files access MySQL.

Connecting to a MySQL Database

Now that you have saved the *login.php* file, you can include it in any PHP files that will need to access the database by using the `require_once` statement. This is preferable to an `include` statement, as it will generate a fatal error if the file is not found—and believe me, not finding the file containing the login details to your database *is* a fatal error.

Also, using `require_once` instead of `require` means that the file will be read in only when it has not previously been included, which prevents wasteful duplicate disk accesses. Example 10-2 shows the code to use.

Example 10-2. Connecting to a MySQL server with mysqli

```php
<?php
  require_once 'login.php';
  $conn = new mysqli($hn, $un, $pw, $db);
  if ($conn->connect_error) die("Fatal Error");
?>
```

This example creates a new object called $conn by calling a new instance of the `mysqli` method, passing all the values retrieved from the *login.php* file. We achieve error checking by referencing the `$conn->connect_error` property.

The `->` operator indicates that the item on the right is a property or method of the object on the left. In this case, if `connect_error` has a value, there was an error, so we call the `die` function to terminate the program.

The $conn object is used in the following examples to access the MySQL database.

The die function is great when you are developing PHP code, but of course you will want more user-friendly error messages on a production server. In this case, you won't abort your PHP program, but will format a message that will be displayed when the program exits normally—perhaps something like this:

```
function mysql_fatal_error()
{
    echo <<< _END
We are sorry, but it was not possible to complete
the requested task. The error message we got was:

    <p>Fatal Error</p>

Please click the back button on your browser
and try again. If you are still having problems,
please <a href="mailto:admin@server.com">email
our administrator</a>. Thank you.
_END;
}
```

You should also never be tempted to output the contents of any error message received from MySQL. Rather than helping your users, you could give away sensitive information to hackers such as login details. Instead, just guide the user with information on how to overcome their difficulty based on what the error message reports to your code.

Building and executing a query

Sending a query to MySQL from PHP is as simple as including the relevant SQL in the query method of a connection object. Example 10-3 shows you how to do this.

Example 10-3. Querying a database with mysqli

```
<?php
  $query  = "SELECT * FROM classics";
  $result = $conn->query($query);
  if (!$result) die("Fatal Error");
?>
```

As you can see, the MySQL query looks just like what you would type directly at the command line, except that there is no trailing semicolon, as none is needed when you are accessing MySQL from PHP.

Here the variable $query is assigned a string containing the query to be made, and then passed to the query method of the $conn object, which returns a result that we place in the object $result. If $result is FALSE, there was a problem and the error property of the connection object will contain the details, so the die function is called to display that error.

All the data returned by MySQL is now stored in an easily interrogable format in the $result object.

Fetching a result

Once you have an object returned in $result, you can use it to extract the data you want, one item at a time, using the fetch_assoc method of the object. Example 10-4 combines and extends the previous examples into a program that you can run yourself to retrieve the results (as depicted in Figure 10-1). Type this script in and save it using the filename *query-mysqli.php*, or download it from the companion website (*http://lpmj.net*).

Example 10-4. Fetching results one cell at a time

```php
<?php // query-mysqli.php
  require_once 'login.php';
  $connection = new mysqli($hn, $un, $pw, $db);

  if ($connection->connect_error) die("Fatal Error");

  $query  = "SELECT * FROM classics";
  $result = $connection->query($query);

  if (!$result) die("Fatal Error");

  $rows = $result->num_rows;

  for ($j = 0 ; $j < $rows ; ++$j)
  {
    $result->data_seek($j);
    echo 'Author: '  .htmlspecialchars($result->fetch_assoc()['author'])  .'<br>';
    $result->data_seek($j);
    echo 'Title: '   .htmlspecialchars($result->fetch_assoc()['title'])   .'<br>';
    $result->data_seek($j);
    echo 'Category: '.htmlspecialchars($result->fetch_assoc()['category']).'<br>';
    $result->data_seek($j);
    echo 'Year: '    .htmlspecialchars($result->fetch_assoc()['year'])    .'<br>';
    $result->data_seek($j);
    echo 'ISBN: '    .htmlspecialchars($result->fetch_assoc()['isbn'])    .'<br><br>';
  }

  $result->close();
  $connection->close();
?>
```

Figure 10-1. *The output from the query-mysqli.php program in Example 10-4*

Here, each time around the loop, we call the `fetch_assoc` method to retrieve the value stored in each cell, and output the result using `echo` statements.

When displaying data in a browser the source of which was (or may have been) user input, there's always a risk of sneaky HTML characters being embedded within it—even if you believe it to have been previously sanitized—which could potentially be used for a cross-site scripting (XSS) attack. The simple way to prevent this possibility is to embed all such output within a call to the function `htmlspecialchars`, which replaces all such characters with harmless HTML entities. This technique was implemented in the preceding example and will be used in many of the following examples.

You will probably agree that all this multiple seeking and so forth is rather cumbersome, and that there ought to be a more efficient method of achieving the same result. And, indeed, there is a better method, which is to extract a row at a time.

In Chapter 9, I talked about First, Second, and Third Normal Form. You may have noticed that the *classics* table doesn't satisfy these, because both author and book details are included within the same table. That's because we created this table before encountering normalization. However, for the purposes of illustrating access to MySQL from PHP, reusing this table avoids the hassle of typing in a new set of test data, so we'll stick with it for the time being.

Fetching a row

To fetch one row at a time, replace the for loop from Example 10-4 with the one highlighted in bold in Example 10-5, and you will find that you get exactly the same result that was displayed in Figure 10-1. You may wish to save this revised file using the name *fetchrow.php*.

Example 10-5. Fetching results one row at a time

```php
<?php // fetchrow.php
  require_once 'login.php';
  $conn = new mysqli($hn, $un, $pw, $db);
  if ($conn->connect_error) die("Fatal Error");

  $query  = "SELECT * FROM classics";
  $result = $conn->query($query);
  if (!$result) die("Fatal Error");

  $rows = $result->num_rows;

  for ($j = 0 ; $j < $rows ; ++$j)
  {
    $row = $result->fetch_array(MYSQLI_ASSOC);

    echo 'Author: '    . htmlspecialchars($row['author'])   . '<br>';
    echo 'Title: '     . htmlspecialchars($row['title'])     . '<br>';
    echo 'Category: '  . htmlspecialchars($row['category'])  . '<br>';
    echo 'Year: '      . htmlspecialchars($row['year'])      . '<br>';
    echo 'ISBN: '      . htmlspecialchars($row['isbn'])      . '<br><br>';
  }

  $result->close();
  $conn->close();
?>
```

In this modified code, only one-fifth of the interrogations of the $result object are made (compared to the previous example), and only one seek into the object is made in each iteration of the loop, because each row is fetched in its entirety via the fetch_array method. This returns a single row of data as an array, which is then assigned to the array $row.

The `fetch_array` method can return three types of array according to the value passed to it:

MYSQLI_NUM

> Numeric array. Each column appears in the array in the order in which you defined it when you created (or altered) the table. In our case, the zeroth element of the array contains the *author* column, element 1 contains the *title* column, and so on.

MYSQLI_ASSOC

> Associative array. Each key is the name of a column. Because items of data are referenced by column name (rather than index number), use this option where possible in your code to make debugging easier and help other programmers better manage your code.

MYSQLI_BOTH

> Associative and numeric array.

Associative arrays are usually more useful than numeric ones because you can refer to each column by name, such as `$row['author']`, instead of trying to remember where it is in the column order. This script uses an associative array, leading us to pass `MYSQLI_ASSOC`.

Closing a connection

PHP will eventually return the memory it has allocated for objects after you have finished with the script, so in small scripts, you don't usually need to worry about releasing memory yourself. However, if you're allocating a lot of result objects or fetching large amounts of data, it can be a good idea to free the memory you have been using to prevent problems later in your script.

This becomes particularly important on higher-traffic pages, because the amount of memory consumed in a session can rapidly grow. Therefore, note the calls to the `close` methods of the objects `$result` and `$conn` in the preceding scripts, as soon as each object is no longer needed, like this:

```
$result->close();
$conn->close();
```

Ideally, you should close each result object when you have finished using it, and then close the connection object when your script will not be accessing MySQL anymore. This best practice ensures that resources are returned to the system as quickly as possible to keep MySQL running optimally, and alleviates doubt over whether PHP will return unused memory in time for when you next need it.

A Practical Example

It's time to write our first example of inserting data in and deleting it from a MySQL table using PHP. I recommend that you type Example 10-6 and save it to your web development directory using the filename *sqltest.php*. You can see an example of the program's output in Figure 10-2.

 Example 10-6 creates a standard HTML form. Chapter 11 explains forms in detail, but in this chapter I take form handling for granted and just deal with database interaction.

Example 10-6. Inserting and deleting using sqltest.php

```php
<?php // sqltest.php
  require_once 'login.php';
  $conn = new mysqli($hn, $un, $pw, $db);
  if ($conn->connect_error) die("Fatal Error");

  if (isset($_POST['delete']) && isset($_POST['isbn']))
  {
    $isbn   = get_post($conn, 'isbn');
    $query  = "DELETE FROM classics WHERE isbn='$isbn'";
    $result = $conn->query($query);
    if (!$result) echo "DELETE failed<br><br>";
  }

  if (isset($_POST['author'])   &&
      isset($_POST['title'])    &&
      isset($_POST['category']) &&
      isset($_POST['year'])     &&
      isset($_POST['isbn']))
  {
    $author   = get_post($conn, 'author');
    $title    = get_post($conn, 'title');
    $category = get_post($conn, 'category');
    $year     = get_post($conn, 'year');
    $isbn     = get_post($conn, 'isbn');
    $query    = "INSERT INTO classics VALUES" .
      "('$author', '$title', '$category', '$year', '$isbn')";
    $result   = $conn->query($query);
    if (!$result) echo "INSERT failed<br><br>";
  }

  echo <<<_END
  <form action="sqltest.php" method="post"><pre>
    Author <input type="text" name="author">
     Title <input type="text" name="title">
  Category <input type="text" name="category">
```

```php
        Year <input type="text" name="year">
        ISBN <input type="text" name="isbn">
              <input type="submit" value="ADD RECORD">
    </pre></form>
_END;

    $query  = "SELECT * FROM classics";
    $result = $conn->query($query);
    if (!$result) die ("Database access failed");

    $rows = $result->num_rows;

    for ($j = 0 ; $j < $rows ; ++$j)
    {
      $row = $result->fetch_array(MYSQLI_NUM);

      $r0 = htmlspecialchars($row[0]);
      $r1 = htmlspecialchars($row[1]);
      $r2 = htmlspecialchars($row[2]);
      $r3 = htmlspecialchars($row[3]);
      $r4 = htmlspecialchars($row[4]);

      echo <<<_END
  <pre>
    Author $r0
     Title $r1
  Category $r2
      Year $r3
      ISBN $r4
  </pre>
  <form action='sqltest.php' method='post'>
  <input type='hidden' name='delete' value='yes'>
  <input type='hidden' name='isbn' value='$r4'>
  <input type='submit' value='DELETE RECORD'></form>
_END;
    }

    $result->close();
    $conn->close();

    function get_post($conn, $var)
    {
      return $conn->real_escape_string($_POST[$var]);
    }
?>
```

Figure 10-2. The output from Example 10-6, sqltest.php

At over 80 lines of code, this program may appear daunting, but don't worry—you've already covered many of those lines in Example 10-5, and what the code does is actually quite simple.

It first checks for any inputs that may have been made and then either inserts new data into the table *classics* of the *publications* database or deletes a row from it, according to the input supplied. Regardless of whether there was input, the program then outputs all rows in the table to the browser. So, let's see how it works.

The first section of new code starts by using the `isset` function to check whether values for all the fields have been posted to the program. Upon confirmation, each line within the `if` statement calls the function `get_post`, which appears at the end of the program. This function has one small but critical job: fetching input from the browser.

For reasons of clarity and brevity, and to explain things as simply as possible, many of the following examples omit certain very sensible security precautions that would have made them longer and possibly detract from explaining their function in the clearest manner. Therefore, it is important that you don't skip past the section later in this chapter on preventing your database from being hacked ("Preventing Hacking Attempts" on page 258), in which you will learn about additional actions you can take with your code to secure it.

The $_POST Array

I mentioned in an earlier chapter that a browser sends user input through either a GET request or a POST request. The POST request is usually preferred (because it avoids placing unsightly data in the browser's address bar), and so we use it here. The web server bundles up all of the user input (even if the form was filled out with a hundred fields) and puts in into an array named $_POST.

$_POST is an associative array, which you encountered in Chapter 6. Depending on whether a form has been set to use the POST or the GET method, either the $_POST or the $_GET associative array will be populated with the form data. They can both be read in exactly the same way.

Each field has an element in the array named after that field. So, if a form contains a field named isbn, the $_POST array contains an element keyed by the word isbn. The PHP program can read that field by referring to either $_POST['isbn'] or $_POST["isbn"] (single and double quotes have the same effect in this case).

If the $_POST syntax still seems complex to you, rest assured that you can just use the convention I've shown in Example 10-6, copy the user's input to other variables, and forget about $_POST after that. This is normal in PHP programs: they retrieve all the fields from $_POST at the beginning of the program and then ignore it.

There is no reason to write to an element in the $_POST array. Its only purpose is to communicate information from the browser to the program, and you're better off copying data to your own variables before altering it.

So, back to the get_post function, which passes each item it retrieves through the real_escape_string method of the connection object to escape any quotes that a hacker may have inserted in order to break into or alter your database, like this:

```
function get_post($conn, $var)
{
  return $conn->real_escape_string($_POST[$var]);
}
```

Deleting a Record

Prior to checking whether new data has been posted, the program checks whether the variable $_POST['delete'] has a value. If so, the user has clicked the DELETE RECORD button to erase a record. In this case, the value of $isbn will also have been posted.

As you'll recall, the ISBN uniquely identifies each record. The HTML form appends the ISBN to the DELETE FROM query string created in the variable $query, which is then passed to the query method of the $conn object to issue it to MySQL.

If $_POST['delete'] is not set (and so there is no record to be deleted), $_POST['author'] and other posted values are checked. If they have all been given values, $query is set to an INSERT INTO command, followed by the five values to be inserted. The string is then passed to the query method, which upon completion returns either TRUE or FALSE. If FALSE is returned an error message is displayed, like this:

```
if (!$result) echo "INSERT failed<br><br>";
```

Displaying the Form

Before displaying the little form (as shown in Figure 10-2), the program sanitizes copies of the elements we will be outputting from the $row array into the variables $r0 through $r4 by passing them to the htmlspecialchars function, to replace any potentially dangerous HTML characters with harmless HTML entities.

Then the part of code that displays the output follows, using an echo <<<_END..._END structure as seen in previous chapters, which outputs everything between the _END tags.

Instead of using the echo command, the program could drop out of PHP using ?>, issue the HTML, and then reenter PHP processing with <?php. Which style is used is a matter of programmer preference, but I always recommend staying within PHP code, for these reasons:

- It makes it very clear when you're debugging (and also for other users) that everything within a *.php* file is PHP code. Therefore, there is no need to go hunting for dropouts to HTML.

- When you wish to include a PHP variable directly within HTML, you can just type it. If you had dropped back to HTML, you would have had to temporarily reenter PHP processing, access the variable, and then drop back out again.

The HTML form section simply sets the form's action to *sqltest.php*. This means that when the form is submitted, the contents of the form fields will be sent to the file *sqltest.php*, which is the program itself. The form is also set up to send the fields as a POST rather than a GET request. This is because GET requests are appended to the URL being submitted and can look messy in your browser. They also allow users to easily modify submissions and try to hack your server (although that can also be achieved with in-browser developer tools). Additionally, avoiding GET requests prevents too much information appearing in server log files. Therefore, whenever possible, you should use POST submissions, which also have the benefit of revealing less posted data.

Having output the form fields, the HTML displays a submit button with the name ADD RECORD and closes the form. Note the <pre> and </pre> tags here, which have been used to force a monospaced font that lines up all the inputs neatly. The carriage returns at the end of each line are also output when inside <pre> tags.

Querying the Database

Next, the code returns to the familiar territory of Example 10-5, where a query is sent to MySQL asking to see all the records in the *classics* table, like this:

```
$query  = "SELECT * FROM classics";
$result = $conn->query($query);
```

After that, $rows is set to a value representing the number of rows in the table:

```
$rows = $result->num_rows;
```

Using the value in $rows, a for loop is then entered to display the contents of each row. Then the program populates the array $row with a row of results by calling the fetch_array method of $result, passing it the constant value MYSQLI_NUM, which forces the return of a numeric (rather than associative) array, like this:

```
$row = $result->fetch_array(MYSQLI_NUM);
```

With the data in $row, it's now a simple matter to display it within the heredoc echo statement that follows, in which I have chosen to use a <pre> tag to line up the display of each record in a pleasing manner.

After the display of each record, there is a second form that also posts to *sqltest.php* (the program itself) but this time contains two hidden fields: delete and isbn. The delete field is set to yes and isbn to the value held in $row[4], which contains the ISBN for the record.

Then a submit button with the name DELETE RECORD is displayed, and the form is closed. A curly brace then completes the for loop, which will continue until all records have been displayed, at which time the $result and $conn object's close methods are closed to release resources back to PHP:

```
$result->close();
$conn->close();
```

Finally, you see the definition for the function get_post, which we've already looked at. And that's it—our first PHP program to manipulate a MySQL database. So, let's check out what it can do.

Once you have typed the program (and corrected any typing errors), try entering the following data into the various input fields to add a new record for the book *Moby Dick* to the database:

```
Herman Melville
Moby Dick
Fiction
1851
9780199535729
```

Running the Program

When you have submitted this data using the ADD RECORD button, scroll down to the bottom of the web page to see the new addition. It should look like Figure 10-3.

```
Category Non-Fiction
        Year 1856
        ISBN 9780517123201

    DELETE RECORD

    Author Charles Dickens
     Title The Old Curiosity Shop
Category Classic Fiction
        Year 1841
        ISBN 9780099533474

    DELETE RECORD

    Author William Shakespeare
     Title Romeo and Juliet
Category Play
        Year 1594
        ISBN 9780192814968

    DELETE RECORD

    Author Herman Melville
     Title Moby Dick
Category Fiction
        Year 1851
        ISBN 9780199535729

    DELETE RECORD
```

Figure 10-3. The result of adding Moby Dick to the database

Now let's look at how deleting a record works by creating a dummy record. Try entering just the number 1 in each of the five fields and clicking the ADD RECORD button. If you now scroll down, you'll see a new record consisting just of 1s. Obviously, this record isn't useful in this table, so now click the DELETE RECORD button and scroll down again to confirm that the record has been deleted.

Assuming that everything worked, you are now able to add and delete records at will. Try doing this a few times, but leave the main records in place (including the new one for *Moby Dick*), as we'll be using them later. You could also try adding the record with all 1s again a couple of times and note the error message that you receive the second time, indicating that there is already an ISBN with the number 1.

Practical MySQL

You are now ready to look at some practical techniques that you can use in PHP to access the MySQL database, including tasks such as creating and dropping tables; inserting, updating, and deleting data; and protecting your database and website from malicious users. Note that the following examples assume that you've already created the *login.php* program discussed earlier in this chapter.

Creating a Table

Let's assume that you are working for a wildlife park and need to create a database to hold details about all the types of cats it houses. You are told that there are nine *families* of cats—Lion, Tiger, Jaguar, Leopard, Cougar, Cheetah, Lynx, Caracal, and Domestic—so you'll need a column for that. Then each cat has been given a *name*, so that's another column, and you also want to keep track of their *ages*, which is another. Of course, you will probably need more columns later, perhaps to hold dietary requirements, inoculations, and other details, but for now that's enough to get going. A unique identifier is also needed for each animal, so you also decide to create a column for that called *id*.

Example 10-7 shows the code you might use to create a MySQL table to hold this data, with the main query assignment in bold text.

Example 10-7. Creating a table called cats

```php
<?php
  require_once 'login.php';
  $conn = new mysqli($hn, $un, $pw, $db);
  if ($conn->connect_error) die("Fatal Error");

  $query = "CREATE TABLE cats (
    id SMALLINT NOT NULL AUTO_INCREMENT,
    family VARCHAR(32) NOT NULL,
    name VARCHAR(32) NOT NULL,
    age TINYINT NOT NULL,
    PRIMARY KEY (id)
  )";

  $result = $conn->query($query);
  if (!$result) die ("Database access failed");
?>
```

As you can see, the MySQL query looks just like what you would type directly at the command line, except without the trailing semicolon.

Describing a Table

When you aren't logged into the MySQL command line, here's a handy piece of code that you can use to verify that a table has been correctly created from inside a browser. It simply issues the query DESCRIBE cats and then outputs an HTML table with four headings—*Column*, *Type*, *Null*, and *Key*—underneath which all columns within the table are shown. To use it with other tables, simply replace the name cats in the query with that of the new table (see Example 10-8).

Example 10-8. Describing the cats table

```php
<?php
  require_once 'login.php';
  $conn = new mysqli($hn, $un, $pw, $db);
  if ($conn->connect_error) die("Fatal Error");

  $query  = "DESCRIBE cats";
  $result = $conn->query($query);
  if (!$result) die ("Database access failed");

  $rows = $result->num_rows;

  echo "<table><tr><th>Column</th><th>Type</th><th>Null</th><th>Key</th></tr>";

  for ($j = 0 ; $j < $rows ; ++$j)
  {
    $row = $result->fetch_array(MYSQLI_NUM);

    echo "<tr>";
    for ($k = 0 ; $k < 4 ; ++$k)
      echo "<td>" . htmlspecialchars($row[$k]) . "</td>";
    echo "</tr>";
  }

  echo "</table>";
?>
```

The output from the program should look like this:

```
Column Type        Null Key
id      smallint(6) NO   PRI
family varchar(32) NO
name    varchar(32) NO
age     tinyint(4)  NO
```

Dropping a Table

Dropping a table is very easy to do and is therefore very dangerous, so be careful. Example 10-9 shows the code that you need. However, I don't recommend that you try it until you have been through the other examples (up to "Performing Additional Queries" on page 257), as it will drop the table *cats* and you'll have to re-create it using Example 10-7.

Example 10-9. Dropping the cats table

```php
<?php
  require_once 'login.php';
  $conn = new mysqli($hn, $un, $pw, $db);
  if ($conn->connect_error) die("Fatal Error");

  $query  = "DROP TABLE cats";
  $result = $conn->query($query);
  if (!$result) die ("Database access failed");
?>
```

Adding Data

Let's add some data to the table now, using the code in Example 10-10.

Example 10-10. Adding data to the cats table

```php
<?php
  require_once 'login.php';
  $conn = new mysqli($hn, $un, $pw, $db);
  if ($conn->connect_error) die("Fatal Error");

  $query  = "INSERT INTO cats VALUES(NULL, 'Lion', 'Leo', 4)";
  $result = $conn->query($query);
  if (!$result) die ("Database access failed");
?>
```

You may wish to add a couple more items of data by modifying $query as follows and
calling up the program in your browser again:

```php
$query = "INSERT INTO cats VALUES(NULL, 'Cougar', 'Growler', 2)";
$query = "INSERT INTO cats VALUES(NULL, 'Cheetah', 'Charly', 3)";
```

By the way, notice the NULL value passed as the first parameter? This is because the *id*
column is of type AUTO_INCREMENT, and MySQL will decide what value to assign
according to the next available number in sequence. So, we simply pass a NULL value,
which will be ignored.

Of course, the most efficient way to populate MySQL with data is to create an array
and insert the data with a single query.

At this point in the book I am concentrating on showing you how to directly insert data into MySQL (and providing some security precautions to keep the process safe). However, later in this book we'll move on to a better method you can employ that involves placeholders (see "Using Placeholders" on page 260), which make it virtually impossible for users to inject malicious hacks into your database. So, as you read this section, do understand that this is the basics of how MySQL insertion works, and remember that we will improve upon it later.

Retrieving Data

Now that some data has been entered into the *cats* table, Example 10-11 shows how you can check that it was correctly inserted.

Example 10-11. Retrieving rows from the cats table

```php
<?php
  require_once 'login.php';
  $conn = new mysqli($hn, $un, $pw, $db);
  if ($conn->connect_error) die("Fatal Error");

  $query  = "SELECT * FROM cats";
  $result = $conn->query($query);
  if (!$result) die ("Database access failed");

  $rows = $result->num_rows;
  echo "<table><tr> <th>Id</th> <th>Family</th><th>Name</th><th>Age</th></tr>";

  for ($j = 0 ; $j < $rows ; ++$j)
  {
    $row = $result->fetch_array(MYSQLI_NUM);

    echo "<tr>";
    for ($k = 0 ; $k < 4 ; ++$k)
      echo "<td>" . htmlspecialchars($row[$k]) . "</td>";
    echo "</tr>";
  }

  echo "</table>";
?>
```

This code simply issues the MySQL query SELECT * FROM cats and then displays all the rows returned. Its output is as follows:

```
Id Family  Name    Age
1  Lion    Leo     4
2  Cougar  Growler 2
3  Cheetah Charly  3
```

Here you can see that the *id* column has correctly auto-incremented.

Updating Data

Changing data that you have already inserted is also quite simple. Did you notice the spelling of *Charly* for the cheetah's name? Let's correct that to *Charlie*, as in Example 10-12.

Example 10-12. Renaming Charly the cheetah to Charlie

```php
<?php
  require_once 'login.php';
  $conn = new mysqli($hn, $un, $pw, $db);
  if ($conn->connect_error) die("Fatal Error");

  $query  = "UPDATE cats SET name='Charlie' WHERE name='Charly'";
  $result = $conn->query($query);
  if (!$result) die ("Database access failed");
?>
```

If you run Example 10-11 again, you'll see that it now outputs the following:

```
Id Family  Name    Age
1  Lion    Leo     4
2  Cougar  Growler 2
3  Cheetah Charlie 3
```

Deleting Data

Growler the cougar has been transferred to another zoo, so it's time to remove him from the database; see Example 10-13.

Example 10-13. Removing Growler the cougar from the cats table

```php
<?php
  require_once 'login.php';
  $conn = new mysqli($hn, $un, $pw, $db);
  if ($conn->connect_error) die("Fatal Error");

  $query  = "DELETE FROM cats WHERE name='Growler'";
  $result = $conn->query($query);
  if (!$result) die ("Database access failed");
?>
```

This uses a standard DELETE FROM query, and when you run Example 10-11, you can see that the row has been removed in the following output:

```
Id Family   Name    Age
1  Lion     Leo     4
3  Cheetah  Charlie 3
```

Using AUTO_INCREMENT

When using AUTO_INCREMENT, you cannot know what value has been given to a column before a row is inserted. Instead, if you need to know it, you must ask MySQL afterward using the mysql_insert_id function. This need is common: for instance, when you process a purchase, you might insert a new customer into a *Customers* table and then refer to the newly created *CustId* when inserting a purchase into the *Purchases* table.

 Using AUTO_INCREMENT is recommended instead of selecting the highest ID in the *id* column and incrementing it by one, because concurrent queries could change the values in that column after the highest value has been fetched and before the calculated value is stored.

Example 10-10 can be rewritten as Example 10-14 to display this value after each insert.

Example 10-14. Adding data to the cats table and reporting the insert ID

```php
<?php
  require_once 'login.php';
  $conn = new mysqli($hn, $un, $pw, $db);
  if ($conn->connect_error) die("Fatal Error");

  $query  = "INSERT INTO cats VALUES(NULL, 'Lynx', 'Stumpy', 5)";
  $result = $conn->query($query);
  if (!$result) die ("Database access failed");

  echo "The Insert ID was: " . $conn->insert_id;
?>
```

The contents of the table should now look like the following (note how the previous *id* value of 2 is *not* reused, as this could cause complications in some instances):

```
Id Family   Name    Age
1  Lion     Leo     4
3  Cheetah  Charlie 3
4  Lynx     Stumpy  5
```

Using insert IDs

It's very common to insert data in multiple tables: a book followed by its author, a customer followed by their purchase, and so on. When doing this with an auto-increment column, you will need to retain the insert ID returned for storing in the related table.

For example, let's assume that these cats can be "adopted" by the public as a means of raising funds, and that when a new cat is stored in the *cats* table, we also want to create a key to tie it to the animal's adoptive owner. The code to do this is similar to that in Example 10-14, except that the returned insert ID is stored in the variable $insertID and is then used as part of the subsequent query:

```
$query   = "INSERT INTO cats VALUES(NULL, 'Lynx', 'Stumpy', 5)";
$result  = $conn->query($query);
$insertID = $conn->insert_id;

$query   = "INSERT INTO owners VALUES($insertID, 'Ann', 'Smith')";
$result  = $conn->query($query);
```

Now the cat is connected to its "owner" through the cat's unique ID, which was created automatically by AUTO_INCREMENT.

Performing Additional Queries

Okay, that's enough feline fun. To explore some slightly more complex queries, we need to revert to using the *customers* and *classics* tables that you created in Chapter 8. There will be two customers in the *customers* table; the *classics* table holds the details of a few books. They also share a common column of ISBNs, called *isbn*, that you can use to perform additional queries.

For example, to display all of the customers along with the titles and authors of the books they have bought, you can use the code in Example 10-15.

Example 10-15. Performing a secondary query

```php
<?php
  require_once 'login.php';
  $conn = new mysqli($hn, $un, $pw, $db);
  if ($conn->connect_error) die("Fatal Error");

  $query  = "SELECT * FROM customers";
  $result = $conn->query($query);
  if (!$result) die ("Database access failed");

  $rows = $result->num_rows;

  for ($j = 0 ; $j < $rows ; ++$j)
  {
```

```
    $row = $result->fetch_array(MYSQLI_NUM);
    echo htmlspecialchars($row[0]) . " purchased ISBN " .
        htmlspecialchars($row[1]) . ":<br>";

    $subquery  = "SELECT * FROM classics WHERE isbn='$row[1]'";
    $subresult = $conn->query($subquery);
    if (!$subresult) die ("Database access failed");

    $subrow = $subresult->fetch_array(MYSQLI_NUM);
    echo "  " . htmlspecialchars("'$subrow[1]'") . " by " .
                    htmlspecialchars( $subrow[0])  . "<br><br>";
  }
?>
```

This program uses an initial query to the *customers* table to look up all the customers and then, given the ISBNs of the books each customer purchased, makes a new query to the *classics* table to find out the title and author for each. The output from this code should be similar to the following:

```
Joe Bloggs purchased ISBN 9780099533474:
  'The Old Curiosity Shop' by Charles Dickens

Jack Wilson purchased ISBN 9780517123201:
  'The Origin of Species' by Charles Darwin

Mary Smith purchased ISBN 9780582506206:
  'Pride and Prejudice' by Jane Austen
```

Of course, although it wouldn't illustrate performing additional queries, in this particular case you could also return the same information using a NATURAL JOIN query (see Chapter 8), like this:

```
SELECT name,isbn,title,author FROM customers
   NATURAL JOIN classics;
```

Preventing Hacking Attempts

If you haven't looked into it, you may find it hard to appreciate just how dangerous it is to pass user input unchecked to MySQL. For example, suppose you have a simple piece of code to verify a user, and it looks like this:

```
$user  = $_POST['user'];
$pass  = $_POST['pass'];
$query = "SELECT * FROM users WHERE user='$user' AND pass='$pass'";
```

At first glance, you might think this code is perfectly fine. If the user enters values of fredsmith and mypass for $user and $pass, respectively, then the query string, as passed to MySQL, will be as follows:

```
SELECT * FROM users WHERE user='fredsmith' AND pass='mypass'
```

This is all well and good, but what if someone enters the following for $user (and doesn't even enter anything for $pass)?

```
admin' #
```

Let's look at the string that would be sent to MySQL:

```
SELECT * FROM users WHERE user='admin' #' AND pass=''
```

Do you see the problem there? An *SQL injection* attack has occurred. In MySQL, the # symbol represents the start of a comment. Therefore, the user will be logged in as *admin* (assuming there is a user *admin*), without having to enter a password. In the following, the part of the query that will be executed is shown in bold; the rest will be ignored.

SELECT * FROM users WHERE user='admin' #' AND pass=''

But you should count yourself very lucky if that's all a malicious user does to you. At least you might still be able to go into your application and undo any changes the user makes as *admin*. But what about the case in which your application code removes a user from the database? The code might look something like this:

```
$user  = $_POST['user'];
$pass  = $_POST['pass'];
$query = "DELETE FROM users WHERE user='$user' AND pass='$pass'";
```

Again, this looks quite normal at first glance, but what if someone entered the following for $user?

```
anything' OR 1=1 #
```

This would be interpreted by MySQL as follows:

DELETE FROM users WHERE user='anything' OR 1=1 #' AND pass=''

Ouch—that SQL query will always be TRUE, and therefore you've lost your whole *users* database! So what can you do about this kind of attack?

Steps You Can Take

The first thing is not to rely on PHP's built-in *magic quotes*, which automatically escape any characters such as single and double quotes by prefacing them with a backslash (\). Why? Because this feature can be turned off. Many programmers do so in order to put their own security code in place, and there is no guarantee that this hasn't happened on the server you are working on. In fact, the feature was deprecated as of PHP 5.3.0 and removed in PHP 5.4.0.

Instead, you should always use the `real_escape_string` method for all calls to MySQL. Example 10-16 is a function you can use that will remove any magic quotes added to a user-inputted string and then properly sanitize it for you.

Example 10-16. How to properly sanitize user input for MySQL

```php
<?php
  function mysql_fix_string($conn, $string)
  {
    if (get_magic_quotes_gpc()) $string = stripslashes($string);
    return $conn->real_escape_string($string);
  }
?>
```

The `get_magic_quotes_gpc` function returns TRUE if magic quotes are active. In that case, any slashes that have been added to a string have to be removed, or the `real_escape_string` method could end up double-escaping some characters, creating corrupted strings. Example 10-17 illustrates how you would incorporate `mysql_fix_string` within your own code.

Example 10-17. How to safely access MySQL with user input

```php
<?php
  require_once 'login.php';
  $conn = new mysqli($hn, $un, $pw, $db);
  if ($conn->connect_error) die("Fatal Error");

  $user = mysql_fix_string($conn, $_POST['user']);
  $pass = mysql_fix_string($conn, $_POST['pass']);
  $query = "SELECT * FROM users WHERE user='$user' AND pass='$pass'";

  // Etc.

  function mysql_fix_string($conn, $string)
  {
    if (get_magic_quotes_gpc()) $string = stripslashes($string);
    return $conn->real_escape_string($string);
  }
?>
```

These precautions are becoming less important, however, because there's a much easier and safer way to access MySQL, which obviates the need for these types of functions—the use of placeholders, explained next.

Using Placeholders

All the methods you have seen so far work with MySQL but had security implications, with strings constantly requiring escaping to prevent security risks. So, now that you know the basics, let me introduce the best and recommended way to interact with MySQL, which is pretty much bulletproof in terms of security. Once you have read this section, you should no longer use direct inserting of data into MySQL (though it was important to show you how to do this), but should always use placeholders instead.

So what are placeholders? They are positions within prepared statements in which data is transferred directly to the database, without the possibility of user-submitted (or other) data being interpreted as MySQL statements (and the potential for hacking that could then result).

The technology works by requiring you to first prepare the statement you wish to be executed in MySQL, but leave all the parts of the statement that refer to data as simple question marks.

In plain MySQL, prepared statements look like Example 10-18.

Example 10-18. MySQL placeholders

```
PREPARE statement FROM "INSERT INTO classics VALUES(?,?,?,?,?)";

SET @author   = "Emily Brontë",
    @title    = "Wuthering Heights",
    @category = "Classic Fiction",
    @year     = "1847",
    @isbn     = "9780553212587";

EXECUTE statement USING @author,@title,@category,@year,@isbn;
DEALLOCATE PREPARE statement;
```

This can be cumbersome to submit to MySQL, so the mysqli extension makes handling placeholders easier for you with a ready-made method called prepare, which you call like this:

```
$stmt = $conn->prepare('INSERT INTO classics VALUES(?,?,?,?,?)');
```

The object $stmt (which is shorthand for *statement*) returned by this method is then used for sending the data to the server in place of the question marks. Its first use is to bind some PHP variables to each of the question marks (the placeholder parameters) in turn, like this:

```
$stmt->bind_param('sssss', $author, $title, $category, $year, $isbn);
```

The first argument to bind_param is a string representing the type of each of the arguments in turn. In this case, it comprises five s characters, representing strings, but any combination of types can be specified here, out of the following:

- i: The data is an integer.
- d: The data is a double.
- s: The data is a string.

- b: The data is a `BLOB` (and will be sent in packets).

With the variables bound to the prepared statement, it is now necessary to populate these variables with the data to be passed to MySQL, like this:

```
$author   = 'Emily Brontë';
$title    = 'Wuthering Heights';
$category = 'Classic Fiction';
$year     = '1847';
$isbn     = '9780553212587';
```

At this point, PHP has everything it needs in order to execute the prepared statement, so you can issue the following command, which calls the `execute` method of the `$stmt` object created earlier:

```
$stmt->execute();
```

Before going any further, it makes sense to verify whether the command was executed successfully. Here's how you can do that by checking the `affected_rows` property of `$stmt`:

```
printf("%d Row inserted.\n", $stmt->affected_rows);
```

In this case, the output should indicate that one row was inserted.

Once you are happy that the statement executed successfully (or you have dealt with any errors), you can close the `$stmt` object, like this:

```
$stmt->close();
```

and finally close the `$conn` object (assuming you have finished with it too), like this:

```
$conn->close();
```

When you put all this together, the result is Example 10-19.

Example 10-19. Issuing prepared statements

```php
<?php
  require_once 'login.php';
  $conn = new mysqli($hn, $un, $pw, $db);
  if ($conn->connect_error) die("Fatal Error");

  $stmt = $conn->prepare('INSERT INTO classics VALUES(?,?,?,?,?)');
  $stmt->bind_param('sssss', $author, $title, $category, $year, $isbn);

  $author   = 'Emily Brontë';
  $title    = 'Wuthering Heights';
  $category = 'Classic Fiction';
  $year     = '1847';
  $isbn     = '9780553212587';

  $stmt->execute();
```

```
    printf("%d Row inserted.\n", $stmt->affected_rows);
    $stmt->close();
    $conn->close();
?>
```

Every time you are able to use prepared statements in place of nonprepared ones, you will be closing a potential security hole, so it's worth spending some time getting to know how to use them.

Preventing HTML Injection

There's another type of injection you need to concern yourself about—not for the safety of your own websites, but for your users' privacy and protection. That's *cross-site scripting*, also referred to as an *XSS attack*.

This occurs when you allow HTML or, more often, JavaScript code to be input by a user and then displayed by your website. One place this is common is in a comment form. What happens most often is that a malicious user will try to write code that steals cookies from your site's users, which sometimes even allows them to discover username and password pairs if those are poorly handled, or other information that could enable session hijacking (in which a user's login is taken over by a hacker, who could then take over that person's account!). Or the malicious user might launch an attack to download a Trojan onto a user's computer.

But preventing this is as simple as calling the `htmlentities` function, which strips out all HTML markup and replaces it with a form that displays the characters, but does not allow a browser to act on them. For example, consider this HTML:

```
<script src='http://x.com/hack.js'>
</script><script>hack();</script>
```

This code loads in a JavaScript program and then executes malicious functions. But if it is first passed through `htmlentities`, it will be turned into the following totally harmless string:

```
&lt;script src='http://x.com/hack.js'&gt; &lt;/script&gt;
&lt;script&gt;hack();&lt;/script&gt;
```

Therefore, if you are ever going to display anything that your users enter, either immediately or after storing it in a database, you need to first sanitize it using the `htmlentities` function. To do this, I recommend that you create a new function, like the first one in Example 10-20, which can sanitize for both SQL and XSS injections.

Example 10-20. Functions for preventing both SQL and XSS injection attacks

```
<?php
  function mysql_entities_fix_string($conn, $string)
  {
```

```
      return htmlentities(mysql_fix_string($conn, $string));
  }

  function mysql_fix_string($conn, $string)
  {
    if (get_magic_quotes_gpc()) $string = stripslashes($string);
    return $conn->real_escape_string($string);
  }
?>
```

The `mysql_entities_fix_string` function first calls `mysql_fix_string` and then passes the result through `htmlentities` before returning the fully sanitized string. To use either of these functions, you must already have an active connection object open to a MySQL database.

Example 10-21 shows the new "higher protection" version of Example 10-17.

Example 10-21. How to safely access MySQL and prevent XSS attacks

```
<?php
  require_once 'login.php';
  $conn = new mysqli($hn, $un, $pw, $db);
  if ($conn->connect_error) die("Fatal Error");

  $user  = mysql_entities_fix_string($conn, $_POST['user']);
  $pass  = mysql_entities_fix_string($conn, $_POST['pass']);
  $query = "SELECT * FROM users WHERE user='$user' AND pass='$pass'";

  // Etc.

  function mysql_entities_fix_string($conn, $string)
  {
    return htmlentities(mysql_fix_string($conn, $string));
  }

  function mysql_fix_string($conn, $string)
  {
    if (get_magic_quotes_gpc()) $string = stripslashes($string);
    return $conn->real_escape_string($string);
  }
?>
```

Using mysqli Procedurally

If you prefer, there is an alternative set of functions you can use to access `mysqli` in a procedural (rather than object-oriented) manner.

So, instead of creating a `$conn` object like this:

```
$conn = new mysqli($hn, $un, $pw, $db);
```

You can use the following:

```
$link = mysqli_connect($hn, $un, $pw, $db);
```

To check that the connection has been made and handle it, you could use code such as this:

```
if (mysqli_connect_errno()) die("Fatal Error");
```

And to make a MySQL query, you would use code such as the following:

```
$result = mysqli_query($link, "SELECT * FROM classics");
```

Upon return, $result will contain the data. You can find out the number of rows returned as follows:

```
$rows = mysqli_num_rows($result);
```

An integer is returned in $rows. You can fetch the actual data one row at a time in the following way, which returns a numeric array:

```
$row = mysqli_fetch_array($result, MYSQLI_NUM);
```

In this instance, $row[0] will contain the first column of data, $row[1] the second, and so on. As described in "Fetching a row" on page 241, rows can also be returned as associative arrays or as both types, depending on the value passed in the second argument.

When you need to know the insert ID of an insert operation, you can always call the mysqli_insert_id function, like this:

```
$insertID = mysqli_insert_id($result);
```

Escaping strings procedurally with mysqli is as easy as using the following:

```
$escaped = mysqli_real_escape_string($link, $val);
```

And preparing a statement with mysqli is as simple as this:

```
$stmt = mysqli_prepare($link, 'INSERT INTO classics VALUES(?,?,?,?,?)');
```

To bind variables to the prepared statement, you would then use the following:

```
mysqli_stmt_bind_param($stmt, 'sssss', $author, $title, $category, $year, $isbn);
```

And to execute the prepared statement after assigning the variables with the required values, you would issue this call:

```
mysqli_stmt_execute($stmt);
```

To close a statement, issue the following command:

```
mysqli_stmt_close($stmt);
```

And to close the connection to MySQL, enter this command:

```
mysqli_close($link);
```

Check out for the documentation in the PHP Manual for complete details on using prepared statements, procedurally or otherwise (*http://tinyurl.com/mysqlistmt*), and for more advice on all aspects of `mysqli` (*http://tinyurl.com/usingmysqli*).

Now that you have learned how to integrate PHP with MySQL in several different ways, the next chapter moves on to creating user-friendly forms and dealing with the data submitted from them.

Questions

1. How do you connect to a MySQL database using `mysqli`?

2. How do you submit a query to MySQL using `mysqli`?

3. How can you retrieve a string containing an error message when a `mysqli` error occurs?

4. How can you determine the number of rows returned by a `mysqli` query?

5. How can you retrieve a particular row of data from a set of `mysqli` results?

6. Which `mysqli` method can be used to properly escape user input to prevent code injection?

7. What negative effects can happen if you do not close the objects created by `mysqli` methods?

See "Chapter 10 Answers" on page 720 in Appendix A for the answers to these questions.

CHAPTER 11

Form Handling

The main way that website users interact with PHP and MySQL is through HTML forms. These were introduced very early on in the development of the World Wide Web, in 1993—even before the advent of ecommerce—and have remained a mainstay ever since, due to their simplicity and ease of use.

Of course, enhancements have been made over the years to add extra functionality to HTML form handling, so this chapter will bring you up to speed on the state of the art and show you the best ways to implement forms for good usability and security. Plus, as you will see a little later on, the HTML5 specification has further improved the use of forms.

Building Forms

Handling forms is a multipart process. First is the creation of a form into which a user can enter the required details. This data is then sent to the web server, where it is interpreted, often with some error checking. If the PHP code identifies one or more fields that require reentering, the form may be redisplayed with an error message. When the code is satisfied with the accuracy of the input, it takes some action that usually involves the database, such as entering details about a purchase.

To build a form, you must have at least the following elements:

- An opening `<form>` and closing `</form>` tag
- A submission type specifying either a GET or POST method
- One or more `input` fields
- The destination URL to which the form data is to be submitted

Example 11-1 shows a very simple form created with PHP, which you should type in and save as *formtest.php*.

Example 11-1. formtest.php—a simple PHP form handler

```
<?php // formtest.php
  echo <<<_END
    <html>
      <head>
        <title>Form Test</title>
      </head>
      <body>
      <form method="post" action="formtest.php">
        What is your name?
        <input type="text" name="name">
        <input type="submit">
      </form>
      </body>
    </html>
_END;
?>
```

The first thing to notice about this example is that, as you have already seen in this book, rather than dropping in and out of PHP code, the echo <<<_END...._END construct is used whenever multiline HTML must be output.

Inside of this multiline output is some standard code for commencing an HTML document, displaying its title, and starting the body of the document. This is followed by the form, which is set to send its data using the POST method to the PHP program *formtest.php*, which is the name of the program itself.

The rest of the program just closes all the items it opened: the form, the body of the HTML document, and the PHP echo <<<_END statement. The result of opening this program in a web browser is shown in Figure 11-1.

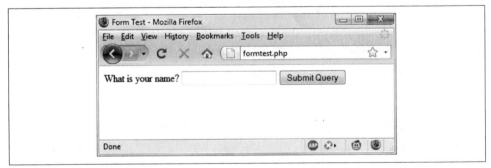

Figure 11-1. The result of opening formtest.php in a web browser

Retrieving Submitted Data

Example 11-1 is only one part of the multipart form-handling process. If you enter a name and click the Submit Query button, absolutely nothing will happen other than the form being redisplayed. So now it's time to add some PHP code to process the data submitted by the form.

Example 11-2 expands on the previous program to include data processing. Type it or modify *formtest.php* by adding in the new lines, save it as *formtest2.php*, and try the program for yourself. The result of running this program and entering a name is shown in Figure 11-2.

Example 11-2. Updated version of formtest.php

```php
<?php // formtest2.php
    if (isset($_POST['name'])) $name = $_POST['name'];
    else $name = "(Not entered)";

    echo <<<_END
        <html>
            <head>
                <title>Form Test</title>
            </head>
            <body>
                Your name is: $name<br>
                <form method="post" action="formtest2.php">
                    What is your name?
                    <input type="text" name="name">
                    <input type="submit">
                </form>
            </body>
        </html>
_END;
?>
```

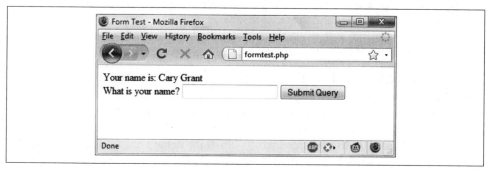

Figure 11-2. formtest.php with data handling

The only changes are a couple of lines at the start that check the `name` field of the `$_POST` associative array and echo it back to the user. Chapter 10 introduced the `$_POST` associative array, which contains an element for each field in an HTML form. In Example 11-2, the input name used was `name` and the form method was POST, so element `name` of the `$_POST` array contains the value in `$_POST['name']`.

The PHP `isset` function is used to test whether `$_POST['name']` has been assigned a value. If nothing was posted, the program assigns the value (`Not entered`); otherwise, it stores the value that was entered. Then a single line has been added after the `<body>` statement to display that value, which is stored in `$name`.

Default Values

Sometimes it's convenient to offer your site visitors a default value in a web form. For example, suppose you put up a loan repayment calculator widget on a real estate website. It could make sense to enter default values of, say, 25 years and 6 percent interest, so that the user can simply type either the principal sum to borrow or the amount that they can afford to pay each month.

In this case, the HTML for those two values would be something like Example 11-3.

Example 11-3. Setting default values

```
<form method="post" action="calc.php"><pre>
     Loan Amount <input type="text" name="principle">
Monthly Repayment <input type="text" name="monthly">
  Number of Years <input type="text" name="years" value="25">
    Interest Rate <input type="text" name="rate"  value="6">
               <input type="submit">
</pre></form>
```

If you wish to try this (and the other HTML code samples), type it and save it with an *.html* (or *.htm*) file extension, such as *test.html* (or *test.htm*), and then load that file into your browser.

Take a look at the third and fourth inputs. By populating the `value` attribute, you display a default value in the field, which the users can then change if they wish. With sensible default values, you can often make your web forms more user-friendly by minimizing unnecessary typing. The result of the previous code looks like Figure 11-3. Of course, this was created to illustrate default values and, because the program *calc.php* has not been written, the form will not do anything if submitted.

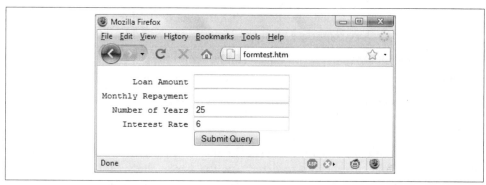

Figure 11-3. Using default values for selected form fields

Default values are also used for hidden fields if you want to pass extra information from your web page to your program, in addition to what users enter. We'll look at hidden fields later in this chapter.

Input Types

HTML forms are very versatile and allow you to submit a wide range of input types, from text boxes and text areas to checkboxes, radio buttons, and more.

Text boxes

The input type you will probably use most often is the text box. It accepts a wide range of alphanumeric text and other characters in a single-line box. The general format of a text box input is as follows:

```
<input type="text" name="name" size="size" maxlength="length" value="value">
```

We've already covered the name and value attributes, but two more are introduced here: size and maxlength. The size attribute specifies the width of the box (in characters of the current font) as it should appear on the screen, and maxlength specifies the maximum number of characters that a user is allowed to enter into the field.

The only required attributes are type, which tells the web browser what type of input to expect, and name, for giving the input a name that will be used to process the field upon receipt of the submitted form.

Text areas

When you need to accept input of more than a short line of text, use a text area. This is similar to a text box, but, because it allows multiple lines, it has some different attributes. Its general format looks like this:

```
<textarea name="name" cols="width" rows="height" wrap="type">
</textarea>
```

The first thing to notice is that `<textarea>` has its own tag and is not a subtype of the `<input>` tag. It therefore requires a closing `</textarea>` to end input.

Instead of a default attribute, if you have default text to display, you must put it before the closing `</textarea>`, and it will then be displayed and be editable by the user:

```
<textarea name="name" cols="width" rows="height" wrap="type">
  This is some default text.
</textarea>
```

To control the width and height, use the `cols` and `rows` attributes. Both use the character spacing of the current font to determine the size of the area. If you omit these values, a default input box will be created that will vary in dimensions depending on the browser used, so you should always define them to be certain about how your form will appear.

Last, you can control how the text entered into the box will wrap (and how any such wrapping will be sent to the server) using the `wrap` attribute. Table 11-1 shows the wrap types available. If you leave out the `wrap` attribute, soft wrapping is used.

Table 11-1. The wrap types available in a <textarea> input

Type	Action
off	Text does not wrap, and lines appear exactly as the user types them.
soft	Text wraps but is sent to the server as one long string without carriage returns and line feeds.
hard	Text wraps and is sent to the server in wrapped format with soft returns and line feeds.

Checkboxes

When you want to offer a number of different options to a user, from which they can select one or more items, checkboxes are the way to go. Here is the format to use:

```
<input type="checkbox" name="name" value="value" checked="checked">
```

By default, checkboxes are square. If you include the `checked` attribute, the box is already checked when the browser is displayed. The string you assign to the attribute should be either a pair of double or single quotes or the value `"checked"`, or there should be no value assigned (just `checked`). If you don't include the attribute, the box is shown unchecked. Here is an example of creating an unchecked box:

```
I Agree <input type="checkbox" name="agree">
```

If the user doesn't check the box, no value will be submitted. But if they do, a value of `"on"` will be submitted for the field named `agree`. If you prefer to have your own value submitted instead of the word *on* (such as the number 1), you could use the following syntax:

```
I Agree <input type="checkbox" name="agree" value="1">
```

On the other hand, if you wish to offer a newsletter to your readers when submitting a form, you might want to have the checkbox already checked as the default value:

```
Subscribe? <input type="checkbox" name="news" checked="checked">
```

If you want to allow groups of items to be selected at one time, assign them all the same name. However, only the last item checked will be submitted, unless you pass an array as the name. For example, Example 11-4 allows the user to select their favorite ice creams (see Figure 11-4 for how it displays in a browser).

Example 11-4. Offering multiple checkbox choices

```
   Vanilla <input type="checkbox" name="ice" value="Vanilla">
 Chocolate <input type="checkbox" name="ice" value="Chocolate">
Strawberry <input type="checkbox" name="ice" value="Strawberry">
```

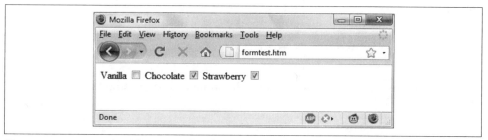

Figure 11-4. Using checkboxes to make quick selections

If only one of the checkboxes is selected, such as the second one, only that item will be submitted (the field named `ice` would be assigned the value `"Chocolate"`). But if two or more are selected, only the last value will be submitted, with prior values being ignored.

If you *want* exclusive behavior—so that only one item can be submitted—then you should use radio buttons instead (see the next section). Otherwise, to allow multiple submissions, you have to slightly alter the HTML, as in Example 11-5 (note the addition of the square brackets, [ ], following the values of `ice`).

Example 11-5. Submitting multiple values with an array

```
   Vanilla <input type="checkbox" name="ice[]" value="Vanilla">
 Chocolate <input type="checkbox" name="ice[]" value="Chocolate">
Strawberry <input type="checkbox" name="ice[]" value="Strawberry">
```

Now when the form is submitted, if any of these items have been checked an array called `ice` will be submitted that contains all the selected values. You can extract either the single submitted value or the array of values to a variable like this:

```
$ice = $_POST['ice'];
```

If the field `ice` has been posted as a single value, `$ice` will be a single string, such as "Strawberry". But if `ice` was defined in the form as an array (like in Example 11-5), `$ice` will be an array, and its number of elements will be the number of values submitted. Table 11-2 shows the seven possible sets of values that could be submitted by this HTML for one, two, or all three selections. In each case, an array of one, two, or three items is created.

Table 11-2. The seven possible sets of values for the array $ice

One value submitted	Two values submitted	Three values submitted
`$ice[0] => Vanilla`	`$ice[0] => Vanilla` `$ice[1] => Chocolate`	`$ice[0] => Vanilla` `$ice[1] => Chocolate`
`$ice[0] => Chocolate`		`$ice[2] => Strawberry`
	`$ice[0] => Vanilla`	
`$ice[0] => Strawberry`	`$ice[1] => Strawberry`	
	`$ice[0] => Chocolate` `$ice[1] => Strawberry`	

If `$ice` is an array, the PHP code to display its contents is quite simple and might look like this:

```
foreach($ice as $item) echo "$item<br>";
```

This uses the standard PHP `foreach` construct to iterate through the array `$ice` and pass each element's value into the variable `$item`, which is then displayed via the `echo` command. The `<br>` is just an HTML formatting device to force a new line after each flavor in the display.

Radio buttons

Radio buttons are named after the push-in preset buttons found on many older radios, where any previously depressed button pops back up when another is pressed. They are used when you want only a single value to be returned from a selection of two or more options. All the buttons in a group must use the same name and, because only a single value is returned, you do not have to pass an array.

For example, if your website offers a choice of delivery times for items purchased from your store, you might use HTML like that in Example 11-6 (see Figure 11-5 to see how it displays). By default, radio buttons are round.

Example 11-6. Using radio buttons

```
8am-Noon<input type="radio" name="time" value="1">
Noon-4pm<input type="radio" name="time" value="2" checked="checked">
 4pm-8pm<input type="radio" name="time" value="3">
```

Figure 11-5. Selecting a single value with radio buttons

Here, the second option of Noon–4pm has been selected by default. This default choice ensures that at least one delivery time will be chosen by the user, which they can change to one of the other two options if they prefer. Had one of the items not been already checked, the user might forget to select an option, and no value would be submitted at all for the delivery time.

Hidden fields

Sometimes it is convenient to have hidden form fields so that you can keep track of the state of form entry. For example, you might wish to know whether a form has already been submitted. You can achieve this by adding some HTML in your PHP code, such as the following:

```
echo '<input type="hidden" name="submitted" value="yes">'
```

This is a simple PHP echo statement that adds an input field to the HTML form. Let's assume the form was created outside the program and displayed to the user. The first time the PHP program receives the input, this line of code has not run, so there will be no field named submitted. The PHP program re-creates the form, adding the input field. So when the visitor resubmits the form, the PHP program receives it with the submitted field set to "yes". The code can simply check whether the field is present:

```
if (isset($_POST['submitted']))
{...
```

Hidden fields can also be useful for storing other details, such as a session ID string that you might create to identify a user, and so on.

Never treat hidden fields as secure—because they are not. Someone could easily view the HTML containing them by using a browser's View Source feature. A malicious attacker could also craft a post that removes, adds, or changes a hidden field.

\<select>

The \<select> tag lets you create a drop-down list of options, offering either single or multiple selections. It conforms to the following syntax:

```
<select name="name" size="size" multiple="multiple">
```

The attribute `size` is the number of lines to display. Clicking on the display causes a list to drop down, showing all the options. If you use the `multiple` attribute, a user can select multiple options from the list by pressing the Ctrl key when clicking. So, to ask a user for their favorite vegetable from a choice of five, you might use HTML like that in Example 11-7, which offers a single selection.

Example 11-7. Using \<select>

```
Vegetables
<select name="veg" size="1">
  <option value="Peas">Peas</option>
  <option value="Beans">Beans</option>
  <option value="Carrots">Carrots</option>
  <option value="Cabbage">Cabbage</option>
  <option value="Broccoli">Broccoli</option>
</select>
```

This HTML offers five choices, with the first one, *Peas*, preselected (due to it being the first item). Figure 11-6 shows the output where the list has been clicked to drop it down, and the option *Carrots* has been highlighted. If you want to have a different default option offered first (such as *Beans*), use the `selected` attribute, like this:

```
<option selected="selected" value="Beans">Beans</option>
```

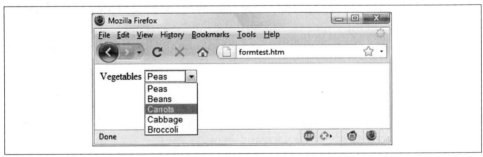

Figure 11-6. Creating a drop-down list with \<select>

You can also allow users to select more than one item, as in Example 11-8.

Example 11-8. Using <select> with the multiple attribute

```
Vegetables
<select name="veg" size="5" multiple="multiple">
  <option value="Peas">Peas</option>
  <option value="Beans">Beans</option>
  <option value="Carrots">Carrots</option>
  <option value="Cabbage">Cabbage</option>
  <option value="Broccoli">Broccoli</option>
</select>
```

This HTML is not very different; the size has been changed to "5" and the attribute multiple has been added. But, as you can see from Figure 11-7, it is now possible for the user to select more than one option by using the Ctrl key when clicking. You can leave out the size attribute if you wish, and the output will be the same; however, with a larger list the drop-down box may display more items, so I recommend that you pick a suitable number of rows and stick with it. I also recommend not using multiple select boxes smaller than two rows in height—some browsers may not correctly display the scroll bars needed to access them.

Figure 11-7. Using a <select> with the multiple attribute

You can also use the selected attribute within a multiple select and can, in fact, have more than one option preselected if you wish.

Labels

You can provide an even better user experience by utilizing the <label> tag. With it, you can surround a form element, making it selectable by clicking any visible part contained between the opening and closing <label> tags.

For example, going back to the example of choosing a delivery time, you could allow the user to click the radio button itself *and* the associated text, like this:

```
<label>8am-Noon<input type="radio" name="time" value="1"></label>
```

The text will not be underlined like a hyperlink when you do this, but as the mouse pointer passes over it will change to an arrow instead of a text cursor, indicating that the whole item is clickable.

The submit button

To match the type of form being submitted, you can change the text of the submit button to anything you like by using the `value` attribute, like this:

```
<input type="submit" value="Search">
```

You can also replace the standard text button with a graphic image of your choice, using HTML such as this:

```
<input type="image" name="submit" src="image.gif">
```

Sanitizing Input

Now we return to PHP programming. It can never be emphasized enough that handling user data is a security minefield, and that it is essential to learn to treat all such data with the utmost caution from the word go. It's actually not that difficult to sanitize user input from potential hacking attempts, but it must be done.

The first thing to remember is that regardless of what constraints you have placed in an HTML form to limit the types and sizes of inputs, it is a trivial matter for a hacker to use their browser's View Source feature to extract the form and modify it to provide malicious input to your website.

Therefore, you must never trust any variable that you fetch from either the `$_GET` or `$_POST` arrays until you have sanitized it. If you don't, users may try to inject JavaScript into the data to interfere with your site's operation, or even attempt to add MySQL commands to compromise your database.

So, instead of just using code such as the following when reading in user input:

```
$variable = $_POST['user_input'];
```

you should also use one or more of the following lines of code. For example, to prevent escape characters from being injected into a string that will be presented to MySQL, use the following. Remember that this function takes into account the current character set of a MySQL connection, so it must be used with a `mysqli` connection object (in this instance, `$connection`), as discussed in Chapter 10:

```
$variable = $connection->real_escape_string($variable);
```

Remember that the safest way to secure MySQL from hacking attempts is to use placeholders and prepared statements, as described in Chapter 10. If you do so for all accesses to MySQL, it becomes unnecessary to escape data being transferred into or out of the database. You will, however, still need to sanitize input when including it within HTML.

To get rid of unwanted slashes, you should first check whether PHP's magic quotes feature is enabled (which will escape quotes by adding slashes), and if so call the `stripslashes` function like this:

```php
if (get_magic_quotes_gpc())
  $variable = stripslashes($variable);
```

And to remove any HTML from a string, use the following:

```php
$variable = htmlentities($variable);
```

For example, this would change a string of interpretable HTML code like hi into <b>hi</b>, which then displays as text, and won't be interpreted as HTML tags.

Finally, if you wish to strip HTML entirely from an input, use the following (but ensure you use it before calling `htmlentities`, which replaces any angle brackets used as part of HTML tags):

```php
$variable = strip_tags($variable);
```

In fact, until you know exactly what sanitization you require for a program, Example 11-9 shows a pair of functions that brings all these checks together to provide a very good level of security.

Example 11-9. The sanitizeString and sanitizeMySQL functions

```php
<?php
  function sanitizeString($var)
  {
    if (get_magic_quotes_gpc())
      $var = stripslashes($var);
    $var = strip_tags($var);
    $var = htmlentities($var);
    return $var;
  }

  function sanitizeMySQL($connection, $var)
  {
    $var = $connection->real_escape_string($var);
    $var = sanitizeString($var);
    return $var;
```

```
    }
?>
```

Add this code to the end of your PHP programs, and you can then call it for each user input to sanitize, like this:

```
$var = sanitizeString($_POST['user_input']);
```

Or, when you have an open MySQL connection and a `mysqli` connection object (in this case, called `$connection`):

```
$var = sanitizeMySQL($connection, $_POST['user_input']);
```

 If you are using the procedural version of the `mysqli` extension, you will need to modify the `sanitizeMySQL` function to call the `mysqli_real_escape_string` function, like this (in which case `$connection` will then be a handle, not an object):

```
$var = mysqli_real_escape_string($connection, $var);
```

An Example Program

Let's look at how a real-life PHP program integrates with an HTML form by creating the program *convert.php* listed in Example 11-10. Type it as shown and try it for yourself.

Example 11-10. A program to convert values between Fahrenheit and Celsius

```php
<?php // convert.php
  $f = $c = '';

  if (isset($_POST['f'])) $f = sanitizeString($_POST['f']);
  if (isset($_POST['c'])) $c = sanitizeString($_POST['c']);

  if (is_numeric($f))
  {
    $c = intval((5 / 9) * ($f - 32));
    $out = "$f &deg;f equals $c &deg;c";
  }
  elseif(is_numeric($c))
  {
    $f = intval((9 / 5) * $c + 32);
    $out = "$c &deg;c equals $f &deg;f";
  }
  else $out = "";

  echo <<<_END
<html>
  <head>
    <title>Temperature Converter</title>
```

```
    </head>
    <body>
      <pre>
        Enter either Fahrenheit or Celsius and click on Convert

        <b>$out</b>
        <form method="post" action="">
          Fahrenheit <input type="text" name="f" size="7">
              Celsius <input type="text" name="c" size="7">
                      <input type="submit" value="Convert">
        </form>
      </pre>
    </body>
</html>
_END;

    function sanitizeString($var)
    {
      if (get_magic_quotes_gpc())
        $var = stripslashes($var);
      $var = strip_tags($var);
      $var = htmlentities($var);
      return $var;
    }
?>
```

When you call up *convert.php* in a browser, the result should look something like
Figure 11-8.

Figure 11-8. The temperature conversion program in action

To break the program down, the first line initializes the variables $c and $f in case
they do not get posted to the program. The next two lines fetch the values of either
the field named f or the one named c, for an input Fahrenheit or Celsius value. If the
user inputs both, the Celsius is simply ignored and the Fahrenheit value is converted.
As a security measure, the new function sanitizeString from Example 11-9 is also
used.

So, having either submitted values or empty strings in both $f and $c, the next portion of code constitutes an if...elseif...else structure that first tests whether $f has a numeric value. If not, it checks $c; if $c does not have a numeric value either, the variable $out is set to the empty string (more on that in a moment).

If $f is found to have a numeric value, the variable $c is assigned a simple mathematical expression that converts the value of $f from Fahrenheit to Celsius. The formula used is Celsius = (5 / 9) × (Fahrenheit − 32). The variable $out is then set to a message string explaining the conversion.

On the other hand, if $c is found to have a numeric value, a complementary operation is performed to convert the value of $c from Celsius to Fahrenheit and assign the result to $f. The formula used is Fahrenheit = (9 / 5) × Celsius + 32. As with the previous section, the string $out is then set to contain a message about the conversion.

In both conversions, the PHP intval function is called to convert the result of the conversion to an integer value. It's not necessary, but looks better.

With all the arithmetic done, the program now outputs the HTML, which starts with the basic head and title and then contains some introductory text before displaying the value of $out. If no temperature conversion was made, $out will have a value of NULL and nothing will be displayed, which is exactly what we want when the form hasn't yet been submitted. But if a conversion was made, $out contains the result, which is displayed.

After this, we come to the form, which is set to submit using the POST method to the program itself (represented by a pair of double quotation marks, so that the file can be saved with any name). Within the form, there are two inputs for either a Fahrenheit or a Celsius value to be entered. A submit button with the text Convert is then displayed, and the form is closed.

After outputting the HTML to close the document, we come finally to the function sanitizeString from Example 11-9. Try playing with the example by inputting different values into the fields; for a bit of fun, can you find a value for which Fahrenheit and Celsius are the same?

 All the examples in this chapter have used the POST method to send form data. I recommend this, as it's the neatest and most secure method. However, the forms can easily be changed to use the GET method, as long as values are fetched from the $_GET array instead of the $_POST array. Reasons to do this might include making the result of a search bookmarkable or directly linkable from another page.

HTML5 Enhancements

With HTML5, developers can draw on a number of useful enhancements to form handling to make using forms easier than ever, including new attributes; color, date, and time pickers; and new input types—although some of these features are not yet implemented across all major browsers.

The autocomplete Attribute

You can apply the `autocomplete` attribute to the `<form>` element, or to any of the `color`, `date`, `email`, `password`, `range`, `search`, `tel`, `text`, or `url` types of the `<input>` element.

With autocomplete enabled, previous user inputs are recalled and automatically entered into fields as suggestions. You can also disable this feature by turning autocomplete off. Here's how to turn autocomplete on for an entire form but disable it for specific fields (highlighted in bold):

```
<form action='myform.php' method='post' autocomplete='on'>
  <input type='text'     name='username'>
  <input type='password' name='password' autocomplete='off'>
</form>
```

The autofocus Attribute

The `autofocus` attribute gives immediate focus to an element when a page loads. It can be applied to any `<input>`, `<textarea>`, or `<button>` element, like this:

```
<input type='text' name='query' autofocus='autofocus'>
```

> Browsers that use touch interfaces (such as Android, iOS, or Windows Phone) usually ignore the `autofocus` attribute, leaving it to the user to tap on a field to give it focus; otherwise, the zooming, focusing, and pop-up keyboards this attribute would generate could quickly become very annoying.

Because this feature will cause the focus to move into an input element, the Backspace key will no longer take the user back a web page (although Alt-Left arrow and Alt-Right arrow will still move backward and forward within the browsing history).

The placeholder Attribute

The `placeholder` attribute lets you place into any blank input field a helpful hint to explain to users what they should enter. You use it like this:

```
<input type='text' name='name' size='50' placeholder='First & Last name'>
```

The input field will display the placeholder text as a prompt until the user starts typing, at which point the placeholder will disappear.

The required Attribute

The `required` attribute ensures that a field has been completed before a form is submitted. Use it like this:

```
<input type='text' name='creditcard' required='required'>
```

When the browser detects an attempted form submission where there's an uncompleted `required` input, a message is displayed, prompting the user to complete the field.

Override Attributes

With override attributes, you can override form settings on an element-by-element basis. So, for example, using the `formaction` attribute, you can specify that a submit button should submit a form to a different URL from the one specified in the form itself, like the following (in which the default and overridden action URLs are bold):

```
<form action='url1.php' method='post'>
  <input type='text' name='field'>
  <input type='submit' formaction='url2.php'>
</form>
```

HTML5 also brings support for the `formenctype`, `formmethod`, `formnovalidate`, and `formtarget` override attributes, which you can use in exactly the same manner as `formaction` to override one of these settings.

The width and height Attributes

Using these new attributes, you can alter the dimensions of an input image, like this:

```
<input type='image' src='picture.png' width='120' height='80'>
```

The min and max Attributes

With the `min` and `max` attributes, you can specify minimum and maximum values for inputs. You use the attributes like this:

```
<input type='time' name='alarm' value='07:00' min='05:00' max='09:00'>
```

The browser will then either offer up and down selectors for the range of values allowed, or simply disallow values outside of that range.

The step Attribute

Often used with `min` and `max`, the `step` attribute supports stepping through number or date values, like this:

```
<input type='time' name='meeting' value='12:00'
    min='09:00' max='16:00' step='3600'>
```

When you are stepping through date or time values, each unit represents 1 second.

The form Attribute

With HTML5, you no longer have to place `<input>` elements within `<form>` elements, because you can specify the form to which an input applies by supplying a `form` attribute. The following code shows a form being created, but with its input outside of the `<form>` and `</form>` tags:

```
<form action='myscript.php' method='post' id='form1'>
</form>

<input type='text' name='username' form='form1'>
```

To do this, you must give the form an ID using the `id` attribute, and refer to this ID in the `form` attribute of the `input` element. This is most useful for adding hidden input fields, because you can't control how the field is laid out inside the form, or for using JavaScript to modify forms and inputs on the fly.

The list Attribute

HTML5 supports attaching lists to inputs to enable users to easily select from a predefined list, which you can use like this:

```
Select destination:
<input type='url' name='site' list='links'>

<datalist id='links'>
  <option label='Google' value='http://google.com'>
  <option label='Yahoo!' value='http://yahoo.com'>
  <option label='Bing'   value='http://bing.com'>
  <option label='Ask'    value='http://ask.com'>
</datalist>
```

The color Input Type

The `color` input type calls up a color picker so that you can simply click the color of your choice. You use it like this:

```
Choose a color <input type='color' name='color'>
```

The number and range Input Types

The `number` and `range` input types restrict input to a number, and optionally also specify an allowed range like this:

```
<input type='number' name='age'>
<input type='range' name='num' min='0' max='100' value='50' step='1'>
```

Date and Time Pickers

When you choose an input type of date, month, week, time, datetime, or datetime-local, a picker will pop up on supported browsers from which the user can make a selection, like this one, which inputs the time:

```
<input type='time' name='time' value='12:34'>
```

The next chapter will show you how to use cookies and authentication to store users' preferences and keep them logged in, and how to maintain a complete user session.

Questions

1. You can submit form data using either the POST or the GET method. Which associative arrays are used to pass this data to PHP?

2. What is the difference between a text box and a text area?

3. If a form has to offer three choices to a user, each of which is mutually exclusive so that only one of the three can be selected, which input type would you use, given a choice between checkboxes and radio buttons?

4. How can you submit a group of selections from a web form using a single field name?

5. How can you submit a form field without displaying it in the browser?

6. Which HTML tag is used to encapsulate a form element and supporting text or graphics, making the entire unit selectable with a mouse-click?

7. Which PHP function converts HTML into a format that can be displayed but will not be interpreted as HTML by a browser?

8. What form attribute can be used to help users complete input fields?

9. How can you ensure that an input is completed before a form gets submitted?

See "Chapter 11 Answers" on page 721 in Appendix A for the answers to these questions.

CHAPTER 12

Cookies, Sessions, and Authentication

As your web projects grow larger and more complicated, you will find an increasing need to keep track of your users. Even if you aren't offering logins and passwords, you will still often need to store details about a user's current session and possibly also recognize them when they return to your site.

Several technologies support this kind of interaction, ranging from simple browser cookies to session handling and HTTP authentication. Between them, they offer the opportunity for you to configure your site to your users' preferences and ensure a smooth and enjoyable transition through it.

Using Cookies in PHP

A *cookie* is an item of data that a web server saves to your computer's hard disk via a web browser. It can contain almost any alphanumeric information (as long as it's under 4 KB) and can be retrieved from your computer and returned to the server. Common uses include session tracking, maintaining data across multiple visits, holding shopping cart contents, storing login details, and more.

Because of their privacy implications, cookies can be read only from the issuing domain. In other words, if a cookie is issued by, for example, *oreilly.com*, it can be retrieved only by a web server using that domain. This prevents other websites from gaining access to details for which they are not authorized.

Because of the way the internet works, multiple elements on a web page can be embedded from multiple domains, each of which can issue its own cookies. When this happens, they are referred to as *third-party cookies*. Most commonly, these are created by advertising companies in order to track users across multiple websites.

Because of this, most browsers allow users to turn cookies off either for the current server's domain, third-party servers, or both. Fortunately, most people who disable cookies do so only for third-party websites.

Cookies are exchanged during the transfer of headers, before the actual HTML of a web page is sent, and it is impossible to send a cookie once any HTML has been transferred. Therefore, careful planning of cookie usage is important. Figure 12-1 illustrates a typical request and response dialog between a web browser and web server passing cookies.

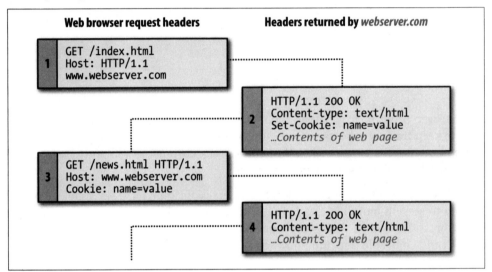

Figure 12-1. A browser/server request/response dialog with cookies

This exchange shows a browser receiving two pages:

1. The browser issues a request to retrieve the main page, *index.html*, at the website *http://www.webserver.com*. The first header specifies the file, and the second header specifies the server.

2. When the web server at *webserver.com* receives this pair of headers, it returns some of its own. The second header defines the type of content to be sent (text/html), and the third one sends a cookie of the name name and with the value value. Only then are the contents of the web page transferred.

3. Once the browser has received the cookie, it will then return it with every future request made to the issuing server until the cookie expires or is deleted. So, when the browser requests the new page */news.html*, it also returns the cookie name with the value value.

4. Because the cookie has already been set, when the server receives the request to send */news.html*, it does not have to resend the cookie, but just returns the requested page.

 It is easy to edit cookies directly from within the browser by using built-in developer tools, or extensions. Therefore, because users can change cookie values, you should not put key information such as usernames in a cookie, or you face the possibility of having your website manipulated in ways you are not expecting. Cookies are best used for storing data such as language or currency settings.

Setting a Cookie

Setting a cookie in PHP is a simple matter. As long as no HTML has yet been transferred, you can call the setcookie function, which has the following syntax (see Table 12-1):

```
setcookie(name, value, expire, path, domain, secure, httponly);
```

Table 12-1. The setcookie parameters

Parameter	Description	Example
name	The name of the cookie. This is the name that your server will use to access the cookie on subsequent browser requests.	location
value	The value of the cookie, or the cookie's contents. This can contain up to 4 KB of alphanumeric text.	USA
expire	(*Optional.*) The Unix timestamp of the expiration date. Generally, you will probably use time() plus a number of seconds. If not set, the cookie expires when the browser closes.	time() + 2592000
path	(*Optional.*) The path of the cookie on the server. If this is a / (forward slash), the cookie is available over the entire domain, such as *www.webserver.com*. If it is a subdirectory, the cookie is available only within that subdirectory. The default is the current directory that the cookie is being set in, and this is the setting you will normally use.	/
domain	(*Optional.*) The internet domain of the cookie. If this is *webserver.com*, the cookie is available to all of *webserver.com* and its subdomains, such as *www.webserver.com* and *images.webserver.com*. If it is *images.webserver.com*, the cookie is available only to *images.webserver.com* and its subdomains, such as *sub.images.webserver.com*, but not, say, to *www.webserver.com*.	webserver.com
secure	(*Optional.*) Whether the cookie must use a secure connection (*https://*). If this value is TRUE, the cookie can be transferred only across a secure connection. The default is FALSE.	FALSE
httponly	(*Optional*; implemented since PHP version 5.2.0.) Whether the cookie must use the HTTP protocol. If this value is TRUE, scripting languages such as JavaScript cannot access the cookie. (Not supported in all browsers.) The default is FALSE.	FALSE

So, to create a cookie with the name `location` and the value `USA` that is accessible across the entire web server on the current domain, and will be removed from the browser's cache in seven days, use the following:

```
setcookie('location', 'USA', time() + 60 * 60 * 24 * 7, '/');
```

Accessing a Cookie

Reading the value of a cookie is as simple as accessing the `$_COOKIE` system array. For example, if you wish to see whether the current browser has the cookie called `location` already stored and, if so, to read its value, use the following:

```
if (isset($_COOKIE['location'])) $location = $_COOKIE['location'];
```

Note that you can read a cookie back only after it has been sent to a web browser. This means that when you issue a cookie, you cannot read it in again until the browser reloads the page (or another with access to the cookie) from your website and passes the cookie back to the server in the process.

Destroying a Cookie

To delete a cookie, you must issue it again and set a date in the past. It is important for all parameters in your new `setcookie` call except the timestamp to be identical to the parameters when the cookie was first issued; otherwise, the deletion will fail. Therefore, to delete the cookie created earlier, you would use the following:

```
setcookie('location', 'USA', time() - 2592000, '/');
```

As long as the time given is in the past, the cookie should be deleted. However, I have used a time of 2,592,000 seconds (one month) in the past in case the client computer's date and time are not correctly set. You may also provide an empty string for the cookie value (or a value of `FALSE`), and PHP will automatically set its time in the past for you.

HTTP Authentication

HTTP authentication uses the web server to manage users and passwords for the application. It's adequate for simple applications that ask users to log in, although most applications will have specialized needs or more stringent security requirements that call for other techniques.

To use HTTP authentication, PHP sends a header request asking to start an authentication dialog with the browser. The server must have this feature turned on in order for it to work, but because it's so common, your server is likely to offer the feature.

Although it is usually installed with Apache, the HTTP authentication module may not necessarily be installed on the server you use. So, attempting to run these examples may generate an error telling you that the feature is not enabled, in which case you must either install the module and change the configuration file to load it, or ask your system administrator to do these fixes.

After entering your URL into the browser or visiting the page via a link, the user will see an "Authentication Required" prompt pop up, requesting two fields: User Name and Password (Figure 12-2 shows how this looks in Firefox).

Figure 12-2. An HTTP authentication login prompt

Example 12-1 shows the code to make this happen.

Example 12-1. PHP authentication

```php
<?php
  if (isset($_SERVER['PHP_AUTH_USER']) &&
      isset($_SERVER['PHP_AUTH_PW']))
  {
    echo "Welcome User: " . htmlspecialchars($_SERVER['PHP_AUTH_USER']) .
        " Password: "    . htmlspecialchars($_SERVER['PHP_AUTH_PW']);
  }
  else
  {
    header('WWW-Authenticate: Basic realm="Restricted Area"');
    header('HTTP/1.0 401 Unauthorized');
    die("Please enter your username and password");
  }
?>
```

The first thing the program does is look for two particular array values: $_SERVER['PHP_AUTH_USER'] and $_SERVER['PHP_AUTH_PW']. If they both exist, they represent the username and password entered by a user into an authentication prompt.

 Notice that when being displayed to the screen, the values that have been returned in the $_SERVER array are first processed through the htmlspecialchars function. This is because these values have been entered by the user and therefore cannot be trusted, as a hacker could make a cross-site scripting attempt by adding HTML characters and other symbols to the input. htmlspecialchars translates any such input into harmless HTML entities.

If either value does not exist, the user has not yet been authenticated and you display the prompt in Figure 12-2 by issuing the following header, where Basic realm is the name of the section that is protected and appears as part of the pop-up prompt:

    WWW-Authenticate: Basic realm="Restricted Area"

If the user fills out the fields, the PHP program runs again from the top. But if the user clicks the Cancel button, the program proceeds to the following two lines, which send the following header and an error message:

    HTTP/1.0 401 Unauthorized

The die statement causes the text "Please enter your username and password" to be displayed (see Figure 12-3).

Figure 12-3. The result of clicking the Cancel button

Once a user has been authenticated, you will not be able to get the authentication dialog to pop up again unless the user closes and reopens all browser windows, because the web browser will keep returning the same username and password to PHP. You may need to close and reopen your browser a few times as you work through this section and try different things out. The easiest way to do this is to open up a new private or anonymous window to run these examples, so you won't need to close the entire browser.

Now let's check for a valid username and password. The code in Example 12-1 doesn't require you to change much to add this check, other than modifying the previous welcome message code to test for a correct username and password, and then issuing a welcome message. A failed authentication causes an error message to be sent (see Example 12-2).

Example 12-2. PHP authentication with input checking

```php
<?php
  $username = 'admin';
  $password = 'letmein';

  if (isset($_SERVER['PHP_AUTH_USER']) &&
      isset($_SERVER['PHP_AUTH_PW']))
  {
    if ($_SERVER['PHP_AUTH_USER'] === $username &&
        $_SERVER['PHP_AUTH_PW']   === $password)
          echo "You are now logged in";
    else die("Invalid username/password combination");
  }
  else
  {
    header('WWW-Authenticate: Basic realm="Restricted Area"');
    header('HTTP/1.0 401 Unauthorized');
    die ("Please enter your username and password");
  }
?>
```

When comparing usernames and passwords the === (identity) operator is used, rather than the == (equals) operator. This is because we are checking whether the two values match *exactly*. For example, '0e123' == '0e456', and this is not a suitable match for either username or password purposes.

A mechanism is now in place to authenticate users, but only for a single username and password. Also, the password appears in clear text within the PHP file, and if someone managed to hack into your server, they would instantly know it. So, let's look at a better way to handle usernames and passwords.

Storing Usernames and Passwords

Obviously, MySQL is the natural way to store usernames and passwords. But again, we don't want to store the passwords as clear text, because our website could be compromised if the database were accessed by a hacker. Instead, we'll use a neat trick called a *one-way function*.

This type of function is easy to use and converts a string of text into a seemingly random string. Because of their one-way nature, such functions are impossible to reverse, so their output can be safely stored in a database—and anyone who steals it will be none the wiser as to the passwords used.

In previous editions of this book, I recommended using the *MD5* hashing algorithm for your data security. Time marches on, however, and now MD5 is considered easily hackable and therefore unsafe. Indeed, even its previously recommended replacement of *SHA-1* can apparently be hacked.

So, now that PHP 5.5 is pretty much the minimum standard everywhere, I have moved on to using its in-built hashing function, which is vastly more secure and handles everything for you in a neat fashion.

Previously, to store a password securely, you would have needed to *salt* the password, which is a term for adding extra characters to a password that the user did not enter (to further obscure it). You then needed to run the result of that through a one-way function to turn it into a seemingly random set of characters, which used to be hard to crack.

For example, code such as the following (which is now very insecure, because modern graphics processing units have such speed and power):

```
echo hash('ripemd128', 'saltstringmypassword');
```

would display this value:

```
9eb8eb0584f82e5d505489e6928741e7
```

Remember that this is not a recommended method you should ever use. Treat this as an example of what *not* to do, as it is very insecure. Instead, please read on.

Using password_hash

From version 5.5 of PHP, there's a far better way to create salted password hashes: the `password_hash` function. Supply `PASSWORD_DEFAULT` as its second (required) argument to ask the function to select the most secure hashing function currently available. `password_hash` will also choose a random salt for every password. (Don't be tempted to add any more salting of your own, as this could compromise the algorithm's security.) So, the following code:

```
echo password_hash("mypassword", PASSWORD_DEFAULT);
```

will return a string such as the following, which includes the salt and all information required for the password to be verified:

```
$2y$10$k0YljbC2dmmCq8WKGf8oteBGiXlM9Zx0ss4PEtb5kz22EoIkXBtbG
```

 If you are letting PHP choose the hashing algorithm for you, you should allow for the returned hash to expand in size over time as better security is implemented. The developers of PHP recommend that you store hashes in a database field that can expand to at least 255 characters (even though 60–72 is the average length right now). Should you wish, you can manually select the BCRYPT algorithm to guarantee a hash string of only 60 characters, by supplying the constant PASSWORD_BCRYPT as the second argument to the function. However, I don't recommend this unless you have a very good reason.

You can supply options (in the form of an optional third argument) to further tailor how hashes are calculated, such as the cost or amount of processor time to allocate to the hashing (more time means more security, but a slower server). The cost has a default value of 10, which is the minimum you should use with BCRYPT.

However, I don't want to confuse you with more information than you need to be able to store password hashes securely with the minimum of fuss, so please refer to the documentation (*http://php.net/password-hash*) if you'd like more details on the available options. You can even choose your own salts (although this is deprecated from PHP 7.0 onward, as it's not considered that secure—so don't be tempted).

Using password_verify

To verify that a password matches a hash, use the password_verify function, passing it the password string a user has just entered, and the stored hash value for that user's password (generally retrieved from your database).

So, assuming your user had previously entered the (very insecure) password of *mypassword*, and you now have their password's hash string (from when the user created their password) stored in the variable $hash, you could verify that they match like this:

```
if (password_verify("mypassword", $hash))
  echo "Valid";
```

If the correct password for the hash has been supplied, password_verify returns the value TRUE, so this if statement will display the word "Valid." If it doesn't match, then FALSE is returned and you can ask the user to try again.

An Example Program

Let's see how these functions work together when combined with MySQL. First you need to create a new table to store password hashes, so type in the program in Example 12-3 and save it as *setupusers.php* (or download it from the companion website (*http://lpmj.net*)), and then open it in your browser.

Example 12-3. Creating a users table and adding two accounts

```php
<?php // setupusers.php
  require_once 'login.php';
  $connection = new mysqli($hn, $un, $pw, $db);

  if ($connection->connect_error) die("Fatal Error");

  $query = "CREATE TABLE users (
    forename VARCHAR(32) NOT NULL,
    surname  VARCHAR(32) NOT NULL,
    username VARCHAR(32) NOT NULL UNIQUE,
    password VARCHAR(255) NOT NULL
  )";

  $result = $connection->query($query);
  if (!$result) die("Fatal Error");

  $forename = 'Bill';
  $surname  = 'Smith';
  $username = 'bsmith';
  $password = 'mysecret';
  $hash     = password_hash($password, PASSWORD_DEFAULT);

  add_user($connection, $forename, $surname, $username, $hash);

  $forename = 'Pauline';
  $surname  = 'Jones';
  $username = 'pjones';
  $password = 'acrobat';
  $hash     = password_hash($password, PASSWORD_DEFAULT);

  add_user($connection, $forename, $surname, $username, $hash);

  function add_user($connection, $fn, $sn, $un, $pw)
  {
    $stmt = $connection->prepare('INSERT INTO users VALUES(?,?,?,?)');
    $stmt->bind_param('ssss', $fn, $sn, $un, $pw);
    $stmt->execute();
    $stmt->close();
  }
?>
```

This program will create the table *users* within your *publications* database (or whichever database you set up for the *login.php* file in Chapter 10). In this table, it will create two users: Bill Smith and Pauline Jones. They have the usernames and passwords of *bsmith/mysecret* and *pjones/acrobat*, respectively.

Using the data in this table, we can now modify Example 12-2 to properly authenticate users, and Example 12-4 shows the code needed to do this. Type it in or download it from the companion website, then make sure it is saved as *authenticate.php*, and call it up in your browser.

Example 12-4. PHP authentication using MySQL

```php
<?php // authenticate.php
  require_once 'login.php';
  $connection = new mysqli($hn, $un, $pw, $db);

  if ($connection->connect_error) die("Fatal Error");

  if (isset($_SERVER['PHP_AUTH_USER']) &&
      isset($_SERVER['PHP_AUTH_PW']))
  {
    $un_temp = mysql_entities_fix_string($connection, $_SERVER['PHP_AUTH_USER']);
    $pw_temp = mysql_entities_fix_string($connection, $_SERVER['PHP_AUTH_PW']);
    $query   = "SELECT * FROM users WHERE username='$un_temp'";
    $result  = $connection->query($query);

    if (!$result) die("User not found");
    elseif ($result->num_rows)
    {
        $row = $result->fetch_array(MYSQLI_NUM);

        $result->close();

        if (password_verify($pw_temp, $row[3])) echo
          htmlspecialchars("$row[0] $row[1] :
          Hi $row[0], you are now logged in as '$row[2]'");
        else die("Invalid username/password combination");
    }
    else die("Invalid username/password combination");
  }
  else
  {
    header('WWW-Authenticate: Basic realm="Restricted Area"');
    header('HTTP/1.0 401 Unauthorized');
    die ("Please enter your username and password");
  }

  $connection->close();

  function mysql_entities_fix_string($connection, $string)
```

```
{
  return htmlentities(mysql_fix_string($connection, $string));
}

function mysql_fix_string($connection, $string)
{
  if (get_magic_quotes_gpc()) $string = stripslashes($string);
  return $connection->real_escape_string($string);
}
?>
```

 Using HTTP authentication will impose approximately an 80 ms penalty when using `password_verify` with passwords hashed with BCRYPT, with the default cost of 10. This slowdown serves as a barrier for attackers to prevent them from trying to crack the passwords at maximum speed. Therefore, HTTP authentication is not a good solution on very busy sites, where you will probably prefer to use sessions (see the next section).

As you might expect at this point in the book, some of these examples are starting to get quite a bit longer. But don't be put off. The final 10 lines are simply from Example 10-21 in Chapter 10. They are there to sanitize the user input—very important.

The only lines to really concern yourself with at this point are the ones highlighted in bold. They start with the assigning of two variables, `$un_temp` and `$pw_temp`, using the submitted username and password. Next, a query is issued to MySQL to look up the user `$un_temp` and, if a result is returned, to assign the first row to `$row`. Because usernames are unique, there will be only one row.

Now all that's necessary is to check the hash value stored in the database, which happens to be in the fourth column—column 3 when you start from 0. `$row[3]` contains the previous hash value calculated with `password_hash` when the user created their password.

If the hash and the password just supplied by the user verify, `password_verify` will return TRUE and a friendly welcome string will be output, calling the user by their first name (see Figure 12-4). Otherwise, an error message is displayed.

You can try this out for yourself by calling up the program in your browser and entering a username of bsmith and password of mysecret (or pjones and acrobat), the values that were saved in the database by Example 12-3.

Figure 12-4. Bill Smith has now been authenticated

By sanitizing input immediately after it is encountered, you will block any malicious HTML, JavaScript, or MySQL attacks before they can get any further, and you will not have to sanitize this data again. If a user has characters such as < or & in their password (for example), these will be expanded to < or & by the htmlenti ties function—but as long as your code allows for strings that may end up larger than the provided input width, and as long as you always run passwords through this sanitization, you'll be just fine.

Using Sessions

Because your program can't tell what variables were set in other programs—or even what values the same program set the previous time it ran—you'll sometimes want to track what your users are doing from one web page to another. You can do this by setting hidden fields in a form, as seen in Chapter 10, and checking the values of the fields after the form is submitted, but PHP provides a much more powerful, more secure, and simpler solution in the form of *sessions*. These are groups of variables that are stored on the server but relate only to the current user. To ensure that the right variables are applied to the right users, PHP saves a cookie in the users' web browsers to uniquely identify them.

This cookie has meaning only to the web server and cannot be used to ascertain any information about a user. You might ask about those users who have cookies turned off. Well, in this day and age, anyone with cookies disabled should not expect to have the best browsing experience, and if you find them disabled you should probably inform such a user that they require cookies enabled if they wish to fully benefit from your site, rather than trying to find ways around the use of cookies, which could create security issues.

Starting a Session

Starting a session requires calling the PHP function session_start before any HTML has been output, similarly to how cookies are sent during header exchanges.

Then, to begin saving session variables, you just assign them as part of the $_SESSION array, like this:

```
$_SESSION['variable'] = $value;
```

They can then be read back just as easily in later program runs, like this:

```
$variable = $_SESSION['variable'];
```

Now assume that you have an application that always needs access to the first name and last name of each user, as stored in the table *users*, which you should have created a little earlier. Let's further modify *authenticate.php* from Example 12-4 to set up a session once a user has been authenticated.

Example 12-5 shows the changes needed. The only difference is the content of the **if (password_verify($pw_temp, $row[3]))** section, which we now start by opening a session and saving these variables into it. Type this program (or modify Example 12-4) and save it as *authenticate2.php*. But don't run it in your browser yet, as you will also need to create a second program in a moment.

Example 12-5. Setting a session after successful authentication

```php
<?php // authenticate2.php
  require_once 'login.php';
  $connection = new mysqli($hn, $un, $pw, $db);

  if ($connection->connect_error) die("Fatal Error");

  if (isset($_SERVER['PHP_AUTH_USER']) &&
      isset($_SERVER['PHP_AUTH_PW']))
  {
    $un_temp = mysql_entities_fix_string($connection, $_SERVER['PHP_AUTH_USER']);
    $pw_temp = mysql_entities_fix_string($connection, $_SERVER['PHP_AUTH_PW']);
    $query   = "SELECT * FROM users WHERE username='$un_temp'";
    $result  = $connection->query($query);

    if (!$result) die("User not found");
    elseif ($result->num_rows)
    {
      $row = $result->fetch_array(MYSQLI_NUM);

      $result->close();

      if (password_verify($pw_temp, $row[3]))
      {
        session_start();
        $_SESSION['forename'] = $row[0];
        $_SESSION['surname']  = $row[1];
        echo htmlspecialchars("$row[0] $row[1] : Hi $row[0],
          you are now logged in as '$row[2]'");
        die ("<p><a href='continue.php'>Click here to continue</a></p>");
```

```
    }
    else die("Invalid username/password combination");
  }
  else die("Invalid username/password combination");
}
else
{
  header('WWW-Authenticate: Basic realm="Restricted Area"');
  header('HTTP/1.0 401 Unauthorized');
  die ("Please enter your username and password");
}

$connection->close();

function mysql_entities_fix_string($connection, $string)
{
  return htmlentities(mysql_fix_string($connection, $string));
}

function mysql_fix_string($connection, $string)
{
  if (get_magic_quotes_gpc()) $string = stripslashes($string);
  return $connection->real_escape_string($string);
}
?>
```

One other addition to the program is the "Click here to continue" link with a destination URL of *continue.php*. This will be used to illustrate how the session will transfer
to another program or PHP web page. So, create *continue.php* by typing the program
in Example 12-6 and saving it.

Example 12-6. Retrieving session variables

```
<?php // continue.php
  session_start();

  if (isset($_SESSION['forename']))
  {
    $forename = htmlspecialchars($_SESSION['forename']);
    $surname  = htmlspecialchars($_SESSION['surname']);

    echo "Welcome back $forename.<br>
          Your full name is $forename $surname.<br>";
  }
  else echo "Please <a href=authenticate2.php>click here</a> to log in.";
?>
```

Now you are ready to call up *authenticate2.php* into your browser. Enter a username
of bsmith and password of mysecret (or pjones and acrobat) when prompted, and

click the link to load in *continue.php*. When your browser calls it up, the result should be something like Figure 12-5.

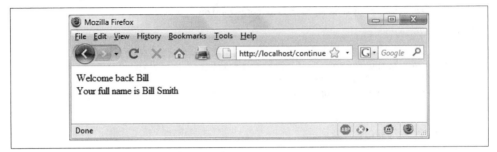

Figure 12-5. Maintaining user data with sessions

Sessions neatly confine to a single program the extensive code required to authenticate and log in a user. Once a user has been authenticated, and you have created a session, your program code becomes very simple indeed. You need only call up `session_start` and look in `$_SESSION` for any variables to which you need access.

In Example 12-6, a quick test of whether `$_SESSION['forename']` has a value is enough to let you know that the current user is authenticated, because session variables are stored on the server (unlike cookies, which are stored in the web browser) and can therefore be trusted.

If `$_SESSION['forename']` has not been assigned a value, no session is active, so the last line of code in Example 12-6 directs users to the login page at *authenticate2.php*.

Ending a Session

When the time comes to end a session, usually when a user requests to log out from your site, you can use the `session_destroy` function, as in Example 12-7. This example provides a useful function for totally destroying a session, logging a user out, and unsetting all session variables.

Example 12-7. A handy function to destroy a session and its data

```php
<?php
  function destroy_session_and_data()
  {
    session_start();
    $_SESSION = array();
    setcookie(session_name(), '', time() - 2592000, '/');
    session_destroy();
  }
?>
```

To see this in action, you could modify *continue.php* as in Example 12-8.

Example 12-8. Retrieving session variables and then destroying the session

```php
<?php
  session_start();

  if (isset($_SESSION['username']))
  {
    $forename = $_SESSION['forename'];
    $surname  = $_SESSION['surname'];

    destroy_session_and_data();

    echo htmlspecialchars("Welcome back $forename.<br>
            Your full name is $forename $surname.");

  }
  else echo "Please <a href='authenticate2.php'>click here</a> to log in.";

  function destroy_session_and_data()
  {
    $_SESSION = array();
    setcookie(session_name(), '', time() - 2592000, '/');
    session_destroy();
  }
?>
```

The first time you navigate from *authenticate2.php* to *continue.php*, it will display all the session variables. But, because of the call to destroy_session_and_data, if you then click your browser's Reload button, the session will have been destroyed and you'll be prompted to return to the login page.

Setting a Timeout

There are other times when you might wish to close a user's session yourself, such as when the user has forgotten or neglected to log out, and you want the program to do so for them for their own security. You do this by setting the timeout after which a logout will automatically occur if there has been no activity.

To do this, use the ini_set function as follows. This example sets the timeout to exactly one day:

```php
ini_set('session.gc_maxlifetime', 60 * 60 * 24);
```

If you wish to know what the current timeout period is, you can display it using the following:

```php
echo ini_get('session.gc_maxlifetime');
```

Session Security

Although I mentioned that once you had authenticated a user and set up a session, you could safely assume that the session variables were trustworthy, this isn't exactly the case. The reason is that it's possible to use *packet sniffing* (sampling of data) to discover session IDs passing across a network. Additionally, if the session ID is passed in the GET part of a URL, it might appear in external site server logs.

The only truly secure way of preventing these from being discovered is to implement *Transport Layer Security* (TLS, the more secure successor to the *Secure Sockets Layer*, or SSL) and run HTTPS instead of HTTP web pages. That's beyond the scope of this book, although you may like to take a look at the Apache documentation (*http://tinyurl.com/apachetls*) for details on setting up a secure web server.

Preventing session hijacking

When SSL is not a possibility, you can further authenticate users by storing their IP addresses along with their other details by adding a line such as the following when you store their sessions:

```
$_SESSION['ip'] = $_SERVER['REMOTE_ADDR'];
```

Then, as an extra check, whenever any page loads and a session is available, perform the following check. It calls the function `different_user` if the stored IP address doesn't match the current one:

```
if ($_SESSION['ip'] != $_SERVER['REMOTE_ADDR']) different_user();
```

What code you place in your `different_user` function is up to you. I recommend that you either delete the current session and ask the user to log in again due to a technical error or, if you have their email address, email them a link to confirm their identity, which will enable them to retain all the data in the session.

Of course, you need to be aware that users on the same proxy server, or sharing the same IP address on a home or business network, will have the same IP address. Again, if this is a problem for you, use HTTPS. You can also store a copy of the browser *user agent string* (a string that developers put in their browsers to identify them by type and version), which might also distinguish users due to the wide variety of browser types, versions, and computer platforms in use (although this is not a perfect solution, and the string will change if the browser auto-updates). Use the following to store the user agent:

```
$_SESSION['ua'] = $_SERVER['HTTP_USER_AGENT'];
```

And use this to compare the current user-agent string with the saved one:

```
if ($_SESSION['ua'] != $_SERVER['HTTP_USER_AGENT']) different_user();
```

Or, better still, combine the two checks like this and save the combination as a `hash` hexadecimal string:

```
$_SESSION['check'] = hash('ripemd128', $_SERVER['REMOTE_ADDR'] .
    $_SERVER['HTTP_USER_AGENT']);
```

And use this to compare the current and stored strings:

```
if ($_SESSION['check'] != hash('ripemd128', $_SERVER['REMOTE_ADDR'] .
    $_SERVER['HTTP_USER_AGENT'])) different_user();
```

Preventing session fixation

Session fixation happens when a malicious third party obtains a valid session ID (which could be server-generated) and makes the user authenticate themselves with that session ID, instead of authenticating with their own. It can happen when an attacker takes advantage of the ability to pass a session ID in the Get part of a URL, like this:

```
http://yourserver.com/authenticate.php?PHPSESSID=123456789
```

In this example, the made-up session ID of 123456789 is being passed to the server. Now, consider Example 12-9, which is susceptible to session fixation. To see how, type it and save it as *sessiontest.php*.

Example 12-9. A session susceptible to session fixation

```
<?php // sessiontest.php
  session_start();

  if (!isset($_SESSION['count'])) $_SESSION['count'] = 0;
  else ++$_SESSION['count'];

  echo $_SESSION['count'];
?>
```

Once it's saved, call it up in your browser using the following URL (prefacing it with the correct pathname, such as *http://localhost*):

```
sessiontest.php?PHPSESSID=1234
```

Press Reload a few times, and you'll see the counter increase. Now try browsing to:

```
sessiontest.php?PHPSESSID=5678
```

Press Reload a few times here, and you should see it count up again from 0. Leave the counter on a different number from the first URL, go back to the first URL, and see how the number changes back. You have created two different sessions of your own choosing here, and you could easily create as many as you needed.

The reason this approach is so dangerous is that a malicious attacker could try to distribute these types of URLs to unsuspecting users, and if any of them followed these links, the attacker would be able to come back and take over any sessions that had not been deleted or expired!

To prevent this, change the session ID using `session_regenerate_id` as soon as you can. This function keeps all current session variable values, but replaces the session ID with a new one that an attacker cannot know.

To do this, check for a special session variable that you arbitrarily invent. If it doesn't exist, you know that this is a new session, so you simply change the session ID and set the special session variable to note the change.

Example 12-10 shows how the code to do this might look, using the session variable `initiated`.

Example 12-10. Session regeneration

```php
<?php
  session_start();

  if (!isset($_SESSION['initiated']))
  {
    session_regenerate_id();
    $_SESSION['initiated'] = 1;
  }

  if (!isset($_SESSION['count'])) $_SESSION['count'] = 0;
  else ++$_SESSION['count'];

  echo $_SESSION['count'];
?>
```

This way, an attacker can come back to your site using any of the session IDs that they generated, but none of them will call up another user's session, as they will all have been replaced with regenerated IDs.

Forcing cookie-only sessions

If you are prepared to require your users to enable cookies on your website, you can use the `ini_set` function, like this:

```php
ini_set('session.use_only_cookies', 1);
```

With that setting, the `?PHPSESSID=` trick will be completely ignored. If you use this security measure, I also recommend that you inform your users that your site requires cookies (but only if the user has cookies disabled), so they know what's wrong if they don't get the results they want.

Using a shared server

On a server shared with other accounts, you will not want to have all your session data saved into the same directory as theirs. Instead, you should choose a directory to which only your account has access (and that is not web-visible) to store your sessions, by placing an `ini_set` call near the start of your program, like this:

```
ini_set('session.save_path', '/home/user/myaccount/sessions');
```

The configuration option will keep this new value only during the program's execution, and the original configuration will be restored at the program's ending.

This sessions folder can fill up quickly; you may wish to periodically clear out older sessions according to how busy your server gets. The more it's used, the less time you will want to keep a session stored.

> Remember that your websites can and will be subject to hacking attempts. There are automated bots running riot around the internet, trying to find sites vulnerable to exploits. So whatever you do, whenever you are handling data that is not 100 percent generated within your own program, you should always treat it with the utmost caution.

At this point, you should now have a very good grasp of both PHP and MySQL, so in the next chapter it's time to introduce the third major technology covered by this book, JavaScript.

Questions

1. Why must a cookie be transferred at the start of a program?
2. Which PHP function stores a cookie in a web browser?
3. How can you destroy a cookie?
4. Where are the username and password stored in a PHP program when you are using HTTP authentication?
5. Why is the `password_hash` function a powerful security measure?
6. What is meant by *salting* a string?
7. What is a PHP session?
8. How do you initiate a PHP session?
9. What is session hijacking?
10. What is session fixation?

See "Chapter 12 Answers" on page 722 in Appendix A for the answers to these .

CHAPTER 13

Exploring JavaScript

JavaScript brings a dynamic functionality to your websites. Every time you see something pop up when you mouse over an item in the browser, or see new text, colors, or images appear on the page in front of your eyes, or grab an object on the page and drag it to a new location—all those things are done through JavaScript. It offers effects that are not otherwise possible, because it runs inside the browser and has direct access to all the elements in a web document.

JavaScript first appeared in the Netscape Navigator browser in 1995, coinciding with the addition of support for Java technology in the browser. Because of the initial incorrect impression that JavaScript was a spin-off of Java, there has been some long-term confusion over their relationship. However, the naming was just a marketing ploy to help the new scripting language benefit from the popularity of the Java programming language.

JavaScript gained new power when the HTML elements of the web page got a more formal, structured definition in what is called the *Document Object Model* (DOM). The DOM makes it relatively easy to add a new paragraph or focus on a piece of text and change it.

Because both JavaScript and PHP support much of the structured programming syntax used by the C programming language, they look very similar to each other. They are both fairly high-level languages, too; for instance, they are weakly typed, so it's easy to change a variable to a new type just by using it in a new context.

Now that you have learned PHP, you should find JavaScript even easier. And you'll be glad you did, because it's at the heart of the asynchronous communication technology that provides the fluid web frontends that (along with HTML5 features) savvy web users expect these days.

JavaScript and HTML Text

JavaScript is a client-side scripting language that runs entirely inside the web browser. To call it up, you place it between opening <script> and closing </script> HTML tags. A typical HTML 4.01 "Hello World" document using JavaScript might look like Example 13-1.

Example 13-1. "Hello World" displayed using JavaScript

```
<html>
  <head><title>Hello World</title></head>
  <body>
    <script type="text/javascript">
      document.write("Hello World")
    </script>
    <noscript>
      Your browser doesn't support or has disabled JavaScript
    </noscript>
  </body>
</html>
```

 You may have seen web pages that use the HTML tag <script language="javascript">, but that usage has now been deprecated. This example uses the more recent and preferred <script type="text/javascript">, or you can just use <script> on its own if you like.

Within the <script> tags is a single line of JavaScript code that uses its equivalent of the PHP echo or print commands, document.write. As you'd expect, it simply outputs the supplied string to the current document, where it is displayed.

You may also have noticed that, unlike with PHP, there is no trailing semicolon (;). This is because a newline serves the same purpose as a semicolon in JavaScript. However, if you wish to have more than one statement on a single line, you do need to place a semicolon after each command except the last one. Of course, if you wish, you can add a semicolon to the end of every statement, and your JavaScript will work fine.

The other thing to note in this example is the <noscript> and </noscript> pair of tags. These are used when you wish to offer alternative HTML to users whose browsers do not support JavaScript or who have it disabled. Using these tags is up to you, as they are not required, but you really ought to use them because it's usually not that difficult to provide static HTML alternatives to the operations you provide using JavaScript. However, the remaining examples in this book will omit <noscript> tags, because we're focusing on what you can do with JavaScript, not what you can do without it.

When Example 13-1 is loaded, a web browser with JavaScript enabled will output the following (see Figure 13-1):

Hello World

Figure 13-1. JavaScript, enabled and working

A browser with JavaScript disabled will display this message (see Figure 13-2):

Your browser doesn't support or has disabled JavaScript

Figure 13-2. JavaScript has been disabled

Using Scripts Within a Document Head

In addition to placing a script within the body of a document, you can put it in the <head> section, which is the ideal place if you wish to execute a script when a page loads. If you place critical code and functions there, you can also ensure that they are ready to use immediately by any other script sections in the document that rely on them.

Another reason for placing a script in the document head is to enable JavaScript to write things such as meta tags into the <head> section, because the location of your script is the part of the document it writes to by default.

Older and Nonstandard Browsers

If you need to support browsers that do not offer scripting (very unlikely in this day and age), you will need to use the HTML comment tags (<!-- and -->) to prevent them from encountering script code that they should not see. Example 13-2 shows how you add them to your script code.

Example 13-2. The "Hello World" example modified for non-JavaScript browsers

```
<html>
  <head><title>Hello World</title></head>
  <body>
    <script type="text/javascript"><!--
      document.write("Hello World")
    // -->
    </script>
  </body>
</html>
```

Here an opening HTML comment tag (`<!--`) has been added directly after the opening `<script>` statement and a closing comment tag (`// -->`) has been added directly before the script is closed with `</script>`.

The double forward slash (`//`) is used by JavaScript to indicate that the rest of the line is a comment. It is there so that browsers that *do* support JavaScript will ignore the following `-->`, but non-JavaScript browsers will ignore the preceding `//` and act on the `-->` by closing the HTML comment.

Although the solution is a little convoluted, all you really need to remember is to use the two following lines to enclose your JavaScript when you wish to support very old or nonstandard browsers:

```
<script type="text/javascript"><!--
  (Your JavaScript goes here...)
// -->
</script>
```

However, the use of these comments is unnecessary for any browser released over the past several years.

 There are a couple of other scripting languages you should know about. These include Microsoft's VBScript, which is based on the Visual Basic programming language, and Tcl, a rapid prototyping language. They are called up in a similar way to JavaScript, except they use types of `text/vbscript` and `text/tcl`, respectively. VBScript works only in Internet Explorer up to version 10, after which it was deprecated; use of it in other browsers requires a plug-in. Tcl always needs a plug-in. Both should be considered nonstandard, and neither is covered in this book.

Including JavaScript Files

In addition to writing JavaScript code directly in HTML documents, you can include files of JavaScript code either from your website or from anywhere on the internet. The syntax for this is as follows:

```
<script type="text/javascript" src="script.js"></script>
```

Or, to pull a file in from the internet, use this:

```
<script type="text/javascript" src="http://someserver.com/script.js">
</script>
```

As for the script files themselves, they must *not* include any `<script>` or `</script>` tags, because they are unnecessary: the browser already knows that a JavaScript file is being loaded. Putting them in the JavaScript files will cause an error.

Including script files is the preferred way for you to use third-party JavaScript files on your website.

It is possible to leave out the `type="text/javascript"` parameter; all modern browsers default to assuming that the script contains JavaScript.

Debugging JavaScript Errors

When you're learning JavaScript, it's important to be able to track typing or other coding errors. Unlike PHP, which displays error messages in the browser, JavaScript handles error messages in a way that changes according to the browser used. Table 13-1 lists how to access JavaScript error messages in the most commonly used browsers.

Table 13-1. Accessing JavaScript error messages in different browsers

Browser	How to access JavaScript error messages
Apple Safari	Safari does not have an Error Console enabled by default, but you can turn it on by selecting Safari → Preferences → Advanced → "Show Developer menu in menu bar." However, you may prefer to use the Firebug Lite JavaScript module (*https://getfire bug.com/firebuglite*), which many people find easier to use.
Google Chrome	Press Ctrl-Shift-J on a PC, or Command-Shift-J on a Mac.
Microsoft Internet Explorer & Edge	Press F12 to call up the DevTools Console.
Mozilla Firefox	Press Ctrl-Shift-J on a PC, or Command-Shift-J on a Mac.
Opera	Select Tools → Advanced → Error Console.

Each of these consoles is quite different, so please refer to the browser developers' documentation on their websites for full details on using them.

Using Comments

Because of their shared inheritance from the C programming language, PHP and JavaScript have many similarities, one of which is commenting. First, there's the single-line comment, like this:

```
// This is a comment
```

This style uses a pair of forward slash characters (//) to inform JavaScript that everything that follows is to be ignored. You also have multiline comments, like this:

```
/* This is a section
   of multiline comments
   that will not be
   interpreted */
```

You start a multiline comment with the sequence /* and end it with */. Just remember that you cannot nest multiline comments, so make sure that you don't comment out large sections of code that already contain multiline comments.

Semicolons

Unlike PHP, JavaScript generally does not require semicolons if you have only one statement on a line. Therefore, the following is valid:

```
x += 10
```

However, when you wish to place more than one statement on a line, you must separate them with semicolons, like this:

```
x += 10; y -= 5; z = 0
```

You can normally leave the final semicolon off, because the newline terminates the final statement.

 There are exceptions to the semicolon rule. If you write JavaScript bookmarklets, or end a statement with a variable or function reference, *and* the first character of the line below is a left parenthesis or bracket, you *must* remember to append a semicolon or the JavaScript will fail. So, when in doubt, use a semicolon.

Variables

No particular character identifies a variable in JavaScript as the dollar sign does in PHP. Instead, variables use the following naming rules:

- A variable may include only the letters a-z, A-Z, 0-9, the $ symbol, and the underscore (_).

- No other characters, such as spaces or punctuation, are allowed in a variable name.

- The first character of a variable name can be only a-z, A-Z, $, or _ (no numbers).

- Names are case-sensitive. Count, count, and COUNT are all different variables.

- There is no set limit on variable name lengths.

And yes, you're right: a $ is there in that list of allowed characters. It *is* allowed by JavaScript and *may* be the first character of a variable or function name. Although I don't recommend keeping the $ characters, this rule lets you port a lot of PHP code more quickly to JavaScript.

String Variables

JavaScript string variables should be enclosed in either single or double quotation marks, like this:

```
greeting = "Hello there"
warning  = 'Be careful'
```

You may include a single quote within a double-quoted string or a double quote within a single-quoted string. But you must escape a quote of the same type by using the backslash character, like this:

```
greeting = "\"Hello there\" is a greeting"
warning  = '\'Be careful\' is a warning'
```

To read from a string variable, you can assign it to another one, like this:

```
newstring = oldstring
```

or you can use it in a function, like this:

```
status = "All systems are working"
document.write(status)
```

Numeric Variables

Creating a numeric variable is as simple as assigning a value, like these examples:

```
count       = 42
temperature = 98.4
```

Like strings, numeric variables can be read from and used in expressions and functions.

Arrays

JavaScript arrays are also very similar to those in PHP, in that an array can contain string or numeric data, as well as other arrays. To assign values to an array, use the following syntax (which in this case creates an array of strings):

```
toys = ['bat', 'ball', 'whistle', 'puzzle', 'doll']
```

To create a multidimensional array, nest smaller arrays within a larger one. So, to create a two-dimensional array containing the colors of a single face of a scrambled Rubik's Cube (where the colors red, green, orange, yellow, blue, and white are represented by their capitalized initial letters), you could use the following code:

```
face =
[
  ['R', 'G', 'Y'],
  ['W', 'R', 'O'],
  ['Y', 'W', 'G']
]
```

The previous example has been formatted to make it obvious what is going on, but it could also be written like this:

```
face = [['R', 'G', 'Y'], ['W', 'R', 'O'], ['Y', 'W', 'G']]
```

or even like this:

```
top = ['R', 'G', 'Y']
mid = ['W', 'R', 'O']
bot = ['Y', 'W', 'G']

face = [top, mid, bot]
```

To access the element two down and three along in this matrix, you would use the following (because array elements start at position 0):

```
document.write(face[1][2])
```

This statement will output the letter **O** for *orange*.

JavaScript arrays are powerful storage structures, so Chapter 15 discusses them in much greater depth.

Operators

Operators in JavaScript, as in PHP, can involve mathematics, changes to strings, and comparison and logical operations (and, or, etc.). JavaScript mathematical operators look a lot like plain arithmetic—for instance, the following statement outputs 15:

```
document.write(13 + 2)
```

The following sections teach you about the various operators.

Arithmetic Operators

Arithmetic operators are used to perform mathematics. You can use them for the main four operations (addition, subtraction, multiplication, and division) as well as to find the modulus (the remainder after a division) and to increment or decrement a value (see Table 13-2).

Table 13-2. Arithmetic operators

Operator	Description	Example
+	Addition	j + 12
-	Subtraction	j - 22
*	Multiplication	j * 7
/	Division	j / 3.13
%	Modulus (division remainder)	j % 6
++	Increment	++j
--	Decrement	--j

Assignment Operators

The *assignment operators* are used to assign values to variables. They start with the very simple =, and move on to +=, -=, and so on. The operator += adds the value on the right side to the variable on the left, instead of totally replacing the value on the left. Thus, if count starts with the value 6, the statement:

```
count += 1
```

sets count to 7, just like the more familiar assignment statement:

```
count = count + 1
```

Table 13-3 lists the various assignment operators available.

Table 13-3. Assignment operators

Operator	Example	Equivalent to
=	j = 99	j = 99
+=	j += 2	j = j + 2
+=	j += 'string'	j = j + 'string'
-=	j -= 12	j = j - 12
*=	j *= 2	j = j * 2
/=	j /= 6	j = j / 6
%=	j %= 7	j = j % 7

Comparison Operators

Comparison operators are generally used inside a construct such as an `if` statement, where you need to compare two items. For example, you may wish to know whether a variable you have been incrementing has reached a specific value, or whether another variable is less than a set value, and so on (see Table 13-4).

Table 13-4. Comparison operators

Operator	Description	Example
==	Is *equal* to	j == 42
!=	Is *not equal* to	j != 17
>	Is *greater than*	j > 0
<	Is *less than*	j < 100
>=	Is *greater than or equal* to	j >= 23
<=	Is *less than or equal* to	j <= 13
===	Is *equal* to (and of the same type)	j === 56
!==	Is *not equal* to (and of the same type)	j !== '1'

Logical Operators

Unlike PHP, JavaScript's *logical operators* do not include and and or equivalents to && and ||, and there is no xor operator (see Table 13-5).

Table 13-5. Logical operators

Operator	Description	Example
&&	And	j == 1 && k == 2
||	Or	j < 100 || j > 0
!	Not	! (j == k)

Incrementing, Decrementing, and Shorthand Assignment

The following forms of post- and pre-incrementing and decrementing you learned to use in PHP are also supported by JavaScript, as are shorthand assignment operators:

```
++x
--y
x += 22
y -= 3
```

String Concatenation

JavaScript handles string concatenation slightly differently from PHP. Instead of the . (period) operator, it uses the plus sign (+), like this:

```
document.write("You have " + messages + " messages.")
```

Assuming that the variable `messages` is set to the value 3, the output from this line of code will be as follows:

You have 3 messages.

Just as you can add a value to a numeric variable with the += operator, you can also append one string to another the same way:

```
name =  "James"
name += " Dean"
```

Escape Characters

Escape characters, which you've seen used to insert quotation marks in strings, can also be used to insert various special characters such as tabs, newlines, and carriage returns. Here is an example using tabs to lay out a heading—it is included here merely to illustrate escapes, because in web pages, there are better ways to do layout:

```
heading = "Name\tAge\tLocation"
```

Table 13-6 details the escape characters available.

Table 13-6. JavaScript's escape characters

Character	Meaning
\b	Backspace
\f	Form feed
\n	Newline
\r	Carriage return
\t	Tab
\'	Single quote (or apostrophe)
\"	Double quote
\\	Backslash
\XXX	An octal number between 000 and 377 that represents the Latin-1 character equivalent (such as \251 for the © symbol)
\xXX	A hexadecimal number between 00 and FF that represents the Latin-1 character equivalent (such as \xA9 for the © symbol)
\uXXXX	A hexadecimal number between 0000 and FFFF that represents the Unicode character equivalent (such as \u00A9 for the © symbol)

Variable Typing

Like PHP, JavaScript is a very loosely typed language; the *type* of a variable is determined only when a value is assigned and can change as the variable appears in different contexts. Usually, you don't have to worry about the type; JavaScript figures out what you want and just does it.

Take a look at Example 13-3, in which:

1. The variable n is assigned the string value `'838102050'`. The next line prints out its value, and the `typeof` operator is used to look up the type.

2. n is given the value returned when the numbers 12345 and 67890 are multiplied together. This value is also 838102050, but it is a number, not a string. The type of the variable is then looked up and displayed.

3. Some text is appended to the number n and the result is displayed.

Example 13-3. Setting a variable's type by assignment

```
<script>
  n = '838102050'        // Set 'n' to a string
  document.write('n = ' + n + ', and is a ' + typeof n + '<br>')

  n = 12345 * 67890;     // Set 'n' to a number
  document.write('n = ' + n + ', and is a ' + typeof n + '<br>')

  n += ' plus some text' // Change 'n' from a number to a string
  document.write('n = ' + n + ', and is a ' + typeof n + '<br>')
</script>
```

The output from this script looks like this:

```
n = 838102050, and is a string
n = 838102050, and is a number
n = 838102050 plus some text, and is a string
```

If there is ever any doubt about the type of a variable, or you need to ensure that a variable has a particular type, you can force it to that type by using statements such as the following (which respectively turn a string into a number and a number into a string):

```
n = "123"
n *= 1     // Convert 'n' into a number

n = 123
n += ""    // Convert 'n' into a string
```

Or, of course, you can always look up a variable's type by using the `typeof` operator.

Functions

As with PHP, JavaScript functions are used to separate out sections of code that perform a particular task. To create a function, declare it in the manner shown in Example 13-4.

Example 13-4. A simple function declaration

```
<script>
  function product(a, b)
  {
    return a*b
  }
</script>
```

This function takes the two parameters passed, multiplies them together, and returns the product.

Global Variables

Global variables are ones defined outside of any functions (or defined within functions, but without the var keyword). They can be defined in the following ways:

```
    a = 123                // Global scope
var b = 456                // Global scope
if (a == 123) var c = 789 // Global scope
```

Regardless of whether you are using the var keyword, as long as a variable is defined outside of a function, it is global in scope. This means that every part of a script can have access to it.

Local Variables

Parameters passed to a function automatically have *local* scope; that is, they can be referenced only from within that function. However, there is one exception. Arrays are passed to a function by reference, so if you modify any elements in an array parameter, the elements of the original array will be modified.

To define a local variable that has scope only within the current function, and has not been passed as a parameter, use the var keyword. Example 13-5 shows a function that creates one variable with global scope and two with local scope.

Example 13-5. A function creating variables with global and local scope

```
<script>
  function test()
```

```
    {
        a = 123                 // Global scope
      var b = 456               // Local scope
      if (a == 123) var c = 789 // Local scope
    }
</script>
```

To test whether scope setting has worked in PHP, we can use the `isset` function. But in JavaScript there is no such function, so Example 13-6 makes use of the `typeof` operator, which returns the string `undefined` when a variable is not defined.

Example 13-6. Checking the scope of the variables defined in the function test

```
<script>
  test()

  if (typeof a != 'undefined') document.write('a = "' + a + '"<br>')
  if (typeof b != 'undefined') document.write('b = "' + b + '"<br>')
  if (typeof c != 'undefined') document.write('c = "' + c + '"<br>')

  function test()
  {
    a    = 123
    var b = 456

    if (a == 123) var c = 789
  }
</script>
```

The output from this script is the following single line:

```
    a = "123"
```

This shows that only the variable a was given global scope, which is exactly what we would expect, since the variables b and c were given local scope by being prefaced with the var keyword.

If your browser issues a warning about b being undefined, the warning is correct but can be ignored.

The Document Object Model

The designers of JavaScript were very smart. Rather than just creating yet another scripting language (which would have still been a pretty good improvement at the time), they had the vision to build it around the already-existing HTML Document Object Model. This breaks down the parts of an HTML document into discrete *objects*, each with its own *properties* and *methods* and each subject to JavaScript's control.

JavaScript separates objects, properties, and methods by using a period (one good reason why + is the string concatenation operator in JavaScript, rather than the period). For example, let's consider a business card as an object we'll call card. This object contains properties such as a name, address, phone number, and so on. In the syntax of JavaScript, these properties would look like this:

```
card.name
card.phone
card.address
```

Its methods are functions that retrieve, change, and otherwise act on the properties. For instance, to invoke a method that displays the properties of the object card, you might use syntax such as this:

```
card.display()
```

Have a look at some of the earlier examples in this chapter and notice where the statement document.write is used. Now that you understand how JavaScript is based around objects, you will see that write is actually a method of the document object.

Within JavaScript, there is a hierarchy of parent and child objects, which is what is known as the Document Object Model (see Figure 13-3).

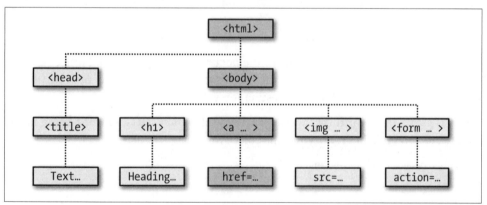

Figure 13-3. Example of DOM object hierarchy

The figure uses HTML tags that you are already familiar with to illustrate the parent/child relationship between the various objects in a document. For example, a URL within a link is part of the body of an HTML document. In JavaScript, it is referenced like this:

```
url = document.links.linkname.href
```

Notice how this follows the central column down. The first part, document, refers to the <html> and <body> tags; links.linkname refers to the <a> tag and href to the href attribute.

Let's turn this into some HTML and a script to read a link's properties. Type Example 13-7 and save it as *linktest.html*; then call it up in your browser.

Example 13-7. Reading a link URL with JavaScript

```html
<html>
  <head>
    <title>Link Test</title>
  </head>
  <body>
    <a id="mylink" href="http://mysite.com">Click me</a><br>
    <script>
      url = document.links.mylink.href
      document.write('The URL is ' + url)
    </script>
  </body>
</html>
```

Note the short form of the `<script>` tags, where I have omitted the parameter `type="text/JavaScript"` to save you some typing. If you wish, just for the purposes of testing this (and other examples), you could also omit everything outside of the `<script>` and `</script>` tags. The output from this example is as follows:

Click me
The URL is http://mysite.com

The second line of output comes from the `document.write` method. Notice how the code follows the document tree down from `document` to `links` to `mylink` (the `id` given to the link) to `href` (the URL destination value).

There is also a short form that works equally well, which starts with the value in the `id` attribute: `mylink.href`. So, you can replace this:

```
url = document.links.mylink.href
```

with the following:

```
url = mylink.href
```

Another Use for the $ Symbol

As mentioned earlier, the $ symbol is allowed in JavaScript variable and function names. Because of this, you may sometimes encounter strange-looking code like this:

```
url = $('mylink').href
```

Some enterprising programmers have decided that the `getElementById` function is so prevalent in JavaScript that they have written a function to replace it called $, like in jQuery (although jQuery uses the $ for much more than that—see Chapter 21), as shown in Example 13-8.

Example 13-8. A replacement function for the getElementById method

```
<script>
  function $(id)
  {
    return document.getElementById(id)
  }
</script>
```

Therefore, as long as you have included the $ function in your code, syntax such as this:

```
$('mylink').href
```

can replace code such as this:

```
document.getElementById('mylink').href
```

Using the DOM

The `links` object is actually an array of URLs, so the `mylink` URL in Example 13-7 can also be safely referred to in all browsers in the following way (because it's the first, and only, link):

```
url = document.links[0].href
```

If you want to know how many links there are in an entire document, you can query the `length` property of the `links` object like this:

```
numlinks = document.links.length
```

You can extract and display all links in a document like this:

```
for (j=0 ; j < document.links.length ; ++j)
  document.write(document.links[j].href + '<br>')
```

The `length` of something is a property of every array, and many objects as well. For example, the number of items in your browser's web history can be queried like this:

```
document.write(history.length)
```

To stop websites from snooping on your browsing history, the `history` object stores only the number of sites in the array: you cannot read from or write to these values. But you can replace the current page with one from the history, if you know what position it has within the history. This can be very useful in cases in which you know that certain pages in the history came from your site, or you simply wish to send the browser back one or more pages, which you do with the `go` method of the `history` object. For example, to send the browser back three pages, issue the following command:

```
history.go(-3)
```

You can also use the following methods to move back or forward a page at a time:

```
history.back()
history.forward()
```

In a similar manner, you can replace the currently loaded URL with one of your choosing, like this:

```
document.location.href = 'http://google.com'
```

Of course, there's a whole lot more to the DOM than reading and modifying links. As you progress through the following chapters on JavaScript, you'll become quite familiar with the DOM and how to access it.

About document.write

When teaching programming it's necessary to have a quick and easy way to display the results of expressions. In PHP (for example) there are the `echo` and `print` statements, which simply send text to the browser, so that's easy. In JavaScript, though, there are the following alternatives.

Using console.log

The `console.log` function will output the result of any value or expression passed to it in the console of the current browser. This is a special mode with a frame or window separate to the browser window, and in which errors and other messages can be made to display. While great for experienced programmers, it is not ideal for beginners because calling up the console is done differently in all browsers, it works differently in all browsers, and the output is not near the web content in the browser.

Using alert

The `alert` function displays values or expressions passed to it in a pop-up window, which requires you to click a button to close. Clearly this can become quite irritating very quickly, and it has the downside of displaying only the current message—previous ones are erased.

Writing into Elements

It is possible to write directly into the text of an HTML element, which is a fairly elegant solution (and the best one for production websites)—except that for this book every example would require such an element to be created, and some lines of JavaScript code to access it. This gets in the way of teaching the core of an example and would make the code look overly cumbersome and confusing.

Using document.write

The `document.write` function writes a value or expression at the current browser location, and is therefore the perfect choice for quickly displaying results. It keeps all the examples short and sweet, by placing the output right there in the browser next to the web content and code.

You may, however, have heard that this function is regarded as unsafe by some developers, because when you call it after a web page is fully loaded, it will overwrite the current document. While this is correct, it doesn't apply to any of the examples in this book, because they all use `document.write` the way it was originally intended: as part of the page creation process, calling it only before the page has completed loading and displaying.

However, although I use `document.write` in this way for simple examples, I never use it in production code (except in the very rarest of circumstances where it actually is necessary). Instead, I almost always use the preceding option of writing directly into a specially prepared element, as per the more complex examples in Chapter 17 onward (which access the `innerHTML` property of elements for program output).

So, please remember that where you see `document.write` being called in this book, it is there only to simplify an example, and I recommend that you also use the function only in this same way—for obtaining quick test results.

With that caveat explained, in the following chapter we'll continue our exploration of JavaScript by looking at how to control program flow and write expressions.

Questions

1. Which tags do you use to enclose JavaScript code?
2. By default, to which part of a document will JavaScript code output?
3. How can you include JavaScript code from another source in your documents?
4. Which JavaScript function is the equivalent of `echo` or `print` in PHP?
5. How can you create a comment in JavaScript?
6. What is the JavaScript string concatenation operator?
7. Which keyword can you use within a JavaScript function to define a variable that has local scope?
8. Give two cross-browser methods to display the URL assigned to the link with an id of `thislink`.
9. Which two JavaScript commands will make the browser load the previous page in its history array?
10. What JavaScript command would you use to replace the current document with the main page at the *oreilly.com* website?

See "Chapter 13 Answers" on page 723 in Appendix A for the answers to these questions.

CHAPTER 14

Expressions and Control Flow in JavaScript

In the previous chapter, I introduced the basics of JavaScript and the DOM. Now it's time to look at how to construct complex expressions in JavaScript and how to control the program flow of your scripts by using conditional statements.

Expressions

JavaScript expressions are very similar to those in PHP. As you learned in Chapter 4, an expression is a combination of values, variables, operators, and functions that results in a value; the result can be a number, a string, or a Boolean value (which evaluates to either true or false).

Example 14-1 shows some simple expressions. For each line, it prints out a letter between a and d, followed by a colon and the result of the expressions. The <br> tag is there to create a line break and separate the output into four lines (remember that both <br> and <br /> are acceptable in HTML5, so I chose to use the former style for brevity).

Example 14-1. Four simple Boolean expressions

```
<script>
  document.write("a: " + (42 > 3) + "<br>")
  document.write("b: " + (91 < 4) + "<br>")
  document.write("c: " + (8 == 2) + "<br>")
  document.write("d: " + (4 < 17) + "<br>")
</script>
```

The output from this code is as follows:

```
a: true
b: false
```

```
c: false
d: true
```

Notice that both expressions a: and d: evaluate to true, but b: and c: evaluate to false. Unlike PHP (which would print the number 1 and nothing, respectively), the actual strings true and false are displayed.

In JavaScript, when you are checking whether a value is true or false, all values evaluate to true except the following, which evaluate to false: the string false itself, 0, -0, the empty string, null, undefined, and NaN (Not a Number, a computer engineering concept for the result of an illegal floating-point operation such as division by zero).

Note how I am referring to true and false in lowercase. This is because, unlike in PHP, these values *must* be in lowercase in JavaScript. Therefore, only the first of the two following statements will display, printing the lowercase word true, because the second will cause a 'TRUE' is not defined error:

```
if (1 == true) document.write('true') // True
if (1 == TRUE) document.write('TRUE') // Will cause an error
```

 Remember that any code snippets you wish to type and try for yourself in an HTML file need to be enclosed within <script> and </script> tags.

Literals and Variables

The simplest form of an expression is a *literal*, which means something that evaluates to itself, such as the number 22 or the string Press Enter. An expression could also be a variable, which evaluates to the value that has been assigned to it. They are both types of expressions, because they return a value.

Example 14-2 shows three different literals and two variables, all of which return values, albeit of different types.

Example 14-2. Five types of literals

```
<script>
  myname = "Peter"
  myage  = 24
  document.write("a: " + 42      + "<br>") // Numeric literal
  document.write("b: " + "Hi"    + "<br>") // String literal
  document.write("c: " + true    + "<br>") // Constant literal
  document.write("d: " + myname  + "<br>") // String variable
  document.write("e: " + myage   + "<br>") // Numeric variable
</script>
```

And, as you'd expect, you see a return value from all of these in the following output:

```
a: 42
b: Hi
c: true
d: Peter
e: 24
```

Operators let you create more complex expressions that evaluate to useful results. When you combine assignment or control-flow constructs with expressions, the result is a *statement*.

Example 14-3 shows one of each. The first assigns the result of the expression 366 - day_number to the variable days_to_new_year, and the second outputs a friendly message only if the expression days_to_new_year < 30 evaluates to true.

Example 14-3. Two simple JavaScript statements

```
<script>
  days_to_new_year = 366 - day_number;
  if (days_to_new_year < 30) document.write("It's nearly New Year")
</script>
```

Operators

JavaScript offers a lot of powerful operators, ranging from arithmetic, string, and logical operators to assignment, comparison, and more (see Table 14-1).

Table 14-1. JavaScript operator types

Operator	Description	Example
Arithmetic	Basic mathematics	a + b
Array	Array manipulation	a + b
Assignment	Assign values	a = b + 23
Bitwise	Manipulate bits within bytes	12 ^ 9
Comparison	Compare two values	a < b
Increment/decrement	Add or subtract one	a++
Logical	Boolean	a && b
String	Concatenation	a + 'string'

Each operator takes a different number of operands:

- *Unary* operators, such as incrementing (a++) or negation (-a), take a single operand.

- *Binary* operators, which represent the bulk of JavaScript operators—including addition, subtraction, multiplication, and division—take two operands.

- The one *ternary* operator, which takes the form ? x : y, requires three operands. It's a terse single-line if statement that chooses between two expressions depending on a third one.

Operator Precedence

Like PHP, JavaScript utilizes operator precedence, in which some operators in an expression are processed before others and are therefore evaluated first. Table 14-2 lists JavaScript's operators and their precedences.

Table 14-2. Precedence of JavaScript operators (high to low)

Operator(s)	Type(s)
( ) [ ] .	Parentheses, call, and member
++ --	Increment/decrement
+ - ~ !	Unary, bitwise, and logical
* / %	Arithmetic
+ -	Arithmetic and string
<< >> >>>	Bitwise
< > <= >=	Comparison
== != === !==	Comparison
& ^ |	Bitwise
&&	Logical
||	Logical
? :	Ternary
= += -= *= /= %=	Assignment
<<= >>= >>>= &= ^= |=	Assignment
,	Separator

Associativity

Most JavaScript operators are processed in order from left to right in an equation. But some operators require processing from right to left instead. The direction of processing is called the operator's *associativity*.

This associativity becomes important where you do not explicitly force precedence. For example, look at the following assignment operators, by which three variables are all set to the value 0:

```
level = score = time = 0
```

This multiple assignment is possible only because the rightmost part of the expression is evaluated first and then processing continues in a right-to-left direction. Table 14-3 lists the JavaScript operators and their associativity.

Table 14-3. Operators and associativity

Operator	Description	Associativity
++ --	Increment and decrement	None
new	Create a new object	Right
+ - ~ !	Unary and bitwise	Right
? :	Ternary	Right
= *= /= %= += -=	Assignment	Right
<<= >>= >>>= &= ^= |=	Assignment	Right
,	Separator	Left
+ - * / %	Arithmetic	Left
<< >> >>>	Bitwise	Left
< <= > >= == != === !==	Arithmetic	Left

Relational Operators

Relational operators test two operands and return a Boolean result of either `true` or `false`. There are three types of relational operators: *equality*, *comparison*, and *logical*.

Equality operators

The equality operator is `==` (which should not be confused with the `=` assignment operator). In Example 14-4, the first statement assigns a value, and the second tests it for equality. As it stands, nothing will be printed out, because `month` is assigned the string value `July`, and therefore the check for it having a value of `October` will fail.

Example 14-4. Assigning a value and testing for equality

```
<script>
  month = "July"
  if (month == "October") document.write("It's the Fall")
</script>
```

If the two operands of an equality expression are of different types, JavaScript will convert them to whatever type makes best sense to it. For example, any strings composed entirely of numbers will be converted to numbers whenever compared with a number. In Example 14-5, `a` and `b` are two different values (one is a number and the other is a string), and we would therefore normally expect neither of the `if` statements to output a result.

Example 14-5. The equality and identity operators

```
<script>
  a = 3.1415927
  b = "3.1415927"
```

```
  if (a == b)  document.write("1")
  if (a === b) document.write("2")
</script>
```

However, if you run the example, you will see that it outputs the number **1**, which means that the first `if` statement evaluated to `true`. This is because the string value of b was first temporarily converted to a number, and therefore both halves of the equation had a numerical value of 3.1415927.

In contrast, the second `if` statement uses the *identity* operator, three equals signs in a row, which prevents JavaScript from automatically converting types. a and b are therefore found to be different, so nothing is output.

As with forcing operator precedence, whenever you're in doubt about how JavaScript will convert operand types, you can use the identity operator to turn this behavior off.

Comparison operators

Using comparison operators, you can test for more than just equality and inequality. JavaScript also gives you > (is greater than), < (is less than), >= (is greater than or equal to), and <= (is less than or equal to) to play with. Example 14-6 shows these operators in use.

Example 14-6. The four comparison operators

```
<script>
  a = 7; b = 11
  if (a > b)  document.write("a is greater than b<br>")
  if (a < b)  document.write("a is less than b<br>")
  if (a >= b) document.write("a is greater than or equal to b<br>")
  if (a <= b) document.write("a is less than or equal to b<br>")
</script>
```

In this example, where a is 7 and b is 11, the following is output (because 7 is less than 11, and also less than or equal to 11):

```
a is less than b
a is less than or equal to b
```

Logical operators

Logical operators produce true or false results, and are also known as *Boolean* operators. There are three of them in JavaScript (see Table 14-4).

Table 14-4. JavaScript's logical operators

Logical operator	Description
&& *(and)*	`true` if both operands are `true`
|| *(or)*	`true` if either operand is `true`
! *(not)*	`true` if the operand is `false`, or `false` if the operand is `true`

You can see how these can be used in Example 14-7, which outputs **0**, **1**, and **true**.

Example 14-7. The logical operators in use

```
<script>
  a = 1; b = 0
  document.write((a && b) + "<br>")
  document.write((a || b) + "<br>")
  document.write(( !b  ) + "<br>")
</script>
```

The && statement requires both operands to be `true` in order to return a value of `true`, the || statement will be `true` if either value is `true`, and the third statement performs a NOT on the value of b, turning it from 0 into a value of `true`.

The || operator can cause unintentional problems, because the second operand will not be evaluated if the first is evaluated as `true`. In Example 14-8, the `getnext` function will never be called if `finished` has a value of 1.

Example 14-8. A statement using the || operator

```
<script>
  if (finished == 1 || getnext() == 1) done = 1
</script>
```

If you *need* `getnext` to be called at each `if` statement, you should rewrite the code as shown in Example 14-9.

Example 14-9. The if...or statement modified to ensure calling of getnext

```
<script>
  gn = getnext()
  if (finished == 1 OR gn == 1) done = 1;
</script>
```

In this case, the code in the function `getnext` will be executed and its return value stored in `gn` before the `if` statement.

Table 14-5 shows all the possible variations of using the logical operators. You should also note that `!true` equals `false`, and `!false` equals `true`.

Table 14-5. All possible logical expressions

Inputs		Operators and results	
a	b	&&	||
true	true	true	true
true	false	false	true
false	true	false	true
false	false	false	false

The with Statement

The `with` statement is not one that you've seen in the earlier chapters on PHP, because it's exclusive to JavaScript. With it (if you see what I mean), you can simplify some types of JavaScript statements by reducing many references to an object to just one reference. References to properties and methods within the `with` block are assumed to apply to that object.

For example, take the code in Example 14-10, in which the `document.write` function never references the variable `string` by name.

Example 14-10. Using the with statement

```
<script>
  string = "The quick brown fox jumps over the lazy dog"

  with (string)
  {
    document.write("The string is " + length + " characters<br>")
    document.write("In upper case it's: " + toUpperCase())
  }
</script>
```

Even though `string` is never directly referenced by `document.write`, this code still manages to output the following:

```
The string is 43 characters
In upper case it's: THE QUICK BROWN FOX JUMPS OVER THE LAZY DOG
```

This is how the code works: the JavaScript interpreter recognizes that the `length` property and `toUpperCase` method have to be applied to some object. Because they stand alone, the interpreter assumes they apply to the `string` object that you specified in the `with` statement.

Using onerror

There are more constructs not available in PHP. Using either the onerror event or a combination of the try and catch keywords, you can catch JavaScript errors and deal with them yourself.

Events are actions that can be detected by JavaScript. Every element on a web page has certain events that can trigger JavaScript functions. For example, the onclick event of a button element can be set to call a function and make it run whenever a user clicks the button.

Example 14-11 illustrates how to use the onerror event.

Example 14-11. A script employing the onerror event

```
<script>
  onerror = errorHandler
  document.writ("Welcome to this website") // Deliberate error

  function errorHandler(message, url, line)
  {
    out  = "Sorry, an error was encountered.\n\n";
    out += "Error: " + message + "\n";
    out += "URL: "   + url     + "\n";
    out += "Line: "  + line    + "\n\n";
    out += "Click OK to continue.\n\n";
    alert(out);
    return true;
  }
</script>
```

The first line of this script tells the error event to use the new errorHandler function from now onward. This function takes three parameters—a message, a url, and a line number—so it's a simple matter to display all these in an alert pop-up.

Then, to test the new function, we deliberately place a syntax error in the code with a call to document.writ instead of document.write (the final e is missing). Figure 14-1 shows the result of running this script in a browser. Using onerror this way can also be quite useful during the debugging process.

Figure 14-1. Using the onerror event with an alert method pop-up

Using try...catch

The `try` and `catch` keywords are more standard and more flexible than the `onerror` technique shown in the previous section. These keywords let you trap errors for a selected section of code, rather than all scripts in a document. However, they do not catch syntax errors, for which you need `onerror`.

The `try...catch` construct is supported by all major browsers and is handy when you want to catch a certain condition that you are aware could occur in a specific part of your code.

For example, in Chapter 17 we'll be exploring Ajax techniques that make use of the `XMLHttpRequest` object. Therefore, we can use `try` and `catch` to trap this case and do something else if the function is not available. Example 14-12 shows how.

Example 14-12. Trapping an error with try and catch

```
<script>
  try
  {
    request = new XMLHTTPRequest()
  }
  catch(err)
  {
    // Use a different method to create an XMLHTTPRequest object
  }
</script>
```

I won't go into how we implement the missing object in Internet Explorer here, but you can see how the system works. There's also another keyword associated with `try` and catch called `finally` that is always executed, regardless of whether an error occurs in the `try` clause. To use it, just add something like the following statements after a `catch` statement:

```
finally
{
  alert("The 'try' clause was encountered")
}
```

Conditionals

Conditionals alter program flow. They enable you to ask questions about certain things and respond to the answers you get in different ways. There are three types of nonlooping conditionals: the `if` statement, the `switch` statement, and the ? operator.

The if Statement

Several examples in this chapter have already made use of `if` statements. The code within such a statement is executed only if the given expression evaluates to `true`. Multiline `if` statements require curly braces around them, but as in PHP, you can omit the braces for single statements. Therefore, the following statements are valid:

```
if (a > 100)
{
  b=2
  document.write("a is greater than 100")
}

if (b == 10) document.write("b is equal to 10")
```

The else Statement

When a condition has not been met, you can execute an alternative by using an `else` statement, like this:

```
if (a > 100)
{
  document.write("a is greater than 100")
}
else
{
  document.write("a is less than or equal to 100")
}
```

Unlike PHP, JavaScript has no `elseif` statement, but that's not a problem because you can use an `else` followed by another `if` to form the equivalent of an `elseif` statement, like this:

```
if (a > 100)
{
  document.write("a is greater than 100")
}
else if(a < 100)
{
  document.write("a is less than 100")
}
else
{
  document.write("a is equal to 100")
}
```

As you can see, you can use another else after the new if, which could equally be
followed by another if statement, and so on. Although I have shown braces on the
statements, because each is a single line, the whole previous example could be written
as follows:

```
if      (a > 100) document.write("a is greater than 100")
else if(a < 100) document.write("a is less than 100")
else              document.write("a is equal to 100")
```

The switch Statement

The switch statement is useful when one variable or the result of an expression can
have multiple values, and you want to perform a different function for each value.

For example, the following code takes the PHP menu system we put together in
Chapter 4 and converts it to JavaScript. It works by passing a single string to the main
menu code according to what the user requests. Let's say the options are Home,
About, News, Login, and Links, and we set the variable page to one of these according
to the user's input.

The code for this written using if...else if... might look like Example 14-13.

Example 14-13. A multiline if...else if... statement

```
<script>
  if      (page == "Home")  document.write("You selected Home")
  else if (page == "About") document.write("You selected About")
  else if (page == "News")  document.write("You selected News")
  else if (page == "Login") document.write("You selected Login")
  else if (page == "Links") document.write("You selected Links")
</script>
```

But using a switch construct, the code could look like Example 14-14.

Example 14-14. A switch construct

```
<script>
  switch (page)
  {
    case "Home":
      document.write("You selected Home")
      break
    case "About":
      document.write("You selected About")
      break
    case "News":
      document.write("You selected News")
      break
    case "Login":
      document.write("You selected Login")
      break
    case "Links":
      document.write("You selected Links")
      break
  }
</script>
```

The variable page is mentioned only once at the start of the switch statement. Thereafter, the case command checks for matches. When one occurs, the matching conditional statement is executed. Of course, a real program would have code here to display or jump to a page, rather than simply telling the user what was selected.

You may also supply multiple cases for a single action. For example:

```
switch (heroName)
{
  case "Superman":
  case "Batman":
  case "Wonder Woman":
    document.write("Justice League")
    break
  case "Iron Man":
  case "Captain America":
  case "Spiderman":
    document.write("The Avengers")
    break
}
```

Breaking out

As you can see in Example 14-14, just as with PHP, the break command allows your code to break out of the switch statement once a condition has been satisfied. Remember to include the break unless you want to continue executing the statements under the next case.

Default action

When no condition is satisfied, you can specify a default action for a switch state-ment by using the default keyword. Example 14-15 shows a code snippet that could be inserted into Example 14-14.

Example 14-15. A default statement to add to Example 14-14

```
default:
  document.write("Unrecognized selection")
  break
```

The ? Operator

The ternary operator (?), combined with the : character, provides a quick way of doing if...else tests. With it you can write an expression to evaluate, and then fol-low it with a ? symbol and the code to execute if the expression is true. After that, place a : and the code to execute if the expression evaluates to false.

Example 14-16 shows the ternary operator being used to print out whether the vari-able a is less than or equal to 5, and prints something either way.

Example 14-16. Using the ternary operator

```
<script>
  document.write(
    a <= 5 ?
    "a is less than or equal to 5" :
    "a is greater than 5"
  )
</script>
```

The statement has been broken up into several lines for clarity, but you would be more likely to use such a statement on a single line, in this manner:

```
size = a <= 5 ? "short" : "long"
```

Looping

Again, you will find many close similarities between JavaScript and PHP when it comes to looping. Both languages support while, do...while, and for loops.

while Loops

A JavaScript while loop first checks the value of an expression and starts executing the statements within the loop only if that expression is true. If it is false, execution skips over to the next JavaScript statement (if any).

Upon completing an iteration of the loop, the expression is again tested to see if it is true, and the process continues until such a time as the expression evaluates to false or until execution is otherwise halted. Example 14-17 shows such a loop.

Example 14-17. A while loop

```
<script>
  counter=0

  while (counter < 5)
  {
    document.write("Counter: " + counter + "<br>")
    ++counter
  }
</script>
```

This script outputs the following:

```
Counter: 0
Counter: 1
Counter: 2
Counter: 3
Counter: 4
```

 If the variable counter were not incremented within the loop, it is quite possible that some browsers could become unresponsive due to a never-ending loop, and the page may not even be easy to terminate with Escape or the Stop button. So, be careful with your JavaScript loops.

do...while Loops

When you require a loop to iterate at least once before any tests are made, use a do...while loop, which is similar to a while loop, except that the test expression is checked only after each iteration of the loop. So, to output the first seven results in the 7 times table, you could use code such as that in Example 14-18.

Example 14-18. A do...while loop

```
<script>
  count = 1

  do
  {
    document.write(count + " times 7 is " + count * 7 + "<br>")
  } while (++count <= 7)
</script>
```

As you might expect, this loop outputs the following:

```
1 times 7 is 7
2 times 7 is 14
3 times 7 is 21
4 times 7 is 28
5 times 7 is 35
6 times 7 is 42
7 times 7 is 49
```

for Loops

A for loop combines the best of all worlds into a single looping construct that allows you to pass three parameters for each statement:

- An initialization expression
- A condition expression
- A modification expression

These are separated by semicolons, like this: for (*expr1* ; *expr2* ; *expr3*). The initialization expression is executed at the start of the first iteration of the loop. In the case of the code for the multiplication table for 7, count would be initialized to the value 1. Then, each time around the loop, the condition expression (in this case, count <= 7) is tested, and the loop is entered only if the condition is true. Finally, at the end of each iteration, the modification expression is executed. In the case of the multiplication table for 7, the variable count is incremented. Example 14-19 shows what the code would look like.

Example 14-19. Using a for loop

```
<script>
  for (count = 1 ; count <= 7 ; ++count)
  {
    document.write(count + "times 7 is " + count * 7 + "<br>");
  }
</script>
```

As in PHP, you can assign multiple variables in the first parameter of a for loop by separating them with a comma, like this:

```
for (i = 1, j = 1 ; i < 10 ; i++)
```

Likewise, you can perform multiple modifications in the last parameter, like this:

```
for (i = 1 ; i < 10 ; i++, --j)
```

Or you can do both at the same time:

```
for (i = 1, j = 1 ; i < 10 ; i++, --j)
```

Breaking Out of a Loop

The break command, which you'll recall is important inside a switch statement, is also available within for loops. You might need to use this, for example, when searching for a match of some kind. Once the match is found, you know that continuing to search will only waste time and make your visitor wait. Example 14-20 shows how to use the break command.

Example 14-20. Using the break command in a for loop

```
<script>
  haystack     = new Array()
  haystack[17] = "Needle"

  for (j = 0 ; j < 20 ; ++j)
  {
    if (haystack[j] == "Needle")
    {
      document.write("<br>- Found at location " + j)
      break
    }
    else document.write(j + ", ")
  }
</script>
```

This script outputs the following:

```
0, 1, 2, 3, 4, 5, 6, 7, 8, 9, 10, 11, 12, 13, 14, 15, 16,
- Found at location 17
```

The continue Statement

Sometimes you don't want to entirely exit from a loop, but instead wish to skip the remaining statements just for this iteration of the loop. In such cases, you can use the continue command. Example 14-21 shows this in use.

Example 14-21. Using the continue command in a for loop

```
<script>
  haystack     = new Array()
  haystack[4]  = "Needle"
  haystack[11] = "Needle"
  haystack[17] = "Needle"

  for (j = 0 ; j < 20 ; ++j)
  {
    if (haystack[j] == "Needle")
    {
      document.write("<br>- Found at location " + j + "<br>")
```

```
        continue
    }

    document.write(j + ", ")
  }
</script>
```

Notice how the second `document.write` call does not have to be enclosed in an `else` statement (as it did before), because the `continue` command will skip it if a match has been found. The output from this script is as follows:

```
0, 1, 2, 3,
- Found at location 4
5, 6, 7, 8, 9, 10,
- Found at location 11
12, 13, 14, 15, 16,
- Found at location 17
18, 19,
```

Explicit Casting

Unlike PHP, JavaScript has no explicit casting of types such as `(int)` or `(float)`. Instead, when you need a value to be of a certain type, use one of JavaScript's built-in functions, shown in Table 14-6.

Table 14-6. JavaScript's type-changing functions

Change to type	Function to use
Int, Integer	parseInt()
Bool, Boolean	Boolean()
Float, Double, Real	parseFloat()
String	String()
Array	split()

So, for example, to change a floating-point number to an integer, you could use code such as the following (which displays the value 3):

```
n = 3.1415927
i = parseInt(n)
document.write(i)
```

Or you can use the compound form:

```
document.write(parseInt(3.1415927))
```

That's it for control flow and expressions. The next chapter focuses on the use of functions, objects, and arrays in JavaScript.

Questions

1. How are Boolean values handled differently by PHP and JavaScript?

2. What characters are used to define a JavaScript variable name?

3. What is the difference between unary, binary, and ternary operators?

4. What is the best way to force your own operator precedence?

5. When would you use the === (identity) operator?

6. What are the simplest two forms of expressions?

7. Name the three conditional statement types.

8. How do if and while statements interpret conditional expressions of different data types?

9. Why is a for loop more powerful than a while loop?

10. What is the purpose of the with statement?

See "Chapter 14 Answers" on page 723 in Appendix A for the answers to these questions.

CHAPTER 15

JavaScript Functions, Objects, and Arrays

Just like PHP, JavaScript offers access to functions and objects. In fact, JavaScript is actually based on objects, because—as you've seen—it has to access the DOM, which makes every element of an HTML document available to manipulate as an object.

The usage and syntax are also quite similar to those of PHP, so you should feel right at home as I take you through using functions and objects in JavaScript, as well as through an in-depth exploration of array handling.

JavaScript Functions

In addition to having access to dozens of built-in functions (or methods), such as write, which you have already seen being used in document.write, you can easily create your own functions. Whenever you have a relatively complex piece of code that is likely to be reused, you have a candidate for a function.

Defining a Function

The general syntax for a function is shown here:

```
function function_name([parameter [, ...]])
{
  statements
}
```

The first line of the syntax indicates the following:

- A definition starts with the word function.

- A name follows that must start with a letter or underscore, followed by any number of letters, digits, dollar signs, or underscores.

- The parentheses are required.

- One or more parameters, separated by commas, are optional (indicated by the square brackets, which are not part of the function syntax).

Function names are case-sensitive, so all of the following strings refer to different functions: `getInput`, `GETINPUT`, and `getinput`.

In JavaScript there is a general naming convention for functions: the first letter of each word in a name is capitalized, except for the very first letter, which is lowercase. Therefore, of the previous examples, `getInput` would be the preferred name used by most programmers. This convention is commonly referred to as *bumpyCaps*, *bumpy-Case*, or *camelCase*.

The opening curly brace starts the statements that will execute when you call the function; a matching curly brace must close it. These statements may include one or more `return` statements, which force the function to cease execution and return to the calling code. If a value is attached to the `return` statement, the calling code can retrieve it.

The arguments array

The `arguments` array is a member of every function. With it, you can determine the number of variables passed to a function and what they are. Take the example of a function called `displayItems`. Example 15-1 shows one way of writing it.

Example 15-1. Defining a function

```
<script>
  displayItems("Dog", "Cat", "Pony", "Hamster", "Tortoise")

  function displayItems(v1, v2, v3, v4, v5)
  {
    document.write(v1 + "<br>")
    document.write(v2 + "<br>")
    document.write(v3 + "<br>")
    document.write(v4 + "<br>")
    document.write(v5 + "<br>")
  }
</script>
```

When you call up this script in your browser, it will display the following:

```
Dog
Cat
Pony
Hamster
Tortoise
```

All of this is fine, but what if you wanted to pass more than five items to the function? Also, reusing the `document.write` call multiple times instead of employing a loop is wasteful programming. Luckily, the `arguments` array gives you the flexibility to handle a variable number of arguments. Example 15-2 shows how you can use it to rewrite the previous example in a much more efficient manner.

Example 15-2. Modifying the function to use the arguments array

```
<script>
  function displayItems()
  {
    for (j = 0 ; j < displayItems.arguments.length ; ++j)
      document.write(displayItems.arguments[j] + "<br>")
  }
</script>
```

Note the use of the `length` property, which you already encountered in the previous chapter, and also how I reference the array `displayItems.arguments` using the variable j as an offset into it. I also chose to keep the function short and sweet by not surrounding the contents of the `for` loop in curly braces, as it contains only a single statement. Remember that the loop must stop when j is one less than `length`, not equal to `length`.

Using this technique, you now have a function that can take as many (or as few) arguments as you like and act on each argument as you desire.

Returning a Value

Functions are not used just to display things. In fact, they are mostly used to perform calculations or data manipulations and then return a result. The function `fixNames` in Example 15-3 uses the `arguments` array (discussed in the previous section) to take a series of strings passed to it and return them as a single string. The "fix" it performs is to convert every character in the arguments to lowercase except for the first character of each argument, which is set to a capital letter.

Example 15-3. Cleaning up a full name

```
<script>
  document.write(fixNames("the", "DALLAS", "CowBoys"))

  function fixNames()
  {
    var s = ""

    for (j = 0 ; j < fixNames.arguments.length ; ++j)
      s += fixNames.arguments[j].charAt(0).toUpperCase() +
```

```
        fixNames.arguments[j].substr(1).toLowerCase() + " "

    return s.substr(0, s.length-1)
  }
</script>
```

When called with the parameters the, DALLAS, and CowBoys, for example, the function returns the string The Dallas Cowboys. Let's walk through the function.

It first initializes the temporary (and local) variable s to the empty string. Then a for loop iterates through each of the passed parameters, isolating the parameter's first character using the charAt method and converting it to uppercase with the toUpperCase method. The various methods shown in this example are all built into JavaScript and available by default.

Then the substr method is used to fetch the rest of each string, which is converted to lowercase via the toLowerCase method. A fuller version of the substr method here would specify how many characters are part of the substring as a second argument:

```
substr(1, (arguments[j].length) - 1 )
```

In other words, this substr method says, "Start with the character at position 1 (the second character) and return the rest of the string (the length minus one)." As a nice touch, though, the substr method assumes that you want the rest of the string if you omit the second argument.

After the whole argument is converted to our desired case, a space character is added to the end and the result is appended to the temporary variable s.

Finally, the substr method is used again to return the contents of the variable s, except for the final space—which is unwanted. We remove this by using substr to return the string up to, but not including, the final character.

This example is particularly interesting in that it illustrates the use of multiple properties and methods in a single expression. For example:

```
fixNames.arguments[j].substr(1).toLowerCase()
```

You have to interpret the statement by mentally dividing it into parts at the periods. JavaScript evaluates these elements of the statement from left to right as follows:

1. Start with the name of the function itself: fixNames.

2. Extract element j from the array arguments representing fixNames arguments.

3. Invoke substr with a parameter of 1 to the extracted element. This passes all but the first character to the next section of the expression.

4. Apply the method toLowerCase to the string that has been passed thus far.

This practice is often referred to as *method chaining*. So, for example, if the string mixedCASE is passed to the example expression, it will go through the following transformations:

```
mixedCASE
ixedCASE
ixedcase
```

In other words, fixNames.arguments[j] produces "mixedCASE", then substr(1) takes "mixedCASE" and produces "ixedCASE", and finally toLowerCase() takes "ixedCASE" and produces "ixedcase".

One final reminder: the s variable created inside the function is local, and therefore cannot be accessed outside the function. By returning s in the return statement, we made its value available to the caller, which could store or use it any way it wanted. But s itself disappears at the end of the function. Although we could make a function operate on global variables (and sometimes that's necessary), it's much better to just return the values you want to preserve and let JavaScript clean up all the other variables used by the function.

Returning an Array

In Example 15-3, the function returned only one parameter—but what if you need to return multiple parameters? You can do this by returning an array, as in Example 15-4.

Example 15-4. Returning an array of values

```
<script>
  words = fixNames("the", "DALLAS", "CowBoys")

  for (j = 0 ; j < words.length ; ++j)
    document.write(words[j] + "<br>")

  function fixNames()
  {
    var s = new Array()

    for (j = 0 ; j < fixNames.arguments.length ; ++j)
      s[j] = fixNames.arguments[j].charAt(0).toUpperCase() +
             fixNames.arguments[j].substr(1).toLowerCase()

    return s
}
</script>
```

Here the variable `words` is automatically defined as an array and populated with the returned result of a call to the function `fixNames`. Then a `for` loop iterates through the array and displays each member.

As for the `fixNames` function, it's almost identical to Example 15-3, except that the variable `s` is now an array; after each word has been processed it is stored as an element of this array, which is returned by the `return` statement.

This function enables the extraction of individual parameters from its returned values, like the following (the output from which is simply **The Cowboys**):

```
words = fixNames("the", "DALLAS", "CowBoys")
document.write(words[0] + " " + words[2])
```

JavaScript Objects

A JavaScript object is a step up from a variable, which can contain only one value at a time. In contrast, objects can contain multiple values and even functions. An object groups data together with the functions needed to manipulate it.

Declaring a Class

When creating a script to use objects, you need to design a composite of data and code called a *class*. Each new object based on this class is called an *instance* (or *occurrence*) of that class. As you've already seen, the data associated with an object is called its *properties*, while the functions it uses are called *methods*.

Let's look at how to declare the class for an object called `User` that will contain details about the current user. To create the class, just write a function named after the class. This function can accept arguments (I'll show later how it's invoked) and can create properties and methods for objects in that class. The function is called a *constructor*.

Example 15-5 shows a constructor for the class `User` with three properties: `forename`, `username`, and `password`. The class also defines the method `showUser`.

Example 15-5. Declaring the User class and its method

```
<script>
  function User(forename, username, password)
  {
    this.forename = forename
    this.username = username
    this.password = password

    this.showUser = function()
    {
      document.write("Forename: " + this.forename + "<br>")
```

```
      document.write("Username: " + this.username + "<br>")
      document.write("Password: " + this.password + "<br>")
    }
  }
</script>
```

The function is different from other functions we've seen so far in several ways:

- Each time the function is called, it creates a new object. Thus, you can call the same function over and over with different arguments to create users with different forenames, for example.

- The function refers to an object named this, which refers to the instance being created. As the example shows, the object uses the name this to set its own properties, which will be different from one User to another.

- A new function named showUser is created within the function. The syntax shown here is new and rather complicated, but its purpose is to tie showUser to the User class. Thus, showUser comes into being as a method of the User class.

The naming convention I have used is to keep all properties in lowercase and to use at least one uppercase character in method names, following the bumpyCaps convention mentioned earlier in the chapter.

Example 15-5 follows the recommended way to write a class constructor, which is to include methods in the constructor function. However, you can also refer to functions defined outside the constructor, as in Example 15-6.

Example 15-6. Separately defining a class and method

```
<script>
  function User(forename, username, password)
  {
    this.forename = forename
    this.username = username
    this.password = password
    this.showUser = showUser
  }

  function showUser()
  {
    document.write("Forename: " + this.forename + "<br>")
    document.write("Username: " + this.username + "<br>")
    document.write("Password: " + this.password + "<br>")
  }
</script>
```

I show you this form because you are certain to encounter it when perusing other programmers' code.

Creating an Object

To create an instance of the class User, you can use a statement such as the following:

```
details = new User("Wolfgang", "w.a.mozart", "composer")
```

Or you can create an empty object, like this:

```
details = new User()
```

and then populate it later, like this:

```
details.forename = "Wolfgang"
details.username = "w.a.mozart"
details.password = "composer"
```

You can also add new properties to an object, like this:

```
details.greeting = "Hello"
```

You can verify that adding such new properties works with the following statement:

```
document.write(details.greeting)
```

Accessing Objects

To access an object, you can refer to its properties, as in the following two unrelated example statements:

```
name = details.forename
if (details.username == "Admin") loginAsAdmin()
```

So, to access the showUser method of an object of class User, you would use the following syntax, in which the object details has already been created and populated with data:

```
details.showUser()
```

Assuming the data supplied earlier, this code would display the following:

```
Forename: Wolfgang
Username: w.a.mozart
Password: composer
```

The prototype Keyword

The prototype keyword can save you a lot of memory. In the User class, every instance will contain the three properties and the method. Therefore, if you have 1,000 of these objects in memory, the method showUser will also be replicated 1,000 times. However, because the method is identical in every case, you can specify that new objects should refer to a single instance of the method instead of creating a copy of it. So, instead of using the following in a class constructor:

```
this.showUser = function()
```

you could replace it with this:

```
User.prototype.showUser = function()
```

Example 15-7 shows what the new constructor would look like.

Example 15-7. Declaring a class using the prototype keyword for a method

```
<script>
  function User(forename, username, password)
  {
    this.forename = forename
    this.username = username
    this.password = password

    User.prototype.showUser = function()
    {
      document.write("Forename: " + this.forename + "<br>")
      document.write("Username: " + this.username + "<br>")
      document.write("Password: " + this.password + "<br>")
    }
  }
</script>
```

This works because all functions have a `prototype` property, designed to hold properties and methods that are not replicated in any objects created from a class. Instead, they are passed to its objects by reference.

This means that you can add a `prototype` property or method at any time, and all objects (even those already created) will inherit it, as the following statements illustrate:

```
User.prototype.greeting = "Hello"
document.write(details.greeting)
```

The first statement adds the `prototype` property of `greeting` with a value of `Hello` to the class `User`. In the second line, the object `details`, which has already been created, correctly displays this new property.

You can also add to or modify methods in a class, as the following statements illustrate:

```
User.prototype.showUser = function()
{
  document.write("Name "   + this.forename +
                 " User " + this.username +
                 " Pass " + this.password)
}

details.showUser()
```

You might add these lines to your script in a conditional statement (such as if), so they run if user activities cause you to decide you need a different showUser method. After these lines run, even if the object details has been created already, further calls to details.showUser will run the new function. The old definition of showUser has been erased.

Static methods and properties

When reading about PHP objects, you learned that classes can have static properties and methods as well as properties and methods associated with a particular instance of a class. JavaScript also supports static properties and methods, which you can conveniently store and retrieve from the class's prototype. Thus, the following statements set and read a static string from User:

```
User.prototype.greeting = "Hello"
document.write(User.prototype.greeting)
```

Extending JavaScript objects

The prototype keyword even lets you add functionality to a built-in object. For example, suppose that you would like to add the ability to replace all spaces in a string with nonbreaking spaces in order to prevent it from wrapping around. You can do this by adding a prototype method to JavaScript's default String object definition, like this:

```
String.prototype.nbsp = function()
{
  return this.replace(/ /g, ' ')
}
```

Here the replace method is used with a regular expression to find and replace all single spaces with the string .

If you are not already familiar with regular expressions, they are a handy means of extracting information from or manipulating strings, and are fully explained in Chapter 16. Suffice it to say that for now, you can copy and paste the preceding examples and they will work as described, illustrating the power of extending JavaScript String objects.

If you then enter the following command:

```
document.write("The quick brown fox".nbsp())
```

it will output the string **The quick brown fox**. Or here's a method you can add that will trim leading and trailing spaces from a string (once again using a regular expression):

```
String.prototype.trim = function()
{
  return this.replace(/^\s+|\s+$/g, '')
}
```

If you issue the following statement, the output will be the string **Please trim me** (with the leading and trailing spaces removed):

```
document.write("  Please trim me    ".trim())
```

If we break down the expression into its component parts, the two / characters mark the start and end of the expression, and the final g specifies a global search. Inside the expression, the ^\s+ part searches for one or more whitespace characters appearing at the start of the search string, while the \s+$ part searches for one or more whitespace characters at the end of the search string. The | character in the middle acts to separate the alternatives.

The result is that when either of these expressions matches, the match is replaced with the empty string, thus returning a trimmed version of the string without any leading or trailing whitespace.

 There is debate about whether extending objects is good or bad practice. Some programmers say that should an object later be extended to officially offer the functionality you have added, it could be implemented another way, or do something quite different to your extension, which could then cause a conflict. However, other programmers, such as the inventor of JavaScript, say that this is a perfectly acceptable practice. My take is to agree with the latter, but in production code to choose extension names that are most unlikely to ever be officially used. So, for example, the trim extension could be renamed as mytrim, and the supporting code might more safely be written as:

```
String.prototype.mytrim = function()
{
  return this.replace(/^\s+|\s+$/g, '')
}
```

JavaScript Arrays

Array handling in JavaScript is very similar to in PHP, although the syntax is a little different. Nevertheless, given all you have already learned about arrays, this section should be relatively straightforward for you.

Numeric Arrays

To create a new array, use the following syntax:

```
arrayname = new Array()
```

Or you can use the shorthand form, as follows:

```
arrayname = []
```

Assigning element values

In PHP, you could add a new element to an array by simply assigning it without specifying the element offset, like this:

```
$arrayname[] = "Element 1";
$arrayname[] = "Element 2";
```

But in JavaScript you use the push method to achieve the same thing, like this:

```
arrayname.push("Element 1")
arrayname.push("Element 2")
```

This allows you to keep adding items to an array without having to keep track of the number of items. When you need to know how many elements are in an array, you can use the length property, like this:

```
document.write(arrayname.length)
```

Alternatively, if you wish to keep track of the element locations yourself and place them in specific locations, you can use syntax such as this:

```
arrayname[0] = "Element 1"
arrayname[1] = "Element 2"
```

Example 15-8 shows a simple script that creates an array, loads it with some values, and then displays them.

Example 15-8. Creating, building, and printing an array

```
<script>
  numbers = []
  numbers.push("One")
  numbers.push("Two")
  numbers.push("Three")

  for (j = 0 ; j < numbers.length ; ++j)
    document.write("Element " + j + " = " + numbers[j] + "<br>")
</script>
```

The output from this script is as follows:

```
Element 0 = One
Element 1 = Two
Element 2 = Three
```

Assignment using the array keyword

You can also create an array together with some initial elements by using the `Array` keyword, like this:

```
numbers = Array("One", "Two", "Three")
```

There is nothing stopping you from adding more elements afterward as well.

You've now seen a couple of ways you can add items to an array, and one way of referencing them. JavaScript offers many more, which I'll get to shortly—but first, we'll look at another type of array.

Associative Arrays

An *associative array* is one in which the elements are referenced by name rather than by an integer offset. However, JavaScript doesn't support such things. Instead, we can achieve the same result by creating an object with properties that will act the same way.

So, to create an "associative array," define a block of elements within curly braces. For each element, place the key on the left and the contents on the right of a colon (`:`). Example 15-9 shows how you might create an associative array to hold the contents of the "balls" section of an online sports equipment retailer.

Example 15-9. Creating and displaying an associative array

```
<script>
  balls = {"golf":    "Golf balls, 6",
           "tennis":  "Tennis balls, 3",
           "soccer":  "Soccer ball, 1",
           "ping":    "Ping Pong balls, 1 doz"}

  for (ball in balls)
    document.write(ball + " = " + balls[ball] + "<br>")
</script>
```

To verify that the array has been correctly created and populated, I have used another kind of `for` loop using the `in` keyword. This creates a new variable to use only within the array (`ball`, in this example) and iterates through all elements of the array to the right of the `in` keyword (`balls`, in this example). The loop acts on each element of `balls`, placing the key value into `ball`.

Using this key value stored in `ball`, you can also get the value of the current element of `balls`. The result of calling up the example script in a browser is as follows:

```
golf = Golf balls, 6
tennis = Tennis balls, 3
soccer = Soccer ball, 1
ping = Ping Pong balls, 1 doz
```

To get a specific element of an associative array, you can specify a key explicitly, in the following manner (in this case, outputting the value **Soccer ball, 1**):

```
document.write(balls['soccer'])
```

Multidimensional Arrays

To create a multidimensional array in JavaScript, just place arrays inside other arrays. For example, to create an array to hold the details of a two-dimensional checkerboard (8 × 8 squares), you could use the code in Example 15-10.

Example 15-10. Creating a multidimensional numeric array

```
<script>
  checkerboard = Array(
    Array(' ', 'o', ' ', 'o', ' ', 'o', ' ', 'o'),
    Array('o', ' ', 'o', ' ', 'o', ' ', 'o', ' '),
    Array(' ', 'o', ' ', 'o', ' ', 'o', ' ', 'o'),
    Array(' ', ' ', ' ', ' ', ' ', ' ', ' ', ' '),
    Array(' ', ' ', ' ', ' ', ' ', ' ', ' ', ' '),
    Array('O', ' ', 'O', ' ', 'O', ' ', 'O', ' '),
    Array(' ', 'O', ' ', 'O', ' ', 'O', ' ', 'O'),
    Array('O', ' ', 'O', ' ', 'O', ' ', 'O', ' '))

  document.write("<pre>")

  for (j = 0 ; j < 8 ; ++j)
  {
    for (k = 0 ; k < 8 ; ++k)
      document.write(checkerboard[j][k] + " ")

    document.write("<br>")
  }

  document.write("</pre>")
</script>
```

In this example, the lowercase letters represent black pieces, and the uppercase white. A pair of nested `for` loops walks through the array and displays its contents.

The outer loop contains two statements, so curly braces enclose them. The inner loop then processes each square in a row, outputting the character at location `[j][k]`, followed by a space (to square up the printout). This loop contains a single statement, so curly braces are not required to enclose it. The `<pre>` and `</pre>` tags ensure that the output displays correctly, like this:

```
 o   o   o   o
o   o   o   o
  o   o   o   o


 O   O   O   O
   O   O   O   O
 O   O   O   O
```

You can also directly access any element within this array by using square brackets:

```
document.write(checkerboard[7][2])
```

This statement outputs the uppercase letter **O**, the eighth element down and the third along—remember that array indexes start at 0, not 1.

Using Array Methods

Given the power of arrays, JavaScript comes ready-made with a number of methods for manipulating them and their data. Here is a selection of the most useful ones.

some

When you need to know whether at least one array element matches a certain criterion, you can use the some function, which will test all the elements and automatically stop and return the required value as soon as one matches. This saves you from having to write your own code to perform such searches, like this:

```
function isBiggerThan10(element, index, array)
{
  return element > 10
}

result = [2, 5, 8, 1, 4].some(isBiggerThan10); // result will be false
result = [12, 5, 8, 1, 4].some(isBiggerThan10); // result will be true
```

indexOf

To find out where an element can be found in an array you can call the indexOf function on the array, which will return the offset of the located element (starting from 0), or -1 if it is not found. For example, the following gives offset the value 2:

```
animals = ['cat', 'dog', 'cow', 'horse', 'elephant']
offset = animals.indexOf('cow')
```

concat

The `concat` method concatenates two arrays, or a series of values within an array. For example, the following code outputs **Banana,Grape,Carrot,Cabbage**:

```
fruit = ["Banana", "Grape"]
veg   = ["Carrot", "Cabbage"]

document.write(fruit.concat(veg))
```

You can specify multiple arrays as arguments, in which case `concat` adds all their elements in the order that the arrays are specified.

Here's another way to use `concat`. This time, plain values are concatenated with the array `pets`, which outputs **Cat,Dog,Fish,Rabbit,Hamster**:

```
pets      = ["Cat", "Dog", "Fish"]
more_pets = pets.concat("Rabbit", "Hamster")

document.write(more_pets)
```

forEach

The `forEach` method in JavaScript is another way of achieving functionality similar to the PHP `foreach` keyword. To use it, you pass it the name of a function, which will be called for each element within the array. Example 15-11 shows how.

Example 15-11. Using the forEach method

```
<script>
  pets = ["Cat", "Dog", "Rabbit", "Hamster"]
  pets.forEach(output)

  function output(element, index, array)
  {
    document.write("Element at index " + index + " has the value " +
      element + "<br>")
  }
</script>
```

In this case, the function passed to `forEach` is called `output`. It takes three parameters: the `element`, its `index`, and the `array`. These can be used as required by your function. This example displays just the `element` and `index` values using the function `document.write`.

Once an array has been populated, the method is called like this:

```
pets.forEach(output)
```

This is the output:

```
Element at index 0 has the value Cat
Element at index 1 has the value Dog
Element at index 2 has the value Rabbit
Element at index 3 has the value Hamster
```

join

With the `join` method, you can convert all the values in an array to strings and then join them together into one large string, placing an optional separator between them. Example 15-12 shows three ways of using this method.

Example 15-12. Using the join method

```
<script>
  pets = ["Cat", "Dog", "Rabbit", "Hamster"]

  document.write(pets.join()      + "<br>")
  document.write(pets.join(' ')   + "<br>")
  document.write(pets.join(' : ') + "<br>")
</script>
```

Without a parameter, `join` uses a comma to separate the elements; otherwise, the string passed to `join` is inserted between each element. The output of Example 15-12 looks like this:

```
Cat,Dog,Rabbit,Hamster
Cat Dog Rabbit Hamster
Cat : Dog : Rabbit : Hamster
```

push and pop

You already saw how the push method can be used to insert a value into an array. The inverse method is pop. It deletes the most recently inserted element from an array and returns it. Example 15-13 shows an example of its use.

Example 15-13. Using the push and pop methods

```
<script>
  sports = ["Football", "Tennis", "Baseball"]
  document.write("Start = "      + sports +  "<br>")

  sports.push("Hockey")
  document.write("After Push = " + sports +  "<br>")

  removed = sports.pop()
  document.write("After Pop = "  + sports +  "<br>")
  document.write("Removed = "    + removed + "<br>")
</script>
```

The three main statements of this script are shown in bold type. First, the script creates an array called sports with three elements and then pushes a fourth element into the array. After that, it pops that element back off. In the process, the various current values are displayed via document.write. The script outputs the following:

```
Start = Football,Tennis,Baseball
After Push = Football,Tennis,Baseball,Hockey
After Pop = Football,Tennis,Baseball
Removed = Hockey
```

The push and pop functions are useful in situations where you need to divert from some activity to do another, and then return. For example, let's suppose you want to put off some activities until later, while you get on with something more important now. This often happens in real life when we're going through "todo" lists, so let's emulate that in code, with tasks number 2 and 5 in a list of 6 items being granted priority status, as in Example 15-14.

Example 15-14. Using push and pop inside and outside of a loop

```
<script>
  numbers = []

  for (j=1 ; j<6 ; ++j)
  {
    if (j == 2 || j == 5)
    {
      document.write("Processing 'todo' #" + j + "<br>")
    }
    else
    {
      document.write("Putting off 'todo' #" + j + " until later<br>")
      numbers.push(j)
    }
  }

  document.write("<br>Finished processing the priority tasks.")
  document.write("<br>Commencing stored tasks, most recent first.<br><br>")

  document.write("Now processing 'todo' #" + numbers.pop() + "<br>")
  document.write("Now processing 'todo' #" + numbers.pop() + "<br>")
  document.write("Now processing 'todo' #" + numbers.pop() + "<br>")
</script>
```

Of course, nothing is actually getting processed here, just text being output to the browser, but you get the idea. The output from this example is as follows:

```
Putting off 'todo' #1 until later
Processing 'todo' #2
Putting off 'todo' #3 until later
Putting off 'todo' #4 until later
```

```
Processing 'todo' #5

Finished processing the priority tasks.
Commencing stored tasks, most recent first.

Now processing 'todo' #4
Now processing 'todo' #3
Now processing 'todo' #1
```

Using reverse

The reverse method simply reverses the order of all elements in an array. Example 15-15 shows this in action.

Example 15-15. Using the reverse method

```
<script>
  sports = ["Football", "Tennis", "Baseball", "Hockey"]
  sports.reverse()
  document.write(sports)
</script>
```

The original array is modified, and the output from this script is as follows:

```
Hockey,Baseball,Tennis,Football
```

sort

With the sort method, you can place all the elements of an array in alphabetical or other order, depending on the parameters used. Example 15-16 shows four types of sort.

Example 15-16. Using the sort method

```
<script>
  // Alphabetical sort
  sports = ["Football", "Tennis", "Baseball", "Hockey"]
  sports.sort()
  document.write(sports + "<br>")

  // Reverse alphabetical sort
  sports = ["Football", "Tennis", "Baseball", "Hockey"]
  sports.sort().reverse()
  document.write(sports + "<br>")

  // Ascending numeric sort
  numbers = [7, 23, 6, 74]
  numbers.sort(function(a,b){return a - b})
  document.write(numbers + "<br>")
```

```
  // Descending numeric sort
  numbers = [7, 23, 6, 74]
  numbers.sort(function(a,b){return b - a})
  document.write(numbers + "<br>")
</script>
```

The first of the four example sections uses the default sort method to perform an *alphabetical sort*, while the second uses the default sort and then applies the reverse method to get a *reverse alphabetical sort*.

The third and fourth sections are a little more complicated; they use a function to compare the relationships between a and b. The function doesn't have a name, because it's used only in the sort. You have already seen the function named function used to create an anonymous function; we used it to define a method in a class (the showUser method).

Here, function creates an anonymous function meeting the needs of the sort method. If the function returns a value greater than zero, the sort assumes that b comes before a. If the function returns a value less than zero, the sort assumes that a comes before b. The sort runs this function across all the values in the array to determine their order. (Of course, if a and b have the same value, the function returns zero and it doesn't matter which value is first.)

By manipulating the value returned (a - b in contrast to b - a), the third and fourth sections of Example 15-16 choose between an *ascending numerical sort* and a *descending numerical sort*.

And, believe it or not, this represents the end of your introduction to JavaScript. You should now have a core knowledge of the three main technologies covered in this book. The next chapter will look at some advanced techniques used across these technologies, such as pattern matching and input validation.

Questions

1. Are JavaScript functions and variable names case-sensitive or case-insensitive?
2. How can you write a function that accepts and processes an unlimited number of parameters?
3. Name a way to return multiple values from a function.
4. When you're defining a class, what keyword do you use to refer to the current object?
5. Do all the methods of a class have to be defined within the class definition?
6. What keyword is used to create an object?

7. How can you make a property or method available to all objects in a class without replicating the property or method within the object?

8. How can you create a multidimensional array?

9. What syntax is used to create an associative array?

10. Write a statement to sort an array of numbers in descending numerical order.

See "Chapter 15 Answers" on page 724 in Appendix A for the answers to these questions.

CHAPTER 16

JavaScript and PHP Validation and Error Handling

With your solid foundation in both PHP and JavaScript, it's time to bring these technologies together to create web forms that are as user-friendly as possible.

We'll be using PHP to create the forms and JavaScript to perform client-side validation to ensure that the data is as complete and correct as it can be before it is submitted. Final validation of the input will then be done by PHP, which will, if necessary, present the form again to the user for further modification.

In the process, this chapter will cover validation and regular expressions in both Java-Script and PHP.

Validating User Input with JavaScript

JavaScript validation should be considered an assistance more to your users than to your websites because, as I have already stressed many times, you cannot trust any data submitted to your server, even if it has supposedly been validated with Java-Script. This is because hackers can quite easily simulate your web forms and submit any data of their choosing.

Another reason you cannot rely on JavaScript to perform all your input validation is that some users disable JavaScript, or use browsers that don't support it.

So, the best types of validation to do in JavaScript are checking that fields have content if they are not to be left empty, ensuring that email addresses conform to the proper format, and ensuring that values entered are within expected bounds.

The validate.html Document (Part 1)

Let's begin with a general signup form, common on most sites that offer memberships or user registration. The inputs requested will be *forename*, *surname*, *username*, *password*, *age*, and *email address*. Example 16-1 provides a good template for such a form.

Example 16-1. A form with JavaScript validation (part 1)

```
<!DOCTYPE html>
<html>
  <head>
    <title>An Example Form</title>
    <style>
      .signup {
        border:1px solid #999999;
        font:  normal 14px helvetica;
        color: #444444;
      }
    </style>
    <script>
      function validate(form)
      {
        fail  = validateForename(form.forename.value)
        fail += validateSurname(form.surname.value)
        fail += validateUsername(form.username.value)
        fail += validatePassword(form.password.value)
        fail += validateAge(form.age.value)
        fail += validateEmail(form.email.value)

        if   (fail == "")    return true
        else { alert(fail); return false }
      }
    </script>
  </head>
  <body>
    <table class="signup" border="0" cellpadding="2"
            cellspacing="5" bgcolor="#eeeeee">
      <th colspan="2" align="center">Signup Form</th>
      <form method="post" action="adduser.php" onsubmit="return validate(this)">
        <tr><td>Forename</td>
          <td><input type="text" maxlength="32" name="forename"></td></tr>
        <tr><td>Surname</td>
          <td><input type="text" maxlength="32" name="surname"></td></tr>
        <tr><td>Username</td>
          <td><input type="text" maxlength="16" name="username"></td></tr>
        <tr><td>Password</td>
          <td><input type="text" maxlength="12" name="password"></td></tr>
        <tr><td>Age</td>
          <td><input type="text" maxlength="3"  name="age"></td></tr>
        <tr><td>Email</td>
          <td><input type="text" maxlength="64" name="email"></td></tr>
```

```
      <tr><td colspan="2" align="center"><input type="submit"
        value="Signup"></td></tr>
      </form>
    </table>
  </body>
</html>
```

As it stands, this form will display correctly but will not self-validate, because the main validation functions have not yet been added. Even so, save it as *validate.html*, and when you call it up in your browser, it will look like Figure 16-1.

Figure 16-1. The output from Example 16-1

Let's look at how this document is made up. The first few lines set up the document and use a little CSS to make the form look a little less plain. The parts of the document related to JavaScript come next and are shown in bold.

Between the `<script>` and `</script>` tags lies a single function called `validate` that itself calls up six other functions to validate each of the form's input fields. We'll get to these functions shortly. For now I'll just explain that they return either an empty string if a field validates, or an error message if it fails. If there are any errors, the final line of the script pops up an alert box to display them.

Upon passing validation, the `validate` function returns a value of `true`; otherwise, it returns `false`. The return values from `validate` are important, because if it returns `false`, the form is prevented from being submitted. This allows the user to close the alert pop-up and make changes. If `true` is returned, no errors were encountered in the form's fields and so the form is submitted.

The second part of this example features the HTML for the form, with each field and its name placed within its own row of a table. This is pretty straightforward HTML, with the exception of the onSubmit="return validate(this)" statement within the opening <form> tag. Using onSubmit, you can cause a function of your choice to be called when a form is submitted. That function can perform some checking and return a value of either true or false to signify whether the form should be allowed to be submitted.

The this parameter is the current object (i.e., this form) and is passed to the validate function just discussed. The validate function receives this parameter as the object form.

As you can see, the only JavaScript used within the form's HTML is the call to return buried in the onSubmit attribute. Browsers with JavaScript disabled or not available will simply ignore the onSubmit attribute, and the HTML will display just fine.

The validate.html Document (Part 2)

Now we come to Example 16-2, a set of six functions that do the actual form-field validation. I suggest that you type all of this second part and save it in the <script>...</script> section of Example 16-1, which you should already have saved as *validate.html*.

Example 16-2. A form with JavaScript validation (part 2)

```
function validateForename(field)
{
  return (field == "") ? "No Forename was entered.\n" : ""
}

function validateSurname(field)
{
  return (field == "") ? "No Surname was entered.\n" : ""
}

function validateUsername(field)
{
  if (field == "") return "No Username was entered.\n"
  else if (field.length < 5)
    return "Usernames must be at least 5 characters.\n"
  else if (/[^a-zA-Z0-9_-]/.test(field))
    return "Only a-z, A-Z, 0-9, - and _ allowed in Usernames.\n"
  return ""
}

function validatePassword(field)
{
  if (field == "") return "No Password was entered.\n"
```

```
  else if (field.length < 6)
    return "Passwords must be at least 6 characters.\n"
  else if (!/[a-z]/.test(field) || ! /[A-Z]/.test(field) ||
          !/[0-9]/.test(field))
    return "Passwords require one each of a-z, A-Z and 0-9.\n"
  return ""
}

function validateAge(field)
{
  if (field == "" || isNaN(field)) return "No Age was entered.\n"
  else if (field < 18 || field > 110)
    return "Age must be between 18 and 110.\n"
  return ""
}

function validateEmail(field)
{
  if (field == "") return "No Email was entered.\n"
    else if (!((field.indexOf(".") > 0) &&
              (field.indexOf("@") > 0)) ||
             /[^a-zA-Z0-9.@_-]/.test(field))
      return "The Email address is invalid.\n"
  return ""
}
```

We'll go through each of these functions in turn, starting with validateForename, so you can see how validation works.

Validating the forename

validateForename is quite a short function that accepts the parameter field, which is the value of the forename passed to it by the validate function.

If this value is the empty string, an error message is returned; otherwise, an empty string is returned to signify that no error was encountered.

If the user entered spaces in this field, it would be accepted by validateForename, even though it's empty for all intents and purposes. You can fix this by adding an extra statement to trim whitespace from the field before checking whether it's empty, use a regular expression to make sure there's something besides whitespace in the field, or—as I do here—just let the user make the mistake and allow the PHP program to catch it on the server.

Validating the surname

The validateSurname function is almost identical to validateForename in that an error is returned only if the surname supplied was an empty string. I chose not to limit the characters allowed in either of the name fields to allow for possibilities such as non-English and accented characters.

Validating the username

The `validateUsername` function is a little more interesting, because it has a more complicated job. It has to allow through only the characters `a-z`, `A-Z`, `0-9`, `_` and `-`, and ensure that usernames are at least five characters long.

The `if...else` statements commence by returning an error if `field` has not been filled in. If it's not the empty string, but is fewer than five characters in length, another error message is returned.

Then the JavaScript `test` function is called, passing a regular expression (which matches any character that is *not* one of those allowed) to be matched against `field` (see "Regular Expressions" on page 377). If even one character that isn't one of the acceptable characters is encountered, the `test` function returns `true`, and so `validateUser` returns an error string.

Validating the password

Similar techniques are used in the `validatePassword` function. First the function checks whether `field` is empty, and if it is, it returns an error. Next, an error message is returned if the password is shorter than six characters.

One of the requirements we're imposing on passwords is that they must have at least one each of a lowercase, uppercase, and numerical character, so the `test` function is called three times, once for each of these cases. If any one of these calls returns `false`, one of the requirements was not met and so an error message is returned. Otherwise, the empty string is returned to signify that the password was OK.

Validating the age

`validateAge` returns an error message if `field` is not a number (determined by a call to the `isNaN` function), or if the age entered is lower than 18 or greater than 110. Your applications may well have different or no age requirements. Again, upon successful validation, the empty string is returned.

Validating the email

In the last and most complicated example, the email address is validated with `validateEmail`. After checking whether anything was actually entered, and returning an error message if it wasn't, the function calls the JavaScript `indexOf` function twice. The first time a check is made to ensure there is a period (`.`) somewhere after the first character of the field, and the second checks that an `@` symbol appears somewhere after the first character.

If those two checks are satisfied, the `test` function is called to see whether any disallowed characters appear in the field. If any of these tests fail, an error message is returned. The allowed characters in an email address are uppercase and lowercase letters, numbers, and the _, -, period, and @ characters, as detailed in the regular expression passed to the `test` method. If no errors are found, the empty string is returned to indicate successful validation. On the last line, the script and document are closed.

Figure 16-2 shows the result of the user clicking the Signup button without having completed any fields.

Figure 16-2. JavaScript form validation in action

Using a separate JavaScript file

Of course, because they are generic in construction and could apply to many types of validations you might require, these six functions make ideal candidates for moving out into a separate JavaScript file. You could name the file something like *validate_functions.js* and include it right after the initial script section in Example 16-1, using the following statement:

```
<script src="validate_functions.js"></script>
```

Regular Expressions

Let's look a little more closely at the pattern matching we have been doing. We've achieved it using *regular expressions*, which are supported by both JavaScript and PHP. They make it possible to construct the most powerful of pattern-matching algorithms within a single expression.

Matching Through Metacharacters

Every regular expression must be enclosed in slashes. Within these slashes, certain characters have special meanings; they are called *metacharacters*. For instance, an asterisk (*) has a meaning similar to what you have seen if you've used a shell or Windows command prompt (but not quite the same). An asterisk means, "The text you're trying to match may have any number of the preceding characters—or none at all."

For instance, let's say you're looking for the name *Le Guin* and know that someone might spell it with or without a space. Because the text is laid out strangely (for instance, someone may have inserted extra spaces to right-justify lines), you could have to search for a line such as this:

```
The    difficulty  of   classifying Le     Guin's    works
```

So you need to match *LeGuin*, as well as *Le* and *Guin* separated by any number of spaces. The solution is to follow a space with an asterisk:

```
/Le *Guin/
```

There's a lot more than the name *Le Guin* in the line, but that's OK. As long as the regular expression matches some part of the line, the `test` function returns a `true` value. What if it's important to make sure the line contains nothing but *Le Guin*? I'll show you how to ensure that later.

Suppose that you know there is always at least one space. In that case, you could use the plus sign (+), because it requires at least one of the preceding characters to be present:

```
/Le +Guin/
```

Fuzzy Character Matching

The dot (.) is particularly useful, because it can match anything except a newline. Suppose that you are looking for HTML tags, which start with < and end with >. A simple way to do so is shown here:

```
/<.*>/
```

The dot matches any character, and the * expands it to match zero or more characters, so this is saying, "Match anything that lies between < and >, even if there's nothing." You will match <>, <em>, <br>, and so on. But if you don't want to match the empty case, <>, you should use + instead of *, like this:

```
/<.+>/
```

The plus sign expands the dot to match one or more characters, saying, "Match anything that lies between < and > as long as there's at least one character between them." You will match <em> and </em>, <h1> and </h1>, and tags with attributes, such as this:

```
<a href="www.mozilla.org">
```

Unfortunately, the plus sign keeps on matching up to the last > on the line, so you might end up with this:

```
<h1><b>Introduction</b></h1>
```

A lot more than one tag! I'll show a better solution later in this section.

 If you use the dot on its own between the angle brackets, without following it with either a + or *, then it matches a single character; you will match <b> and <i> but *not* <em> or <textarea>.

If you want to match the dot character itself (.), you have to escape it by placing a backslash (\) before it, because otherwise it's a metacharacter and matches anything. As an example, suppose you want to match the floating-point number 5.0. The regular expression is as follows:

```
/5\.0/
```

The backslash can escape any metacharacter, including another backslash (in case you're trying to match a backslash in text). However, to make things a bit confusing, you'll see later how backslashes sometimes give the following character a special meaning.

We just matched a floating-point number. But perhaps you want to match 5. as well as 5.0, because both mean the same thing as a floating-point number. You also want to match 5.00, 5.000, and so forth—any number of zeros is allowed. You can do this by adding an asterisk, as you've seen:

```
/5\.0*/
```

Grouping Through Parentheses

Suppose you want to match powers of increments of units, such as kilo, mega, giga, and tera. In other words, you want all the following to match:

```
1,000
1,000,000
1,000,000,000
1,000,000,000,000
...
```

The plus sign works here, too, but you need to group the string ,000 so the plus sign matches the whole thing. The regular expression is as follows:

```
/1(,000)+ /
```

The parentheses mean "treat this as a group when you apply something such as a plus sign." `1,00,000` and `1,000,00` won't match because the text must have a 1 followed by one or more complete groups of a comma followed by three zeros.

The space after the `+` character indicates that the match must end when a space is encountered. Without it, `1,000,00` would incorrectly match because only the first `1,000` would be taken into account, and the remaining `,00` would be ignored. Requiring a space afterward ensures that matching will continue right through to the end of a number.

Character Classes

Sometimes you want to match something fuzzy, but not so broad that you want to use a dot. Fuzziness is the great strength of regular expressions: they allow you to be as precise or vague as you want.

One of the key features supporting fuzzy matching is the pair of square brackets, `[]`. It matches a single character, like a dot, but inside the brackets you put a list of things that can match. If any of those characters appears, the text matches. For instance, if you wanted to match both the American spelling *gray* and the British spelling *grey*, you could specify the following:

    /gr[ae]y/

After the `gr` in the text you're matching, there can be either an `a` or an `e`. But there must be only one of them: whatever you put inside the brackets matches exactly one character. The group of characters inside the brackets is called a *character class*.

Indicating a Range

Inside the brackets, you can use a hyphen (`-`) to indicate a range. One very common task is matching a single digit, which you can do with a range as follows:

    /[0-9]/

Digits are such a common item in regular expressions that a single character is provided to represent them: `\d`. You can use it in place of the bracketed regular expression to match a digit:

    /\d/

Negation

One other important feature of the square brackets is *negation* of a character class. You can turn the whole character class on its head by placing a caret (`^`) after the opening bracket. Here it means, "Match any characters *except* the following." So let's say you want to find instances of *Yahoo* that lack the following exclamation point.

(The name of the company officially contains an exclamation point!) You could do it as follows:

```
/Yahoo[^!]/
```

The character class consists of a single character—an exclamation point—but it is inverted by the preceding ^. This is actually not a great solution to the problem—for instance, it fails if *Yahoo* is at the end of the line, because then it's not followed by *anything*, whereas the brackets must match a character. A better solution involves negative *lookahead* (matching something that is not followed by anything else), but that's beyond the scope of this book.

Some More Complicated Examples

With an understanding of character classes and negation, you're ready now to see a better solution to the problem of matching an HTML tag. This solution avoids going past the end of a single tag, but still matches tags such as <em> and </em> as well as tags with attributes such as this:

```
<a href="www.mozilla.org">
```

Here is one solution:

```
/<[^>]+>/
```

That regular expression may look like I just dropped my teacup on the keyboard, but it is perfectly valid and very useful. Let's break it apart. Figure 16-3 shows the various elements, which I'll describe one by one.

Figure 16-3. Breakdown of a typical regular expression

The elements are as follows:

/

Opening slash that indicates this is a regular expression.

<

Opening bracket of an HTML tag. This is matched exactly; it's not a metachar-acter.

[^>]

Character class. The embedded ^> means "match anything except a closing angle bracket."

+

Allows any number of characters to match the previous [^>], as long as there is at least one of them.

>

Closing bracket of an HTML tag. This is matched exactly.

/

Closing slash that indicates the end of the regular expression.

 Another solution to the problem of matching HTML tags is to use a nongreedy operation. By default, pattern matching is greedy, returning the longest match possible. Nongreedy (or lazy) matching finds the shortest possible match. Its use is beyond the scope of this book, but there are more details on the JavaScript.info website (*https://javascript.info/regexp-greedy-and-lazy*).

We are going to look now at one of the expressions from Example 16-1, where the `validateUsername` function is used:

```
/[^a-zA-Z0-9_-]/
```

Figure 16-4 shows the various elements.

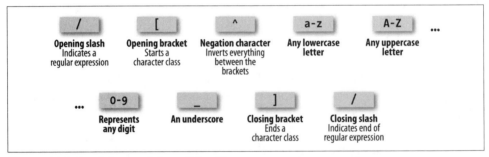

Figure 16-4. Breakdown of the validateUsername regular expression

Let's look at these elements in detail:

/

Opening slash that indicates this is a regular expression.

[

Opening bracket that starts a character class.

^

Negation character: inverts everything else between the brackets.

```
a-z
```
> Represents any lowercase letter.

```
A-Z
```
> Represents any uppercase letter.

```
0-9
```
> Represents any digit.

```
_
```
> An underscore.

```
-
```
> A dash.

```
]
```
> Closing bracket that ends a character class.

```
/
```
> Closing slash that indicates the end of the regular expression.

There are two other important metacharacters. They "anchor" a regular expression by requiring that it appear in a particular place. If a caret (^) appears at the beginning of the regular expression, the expression has to appear at the beginning of a line of text; otherwise, it doesn't match. Similarly, if a dollar sign ($) appears at the end of the regular expression, the expression has to appear at the end of a line of text.

> It may be somewhat confusing that ^ can mean "negate the character class" inside square brackets and "match the beginning of the line" if it's at the beginning of the regular expression. Unfortunately, the same character is used for two different things, so take care when using it.

We'll finish our exploration of regular expression basics by answering a question raised earlier: suppose you want to make sure there is nothing extra on a line besides the regular expression? What if you want a line that has "Le Guin" and nothing else? We can do that by amending the earlier regular expression to anchor the two ends:

```
/^Le *Guin$/
```

Summary of Metacharacters

Table 16-1 shows the metacharacters available in regular expressions.

Table 16-1. Regular expression metacharacters

Metacharacters	Description
/	Begins and ends the regular expression
.	Matches any single character except the newline
element*	Matches *element* zero or more times
element+	Matches *element* one or more times
element?	Matches *element* zero or one times
[characters]	Matches a character out of those contained within the brackets
[^characters]	Matches a single character that is not contained within the brackets
(regex)	Treats the *regex* as a group for counting or a following *, +, or ?
left|right	Matches either *left* or *right*
[l-r]	Matches a range of characters between *l* and *r*
^	Requires match to be at the string's start
$	Requires match to be at the string's end
\b	Matches a word boundary
\B	Matches where there is not a word boundary
\d	Matches a single digit
\D	Matches a single nondigit
\n	Matches a newline character
\s	Matches a whitespace character
\S	Matches a nonwhitespace character
\t	Matches a tab character
\w	Matches a word character (a-z, A-Z, 0-9, and _)
\W	Matches a nonword character (anything but a-z, A-Z, 0-9, and _)
\x	Matches *x* (useful if *x* is a metacharacter, but you really want *x*)
{n}	Matches exactly *n* times
{n,}	Matches *n* times or more
{min,max}	Matches at least *min* and at most *max* times

Provided with this table, and looking again at the expression /[^a-zA-Z0-9_]/, you can see that it could easily be shortened to /[^\w]/ because the single metacharacter \w (with a lowercase w) specifies the characters a-z, A-Z, 0-9, and _.

In fact, we can be cleverer than that, because the metacharacter \W (with an uppercase W) specifies all characters *except* for a-z, A-Z, 0-9, and _. Therefore, we could also drop the ^ metacharacter and simply use /[\W]/ for the expression, or even go a step further and drop the square brackets, as in /\W/, because it's single character.

To give you more ideas of how this all works, Table 16-2 shows a range of expressions and the patterns they match.

Table 16-2. Some example regular expressions

Example	Matches
r	The first *r* in *The quick brown*
rec[ei][ei]ve	Either of *receive* or *recieve* (but also *receeve* or *reciive*)
rec[ei]{2}ve	Either of *receive* or *recieve* (but also *receeve* or *reciive*)
rec(ei|ie)ve	Either of *receive* or *recieve* (but not *receeve* or *reciive*)
cat	The word *cat* in *I like cats and dogs*
cat|dog	The word *cat* in *I like cats and dogs* (matches either *cat* or *dog*, whichever is encountered first)
\.	. (the \ is necessary because . is a metacharacter)
5\.0*	*5., 5.0, 5.00, 5.000*, etc.
[a-f]	Any of the characters *a, b, c, d, e,* or *f*
cats$	Only the final *cats* in *My cats are friendly cats*
^my	Only the first *my* in *my cats are my pets*
\d{2,3}	Any two- or three-digit number (*00* through *999*)
7(,000)+	*7,000; 7,000,000; 7,000,000,000; 7,000,000,000,000*; etc.
[\w]+	Any word of one or more characters
[\w]{5}	Any five-letter word

General Modifiers

Some additional modifiers are available for regular expressions:

- /g enables *global* matching. When using a replace function, specify this modifier to replace all matches, rather than only the first one.

- /i makes the regular expression match case-insensitive. Thus, instead of /[a-zA-Z]/, you could specify /[a-z]/i or /[A-Z]/i.

- /m enables multiline mode, in which the caret (^) and dollar sign ($) match before and after any newlines in the subject string. Normally, in a multiline string, ^ matches only at the start of the string, and $ matches only at the end of the string.

For example, the expression /cats/g will match both occurrences of the word *cats* in the sentence *I like cats, and cats like me*. Similarly, /dogs/gi will match both occurrences of the word *dogs* (*Dogs* and *dogs*) in the sentence *Dogs like other dogs*, because you can use these specifiers together.

Using Regular Expressions in JavaScript

In JavaScript, you will use regular expressions mostly in two methods: test (which you have already seen) and replace. Whereas test just tells you whether its argument matches the regular expression, replace takes a second parameter: the string to replace the text that matches. Like most functions, `replace` generates a new string as a return value; it does not change the input.

To compare the two methods, the following statement just returns `true` to let us know that the word *cats* appears at least once somewhere within the string:

```
document.write(/cats/i.test("Cats are funny. I like cats."))
```

But the following statement replaces both occurrences of the word *cats* with the word *dogs*, printing the result. The search has to be global (`/g`) to find all occurrences, and case-insensitive (`/i`) to find the capitalized *Cats*:

```
document.write("Cats are friendly. I like cats.".replace(/cats/gi,"dogs"))
```

If you try out the statement, you'll see a limitation of `replace`: because it replaces text with exactly the string you tell it to use, the first word *Cats* is replaced by *dogs* instead of *Dogs*.

Using Regular Expressions in PHP

The most common regular expression functions that you are likely to use in PHP are `preg_match`, `preg_match_all`, and `preg_replace`.

To test whether the word *cats* appears anywhere within a string, in any combination of upper- and lowercase, you could use `preg_match` like this:

```
$n = preg_match("/cats/i", "Cats are crazy. I like cats.");
```

Because PHP uses 1 for TRUE and 0 for FALSE, the preceding statement sets `$n` to 1. The first argument is the regular expression, and the second is the text to match. But `preg_match` is actually a good deal more powerful and complicated, because it takes a third argument that shows what text matched:

```
$n = preg_match("/cats/i", "Cats are curious. I like cats.", $match);
echo "$n Matches: $match[0]";
```

The third argument is an array (here, given the name `$match`). The function puts the matching text into the first element, so if the match is successful, you can find the text that matched in `$match[0]`. In this example, the output lets us know that the matched text was capitalized:

```
1 Matches: Cats
```

If you wish to locate all matches, you use the `preg_match_all` function, like this:

```
$n = preg_match_all("/cats/i", "Cats are strange. I like cats.", $match);
echo "$n Matches: ";
for ($j=0 ; $j < $n ; ++$j) echo $match[0][$j]." ";
```

As before, $match is passed to the function and the element $match[0] is assigned the matches made, but this time as a subarray. To display the subarray, this example iterates through it with a for loop.

When you want to replace part of a string, you can use preg_replace as shown here. This example replaces all occurrences of the word *cats* with the word *dogs*, regardless of case:

```
echo preg_replace("/cats/i", "dogs", "Cats are furry. I like cats.");
```

 The subject of regular expressions is a large one, and entire books have been written about it. If you would like further information, I suggest the Wikipedia entry (*http://bit.ly/regex-wiki*), or *Regular-Expressions.info (https://www.regular-expressions.info)*.

Redisplaying a Form After PHP Validation

OK, back to form validation. So far we've created the HTML document *validate.html*, which will post through to the PHP program *adduser.php*, but only if JavaScript validates the fields or if JavaScript is disabled or unavailable.

So now it's time to create *adduser.php* to receive the posted form, perform its own validation, and then present the form again to the visitor if the validation fails. Example 16-3 contains the code that you should type and save (or download from the companion website).

Example 16-3. The adduser.php program

```
<?php // adduser.php

    // The PHP code

    $forename = $surname = $username = $password = $age = $email = "";

    if (isset($_POST['forename']))
      $forename = fix_string($_POST['forename']);
    if (isset($_POST['surname']))
      $surname  = fix_string($_POST['surname']);
    if (isset($_POST['username']))
      $username = fix_string($_POST['username']);
    if (isset($_POST['password']))
      $password = fix_string($_POST['password']);
    if (isset($_POST['age']))
      $age      = fix_string($_POST['age']);
    if (isset($_POST['email']))
      $email    = fix_string($_POST['email']);
```

```php
$fail  = validate_forename($forename);
$fail .= validate_surname($surname);
$fail .= validate_username($username);
$fail .= validate_password($password);
$fail .= validate_age($age);
$fail .= validate_email($email);

echo "<!DOCTYPE html>\n<html><head><title>An Example Form</title>";

if ($fail == "")
{
  echo "</head><body>Form data successfully validated:
    $forename, $surname, $username, $password, $age, $email.</body></html>";

  // This is where you would enter the posted fields into a database,
  // preferably using hash encryption for the password.

  exit;
}

echo <<<_END

  <!-- The HTML/JavaScript section -->

  <style>
    .signup {
      border: 1px solid #999999;
    font:    normal 14px helvetica; color:#444444;
    }
  </style>

  <script>
    function validate(form)
    {
      fail  = validateForename(form.forename.value)
      fail += validateSurname(form.surname.value)
      fail += validateUsername(form.username.value)
      fail += validatePassword(form.password.value)
      fail += validateAge(form.age.value)
      fail += validateEmail(form.email.value)

      if (fail == "")      return true
      else { alert(fail); return false }
    }

    function validateForename(field)
    {
      return (field == "") ? "No Forename was entered.\\n" : ""
    }

    function validateSurname(field)
    {
```

```
      return (field == "") ? "No Surname was entered.\\n" : ""
    }

    function validateUsername(field)
    {
      if (field == "") return "No Username was entered.\\n"
      else if (field.length < 5)
        return "Usernames must be at least 5 characters.\\n"
      else if (/[^a-zA-Z0-9_-]/.test(field))
        return "Only a-z, A-Z, 0-9, - and _ allowed in Usernames.\\n"
      return ""
    }

    function validatePassword(field)
    {
      if (field == "") return "No Password was entered.\\n"
      else if (field.length < 6)
        return "Passwords must be at least 6 characters.\\n"
      else if (!/[a-z]/.test(field) || ! /[A-Z]/.test(field) ||
               !/[0-9]/.test(field))
        return "Passwords require one each of a-z, A-Z and 0-9.\\n"
      return ""
    }

    function validateAge(field)
    {
      if (isNaN(field)) return "No Age was entered.\\n"
      else if (field < 18 || field > 110)
        return "Age must be between 18 and 110.\\n"
      return ""
    }

    function validateEmail(field)
    {
      if (field == "") return "No Email was entered.\\n"
        else if (!((field.indexOf(".") > 0) &&
                   (field.indexOf("@") > 0)) ||
                  /[^a-zA-Z0-9.@_-]/.test(field))
          return "The Email address is invalid.\\n"
      return ""
    }
  </script>
</head>
<body>

  <table border="0" cellpadding="2" cellspacing="5" bgcolor="#eeeeee">
    <th colspan="2" align="center">Signup Form</th>

      <tr><td colspan="2">Sorry, the following errors were found<br>
       in your form: <p><font color=red size=1><i>$fail</i></font></p>
      </td></tr>
```

```
        <form method="post" action="adduser.php" onSubmit="return validate(this)">
          <tr><td>Forename</td>
            <td><input type="text" maxlength="32" name="forename" value="$forename">
          </td></tr><tr><td>Surname</td>
            <td><input type="text" maxlength="32" name="surname"  value="$surname">
          </td></tr><tr><td>Username</td>
            <td><input type="text" maxlength="16" name="username" value="$username">
          </td></tr><tr><td>Password</td>
            <td><input type="text" maxlength="12" name="password" value="$password">
          </td></tr><tr><td>Age</td>
            <td><input type="text" maxlength="3"  name="age"        value="$age">
          </td></tr><tr><td>Email</td>
            <td><input type="text" maxlength="64" name="email"     value="$email">
          </td></tr><tr><td colspan="2" align="center"><input type="submit"
            value="Signup"></td></tr>
        </form>
      </table>
    </body>
</html>

_END;

  // The PHP functions

  function validate_forename($field)
  {
    return ($field == "") ? "No Forename was entered<br>": "";
  }

  function validate_surname($field)
  {
    return($field == "") ? "No Surname was entered<br>" : "";
  }

  function validate_username($field)
  {
    if ($field == "") return "No Username was entered<br>";
    else if (strlen($field) < 5)
      return "Usernames must be at least 5 characters<br>";
    else if (preg_match("/[^a-zA-Z0-9_-]/", $field))
      return "Only letters, numbers, - and _ in usernames<br>";
    return "";
  }

  function validate_password($field)
  {
    if ($field == "") return "No Password was entered<br>";
    else if (strlen($field) < 6)
      return "Passwords must be at least 6 characters<br>";
    else if (!preg_match("/[a-z]/", $field) ||
             !preg_match("/[A-Z]/", $field) ||
             !preg_match("/[0-9]/", $field))
```

```
      return "Passwords require 1 each of a-z, A-Z and 0-9<br>";
    return "";
}

function validate_age($field)
{
  if ($field == "") return "No Age was entered<br>";
  else if ($field < 18 || $field > 110)
    return "Age must be between 18 and 110<br>";
  return "";
}

function validate_email($field)
{
  if ($field == "") return "No Email was entered<br>";
    else if (!((strpos($field, ".") > 0) &&
               (strpos($field, "@") > 0)) ||
               preg_match("/[^a-zA-Z0-9.@_-]/", $field))
      return "The Email address is invalid<br>";
  return "";
}

function fix_string($string)
{
  if (get_magic_quotes_gpc()) $string = stripslashes($string);
  return htmlentities ($string);
}
?>
```

In this example, all input is sanitized prior to use—even passwords, which, since they may contain characters used to format HTML, will be changed into HTML entities. For example, & will become &, < will become <, and so on. If you will be using a hash function to store encrypted passwords, this will not be an issue as long as when you later check the password entered it is sanitized in the same way, so that the same inputs will be compared.

The result of submitting the form with JavaScript disabled (and two fields incorrectly completed) is shown in Figure 16-5.

Figure 16-5. The form as represented after PHP validation fails

I have put the PHP section of this code (and changes to the HTML section) in a bold typeface so that you can more clearly see the difference between this and Examples 16-1 and 16-2.

If you browsed through this example (or typed it in or downloaded it from the book's companion website (*http://lpmj.net*)), you'll have seen that the PHP code is almost a clone of the JavaScript code; the same regular expressions are used to validate each field in very similar functions.

But there are a couple of things to note. First, the fix_string function (right at the end) is used to sanitize each field and prevent any attempts at code injection from succeeding.

Also, you will see that the HTML from Example 16-1 has been repeated in the PHP code within an <<<_END..._END; structure, displaying the form with the values that the visitor entered the previous time. You do this by simply adding an extra value parameter to each <input> tag (such as value="$forename"). This courtesy is highly recommended so that the user only has to edit the previously entered values, and doesn't have to type the values in the fields all over again.

In the real world, you probably wouldn't start with an HTML form such as the one in Example 16-1. Instead, you'd be more likely to go straight ahead and write the PHP program in Example 16-3, which incorporates all the HTML. And, of course, you'd also need to make a minor tweak for the case when it's the first time the program is called up, to prevent it from displaying errors when all the fields are empty. You also might drop the six JavaScript functions into their own *.js* file for separate inclusion, as mentioned in "Using a separate JavaScript file" on page 377.

Now that you've seen how to bring PHP, HTML, and JavaScript together, the next chapter will introduce *Ajax* (Asynchronous JavaScript and XML), which uses JavaScript calls to the server in the background to seamlessly update portions of a web page, without having to resubmit the entire page to the web server.

Questions

1. What JavaScript method can you use to send a form for validation prior to submitting it?

2. What JavaScript method is used to match a string against a regular expression?

3. Write a regular expression to match any characters that are *not* in a word, as defined by regular expression syntax.

4. Write a regular expression to match either of the words *fox* or *fix*.

5. Write a regular expression to match any single word followed by any nonword character.

6. Using regular expressions, write a JavaScript function to test whether the word *fox* exists in the string The quick brown fox.

7. Using regular expressions, write a PHP function to replace all occurrences of the word *the* in The cow jumps over the moon with the word *my*.

8. What HTML attribute is used to precomplete form fields with a value?

See "Chapter 16 Answers" on page 725 in Appendix A for the answers to these questions.

CHAPTER 17

Using Asynchronous Communication

The term *Ajax* was first coined in 2005. It stands for *Asynchronous JavaScript and XML*, which, in simple terms, means using a set of methods built into JavaScript to transfer data between the browser and a server in the background. This term has now been mostly abandoned in favor of simply talking about asynchronous communication.

An excellent example of this technology is Google Maps (see Figure 17-1), in which new sections of a map are downloaded from the server when needed, without requiring a page refresh.

Using asynchronous communication not only substantially reduces the amount of data that must be sent back and forth, but also makes web pages seamlessly dynamic —allowing them to behave more like self-contained applications. The results are a much improved user interface and better responsiveness.

Figure 17-1. Google Maps is an excellent example of asynchronous communication

What Is Asynchronous Communication?

Asynchronous communication as used today had its beginning with the release of Internet Explorer 5 in 1999, which introduced a new ActiveX object, XMLHttpRequest. ActiveX is Microsoft's technology for signing plug-ins that install additional software on your computer. Other browser developers later followed suit, but rather than using ActiveX, they all implemented the feature as a native part of the JavaScript interpreter.

However, even before then, an early form of the technology had already surfaced that used hidden frames on a page that interacted with the server in the background. Chat rooms were early adopters, using it to poll for and display new message posts without requiring page reloads.

So, let's see how to implement asynchronous communication by using JavaScript.

Using XMLHttpRequest

Because of the differences between browser implementations of XMLHttpRequest, you must create a special function in order to ensure that your code will work in all major browsers.

To do this, you must understand the three ways of creating an XMLHttpRequest object:

- IE 5: `request = new ActiveXObject("Microsoft.XMLHTTP")`
- IE 6+: `request = new ActiveXObject("Msxml2.XMLHTTP")`
- All others: `request = new XMLHttpRequest()`

This is the case because Microsoft chose to implement a change with the release of Internet Explorer 6, while all other browsers use a slightly different method. Therefore, the code in Example 17-1 will work for all major browsers released over the last few years.

Example 17-1. A cross-browser asynchronous function

```
<script>
  function asyncRequest()
  {
    try // Non-IE browser?
    {   // Yes
      var request = new XMLHttpRequest()
    }
    catch(e1)
    {
      try // IE 6+?
      {   // Yes
        request = new ActiveXObject("Msxml2.XMLHTTP")
      }
      catch(e2)
      {
        try // IE 5?
        {   // Yes
          request = new ActiveXObject("Microsoft.XMLHTTP")
        }
        catch(e3) // There is no asynchronous support
        {
          request = false
        }
      }
    }
    return request
  }
</script>
```

You may remember the introduction to error handling in Chapter 14, using the `try...catch` construct. Example 17-1 is a perfect illustration of its utility, because it uses the `try` keyword to execute the non-IE command and, upon success, jumps on to the final `return` statement, where the new object is returned.

Otherwise, a `catch` traps the error, and the subsequent command is executed. Again, upon success, the new object is returned; otherwise, the final of the three commands is tried. If that attempt fails, then the browser doesn't support asynchronous communication and the request object is set to false; otherwise, the object is returned. So there you have it: a cross-browser request function that you may wish to add to your library of useful JavaScript functions.

OK, so now you have a means of creating an XMLHttpRequest object, but what can you do with these objects? Well, each one comes with a set of properties (variables) and methods (functions), which are detailed in Tables 17-1 and 17-2.

Table 17-1. An XMLHttpRequest object's properties

Property	Description
onreadystatechange	Specifies an event-handling function to be called whenever the readyState property of an object changes.
readyState	An integer property that reports on the status of a request. It can have any of these values: 0 = Uninitialized, 1 = Loading, 2 = Loaded, 3 = Interactive, or 4 = Completed.
responseText	The data returned by the server in text format.
responseXML	The data returned by the server in XML format.
status	The HTTP status code returned by the server.
statusText	The HTTP status text returned by the server.

Table 17-2. An XMLHttpRequest object's methods

Method	Description
abort()	Aborts the current request
getAllResponseHeaders()	Returns all headers as a string
getResponseHeader(*param*)	Returns the value of *param* as a string
open('*method*', '*url*', '*async*')	Specifies the HTTP method to use (GET or POST), the target URL, and whether the request should be handled asynchronously (true or false)
send(*data*)	Sends *data* to the target server using the specified HTTP method
setRequestHeader('*param*', '*value*')	Sets a header with a parameter/value pair

These properties and methods give you control over what data you send to the server and receive back, as well as a choice of send and receive methods. For example, you can choose whether to request data in plain text (which could include HTML and other tags) or in XML format. You can also decide whether you wish to use the POST or GET method to send to the server.

Let's look at the POST method first by creating a very simple pair of documents: a combination of HTML and JavaScript, and a PHP program to interact asynchronously with the first file. With a few lines of JavaScript, they request a web document from a third-party web server, which is then returned to the browser by your server and placed within a section of the current document.

Your First Asynchronous Program

Type and save the code in Example 17-2 as *urlpost.html*, but don't load it into your browser yet.

Example 17-2. urlpost.html

```
<!DOCTYPE html>
<html> <!-- urlpost.html -->
  <head>
    <title>Asynchronous Communication Example</title>
  </head>
  <body style='text-align:center'>
    <h1>Loading a web page into a DIV</h1>
    <div id='info'>This sentence will be replaced</div>

    <script>
      params  = "url=news.com"
      request = new asyncRequest()

      request.open("POST", "urlpost.php", true)
      request.setRequestHeader("Content-type",
        "application/x-www-form-urlencoded")
      request.setRequestHeader("Content-length", params.length)
      request.setRequestHeader("Connection", "close")

      request.onreadystatechange = function()
      {
        if (this.readyState == 4)
        {
          if (this.status == 200)
          {
            if (this.responseText != null)
            {
              document.getElementById('info').innerHTML =
                this.responseText
            }
            else alert("Communication error: No data received")
          }
          else alert( "Communication error: " + this.statusText)
        }
      }

      request.send(params)

      function asyncRequest()
      {
        try
        {
          var request = new XMLHttpRequest()
        }
```

```
      catch(e1)
      {
        try
        {
          request = new ActiveXObject("Msxml2.XMLHTTP")
        }
        catch(e2)
        {
          try
          {
            request = new ActiveXObject("Microsoft.XMLHTTP")
          }
          catch(e3)
          {
            request = false
          }
        }
      }
      return request
    }
  </script>
 </body>
</html>
```

Let's go through this document and look at what it does, starting with the first six lines, which simply set up an HTML document and display a heading. The next line creates a <div> with the ID info, containing the text This sentence will be replaced by default. Later on, the text returned from the call will be inserted here.

The next six lines are required for making an HTTP POST request. The first sets the variable params to a *parameter=value* pair, which is what we'll send to the server. Then the object request is created. After this, the open method is called to set the object to make a POST request to *urlpost.php* in asynchronous mode. The last three lines in this group set up headers that are required for the receiving server to know that a POST request is coming.

The readyState property

Now we get to the nitty-gritty of an asynchronous call, which all hangs on the ready State property. This allows the browser to keep accepting user input and changing the screen, while our program sets the onreadystatechange property to call a function of our choice each time readyState changes. In this case, a nameless (or anonymous) inline function has been used, as opposed to a separate, named function. This type of function is known as a *callback* function, as it is called back each time ready State changes.

The syntax to set up the callback function using an inline, anonymous function is as follows:

```
request.onreadystatechange = function()
{
  if (this.readyState == 4)
  {
    // do something
  }
}
```

If you wish to use a separate, named function, the syntax is slightly different:

```
request.onreadystatechange = asyncCallback

function asyncCallback()
{
  if (this.readyState == 4)
  {
    // do something
  }
}
```

Looking at Table 17-1, you'll see that `readyState` can have five values. But only one concerns us: the value 4, which represents a completed call. Therefore, each time the new function gets called, it returns without doing anything until `readyState` has a value of 4. When our function detects that value, it next inspects the `status` of the call to ensure it has a value of `200`, which means that the call succeeded. If it's not `200`, an alert pop-up displays the error message contained in `statusText`.

 You will notice that all of these object properties are referenced using `this.readyState`, `this.status`, and so on, rather than the object's current name, `request`, as in `request.readyState` or `request.status`. This is so that you can easily copy and paste the code and it will work with any object name, because the `this` keyword always refers to the current object.

So, having ascertained that the `readyState` is 4 and the `status` is `200`, we test the `responseText` value to see whether it contains a value. If not, an error message is displayed in an alert box. Otherwise, the inner HTML of the `<div>` is assigned the value of `responseText`, like this:

```
document.getElementById('info').innerHTML = this.responseText
```

In this line, the element `info` is referenced via the `getElementById` method, and then its `innerHTML` property is assigned the value that was returned by the call. The effect is that this element of the web page changes, while everything else remains the same.

After all this setting up and preparation, the asynchronous request is finally sent to the server via the following command, which passes the parameters already defined in the variable `params`:

```
request.send(params)
```

After that, all the preceding code is activated each time readyState changes.

The remainder of the document is the asyncRequest function from Example 17-1, and the closing </script> and HTML tags.

The server half of the asynchronous process

Now we get to the PHP half of the equation, which you can see in Example 17-3. Type this code and save it as *urlpost.php*.

Example 17-3. urlpost.php

```php
<?php // urlpost.php
  if (isset($_POST['url']))
  {
    echo file_get_contents('http://' . SanitizeString($_POST['url']));
  }

  function SanitizeString($var)
  {
    $var = strip_tags($var);
    $var = htmlentities($var);
    return stripslashes($var);
  }
?>
```

As you can see, this is short and sweet, and also makes use of the ever-important SanitizeString function, as should be done with all posted data. In this instance, unsanitized data could result in the user inserting JavaScript and gaining an advantage over your code.

This program uses the file_get_contents PHP function to load in the web page at the URL supplied to it in the variable $_POST['url']. The file_get_contents function is versatile in that it loads in the entire contents of a file or web page from either a local or a remote server; it even takes into account moved pages and other redirects.

Once you have typed the program, you are ready to call up *urlpost.html* in your web browser, and after a few seconds you should see the contents of the *news.com* front page loaded into the <div> that we created for that purpose. It won't be as fast as directly loading the web page, because it is transferred twice: once to the server and again from the server to your browser. The result should look like Figure 17-2.

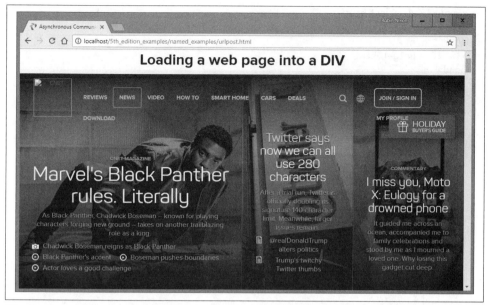

Figure 17-2. The news.com front page has been loaded into a div element

Not only have we succeeded in making an asynchronous call and having a response returned to JavaScript, but we've also harnessed the power of PHP to merge in a totally unrelated web object. Incidentally, if we had tried to find a way to asynchronously fetch this web page directly (without recourse to the PHP server-side module), we wouldn't have succeeded, because there are security blocks preventing cross-domain asynchronous communication. So, this example also illustrates a handy solution to a practical problem.

Using GET Instead of POST

As when you submit any data from a form, you have the option of submitting your data in the form of GET requests, and you will save a few lines of code if you do so. However, there is a downside: some browsers may cache GET requests, whereas POST requests will never be cached. You don't want to cache a request, because the browser will just redisplay what it got the last time instead of going to the server for fresh input. The solution to this is to use a workaround that adds a random parameter to each request, ensuring that each URL requested is unique.

Example 17-4 shows how you would achieve the same result as with Example 17-2, but using a GET request instead of POST.

Example 17-4. urlget.html

```html
<!DOCTYPE html>
<html> <!-- urlget.html -->
  <head>
    <title>Asynchronous Communication Example</title>
  </head>
  <body style='text-align:center'>
    <h1>Loading a web page into a DIV</h1>
    <div id='info'>This sentence will be replaced</div>

    <script>
      nocache = "&nocache=" + Math.random() * 1000000
      request = new asyncRequest()
      request.open("GET", "urlget.php?url=news.com" + nocache, true)

      request.onreadystatechange = function()
      {
        if (this.readyState == 4)
        {
          if (this.status == 200)
          {
            if (this.responseText != null)
            {
              document.getElementById('info').innerHTML =
                this.responseText
            }
            else alert("Communication error: No data received")
          }
          else alert( "Communication error: " + this.statusText)
        }
      }

      request.send(null)

      function asyncRequest()
      {
        try
        {
          var request = new XMLHttpRequest()
        }
        catch(e1)
        {
          try
          {
            request = new ActiveXObject("Msxml2.XMLHTTP")
          }
          catch(e2)
          {
            try
            {
              request = new ActiveXObject("Microsoft.XMLHTTP")
```

```
            }
            catch(e3)
            {
              request = false
            }
          }
        }
        return request
      }
    </script>
  </body>
</html>
```

The differences to note between the two documents are highlighted in bold, and described as follows:

- It is not necessary to send headers for a GET request.

- We call the open method using a GET request, supplying a URL with a string comprising a ? symbol followed by the parameter/value pair url=news.com.

- We start a second parameter/value pair using an & symbol, and then set the value of the parameter nocache to a random value between 0 and 1 million. This is done to ensure that each URL requested is different, and therefore that no requests will be cached.

- The call to send now contains only a parameter of null, as no parameters are being passed via a POST request. Note that leaving the parameter out is not an option, as it would result in an error.

To accompany this new document, the PHP program must be modified to respond to a GET request, as in Example 17-5, *urlget.php*.

Example 17-5. urlget.php

```php
<?php
  if (isset($_GET['url']))
  {
    echo file_get_contents("http://".sanitizeString($_GET['url']));
  }

  function sanitizeString($var)
  {
    $var = strip_tags($var);
    $var = htmlentities($var);
    return stripslashes($var);
  }
?>
```

The only difference between this and Example 17-3 is that the references to `$_POST` have been replaced with `$_GET`. The end result of calling up *urlget.html* in your browser is identical to loading *urlpost.html*.

Sending XML Requests

Although the objects we've been creating are called `XMLHttpRequest` objects, so far we have made absolutely no use of XML. As you have seen, we have been able to asynchronously request an entire HTML document, but we could equally have asked for a text page, a string or number, or even spreadsheet data.

So, let's modify the previous example document and PHP program to fetch some XML data. To do this, first take a look at the PHP program, *xmlget.php*, shown in Example 17-6.

Example 17-6. xmlget.php

```php
<?php
  if (isset($_GET['url']))
  {
    header('Content-Type: text/xml');
    echo file_get_contents("http://".sanitizeString($_GET['url']));
  }

  function sanitizeString($var)
  {
    $var = strip_tags($var);
    $var = htmlentities($var);
    return stripslashes($var);
  }
?>
```

This program has been very slightly modified (shown in bold highlighting) to output the correct XML header before returning a fetched document. No checking is done here, as it is assumed that the calling code will request an actual XML document.

Now on to the HTML document, *xmlget.html*, shown in Example 17-7.

Example 17-7. xmlget.html

```html
<!DOCTYPE html>
<html> <!-- xmlget.html -->
  <head>
    <title>Asynchronous Communication Example</title>
  </head>
  <body>
    <h1>Loading XML data into a DIV</h1>
    <div id='info'>This sentence will be replaced</div>
```

```
<script>
  nocache = "&nocache=" + Math.random() * 1000000
  url     = "rss.news.yahoo.com/rss/topstories"
  out     = "";

  request = new asyncRequest()
  request.open("GET", "xmlget.php?url=" + url + nocache, true)

  request.onreadystatechange = function()
  {
    if (this.readyState == 4)
    {
      if (this.status == 200)
      {
        if (this.responseText != null)
        {
          titles = this.responseXML.getElementsByTagName('title')

          for (j = 0 ; j < titles.length ; ++j)
          {
            out += titles[j].childNodes[0].nodeValue + '<br>'
          }
          document.getElementById('info').innerHTML = out
        }
        else alert("Communication error: No data received")
      }
      else alert( "Communication error: " + this.statusText)
    }
  }

  request.send(null)

  function asyncRequest()
  {
    try
    {
      var request = new XMLHttpRequest()
    }
    catch(e1)
    {
      try
      {
        request = new ActiveXObject("Msxml2.XMLHTTP")
      }
      catch(e2)
      {
        try
        {
          request = new ActiveXObject("Microsoft.XMLHTTP")
        }
        catch(e3)
```

```
            {
                request = false
            }
        }
    }
    return request
}
    </script>
  </body>
</html>
```

Again, the differences have been highlighted in bold. As you can see, this code is substantially similar to the previous versions, except that the URL now being requested, *rss.news.yahoo.com/rss/topstories*, contains an XML document, the *Yahoo! News Top Stories* feed.

The other big change is the use of the `responseXML` property, which replaces the `responseText` property. Whenever a server returns XML data, `responseXML` will contain the XML returned.

However, `responseXML` doesn't simply contain a string of XML text: it is actually a complete XML document object that we can examine and parse using DOM tree methods and properties. This means it is accessible, for example, by the JavaScript `getElementsByTagName` method.

About XML

An XML document will generally take the form of the RSS feed shown in Example 17-8. However, the beauty of XML is that we can store this type of structure internally in a DOM tree (see Figure 17-3) to make it quickly searchable.

Example 17-8. An XML document

```
<?xml version="1.0" encoding="UTF-8"?>
<rss version="2.0">
  <channel>
    <title>RSS Feed</title>
    <link>http://website.com</link>
    <description>website.com's RSS Feed</description>
    <pubDate>Mon, 11 May 2020 00:00:00 GMT</pubDate>
    <item>
      <title>Headline</title>
      <guid>http://website.com/headline</guid>
      <description>This is a headline</description>
    </item>
    <item>
      <title>Headline 2</title>
      <guid>http://website.com/headline2</guid>
      <description>The 2nd headline</description>
```

```
    </item>
  </channel>
</rss>
```

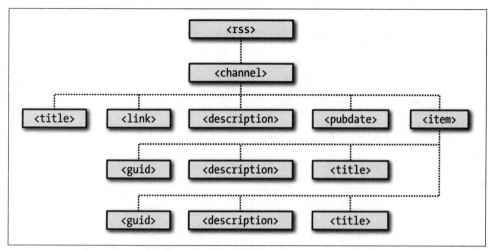

Figure 17-3. The DOM tree of Example 17-8

Then, using the `getElementsByTagName` method, we can quickly extract the values associated with various tags without a lot of string searching. This is exactly what we do in Example 17-7, where the following command is issued:

```
titles = this.responseXML.getElementsByTagName('title')
```

This single command has the effect of placing all the values of the `<title>` elements into the array `titles`. From there, it is a simple matter to extract them with the following expression (where `j` has been assigned to an integer that represents the title to access):

```
titles[j].childNodes[0].nodeValue
```

All the titles are then appended to the string variable `out`, and once they've all been processed, the result is inserted into the empty `<div>` at the document start. When you call up *xmlget.html* in your browser, the result will be something like Figure 17-4.

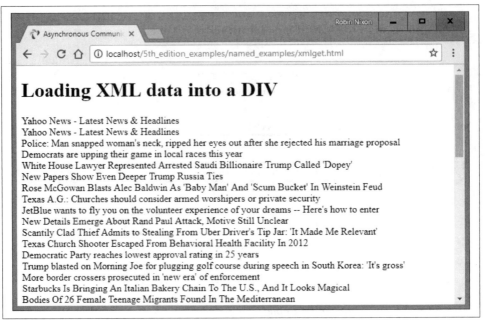

Figure 17-4. Asynchronously fetching a Yahoo! XML news feed

To recap, each entity such as `title` is a node, and so, for example, the title text is considered a node inside the title. But even after you get the child node, you have to ask for it as text, which is the purpose of `.nodeValue`. Also, as with all form data, remember that you can use either the POST or the GET method when requesting XML data; your choice will make little difference to the result.

Why use XML?

You may ask why you would use XML other than for fetching XML documents such as RSS feeds. Well, the simple answer is that you don't have to, but if you wish to pass structured data back to your applications, it could be a real pain to send a simple, unorganized jumble of text that would need complicated processing in JavaScript.

Instead, you can create an XML document and pass that back to the calling function, which will automatically place it into a DOM tree, as easily accessible as the HTML DOM object with which you are now familiar.

These days programmers are more likely to use JavaScript Object Notation (*http://json.org*) (JSON) as their preferred data-interchange format, as it's a simple subset of JavaScript.

Using Frameworks for Asynchronous Communication

Now that you know how to code your own asynchronous routines, you might like to investigate some of the free frameworks that are available to make it even easier, and which offer many more advanced features. In particular, I would suggest you check out jQuery, probably the most commonly used framework, which I introduce in Chapter 21. In the following chapter, though, we'll look at how to apply styling to your websites with CSS.

Questions

1. Why is it necessary to write a function for creating new XMLHttpRequest objects?

2. What is the purpose of the try...catch construct?

3. How many properties and how many methods does an XMLHttpRequest object have?

4. How can you tell when an asynchronous call has completed?

5. How do you know whether an asynchronous call completed successfully?

6. What XMLHttpRequest object property returns an asynchronous call's text response?

7. What XMLHttpRequest object property returns an asynchronous call's XML response?

8. How can you specify a callback function to handle asynchronous responses?

9. What XMLHttpRequest method is used to initiate an asynchronous request?

10. What are the main differences between an asynchronous GET and POST request?

See "Chapter 17 Answers" on page 726 in Appendix A for the answers to these questions.

CHAPTER 18

Introduction to CSS

Using Cascading Style Sheets (CSS), you can apply styles to your web pages to make them look exactly how you want. This works because CSS is connected to the Document Object Model (DOM), which I explained in Chapter 13.

With CSS and its integration with the DOM, you can quickly and easily restyle any element. For example, if you don't like the default look of the <h1>, <h2>, and other heading tags, you can assign new styles to override the default settings for the font family and size used, or whether bold or italics should be set, and many more properties too.

One way you can add styling to a web page is by inserting the required statements into the head of the page, between the <head> and </head> tags. So, to change the style of the <h1> tag, you might use the following code (I'll explain the syntax later):

```
<style>
  h1 { color:red; font-size:3em; font-family:Arial; }
</style>
```

Within an HTML page, this might look like Example 18-1 (see Figure 18-1), which, like all the examples in this chapter, uses the standard HTML5 DOCTYPE declaration.

Example 18-1. A simple HTML page

```
<!DOCTYPE html>
<html>
  <head>
    <title>Hello World</title>
    <style>
      h1 { color:red; font-size:3em; font-family:Arial; }
    </style>
  </head>
  <body>
```

```
    <h1>Hello there</h1>
  </body>
</html>
```

Figure 18-1. Styling a tag, with the original style shown in the inset

Importing a Stylesheet

When you wish to style a whole site, rather than a single page, a better way to manage stylesheets is to move them completely out of your web pages into separate files, and then import the ones you need. This lets you apply different stylesheets for different layouts (such as web and print), without changing the HTML.

There are a couple of different ways you can achieve this. The first is to use the CSS @import directive, like this:

```
<style>
  @import url('styles.css');
</style>
```

This statement tells the browser to fetch a stylesheet with the name *styles.css*. The @import command is quite flexible because you can put it in a stylesheet, so stylesheets can pull in other stylesheets, and so on. Just make sure that there are no <style> or </style> tags in any of your external stylesheets, or they will not work.

Importing CSS from Within HTML

You can also include a stylesheet with the HTML <link> tag, like this:

```
<link rel='stylesheet' href='styles.css'>
```

This has the exact same effect as the @import directive, except that <link> is an HTML-only tag and is not a valid style directive, so it cannot be used from within one stylesheet to pull in another, and also cannot be placed within a pair of <style>...</style> tags.

Just as you can use multiple @import directives within your CSS to include multiple external stylesheets, you can also use as many <link> elements as you like in your HTML.

Embedded Style Settings

There's also nothing stopping you from individually setting or overriding certain styles for the current page on a case-by-case basis by inserting style declarations directly within HTML, like this (which results in italic, blue text within the tags):

```
<div style='font-style:italic; color:blue;'>Hello there</div>
```

But this should be reserved only for the most exceptional circumstances, as it breaks the separation of content and presentation.

Using IDs

A better solution for setting the style of an element is to assign an ID to it in the HTML, like this:

```
<div id='welcome'>Hello there</div>
```

This states that the contents of the <div> with the ID welcome should have applied to them the style defined in the welcome style setting. The matching CSS statement for this might look like the following:

```
#welcome { font-style:italic; color:blue; }
```

Note the use of the # symbol, which specifies that only the ID with the name welcome should be styled with this statement.

Using Classes

The value of an id element must be unique within the web page, because that's what lets it serve as an identifier. If you would like to apply the same style to many elements, you do not have to give each one a different ID because you can specify a class to manage them all, like this:

```
<div class='welcome'>Hello</div>
```

This states that the contents of this element (and any others that use the class) should have applied to them the style defined in the welcome class. Once a class is applied, you can use the following rule, either in the page header or within an external stylesheet, for setting the styles for the class:

```
.welcome { font-style:italic; color:blue; }
```

Instead of the # symbol, which is reserved for IDs, class statements are prefaced with a . (period).

Using Semicolons

In CSS, semicolons are used to separate multiple CSS statements on the same line. But if there is only one statement in a rule (or in an inline style setting within an HTML tag), you can omit the semicolon, as you can for the final statement in a group.

However, to avoid hard-to-find CSS errors, you may prefer to always use a semicolon after every CSS setting. You can then copy and paste them, and otherwise modify properties, without worrying about removing semicolons where they aren't strictly necessary or having to add them where they are required.

CSS Rules

Each statement in a CSS rule starts with a *selector*, which is the item to which the rule will be applied. For example, in this assignment, h1 is the selector being given a font size 240 percent larger than the default:

```
h1 { font-size:240%; }
```

font-size is a *property*. Providing a value of 240% to the font-size property of the selector ensures that the contents of all <h1>...</h1> pairs of tags will be displayed at a font size that is 240 percent of the default size. All changes in rules must be within the { and } symbols that follow the selector. In font-size:240%; the part before the : (colon) is the property, while the remainder is the value applied to it.

Last comes a ; (semicolon) to end the statement. In this instance, because font-size is the last property in the rule, the semicolon is not required (but it would be if another assignment were to follow).

Multiple Assignments

You can create multiple style declarations in a couple of different ways. First, you can concatenate them on the same line, like this:

```
h1 { font-size:240%; color:blue; }
```

This adds a second assignment that changes the color of all <h1> headings to blue. You can also place the assignments one per line, like the following:

```
h1 { font-size:240%;
color:blue; }
```

Or you can space out the assignments a little more, so that they line up below each other in a column at the colons, like this:

```
h1 {
  font-size:240%;
  color    :blue;
}
```

This way, you can easily see where each new set of rules begins, because the selector is always in the first column, and the assignments that follow are neatly lined up with all property values starting at the same horizontal offset. In the preceding examples, the final semicolon is unnecessary, but should you ever want to concatenate any such groups of statements into a single line, it is very quick to do with all the semicolons already in place.

You can specify the same selector as many times as you want, and CSS combines all the properties. So, the previous example could also be specified as follows:

```
h1 { font-size: 240%; }
h1 { color    : blue; }
```

 There is no right or wrong way to lay out your CSS, but I recommend that you at least try to keep each block of CSS consistent with itself in terms of visual layout, so that other people can take it in at a glance.

What if you specified the same property to the same selector twice?

```
h1 { color : red; }
h1 { color : blue; }
```

The last value specified—in this case, blue—would apply. In a single file, repeating the same property for the same selector would be pointless, but such repetition happens frequently in real-life web pages when multiple stylesheets are applied. It's one of the valuable features of CSS, and where the term *cascading* comes from.

Using Comments

It is a good idea to comment your CSS rules, even if you describe only the main groups of statements rather than all or most of them. Do this by placing a comment within a pair of /*...*/ tags, like this:

```
/* This is a CSS comment */
```

You can extend a comment over many lines, like this:

```
/*
    A multi-
    line
    comment
*/
```

 When using multiline comments, note that you cannot nest single-line (or any other) comments within them. Doing so can lead to unpredictable errors.

Style Types

There are a number of different style types, ranging from the default styles set up by your browser (and any user styles you may have applied in your browser to override its defaults), through inline or embedded styles, to external stylesheets. The styles defined in each type have a hierarchy of precedence, from low to high.

We'll talk more about the *Cascading* part of Cascading Style Sheets, which is explained in "The CSS Cascade" on page 425. But before we go into the details, it helps to first have a brief introduction.

Default Styles

The lowest level of style precedence is the default styling applied by a web browser. These styles are created as a fallback for when a web page doesn't have any styles, and they are intended to be a generic set of styles that will display reasonably well in most instances.

Pre-CSS, these were the only styles applied to a document, and only a handful of them could be changed by a web page (such as font face, color, and a few element sizing arguments).

User Styles

User styles have the next highest precedence. They are supported by most modern browsers but are implemented differently by each, so the easiest way for you to create your own preferred browsing styles these days is to use a plug-in such as Stylish (*http://userstyles.org*). This is available for most popular browsers, except for the Microsoft Internet Explorer and Edge browsers, with which you must load your own user stylesheet from the Internet Options menu.

If you would like to learn how to create your own default styles for browsing, enter your browser's name followed by "user styles" in a search engine (for example, "Firefox user styles" or "Opera user styles"). Figure 18-2 shows a user stylesheet being applied to Internet Explorer.

Figure 18-2. Applying a user stylesheet to Internet Explorer

If a user style is assigned that has already been defined as a browser default, it will override the browser's default setting. Any styles not defined in a user stylesheet will retain their default values as set up in the browser.

External Stylesheets

The next type of styles are those assigned in an external stylesheet. These settings will override any assigned either by the user or by the browser. External stylesheets are the recommended way to create your styles because you can produce different stylesheets for different purposes, such as styling for general web use, for viewing on a mobile browser with a smaller screen, for printing purposes, and so on. Just apply the one needed for each type of media when you create the web page.

Internal Styles

Then there are internal styles, which you create within <style>...</style> tags, and which take precedence over all the preceding style types. At this point, though, you are beginning to break the separation between styling and content, as any external stylesheets loaded in at the same time will have a lower precedence.

Inline Styles

Finally, inline styles are where you assign a property directly to an element. They have the highest precedence of any style type, and are used like this:

```
<a href="http://google.com" style="color:green;">Visit Google</a>
```

In this example, the link specified will be displayed in green, regardless of any default or other color settings applied by any other type of stylesheet, whether directly to this link or generically for all links.

 When you use this type of styling, you are breaking the separation between layout and content; therefore, it is recommended that you do so only when you have a very good reason.

CSS Selectors

The means by which you access one or more elements is called *selection*, and the part of a CSS rule that does this is known as a *selector*. As you might expect, there are many varieties of selector.

The Type Selector

The type selector works on types of HTML elements such as `<p>` or `<i>`. For example, the following rule will ensure that all text within `<p>...</p>` tags is fully justified:

```
p { text-align:justify; }
```

The Descendant Selector

Descendant selectors let you apply styles to elements that are contained within other elements. For example, the following rule sets all text within `<b>...</b>` tags to red, but only if those tags occur within `<p>...</p>` tags (like this: `<p><b>Hello</b> there</p>`):

```
p b { color:red; }
```

Descendant selectors can continue nesting indefinitely, so the following is a perfectly valid rule to make the text blue within bold text, inside a list element of an unordered list:

```
ul li b { color:blue; }
```

As a practical example, suppose you want to use a different numbering system for an ordered list that is nested within another ordered list. You can achieve this in the following way, which will replace the default numeric numbering (starting from 1) with lowercase letters (starting from a):

```
<!DOCTYPE html>
<html>
  <head>
    <style>
      ol ol { list-style-type:lower-alpha; }
    </style>
  </head>
  <body>
    <ol>
      <li>One</li>
      <li>Two</li>
      <li>Three
        <ol>
          <li>One</li>
          <li>Two</li>
          <li>Three</li>
        </ol>
      </li>
    </ol>
  </body>
</html>
```

The result of loading this HTML into a web browser is as follows, in which you can see that the second list of elements displays differently:

```
1. One
2. Two
3. Three
   a. One
   b. Two
   c. Three
```

The Child Selector

The child selector is similar to the descendant selector but is more restrictive about when the style will be applied, by selecting only those elements that are direct children of another element. For example, the following code uses a descendant selector that will change any bold text within a paragraph to red, even if the bold text is itself within a section of italic text (like this `<p><i><b>Hello</b> there</i></p>`):

```
p b { color:red; }
```

In this instance, the word Hello displays in red. However, when this more general type of behavior is not required, a child selector can be used to narrow the scope of the selector. For example, the following rule inserts a greater-than sign (>) to create a child selector, which sets bold text to red only if the element is a direct child of a paragraph, and is not itself contained within another element:

```
p > b { color:red; }
```

Now Hello will not change color because <b> is not a direct child of <p>.

For a practical example, suppose you wish to make bold only those <li> elements that are direct children of <ol> elements. You can achieve this as follows, where the <li> elements that are direct children of <ul> elements are not made bold:

```
<!DOCTYPE html>
<html>
  <head>
    <style>
      ol > li { font-weight:bold; }
    </style>
  </head>
  <body>
    <ol>
      <li>One</li>
      <li>Two</li>
      <li>Three</li>
    </ol>
    <ul>
      <li>One</li>
      <li>Two</li>
      <li>Three</li>
    </ul>
  </body>
</html>
```

The result of loading this HTML into a browser will be as follows:

1. **One**
2. **Two**
3. **Three**

- One
- Two
- Three

The ID Selector

If you give an element an ID name (like this: <div id='mydiv'>), you can directly access it from CSS in the following way, which changes all text in the element to italic:

```
#mydiv { font-style:italic; }
```

Each ID can be used only once within a document, so only the first occurrence found will receive the new property value assigned by a CSS rule. But in CSS you can directly reference any IDs that have the same name, as long as they occur within different element types, like this:

```
<div id='myid'>Hello</div> <span id='myid'>Hello</span>
```

Because IDs normally apply only to unique elements, the following rule will apply an underline to only the first occurrence of `myid`:

```
#myid { text-decoration:underline; }
```

However, you can ensure that CSS applies the rule to both occurrences like this:

```
span#myid { text-decoration:underline; }
div#myid  { text-decoration:underline; }
```

Or more succinctly, like this (see "Selecting by Group" on page 425):

```
span#myid, div#myid { text-decoration:underline; }
```

I don't recommend using this form of selection because it raises barriers to the use of JavaScript. Any JavaScript that also must access these elements cannot easily do so because the commonly used `getElementById` function will return only the first occurrence. To reference any other instances, a program would have to search through the whole list of elements in the document—a trickier task to undertake. So, it's generally better to always use unique ID names.

The Class Selector

When you want to share the same styling among a number of elements in a page, you can assign them all the same class name (like this: `<span class='myclass'>`). Then create a single rule to modify all those elements at once, as in the following rule, which creates a 10-pixel left margin offset for all elements using the class:

```
.myclass { margin-left:10px; }
```

In modern browsers, you can have HTML elements use more than one class by separating the class names with spaces, like this: `<span class='class1 class2 class3'>`. Remember, though, that some very old browsers allow only a single class name in a `class` argument.

You can narrow the scope of action of a class by specifying the types of elements to which it should apply. For example, the following rule applies the setting only to paragraphs that use the class `main`:

```
p.main { text-indent:30px; }
```

In this example, only paragraphs using the class main (like this: `<p class="main">`) will receive the new property value. Any other element types that may try to use the class (such as `<div class="main">`) will not be affected by this rule.

The Attribute Selector

Many HTML tags support attributes, and using this type of selector can save you from having to use IDs and classes to refer to them. For example, you can directly reference attributes in the following manner, which sets all elements with the attribute `type="submit"` to a width of 100 pixels:

```
[type="submit"] { width:100px; }
```

If you wish to narrow down the scope of the selector to, for example, only `<form>` input elements with that attribute type, you could use the following rule instead:

```
form input[type="submit"] { width:100px; }
```

 Attribute selectors also work on IDs and classes, so for example, `[class~="classname"]` works exactly like the class selector `.class name` (except that the latter has a higher precedence). Likewise, `[id="idname"]` is equivalent to using the ID selector `#idname`. The class and ID selectors prefaced by # and . can therefore be viewed as shorthand for attribute selectors, but with a higher precedence. The ~= operator matches an attribute even if it is one of a space-separated group of attributes.

The Universal Selector

The * wildcard or universal selector matches any element, so the following rule will make a complete mess of a document by giving a green border to all of its elements:

```
* { border:1px solid green; }
```

It's therefore unlikely that you will use the * on its own, but as part of a compound rule it can be very powerful. For example, the following rule will apply the same styling as the preceding one, but only to all paragraphs that are subelements of the element with the ID boxout, and only as long as they are not direct children:

```
#boxout * p {border:1px solid green; }
```

Let's look at what's going on here. The first selector following #boxout is a * symbol, so it refers to any element within the boxout object. The following p selector then narrows down the selection focus by changing the selector to apply only to paragraphs (as defined by the p) that are subelements of elements returned by the * selector. Therefore, this CSS rule performs the following actions (in which I use the terms *object* and *element* interchangeably):

1. Find the object with the ID of boxout.

2. Find all subelements of the object returned in step 1.

3. Find all p subelements of the objects returned in step 2 and, since this is the final selector in the group, also find all p sub- and sub-subelements (and so on) of the objects returned in step 2.

4. Apply the styles within the { and } characters to the objects returned in step 3.

The net result of this is that the green border is applied only to paragraphs that are grandchildren (or great-grandchildren, and so on) of the main element.

Selecting by Group

Using CSS, you can apply a rule to more than one element, class, or any other type of selector at the same time by separating the selectors with commas. So, for example, the following rule will place a dotted orange line underneath all paragraphs, the element with the ID of idname, and all elements that use the class classname:

```
p, #idname, .classname { border-bottom:1px dotted orange; }
```

Figure 18-3 shows various selectors in use, with the rules applied to them alongside.

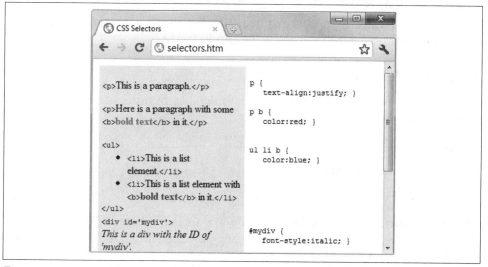

Figure 18-3. Some HTML and the CSS rules used by it

The CSS Cascade

As already briefly discussed, one of the most fundamental things about CSS properties is that they cascade—hence the name Cascading Style Sheets. But what does this mean?

Cascading is a method used to resolve potential conflicts between the various types of stylesheet a browser supports, and apply them in order of precedence by who created them, the method used to create the style, and the types of properties selected.

Stylesheet Creators

There are three main types of stylesheet supported by all modern browsers. In order of precedence from high to low, they are as follows:

1. Those created by a document's author
2. Those created by the user
3. Those created by the browser

These three sets of stylesheets are processed in reverse order. First, the defaults in the web browser are applied to the document. Without these defaults, web pages that don't use stylesheets would look terrible. They include the font face, size, and color; element spacing; table borders and spacing; and all the other reasonable standards a user would expect.

Next, if the user has created any styles to use instead of the standard ones, these are applied, replacing any of the browser's default styles that may conflict.

Last, any styles created by the current document's author are applied, replacing any that have been created either as browser defaults or by the user.

Stylesheet Methods

Stylesheets can be created via three different methods. In order of precedence from high to low, they are as follows:

1. As inline styles
2. In an embedded stylesheet
3. In an external stylesheet

Again, these methods of stylesheet creation are applied in reverse order of precedence. Therefore, all external stylesheets are processed first, and their styles are applied to the document.

Next, any embedded styles (within `<style>...</style>` tags) are processed, and any that conflict with external rules are given precedence and will override them.

Last, any styles applied directly to an element as an inline style (such as `<div style="...">...</div>`) are given the highest precedence, and override all previously assigned properties.

Stylesheet Selectors

There are three different ways of selecting elements to be styled. Going from highest to lowest order of precedence, they are as follows:

1. Referencing by individual ID or attribute selector

2. Referencing in groups by class

3. Referencing by element tags (such as <p> or <b>)

Selectors are processed according to the number and types of elements affected by a rule, which is a little different from the previous two methods for resolving conflicts. This is because rules do not have to apply only to one type of selector at a time, and may reference many different selectors.

Therefore, we need a method to determine the precedence of rules that can contain any combination of selectors. CSS does this by calculating the specificity of each rule by ordering them from the widest to narrowest scope of action.

Calculating specificity

We calculate the specificity of a rule by creating three-part numbers based on the selector types in the preceding numbered list. These compound numbers start off looking like [0,0,0]. When processing a rule, each selector that references an ID increments the first number by 1, so that the compound number would become [1,0,0].

Let's look at the following rule, which has seven references. Three of them are to the IDs #heading, #main, and #menu, so the compound number becomes [3,0,0]:

```
#heading #main #menu .text .quote p span {
    // Rules go here;
}
```

Then the number of classes in the selector is placed in the second part of the compound number. In this example, there are two of them (.text and .quote), so the compound number becomes [3,2,0].

Finally, all selectors that reference element tags are counted, and this number is placed in the last part of the compound number. In the example, there are two (p and span), so the final compound number becomes [3,2,2].

This is all that is needed to compare this rule's specificity with that of another. In cases such as this one where there are nine or fewer of each type in a compound number, you can convert it directly to a decimal number, which in this case is 322. Rules with a lower number than this will have lower precedence, and those with a higher number will have greater precedence. Where two rules share the same value, the most recently applied one wins.

For example, suppose we also have the following rule:

```
#heading #main .text .quote .news p span {
  // Rules go here;
}
```

Here, although seven elements are also referenced, there are now only two ID references but three class references, which results in the compound number [2,3,2]. Since 322 is greater than 232, the former example has precedence over the latter.

Using a different number base.   Where there are more than nine of a type in a compound number, you have to work in a higher number base. For example, you can't convert the compound number [11,7,19] to decimal by simply concatenating the three parts. Instead, you must convert the number to a higher base, such as base 20 (or higher if there are more than 19 of any type).

To do this, multiply the three parts out and add the results like this, starting with the rightmost number and working left:

```
        20 ×  19 =   380
      20×20 ×   7 =  2800
    20×20×20 × 11 = 88000
    Total in decimal = 91180
```

On the left, replace the values of 20 with the base you are using, as needed. Once all of the compound numbers of a set of rules are converted from this base to decimal, it is easy to determine the specificity, and therefore the precedence, of each.

Thankfully, the CSS processor handles all of this for you, but knowing how it works helps you to properly construct rules and understand what precedence they will have.

 If all this precedence calculation sounds rather complicated, you'll be pleased to know that in most cases you can usually get by with this simple rule of thumb: in general, the fewer elements there are to be modified, and the more specific they are, the greater the precedence that is given to a rule.

Some rules are more equal than others.   Where two or more style rules are exactly equivalent, only the most recently processed rule will take precedence. However, you can force a rule to a higher precedence than other equivalent rules by using the !impor tant declaration, like this:

```
p { color:#ff0000 !important; }
```

When you do this, all previous equivalent settings are overridden (even ones using `!important`), and any equivalent rules that are processed later will be ignored. So, for example, the second of the two following rules would normally take precedence, but because of the use of `!important` in the prior assignment, the second one is ignored:

```
p { color:#ff0000 !important; }
p { color:#ffff00 }
```

 User stylesheets can be created for specifying default browser styles, and they may use the `!important` declaration, in which case the user's style setting will take precedence over the same properties specified in the current web page. However, on very old browsers using CSS1, this feature isn't supported. You should also note that non-`!important` user style settings will be overwritten by any `!important` styles in web pages.

The Difference Between div and span Elements

Both `<div>` and `<span>` elements are types of containers, but with some different qualities. By default, a `<div>` element has infinite width (at least to the browser edge), which you can see by applying a border to one, like this:

```
<div style="border:1px solid green;">Hello</div>
```

A `<span>` element, however, is only as wide as the text it contains. Therefore, the following line of HTML creates a border only around the word Hello, which does not extend to the righthand edge of the browser:

```
<span style="border:1px solid green;">Hello</span>
```

Also, `<span>` elements follow text or other objects as they wrap around them, and can therefore have complicated borders. For example, in Example 18-2, I used CSS to make the background of all `<div>` elements yellow, to make all `<span>` elements cyan, and to add a border to both, before then creating a few example `<span>` and `<div>` sections.

Example 18-2. <div> and <span> example

```
<!DOCTYPE html>
<html>
  <head>
    <title>Div and span example</title>
    <style>
      div, span { border            :1px solid black; }
      div       { background-color:yellow;         }
      span      { background-color:cyan;           }
```

```
    </style>
  </head>
  <body>
    <div>This text is within a div tag</div>
    This isn't. <div>And this is again.</div><br>

    <span>This text is inside a span tag.</span>
    This isn't. <span>And this is again.</span><br><br>

    <div>This is a larger amount of text in a div that wraps around
    to the next line of the browser</div><br>

    <span>This is a larger amount of text in a span that wraps around
    to the next line of the browser</span>
  </body>
</html>
```

Figure 18-4 shows what this example looks like in a web browser. Although it appears only in shades of gray in the printed book, the figure clearly shows how <div> elements extend to the righthand edge of the browser window and force the following content to appear at the start of the first available position below them.

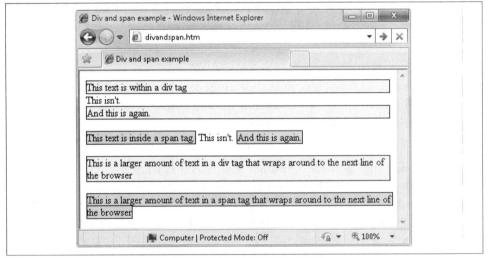

Figure 18-4. A variety of elements of differing width

The figure also shows how <span> elements keep to themselves and take up only the space required to hold their content, without forcing subsequent content to appear below them.

Additionally, in the bottom two examples in the figure you can see that when <div> elements wrap at the screen's edge, they retain a rectangular shape, whereas <span> elements simply follow the flow of the text (or other content) they contain.

Since `<div>` elements can only be rectangular, they are better suited for containing objects such as images, boxouts, quotations, and so on, whereas `<span>` tags are best used for holding text or other attributes that are placed one after another inline, and which should flow from left to right (or right to left in some languages).

Measurements

CSS supports an impressive range of units of measurement, enabling you to tailor your web pages precisely to specific values, or by relative dimensions. The ones I generally use (and believe you will also find the most useful) are pixels, points, ems, and percent, but here's the complete list:

Pixels

The size of a pixel varies according to the dimensions and pixel depth of the user's screen. One pixel equals the width/height of a single dot on the screen, and so this measurement is best suited to screens rather than print. For example:

```
.classname { margin:5px; }
```

Points

A point is equivalent in size to 1/72 of an inch. The measurement comes from a print design background and is best suited for that medium, but is also commonly used for on-screen display. For example:

```
.classname { font-size:14pt; }
```

Inches

An inch is the equivalent of 72 points and is also a measurement type best suited for print. For example:

```
.classname { width:3in; }
```

Centimeters

Centimeters are another unit of measurement best suited for print. One centimeter is a little over 28 points. For example:

```
.classname { height:2cm; }
```

Millimeters

A millimeter is 1/10 of a centimeter (or almost 3 points). Millimeters are another measure best suited to print. For example:

```
.classname { font-size:5mm; }
```

Picas

A pica is another print typographic measurement, which is equivalent to 12 points. For example:

```
.classname { font-size:1pc; }
```

Ems

An em is equal to the current font size and is therefore one of the more useful measurements for CSS since it is used to describe relative dimensions. For example:

```
.classname { font-size:2em; }
```

Exs

An ex is also related to the current font size; it is equivalent to the height of a lowercase letter *x*. This is a less popular unit of measurement that is most often used as a good approximation for helping to set the width of a box that will contain some text. For example:

```
.classname { width:20ex; }
```

Percent

This unit is related to the em in that it is exactly 100 times greater (when used on a font). Whereas 1 em equals the current font size, the same size is 100 in percent. When not relating to a font, this unit is relative to the size of the container of the property being accessed. For example:

```
.classname { height:120%; }
```

Figure 18-5 shows each of these measurement types in turn being used to display text in almost identical sizes.

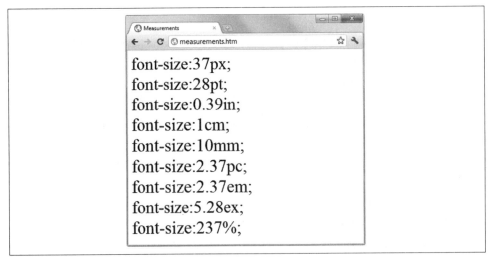

Figure 18-5. Different measurements that display almost the same

Fonts and Typography

You can change four main font properties using CSS: `font-family`, `font-style`, `font-size`, and `font-weight`. Between them, you can fine-tune the way text displays in your web pages and/or when printed.

font-family

The `font-family` property assigns the font to use. Here you can list a variety of fonts in order of preference from left to right, so that styling can fall back gracefully when the user doesn't have the preferred font installed. For example, to set the default font for paragraphs, you might use a CSS rule such as this:

```
p { font-family:Verdana, Arial, Helvetica, sans-serif; }
```

Where a font name is made up of two or more words, you must enclose the name in quotation marks, like this:

```
p { font-family:"Times New Roman", Georgia, serif; }
```

 Because they should be available in virtually all web browsers and operating systems, the safest font families to use on a web page are *Arial, Helvetica, Times New Roman, Times, Courier New*, and *Courier*. The *Verdana, Georgia, Comic Sans MS, Trebuchet MS, Arial Black*, and *Impact* fonts are safe for Mac and PC use, but may not be installed on other operating systems such as Linux. Other common but less safe fonts are *Palatino, Garamond, Bookman*, and *Avant Garde*. If you use one of the less safe fonts, make sure you offer fallbacks of one or more safer fonts in your CSS so that your web pages will degrade gracefully on browsers without your preferred fonts.

Figure 18-6 shows these two sets of CSS rules being applied.

Figure 18-6. Selecting font families

font-style

With the `font-style` property, you can choose to display a font normally, in italics, or obliquely. The following rules create three classes (`normal`, `italic`, and `oblique`) that can be applied to elements to create these effects:

```
.normal  { font-style:normal;  }
.italic  { font-style:italic;  }
.oblique { font-style:oblique; }
```

font-size

As described in the earlier section on measurements, there are a large number of ways you can change a font's size. But these all boil down to two main types: fixed and relative. A fixed setting looks like the following rule, which sets the default paragraph font size to 14 points:

```
p { font-size:14pt; }
```

Alternatively, you may wish to work with the current default font size, using it to style various types of text such as headings. In the following rules, relative sizes of some headers are defined, with the `<h4>` tag starting off 20 percent bigger than the default, and with each greater size another 40 percent larger than the previous one:

```
h1 { font-size:240%; }
h2 { font-size:200%; }
h3 { font-size:160%; }
h4 { font-size:120%; }
```

Figure 18-7 shows a selection of font sizes in use.

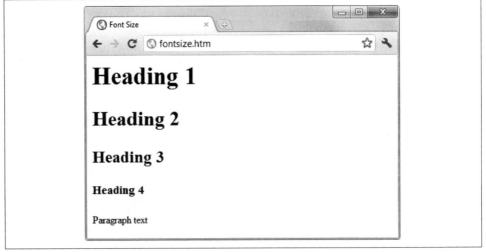

Figure 18-7. Setting four heading sizes and the default paragraph size

font-weight

Using the `font-weight` property, you can choose how boldly to display a font. It supports a number of values, but the main ones you will use are likely to be `normal` and `bold`, like this:

```
.bold { font-weight:bold; }
```

Managing Text Styles

Regardless of the font in use, you can further modify the way text displays by altering its decoration, spacing, and alignment. There is a crossover between the text and font properties, though, in that effects such as italics or bold text are achieved via the `font-style` and `font-weight` properties, while others such as underlining require the `text-decoration` property.

Decoration

With the `text-decoration` property, you can apply effects to text such as `underline`, `line-through`, `overline`, and `blink`. The following rule creates a new class called over that applies overlines to text (the weight of over, under, and through lines will match that of the font):

```
.over { text-decoration:overline; }
```

In Figure 18-8 you can see a selection of font styles, weights, and decorations.

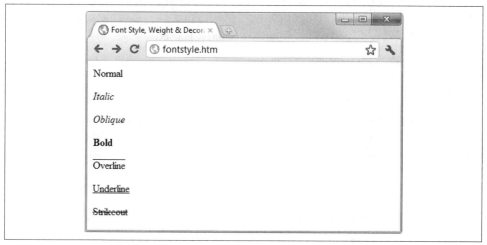

Figure 18-8. Examples of the styles and decoration rules available

Spacing

A number of different properties allow you to modify line, word, and letter spacing. For example, the following rules change the line spacing for paragraphs by modifying the `line-height` property to be 25 percent greater, set the `word-spacing` property to 30 pixels, and set `letter-spacing` to 3 pixels:

```
p {
  line-height    :125%;
  word-spacing   :30px;
  letter-spacing:3px;
}
```

You can equally choose to use a percentage value with `word-spacing` or `letter-spacing` to decrease or increase the default amount of space applied to a font by using values less than or greater than 100%, which will work with proportional and non-proportional fonts.

Alignment

There are four types of text alignment available in CSS: `left`, `right`, `center`, and `justify`. In the following rule, the default paragraph text is set to full justification:

```
p { text-align:justify; }
```

Transformation

There are four properties available for transforming your text: `none`, `capitalize`, `uppercase`, and `lowercase`. The following rule creates a class called `upper` that will ensure that all text is displayed in uppercase when it is used:

```
.upper { text-transform:uppercase; }
```

Indenting

Using the `text-indent` property, you can indent the first line of a block of text by a specified amount. The following rule indents the first line of every paragraph by 20 pixels, although a different unit of measurement or a percent increase could also be applied:

```
p { text-indent:20px; }
```

In Figure 18-9 the following rules have been applied to a section of text:

```
p {          line-height    :150%;
             word-spacing   :10px;
             letter-spacing:1px;
}
.justify    { text-align     :justify;   }
```

```
.uppercase { text-transform:uppercase; }
.indent    { text-indent   :20px;      }
```

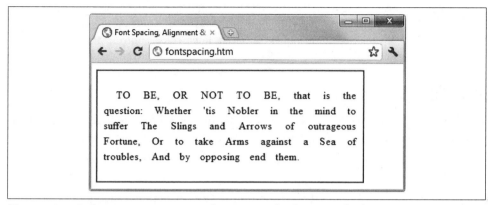

Figure 18-9. Indenting, uppercase, and spacing rules being applied

CSS Colors

You can apply colors to the foreground and background of text and objects by using the color and background-color properties (or by supplying a single argument to the background property). The colors specified can be one of the named colors (such as red or blue), colors created from hexadecimal RGB triplets (such as #ff0000 or #0000ff), or colors created using the rgb CSS function.

The standard 16 color names as defined by the W3C standards organization (*http://www.w3.org*) are aqua, black, blue, fuchsia, gray, green, lime, maroon, navy, olive, purple, red, silver, teal, white, and yellow. The following rule uses one of these names to set the background color for an object with the ID of object:

```
#object { background-color:silver; }
```

In this rule, the foreground color of text in all <div> elements is set to yellow (because on a computer display, hexadecimal levels of ff red, plus ff green, plus 00 blue create the color yellow):

```
div { color:#ffff00; }
```

Or, if you don't wish to work in hexadecimal, you can specify your color triplets by using the rgb function, as in the following rule, which changes the background color of the current document to aqua:

```
body { background-color:rgb(0, 255, 255); }
```

If you prefer not to work in ranges of 256 levels per color, you can use percentages in the `rgb` function instead, with values from 0 to 100 ranging from the lowest (0) amount of a primary color through to the highest (100), like this: `rgb(58%, 95%, 74%)`. You can also use floating-point values for even finer color control, like this: `rgb(23.4%, 67.6%, 15.5%)`.

Short Color Strings

There is also a short form of the hex digit string in which only the first of each 2-byte pair is used for each color. For example, instead of assigning the color #fe4692, you use #f49, omitting the second hex digit from each pair, which equates to a color value of #ff4499.

This results in almost the same color and is useful where exact colors are not required. The difference between a 6-digit and 3-digit string is that the former supports 16 million different colors, while the latter supports 4,000.

Wherever you intend to use a color such as #883366, this is the direct equivalent of #836 (since the repeated digits are implied by the shorter version), and you can use either string to create the exact same color.

Gradients

In place of using a solid background color, you can choose to apply a gradient, which will then automatically flow from a given initial color to a final color of your choice. It is best used in conjunction with a simple color rule so that browsers that don't support gradients will at least display a solid color.

Example 18-3 uses a rule to display an orange gradient (or simply plain orange on nonsupporting browsers), as shown in the middle section of Figure 18-10.

Example 18-3. Creating a linear gradient

```
<!DOCTYPE html>
<html>
  <head>
    <title>Creating a linear gradient</title>
    <style>
      .orangegrad {
        background:orange;
        background:linear-gradient(top, #fb0, #f50);
        background:-moz-linear-gradient(top, #fb0, #f50);
        background:-webkit-linear-gradient(top, #fb0, #f50);
        background:-o-linear-gradient(top, #fb0, #f50);
        background:-ms-linear-gradient(top, #fb0, #f50); }
    </style>
```

```
  </head>
  <body>
    <div class='orangegrad'>Black text<br>
    on an orange<br>linear gradient</div>
  </body>
</html>
```

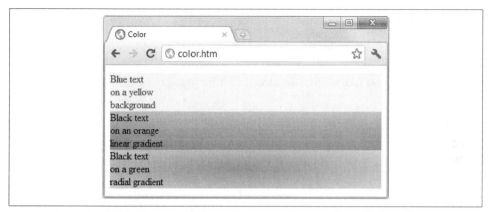

Figure 18-10. A solid background color, a linear gradient, and a radial gradient

 As shown in the preceding example, many CSS rules require browser-specific prefixes such as `-moz-`, `-webkit-`, `-o-`, and `-ms-` (for Mozilla-based browsers such as Firefox; WebKit-based browsers such as Apple Safari, Google Chrome, and the iOS and Android browsers; and the Opera and Microsoft browsers, respectively). The Can I use... website (*http://caniuse.com*) lists the major CSS rules and attributes, and whether browser-specific versions are required. If in doubt, include all the browser-specific prefixes as well as the standard rule name and your styles should apply correctly on all browsers (that support the rules you are using).

To create a gradient, choose where it will begin out of `top`, `bottom`, `left`, `right`, and `center` (or any combination, such as `top left` or `center right`), enter the start and end colors you require, and then apply either the `linear-gradient` or `radial-gradient` rule, making sure you also supply rules for all browsers you are targeting.

You can also use more than just a start and end color by supplying what are termed *stop* colors in between as additional arguments. For example, if five arguments are supplied, each argument will control the color change over a fifth of the area, determined by its location in the argument list.

In addition to gradients you can also apply transparency to CSS objects, as detailed in Chapter 19.

Positioning Elements

Elements within a web page fall where they are placed in the document, but you can move them about by changing an element's `position` property from the default of `static` to one of `absolute`, `relative`, `sticky`, or `fixed`.

Absolute Positioning

An element with absolute positioning is removed from the document, and any other elements that are capable will flow into its released space. You can then position the object anywhere you like within the document by using the `top`, `right`, `bottom`, and `left` properties.

So, for example, to move an object with the ID of `object` to the absolute location of 100 pixels down from the document start and 200 pixels in from the left, you would apply the following rules to it (you can also use any of the other units of measurement supported by CSS):

```
#object {
  position:absolute;
  top     :100px;
  left    :200px;
}
```

The object will rest either on top of or behind other elements that it overlaps, depending on the value assigned to the `z-index` property (which works only on positioned elements). The default `z-index` value of an element is `auto`, where the browser will work it out for you. Alternatively, you can give the property an integer value (which may be negative), like this:

```
#object {
  position:absolute;
  top :100px;
  left :200px;
  z-index:100;
}
```

Objects then appear in order from the lowest to highest `z-index` level, with higher values displaying on top of lower ones.

Relative Positioning

Likewise, you can move the object relative to the location it would occupy in the normal document flow. So, for example, to move `object` 10 pixels down and 10 pixels to the right of its normal location, you would use the following rules:

```
#object {
  position:relative;
```

```
    top     :10px;
    left    :10px;
  }
```

Fixed Positioning

The final `position` property setting lets you move an object to an absolute location, but only within the current browser viewport. Then, when the document is scrolled, the object remains exactly where it has been placed, with the main document scrolling beneath it—a great way to create dock bars and other similar devices. To fix the object to the top-left corner of the browser window, use the following rules:

```
#object {
  position:fixed;
  top      :0px;
  left     :0px;
}
```

Example 18-4 demonstrates applying different positioning values to objects on a page.

Example 18-4. Applying different positioning values

```
<!DOCTYPE html>
<html>
  <head>
    <title>Positioning</title>
    <style>
      #container {
        position   :absolute;
        top        :50px;
        left       :0px;
      }
      #object1 {
        position   :absolute;
        background:pink;
        width      :100px;
        height     :100px;
        top        :0px;
        left       :0px;
      }
      #object2 {
        position   :relative;
        background:lightgreen;
        width      :100px;
        height     :100px;
        top        :0px;
        left       :110px;
      }
      #object3 {
        position   :fixed;
```

```
        background:yellow;
        width      :100px;
        height     :100px;
        top        :50px;
        left       :220px;
      }
    </style>
  </head>
  <body>
    <br><br><br><br><br>
    <div id='container'>
      <div id='object1'>Absolute Positioning</div>
      <div id='object2'>Relative Positioning</div>
      <div id='object3'>Fixed Positioning</div>
    </div>
  </body>
</html>
```

In Figure 18-11, Example 18-4 has been loaded into a browser, and the browser window has been reduced in width and height so that you must scroll down to see all of the web page.

Figure 18-11. Using different positioning values

When this is done, it is immediately obvious that the element with fixed positioning (object3) remains in place even through scrolling. You can also see that the container element (with the name container) has absolute positioning and is located exactly at 50 pixels down, with 0 pixels horizontal offset, so that object1 (which has absolute positioning within container) appears at that location. Meanwhile, object2 has relative positioning and so is offset from the left margin of container by 110 pixels, to line up alongside object1 .

In the figure, object3, even though it appears within the container element in the HTML, has fixed positioning and therefore is actually totally independent from the other objects and not constricted to stay within the bounds of container. It is set to initially line up alongside object1 and object2, but has stayed put while the others have been scrolled up the page, and now appears offset below them.

Pseudoclasses

A number of selectors and classes are used only within a stylesheet and do not have any matching tags or attributes within HTML. Their task is to classify elements using characteristics other than their name, attributes, or content—that is, characteristics that cannot be deduced from the document tree. These include pseudoclasses such as link and visited. There are also pseudoelements that make a selection, which may consist of partial elements such as first-line or first-letter.

Pseudoclasses and pseudoelements are separated by a : (colon) character. For example, to create a class called bigfirst for emphasizing the first letter of an element, you would use a rule such as the following:

```
.bigfirst:first-letter {
  font-size:400%;
  float     :left;
}
```

When the bigfirst class is applied to an element, the first letter will be displayed much enlarged, with the remaining text shown at normal size, neatly flowing around it (due to the float property) as if the first letter were an image or other object. Pseudoclasses include hover, link, active, and visited, all of which are mostly useful for applying to anchor elements—as in the following rules, which set the default color of all links to blue, and that of links that have already been visited to light blue:

```
a:link    { color:blue;     }
a:visited { color:lightblue; }
```

The following rules are interesting in that they use the hover pseudoclass so that they are applied only when the mouse pointer is positioned over the element. In this example, they change the link to white text on a red background, providing a dynamic effect you would normally expect only from using JavaScript code:

```
a:hover {
  color     :white;
  background:red;
}
```

Here I have used the background property with a single argument, instead of the longer background-color property.

The active pseudoclass is also dynamic in that it effects a change to a link during the time between the mouse button being clicked and released, as with this rule, which changes the link color to dark blue:

```
a:active { color:darkblue; }
```

Another interesting dynamic pseudoclass is focus, which is applied only when an element is given focus by the user selecting it with the keyboard or mouse. The following rule uses the universal selector to always place a mid-gray, dotted, 2-pixel border around the currently focused object:

```
*:focus { border:2px dotted #888888; }
```

 This discussion applies to traditional web development, not development for mobile/touch devices. We'll focus more on that topic in Chapter 22, where we look at jQuery Mobile.

Example 18-5 displays two links and an input field, as shown in Figure 18-12. The first link shows up as gray since it has already been visited in this browser, but the second link has not and displays in blue. The Tab key has been pressed, and the focus of input is now the input field, so its background has changed to yellow. When either link is clicked, it will display in purple, and when hovered over, it will appear red.

Example 18-5. Link and focus pseudoclasses

```
<!DOCTYPE html>
<html>
  <head>
    <title>Pseudoclasses</title>
    <style>
      a:link    { color:blue; }
      a:visited { color:gray; }
      a:hover   { color:red; }
      a:active  { color:purple; }
      *:focus   { background:yellow; }
    </style>
  </head>
  <body>
    <a href='http://google.com'>Link to Google'</a><br>
    <a href='nowhere'>Link to nowhere'</a><br>
    <input type='text'>
  </body>
</html>
```

Figure 18-12. Pseudoclasses applied to a selection of elements

Other pseudoclasses are also available; for more information, see the HTML Dog "Pseudo Classes" tutorial (*https://htmldog.com/guides/css/intermediate/pseudoclasses/*).

> Beware of applying the focus pseudoclass to the universal selector, *, as shown in this example; Internet Explorer regards an unfocused document as having focus applied to the entire web page, and (in this instance) the whole page will turn yellow until Tab is pressed or focus is otherwise applied to one of the page's elements.

Shorthand Rules

To save space, groups of related CSS properties can be concatenated into a single shorthand assignment. For example, I have already used the shorthand for creating a border a few times, as in the focus rule in the previous section:

```
*:focus { border:2px dotted #ff8800; }
```

This is actually a shorthand concatenation of the following rule set:

```
*:focus {
  border-width:2px;
  border-style:dotted;
  border-color:#ff8800;
}
```

When using a shorthand rule, you need only apply the properties up to the point where you wish to change values. So, you could use the following to set only a border's width and style, choosing not to set its color:

```
*:focus { border:2px dotted; }
```

The order in which the properties are placed in a shorthand rule can be important, and misplacing them is a common way to get unexpected results. Since there are far too many to detail in this chapter, if you wish to use shorthand CSS, you will need to look up the default properties and their order of application using a CSS manual or search engine. To get you started, I recommend reading Trenton Moss's article (*https://www.webcredible.com/blog/css-shorthand-properties/*) on the topic.

The Box Model and Layout

The CSS properties affecting the layout of a page are based around the *box model*, a nested set of properties surrounding an element. Virtually all elements have (or can have) these properties, including the document body, whose margin you can (for example) remove with the following rule:

```
body { margin:0px; }
```

The box model of an object starts at the outside, with the object's margin. Inside this is the border, then there is padding between the border and the inner contents, and finally you have the object's contents.

Once you have the hang of the box model, you will be well on your way to creating professionally laid-out pages, since these properties alone will make up much of your page styling.

Setting Margins

The margin is the outermost level of the box model. It separates elements from each other, and its use is quite smart. For example, assume you give a number of elements a default margin of 10 pixels around each. This is the amount of space you would like to appear between two elements positioned one below the other—but if they each have a margin of 10 pixels, won't the result be a gap of 20 pixels?

In fact, CSS overcomes this potential issue: when two elements with margins defined are positioned directly one after the other, only the larger of the two margins is used to separate them. If both margins are the same width, just one of the widths is used. This way, you are much more likely to get the result you want. But you should note that the margins of absolutely positioned or inline elements do not collapse in this way.

The margins of an element can be changed en masse with the `margin` property, or individually with `margin-left`, `margin-top`, `margin-right`, and `margin-bottom`. When setting the `margin` property, you can supply one, two, three, or four arguments, which have the effects commented in the following rules:

```
/* Set all margins to 1 pixel */
margin:1px;

/* Set top and bottom to 1 pixel, and left and right to 2 */
margin:1px 2px;

/* Set top to 1 pixel, left and right to 2, and bottom to 3 */
margin:1px 2px 3px;

/* Set top to 1 pixel, right to 2, bottom to 3, and left to 4 */
margin:1px 2px 3px 4px;
```

In Example 18-6, a `margin` property rule (highlighted in bold) is applied to a square element that has been placed inside a `table` element. Figure 18-13 shows this example loaded into a browser. The table has been given no dimensions, so it will simply wrap as closely around the inner <div> element as it can. As a consequence, there is a margin of 10 pixels above it, 20 pixels to its right, 30 pixels below it, and 40 pixels to its left.

Example 18-6. How margins are applied

```
<!DOCTYPE html>
<html>
  <head>
    <title>CSS Margins</title>
    <style>
      #object1 {
        background  :lightgreen;
        border-style:solid;
        border-width:1px;
        font-family :"Courier New";
        font-size   :9px;
        width       :100px;
        height      :100px;
        padding     :5px;
        margin      :10px 20px 30px 40px;
      }
      table {
        padding     :0;
        border      :1px solid black;
        background  :cyan;
      }
    </style>
  </head>
<body>
  <table>
    <tr>
      <td>
        <div id='object1'>margin:<br>10px 20px 30px 40px;</div>
      </td>
```

```
      </tr>
    </table>
  </body>
</html>
```

Figure 18-13. The outer table expands according to the margin widths

Applying Borders

The border level of the box model is similar to the margin, except that there is no collapsing. It is the next level as we move into the box model. The main properties used to modify borders are `border`, `border-left`, `border-top`, `border-right`, and `border-bottom`, and each of these can have other subproperties added as suffixes, such as `-color`, `-style`, and `-width`.

The four ways of accessing individual property settings used for the `margin` property also apply with the `border-width` property, so all the following are valid rules:

```
/* All borders */
border-width:1px;

/* Top/bottom and left/right */
border-width:1px 5px;

/* Top, left/right, and bottom */
border-width:1px 5px 10px;

/* Top, right, bottom, and left */
border-width:1px 5px 10px 15px;
```

Figure 18-14 shows each of these rules applied in turn to a group of square elements. In the first one, you can clearly see that all borders have a width of 1 pixel. The second element, however, has a top and bottom border width of 1 pixel, while its side borders are each 5 pixels wide. The third element has a 1-pixel-wide top border, while its sides are 5 pixels wide and its bottom is 10 pixels wide. The fourth element has a 1-

pixel top border width, a 5-pixel right border width, a 10-pixel bottom border width, and a 15-pixel left border width.

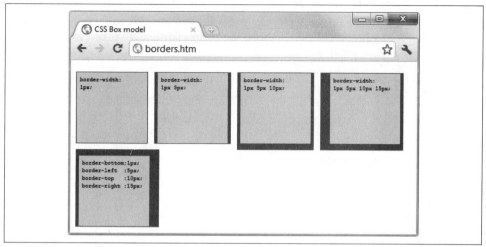

Figure 18-14. Applying long- and shorthand border rule values

The final element, under the previous ones, doesn't use the shorthand rules; instead, it sets each of the border widths separately. As you can see, it takes a lot more typing to achieve the same result.

Adjusting Padding

The deepest of the box model levels (other than the contents of an element) is the padding, which is applied inside any borders and/or margins. The main properties used to modify padding are `padding`, `padding-left`, `padding-top`, `padding-right`, and `padding-bottom`.

The four ways of accessing individual property settings used for the `margin` and `bor der` properties also apply with the `padding` property, so all the following are valid rules:

```
/* All padding */
padding:1px;

/* Top/bottom and left/right */
padding:1px 2px;

/* Top, left/right, and bottom */
padding:1px 2px 3px;

/* Top, right, bottom, and left */
padding:1px 2px 3px 4px;
```

Figure 18-15 shows the padding rule (shown in bold) in Example 18-7 applied to some text within a table cell (as defined by the rule `display:table-cell;`, which makes the encapsulating <div> element display like a table cell), which has been given no dimensions so it will simply wrap as closely around the text as it can. As a consequence, there is padding of 10 pixels above the inner element, 20 pixels to its right, 30 pixels below it, and 40 pixels to its left.

Example 18-7. Applying padding

```
<!DOCTYPE html>
<html>
  <head>
    <title>CSS Padding</title>
    <style>
      #object1 {
        border-style:solid;
        border-width:1px;
        background  :orange;
        color       :darkred;
        font-family :Arial;
        font-size   :12px;
        text-align  :justify;
        display     :table-cell;
        width       :148px;
        padding     :10px 20px 30px 40px; }
    </style>
  </head>
  <body>
    <div id='object1'>To be, or not to be that is the question:
    Whether 'tis Nobler in the mind to suffer
    The Slings and Arrows of outrageous Fortune,
    Or to take Arms against a Sea of troubles,
    And by opposing end them.</div>
  </body>
</html>
```

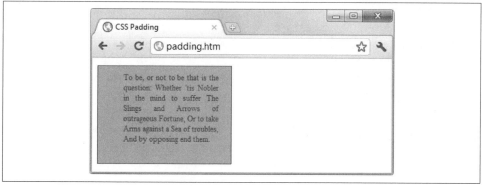

Figure 18-15. Applying different padding values to an object

Object Contents

Finally, deep within the box model levels, at its center, lies an element that can be styled in all the ways discussed in this chapter. As you now know, this element can (and usually will) contain further subelements, which in turn may contain sub-subelements, and so on, each with its own styling and box model settings.

Questions

1. Which directive do you use to import one stylesheet into another (or the `<style>` section of some HTML)?

2. What HTML tag can you use to import a stylesheet into a document?

3. Which HTML tag attribute is used to directly embed a style into an element?

4. What is the difference between a CSS ID and a CSS class?

5. Which characters are used to prefix (a) IDs and (b) class names in a CSS rule?

6. In CSS rules, what is the purpose of the semicolon?

7. How can you add a comment to a stylesheet?

8. Which character is used by CSS to represent any element?

9. How can you select a group of different elements and/or element types in CSS?

10. Given a pair of CSS rules with equal precedence, how can you make one have greater precedence than the other?

See "Chapter 18 Answers" on page 727 in Appendix A for the answers to these questions.

CHAPTER 19

Advanced CSS with CSS3

The first implementation of CSS was drawn up in 1996, and released in 1999; it has been supported by all browser releases since 2001. The standard for this version (CSS1) was revised in 2008. Then, beginning in 1998, developers began drawing up the second specification (CSS2); its standard was completed in 2007 and revised in 2009.

Development for the CSS3 specification commenced in 2001, with some features being proposed in 2009, and the latest recommendations being included as recently as 2016.

A CSS4 is already being proposed by the CSS working group, although this is not a major leap forward. Rather, it's simply a development of one part of CSS—the selectors—and its contents are beyond the scope of this book, given that the first draft discussion documents (*https://drafts.csswg.org/selectors-4/*) are only just being published as I write this edition.

Thankfully, though, the CSS working group publishes regular snapshots of the CSS modules that it considers stable. So far, four such best-current-practices documents have been published as Notes, with the most recent being in 2017 (*https://www.w3.org/TR/css-2017/*). This is the best place to gauge the current state of play in the world of CSS.

In this chapter, I'll take you through the most important CSS3 features that have been adopted by the major browsers, many of which provide functionality that hitherto could be attained only with JavaScript.

I recommend using CSS3 to implement dynamic features where you can, instead of JavaScript. The features provided by CSS make document attributes part of the document itself, instead of being tacked on through JavaScript. Making them part of the document is a cleaner design.

It has to be said that there's an awful lot to CSS, and browsers implement the various features differently (if at all). Therefore, I recommend that whenever you wish to ensure that the CSS you are creating will work in all browsers, you first take a look at the Can I use... website (*http://caniuse.com*). It maintains a record of what features are available in which browsers, so it will always be more up-to-date than this book, which sees a new edition only every couple of years or so—and CSS can move a long way in that time.

Attribute Selectors

In the previous chapter, I detailed the various CSS attribute selectors, which I will now quickly recap. Selectors are used in CSS to match HTML elements, and there are 10 different types, as listed in Table 19-1.

Table 19-1. CSS selectors, pseudoclasses, and pseudoelements

Selector type	Example
Universal selector	`* { color:#555; }`
Type selectors	`b { color:red; }`
Class selectors	`.classname { color:blue; }`
ID selectors	`#id { background:cyan; }`
Descendant selectors	`span em { color:green; }`
Child selectors	`div > em { background:lime; }`
Adjacent sibling selectors	`i + b { color:gray; }`
Attribute selectors	`a[href='info.htm'] { color:red; }`
Pseudoclasses	`a:hover { font-weight:bold; }`
Pseudoelements	`P::first-letter { font-size:300%; }`

The CSS3 designers decided that most of these selectors worked just fine the way they were, but three enhancements have been made so that you can more easily match elements based on the contents of their attributes. The following sections examine these.

Matching Parts of Strings

In CSS2 you can use a selector such as `a[href='info.htm']` to match the string `info.htm` when found in an `href` attribute, but there's no way to match only a *portion* of a string. CSS3 comes to the rescue with three new operators: `^`, `$`, and `*`. If one directly precedes the = symbol, you can match the start, end, or any part of a string, respectively.

The ^= operator

This operator matches at the start of a string. So, for example, the following will match any `href` attribute whose value begins with the string `http://website`:

```
a[href^='http://website']
```

Therefore, the following element will match:

```
<a href='http://website.com'>
```

But this will not:

```
<a href='http://mywebsite.com'>
```

The $= operator

To match only at the end of a string, you can use a selector such as the following, which will match any `img` tag whose `src` attribute ends with `.png`:

```
img[src$='.png']
```

For example, the following will match:

```
<img src='photo.png'>
```

But this will not:

```
<img src='snapshot.jpg'>
```

The *= operator

To match any substring anywhere in the attribute, you can use a selector such as the following, which finds any links on a page that have the string `google` anywhere within them:

```
a[href*='google']
```

For example, the HTML segment `<a href='http://google.com'>` will match, while the segment `<a href='http://gmail.com'>` will not.

The box-sizing Property

The W3C box model specifies that the width and height of an object should refer only to the dimensions of an element's content, ignoring any padding or border. But some web designers have expressed a desire to specify dimensions that refer to an entire element, including any padding and border.

To provide this feature, CSS3 lets you choose the box model you wish to use with the `box-sizing` property. For example, to use the total width and height of an object including padding and borders, use this declaration:

```
box-sizing:border-box;
```

Or, to have an object's width and height refer only to its content, use this declaration (the default):

```
box-sizing:content-box;
```

CSS3 Backgrounds

CSS3 provides two new properties: `background-clip` and `background-origin`. Between them, you can specify where a background should start within an element, and how to clip the background so that it doesn't appear in parts of the box model where you don't want it to.

To accomplish this, both properties support the following values:

`border-box`
Refers to the outer edge of the border

`padding-box`
Refers to the outer edge of the padding area

`content-box`
Refers to the outer edge of the content area

The background-clip Property

The `background-clip` property specifies whether the background should be ignored (clipped) if it appears within either the border or padding area of an element. For example, the following declaration states that the background may display in all parts of an element, all the way to the outer edge of the border:

```
background-clip:border-box;
```

To keep the background from appearing within the border area of an element, you can restrict it to only the section of an element inside the outer edge of its padding area, like this:

```
background-clip:padding-box;
```

Or to restrict the background to display only within the content area of an element, use this declaration:

```
background-clip:content-box;
```

Figure 19-1 shows three rows of elements displayed in the Safari web browser, in which the first row uses `border-box` for the `background-clip` property, the second uses `padding-box`, and the third uses `content-box`.

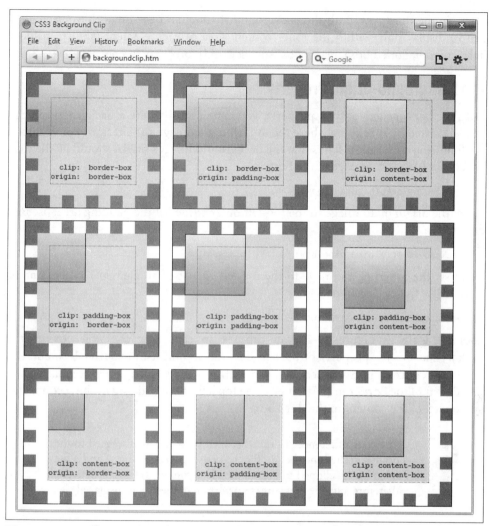

Figure 19-1. Different ways of combining CSS3 background properties

In the first row, the inner box (an image file that has been loaded into the top left of the element, with repeating disabled) is allowed to display anywhere in the element. You can also clearly see it displayed in the border area of the first box because the border has been set to dotted.

In the second row, neither the background image nor the background shading displays in the border area, because they have been clipped to the padding area with a background-clip property value of padding-box.

Then, in the third row, both the background shading and the image have been clipped to display only within the inner content area of each element (shown inside a light-colored, dotted box), using a `background-clip` property of `content-box`.

The background-origin Property

With the `background-origin` property, you can control where a background image will be located by specifying where the top left of the image should start. For example, the following declaration states that the background image's origin should be the top-left corner of the outer edge of the border:

```
background-origin:border-box;
```

To set the origin of an image to the top-left outer corner of the padding area, use this declaration:

```
background-origin:padding-box;
```

Or to set the origin of an image to the top-left corner of an element's inner content section, use this declaration:

```
background-origin:content-box;
```

Looking again at Figure 19-1, you can see in each row the first box uses a `background-origin` property of `border-box`, the second uses `padding-box`, and the third uses `content-box`. Consequently, in each row the smaller inner box displays at the top left of the border in the first box, the top left of the padding in the second, and the top left of the content in the third box.

 The only differences to note between the rows, with regard to the origins of the inner box in Figure 19-1, are that in rows 2 and 3 the inner box is clipped to the padding and content areas, respectively; therefore, outside these areas no portion of the box is displayed.

The background-size Property

In the same way that you can specify the width and height of an image when used in the `<img>` tag, you can now also do so for background images in the latest versions of all browsers.

You apply the property as follows (where *ww* is the width and *hh* is the height):

```
background-size:wwpx hhpx;
```

If you prefer, you can use only one argument, and then both dimensions will be set to that value. Also, if you apply this property to a block-level element such as a `<div>` (rather than one that is inline, such as a `<span>`), you can specify the width and/or height as a percentage, instead of a fixed value.

Using the auto Value

If you wish to scale only one dimension of a background image, and then have the other one scale automatically to retain the same proportions, you can use the value auto for the other dimension, like this:

```
background-size:100px auto;
```

This sets the width to 100 pixels, and the height to a value proportionate to the increase or decrease in width.

 Different browsers may require different versions of the various background property names, so please refer to the Can I use... website (*http://caniuse.com*) when using them to ensure you are applying all the versions required for the browsers you are targeting.

Multiple Backgrounds

With CSS3 you can attach multiple backgrounds to an element, each of which can use the previously discussed CSS3 background properties. Figure 19-2 shows an example of this; eight different images have been assigned to the background, to create the four corners and four edges of the certificate border.

To display multiple background images in a single CSS declaration, separate them with commas. Example 19-1 shows the HTML and CSS used to create the background in Figure 19-2.

Example 19-1. Using multiple images in a background

```
<!DOCTYPE html>
<html> <!-- backgroundimages.html -->
  <head>
    <title>CSS3 Multiple Backgrounds Example</title>
    <style>
      .border {
        font-family:'Times New Roman';
        font-style :italic;
        font-size  :170%;
        text-align :center;
        padding    :60px;
        width      :350px;
        height     :500px;
        background :url('b1.gif') top    left  no-repeat,
                    url('b2.gif') top    right no-repeat,
                    url('b3.gif') bottom left  no-repeat,
                    url('b4.gif') bottom right no-repeat,
                    url('ba.gif') top          repeat-x,
                    url('bb.gif') left         repeat-y,
```

```
                    url('bc.gif') right        repeat-y,
                    url('bd.gif') bottom       repeat-x
      }
    </style>
  </head>
  <body>
    <div class='border'>
      <h1>Employee of the month</h1>
      <h2>Awarded To:</h2>
      <h3>_____</h3>
      <h2>Date:</h2>
      <h3>___/___/____</h3>
    </div>
  </body>
</html>
```

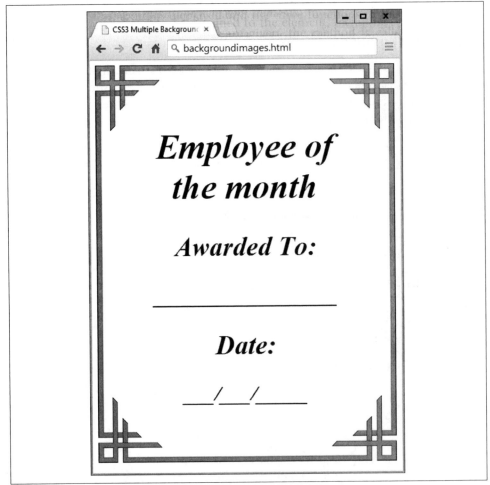

Figure 19-2. A background created with multiple images

Looking at the CSS section, you see that the first four lines of the `background` declaration place the corner images into the four corners of the element, and the final four place the edge images, which are handled last because the order of priority for background images goes from top to bottom. In other words, where they overlap, additional background images will appear behind already placed images. If the GIFs were in the reverse order, the repeating edge images would display on top of the corners, which would be incorrect.

 Using this CSS, you can resize the containing element to any dimensions, and the border will always correctly resize to fit, which is much easier than using tables or multiple elements for the same effect.

CSS3 Borders

CSS3 also brings a lot more flexibility to the way borders can be presented, by allowing you to independently change the colors of all four border edges, to display images for the edges and corners, to provide a radius value for applying rounded corners to borders, and to place box shadows underneath elements.

The border-color Property

There are two ways you can apply colors to a border. First, you can pass a single color to the property, as follows:

```
border-color:#888;
```

This property sets all the borders of an element to mid-gray. You can also set border colors individually, like this (which sets the border colors to various shades of gray):

```
border-top-color    :#000;
border-left-color   :#444;
border-right-color  :#888;
border-bottom-color:#ccc;
```

Or you can set all the colors individually with a single declaration, as follows:

```
border-color:#f00 #0f0 #880 #00f;
```

This declaration sets the top border color to #f00, the right one to #0f0, the bottom one to #880, and the left one to #00f (red, green, orange, and blue, respectively). You can also use color names for the arguments.

The border-radius Property

Prior to CSS3, talented web developers came up with numerous tweaks and fixes in order to achieve rounded borders, generally using <table> or <div> tags.

But now adding rounded borders to an element is really simple, and it works in the latest versions of all major browsers, as shown in Figure 19-3, in which a 10-pixel border is displayed in different ways. Example 19-2 shows the HTML for this.

Example 19-2. The border-radius property

```
<!DOCTYPE html>
<html> <!-- borderradius.html -->
  <head>
    <title>CSS3 Border Radius Examples</title>
    <style>
      .box {
        margin-bottom:10px;
        font-family :'Courier New', monospace;
        font-size   :12pt;
        text-align  :center;
        padding     :10px;
        width       :380px;
        height      :75px;
        border      :10px solid #006;
      }
      .b1 {
        -moz-border-radius   :40px;
        -webkit-border-radius:40px;
        border-radius        :40px;
      }
      .b2 {
        -moz-border-radius   :40px 40px 20px 20px;
        -webkit-border-radius:40px 40px 20px 20px;
        border-radius        :40px 40px 20px 20px;
      }
      .b3 {
        -moz-border-radius-topleft        :20px;
        -moz-border-radius-topright       :40px;
        -moz-border-radius-bottomleft     :60px;
        -moz-border-radius-bottomright    :80px;
        -webkit-border-top-left-radius    :20px;
        -webkit-border-top-right-radius   :40px;
        -webkit-border-bottom-left-radius :60px;
        -webkit-border-bottom-right-radius:80px;
        border-top-left-radius     :20px;
        border-top-right-radius    :40px;
        border-bottom-left-radius  :60px;
        border-bottom-right-radius :80px;
      }
      .b4 {
        -moz-border-radius-topleft        :40px 20px;
        -moz-border-radius-topright       :40px 20px;
        -moz-border-radius-bottomleft     :20px 40px;
        -moz-border-radius-bottomright    :20px 40px;
        -webkit-border-top-left-radius    :40px 20px;
```

```
        -webkit-border-top-right-radius   :40px 20px;
        -webkit-border-bottom-left-radius :20px 40px;
        -webkit-border-bottom-right-radius:20px 40px;
        border-top-left-radius            :40px 20px;
        border-top-right-radius           :40px 20px;
        border-bottom-left-radius         :20px 40px;
        border-bottom-right-radius        :20px 40px;
      }
    </style>
  </head>
  <body>
    <div class='box b1'>
      border-radius:40px;
    </div>

    <div class='box b2'>
      border-radius:40px 40px 20px 20px;
    </div>

    <div class='box b3'>
      border-top-left-radius    :20px;<br>
      border-top-right-radius   :40px;<br>
      border-bottom-left-radius :60px;<br>
      border-bottom-right-radius:80px;
    </div>

    <div class='box b4'>
      border-top-left-radius    :40px 20px;<br>
      border-top-right-radius   :40px 20px;<br>
      border-bottom-left-radius :20px 40px;<br>
      border-bottom-right-radius:20px 40px;
    </div>
  </body>
</html>
```

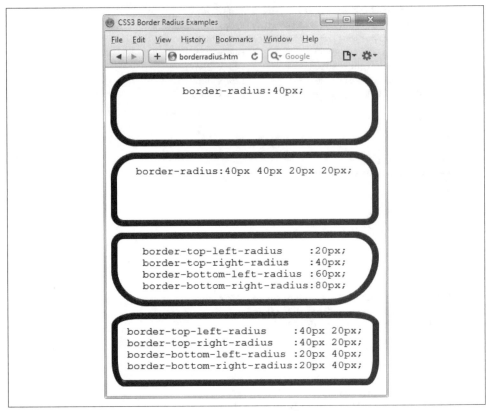

Figure 19-3. Mixing and matching various border radius properties

So, for example, to create a rounded border with a radius of 20 pixels, you could simply use the following declaration:

```
border-radius:20px;
```

 Although most browsers will work fine with border radius properties (including IE), some current (and many older) versions of the major browsers use different property names. So, if you wish to support them all, you will need to also use the relevant browser-specific prefixes for them, such as `-moz-` and `-webkit-`. To ensure that Example 19-2 works in all browsers, I have included all the required prefixes.

You can specify a separate radius for each of the four corners, like this (applied in a clockwise direction starting from the top-left corner):

```
border-radius:10px 20px 30px 40px;
```

If you prefer, you can also address each corner of an element individually, like this:

```
border-top-left-radius     :20px;
border-top-right-radius    :40px;
border-bottom-left-radius  :60px;
border-bottom-right-radius :80px;
```

And, when referencing individual corners, you can supply two arguments to choose a different vertical and horizontal radius (giving more interesting and subtle borders), like this:

```
border-top-left-radius     :40px 20px;
border-top-right-radius    :40px 20px;
border-bottom-left-radius  :20px 40px;
border-bottom-right-radius :20px 40px;
```

The first argument is the horizontal and the second is the vertical radius.

Box Shadows

To apply a box shadow, specify a horizontal and vertical offset from the object, the amount of blurring to add to the shadow, and the color to use, like this:

```
box-shadow:15px 15px 10px #888;
```

The two instances of 15px specify the vertical and horizontal offset from the element, and these values can be negative, zero, or positive. The 10px specifies the amount of blurring, with smaller values resulting in less blurring, and the #888 is the color for the shadow, which can be any valid color value. The result of this declaration can be seen in Figure 19-4.

Figure 19-4. A box shadow displayed under an element

Also use the WebKit (-webkit-) and Mozilla (-moz-) prefixes to this property for those browsers, to ensure compatibility with all recent versions.

Element Overflow

In CSS2, you can indicate what to do when one element is too large to be fully contained by its parent by setting the overflow property to hidden, visible, scroll, or auto. But with CSS3, you can now separately apply these values in the horizontal or vertical directions, too, as with these example declarations:

```
overflow-x:hidden;
overflow-x:visible;
overflow-y:auto;
overflow-y:scroll;
```

Multicolumn Layout

One of the features most requested by web developers is multiple columns, and this has finally been realized in CSS3, with Internet Explorer 10 being the last major browser to adopt it.

Now, flowing text over multiple columns is as easy as specifying the number of columns and then (optionally) choosing the spacing between them and the type of dividing line (if any), as shown in Figure 19-5 (created with Example 19-3).

Figure 19-5. Flowing text in multiple columns

Example 19-3. Using CSS to create multiple columns

```
<!DOCTYPE html>
<html> <!-- multiplecolumns.html -->
```

```
<head>
  <title>Multiple Columns</title>
  <style>
    .columns {
      text-align           :justify;
      font-size            :16pt;
      -moz-column-count    :3;
      -moz-column-gap      :1em;
      -moz-column-rule     :1px solid black;
      -webkit-column-count:3;
      -webkit-column-gap   :1em;
      -webkit-column-rule :1px solid black;
      column-count         :3;
      column-gap           :1em;
      column-rule          :1px solid black;
    }
  </style>
</head>
<body>
  <div class='columns'>
    Now is the winter of our discontent
    Made glorious summer by this sun of York;
    And all the clouds that lour'd upon our house
    In the deep bosom of the ocean buried.
    Now are our brows bound with victorious wreaths;
    Our bruised arms hung up for monuments;
    Our stern alarums changed to merry meetings,
    Our dreadful marches to delightful measures.
    Grim-visaged war hath smooth'd his wrinkled front;
    And now, instead of mounting barded steeds
    To fright the souls of fearful adversaries,
    He capers nimbly in a lady's chamber
    To the lascivious pleasing of a lute.
  </div>
</body>
</html>
```

Within the .columns class, the first two lines simply tell the browser to right-justify the text and to set it to a font size of 16pt. These declarations aren't needed for multiple columns, but they improve the text display. The remaining lines set up the element so that, within it, text will flow over three columns, with a gap of 1em between the columns and with a single-pixel border down the middle of each gap.

 In Example 19-3, Mozilla- and WebKit-based browsers may require their browser-specific prefixes to the declarations.

Colors and Opacity

The ways in which you can define colors have been greatly expanded with CSS3, and you can now also use CSS functions to apply colors in the common formats RGB (red, green, and blue), RGBA (red, green, blue, and alpha), HSL (hue, saturation, and luminance), and HSLA (hue, saturation, luminance, and alpha). The alpha value specifies a color's transparency, which allows underlying elements to show through.

HSL Colors

To define a color with the `hsl` function, you must first choose a value for the hue between `0` and `359` from a color wheel. Any higher color numbers simply wrap around to the beginning again, so the value of `0` is red, and so are the values `360` and `720`.

In a color wheel, the primary colors of red, green, and blue are separated by 120 degrees, so that pure red is `0`, green is `120`, and blue is `240`. The numbers between these values represent shades comprising different proportions of the primary colors on either side.

Next you need the saturation level, which is a value between 0 and 100 percent. This specifies how washed out or vibrant a color will appear. The saturation values commence in the center of the wheel with a mid-gray color (a saturation of 0 percent) and then become more and more vivid as they progress to the outer edge (a saturation of 100 percent).

All that's left then is for you to decide how bright you want the color to be, by choosing a luminance value of between 0 and 100 percent. A value of `50%` for the luminance gives the fullest, brightest color; decreasing the value (down to a minimum of `0%`) darkens the color until it displays as black; and increasing the value (up to a maximum of `100%`) lightens the color until it shows as white. You can visualize this as if you are mixing levels of either black or white into the color.

Therefore, for example, to choose a fully saturated yellow color with standard percent brightness, you would use a declaration such as this:

```
color:hsl(60, 100%, 50%);
```

Or, for a darker blue color, you might use a declaration such as this:

```
color:hsl(240, 100%, 40%);
```

You can also use this (and all other CSS color functions) with any property that expects a color, such as `background-color` and so on.

HSLA Colors

To provide even further control over how colors will appear, you can use the `hsla` function, supplying it with a fourth (alpha) level for a color, which is a floating-point value between `0` and `1`. A value of `0` specifies that the color is totally transparent, while `1` means it is fully opaque.

Here's how you would choose a fully saturated yellow color with standard brightness and 30 percent opacity:

```
color:hsla(60, 100%, 50%, 0.3);
```

Or, for a fully saturated but lighter blue color with 82 percent opacity, you might use this declaration:

```
color:hsla(240, 100%, 60%, 0.82);
```

RGB Colors

You will probably be more familiar with the RGB system of selecting a color, as it's similar to the *#nnnnnn* and *#nnn* color formats. For example, to apply a yellow color to a property, you can use either of the following declarations (the first supporting 16 million colors, and the second supporting 4,000):

```
color:#ffff00;
color:#ff0;
```

You can also use the CSS `rgb` function to achieve the same result, but with decimal numbers instead of hexadecimal (where 255 decimal is `ff` hexadecimal):

```
color:rgb(255, 255, 0);
```

But even better than that, you don't even have to think in amounts of up to 256 anymore, because you can specify percentage values, like this:

```
color:rgb(100%, 100%, 0);
```

In fact, you can now get very close to a desired color by simply thinking about its primary colors. For example, green and blue make cyan, so to create a color close to cyan, but with more blue in it than green, you could make a good first guess at 0% red, 40% green, and 60% blue, and try a declaration such as this:

```
color:rgb(0%, 40%, 60%);
```

RGBA Colors

As with the `hsla` function, the `rgba` function supports a fourth alpha argument, so you can, for example, apply the previous cyan-like color with an opacity of 40 percent by using a declaration such as this:

```
color:rgba(0%, 40%, 60%, 0.4);
```

The opacity Property

The `opacity` property provides the same alpha control as the `hsla` and `rgba` functions, but lets you modify an object's opacity (or transparency if you prefer) separately from its color.

To use it, apply a declaration such as the following to an element (which in this example sets the opacity to 25 percent, or 75 percent transparent):

```
opacity:0.25;
```

 WebKit- and Mozilla-based browsers require browser-specific prefixes to this property. And for backward compatibility with releases of Internet Explorer prior to version 9, you should add the following declaration (in which the opacity value is multiplied by 100):

```
filter:alpha(opacity='25');
```

Text Effects

A number of new effects can now be applied to text with the help of CSS3, including text shadows, text overlapping, and word wrapping.

The text-shadow Property

The `text-shadow` property is similar to the `box-shadow` property and takes the same set of arguments: a horizontal and vertical offset, an amount for the blurring, and the color to use. For example, the following declaration offsets the shadow by 3 pixels both horizontally and vertically, and displays the shadow in dark gray, with a blurring of 4 pixels:

```
text-shadow:3px 3px 4px #444;
```

The result of this declaration looks like Figure 19-6, and works in all recent versions of all major browsers (but not IE 9 or lower).

This is shadowed text

Figure 19-6. Applying a shadow to text

The text-overflow Property

When using any of the CSS overflow properties with a value of `hidden`, you can also use the `text-overflow` property to place an ellipsis (three dots) just before the cutoff to indicate that some text has been truncated, like this:

```
text-overflow:ellipsis;
```

Without this property, when the text "To be, or not to be. That is the question." is truncated, the result will look like Figure 19-7; with the declaration applied, however, the result is like Figure 19-8.

Figure 19-7. The text is automatically truncated

Figure 19-8. Instead of being cut off, the text trails off using an ellipsis

For this to work, three things are required:

- The element should have an `overflow` property that is not visible, such as `overflow:hidden`.
- The element must have the `white-space:nowrap` property set to constrain the text.
- The width of the element must be less than that of the text to truncate.

The word-wrap Property

When you have a really long word that is wider than the element containing it, it will either overflow or be truncated. But as an alternative to using the `text-overflow` property and truncating text, you can use the `word-wrap` property with a value of `break-word` to wrap long lines, like this:

```
word-wrap:break-word;
```

For example, in Figure 19-9 the word *Honorificabilitudinitatibus* is too wide for the containing box (whose righthand edge is shown as a solid vertical line between the letters *t* and *a*) and, because no overflow properties have been applied, it has overflowed its bounds.

Figure 19-9. The word is too wide for its container and has overflowed

But in Figure 19-10, the word-wrap property of the element has been assigned a value of break-word, so the word has neatly wrapped around to the next line.

Figure 19-10. The word now wraps at the righthand edge

Web Fonts

The use of CSS3 web fonts vastly increases the typography available to web designers by allowing fonts to be loaded in and displayed from across the web, not just from the user's computer. To achieve this, declare a web font by using @font-face, like this:

```
@font-face
{
  font-family:FontName;
  src:url('FontName.otf');
}
```

The url function requires a value containing the path or URL of a font. On most browsers, you can use either TrueType (*.ttf*) or OpenType (*.otf*) fonts, but Internet Explorer restricts you to TrueType fonts that have been converted to Embedded Open Type (*.eot*).

To tell the browser the type of font, you can use the format function, like this for OpenType fonts:

```
@font-face
{
  font-family:FontName;
  src:url('FontName.otf') format('opentype');
}
```

Or this for TrueType fonts:

```
@font-face
{
  font-family:FontName;
  src:url('FontName.ttf') format('truetype');
}
```

However, because Internet Explorer accepts only EOT fonts, it ignores @font-face declarations that contain the format function.

Google Web Fonts

One of the best ways to use web fonts is to load them in for free from Google's servers. To find out more about this, check out the Google Fonts website (*http://google.com/fonts*), seen in Figure 19-11, where you can get access to over 848 font families, and counting!

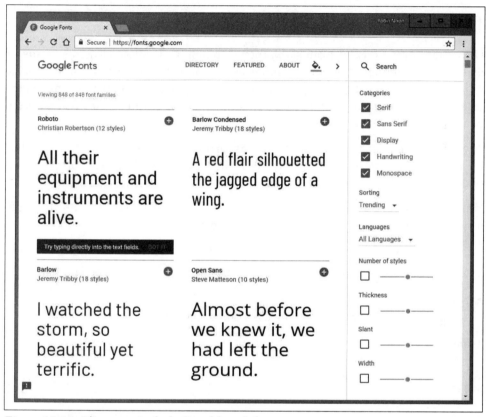

Figure 19-11. It's easy to include Google's web fonts

To show you how easy it is to use one of these fonts, here's how you load a Google font (in this case, Lobster) into your HTML for use in `<h1>` headings:

```
<!DOCTYPE html>
<html>
  <head>
    <style>
      h1 { font-family:'Lobster', arial, serif; }
    </style>
    <link href='http://fonts.googleapis.com/css?family=Lobster'
      rel='stylesheet'>
  </head>
```

```
    <body>
      <h1>Hello</h1>
    </body>
  </html>
```

When you select a font from the website, Google provides the `<link>` tag to copy and paste into the `<head>` of your web page.

Transformations

Using transformations, you can skew, rotate, stretch, and squash elements in any of up to three dimensions (yes, 3D is supported, but only in WebKit-based browsers for now). This makes it easy to create great effects by stepping out of the uniform rectangular layout of `<div>` and other elements, because now they can be shown at a variety of angles and in many different forms.

To perform a transformation, use the `transform` property (which unfortunately has browser-specific prefixes for Mozilla, WebKit, Opera, and Microsoft browsers, so once again you'll need to refer to *http://caniuse.com*).

You can apply various properties to the `transform` property, starting with the value `none`, which resets an object to a nontransformed state:

```
transform:none;
```

You can supply one or more of the following functions to the `transform` property:

`matrix`
Transforms an object by applying a matrix of values to it

`translate`
Moves an element's origin

`scale`
Scales an object

`rotate`
Rotates an object

`skew`
Skews an object

The only one of these that may cause you to scratch your head is `skew`. With this function, one coordinate is displaced in one direction in proportion to its distance from a coordinate plane or axis. So, a rectangle, for example, is transformed into a parallelogram when skewed.

There are also single versions of many of these functions, such as `translateX`, `scaleY`, and so on.

So, for example, to rotate an element clockwise by 45 degrees, you could apply this declaration to it:

```
transform:rotate(45deg);
```

At the same time, you could enlarge this object, as in the following declaration, which enlarges its width by 1.5 times and its height by 2 times and then performs the rotation. Figure 19-12 shows an object before the transformations are applied, and then afterward:

```
transform:scale(1.5, 2) rotate(45deg);
```

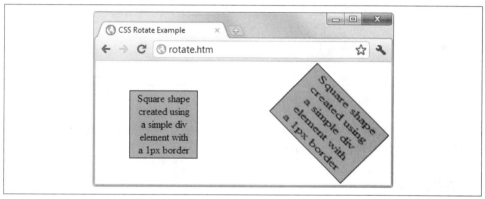

Figure 19-12. An object before and after transformation

3D Transformations

You can also transform objects in three dimensions by using the following CSS3 3D transformation features:

`perspective`
Releases an element from 2D space and creates a third dimension within which it can move. Required to work with 3D CSS functions.

`transform-origin`
Exploits perspective, setting the location at which all lines converge to a single point.

`translate3d`
Moves an element to another location in its 3D space.

`scale3d`
Rescales one or more dimensions.

`rotate3d`

Rotates an element around any of the x-, y-, and z-axes.

Figure 19-13 shows a 2D object that has been rotated in 3D space with a CSS rule such as the following:

```
transform:perspective(200px) rotateX(10deg) rotateY(20deg) rotateZ(30deg);
```

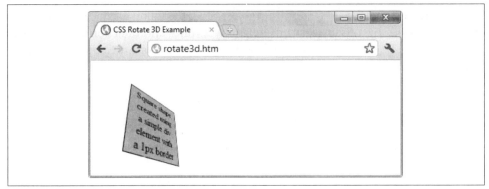

Figure 19-13. A figure rotated in 3D space

For more information, please refer to David DeSandro's "An Introduction to CSS 3-D Transforms" tutorial (*http://tinyurl.com/3dcsstransforms*).

Transitions

Also appearing in all the latest versions of the major browsers (including Internet Explorer 10, but not lower versions) is a dynamic new feature called *transitions*. These specify an animation effect you want to occur when an element is transformed, and the browser will automatically take care of all the in-between frames for you.

There are four properties you should supply in order to set up a transition, as follows:

```
transition-property         :property;
transition-duration         :time;
transition-delay            :time;
transition-timing-function:type;
```

 You must preface these properties with the relevant browser prefixes for Mozilla, WebKit, Opera, and Microsoft browsers.

Properties to Transition

Transitions have properties such as `height` and `border-color`. Specify the properties you want to change in the CSS property named `transition-property`. (I'm using the word *property* here in two different ways: for a CSS property, and for the transition properties it sets.) You can include multiple properties by separating them with commas, like this:

```
transition-property:width, height, opacity;
```

Or, if you want absolutely everything about an element to transition (including colors), use the value `all`, like this:

```
transition-property:all;
```

Transition Duration

The `transition-duration` property requires a value of 0 seconds or greater, like the following, which specifies that the transition should take 1.25 seconds to complete:

```
transition-duration:1.25s;
```

Transition Delay

If the `transition-delay` property is given a value greater than 0 seconds (the default), it introduces a delay between the initial display of the element and the beginning of the transition. The following starts the transition after a 0.1-second delay:

```
transition-delay:0.1s;
```

If the `transition-delay` property is given a value of less than 0 seconds (in other words, a negative value), the transition will execute the moment the property is changed, but will appear to have begun execution at the specified offset, partway through its cycle.

Transition Timing

The `transition-timing` function property requires one of the following values:

ease
: Start slowly, get faster, and then end slowly.

linear
: Transition at constant speed.

ease-in
: Start slowly, and then go quickly until finished.

`ease-out`
> Start quickly, stay fast until near the end, and then end slowly.

`ease-in-out`
> Start slowly, go fast, and then end slowly.

Using any of the values containing the word *ease* ensures that the transition looks extra fluid and natural, unlike a linear transition that somehow seems more mechanical. And if these aren't sufficiently varied for you, you can also create your own transitions using the `cubic-bezier` function.

For example, following are the declarations used to create the preceding five transition types, illustrating how you can easily create your own:

```
transition-timing-function:cubic-bezier(0.25, 0.1, 0.25, 1);
transition-timing-function:cubic-bezier(0,    0,   1,    1);
transition-timing-function:cubic-bezier(0.42, 0,   1,    1);
transition-timing-function:cubic-bezier(0,    0,   0.58, 1);
transition-timing-function:cubic-bezier(0.42, 0,   0.58, 1);
```

Shorthand Syntax

You may find it easier to use the shorthand version of this property and include all the values in a single declaration like the following, which will transition all properties in a linear fashion, over a period of 0.3 seconds, after an initial (optional) delay of 0.2 seconds:

```
transition:all .3s linear .2s;
```

Doing so will save you the trouble of entering many very similar declarations, particularly if you are supporting all the major browser prefixes.

Example 19-4 illustrates how you might use transitions and transformations together. The CSS creates a square, orange element with some text in it, and a hover pseudoclass specifying that when the mouse passes over the object, it should rotate by 180 degrees and change from orange to yellow (see Figure 19-14).

Example 19-4. A transition on hover effect

```
<!DOCTYPE html>
<html>
  <head>
    <title>Transitioning on hover</title>
    <style>
      #square {
        position        :absolute;
        top             :50px;
        left            :50px;
        width           :100px;
```

```
          height              :100px;
          padding             :2px;
          text-align          :center;
          border-width        :1px;
          border-style        :solid;
          background          :orange;
          transition          :all .8s ease-in-out;
          -moz-transition     :all .8s ease-in-out;
          -webkit-transition:all .8s ease-in-out;
          -o-transition       :all .8s ease-in-out;
          -ms-transition      :all .8s ease-in-out;
        }
        #square:hover {
          background          :yellow;
          -moz-transform      :rotate(180deg);
          -webkit-transform :rotate(180deg);
          -o-transform        :rotate(180deg);
          -ms-transform       :rotate(180deg);
          transform           :rotate(180deg);
        }
    </style>
  </head>
  <body>
    <div id='square'>
      Square shape<br>
      created using<br>
      a simple div<br>
      element with<br>
      a 1px border
    </div>
  </body>
</html>
```

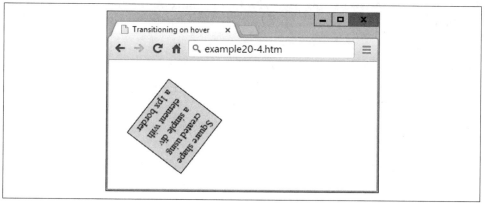

Figure 19-14. The object rotates and changes color when hovered over

The sample code caters to all browsers by providing browser-specific versions of the declarations. In all the latest browsers (including IE 10 or higher), the object will rotate clockwise when hovered over, while slowly changing from orange to yellow.

CSS transitions are smart in that when they are canceled, they smoothly return to their original value. So, if you move the mouse away before the transition has completed, it will instantly reverse and transition back to its initial state.

Questions

1. What do the CSS3 attribute selector operators ^=, $=, and *= do?
2. What property do you use to specify the size of a background image?
3. With which property can you specify the radius of a border?
4. How can you flow text over multiple columns?
5. Name the four functions with which you can specify CSS colors.
6. How would you create a gray shadow under some text, offset diagonally to the bottom right by 5 pixels, with a blurring of 3 pixels?
7. How can you indicate with an ellipsis that text is truncated?
8. How can you include a Google web font in a web page?
9. What CSS declaration would you use to rotate an object by 90 degrees?
10. How do you set up a transition on an object so that when any of its properties are changed, the change will transition immediately in a linear fashion over the course of half a second?

See "Chapter 19 Answers" on page 727 in Appendix A for the answers to these questions.

Accessing CSS from JavaScript

With a good understanding of the DOM and CSS now under your belt, you'll learn in this chapter how to access both the DOM and CSS directly from JavaScript, enabling you to create highly dynamic and responsive websites.

I'll also show you how to use interrupts so you can create animations or provide any code that must continue running (such as a clock). Finally, I'll explain how you can add new elements to or remove existing ones from the DOM so you don't have to precreate elements in HTML just in case JavaScript may need to access them later.

Revisiting the getElementById Function

To help with the examples in the rest of this book, I would like to provide an enhanced version of the `getElementById` function, for handling DOM elements and CSS styles quickly and efficiently, without the need for including a framework such as jQuery.

However, to avoid conflicting with frameworks that use the `$` character, I'll use the uppercase O, because it's the first letter of *Object*, which is what will be returned when the function is called (the object represented by the ID passed to the function).

The O function

Here's what the bare-bones O function looks like:

```
function O(i)
{
  return document.getElementById(i)
}
```

This alone saves 22 characters of typing each time it's called. But I've chosen to extend the function a little by allowing either an ID name or an object to be passed to the function, as shown in the complete version in Example 20-1.

Example 20-1. The O function

```
function O(i)
{
  return typeof i == 'object' ? i : document.getElementById(i)
}
```

If an object is passed to the function, it just returns that object back again. Otherwise, it assumes that an ID has been passed and returns the object to which the ID refers.

But why on Earth would I want to add this first statement, which simply returns the object passed to it?

The S Function

The answer to this question becomes clear when you look at a partner function called S, which gives you easy access to the style (or CSS) properties of an object, as shown in Example 20-2.

Example 20-2. The S function

```
function S(i)
{
  return O(i).style
}
```

The S in this function name is the first letter of *Style*, and the function performs the task of returning the style property (or subobject) of the element referred to. Because the embedded O function accepts either an ID or an object, you can pass either an ID or an object to S as well.

Let's look at what's going on here by taking a `<div>` element with the ID of `myobj` and setting its text color to green, like this:

```
<div id='myobj'>Some text</div>

<script>
  O('myobj').style.color = 'green'
</script>
```

The preceding code will do the job, but it's much simpler to call the new S function, like this:

```
S('myobj').color = 'green'
```

Now consider the case in which the object returned by calling O is stored in, for example, an object called fred, like this:

```
fred = O('myobj')
```

Because of the way the S function works, we can still call it to change the text color to green, like this:

```
S(fred).color = 'green'
```

This means that whether you wish to access an object directly or via its ID, you can do so by passing it to either the O or S function as required. Just remember that when you pass an object (rather than an ID), you must not place it in quotation marks.

The C Function

So far I've provided you with two simple functions that make it easy for you to access any element on a web page, and any style property of an element. Sometimes, though, you will want to access more than one element at a time. You can do this by assigning a CSS class name to each such element, like in these examples, which both employ the class myclass:

```
<div class='myclass'>Div contents</div>
<p class='myclass'>Paragraph contents</p>
```

If you want to access all elements on a page that use a particular class, you can use the C function (for the first letter of *Class*), shown in Example 20-3, to return an array containing all the objects that match the class name provided.

Example 20-3. The C function

```
function C(i)
{
  return document.getElementsByClassName(i)
}
```

To use this function, simply call it as follows, saving the returned array so that you can access each of the elements individually as required or (more likely to be the case) en masse via a loop:

```
myarray = C('myclass')
```

Now you can do whatever you like with the objects returned, such as (for example) setting their textDecoration style property to underline, as follows:

```
for (i = 0 ; i < myarray.length ; ++i)
  S(myarray[i]).textDecoration = 'underline'
```

This code iterates through the objects in myarray[] and then uses the S function to reference each one's style property, setting its textDecoration property to underline.

Including the Functions

I use the O and S functions in the examples for the remainder of this chapter, as they make the code shorter and easier to follow. Therefore, I have saved them in the file *OSC.js* (along with the C function, which I think you'll find extremely useful) in the Chapter 20 folder of the accompanying archive of examples, freely downloadable from the book's companion website (*http://lpmj.net*).

You can include these functions in any web page by using the following statement—preferably in its <head> section, anywhere before any script that relies on calling them:

```
<script src='OSC.js'></script>
```

The contents of *OSC.js* are shown in Example 20-4, where everything is neatened into just three lines.

Example 20-4. The OSC.js file

```
function O(i) { return typeof i == 'object' ? i : document.getElementById(i) }
function S(i) { return O(i).style                                            }
function C(i) { return document.getElementsByClassName(i)                    }
```

Accessing CSS Properties from JavaScript

The textDecoration property I used in an earlier example represents a CSS property that is normally hyphenated like this: text-decoration. But since JavaScript reserves the hyphen character for use as a mathematical operator, whenever you access a hyphenated CSS property, you must omit the hyphen and set the character immediately following it to uppercase.

Another example of this is the font-size property, which is referenced in JavaScript as fontSize when placed after a period operator, like this:

```
myobject.fontSize = '16pt'
```

An alternative to this is to be more long-winded and use the setAttribute function, which *does* support (and in fact requires) standard CSS property names, like this:

```
myobject.setAttribute('style', 'font-size:16pt')
```

 Some older versions of Microsoft Internet Explorer are picky in certain instances about using the JavaScript-style CSS property names when applying the browser-specific -ms- prefixed versions of the rules. If you encounter this, use the setAttribute function and you should be all right.

Some Common Properties

Using JavaScript, you can modify any property of any element in a web document, in a similar manner to using CSS. I've already shown you how to access CSS properties using either the JavaScript short form or the `setAttribute` function to use exact CSS property names, so I won't bore you by detailing all of the hundreds of properties. Rather, I'd like to show you how to access just a few of the CSS properties as an overview of some of the things you can do.

First, then, let's look at modifying a few CSS properties from JavaScript using Example 20-5, which loads in the three earlier functions, creates a `<div>` element, and then issues JavaScript statements within a `<script>` section of HTML to modify some of its attributes (see Figure 20-1).

Example 20-5. Accessing CSS properties from JavaScript

```
<!DOCTYPE html>
<html>
  <head>
    <title>Accessing CSS Properties</title>
    <script src='OSC.js'></script>
  </head>
  <body>
    <div id='object'>Div Object</div>

    <script>
      S('object').border     = 'solid 1px red'
      S('object').width      = '100px'
      S('object').height     = '100px'
      S('object').background = '#eee'
      S('object').color      = 'blue'
      S('object').fontSize   = '15pt'
      S('object').fontFamily = 'Helvetica'
      S('object').fontStyle  = 'italic'
    </script>
  </body>
</html>
```

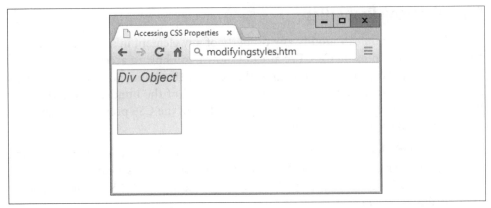

Figure 20-1. Modifying styles from JavaScript

You gain nothing by modifying properties like this, because you could just as easily have included some CSS directly, but shortly we'll be modifying properties in response to user interaction—and then you'll see the real power of combining Java-Script and CSS.

Other Properties

JavaScript also opens up access to a very wide range of other properties, such as the width and height of the browser window and of any pop-up or in-browser windows or frames, plus handy information such as the parent window (if there is one) and the history of URLs visited in this session.

All these properties are accessed from the `window` object via the period operator (for example, `window.name`), and Table 20-1 lists them all, along with descriptions of each.

Table 20-1. The window properties

Property	Description
closed	Returns a Boolean value indicating whether a window has been closed or not
defaultStatus	Sets or returns the default text in the status bar of a window
document	Returns the `document` object for the window
frameElement	Returns the `iframe` element in which the current window is inserted
frames	Returns an array of all the frames and iframes in the window
history	Returns the `history` object for the window
innerHeight	Sets or returns the inner height of a window's content area
innerWidth	Sets or returns the inner width of a window's content area
length	Returns the number of frames and iframes in a window
localStorage	Allows saving of key/value pairs in a web browser
location	Returns the `location` object for the window

Property	Description
name	Sets or returns the name of a window
navigator	Returns the navigator object for the window
opener	Returns a reference to the window that created the window
outerHeight	Sets or returns the outer height of a window, including tool- and scrollbars
outerWidth	Sets or returns the outer width of a window, including tool- and scrollbars
pageXOffset	Returns the number of pixels the document has been scrolled horizontally from the left of the window
pageYOffset	Returns the number of pixels the document has been scrolled vertically from the top of the window
parent	Returns the parent window of a window
screen	Returns the screen object for the window
screenLeft	Returns the x coordinate of the window relative to the screen
screenTop	Returns the y coordinate of the window relative to the screen
screenX	Returns the x coordinate of the window relative to the screen
screenY	Returns the y coordinate of the window relative to the screen
sessionStorage	Allows saving of key/value pairs in a web browser
self	Returns the current window
status	Sets or returns the text in the status bar of a window
top	Returns the top browser window

There are a few points to note about some of these properties:

- The defaultStatus and status properties can be set only if users have modified their browsers to allow it (very unlikely).

- The history object cannot be read from (so you cannot see where your visitors have been surfing). But it supports the length property to determine how long the history is, and the back, forward, and go methods to navigate to specific pages in the history.

- When you need to know how much space there is available in a current window of the web browser, just read the values in window.innerHeight and window.innerWidth. I often use these values for centering in-browser pop-up alert or "confirm dialog" windows.

- The screen object supports the read-only properties availHeight, availWidth, colorDepth, height, pixelDepth, and width, and is therefore great for determining information about the user's display.

- Mozilla Firefox does not support the screenLeft and screenTop properties. For that browser, use screenX and screenY instead.

Many of these properties can be invaluable when you're targeting mobile phones and tablet devices, as they will tell you exactly how much screen space you have to work with, the type of browser being used, and more.

These few items of information will get you started and provide you with an idea of the many new and interesting things you can do with JavaScript. There are far more properties and methods available than can be covered in this chapter, but now that you know how to access and use properties, all you need is a resource listing them all. I recommend that you check out JavaScript Kit's DOM Reference (*http://www.javas criptkit.com/domref/index.shtml*) as a good starting point.

Inline JavaScript

Using `<script>` tags isn't the only way you can execute JavaScript statements; you can also access JavaScript from within HTML tags, which makes for great dynamic inter-activity. For example, to add a quick effect when the mouse passes over an object, you can use code such as that in the `<img>` tag in Example 20-6, which displays an apple by default, but replaces it with an orange when the mouse passes over the object and restores the apple again when the mouse leaves.

Example 20-6. Using inline JavaScript

```
<!DOCTYPE html>
<html>
  <head>
    <title>Inline JavaScript</title>
  </head>
  <body>
    <img src='apple.png'
      onmouseover="this.src='orange.png'"
      onmouseout="this.src='apple.png'">
  </body>
</html>
```

The this Keyword

In the preceding example, you see the `this` keyword in use. It tells the JavaScript to operate on the calling object, namely the `<img>` tag. You can see the result in Figure 20-2, where the mouse has yet to pass over the apple.

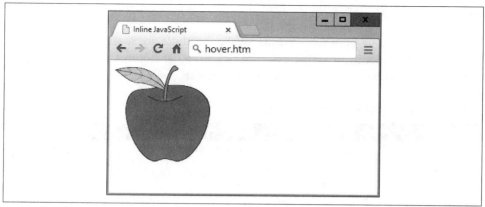

Figure 20-2. Inline mouse hover JavaScript example

When supplied from an inline JavaScript call, the this keyword represents the calling object. When used in class methods, it represents an object to which the method applies.

Attaching Events to Objects in a Script

The preceding code is the equivalent of providing an ID to the `<img>` tag and then attaching the actions to the tag's mouse events, like in Example 20-7.

Example 20-7. Non-inline JavaScript

```
<!DOCTYPE html>
<html>
  <head>
    <title>Non-inline JavaScript</title>
    <script src='OSC.js'></script>
  </head>
  <body>
    <img id='object' src='apple.png'>

    <script>
      O('object').onmouseover = function() { this.src = 'orange.png' }
      O('object').onmouseout  = function() { this.src = 'apple.png'  }
    </script>
  </body>
</html>
```

In the HTML section, this example gives the `<img>` element an ID of object, and it then proceeds to manipulate it separately in the JavaScript section by attaching anonymous functions to each event.

Attaching to Other Events

Whether you're using inline or separate JavaScript, there are several events to which you can attach actions, providing a wealth of additional features you can offer your users. Table 20-2 lists these events and details when they will be triggered.

Table 20-2. Events and when they are triggered

Event	Occurs
onabort	When an image's loading is stopped before completion
onblur	When an element loses focus[a]
onchange	When any part of a form has changed
onclick	When an object is clicked
ondblclick	When an object is double-clicked
onerror	When a JavaScript error is encountered
onfocus	When an element gets focus
onkeydown	When a key is being pressed (including Shift, Alt, Ctrl, and Esc)
onkeypress	When a key is being pressed (not including Shift, Alt, Ctrl, and Esc)
onkeyup	When a key is released
onload	When an object has loaded
onmousedown	When the mouse button is pressed over an element
onmousemove	When the mouse is moved over an element
onmouseout	When the mouse leaves an element
onmouseover	When the mouse passes over an element from outside it
onmouseup	When the mouse button is released
onreset	When a form is reset
onresize	When the browser is resized
onscroll	When the document is scrolled
onselect	When some text is selected
onsubmit	When a form is submitted
onunload	When a document is removed

[a] An element that has *focus* is one that has been clicked or otherwise entered into, such as an input field.

Make sure you attach events to objects that make sense. For example, an object that is not a form will not respond to the onsubmit event.

Adding New Elements

With JavaScript, you are not limited to manipulating the elements and objects supplied to a document in its HTML. In fact, you can create objects at will by inserting them into the DOM.

For example, suppose you need a new `<div>` element. Example 20-8 shows one way you can add it to a web page.

Example 20-8. Inserting an element into the DOM

```
<!DOCTYPE html>
<html>
  <head>
    <title>Adding Elements</title>
    <script src='OSC.js'></script>
  </head>
  <body>
    This is a document with only this text in it.<br><br>

    <script>
      alert('Click OK to add an element')

      newdiv    = document.createElement('div')
      newdiv.id = 'NewDiv'
      document.body.appendChild(newdiv)

      S(newdiv).border = 'solid 1px red'
      S(newdiv).width  = '100px'
      S(newdiv).height = '100px'
      newdiv.innerHTML = "I'm a new object inserted in the DOM"
      tmp              = newdiv.offsetTop

      alert('Click OK to remove the element')
      pnode = newdiv.parentNode
      pnode.removeChild(newdiv)
      tmp = pnode.offsetTop
    </script>
  </body>
</html>
```

Figure 20-3 shows this code being used to add a new `<div>` element to a web document. First, the new element is created with `createElement`; then the `appendChild` function is called, and the element gets inserted into the DOM.

Figure 20-3. Inserting a new element into the DOM

After this, various properties are assigned to the element, including some text for its inner HTML. And then, in order to make sure the new element is instantly revealed, its `offsetTop` property is read into the throwaway variable `tmp`. This forces a DOM refresh and makes the element display in any browser that might otherwise delay before doing so—particularly Internet Explorer.

This new element that's created is exactly the same as if it had been included in the original HTML, and has all the same properties and methods available.

I sometimes use the technique of creating new elements when I want to create in-browser pop-up windows, because it doesn't rely on there being a spare `<div>` element available in the DOM.

Removing Elements

You can also remove elements from the DOM, including ones that you didn't insert using JavaScript; it's even easier than adding an element. It works like this, assuming the element to remove is in the object `element`:

```
element.parentNode.removeChild(element)
```

This code accesses the element's `parentNode` object so that it can remove the element from that node. Then it calls the `removeChild` method on that parent object, passing the object to be removed. However, to ensure the DOM instantly refreshes in all browsers, you may prefer to replace the preceding single statement with something like this:

```
pnode = element.parentNode
pnode.removeChild(element)
tmp   = pnode.offsetTop
```

The first statement makes a copy of `element.parentNode` (the parent element of the object) in `pnode`. The third statement (after the child element is removed in the second statement) looks up the parent objects' `offsetTop` property (using the throw-away variable `tmp`), to ensure that the DOM is fully refreshed.

Alternatives to Adding and Removing Elements

Inserting an element is intended for adding totally new objects into a web page. But if all you intend to do is hide and reveal objects according to an `onmouseover` or other event, don't forget that there are a couple of CSS properties you can use for this purpose, without taking such drastic measures as creating and deleting DOM elements.

For example, when you want to make an element invisible but leave it in place (and with all the elements surrounding it remaining in their positions), you can simply set the object's `visibility` property to `hidden`, like this:

```
myobject.visibility = 'hidden'
```

And to redisplay the object, you can use the following:

```
myobject.visibility = 'visible'
```

You can also collapse an element down to occupy zero width and height (with all the objects around it filling in the freed-up space), like this:

```
myobject.display = 'none'
```

To then restore the element to its original dimensions, you would use the following:

```
myobject.display = 'block'
```

And, of course, there's always the `innerHTML` property, with which you can change the HTML applied to an element, like this, for example:

```
mylement.innerHTML = '<b>Replacement HTML</b>'
```

Or, to use the O function I outlined earlier:

```
O('someid').innerHTML = 'New contents'
```

Or you can make an element seem to disappear, like this:

```
O('someid').innerHTML = ''
```

 Don't forget the other useful CSS properties you can access from JavaScript, such as `opacity` for setting the visibility of an object to somewhere between visible and invisible, or `width` and `height` for resizing an object. And, of course, using the `position` property with values of `absolute`, `static`, `fixed`, `sticky`, or `relative`, you can even locate an object anywhere in (or outside) the browser window that you like.

Using Interrupts

JavaScript provides access to *interrupts*, a method by which you can ask the browser to call your code after a set period of time, or even to keep calling it at specified intervals. This gives you a means of handling background tasks such as asynchronous communications, or even things like animating web elements.

There are two types of interrupt: `setTimeout` and `setInterval`, which have accompanying `clearTimeout` and `clearInterval` functions for turning them off again.

Using setTimeout

When you call `setTimeout`, you pass it some JavaScript code or the name of a function, and a value in milliseconds representing how long to wait before the code should be executed, like this:

```
setTimeout(dothis, 5000)
```

Your `dothis` function might look like this:

```
function dothis()
{
  alert('This is your wakeup alert!');
}
```

 In case you're wondering, you cannot simply specify `alert()` (with empty parentheses) as a function to be called by `setTimeout`, because the function would be executed immediately. Only when you provide a function name without parentheses (for example, `alert`) can you safely pass the function name so that its code will be executed only when the timeout occurs.

Passing a string

When you need to provide an argument to a function, you can also pass a string value to the `setTimeout` function, which will not be executed until the correct time. For example:

```
setTimeout("alert('Hello!')", 5000)
```

In fact, you can provide as many lines of JavaScript code as you like if you place a semicolon after each statement, like this:

```
setTimeout("document.write('Starting'); alert('Hello!')", 5000)
```

Repeating timeouts

One technique some programmers use to provide repeating interrupts is to call the setTimeout function from the code called by it, as in the following example, which will initiate a never-ending loop of alert windows:

```
setTimeout(dothis, 5000)

function dothis()
{
  setTimeout(dothis, 5000)
  alert('I am annoying!')
}
```

Now the alert will pop up every five seconds. I don't recommend you run this actual example (even as a test), or you'll probably have to close your browser to stop it!

 Another option is to use the setInterval function, as described shortly.

Canceling a Timeout

Once a timeout has been set up, you can cancel it if you previously saved the value returned from the initial call to setTimeout, like this:

```
handle = setTimeout(dothis, 5000)
```

Armed with the value in handle, you can now cancel the interrupt at any point up until its due time, like this:

```
clearTimeout(handle)
```

When you do this, the interrupt is completely forgotten, and the code assigned to it will not get executed.

Using setInterval

An easier way to set up regular interrupts is to use the setInterval function. It works in the same way as setTimeout, except that having popped up after the interval you specify in milliseconds, it will do so again after that interval again passes, and so on forever, unless you cancel it.

Example 20-9 uses this function to display a simple clock in the browser, as shown in Figure 20-4.

Example 20-9. A clock created using interrupts

```html
<!DOCTYPE html>
<html>
  <head>
    <title>Using setInterval</title>
    <script src='OSC.js'></script>
  </head>
  <body>
    The time is: <span id='time'>00:00:00</span><br>

    <script>
      setInterval("showtime(O('time'))", 1000)

      function showtime(object)
      {
        var date = new Date()
        object.innerHTML = date.toTimeString().substr(0,8)
      }
    </script>
  </body>
</html>
```

Figure 20-4. Maintaining the correct time with interrupts

Every time ShowTime is called, it sets the object date to the current date and time with a call to Date:

```
var date = new Date()
```

Then the innerHTML property of the object passed to showtime (namely, object) is set to the current time in hours, minutes, and seconds, as determined by a call to the function toTimeString. This returns a string such as 09:57:17 UTC+0530, which is then truncated to just the first eight characters with a call to the substr function:

```
object.innerHTML = date.toTimeString().substr(0,8)
```

Using the function

To use this function, you first have to create an object whose innerHTML property will be used for displaying the time, like with this HTML:

```
The time is: <span id='time'>00:00:00</span>
```

Then, from a <script> section of code, call the setInterval function like this:

```
setInterval("showtime(O('time'))", 1000)
```

The script then passes a string to setInterval containing the following statement, which is set to execute once a second (every 1,000 milliseconds):

```
showtime(O('time'))
```

In the rare situation where somebody has disabled JavaScript (which people sometimes do for security reasons), your JavaScript will not run and the user will just see the original 00:00:00.

Canceling an interval

To stop a repeating interval, when you first set up the interval with a call to the function setInterval, you must make a note of the interval's handle, like this:

```
handle = setInterval("showtime(O('time'))", 1000)
```

Now you can stop the clock at any time by issuing the following call:

```
clearInterval(handle)
```

You can even set up a timer to stop the clock after a certain amount of time, like this:

```
setTimeout("clearInterval(handle)", 10000)
```

This statement will issue an interrupt in 10 seconds that will clear the repeating intervals.

Using Interrupts for Animation

By combining a few CSS properties with a repeating interrupt, you can produce all manner of animations and effects.

For example, the code in Example 20-10 moves a square shape across the top of the browser window, all the time ballooning in size, as shown in Figure 20-5; when LEFT is reset to 0, the animation restarts.

Example 20-10. A simple animation

```
<!DOCTYPE html>
<html>
  <head>
    <title>Simple Animation</title>
    <script src='OSC.js'></script>
    <style>
      #box {
        position  :absolute;
```

```
        background:orange;
        border     :1px solid red;
      }
    </style>
  </head>
  <body>
    <div id='box'></div>

    <script>
      SIZE = LEFT = 0

      setInterval(animate, 30)

      function animate()
      {
        SIZE += 10
        LEFT += 3

        if (SIZE == 200) SIZE = 0
        if (LEFT == 600) LEFT = 0

        S('box').width  = SIZE + 'px'
        S('box').height = SIZE + 'px'
        S('box').left   = LEFT + 'px'
      }
    </script>
  </body>
</html>
```

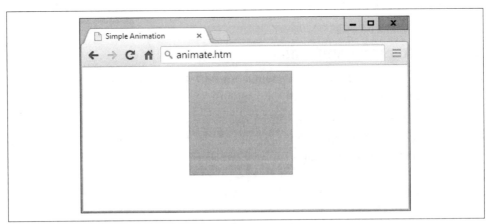

Figure 20-5. This object slides in from the left while changing size

In the <head> section of the document, the box object is set to a background color of
orange with a border value of 1px solid red, and its position property is set to
absolute so that the animation code that follows can position it in the precise ways
you want.

Then, in the `animate` function, the global variables `SIZE` and `LEFT` are continuously updated and applied to the `width`, `height`, and `left` style attributes of the box object (with `'px'` added after each to specify that the values are in pixels), thus animating it at a frequency of once every 30 milliseconds. This results in an animation rate of 33.33 frames per second (1,000/30 milliseconds).

Questions

1. What are the O, S, and C functions provided to do?

2. Name two ways to modify a CSS attribute of an object.

3. Which properties provide the width and height available in a browser window?

4. How can you make something happen when the mouse passes both over and out of an object?

5. Which JavaScript function creates new elements, and which appends them to the DOM?

6. How can you make an element (a) invisible and (b) collapse to zero dimensions?

7. Which function creates a single event at a future time?

8. Which function sets up repeating events at set intervals?

9. How can you release an element from its location in a web page to enable it to be moved around?

10. What delay between events should you set (in milliseconds) to achieve an animation rate of 50 frames per second?

See "Chapter 20 Answers" on page 728 in Appendix A for the answers to these questions.

Introduction to jQuery

Powerful and flexible as JavaScript is, with its plethora of built-in functions, you still need additional layers of code for simple things that cannot be achieved natively or with CSS, such as animations, event handling, and asynchronous communication.

What's more, as a consequence of the various browser wars over the years, frustrating and annoying browser incompatibilities have come and gone, rearing their heads at different times on different platforms and programs.

As a result, ensuring your web pages look the same on all devices can sometimes be achieved only through tedious JavaScript code that accounts for all the discrepancies across the range of browsers and versions released over recent years. In a word— nightmare.

To fill these gaps, a number of libraries of functions (many of which also provide easy hooks into the DOM) have been developed to minimize the differences between browsers and to facilitate asynchronous communication and event and animation handling. These include the likes of *AngularJS*, *jQuery*, *MooTools*, *Prototype*, *script.aculo.us*, and *YUI* (among many others).

Why jQuery?

There's room to cover only one library in this book, however, so I have opted for the most widely used: jQuery, which is now installed on over 73 percent of all websites, according to W3Techs (*http://w3techs.com*), and (as far as I can tell from their graphs) is more used than all its major competitors combined. Incidentally, if you ever want to see how the various libraries stack up at any point, search for *javascript* at Similar-Tech's website (*http://www.similartech.com*).

With jQuery, not only do you get a very high level of cross-browser compatibility (yes, even including Internet Explorer), but you also have quick and easy access to HTML and DOM manipulation, special functions to interact directly with CSS, the ability to control events, powerful tools to create professional effects and animations, and functions for conducting asynchronous communications with the web server. jQuery is also the base for a wide range of plug-ins and other utilities.

Of course, you don't *need* to use jQuery, and some programming purists would never touch a library, preferring to create their own bespoke collections of functions (and there can be good reasons for this, such as not having to wait on others to correct bugs you find, implementing your own security features, and so on). But jQuery has definitely stood the test of time, and if you would like to take advantage of its gentle learning curve and be developing quality web pages as quickly as possible, this chapter will show how you can get started using it.

Including jQuery

There are two ways to include jQuery in your web pages. You can go to the download page (*https://code.jquery.com/jquery/*), download the version you need, upload it to your web server, and reference it from a `script` tag in your HTML files. Or you can take advantage of a free content delivery network (CDN) and simply link to the version you require.

 jQuery is released under the terms of the MIT license, which places almost no restrictions on what you can do with it. You are free to use any jQuery project in any other project (even commercial projects) as long as the copyright header is left intact.

Choosing the Right Version

Before deciding whether to download and host jQuery directly or to use a CDN, you must pick a version of jQuery. In most cases this is straightforward, because you'll simply opt for the latest release. However, if you are targeting particular browsers, or if you are maintaining a legacy website that relies on a particular version of jQuery, the latest one may not be right for you.

Unlike most software, where you simply download and install the newest available version, jQuery has evolved over time to take account of the changing dynamics in the market of differing browser versions, with different features and bugs.

At the same time, improvements to jQuery have been made that might make newer versions operate differently on sites that have been specially tailored to a particular version (and the quirks surrounding it).

Of course, each newer version is an improvement over the previous one, and is more and more likely to cover all the bases. But where identical operation is critical for a website, until you have fully tested a new version, it is often best to stick with an earlier one.

Different flavors of jQuery

There are now three branches of jQuery, called 1.x, 2.x, and 3.x, each designed for different environments.

Version 1.x was the first stable release of jQuery. This release supports older web browsers that aren't even supported by their respective developers any longer. If you expect a large amount of visitors with older web browsers, this is the version to go for (as I write, version 1.12 is probably the best).

Version 2.x dropped support for Internet Explorer 6–8 to increase jQuery's overall performance and reduce the library's file size. It is faster and smaller than version 1.x, but doesn't support older web browsers. Since Microsoft dropped support for Windows XP, it may be safe to assume that your visitors will be using a browser compatible with version 2.x, unless you know otherwise.

Generally speaking, each new version of jQuery supports these browser versions:

- Chrome: (Current – 1) and Current
- Edge: (Current – 1) and Current
- Firefox: (Current – 1) and Current
- Internet Explorer: 9+
- Safari: (Current – 1) and Current
- Opera: Current

If you need to support older browsers like Internet Explorer 6–8, Opera 12.1x, or Safari 5.1+, the jQuery developers recommend using version 1.12. For full details on the different versions supported, please refer to the website (*http://jquery.com/browser-support/*). In this edition of the book I have settled on version 3.2.1.

Compressed or editable

You also must decide whether to use a version of jQuery that has been minified (compressed in size to minimize bandwidth and decrease loading time) or an uncompressed version (perhaps because you want to make an edit to it yourself—which you are fully entitled to do). Generally, a minified version is best, but most web servers support *gzip* for on-the-fly compression and decompression, so this is becoming less important (although minification does remove comments too).

Downloading

The most recent released version of jQuery is available in both uncompressed and minified forms on the download page (*http://jquery.com/download*). You can also find all of the past releases on the jQuery CDN (*https://code.jquery.com/jquery/*). The slim versions of jQuery that appear on the download page omit the asynchronous communication functions to save on space, so you should avoid these if you wish to make use of any AJAX functionality using jQuery.

All you need to do is choose the version you need, right-click the link displayed alongside it, and save it to your hard disk. From there, you can upload it to your web server and then include it within `<script>` tags, like this (for the minified version of release 3.2.1):

```
<script src='http://myserver.com/jquery-3.2.1.min.js'></script>
```

 If you have never used jQuery before (and have no special requirements), then just download the latest minified version, or link to it via a CDN, as described in the following section.

Using a Content Delivery Network

Several CDNs support jQuery. If you use one of them, you can save yourself the hassle of having to download new versions and then upload them to your server by simply linking directly to the URLs supplied by these networks.

Not only that, but they provide this service free of charge, and usually on high-capacity backbones that are probably the fastest in the world. Additionally, CDNs usually hold their content in a number of different geographic locations and then supply the required file from the server closest to a surfer, ensuring the quickest possible delivery.

Overall, if you don't need to modify the jQuery source code (requiring you to host it on your own web servers), and your users are certain to have a live internet connection, using a CDN is probably the way to go. And it's very easy. All you need to know is the filename you wish to access and the root folder the CDN is using. For example, all current and previous versions can be accessed though the CDN that jQuery uses, like this:

```
<script src='http://code.jquery.com/jquery-3.2.1.min.js'></script>
```

The base directory is at *http://code.jquery.com/*, and you simply follow this with the name of the file you need to include (in this case, *jquery-3.2.1.min.js*).

Both Microsoft and Google offer jQuery on their networks, so you can also include it in either of the following ways:

```
<script src='http://ajax.aspnetcdn.com/ajax/jQuery/jquery-3.2.1.min.js'></script>
<script src='http://ajax.googleapis.com/ajax/libs/jquery/3.2.1/jquery.min.js'>
</script>
```

In the case of the Microsoft CDN (*aspnetcdn.com*), you should begin the URL with the base directory of *ajax.aspnetcdn.com/ajax/jQuery/*, and then follow that with the filename you require.

For Google, however, you must split the filename (for example, *jquery-3.2.1.min.js*) into a folder and filename (like this: *3.2.1/jquery.min.js*). Then precede that with *ajax.googleapis.com/ajax/libs/jquery/*.

 An added benefit of using a CDN is that most other websites also do this, so jQuery may well already be cached in the user's browser and might not even require redelivery. With 73 percent or more of websites using jQuery, this can be a lot of valuable bandwidth and time saved.

Customizing jQuery

If it's absolutely critical that you keep the amount of data downloaded by a web page to the minimum, then you may still be able to use jQuery by making a special build of it that includes only the features your website will be using. You won't be able to rely on a CDN to deliver it, but in this circumstance you probably weren't planning on using one anyway.

To create your own custom build of jQuery, try jQuery Builder (*http://projects.jga.me/ jquery-builder*). Simply check the boxes you want and uncheck those that you don't. The bespoke version of jQuery will then be loaded into a separate tab or window, from where you can copy and paste it as required.

jQuery Syntax

The most striking thing about jQuery to people who are new to it is the $ symbol, which acts as the jQuery factory method. It was chosen because the symbol is legal in JavaScript, is short, and is different from customary variable, object, or function/ method names.

This symbol takes the place of making a call to the `jQuery` function (which you can also do if you wish). The idea is to keep your code short and sweet, and to save on unnecessary extra typing each time you access jQuery. It also immediately shows other developers new to your code that jQuery (or a similar library) is in use.

A Simple Example

At its simplest, you access jQuery by typing a $ symbol, followed by a selector in parentheses, and then a period and a method to apply to the selected element(s).

For example, to change the font family of all paragraphs to monospace, you could use this statement:

```
$('p').css('font-family', 'monospace')
```

Or to add a border to a <code> element, you could use this:

```
$('code').css('border', '1px solid #aaa')
```

Let's look at that as part of a complete example (see Example 21-1, where the jQuery parts are highlighted in bold).

Example 21-1. A simple jQuery example

```
<!DOCTYPE html>
<html>
  <head>
    <title>First jQuery Example</title>
    <script src='jquery-3.2.1.min.js'></script>
  </head>
  <body>
    The jQuery library uses either the <code>$()</code>
      or <code>jQuery()</code> function names.
    <script>
      $('code').css('border', '1px solid #aaa')
    </script>
  </body>
</html>
```

When you load this example into a browser, the result will be similar to Figure 21-1. Of course, this particular instruction simply replicates what you can do with normal CSS, but the idea is to illustrate jQuery syntax, so I'm keeping things simple for now.

Another way of issuing this command is by calling the jQuery function (which works in the same way as $), like this:

```
jQuery('code').css('border', '1px solid #aaa')
```

Figure 21-1. Modifying elements with jQuery

Avoiding Library Conflicts

If you use other libraries alongside jQuery, you may find that they define their own $ functions. To resolve this issue, you can call the noConflict method on the symbol, which releases control so that the other library can take over, like this:

```
$.noConflict()
```

Once you do this, to access jQuery thereafter, you must call the jQuery function. Or you can replace use of the $ symbol with an object name of your choice, like this:

```
jq = $.noConflict()
```

Now you can use the keyword jq to call jQuery, wherever you had previously used $.

> To distinguish and keep track of jQuery objects separately from standard element objects, some developers prefix a $ to any object created with jQuery (so that they end up looking like PHP variables!).

Selectors

Now that you've seen how easy it is to include jQuery in a web page and access its features, let's move on to looking at its selectors, which (I'm sure you'll be pleased to learn) work in exactly the same way as in CSS. In fact, selectors are at the heart of how most of jQuery operates.

All you have to do is think about how you would style one or more elements using CSS, and then you can use the same selector(s) to apply jQuery operations on these selected elements. This means you can make use of element selectors, ID selectors, class selectors, and any combinations thereof.

The css Method

To explain jQuery's use of selectors, let's first look at one of the more fundamental jQuery methods, `css`, with which you can dynamically alter any CSS property. It takes two arguments, the property name to be accessed and a value to be applied, like this:

```
css('font-family', 'Arial')
```

As you will see in the following sections, you cannot use this method on its own; you must append it to a jQuery selector, which will select one or more elements whose properties should be changed by the method. The following, which sets the content of all `<p>` elements to display with full justification, is an example:

```
$('p').css('text-align', 'justify')
```

You can also use the `css` method to return (rather than set) a computed value by supplying only a property name (and no second argument). In this case, the value of the first element that matches the selector is returned. For example, the following will return the text color of the element with the ID of `elem`, as an `rgb` method:

```
color = $('#elem').css('color')
```

Remember that the value returned is the *computed* value. In other words, jQuery will compute and return the value as used by the browser at the moment the method is called, not the original value that may have been assigned to the property via a stylesheet or in any other way.

So, if the text color is blue (for example), the value assigned to the variable `color` in the preceding statement will be `rgb(0, 0, 255)`, even if the color was originally set with the color name `blue`, or the hex strings `#00f` or `#0000ff`. This computed value, though, will always be in a form that can be assigned back to the element (or any other element) via the second argument of the `css` method.

 Be wary of any computed dimensions returned by this method because, depending on the current `box-sizing` setting (see Chapter 19), they may or may not necessarily be what you expect. When you need to get or set widths and heights without consideration for `box-sizing`, you should use the `width` and `height` methods (and their siblings), as described in the section "Modifying Dimensions" on page 537.

The Element Selector

To select an element to be manipulated by jQuery, just list its name within the parentheses following the `$` symbol (or jQuery function name). For example, if you wanted to change the background color of all `<blockquote>` elements, you could use a statement such as the following:

```
$('blockquote').css('background', 'lime')
```

The ID Selector

You can also refer to elements by their IDs if you place a # character in front of the ID name. So, to add a border to the element with the ID of advert (for example), you could use this:

```
$('#advert').css('border', '3px dashed red')
```

The Class Selector

And you can manipulate groups of elements according to the class they use. For example, to underline all elements that use the class new, you could use this:

```
$('.new').css('text-decoration', 'underline')
```

Combining Selectors

Just as with CSS, you may combine selectors into a single jQuery selection using commas, as with the following example:

```
$('blockquote, #advert, .new').css('font-weight', 'bold')
```

Example 21-2 brings all these types of selectors together into a single example (with the jQuery statements shown in bold), the result of which you can see in Figure 21-2.

Example 21-2. Using jQuery with different selectors

```
<!DOCTYPE html>
<html>
  <head>
    <title>Second jQuery Example</title>
    <script src='jquery-3.2.1.min.js'></script>
  </head>
  <body>
    <blockquote>Powerful and flexible as JavaScript is, with a plethora of
      built-in functions, it is still necessary to use additional code for
      simple things that cannot be achieved natively or with CSS, such as
      animations, event handling, and asynchronous communication.</blockquote>
    <div id='advert'>This is an ad</div>
    <p>This is my <span class='new'>new</span> website</p>
    <script>
      $('blockquote').css('background', 'lime')
      $('#advert').css('border', '3px dashed red')
      $('.new').css('text-decoration', 'underline')
      $('blockquote, #advert, .new').css('font-weight', 'bold')
    </script>
  </body>
</html>
```

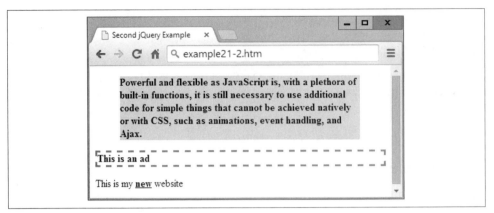

Figure 21-2. Manipulating multiple elements

Handling Events

If all jQuery could do was alter CSS styles, it wouldn't be a great deal of help—but of course, it can do far more than that. Let's further investigate by seeing how it handles events.

As you will recall, most events are triggered by user interaction: when a mouse passes over an element, the mouse button is clicked, or a key is pressed. But there are also other events that can be triggered, such as when a document completes loading.

With jQuery, it's a simple matter to attach your own code to these events in a safe way that doesn't block other code from also gaining access to these events. For example, here's how to get jQuery to respond to an element being clicked:

```
$('#clickme').click(function()
{
  $('#result').html('You clicked the button!')
})
```

When the element with the ID of clickme is clicked, the innerHTML property of the element with the ID of result is updated via the jQuery html function.

 jQuery objects (created with either the $ or jQuery methods) are *not* the same as JavaScript objects created with getElementById. In plain JavaScript, you can use a statement like object = document.getElementById('result') followed by (for example) object.innerHTML = 'something'. But in the preceding example, $('#result').innerHTML would not work, because innerHTML is not a property of a jQuery object—hence the use of the jQuery method html to achieve the required result.

Example 21-3 fleshes out the idea; you can see it running in Figure 21-3.

Example 21-3. Processing an event

```html
<!DOCTYPE html>
<html>
  <head>
    <title>jQuery Events</title>
    <script src='jquery-3.2.1.min.js'></script>
  </head>
  <body>
    <button id='clickme'>Click Me</button>
    <p id='result'>I am a paragraph</p>
    <script>
      $('#clickme').click(function()
      {
        $('#result').html('You clicked the button!')
      })
    </script>
  </body>
</html>
```

Figure 21-3. Processing a click event

 When accessing an event with jQuery, omit the on prefix that you would use in standard JavaScript. So, for example, the onmouseover event name becomes the mouseover function in jQuery, onclick becomes click, and so on.

Waiting Until the Document Is Ready

Since jQuery is so closely related to the DOM in what it lets you achieve, more often than not you will need to wait until a web page has loaded before manipulating parts of it. Without jQuery, this can be achieved with the onload event, but there's a more efficient, cross-browser jQuery method called ready that you can call to enable it at the earliest possible moment (even sooner than with onload). This means jQuery can get working on a page that much more quickly, and user-unfriendly delays are minimized.

To make use of this feature, place your jQuery code within the following structure:

```
$('document').ready(function()
{
  // Your code goes here
})
```

The code will wait there until the document is ready, and only then will it be called by the `ready` method. In fact, there's a shorter version you can use that takes even less typing, as shown in Example 21-4.

Example 21-4. The smallest jQuery "ready" code encapsulation function

```
$(function()
{
  // Your code goes here
})
```

If you get used to encapsulating your jQuery statements in one of these two structures, you won't encounter the types of errors that can be generated by trying to access the DOM too soon.

 Alternatively, another approach is to always place your JavaScript at the *end* of every HTML page, so that it is executed only after the entire document has loaded. There is a secondary advantage too, in that this ensures the web page contents get priority with loading—thus, you may well see improvements in user experience.

The only time end-of-page scripts may not be a good idea is if a document could appear to be ready when it isn't, or if all external stylesheets have not yet loaded (which can really be identified only by testing), causing users to think they can interact with it before your script is ready. In such cases, implement the `ready` function and all will be well. In fact, if in doubt, place your script at the page end *and* place its jQuery calls within the `ready` function, and you'll get the best of both worlds.

Event Functions and Properties

You've just seen the `ready` event method, but you can access several dozen jQuery event methods and associated properties (far too many to detail here). However, the following are some of the ones that are more commonly used, and they'll get you started for most projects. For a comprehensive summary of all available events, please see the documentation (*http://api.jquery.com/category/events*).

The blur and focus Events

The `blur` event triggers when focus is removed from an element, causing it to blur, and is a good partner for the `focus` event. The `blur` and `focus` methods can be used to add a handler to the event. They will trigger the event if you omit any arguments from the method's parentheses.

In Example 21-5, there are four input fields. The first is given immediate focus with a quick call to the `focus` method, applying it to the element with the ID of `first`. Then a pair of handlers is added to all `input` elements. The `focus` handler sets their background to yellow when focus is given, and the `blur` handler sets their background to light gray when focus is removed (or blurred).

Example 21-5. Using the focus and blur events

```
<!DOCTYPE html>
<html>
  <head>
    <title>Events: blur</title>
    <script src='jquery-3.2.1.min.js'></script>
  </head>
  <body>
    <h2>Click in and out of these fields</h2>
    <input id='first'> <input> <input> <input>
    <script>
      $('#first').focus()
      $('input').focus(function() { $(this).css('background', '#ff0') } )
      $('input') .blur(function() { $(this).css('background', '#aaa') } )
    </script>
  </body>
</html>
```

 You are allowed to include whitespace characters between the closing parenthesis of a method and the period operator used to attach another method to it (and after the period too, if you like), as in the previous example where I have right-aligned the `blur` event name under `focus`, to help the rest of the statements also line up in columns.

In Figure 21-4, you can see how this code gives any input fields that have ever had focus a light gray background color. If one currently has focus, its background color is set to yellow, while unvisited fields remain with a white background color.

Figure 21-4. Attaching event handlers to the blur and focus events

The this Keyword

This example also serves to illustrate the use of the this keyword. When an event is called, the element on which it was triggered is passed in the object this, which can then be given to the $ method for processing. Or, since this is a standard JavaScript object (and not a jQuery object), it can be used as such. So, if you prefer, you could replace this:

```
$(this).css('background', '#ff0')
```

with this:

```
this.style.background = '#ff0'
```

The click and dblclick Events

You saw the click event a little earlier, but there's an event for handling double-clicks too. To use either, attach the event's method to a jQuery selection, and for its argument provide a jQuery method to invoke when the event triggers, like this:

```
$('.myclass')   .click( function() { $(this).slideUp() })
$('.myclass').dblclick( function() { $(this).hide()    })
```

Here I have opted to use inline anonymous functions, but you can use named ones instead if you like (just remember to supply only the name of the function, without parentheses, or it will be called at the wrong time). The this object will pass through as expected and be made available to the named function, like this:

```
$('.myclass').click(doslide)

function doslide()
{
  $(this).slideUp()
}
```

The slideUp and hide methods are detailed in the section "Special Effects" on page 523. For now, though, just try running Example 21-6 and either clicking or double-clicking the buttons to see how they sometimes disappear with an animation (using slideUp) and sometimes just vanish (using hide), as shown in Figure 21-5.

Example 21-6. Attaching to the click and dblclick events

```
<!DOCTYPE html>
<html>
  <head>
    <title>Events: click & dblclick</title>
    <script src='jquery-3.2.1.min.js'></script>
  </head>
  <body>
    <h2>Click and double click the buttons</h2>
    <button class='myclass'>Button 1</button>
    <button class='myclass'>Button 2</button>
    <button class='myclass'>Button 3</button>
    <button class='myclass'>Button 4</button>
    <button class='myclass'>Button 5</button>
    <script>
      $('.myclass').click(    function() { $(this).slideUp() })
      $('.myclass').dblclick( function() { $(this).hide()    })
    </script>
  </body>
</html>
```

Figure 21-5. Button 3 has been clicked once and is sliding up

The keypress Event

From time to time, you'll need better control over user keyboard interaction, particularly when processing complex forms or when writing games. For cases such as these, you can use the keypress method, which can be attached to anything that accepts keyboard input, such as an input field or even the document itself.

In Example 21-7, the method has been attached to the document in order to intercept all key presses. The result of running it can be seen in Figure 21-6.

Example 21-7. Intercepting key presses

```
<!DOCTYPE html>
<html>
  <head>
    <title>Events: keypress</title>
    <script src='jquery-3.2.1.min.js'></script>
  </head>
  <body>
    <h2>Press some keys</h2>
    <div id='result'></div>
    <script>
      $(document).keypress(function(event)
      {
        key = String.fromCharCode(event.which)

        if (key >= 'a' && key <= 'z' ||
            key >= 'A' && key <= 'Z' ||
            key >= '0' && key <= '9')
        {
          $('#result').html('You pressed: ' + key)
          event.preventDefault()
        }
      })
    </script>
  </body>
</html>
```

Figure 21-6. Processing key presses from the keyboard

There are a few things of note in this example that you will need to bear in mind when writing your own keyboard handlers. For example, because browsers return differing values for this event, the which property of the event object is normalized by jQuery to return the same character codes across all browsers. So, this is where to look for which key was pressed.

Being a character code, though, the value in which is a number. You can turn it into a single-letter string by passing it through String.fromCharCode. You don't have to do this, because you can easily respond to ASCII values in your code, but this method is useful when you need to work with characters.

Within the `if` block, when a key press is recognized, the example code inserts a simple statement to that effect into the `innerHTML` property of the `<div>` element with the ID of `result`.

 This is a good example of where the `document.write` function should not be used, because the document will have already fully loaded by the time the user presses a key. If `document.write` were called to display the information at this time, it would erase the current document. Writing into the HTML of an element instead is a perfect, nondestructive means of supplying user feedback, as explained in "About document.write" on page 326 in Chapter 13.

Considerate Programming

When you are anticipating user input, you should decide which values you will respond to and then ignore all others, just in case another event handler needs access to them. This is considerate practice for any other utilities (and the main browser itself) that may also be running. For example, in the preceding example I have chosen to accept only the characters a–z, A–Z, and 0–9, ignoring all others.

There are two ways you can pass keyboard interrupts on to (or deny them from) other handlers. First, do nothing; when your code exits, other handlers will also see and be able to react to the same key presses. This can cause confusion, though, if multiple actions occur from a single key press.

Alternatively, when you don't want the event to trigger any other handlers, you can make a call to the `preventDefault` method of `event`, which then keeps the event from "bubbling up" to other handlers.

 Be careful where you place your call to `preventDefault`—if it's outside the part of the code in which you process the key presses, it will prevent all other keyboard events from bubbling up, and you may lock the user out of the browser (or at least out of using certain features).

The mousemove Event

Some of the most commonly intercepted events are for mouse handling. I've already covered mouse button clicks, but now let's take a look at attaching to mouse movement events.

It's time, I think, for a slightly more interesting example, so in Example 21-8 I have put together a rudimentary drawing program using jQuery in conjunction with an HTML5 canvas. Although the canvas is not fully explained until Chapter 24, don't worry because the code is very simple.

Example 21-8. Intercepting mouse movement and mouse key events

```html
<!DOCTYPE html>
<html>
  <head>
    <title>Events: Mouse Handling</title>
    <script src='jquery-3.2.1.min.js'></script>
    <style>
      #pad {
        background:#def;
        border     :1px solid #aaa;
      }
    </style>
  </head>
  <body>
    <canvas id='pad' width='480' height='320'></canvas>
    <script>
      canvas  = $('#pad')[0]
      context = canvas.getContext("2d")
      pendown = false

      $('#pad').mousemove(function(event)
      {
        var xpos = event.pageX - canvas.offsetLeft
        var ypos = event.pageY - canvas.offsetTop

        if (pendown) context.lineTo(xpos, ypos)
        else         context.moveTo(xpos, ypos)

        context.stroke()
      })

      $('#pad').mousedown(function() { pendown = true  } )
      $('#pad') .mouseup(function() { pendown = false } )
    </script>
  </body>
</html>
```

In Figure 21-7, you can see how this fairly simple set of instructions can be used to create line drawings (well, if you have artistic ability, that is :). Here's how it works. First, the program creates a canvas object by referencing the first (or zeroth) element of the jQuery selector, like this:

```
canvas = $('#pad')[0]
```

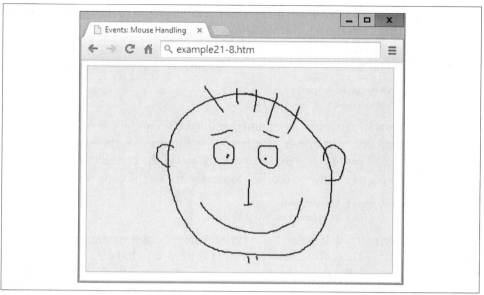

Figure 21-7. Capturing mouse movement and mouse key events

This is one way you can quickly take a jQuery object and extract a standard JavaScript element object. Another would be to use the get method, like this:

```
canvas  = $('#pad').get(0)
```

The two are interchangeable, but get has the edge because, without any argument passed, it will return all the element node objects from a jQuery object as an array.

Anyway, as you'll learn in Chapter 24, the canvas will be written to using a special context object, which is now created:

```
context = canvas.getContext("2d")
```

There's one more thing to initialize, which is a Boolean variable called pendown to track the status of the mouse button (initially false because the pen is up):

```
pendown = false
```

After this, the canvas (with the ID of pad) has its mousemove event intercepted by the anonymous function that follows, within which three sets of things happen:

```
$('#pad').mousemove(function(event)
{
  ...
})
```

First, the xpos and ypos local variables (local because of the var keywords) are assigned values representing the position of the mouse within the canvas area.

These values are taken from the jQuery `pageX` and `pageY` properties, which refer to the mouse pointer's offset from the top-lefthand corner of the containing document. Therefore, since the canvas is itself offset slightly from that location, the canvas offset values (in `offsetLeft` and `offsetTop`) are subtracted from `pageX` and `pageY`:

```
var xpos = event.pageX - canvas.offsetLeft
var ypos = event.pageY - canvas.offsetTop
```

Now that we know where the mouse pointer is in relation to the canvas, the next pair of lines tests the value of `pendown`. If it is `true`, we know that the mouse button is being pressed, so a `lineTo` call is made to draw a line to the current location. Otherwise, the pen is up, and so `moveTo` is called to simply update the current location:

```
if (pendown) context.lineTo(xpos, ypos)
else         context.moveTo(xpos, ypos)
```

Then the `stroke` method is called to apply whichever drawing command was just made to the canvas. These five lines are all that is needed to handle drawing, but it's still necessary to track the mouse button state, so the final two lines of code intercept the `mousedown` and `mouseup` events, setting `pendown` to `true` when the mouse button is pressed and `false` when it's released:

```
$('#pad').mousedown(function() { pendown = true  } )
$('#pad') .mouseup(function() { pendown = false } )
```

In this example, you see the combination of three different event handlers working together to create a simple utility, using both local variables for internal expressions and global variables where an object or the state of something must be made available across multiple functions.

Other Mouse Events

The `mouseenter` and `mouseleave` events trigger whenever the mouse passes into an element or leaves it. No position values are supplied because the functions assume you simply want to make a Boolean decision about what to do when one of these events is triggered.

In Example 21-9, a pair of anonymous functions is attached to these events, altering the HTML of an element accordingly, as shown in Figure 21-8.

Example 21-9. Detecting the mouse entering and leaving an element

```
<!DOCTYPE html>
<html>
  <head>
    <title>Events: Further Mouse Handling</title>
    <script src='jquery-3.2.1.min.js'></script>
  </head>
```

```
    <body>
      <h2 id='test'>Pass the mouse over me</h2>
      <script>
        $('#test').mouseenter(function() { $(this).html('Hey, stop tickling!') } )
        $('#test').mouseleave(function() { $(this).html('Where did you go?')   } )
      </script>
    </body>
</html>
```

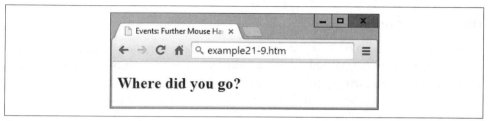

Figure 21-8. Detecting when the mouse enters and leaves an element

When the mouse enters the bounds of the selected element, that element's `innerHTML` property is updated (with a call to `html`). Then, when the mouse leaves again, a further update is made to the element's HTML.

Alternative Mouse Methods

A number of other jQuery mouse event functions are available to cover a wide range of circumstances, all of which are detailed in the mouse events documentation (*http://api.jquery.com/category/events/mouse-events*). For example, you can use the following alternative `mouseover` and `mouseout` methods to achieve similar results to the code in the preceding section:

```
$('#test').mouseover(function() { $(this).html('Cut it out!')       } )
$('#test') .mouseout(function() { $(this).html('Try it this time...') } )
```

Or you could use the `hover` method to bind two handlers with a single function call, like this:

```
$('#test').hover(function() { $(this).html('Cut it out!')       },
                 function() { $(this).html('Try it this time...') } )
```

If you are planning on creating `mouseover` and `mouseout` combined effects, clearly the hover method is the logical function to choose—but there's also another way you can achieve the same result, which is *chaining* (explained in the section "Method chaining" on page 531), using code like this:

```
$('#test').mouseover(function() { $(this).html('Cut it out!')       } )
          .mouseout(function() { $(this).html('Try it this time...') } )
```

Here the period operator at the start of the second statement attaches it to the first, creating a chain of methods.

The preceding examples show how to capture mouse click, mouse movement, and keyboard events, and therefore they are mostly suitable for desktop environments—which is what jQuery is primarily targeted at. However, there is a version of jQuery for mobile devices that provides all the touch-handling event control you could wish for (and much more), called jQuery Mobile (*http://jquerymobile.com*). We'll take a closer look at this in the next chapter.

The submit Event

When a form is submitted, you may want to perform some error checking on the data entered before it gets sent to the server. One way to do this is to intercept the submit event of the form, as in Example 21-10. Figure 21-9 shows the result of loading this document and then submitting the form with one or more fields left empty.

Example 21-10. Intercepting the submit event of a form

```
<!DOCTYPE html>
<html>
  <head>
    <title>Events: submit</title>
    <script src='jquery-3.2.1.min.js'></script>
  </head>
  <body>
    <form id='form'>
      First name: <input id='fname' type='text' name='fname'><br>
      Last name:  <input id='lname' type='text' name='lname'><br>
      <input type='submit'>
    </form>
    <script>
      $('#form').submit(function()
      {
        if ($('#fname').val() == '' ||
            $('#lname').val() == '')
        {
          alert('Please enter both names')
          return false
        }
      })
    </script>
  </body>
</html>
```

Figure 21-9. Checking user input upon submission

The key parts of this example are where the event is attached to an anonymous function, like this:

```
$('#form').submit(function()
```

and where the values of the two input fields are tested for being empty:

```
if ($('#fname').val() == '' ||
    $('#lname').val() == '')
```

Here the jQuery `val` method is used to retrieve the value in the `value` property of each field. This is neater than using `$('#fname')[0]` (as in Example 21-8) to get access to the DOM object and then appending `value` to it to read the field's value, like this: `$('#fname')[0].value`.

In this example, by returning the value `false` if one or more fields are empty, the `if` test cancels the normal submission process. To enable the submission to proceed, you can return `true`, or just not return anything.

Special Effects

jQuery really begins to come into its own when processing special effects. Although you can use CSS3 transitions, they are not so easy to manage dynamically from Java-Script—but with jQuery it really is as simple as selecting one or more elements and then applying one or more effects to them.

The core effects available are hiding and showing, fading in and out, sliding, and animations. These can be used singly, together in synchronization, or in sequence. They also support the use of callbacks, which are functions or methods that get called only once an operation has completed.

The following sections describe some of the more useful jQuery effects, each of which supports up to three arguments, as follows:

Duration
> When a duration value is supplied, the effect will take place over the assigned time, which can be a value in milliseconds, or the strings `fast` or `slow`.

Easing
> There are only two easing options in the jQuery library, `swing` and `linear`. The default is `swing`, which gives a more natural effect than `linear`. For more easing options, you can check out plug-ins like jQuery UI (*http://jqueryui.com/easing/*).

Callback
> If you supply a callback function, it will be called after the effect method completes.

This means that when no arguments are given, the method is called immediately without being placed in the animation queue.

So, for example, you can call the `hide` method in a variety of ways, such as these:

```
$('#object').hide()
$('#object').hide(1000)
$('#object').hide('fast')
$('#object').hide('linear')
$('#object').hide('slow', 'linear')
$('#object').hide(myfunction)
$('#object').hide(333, myfunction)
$('#object').hide(200, 'linear', function() { alert('Finished!') } )
```

As you'll see in the section "Method chaining" on page 531, you can attach function calls (with arguments) to each other and they will then be animated in turn, like in the following example, which will hide and then reveal an element:

```
$('#object').hide(1000).show(1000)
```

Other less commonly used arguments are also supported by many of these methods, and you can get full details on them (and all the other supported effects methods) by visiting the documentation on effects (*http://api.jquery.com/category/effects*).

Hiding and Showing

Probably the simplest effect is to hide and show elements in response to user interaction. As described in the previous section, you can provide no arguments or a variety of arguments to the `hide` and `show` methods. By default, when none are supplied, the result is to instantly hide or reveal an element.

When arguments are supplied, these two methods modify the `width`, `height`, and `opacity` properties of an element simultaneously, until they reach 0 for `hide` or their original values for show. The `hide` function sets the `display` property of the element to `none` when it is fully hidden, and the `show` function reassigns its previous value to it once the element is fully restored.

Example 21-11 lets you try `hide` and `show` for yourself (as shown in Figure 21-10).

Example 21-11. Hiding and showing an element

```
<!DOCTYPE html>
<html>
  <head>
    <title>Effects: hide & show</title>
    <script src='jquery-3.2.1.min.js'></script>
  </head>
  <body>
    <button id='hide'>Hide</button>
    <button id='show'>Show</button>
    <p id='text'>Click the Hide and Show buttons</p>
    <script>
      $('#hide').click(function() { $('#text').hide('slow', 'linear') })
      $('#show').click(function() { $('#text').show('slow', 'linear') })
    </script>
  </body>
</html>
```

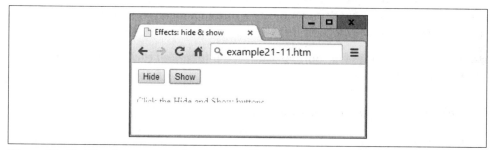

Figure 21-10. The element is in the process of being revealed

The toggle Method

As an alternative to calling both the `hide` and `show` methods, you can use the `toggle` method, which enables you to replace the previous example with Example 21-12.

Example 21-12. Using the toggle method

```
<!DOCTYPE html>
<html>
  <head>
    <title>Effects: toggle</title>
    <script src='jquery-3.2.1.min.js'></script>
```

```
    </head>
    <body>
      <button id='toggle'>Toggle</button>
      <p id='text'>Click the Toggle button</p>
      <script>
        $('#toggle').click(function() { $('#text').toggle('slow', 'linear') })
      </script>
    </body>
</html>
```

The `toggle` method takes the same arguments as `hide` and `show` but keeps track of
the state of the element internally so that it knows whether to hide or show it.

 There are four main jQuery methods that set either one state or
another, and which offer toggling versions to simplify coding. In
addition to `toggle`, there's `fadeToggle`, `slideToggle`, and
`toggleClass`, all described in this chapter.

Fading In and Out

Four methods manage fades: `fadeIn`, `fadeOut`, `fadeToggle`, and `fadeTo`. You should
be getting the idea of how jQuery works by now, and realize that the first three are
similar to `show`, `hide`, and `toggle`, respectively. The last one, though, is a little different in that it lets you specify an opacity value to which an element (or elements)
should be faded, between 0 and 1.

Example 21-13 provides four buttons with which to try out each of these methods, as
shown in Figure 21-11.

Example 21-13. The four fade methods

```
<!DOCTYPE html>
<html>
  <head>
    <title>Effects: Fading</title>
    <script src='jquery-3.2.1.min.js'></script>
  </head>
  <body>
    <button id='fadeout'>fadeOut</button>
    <button id='fadein'>fadeIn</button>
    <button id='fadetoggle'>fadeToggle</button>
    <button id='fadeto'>fadeTo</button>
    <p id='text'>Click the buttons above</p>
    <script>
      $('#fadeout')   .click(function() { $('#text').fadeOut(   'slow'      ) })
      $('#fadein')    .click(function() { $('#text').fadeIn(    'slow'      ) })
      $('#fadetoggle').click(function() { $('#text').fadeToggle('slow'      ) })
      $('#fadeto')    .click(function() { $('#text').fadeTo(    'slow', 0.5) })
```

```
      </script>
    </body>
  </html>
```

Figure 21-11. The text has been faded to 50 percent opacity

Sliding Elements Up and Down

Another way to make elements disappear and reappear is to alter their height over time to make them appear to slide up and down. There are three jQuery methods to do this: slideDown, slideUp, and slideToggle. They work in a similar way to the previous functions, as coded in Example 21-14 and shown in Figure 21-12.

Example 21-14. Using the slide methods

```
<!DOCTYPE html>
<html>
  <head>
    <title>Effects: Sliding</title>
    <script src='jquery-3.2.1.min.js'></script>
  </head>
  <body>
    <button id='slideup'>slideUp</button>
    <button id='slidedown'>slideDown</button>
    <button id='slidetoggle'>slideToggle</button>
    <div id='para' style='background:#def'>
      <h2>From A Tale of Two Cities - By Charles Dickens</h2>
      <p>It was the best of times, it was the worst of times, it was the age of
      wisdom, it was the age of foolishness, it was the epoch of belief, it was
      the epoch of incredulity, it was the season of Light, it was the season of
      Darkness, it was the spring of hope, it was the winter of despair, we had
      everything before us, we had nothing before us, we were all going direct to
      Heaven, we were all going direct the other way - in short, the period was so
      far like the present period, that some of its noisiest authorities insisted
      on its being received, for good or for evil, in the superlative degree of
      comparison only</p>
    </div>
    <script>
      $('#slideup')     .click(function() { $('#para').slideUp(     'slow') })
      $('#slidedown')   .click(function() { $('#para').slideDown(   'slow') })
```

```
      $('#slidetoggle').click(function() { $('#para').slideToggle('slow') })
    </script>
  </body>
</html>
```

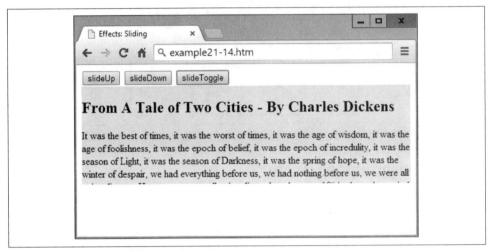

Figure 21-12. The paragraph is sliding up

These methods work well when you have menus and submenus that you want to open up or close dynamically, according to the sections clicked by the user.

Animations

Now we can really start to have some fun by actually moving elements around in the browser. To do this, though, because the default value of static will not allow them to move, you must remember to first give your elements' position properties the values of relative, fixed, or absolute.

To animate an element, all you do is supply a list of CSS properties (excluding colors) to the animate method. Unlike the previous effects methods, animate requires this list of properties first, and then you can supply any duration, easing, and callback arguments you need.

So, for example, to animate a bouncing ball, you could use code such as that in Example 21-15 (which displays like Figure 21-13).

Example 21-15. Creating a bouncing ball animation

```html
<!DOCTYPE html>
<html>
  <head>
    <title>Effects: Animation</title>
    <script src='jquery-3.2.1.min.js'></script>
    <style>
      #ball {
        position  :relative;
      }
      #box {
        width     :640px;
        height    :480px;
        background:green;
        border    :1px solid #444;
      }
    </style>
  </head>
  <body>
    <div id='box'>
      <img id='ball' src='ball.png'>
    </div>
    <script>
      bounce()

      function bounce()
      {
        $('#ball')
          .animate( { left:'270px', top :'380px' }, 'slow', 'linear')
          .animate( { left:'540px', top :'190px' }, 'slow', 'linear')
          .animate( { left:'270px', top :'0px'   }, 'slow', 'linear')
          .animate( { left:'0px',   top :'190px' }, 'slow', 'linear')
      }
    </script>
  </body>
</html>
```

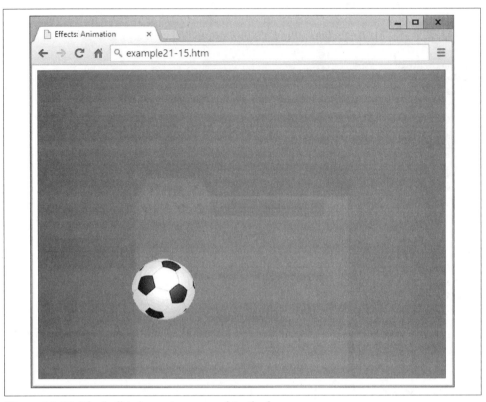

Figure 21-13. The ball is bouncing around in the browser

In the `<style>` section of this example, the `position` property of the ball is set relative to its container, which is a `<div>` element that has been given a border and a green background.

Then the `<script>` section features a function called `bounce`, which concatenates four calls to `animate`. Notice how the names of the properties to animate (`left` and `top` in this example) are supplied without quotation marks and are separated from the values to which they should be changed (such as `'270px'`) with colons—in other words, in the form of associative arrays.

You can also supply relative values in place of absolute ones by using the `+=` and `-=` operators. So, for example, the following will animate the ball to the right and up by 50 pixels relative to its current position:

```
.animate( { left:'+=50px', top:'-=50px' }, 'slow', 'linear')
```

And you can even use the string values of `hide`, `show`, and `toggle` to update a property, like this:

```
.animate( { height:'hide', width:'toggle' }, 'slow', 'linear')
```

If you wish to modify any hyphenated CSS properties and they're not being passed within quotation marks (as with `height` and `width` in the previous example), you must convert their names to camelCase by removing the hyphens and capitalizing the letter following. For example, to animate the `left-margin` property of an element, you would supply the name of `leftMargin`. However, when supplying a hyphenated property name within a string—for example, `css('font-weight', 'bold')`, you shouldn't convert it to camelCase.

Method chaining

Because of the way that method chaining works, when jQuery methods have been given arguments, they will run sequentially. So, each of these methods is called only after the previous one has finished animating. Any methods you call without arguments, however, will run immediately and quickly, without animation.

When you load Example 21-15 into a web browser, the animation is kicked off (so to speak) with a single call to bounce, causing the ball to bounce off the bottom, right, and top edges of its container, and then come to rest back at the middle of the left-hand edge. Looking again at the bounce function in this example, you can see there are four chained calls to the `animate` function.

Using callbacks

As it stands, the preceding example stops after four animations, but you can use a callback function to make the animation start over again every time it completes. This is why I chose to place the animation in a named function.

With the animation in the bounce function, it is necessary only to add that name as a callback to the fourth animation in the group in order to make the animation repeat forever, as shown in bold here:

```
.animate( { left:'0px', top :'190px' }, 'slow', 'linear', bounce)
```

Using the `animate` method, you can animate many CSS properties, with the notable exception of colors. However, even color animation is possible with the addition of the jQuery UI add-in, which provides the facility to create very eye-pleasing color-changing effects (plus many more goodies). Please refer to the jQuery UI page (*http://jqueryui.com*) for details.

Stopping Animations

There are several methods available for cutting off animations midway through, or ending a chain of animations. For example, `clearQueue` can empty all stored animations from the queue, `stop` can immediately stop any animation currently in progress, and `finish` will stop the currently running animation and remove any that are queued.

Let's turn the previous example into a sort of game by making the ball clickable, such that when the click event triggers, the animation will cease. To do this, all that's required is to add the following single line of code underneath the bounce function:

```
$('#ball').click(function() { $(this).finish() })
```

If you successfully manage to click the ball, the `finish` method will stop the current animation, empty the queue, and ignore any callbacks—in other words, the ball will come to rest.

For more information on managing jQuery queues, check out the documentation for the `queue` method (*http://api.jquery.com/queue*), where you'll also learn how to directly manipulate the contents of queues to get exactly the effects you need.

Manipulating the DOM

Because jQuery is so tightly linked with the DOM, of necessity the examples in this chapter have already utilized some of its DOM-accessing methods, such as `html` and `val`. But let's now look at all the DOM methods in detail to discover exactly what you can get access to with jQuery, and how.

In Example 21-3, you saw how to use the `html` method to change the `innerHTML` property of an element. This method can be used either to set the HTML or retrieve it from an HTML document. Example 21-16 (with the jQuery highlighted in bold) shows how to retrieve the HTML content of an element (as shown in Figure 21-14).

Example 21-16. Displaying the HTML of an element using an alert window

```html
<!DOCTYPE html>
<html>
  <head>
    <title>The DOM: html & text</title>
    <script src='jquery-3.2.1.min.js'></script>
  </head>
  <body>
    <h2>Example Document</h2>
    <p id='intro'>This is an example document</p>
    <script>
      alert($('#intro').html())
    </script>
  </body>
</html>
```

Figure 21-14. Retrieving and displaying the HTML of an element

When you issue this method without arguments, the result is to read rather than set the HTML of the element.

The Difference Between the text and html Methods

When you are working with XML documents, you cannot use the `html` method because it simply won't work (it's designed for use only with HTML). But you can use the `text` method to achieve a similar result (in XML or HTML documents), like this:

```
text = $('#intro').text()
```

The difference between the two is quite simply that `html` treats the content as HTML and `text` treats it as text. So, for example, let's assume you wish to assign the following string to an element:

```
<a href='http://google.com'>Visit Google</a>
```

If you assign it to an HTML element using the `html` method, the DOM will be updated with the new `<a>` element and the link will become clickable. But if you do so to either an XML or HTML document using the `text` method, that string will first be escaped into text (for example, by converting HTML characters such as `<` into the `&lt;` entity, and so on), and then inserted into the element—no element is added to the DOM.

The val and attr Methods

There are a couple more methods for interacting with the content of elements. First, you can set and get the value of an input element with the `val` method, as illustrated in Example 21-10, in which the first and last name fields are read. To set a value, simply provide it as an argument to the method, like this:

```
$('#password').val('mypass123')
```

With the `attr` method, you can get and set the attributes of elements, as shown in Example 21-17, in which a link to the Google website has been completely replaced with one to Yahoo!

Example 21-17. Modifying attributes with the attr method

```html
<!DOCTYPE html>
<html>
  <head>
    <title>The DOM: attr</title>
    <script src='jquery-3.2.1.min.js'></script>
  </head>
  <body>
    <h2>Example Document</h2>
    <p><a id='link' href='http://google.com' title='Google'>Visit Google</a></p>
    <script>
      $('#link').text('Visit Yahoo!')
      $('#link').attr( { href :'http://yahoo.com', title:'Yahoo!' } )
      alert('The new HTML is:\n' + $('p').html())
    </script>
  </body>
</html>
```

The first jQuery statement uses the `text` method to change the text inside the `<a>` element, and the second one changes the `href` and `title` attribute values to match by supplying the data in the form of an associative array. The third statement displays the changed element's contents in an alert window by first retrieving it with the `html` method, as shown in Figure 21-15.

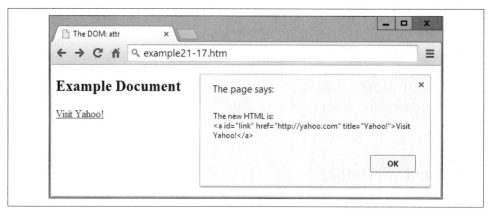

Figure 21-15. The link has now been completely modified

You can also read the value of an attribute like this:

```
url = $('#link').attr('href')
```

Adding and Removing Elements

While it is possible to insert elements into the DOM using the `html` method, this is suitable only for creating child elements of a particular element. Therefore, jQuery provides a number of methods for manipulating any part of the DOM.

These methods are `append`, `prepend`, `after`, `before`, `remove`, and `empty`. An example of each appears in Example 21-18.

Example 21-18. Adding and removing elements

```html
<!DOCTYPE html>
<html>
  <head>
    <title>Modifying The DOM</title>
    <script src='jquery-3.2.1.min.js'></script>
  </head>
  <body>
    <h2>Example Document</h2>
    <a href='http://google.com' title='Google'>Visit Google</a>
    <code>
      This is a code section
    </code>
    <p>
      <button id='a'>Remove the image</button>
      <button id='b'>Empty the quote</button>
    </p>
    <img id='ball' src='ball.png'>
    <blockquote id='quote' style='border:1px dotted #444; height:20px;'>
      test
    </blockquote>
    <script>
      $('a').prepend('Link: ')
      $("[href^='http']").append(" <img src='link.png'>")
      $('code').before('<hr>').after('<hr>')
      $('#a').click(function() { $('#ball').remove() } )
      $('#b').click(function() { $('#quote').empty() } )
    </script>
  </body>
</html>
```

In Figure 21-16, you can see the result of applying the `prepend`, `append`, `before`, and `after` methods to some elements.

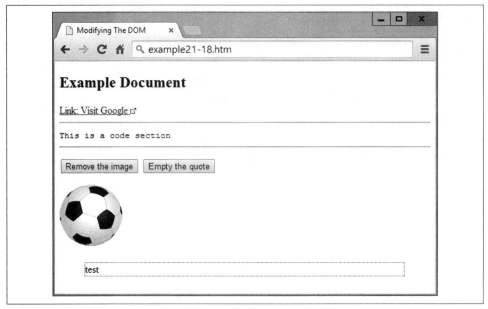

Figure 21-16. A document with a variety of elements

The prepend method has been used to insert the string Link: before the inner text or HTML of all <a> elements, like this:

```
$('a').prepend('Link: ')
```

Then an attribute selector is used to select all elements that have an href attribute starting with http. The string http appearing at the beginning of the URL (because of the ^= operator) denotes links that are not relative and therefore are absolute. In these cases, an external link icon is appended to the end of the inner text or HTML of all matching elements, like this:

```
$("[href^='http']").append(" <img src='link.png'>")
```

The ^= operator is how only the start of the string is matched. If just the = operator were used, only entire strings that matched would be selected. CSS selectors are covered in detail in Chapters 18 and 19.

Next, using chained methods, the before and after methods are employed to place sibling elements either before or after another one. In this instance, I have chosen to place an <hr> element both before and after <code> elements, like this:

```
$('code').before('<hr>').after('<hr>')
```

Then I added a little user interaction with a couple of buttons. When clicked, using the `remove` method, the first button removes the `<img>` element containing the ball, like this:

```
$('#a').click(function() { $('#ball').remove() } )
```

 The image is now no longer in the DOM, which you can verify if you highlight the browser window's contents, right-click, and choose Inspect Element in most major desktop browsers, or press F12 in Internet Explorer.

Finally, the `empty` method is applied to the `<blockquote>` element when the second button is clicked, like this:

```
$('#b').click(function() { $('#quote').empty() } )
```

This empties out the element's contents but leaves the element in the DOM.

Dynamically Applying Classes

Sometimes it can be convenient to change the class applied to an element, or maybe just add a class to an element or remove it from one. For example, suppose you have a class called `read` that you use to style blog posts that have been read. Using the `add Class` method, it's a simple matter to add a class to that post, like this:

```
$('#post23').addClass('read')
```

You can add more than one class at a time by separating them with spaces, like this:

```
$('#post23').addClass('read liked')
```

But what if a reader chooses to mark a post as unread again, perhaps to be reminded to read it again later? In this case, all you need to do is use `removeClass`, like this:

```
$('#post23').removeClass('read')
```

All other classes that the post uses remain unaffected when you do this.

Where you are supporting the ability of a class to be continuously added or removed, however, you might find it simpler to use the `toggleClass` method, like this:

```
$('#post23').toggleClass('read')
```

Now, if the post doesn't already use the class, it is added; otherwise, it is removed.

Modifying Dimensions

Working with dimensions is always a tricky web development task because different browsers tend to utilize slightly differing values. One of jQuery's big strengths, therefore, is that it does a great job of normalizing these types of values, so that your pages will look how you intend them to appear in all major browsers.

There are three types of dimensions: element width and height, inner width and height, and outer width and height. Let's look at these in turn.

The width and height Methods

Both the `width` and `height` methods can get the width or height of the first element that matches a selector, or set the width or height of all matching elements. For example, to get the width of an element with the ID of `elem`, you could use this statement:

```
width = $('#elem').width()
```

The value returned to the variable `width` is a plain numeric value, which is different from returning the CSS value from a call to the `css` method, as in the following example, which would return (for example) `230px` rather than just the number `230`:

```
width = $('#elem').css('width')
```

You can also obtain the width of either the current window or the document, like this:

```
width = $(window).width()
width = $(document).width()
```

 When you pass the `window` or `document` objects to jQuery, you cannot fetch their width or height with the `css` method. Instead, you must use the `width` or `height` methods.

The value returned is independent of the `box-sizing` setting (see Chapter 19). If you need to take `box-sizing` into account, use the `css` method with an argument of `width` instead, like this (but remember to remove from the returned value the `px` that will be added after the numeric part, if you intend to work with the values returned):

```
width = $('#elem').css('width')
```

Setting values is just as easy. For example, to set all elements that use the class `box` to 100 × 100 pixels, you could use this statement:

```
$('.box').width(100).height(100)
```

Example 21-19 combines these actions into a single program that displays as Figure 21-17.

Example 21-19. Getting and setting element dimensions

```
<!DOCTYPE html>
<html>
```

```
<head>
  <title>Dimensions</title>
  <script src='jquery-3.2.1.min.js'></script>
</head>
<body>
  <p>
    <button id='getdoc'>Get document width</button>
    <button id='getwin'>Get window width</button>
    <button id='getdiv'>Get div width</button>
    <button id='setdiv'>Set div width to 150 pixels</button>
  </p>
  <div id='result' style='width:300px; height:50px; background:#def;'></div>
  <script>
    $('#getdoc').click(function()
    {
      $('#result').html('Document width: ' + $(document).width())
    } )

    $('#getwin').click(function()
    {
      $('#result').html('Window width: ' + $(window).width())
    } )

    $('#getdiv').click(function()
    {
      $('#result').html('Div width: ' + $('#result').width())
    } )

    $('#setdiv').click(function()
    {
      $('#result').width(150)
      $('#result').html('Div width: ' + $('#result').width())
    } )
  </script>
</body>
</html>
```

Figure 21-17. Getting and setting element dimensions

At the start of the <body>, there are four buttons: three for reporting the widths of the document, window, and a <div> element that appears just below the buttons; and one to set the <div>'s width to a new value. In the <script> section, there are four jQuery statements, the first three of which simply fetch the widths of the objects given and then report these values by writing into the HTML of the <div>.

The final statement has two parts: the first reduces the width of the <div> element to 150 pixels, and the second displays the new width value within the <div> by fetching it using the width method, to ensure the computed value is displayed.

 When the page has been zoomed (either in or out) by the user, this event is not noted in any major browser, in any way that JavaScript can reliably detect. Therefore, jQuery cannot take zooming into account when it applies or returns dimensional values, so it is possible to get unexpected results in this circumstance.

The innerWidth and innerHeight Methods

It's often necessary to also take borders, padding, and other properties into account when working with dimensions. For these purposes, you can use the innerWidth and innerHeight methods to return the width and height of the first element that matches the selector, *including* the padding but *not including* any border.

For example, the following returns the innerWidth of the element with an ID of elem, including padding:

```
iwidth = $('#elem').innerWidth()
```

The outerWidth and OuterHeight Methods

To return the dimensions of an element including *both* padding and border, you can call the outerWidth and outerHeight methods, like this:

```
owidth = $('#elem').outerWidth()
```

If you wish to *also* include any margin in the returned value, you can pass the value of true when you call either of these methods, like this:

```
owidth = $('#elem').outerWidth(true)
```

 The values returned for any of the inner... or outer... methods are not necessarily integers and may be fractional in some cases. User page zooming is not detected by these methods, and you cannot use these methods on window or document objects—for those, use the width or height methods instead.

DOM Traversal

If you refer back to the section on the Document Object Model in Chapter 13, you'll recall that all web pages are constructed in much the same way as extended families. There are parent and child objects, siblings, grandparents, grandchildren, and even element relationships that could be referred to as cousins, aunts, and so forth. For example, in the following snippet, the `<li>` elements are children of the `<ul>` element, which, in turn, is parent to the `<li>` elements:

```
<ul>
  <li>Item 1</li>
  <li>Item 2</li>
  <li>Item 3</li>
</ul>
```

And, like in families, there are multiple ways you can refer to HTML elements, such as with absolute specifications, or by starting at the window level and moving on down (also known as *traversing the DOM*). You can also use the relationship between one element and another to refer to elements. Really, it's a matter of what makes sense for your particular project—for example, if you want a web page to be as self-contained as possible so that you have a better chance of cutting and pasting elements into other web documents without having to change the pasted HTML to match that of the destination. Whatever you choose, though, jQuery offers a wide range of functions to help you accurately address elements.

Parent Elements

To refer to an element's direct parent, use the `parent` method like this:

```
my_parent = $('#elem').parent()
```

Whatever type of element `elem` may be, the `my_parent` object now contains a jQuery object that refers to its parent element. In fact, since selectors can refer to multiple elements, this call actually returns an object that refers to a list of parent elements (although the list can have only one item), one for each matching element.

Since a parent may have many children, you might wonder whether more elements can be returned by this method than there are parents. Take the preceding snippet with three `<li>` elements. If we do this:

```
my_parent = $('li').parent()
```

will three parent elements be returned (because three matches will be made), even though there is just a single `<ul>` parent? The answer is no, because jQuery is smart enough to recognize all duplicates and filter them out. To verify this, if you ask for the number of elements returned like this, the result will be 1:

```
alert($('li').parent().length)
```

Let's now make something happen when the selector matches, such as changing the `font-weight` property of the parent element in the previous snippet to `bold`, like this:

```
$('li').parent().css('font-weight', 'bold')
```

Using a filter

Optionally, a selector can be passed to `parent` to filter out which of the parents should reflect the desired changes. To illustrate, Example 21-20 has three small lists and a couple of jQuery statements.

Example 21-20. Accessing parent elements

```html
<!DOCTYPE html>
<html>
  <head>
    <title>DOM Traversal: Parent</title>
    <script src='jquery-3.2.1.min.js'></script>
  </head>
  <body>
    <ul>
      <li>Item 1</li>
      <li>Item 2</li>
      <li>Item 3</li>
    </ul>
    <ul class='memo'>
      <li>Item 1</li>
      <li>Item 2</li>
      <li>Item 3</li>
    </ul>
    <ul>
      <li>Item 1</li>
      <li>Item 2</li>
      <li>Item 3</li>
    </ul>
    <script>
      $('li').parent()       .css('font-weight',     'bold')
      $('li').parent('.memo').css('list-style-type', 'circle')
    </script>
  </body>
</html>
```

The three lists are all the same, except that the middle one's `<ul>` element uses a class of `memo`. In the `<script>` section, the first statement applies a value of `bold` to the `font-weight` property of all parents of `<li>` elements. In this instance, it causes all the `<ul>` elements to display in bold.

The second statement is similar, but also passes the class name `memo` to the parent method, so that only that parent will be selected. Then the `css` method is called to set the `list-style-type` property of the selected list to `circle`. Figure 21-18 shows the effect of these two statements.

Figure 21-18. Accessing parent elements with and without filters

Selecting all ancestor elements

We've just seen how to select direct parents of elements, but you can also select ancestors, all the way back to the `<html>` root element, by using the `parents` method. But why might you want to do this? Well, how about wanting to access the first `<div>` element up the ancestry chain in order to style it according to something dynamic that has gone on further down the chain?

This type of selection may be slightly too advanced for any purpose you can think of right now, but you'll be pleased it's there when you need it, and here's how you might proceed:

```
$('#elem').parents('div').css('background', 'yellow')
```

Actually, that may not be exactly what you want, because it will select all `<div>` elements in the ancestry chain, and there may be others further up that you don't want to style. So, for this type of eventuality, you can further filter the selection by using the `parentsUntil` method instead.

The `parentsUntil` method traverses up the ancestry chain in the same way as `parents`, but stops at the first element that matches the selection filter (in this case, it's a `<div>` element), so you can use it in the same way as the preceding statement, certain in the knowledge that you will select only the closest matching element you want:

```
$('#elem').parentsUntil('div').css('background', 'yellow')
```

To illustrate the difference between these two methods, take a look at Example 21-21, which contains two sets of nested elements, both of which are within one parent

`<div>` element. The `<script>` section calls one example each of the parents and parentsUntil methods.

Example 21-21. Using the parents and parentsUntil methods

```html
<!DOCTYPE html>
<html>
  <head>
    <title>DOM Traversal: Parents</title>
    <script src='jquery-3.2.1.min.js'></script>
  </head>
  <body>
    <div>
      <div>
        <section>
          <blockquote>
            <ul>
              <li>Item 1</li>
              <li id='elem'>Item 2</li>
              <li>Item 3</li>
            </ul>
          </blockquote>
        </section>
      </div>
      <div>
        <section>
          <blockquote>
            <ul>
              <li>Item 1</li>
              <li>Item 2</li>
              <li>Item 3</li>
            </ul>
          </blockquote>
        </section>
      </div>
    </div>
    <script>
      $('#elem').parents('div')      .css('background',       'yellow')
      $('#elem').parentsUntil('div').css('text-decoration', 'underline')
    </script>
  </body>
</html>
```

If you take a look at Figure 21-19, you'll see that the first jQuery statement has set the background color of all the contents to yellow. This is because the ancestry tree has been traversed all the way up to the `<html>` element using the parents method, and both `<div>` elements encountered on the way up the tree have been selected (the one containing the list with the `<li>` element—highlighted in bold—with the ID of elem, *and* its parent `<div>`, which contains both sets of nested elements).

Figure 21-19. Comparing the parents and parentsUntil methods

However, the second statement uses parentsUntil so that the selection stops at the first <div> element encountered. This means that when the underline styling is applied, it is applied only to the closest parent <div> that contains the <li> element with the ID of elem. The outer <div> is not reached, and because it doesn't get styled, the second list isn't underlined.

Child Elements

To access the children of an element, use the children method, like this:

```
my_children = $('#elem').children()
```

Like the parent method, this goes down only one level and returns a list of zero, one, or more matching selections. You can also pass a filter argument to it to select between the children, like this:

```
li_children = $('#elem').children('li')
```

Here only children that are <li> elements will be selected.

To delve deeper down the generations, you need to use the find method, which is the inverse of parents, like this:

```
li_descendants = $('#elem').find('li')
```

However, unlike with parents, you *must* provide a filter selector to the find method. If you need to select all descendants, you can use the universal selector, like this:

```
all_descendants = $('#elem').find('*')
```

Sibling Elements

When it comes to selecting siblings, there's an even wider range of methods available, starting with siblings.

The `siblings` method will return all the matching elements that are children of the same parent, *except* for the element used for selecting. So, taking the example of the following snippet, if you look up the siblings of the `<li>` element with the ID of `two`, it will return only the first and third `<li>` elements:

```html
<ul>
  <li>Item 1</li>
  <li id='two'>Item 2</li>
  <li>Item 3</li>
</ul>
```

For example, the following statement will cause the first and third sibling elements to be bold:

```
$('#two').siblings().css('font-weight', 'bold')
```

You can also use a filter in the `siblings` method to further narrow down the siblings returned. For example, to select only those siblings that use the class `new`, you might use a statement such as this:

```
$('#two').siblings('.new').css('font-weight', 'bold')
```

Example 21-22 (liberally whitespaced to line up the attributes in columns) displays an unordered list of seven items, of which four use the class `new`. The second item also has the ID of `two`.

Example 21-22. Selecting and filtering sibling elements

```html
<!DOCTYPE html>
<html>
  <head>
    <title>DOM Traversal: Siblings</title>
    <script src='jquery-3.2.1.min.js'></script>
  </head>
  <body>
    <ul>
      <li            class='new'>Item 1</li>
      <li id='two'  class='new'>Item 2</li>
      <li                       >Item 3</li>
      <li            class='new'>Item 4</li>
      <li            class='new'>Item 5</li>
      <li                       >Item 6</li>
      <li                       >Item 7</li>
    </ul>
    <script>
      $('#two').siblings('.new').css('font-weight', 'bold')
    </script>
  </body>
</html>
```

When loaded into a browser, the jQuery statement results in Figure 21-20, in which only Item 1, Item 4, and Item 5 are in bold, even though Item 2 also uses the class new (because the method is called on that element, and so it is excluded from the selection).

Figure 21-20. Selecting sibling elements

 Since the `siblings` method omits the element on which it is called (which I will refer to as the *callee*), it cannot be used to select from *all* children of a parent element. However, to achieve that with the preceding example, you could use a statement such as the following, which will return all siblings (including the callee) that use the class new:

```
$('#two').parent().children('.new')
.css('font-weight', 'bold')
```

You can alternatively add the `addBack` method to the selection to achieve the same result, like this:

```
$('#two').siblings('.new').addBack()
.css('font-weight', 'bold')
```

Selecting the Next and Previous Elements

When you need finer control over the selection of siblings, you can further narrow down the elements returned using the `next` and `prev` methods and their extended versions. For example, to refer to the element immediately following a selector, you can use a statement such as this (which sets the matched element(s) to display in bold):

```
$('#new').next().css('font-weight', 'bold')
```

In the case of the following liberally whitespaced snippet, for example, the third item has the ID new, and therefore the fourth item is returned:

```
<ul>
  <li           >Item 1</li>
  <li           >Item 2</li>
  <li id='new'>Item 3</li>
  <li           >Item 4</li>
  <li           >Item 5</li>
</ul>
```

So far, so simple. But what if you would like to reference *all* the siblings following a particular element? Well, you can do that with the nextAll method, like this (which in the preceding snippet would style the last two items):

```
$('#new').nextAll().css('font-weight', 'bold')
```

When calling nextAll, you can also supply a filter to select from the elements that are matched, such as in the following example, which will style only the following siblings that use the class info (in the previous snippet, however, there are no elements that use that class, so the statement will do nothing):

```
$('#new').nextAll('.info').css('font-weight', 'bold')
```

Or consider the case of this snippet, in which one item has the ID new and another has the ID old:

```
<ul>
  <li           >Item 1</li>
  <li id='new'>Item 2</li>
  <li           >Item 3</li>
  <li id='old'>Item 4</li>
  <li           >Item 5</li>
</ul>
```

Now it's possible to select only those siblings following the one with the ID of new, up to (but not including) the one with the ID of old, like this (in which just the third item will be styled):

```
$('#new').nextUntil('#old').css('font-weight', 'bold')
```

If no argument is supplied to nextUntil, it behaves exactly like nextAll, returning all the following siblings. You can also supply a second argument to nextUntil to act as a filter for selecting from the elements that are matched by it, like this:

```
$('#new').nextUntil('#old', '.info').css('font-weight', 'bold')
```

In this statement, only those elements that use the class info will be styled, which in the case of the preceding snippet is none of them, so no action will be taken.

You can do exactly the same, working backward through groups of siblings, by using the prev, prevAll, and prevUntil methods.

Traversing jQuery Selections

In addition to traversing the DOM, once you have returned a set of elements as a jQuery selection you can also traverse those elements, choosing which ones to act on.

For example, to style just the first element returned by a selection, you can use the `first` method, like this (to set the first list item in the first unordered list to display underlined):

```
$('ul>li').first().css('text-decoration', 'underline')
```

Or you can choose to style only the last item by using the `last` method, like this:

```
$('ul>li').last().css('font-style', 'italic')
```

Or, to access an element by index (starting from 0), you can use the `eq` method, like this (which styles the second item in the list, because numbering starts at 0):

```
$('ul>li').eq(1).css('font-weight', 'bold')
```

You can also apply a filter to a selection using the `filter` method, like this (which changes the background color of every other element starting with the first, element 0):

```
$('ul>li').filter(':even').css('background', 'cyan')
```

 Remember that when you are indexing into jQuery selections, the first element is the zeroth. So, for example, when you use the selector `:even` in this manner, elements 1, 3, 5, and so on will be selected (not 2, 4, 6, etc.).

To exclude one or more elements you can apply the `not` method, like this (where elements that *don't* use the ID new are styled in blue):

```
$('ul>li').not('#new').css('color', 'blue')
```

You can also select an element depending on what descendants it has. To select only elements that have descendant <ol> elements, for example, you could use this statement, to place a line through those that match:

```
$('ul>li').has('ol').css('text-decoration', 'line-through')
```

Example 21-23 brings all these together to style an unordered list, one of whose elements also contains an ordered list.

Example 21-23. Traversing a jQuery selection

```
<!DOCTYPE html>
<html>
  <head>
```

```
    <title>Selection Traversal</title>
    <script src='jquery-3.2.1.min.js'></script>
  </head>
  <body>
    <ul>
      <li>Item 1</li>
      <li>Item 2</li>
      <li id='new'>Item 3</li>
      <li>Item 4
        <ol type='a'>
          <li>Item 4a</li>
          <li>Item 4b</li>
        </ol></li>
      <li>Item 5</li>
    </ul>
    <script>
      $('ul>li').first()          .css('text-decoration', 'underline')
      $('ul>li').last()           .css('font-style',       'italic')
      $('ul>li').eq(1)            .css('font-weight',      'bold')
      $('ul>li').filter(':even').css('background',       'cyan')
      $('ul>li').not('#new')      .css('color',            'blue')
      $('ul>li').has('ol')        .css('text-decoration', 'line-through')
    </script>
  </body>
</html>
```

As you will see from studying Figure 21-21, every element in each list has been styled by one or more of the jQuery statements.

Figure 21-21. Uniquely addressing elements in a jQuery selection

The is Method

There is also a jQuery selector that returns a Boolean value for use in plain JavaScript: the is method. Unlike the jQuery filtering methods shown in earlier sections, this function doesn't create a new jQuery object that can then have other methods appended to it, or that can then be further filtered. Instead, it returns just `true` or `false`, making the method most suitable for use in conditional statements.

Example 21-24 uses the `is` method attached to a call to `parent` in an event handler for a set of buttons. When any button is clicked, the handler is called, and the `is` method returns a value of `true` or `false` when asked whether the parent element is a `<div>` (Figure 21-22).

Example 21-24. Reporting the parent element with is

```
<!DOCTYPE html>
<html>
  <head>
    <title>Using is</title>
    <script src='jquery-3.2.1.min.js'></script>
  </head>
  <body>
    <div><button>Button in a div</button></div>
    <div><button>Button in a div</button></div>
    <span><button>Button in a span</button></span>
    <div><button>Button in a div</button></div>
    <span><button>Button in a span</button></span>
    <p id='info'></p>
    <script>
      $('button').click(function()
      {
        var elem = ''

        if ($(this).parent().is('div')) elem = 'div'
        else                            elem = 'span'

        $('#info').html('You clicked a ' + elem)
      })
    </script>
  </body>
</html>
```

Figure 21-22. Using the is method to report the parent element

Using jQuery Without Selectors

A couple of jQuery methods are provided for use with standard JavaScript objects, rendering their handling a lot simpler. These are $.each and $.map, which are similar but have subtle differences.

The $.each Method

Using $.each, you can iterate through arrays or array-like objects by simply attaching a function to be called for each iteration. Example 21-25 shows an array of pet names and types (called pets), from which another array (called guineapigs) needs to be extracted, containing only the names of the guinea pigs.

Example 21-25. Calling the $.each method

```
<!DOCTYPE html>
<html>
  <head>
    <title>Using each</title>
    <script src='jquery-3.2.1.min.js'></script>
  </head>
  <body>
    <div id='info'></div>
    <script>
      pets =
      {
        Scratchy : 'Guinea Pig',
        Squeeky  : 'Guinea Pig',
        Fluffy   : 'Rabbit',
        Thumper  : 'Rabbit',
        Snoopy   : 'Dog',
        Tiddles  : 'Cat'
```

```
    }

    guineapigs = []

    $.each(pets, function(name, type)
    {
      if (type == 'Guinea Pig') guineapigs.push(name)
    })

    $('#info').html('The guinea pig names are: ' + guineapigs.join(' & '))
  </script>
  </body>
</html>
```

To do this, the $.each method is passed the array, along with an anonymous function to process it. The function takes two arguments, the index into the array (called name) and the contents of each element (called type).

The value in type is then tested to see whether it is Guinea Pig, and if so, the value in name is pushed onto the guineapigs array. Upon completion, the code displays the contents of the guineapigs array by writing them into the <div> element with the ID of info. To separate the items in the array, the JavaScript join method is used with the & symbol as a separator. The result of loading this example into a browser is simply to display the text "The guinea pig names are: Scratchy & Squeeky."

The $.map Method

Another way to achieve this is with the $.map method, which returns all the values that your function returns in an array.

This function saves you the trouble of creating an array, as we had to in the preceding example. Instead, you can create and populate the array at the same time, by assigning the array returned by $.map to a variable, like this (the end result being the same but with less code):

```
guineapigs = $.map(pets, function(type, name)
{
  if (type == 'Guinea Pig') return name
})
```

Watch out when you change between using the $.each and $.map methods, because $.each passes arguments to the function in the order *index, value*, but map uses the order *value, index*. This is why the two arguments are swapped in the preceding $.map example.

Using Asynchronous Communication

In Chapter 17, I showed in detail how to implement asynchronous communications between JavaScript in a browser and PHP running on a web server. I also provided some handy and compact functions you can call to simplify the process.

But if you have jQuery loaded, you can use its asynchronous functionality instead, if you prefer—it works in a very similar way, in that you choose whether to make a POST or a GET request, and then take it from there.

Using the POST Method

Example 21-26 (which loads the Amazon Mobile website into a `<div>` element) is the direct jQuery equivalent to Example 17-2, but since all the asynchronous communication–handling code is tidied away in the jQuery library file, it's much shorter. It requires just a single call to the `$.post` method, passing it the following three items:

- The URL of a PHP program on the server to access
- The data to pass to that URL
- An anonymous function to process the returned data

Example 21-26. Sending a POST asynchronous request

```
<!DOCTYPE html>
<html> <!-- jqueryasyncpost.htm -->
  <head>
    <title>jQuery Asynchronous Post</title>
    <script src='jquery-3.2.1.min.js'></script>
  </head>
  <body style='text-align:center'>
    <h1>Loading a web page into a DIV</h1>
    <div id='info'>This sentence will be replaced</div>

    <script>
      $.post('urlpost.php', { url : 'amazon.com/gp/aw' }, function(data)
      {
        $('#info').html(data)
      } )
    </script>
  </body>
</html>
```

The *urlpost.php* program remains unchanged from Example 17-3, because this example and Example 17-2 are interchangeable.

Using the GET Method

Communicating asynchronously using the GET method is just as easy, requiring only the following two arguments:

- The URL of a PHP program on the server to access (including a query string containing the data to pass to it)
- An anonymous function to process the returned data

Example 21-27 is therefore the jQuery equivalent to Example 17-4.

Example 21-27. Sending a GET asynchronous request

```
<!DOCTYPE html>
<html> <!-- jqueryasyncget.htm -->
  <head>
    <title>jQuery Asynchronous GET</title>
    <script src='jquery-3.2.1.min.js'></script>
  </head>
  <body style='text-align:center'>
    <h1>Loading a web page into a DIV</h1>
    <div id='info'>This sentence will be replaced</div>

    <script>
      $.get('urlget.php?url=amazon.com/gp/aw', function(data)
      {
        $('#info').html(data)
      } )
    </script>
  </body>
</html>
```

The *urlget.php* program remains unchanged from Example 17-5, because this example and Example 17-4 are interchangeable.

 Remember that the security restrictions of asynchronous communication require that the communication takes place with the same server that supplied the main web document. You must also use a web server for asynchronous communication, not a local filesystem. These examples are therefore best tested with a production or development server, as described in Chapter 2.

Plug-ins

There's room in this chapter to cover only the core jQuery library, and while that's more than enough for a beginner to accomplish a lot, the time will come when you'll find you need even more features and functionality. Thankfully, other jQuery projects can help you there, because a range of official and third-party plug-ins are now available to provide just about any features you can imagine.

jQuery User Interface

First, there's the jQuery User Interface plug-in, known as jQuery UI (*http://jquer yui.com*), which takes over directly where jQuery leaves off. With it, you can add dragging and dropping, resizing, and sorting methods to your web pages, as well as more animations and effects, animated color transitions, and more easing effects. It also provides a bunch of widgets to create menus and other features such as accordions, buttons, pickers, progress bars, sliders, spinners, tabs, tooltips, and much more.

If you want to see some demos before deciding whether to download it, check out the jQuery UI Demos page (*http://jqueryui.com/demos*).

The whole package is under 400 KB zipped and is usable with almost no restrictions (just the very generous MIT license).

Other Plug-ins

The jQuery Plugin Registry (*http://plugins.jquery.com*) brings together a wide variety of free, ready-made plug-ins to jQuery from numerous developers. These include plug-ins for form handling and verification, slideshows, responsive layout, image manipulation, additional animations, and much more.

If you are using jQuery and developing for mobile browsers, you will also want to take a look at jQuery Mobile (see Chapter 22), which offers sophisticated, touch-optimized ways to navigate the wide range of different types of mobile hard- and software, to provide the best possible user experience.

You've come a long way in this chapter, learning material that sometimes takes up entire books. I hope you've found everything clear, though, because jQuery is very easy to learn and use. Please take a moment now to peruse Appendix E, which lists all the main jQuery objects, events, and methods, and should serve as a handy reference. If you need any other information, check out the *jQuery website (http://jquery.com)*.

Questions

1. What is the symbol commonly used as the factory method for creating jQuery objects, and what is the alternative method name?

2. How would you link to the minified release 3.2.1 of jQuery from the Google CDN?

3. What types of argument does the jQuery factory method accept?

4. With which jQuery method can you get or set a CSS property value?

5. What statement would you use to attach a method to the click event of an element with the ID of elem, to make it slowly hide?

6. What element property must you modify in order to allow it to be animated, and what are the acceptable values?

7. How can you cause several methods to run at once (or sequentially, in the case of animations)?

8. How can you retrieve an element node object from a jQuery selection object?

9. What statement would set the sibling element immediately preceding one with the ID of news to display in bold?

10. With which method can you make a jQuery asynchronous GET request?

See "Chapter 21 Answers" on page 729 in Appendix A for the answers to these questions.

CHAPTER 22

Introduction to jQuery Mobile

Now that you've realized the time you can save and the tremendous power you can harness from jQuery, as discussed in Chapter 21, I think you'll be delighted to learn that you can do even more with the jQuery Mobile library.

Created to complement jQuery, jQuery Mobile requires you to include both jQuery and jQuery Mobile in a web page (along with a CSS file and accompanying images you will also need) in order to transform it into a fully interactive experience when viewed on phones and other mobile devices.

The jQuery Mobile library enables you to adapt ordinary web pages to become mobile web pages using a technique called "progressive enhancement" (in which basic browser features are made to display well first, and then more and more functionality is added when more capability is encountered within a browser). It also features what is called "responsive web design" (in which web pages render well on a variety of devices and window or screen sizes).

The point of this chapter isn't to teach you absolutely everything there is to know about jQuery Mobile—that could take up a whole book in itself! Rather, I want to give you enough information to let you refashion any not-too-large set of web pages into a coherent, fast, and good-looking web app, with all the page slides and other transitions you would expect from a modern touch device, as well as bigger and easier-to-use icons, input fields, and other enhanced aspects of input and navigation.

To this end, I introduce just a few of the main features of jQuery Mobile that will let you get up and running with a clean and workable solution that runs well on both desktop and mobile platforms. Along the way, I point out a few pitfalls that you may face when adapting web pages to mobile this way, and how to avoid them. Once you've mastered using jQuery Mobile, you'll then find it a simple matter to peruse the online documentation to find just the features you need for your own projects.

In addition to progressively enhancing the way your HTML displays, depending on the capabilities of the browser in which it finds itself running, jQuery Mobile also progressively enhances regular HTML markup based on the tags used and a set of custom data attributes. Some elements are automatically enhanced without the need for any data attributes (for example, `select` elements are automatically upgraded to menus), while other elements require the presence of a data attribute in order to be enhanced. The full list of supported data attributes can be viewed in the API documentation (*http://api.jquerymobile.com/data-attribute/*).

Including jQuery Mobile

There are two ways to include jQuery Mobile in your web pages. First, you can go to the download page (*http://jquerymobile.com/download/*), choose the version you need, download the files to your web server (including the stylesheet and accompanying images that go with the library), and serve them up from there.

For example, if you have downloaded jQuery Mobile 1.4.5 (the current version as I write) and its CSS file to the document root of your server, you could include them—and the accompanying jQuery JavaScript, which *must* be version 2.2.4 as I write, because jQuery Mobile doesn't yet support version 3 (although jQuery Mobile 1.5 *is* planned to support jQuery 3)—in a web page like this:

```
<link href="http://myserver.com/jquery.mobile-1.4.5.min.css" rel="stylesheet">
<script src='http://myserver.com/jquery-2.2.4.min.js'></script>
<script src='http://myserver.com/jquery.mobile-1.4.5.min.js'></script>
```

Or, as with jQuery, you can take advantage of a free content delivery network (CDN) and simply link to the version(s) you require. There are three main CDNs to choose from (Max CDN, Google CDN, and Microsoft CDN), and you can retrieve the files you need from them in the following ways:

```
<!-- Retrieving jQuery & Mobile via Max CDN -->
<link rel="stylesheet"
  href="http://code.jquery.com/mobile/1.4.5/jquery.mobile-1.4.5.min.css">
<script src="http://code.jquery.com/jquery-2.2.4.min.js"></script>
<script src="http://code.jquery.com/mobile/1.4.5/jquery.mobile-1.4.5.min.js">
</script>

<!-- Retrieving jQuery & Mobile via Google CDN -->
<link rel="stylesheet" href=
 "http://ajax.googleapis.com/ajax/libs/jquerymobile/1.4.5/jquery.mobile.min.css">
<script src=
"http://ajax.googleapis.com/ajax/libs/jquery/2.2.4/jquery.min.js"></script>
<script src=
"http://ajax.googleapis.com/ajax/libs/jquerymobile/1.4.5/jquery.mobile.min.js">
</script>
```

```
<!-- Retrieving jQuery & Mobile via Microsoft CDN -->
<link rel="stylesheet" href=
   "http://ajax.aspnetcdn.com/ajax/jquery.mobile/1.4.5/jquery.mobile-1.4.5.min.css">
<script src=
"http://ajax.aspnetcdn.com/ajax/jQuery/jquery-2.2.4.min.js"></script>
<script src=
"http://ajax.aspnetcdn.com/ajax/jquery.mobile/1.4.5/jquery.mobile-1.4.5.min.js">
</script>
```

You will probably want to place one set of these statements within the `<head>` section of a page.

 To ensure you can use these examples when offline, I have downloaded all the required jQuery files and included them along with the archive of example files, which you may freely download from the book's companion website (*http://lpmj.net*). Therefore, all these examples show the files being served locally.

Getting Started

Let's dive right in by seeing what a jQuery Mobile web page will generally look like, with Example 22-1. It's really quite simple, and if you give it a quick once-over, it will help the rest of this chapter to fall quickly into place.

Example 22-1. A jQuery Mobile single page template

```
<!DOCTYPE html>
<html>
  <head>
    <meta charset="utf-8">
    <meta name="viewport" content="width=device-width, initial-scale=1">
    <title>Single page template</title>
    <link rel="stylesheet" href="jquery.mobile-1.4.5.min.css">
    <script src="jquery-2.2.4.min.js"></script>
    <script src="jquery.mobile-1.4.5.min.js"></script>
  </head>
  <body>
    <div data-role="page">
      <div data-role="header">
        <h1>Single page</h1>
      </div>
      <div data-role="content">
        <p>This is a single page boilerplate template</p>
      </div>
      <div data-role="footer">
        <h4>Footer content</h4>
      </div>
    </div>
```

```
    </body>
</html>
```

Upon examining the previous example, you'll see that it starts with the standard HTML5 elements you would expect. The first unusual item you may notice is in the `<head>` section, namely the `viewport` setting within the `<meta>` tag. This line tells mobile browsers to set the width of the displayed document to that of the web browser, and to start off without the document zoomed either in or out. When displayed in a browser, the page looks like Figure 22-1.

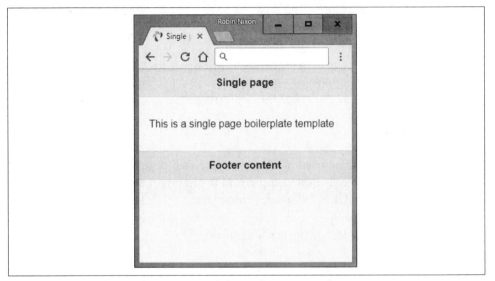

Figure 22-1. Displaying the jQuery Mobile single page template

After specifying a page title, the CSS for jQuery Mobile is loaded, followed by the jQuery 2.2.4 library and the jQuery Mobile 1.4.5 library. As explained in "Including jQuery Mobile" on page 560, these can all be downloaded from a CDN if you prefer.

> The examples accompanying this chapter contain a folder called *images*, which contains all the icons and other images required by the CSS. If you use a CDN to download the CSS and JavaScript library files, you may not need to include this folder in your own projects, as the CDN's own *images* folder should be used instead.

Moving on to the `<body>` section, you'll note that the main web page is contained within a `<div>` element, which bears the jQuery Mobile `data-role` property value of `page` and consists of three further `<div>` elements for the page's header, content, and footer, each with `data-role` properties to match.

And there you have the basic structure of a jQuery Mobile web page. When you link between pages, new ones will be loaded in and added to the DOM using asynchronous communication. Once loaded, the page can then be transitioned into view in any number of ways, including instant replace, fade, dissolve, slide, and so on.

 Due to the asynchronous loading of web pages, you should always test your jQuery Mobile code on a web server rather than a local filesystem. This is because a web server knows how to handle the asynchronous loading of web pages, which is necessary for communication to work correctly.

Linking Pages

With jQuery Mobile you can link to pages in the normal way, and it will automatically handle these page requests asynchronously (where possible) to ensure that any transitions you have selected will be applied.

This allows you to focus on simply creating your web pages and let jQuery Mobile deal with making them look good and display quickly and professionally.

To enable animated page transitions, all links that point to an external page will be loaded asynchronously. jQuery Mobile achieves this by transforming all `<a href...>` links into asynchronous communication (also known as Ajax) requests, and then displaying a loading spinner while the requests are made.

 The way jQuery Mobile achieves its page transitions when you click a link is via "hijacking" clicks by accessing the `event.prevent Default` event and then providing its special jQuery Mobile code.

If the request is successful, the new page content is added to the DOM, and the selected new page is then animated into view, using either a default page transition or one of your choosing.

Should the asynchronous request fail, a small and unobtrusive error message will briefly appear to let you know, but will not interfere with the navigational flow.

Linking Synchronously

Links that point to other domains or that have `rel="external"`, `data-ajax="false"`, or `target` attributes will be loaded synchronously, causing a full page refresh with no animated transition.

Both `rel="external"` and `data-ajax="false"` have the same effect, but the former is intended for linking to another site or domain, while the latter is useful for preventing any page from being loaded asynchronously.

Because of security restrictions, jQuery Mobile loads pages from all external domains synchronously.

> You will need to disable asynchronous page loading when using HTML file upload, because this way of fetching a web page conflicts with jQuery Mobile's ability to receive an uploaded file. For this particular case, the best course is probably to place a `data-ajax="false"` attribute in the `<form>` element, like this:

```
<form data-ajax='false' method='post'
  action='dest_file' enctype='multipart/form-data'>
```

Linking Within a Multipage Document

A single HTML document can contain one or many pages. The latter involves stacking multiple `<div>` elements with a `data-role` of `page`. This allows you to build a small site or application within a *single* HTML document; jQuery Mobile will simply display the first page it finds in the source order when the page loads.

If a link in a multipage document points to an anchor (such as `#page2`), the framework will look for a page wrapper `<div>` with a `data-role` attribute of `page` and the given id (`id="page2"`). If found, it will transition the new page into view.

Users can seamlessly navigate between all types of web pages (whether internal, local, or external) in jQuery Mobile. All will look the same to the end user, except that external pages will display the Ajax spinner while loading. In all situations, jQuery Mobile updates the page's URL hash to enable Back button support. This also means that jQuery Mobile pages are indexable by search engines, and not walled off somewhere in a native app.

> When linking from a mobile page that was loaded asynchronously to one that contains multiple internal pages, you must add either `rel="external"` or `data-ajax="false"` to the link in order to force a full page reload, clearing out the asynchronous hash from the URL. Asynchronous pages use the hash (#) to track their history, while multiple internal pages use this symbol to indicate internal pages.

Page Transitions

By using CSS transitions, jQuery Mobile can apply effects to any page link or form submission, as long as asynchronous navigation is being used (the default).

To apply a transition, you use the `data-transition` attribute within an `<a>` or `&lt;form&gt;` tag, like this:

```
<a data-transition="slide" href="destination.html">Click me</a>
```

This attribute supports the values `fade` (the default since version 1.1), `pop`, `flip`, `turn`, `flow`, `slidefade`, `slide` (the default prior to version 1.1), `slideup`, `slidedown`, and `none`.

For example, the value `slide` causes the new page to slide in from the right, with the current one sliding off to the left at the same time. The other values are similarly obvious in their effect.

Loading a page as a dialog

You can display a new page as a dialog window using the `data-rel` attribute with a value of `dialog`, like this:

```
<a data-rel="dialog" href="dialog.html">Open dialog</a>
```

Example 22-2 demonstrates how to apply the various page transitions to both page loads and dialogs, loading the jQuery libraries locally rather than via a CDN. It consists of a bare-bones table with two columns, the first for loading a dialog and the other for loading a new page. Each of the available transition types is listed. To display the links as buttons, I've supplied the `data-role` attribute of each a value of `button` (buttons are covered in "Styling Buttons" on page 568).

Example 22-2. jQuery Mobile page transitions

```
<!DOCTYPE html>
<html>
  <head>
    <meta charset="utf-8">
    <meta name="viewport" content="width=device-width, initial-scale=1">
    <title>Page Transitions</title>
    <link rel="stylesheet" href="jquery.mobile-1.4.5.min.css">
    <script src="jquery-2.2.4.min.js"></script>
    <script src="jquery.mobile-1.4.5.min.js"></script>
  </head>
  <body>
    <div data-role="page">
      <div data-role="header">
        <h1>jQuery Mobile Page Transitions</h1>
      </div>
```

```
<div data-role="content"><table>
  <tr><th><h3>fade</h3></th>
    <td><a href="page-template.html" data-rel="dialog"
    data-transition="fade" data-role='button'>dialog</a></td>
    <td><a href="page-template.html" data-transition="fade"
    data-role='button'>page</a></td>
  </tr><tr><th><h3>pop</h3></th>
    <td><a href="page-template.html" data-rel="dialog"
    data-transition="pop" data-role='button'>dialog</a></td>
    <td><a href="page-template.html" data-transition="pop"
    data-role='button'>page</a></td>
  </tr><tr><th><h3>flip</h3></th>
    <td><a href="page-template.html" data-rel="dialog"
    data-transition="flip" data-role='button'>dialog</a></td>
    <td><a href="page-template.html" data-transition="flip"
    data-role='button'>page</a></td>
  </tr><tr><th><h3>turn</h3></th>
    <td><a href="page-template.html" data-rel="dialog"
    data-transition="turn" data-role='button'>dialog</a></td>
    <td><a href="page-template.html" data-transition="turn"
    data-role='button'>page</a></td>
  </tr><tr><th><h3>flow</h3></th>
    <td><a href="page-template.html" data-rel="dialog"
    data-transition="flow" data-role='button'>dialog</a></td>
    <td><a href="page-template.html" data-transition="flow"
    data-role='button'>page</a></td>
  </tr><tr><th><h3>slidefade</h3></th>
    <td><a href="page-template.html" data-rel="dialog"
    data-transition="slidefade" data-role='button'>dialog</a></td>
    <td><a href="page-template.html" data-transition="slidefade"
    data-role='button'>page</a></td>
  </tr><tr><th><h3>slide</h3></th>
    <td><a href="page-template.html" data-rel="dialog"
    data-transition="slide" data-role='button'>dialog</a></td>
    <td><a href="page-template.html" data-transition="slide"
    data-role='button'>page</a></td>
  </tr><tr><th><h3>slideup</h3></th>
    <td><a href="page-template.html" data-rel="dialog"
    data-transition="slideup" data-role='button'>dialog</a></td>
    <td><a href="page-template.html" data-transition="slideup"
    data-role='button'>page</a></td>
  </tr><tr><th><h3>slidedown</h3></th>
    <td><a href="page-template.html" data-rel="dialog"
    data-transition="slidedown" data-role='button'>dialog</a></td>
    <td><a href="page-template.html" data-transition="slidedown"
    data-role='button'>page</a></td>
  </tr><tr><th><h3>none</h3></th>
    <td><a href="page-template.html" data-rel="dialog"
    data-transition="none" data-role='button'>dialog</a></td>
    <td><a href="page-template.html" data-transition="none"
    data-role='button'>page</a></td></tr></table>
</div>
```

```
        <div data-role="footer">
          <h4><a href="http://tinyurl.com/jqm-trans">Official Demo</a></h4>
        </div>
      </div>
    </body>
</html>
```

Figure 22-2 shows the result of loading this example (saved using the filename *page-template.html*) into a browser, and Figure 22-3 demonstrates a flip transition in action. Incidentally, if you follow the link (*http://demos.jquerymobile.com/1.4.4/transitions/*) in the footer of the example it will take you to the official demo site, where you can explore these effects in greater detail.

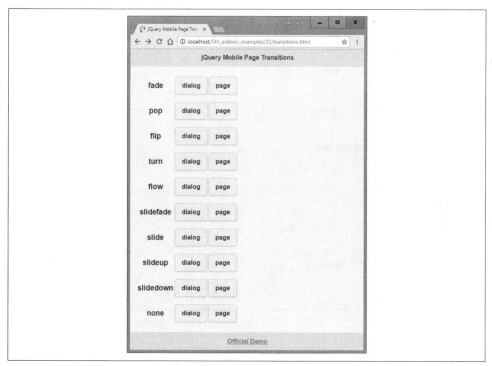

Figure 22-2. Applying transitions to pages and dialogs

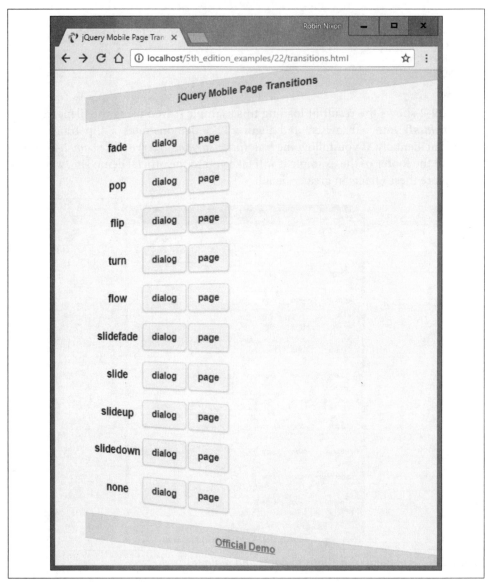

Figure 22-3. A flip transition in progress

Styling Buttons

You can easily display a simple link as a button without adding your own CSS. All you need to do is provide the value button to an element's data-role attribute, like this:

```
<a data-role="button" href="news.html">Latest news</a>
```

You can decide whether to have such a button expand to the full width of the window (the default), like a <div> element, or opt to make the button display inline, like a <span> element. To display the button inline, supply the value true to the data-inline attribute, like this:

```
<a data-role="button" data-inline="true" href="news.html">Latest news</a>
```

And whether you create a button from a link or use one from a form, you can modify the way it displays by choosing between rounded corners (the default) or straight corners, and make it shadowed (the default) or non-shadowed. Turn these features off by supplying a value of false to the data-corners and data-shadow attributes, respectively, like this:

```
<a data-role="button" data-inline="true" data-corners="false"
   data-shadow="false" href="news.html">Latest news</a>
```

What's more, you can even choose to add icons to your buttons with the data-icon attribute, like this:

```
<a data-role="button" data-inline="true" data-icon="home"
   href="home.html">Home page</a>
```

There are over 50 ready-made icons to choose from. They are all created using a powerful graphical language called Scalable Vector Graphics (SVG), and they fall back to PNG for devices that don't support SVG, making the icons look great on Retina displays. Take a look at the Icons demo (*http://tinyurl.com/jqmicons*) to see what's available.

Icons appear to the left of button text by default, but you can choose to place them to the right, above, or below the text, or to remove any text by applying the values right, top, bottom, or notext to the data-iconpos attribute, like this:

```
<a data-role="button" data-inline="true" data-icon="home"
   data-iconpos="right" href="home.html">Home page</a>
```

If you choose not to display any button text, the icon displayed will be round by default.

Finally in this brief roundup of button styling, you can choose to display smaller buttons (including the button text) by supplying a value of true to the data-mini attribute, like this:

```
<a data-role="button" data-inline="true" data-icon="home"
   data-mini="true" href="home.html">Home page</a>
```

Example 22-3 demonstrates a selection of buttons being created with a variety of these button styles (with no href attributes for brevity), as shown in Figure 22-4.

Example 22-3. A variety of button elements

```
<a data-role="button">Default</a>
<a data-role="button" data-inline="true">In-line</a>
<a data-role="button" data-inline="true"
                      data-corners="false">Squared corners</a>
<a data-role="button" data-inline="true"
                      data-shadow="false">Unshadowed</a>
<a data-role="button" data-inline="true" data-corners="false"
                      data-shadow="false">Both</a><br>
<a data-role="button" data-inline="true"
                      data-icon="home">Left icon</a>
<a data-role="button" data-inline="true" data-icon="home"
                      data-iconpos="right">Right icon</a>
<a data-role="button" data-inline="true" data-icon="home"
                      data-iconpos="top">Top icon</a>
<a data-role="button" data-inline="true" data-icon="home"
                      data-iconpos="bottom">Bottom icon</a><br>
<a data-role="button" data-mini="true">Default Mini</a>
```

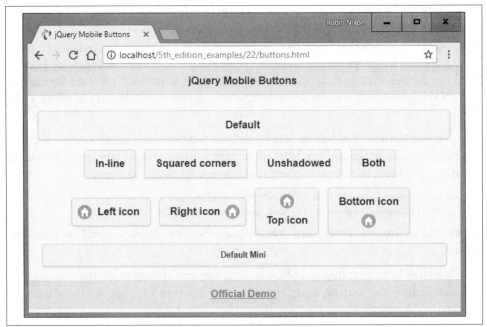

Figure 22-4. An assortment of button styles

There's actually a great deal more styling you can do with buttons, and you can get all the details you need in the Buttons demo (*http://tinyurl.com/jqmbuttons*). But for now, this introduction will stand you in good stead.

List Handling

When it comes to list handling, jQuery Mobile really makes things easy for you with a wide range of easy-to-use features, all of which you can access by supplying a value of listview to the data-role attribute of a <ul> or <ol> element.

So, for example, to create a simple unordered list, you could use code such as this:

```
<ul data-role="listview">
  <li>Brocolli</li>
  <li>Carrots</li>
  <li>Lettuce</li>
</ul>
```

For an ordered list, simply replace the <ul> opening and closing tags with <ol>, and the list will be numbered.

Any links within a list will automatically have an arrow icon embedded and be displayed as buttons. You can also inset a list, to mix it with other content on a page, by giving the data-inset attribute a value of true.

Example 22-4 demonstrates how these various features work in practice; the result is displayed in Figure 22-5.

Example 22-4. A selection of lists

```
<ul data-role="listview">
  <li>An</li>
  <li>Unordered</li>
  <li>List</li>
</ul><br><br>

<ol data-role="listview">
  <li>An</li>
  <li>Ordered</li>
  <li>List</li>
</ol><br>

<ul data-role="listview" data-inset="true">
  <li>An</li>
  <li>Inset Unordered</li>
  <li>List</li>
</ul>

<ul data-role="listview" data-inset="true">
  <li><a href='#'>An</a></li>
  <li><a href='#'>Inset Unordered</a></li>
  <li><a href='#'>Linked List</a></li>
</ul>
```

Figure 22-5. Ordered and unordered plain and inset lists

Filterable Lists

You can make lists filterable by setting the `data-filter` attribute to `true`, which will place a search box above the list and, as the user types, will automatically remove from view any list elements that do not match the search term being entered. You can also set `data-filter-reveal` to `true` so that no fields are displayed until at least one character of filter input has been entered, and only those fields that match the input are then displayed.

Example 22-5 demonstrates the use of these two types of filtered lists, which differ only by the addition of data-filter-reveal="true" to the latter.

Example 22-5. Filtered and filter-reveal lists

```
<ul data-role="listview" data-filter="true"
    data-filter-placeholder="Search big cats..." data-inset="true">
  <li>Cheetah</li>
  <li>Cougar</li>
  <li>Jaguar</li>
  <li>Leopard</li>
  <li>Lion</li>
  <li>Snow Leopard</li>
  <li>Tiger</li>
</ul>

<ul data-role="listview" data-filter="true" data-filter-reveal="true"
    data-filter-placeholder="Search big cats..." data-inset="true">
  <li>Cheetah</li>
  <li>Cougar</li>
  <li>Jaguar</li>
  <li>Leopard</li>
  <li>Lion</li>
  <li>Snow Leopard</li>
  <li>Tiger</li>
</ul>
```

Note the use of the data-filter-placeholder attribute to offer a prompt to the user when the input field is blank.

In Figure 22-6 you can see how the former list type has had the letter a entered into the filter field, so only those fields that have an a in them are currently displayed, while none of the fields in the second list are shown because nothing has yet been entered into the filter field.

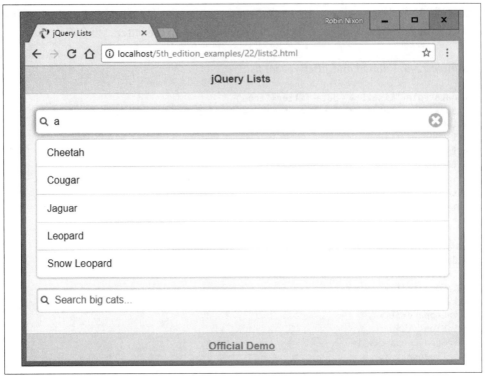

Figure 22-6. Displaying a filtered and a filter-reveal list

List Dividers

To enhance the way lists are displayed, you can also place manual or automatic dividers within them. You create manual list dividers by supplying a list element with a `data-role` attribute value of `list-divider`, as shown in Example 22-6, which displays as Figure 22-7.

Example 22-6. Manual list dividers

```
<ul data-role="listview" data-inset="true">
  <li data-role="list-divider">Big Cats</li>
  <li>Cheetah</li>
  <li>Cougar</li>
  <li>Jaguar</li>
  <li>Lion</li>
  <li>Snow Leopard</li>
  <li data-role="list-divider">Big Dogs</li>
  <li>Bloodhound</li>
  <li>Doberman Pinscher</li>
  <li>Great Dane</li>
  <li>Mastiff</li>
```

```
      <li>Rottweiler</li>
</ul>
```

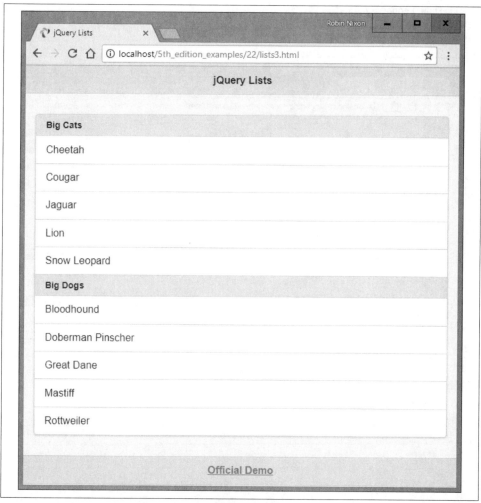

Figure 22-7. The list is divided into categories

To let jQuery Mobile determine the division in a convenient way, you can supply the
value true to the data-autodividers attribute, as in Example 22-7, which divides the
fields alphabetically and displays as Figure 22-8.

Example 22-7. Using autodividers

```
<ul data-role="listview" data-inset="true" data-autodividers="true">
   <li>Cheetah</li>
   <li>Cougar</li>
```

```
    <li>Jaguar</li>
    <li>Leopard</li>
    <li>Lion</li>
    <li>Snow Leopard</li>
    <li>Tiger</li>
</ul>
```

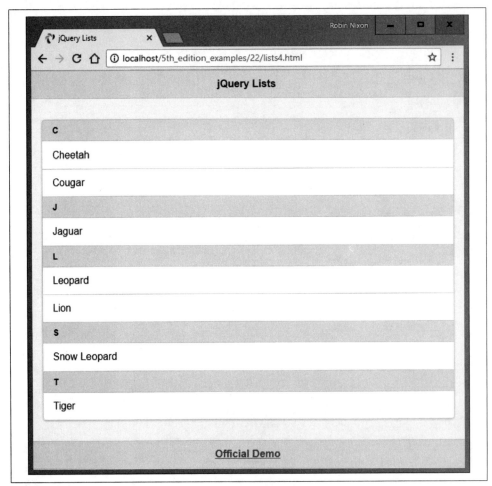

Figure 22-8. Automatically dividing a list alphabetically

As with buttons (see "Styling Buttons" on page 568), you can also add icons to linked list fields using the data-icon attribute along with a value representing the icon to display, like this:

```
<li data-icon="gear"><a href="settings.html">Settings</a></li>
```

In this example, the default right angle bracket of a linked list will be replaced with the icon you select (in this case, a gear icon).

In addition to all these great features, you can also add icons and thumbnails within list fields and they will be scaled to look good when displayed. For details on how to do this and on many other list features, please refer to the official documentation (*http://tinyurl.com/jqmlists*).

What Next?

As I mentioned at the start, the purpose of this chapter has been to get you up to speed quickly with jQuery Mobile, so that you can easily repackage websites into web apps that look good on all devices, whether desktop or mobile.

To this end, I have introduced only jQuery Mobile's very best and most important features, so I've really only scratched the surface of what you can do with it. For example, there's a tremendous variety of ways you can enhance and make forms work well on mobile devices. You can build responsive tables, create collapsible content, invoke pop-ups, design your own themes, and much more.

 You may be interested to learn that you can use jQuery Mobile in conjunction with a product by Adobe called PhoneGap (*https:// phonegap.com*) to build standalone apps for Android and iOS. It's not entirely straightforward, and doing so is outside the remit of this book to explain, but most of the hard work has already been done for you by the jQuery and PhoneGap teams. For more information, please refer to the jQuery Mobile guide (*http://bit.ly/ 2HHx1zR*) to building PhoneGap apps.

Once you've got the hang of everything in this chapter, if you would like to see what else jQuery Mobile can do for you, I recommend you check out the official demos and documentation on the website (*http://demos.jquerymobile.com*).

Also, the example social networking app in Chapter 27 applies many of these features in a close-to-real-world scenario, and is a great way to really see how you can mobile up your web pages. Before we get to that, though, in the following chapters we'll turn our gaze to all the goodies available in HTML5.

Questions

1. Name a couple of major benefits and one downside to using a CDN for delivering jQuery Mobile to a web browser.

2. What HTML would you use to define a page of content to jQuery Mobile?

3. What are the three main parts that make up a jQuery page, and how are they denoted?

4. How can you put more than one jQuery Mobile page within an HTML document?

5. How can you prevent a web page from being loaded asynchronously?

6. How would you set the page transition of an anchor to flip, rather than using the default of fade?

7. How can you load a page so that it displays as a dialog rather than a web page?

8. How can you easily make an anchor link display as a button?

9. How can you make a jQuery Mobile element display inline like a <span> element, rather than full width like a <div>?

10. How can you add an icon to a button?

See "Chapter 22 Answers" on page 730 in Appendix A for the answers to these questions.

CHAPTER 23

Introduction to HTML5

HTML5 represents a substantial leap forward in web design, layout, and usability. It provides a simple way to manipulate graphics in a web browser without resorting to plug-ins such as Flash, offers methods to insert audio and video into web pages (again without plug-ins), and irons out several annoying inconsistencies that crept into HTML during its evolution.

In addition, HTML5 includes numerous other enhancements such as geolocation handling, web workers to manage background tasks, improved form handling, and access to bundles of local storage (far in excess of the limited capabilities of cookies).

What's interesting about HTML5, though, is that it has been an ongoing evolution, in which browsers have adopted different features at different times. Fortunately, all the biggest and most popular HTML5 additions are now supported by all major browsers (those with more than 1 percent or so of the market, such as Chrome, Internet Explorer, Edge, Firefox, Safari, Opera, and the Android and iOS browsers).

The Canvas

Originally introduced by Apple for the WebKit rendering engine (which had itself originated in the KDE HTML layout engine) for its Safari browser (and now also implemented in the iOS, Android, Kindle, Chrome, BlackBerry, Opera, and Tizen browsers), the *canvas* element enables us to draw graphics in a web page without having to rely on a plug-in such as Java or Flash. After being standardized, the canvas was adopted by all other browsers and is now a mainstay of modern web development.

Like other HTML elements, a canvas is simply an element within a web page with defined dimensions, and within which you can use JavaScript to insert content—in this case, to draw graphics. You create a canvas by using the <canvas> tag, to which you must assign an ID so that JavaScript will know which canvas it is accessing (as you can have more than one canvas on a page).

In Example 23-1 I've created a canvas element, with the ID mycanvas, that contains some text that is displayed only in browsers that don't support the canvas. Beneath this there is a section of JavaScript that draws the Japanese flag on the canvas (as shown in Figure 23-1).

Example 23-1. Using the HTML5 canvas element

```
<!DOCTYPE html>
<html>
  <head>
    <title>The HTML5 Canvas</title>
    <script src='OSC.js'></script>
  </head>
  <body>
    <canvas id='mycanvas' width='320' height='240'>
      This is a canvas element given the ID <i>mycanvas</i>
      This text is visible only in non-HTML5 browsers
    </canvas>

    <script>
      canvas             = O('mycanvas')
      context            = canvas.getContext('2d')
      context.fillStyle = 'red'
      S(canvas).border  = '1px solid black'

      context.beginPath()
      context.moveTo(160, 120)
      context.arc(160, 120, 70, 0, Math.PI * 2, false)
      context.closePath()
      context.fill()
    </script>
  </body>
</html>
```

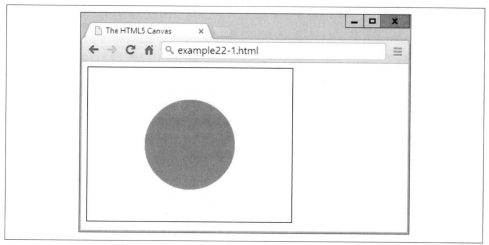

Figure 23-1. Drawing the Japanese flag using an HTML5 canvas

At this point, it's not necessary to detail exactly what is going on—I explain that in Chapter 24—but you should already see that using the canvas is not hard, although it does require learning a few new JavaScript functions. Note that this example draws on the *OSC.js* set of functions from Chapter 20 to help keep the code neat and compact.

Geolocation

Using *geolocation*, your browser can return information to a web server about your location. This information can come from a GPS chip in the computer or mobile device you're using, from your IP address, or from analysis of nearby WiFi hotspots. For security purposes, the user is always in control and can refuse to provide this information on a one-off basis, or can enable settings to either permanently block or allow access to this data from one or all websites.

There are numerous uses for this technology, including giving you turn-by-turn navigation; providing local maps; notifying you of nearby restaurants, WiFi hotspots, or other places; letting you know which friends are near you; directing you to the nearest gas station; and more.

Example 23-2 will display a Google map of the user's location, as long as the browser supports geolocation and the user grants access to location data (as shown in Figure 23-2). Otherwise, it will display an error.

Example 23-2. Displaying a map of the user's location

```
<!DOCTYPE html>
<html>
  <head>
```

```
    <title>Geolocation Example</title>
  </head>
  <body>
    <script>
      if (typeof navigator.geolocation == 'undefined')
        alert("Geolocation not supported.")
      else
        navigator.geolocation.getCurrentPosition(granted, denied)

      function granted(position)
      {
        var lat = position.coords.latitude
        var lon = position.coords.longitude

        alert("Permission Granted. You are at location:\n\n"
          + lat + ", " + lon +
          "\n\nClick 'OK' to load Google Maps with your location")

        window.location.replace("https://www.google.com/maps/@"
          + lat + "," + lon + ",14z")
      }

      function denied(error)
      {
        var message

        switch(error.code)
        {
          case 1: message = 'Permission Denied'; break;
          case 2: message = 'Position Unavailable'; break;
          case 3: message = 'Operation Timed Out'; break;
          case 4: message = 'Unknown Error'; break;
        }

        alert("Geolocation Error: " + message)
      }
    </script>
  </body>
</html>
```

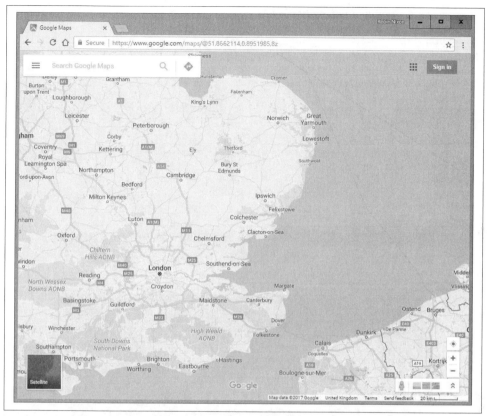

Figure 23-2. The user's location has been used to display a map

Again, here is not the place to describe how this all works; I will detail that in Chapter 26. For now, though, this example serves to show you how easy managing geolocation can be.

Audio and Video

Another great addition to HTML5 is support for in-browser audio and video. While playing these types of media can be a little complicated due to the variety of encoding types and licenses, the `<audio>` and `<video>` elements provide the flexibility you need to display the types of media you have available.

In Example 23-3, the same video file has been encoded in different formats to ensure that all major browsers are accounted for. Browsers will simply select the first type they recognize and play it, as shown in Figure 23-3.

Example 23-3. Playing a video with HTML5

```html
<!DOCTYPE html>
<html>
  <head>
    <title>HTML5 Video</title>
  </head>
  <body>
    <video width='560' height='320' controls>
      <source src='movie.mp4'  type='video/mp4'>
      <source src='movie.webm' type='video/webm'>
      <source src='movie.ogv'  type='video/ogg'>
    </video>
  </body>
</html>
```

Figure 23-3. Displaying video using HTML5

Inserting audio into a web page is just as easy, as you will discover in Chapter 25.

Forms

As you already saw in Chapter 11, HTML5 forms are in the process of being enhanced, but support across all browsers remains patchy. What you *can* safely use today has been detailed in Chapter 11.

Local Storage

With local storage, the amount and complexity of data you can save on a local device is substantially increased from the meager space provided by cookies. This opens up the possibility of using web apps to work on documents offline and then syncing them with the web server only when an internet connection is available. It also raises the prospect of storing small databases locally for access with WebSQL, perhaps for keeping a copy of your music collection's details, or all your personal statistics as part of a diet or weight loss plan, for example. In Chapter 26, I show you how to make the most of this new facility in your web projects.

Web Workers

It has been possible to run interrupt-driven applications in the background using JavaScript for many years, but only through a clumsy and inefficient process. It makes much more sense to let the underlying browser technology run background tasks on your behalf, which it can do far more quickly than you can by continuously interrupting the browser to check how things are going.

Instead, with *web workers* you set everything up and pass your code to the web browser, which then runs it. When anything significant occurs, your code simply has to notify the browser, which then reports back to your main code. In the meantime, your web page can be doing nothing or a number of other tasks, and can forget about the background task until it makes itself known.

In Chapter 26, I demonstrate how you can use web workers to create a simple clock and to calculate prime numbers.

Microdata

In Chapter 26, I also show how you can mark up your code with *microdata* to make it totally understandable to any browser or other technology that needs to access it. Microdata is sure to become more and more important to search engine optimization too, so it's important that you begin to incorporate it or at least understand what information it can provide about your websites.

As you can see, there's quite a lot to HTML5—many people have waited a long time for these goodies, but they're finally here. Starting with the canvas, the following few chapters will explain these features to you in glorious detail, so you can be up and running with them, and enhancing your websites, in no time.

Questions

1. What new HTML5 element enables drawing of graphics in web pages?

2. What programming language is required to access many of the advanced HTML5 features?

3. Which HTML5 tags would you use to incorporate audio and video in a web page?

4. What feature is new in HTML5 and offers greater capability than cookies?

5. Which HTML5 technology supports running background JavaScript tasks?

See "Chapter 23 Answers" on page 731 in Appendix A for the answers to these questions.

CHAPTER 24

The HTML5 Canvas

Although the collective term given to the new web technologies is *HTML5*, they are not all simply HTML tags and properties. Such is the case with the canvas element. Yes, you create a canvas by using the <canvas> tag, and maybe supply a width and height, and can modify it a little with CSS, but to actually write to (or read from) a canvas, you must use JavaScript.

Thankfully, the JavaScript you need to learn is minimal and very easy to implement, plus I've already provided you with a set of three ready-made functions in Chapter 20 (in the file *OSC.js*) to make accessing objects such as the canvas even more straightforward. So, let's dive right in and start using the new <canvas> tag.

Creating and Accessing a Canvas

In Chapter 23, I showed you how to draw a simple circle to display the Japanese flag, as in Example 24-1. Let's now look at what exactly is going on here.

Example 24-1. Displaying the Japanese flag by using a canvas

```
<!DOCTYPE html>
<html>
  <head>
    <title>The HTML5 Canvas</title>
    <script src='OSC.js'></script>
  </head>
  <body>
    <canvas id='mycanvas' width='320' height='240'>
      This is a canvas element given the ID <i>mycanvas</i>
      This text is only visible in non-HTML5 browsers
    </canvas>
```

```
    <script>
      canvas              = O('mycanvas')
      context             = canvas.getContext('2d')
      context.fillStyle = 'red'
      S(canvas).border  = '1px solid black'

      context.beginPath()
      context.moveTo(160, 120)
      context.arc(160, 120, 70, 0, Math.PI * 2, false)
      context.closePath()
      context.fill()
    </script>
  </body>
</html>
```

First, the `<!DOCTYPE html>` declaration tells the browser that the document will use HTML5. After this, a title is displayed and the three functions in the *OSC.js* file are loaded in.

The body of the document defines a canvas element, gives it an ID of `mycanvas`, and gives it a width and height of 320 × 240 pixels. The text of the canvas, as explained in the previous chapter, will not appear in browsers that support the canvas element, but will appear in older browsers that don't.

This is followed by a section of JavaScript that styles and draws on the canvas. We begin by creating a `canvas` object by calling the `O` function on the canvas element. As you will recall, this calls the `document.getElementById` function, and is therefore a much shorter way of referencing the element.

This is all stuff you've seen before, but next comes something new:

```
context = canvas.getContext('2d')
```

This command calls the `getContext` method of the new `canvas` object just created, requesting two-dimensional access to the canvas by passing the value 2d.

 If you want to display 3D on a canvas, you can either do the math yourself and "fake" it in 2D, or you can use WebGL (which is based on OpenGL ES), in which case you would create a `context` for it by calling `canvas.getContext('webgl')`. There's no room to cover the subject any further here, but you can find a great tutorial on the WEBGL Tutorials site (*http://www.webgltutorials.org*). Alternatively, check out the Three.js (*https://threejs.org*) JavaScript library of 3D functions, which also uses WebGL.

Armed with this context in the object `context`, we prime the subsequent drawing commands by setting the `fillStyle` property of `context` to the value `red`:

```
context.fillStyle = 'red'
```

Then the S function is called to set the `border` property of the canvas to a 1-pixel, solid black line to outline the flag image:

```
S(canvas).border = '1px solid black'
```

With everything prepared, a path is opened on the context and the drawing position is moved to the location (160,120):

```
context.beginPath()
context.moveTo(160, 120)
```

After that, an arc is drawn centered on that coordinate, with a radius of 70 pixels, beginning at an angle of 0 degrees (which is the righthand edge of the circle as you look at it) and continuing all the way around the circle in radians as determined by a value of $2 \times \pi$:

```
context.arc(160, 120, 70, 0, Math.PI * 2, false)
```

The final value of `false` indicates a clockwise direction for drawing the arc; a value of `true` would indicate that the drawing should occur in a counterclockwise direction.

Finally, we close and fill the path, using the preselected value in the `fillStyle` property that we set to `red` a few lines earlier:

```
context.closePath()
context.fill()
```

The result of loading this document into a web browser looks like Figure 23-1 in the previous chapter.

The toDataURL Function

After you have created an image in a canvas, you will sometimes want to make a copy of it, perhaps to repeat elsewhere on a web page, for animation purposes, to save to local storage, or to upload to a web server. This is particularly handy since users cannot use drag and drop to save a canvas image.

To illustrate how you do this, I have added a few lines of code to the previous example in Example 24-2 (highlighted in bold). These create a new `<img>` element with the ID `myimage`, give it a solid black border, and then copy the canvas image into the `<img>` element (see Figure 24-1).

Example 24-2. Copying a canvas image

```
<!DOCTYPE html>
<html>
  <head>
    <title>Copying a Canvas</title>
    <script src='OSC.js'></script>
  </head>
```

```
<body>
  <canvas id='mycanvas' width='320' height='240'>
    This is a canvas element given the ID <i>mycanvas</i>
    This text is only visible in non-HTML5 browsers
  </canvas>

  <img id='myimage'>

  <script>
    canvas             = O('mycanvas')
    context            = canvas.getContext('2d')
    context.fillStyle = 'red'
    S(canvas).border   = '1px solid black'

    context.beginPath()
    context.moveTo(160, 120)
    context.arc(160, 120, 70, 0, Math.PI * 2, false)
    context.closePath()
    context.fill()

    S('myimage').border = '1px solid black'
    O('myimage').src    = canvas.toDataURL()
  </script>
</body>
</html>
```

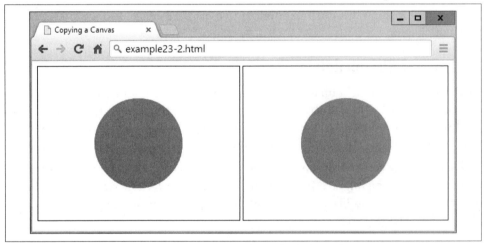

Figure 24-1. The image on the right is copied from the lefthand canvas

If you try this code for yourself, you will notice that although you cannot drag and drop the lefthand canvas image, you can do so with the righthand picture, which you could also save to local storage or upload to a web server using the right JavaScript (and PHP on the server end).

Specifying an Image Type

When creating an image from a canvas, you can specify the type of image you want as either JPEG (*.jpg* or *.jpeg* files) or PNG (*.png* files). The default is PNG (image/png), but should you prefer JPEG, you can alter the call to toDataURL. At the same time, you can also specify the amount of compression to use, between 0 (for lowest quality) and 1 (for highest quality). The following uses a compression value of 0.4, and should generate a reasonably good-looking image at a fairly low file size:

```
O('myimage').src = canvas.toDataURL('image/jpeg', 0.4)
```

 Remember that the toDataURL method applies to a canvas object, not to any context created from that object.

Now that you know how to create canvas images and then copy or otherwise use them, it's time to look at the drawing commands available, starting with rectangles.

The fillRect Method

There are two different methods you can call for drawing rectangles, the first of which is fillRect. To use it, you simply supply the top-left coordinates of your rectangle, followed by the width and height in pixels, like this:

```
context.fillRect(20, 20, 600, 200)
```

By default, the rectangle will be filled with black, but you can use any other color you like by first issuing a command such as the following, where the argument can be any acceptable CSS color, name, or value:

```
context.fillStyle = 'blue'
```

The clearRect Method

You can also draw a rectangle in which all the color values (red, green, blue, and alpha transparency) have been set to 0, like in the following example, which uses the same order of coordinates and width and height arguments:

```
context.clearRect(40, 40, 560, 160)
```

Once the clearRect method is applied, the new clear rectangle will strip all color from the area it covers, leaving only any underlying CSS color that has been applied to the canvas element.

The strokeRect Method

When you want only an outlined rectangle, you can use a command such as the following, which will use the default of black or the currently selected stroke color:

```
context.strokeRect(60, 60, 520, 120)
```

To change the color used, you can first issue a command such as the following, supplying any valid CSS color argument:

```
context.strokeStyle = 'green'
```

Combining These Commands

In Example 24-3, the preceding rectangle-drawing commands have been combined to display the image shown in Figure 24-2.

Example 24-3. Drawing several rectangles

```
<!DOCTYPE html>
<html>
  <head>
    <title>Drawing Rectangles</title>
    <script src='OSC.js'></script>
  </head>
  <body>
    <canvas id='mycanvas' width='640' height='240'></canvas>

    <script>
      canvas               = O('mycanvas')
      context              = canvas.getContext('2d')
      S(canvas).background = 'lightblue'
      context.fillStyle    = 'blue'
      context.strokeStyle  = 'green'

      context.fillRect(  20, 20, 600, 200)
      context.clearRect( 40, 40, 560, 160)
      context.strokeRect(60, 60, 520, 120)
    </script>
  </body>
</html>
```

Figure 24-2. Drawing concentric rectangles

Later in this chapter, you'll see how you can further modify the output by changing stroke types and widths—but first, let's turn to modifying fills by applying gradients (which were introduced in "Gradients" on page 438 as part of CSS).

The createLinearGradient Method

There are a couple of ways to apply a gradient to a fill, but the simplest is with the `createLinearGradient` method. You specify start and end *x* and *y* coordinates relative to the canvas (not the object being filled). This allows for greater subtlety. For example, you can specify that a gradient begin at the far left and end at the far right of a canvas, but apply it only within the area defined in a fill command, as shown in Example 24-4.

Example 24-4. Applying a gradient fill

```
gradient = context.createLinearGradient(0, 80, 640,80)
gradient.addColorStop(0, 'white')
gradient.addColorStop(1, 'black')
context.fillStyle = gradient
context.fillRect(80, 80, 480,80)
```

For brevity and clarity in this and many of the following examples, only salient lines of code are shown. Complete examples with the surrounding HTML, setup, and other sections of code are available to freely download from the companion website (*http://lpmj.net*).

In this example, we create a gradient fill object named `gradient` by making a call to the `createLinearGradient` method of the `context` object. The start position of (0,80) is halfway down the lefthand canvas edge, while the end of (640,80) is halfway down the righthand edge.

To create your gradient, determine the direction in which you want it to flow and then locate two points to represent the start and end. No matter what values you supply for these points, the gradient will smoothly transition in the direction given, even if the points are outside the fill area.

Next, a couple of color stops are provided to specify that the very first color of the gradient is white, and the final color is black. The gradient will then transition smoothly between these colors across the canvas from left to right.

With the `gradient` object now ready, it is applied to the `fillStyle` property of the `context` object, so that the final `fillRect` call can use it. In this call, the fill is applied only in a central rectangular area of the canvas, so although the gradient goes from the far left to the far right of the canvas, the portion of it shown is only from 80 pixels in and down from the top-left corner, to a width of 480 and depth of 80 pixels. The result (when added to the previous example code) looks like Figure 24-3.

Figure 24-3. The central rectangle has a horizontal gradient fill

By specifying different start and end coordinates for a gradient, you can make it slant in any direction, as demonstrated with Example 24-5 and shown in Figure 24-4.

Example 24-5. A variety of gradients at different angles and colors

```
gradient = context.createLinearGradient(0, 0, 160, 0)
gradient.addColorStop(0, 'white')
gradient.addColorStop(1, 'black')
```

```
context.fillStyle = gradient
context.fillRect(20, 20, 135, 200)

gradient = context.createLinearGradient(0, 0, 0, 240)
gradient.addColorStop(0, 'yellow')
gradient.addColorStop(1, 'red')
context.fillStyle = gradient
context.fillRect(175, 20, 135, 200)

gradient = context.createLinearGradient(320, 0, 480, 240)
gradient.addColorStop(0, 'green')
gradient.addColorStop(1, 'purple')
context.fillStyle = gradient
context.fillRect(330, 20, 135, 200)

gradient = context.createLinearGradient(480, 240, 640, 0)
gradient.addColorStop(0, 'orange')
gradient.addColorStop(1, 'magenta')
context.fillStyle = gradient
context.fillRect(485, 20, 135, 200)
```

Figure 24-4. A range of different linear gradients

In this example, I chose to place the gradients directly on top of the areas to be filled in order to more clearly show the maximum variation in color from start to end.

The addColorStop Method in Detail

You can use as many color stops in a gradient as you like, not just the two start and end colors used so far in these examples. This makes it possible to clearly describe almost any type of gradient effect you can imagine. To do this, you must specify the percent of the gradient that each color should take up, by allocating a floating-point start position along the gradient range between 0 and 1. You do not enter a color's end position, because it is deduced from the start position of the next color stop, or the gradient end if the position is the last one you specify.

In the preceding examples, only the two start and end values were chosen, but to create a rainbow effect, you could set up your color stops as shown in Example 24-6 (displayed in Figure 24-5).

Example 24-6. Adding multiple color stops

```
gradient.addColorStop(0.00, 'red')
gradient.addColorStop(0.14, 'orange')
gradient.addColorStop(0.28, 'yellow')
gradient.addColorStop(0.42, 'green')
gradient.addColorStop(0.56, 'blue')
gradient.addColorStop(0.70, 'indigo')
gradient.addColorStop(0.84, 'violet')
```

Figure 24-5. A rainbow effect with seven stop colors

In Example 24-6, all the colors are spaced roughly equidistantly (with each color given 14 percent of the gradient, and the final one 16), but you don't have to stick to that; you can squish several colors near each other, while spacing others out. It's entirely up to you as to how many colors you use and where in the gradient they start and end.

The createRadialGradient Method

You aren't restricted to only linear gradients in HTML; you can create radial gradients on a canvas too. It's a little more complex than with a linear gradient, but not much more so.

What you need to do is pass the center location as a pair of *x* and *y* coordinates, along with a radius in pixels. These are used as the start of the gradient and outer circumference, respectively. Then you also pass another set of coordinates and a radius to specify the end of the gradient.

So, for example, to create a gradient that simply starts at the center of a circle and then expands out, you could issue a command such as the one in Example 24-7 (displayed in Figure 24-6). The coordinates for the start and end are the same, but the radius is 0 for the start and encompasses the entire gradient for the end.

Example 24-7. Creating a radial gradient

```
gradient = context.createRadialGradient(320, 120, 0, 320, 120, 320)
```

Figure 24-6. A centered radial gradient

Or you can be fancy and move the location of the start and end of a radial gradient, as in Example 24-8 (and displayed in Figure 24-7), which starts centered on location (0,120) with a radius of 0 pixels, and ends centered at (480,120) with a radius of 480 pixels.

Example 24-8. Stretching a radial gradient

```
gradient = context.createRadialGradient(0, 120, 0, 480, 120, 480)
```

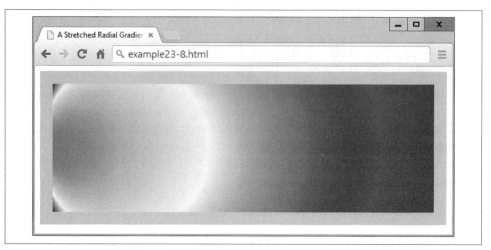

Figure 24-7. A stretched radial gradient

By manipulating the figures supplied to this method, you can create a wide range of weird and wonderful effects—try it for yourself with the supplied examples.

Using Patterns for Fills

In a similar manner to gradient fills, you can also apply an image as a fill pattern. This can be an image anywhere in the current document, or even one created from a canvas via the toDataURL method (explained earlier in this chapter).

Example 24-9 loads a 100 × 100–pixel image (the yin-yang symbol) into the new image object image. The following statement attaches to the onload event a function that creates a repeating pattern for the fillStyle property of the context. This is then used to fill a 600 × 200–pixel area within the canvas, as shown in Figure 24-8.

Example 24-9. Using an image for a pattern fill

```
image     = new Image()
image.src = 'image.png'

image.onload = function()
{
  pattern           = context.createPattern(image, 'repeat')
  context.fillStyle = pattern
  context.fillRect(20, 20, 600, 200)
}
```

Pattern Fill   ×   example23-9.html

Figure 24-8. Tiling an image by using it as a pattern fill

We create the pattern by using the `createPattern` method, which also supports non-repeating patterns, or ones that just repeat in the x- or y-axes. We achieve this by passing one of the following values to it as the second argument, after the image to use:

`repeat`
> Repeat the image both vertically and horizontally.

`repeat-x`
> Repeat the image horizontally.

`repeat-y`
> Repeat the image vertically.

`no-repeat`
> Do not repeat the image.

The fill pattern is based on the entire canvas area, so where the fill command is set to apply only to a smaller area within the canvas, the images appear cut off at the top and left.

> If the `onload` event had not been used in this example and, instead, the code was simply executed as soon as encountered, the image might not have already loaded by the time the web page was displayed and might not appear in the display. Attaching to this event ensures that the image is available for use in the canvas, because the event triggers only upon successful loading of an image.

Writing Text to the Canvas

As you would expect from a set of graphics features, writing to the canvas with text is fully supported with a variety of font, alignment, and fill methods. But why would you want to write text to the canvas when there's already such good support for web fonts in CSS these days?

Well, suppose you wish to display a graph or table with graphical elements. You'll surely also want to label parts of it. What's more, using the available commands, you can produce much more than simply a colored font. So, let's start by assuming you've been tasked to create a header for a website on basket weaving, called WickerpediA (actually there's already one of these, but let's go ahead anyway).

To start with, you need to select a suitable font and size it appropriately, perhaps as in Example 24-10, in which a font style of bold, a size of 140 pixels, and a typeface of Times have been selected. Also, the `textBaseline` property has been set to `top` so that the `strokeText` method can pass coordinates of (0,0) for the top-left origin of the text, placing it at the top left of the canvas. Figure 24-9 shows what this looks like.

Example 24-10. Writing text to the canvas

```
context.font        = 'bold 140px Times'
context.textBaseline = 'top'
context.strokeText('WickerpediA', 0, 0)
```

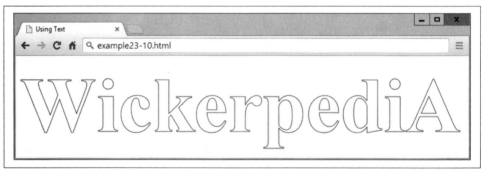

Figure 24-9. The text has been written to the canvas

The strokeText Method

To write text to the canvas, you send the text string and a pair of coordinates to the `strokeText` method, like this:

```
context.strokeText('WickerpediA', 0, 0)
```

The *x* and *y* coordinates supplied will be used as a relative reference by the `textBase Line` and `textAlign` properties.

This method—using line drawing—is only one way of drawing text to the canvas. So, in addition to all the following properties that affect text, line-drawing properties such as lineWidth (detailed later in this chapter) will also affect how text displays.

The textBaseLine Property

The textBaseLine property can be given any of the following values:

top
> Aligns to the top of the text

middle
> Aligns to the middle of the text

alphabetic
> Aligns to the alphabetic baseline of the text

bottom
> Aligns to the bottom of the text

The font Property

The font style can be any of bold, italic, or normal (the default), or a combination of italic bold, and the size values can be specified in em, ex, px, %, in, cm, mm, pt, or pc measures, just as with CSS. The font should be one available to the current browser, which generally means one of Helvetica, Impact, Courier, Times, or Arial, or you can choose the default Serif or Sans-serif font of the user's system. If you're confident that another font you want to use will be available to the browser, you can specify that, too, but it's a good idea to include at least one of the more common or default options after it so styling can fall back gracefully if the user doesn't have your preferred font installed.

 If you want to use a font such as Times New Roman, which incorporates spaces in its name, you should change the relevant line to something like this, in which the outer quotes are different from the ones surrounding the font name:

```
context.font = 'bold 140px "Times New Roman"'
```

The textAlign Property

In addition to choosing how to align your text vertically, you can specify horizontal alignment by giving the textAlign property one of the following values:

start
>   Aligns the text to the left if the document direction is left to right, or otherwise to the right. This is the default setting.

end
>   Aligns the text to the right if the document direction is left to right, or otherwise to the left.

left
>   Aligns the text to the left.

right
>   Aligns the text to the right.

center
>   Centers the text.

You use the property like this:

```
context.textAlign = 'center'
```

In the case of the current example, you need the text left-aligned so that it butts up neatly to the edge of the canvas, so the `textAlign` property is not used, and therefore the default left alignment occurs.

The fillText Method

You can also choose to use a fill property to fill in canvas text, which can be any of a solid color, a linear or radial gradient, or a pattern fill. Let's try a pattern fill for our heading based on the texture of a wicker basket, as in Example 24-11, the result of which is shown in Figure 24-10.

Example 24-11. Filling in the text with a pattern

```
image     = new Image()
image.src = 'wicker.jpg'

image.onload = function()
{
  pattern           = context.createPattern(image, 'repeat')
  context.fillStyle = pattern
  context.fillText(  'WickerpediA', 0, 0)
  context.strokeText('WickerpediA', 0, 0)
}
```

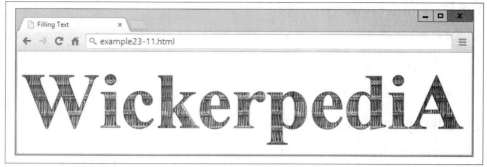

Figure 24-10. The text now has a pattern fill

For good measure, I also kept the strokeText call in this example to ensure a black outline to the text; without it, there wasn't enough definition at the edges.

A wide variety of other fill types or patterns can also be used here, and the simplicity of the canvas makes it easy to experiment. What's more, if you wish, once you have the heading just right, you can also choose to save a copy by issuing a call toDataURL, as detailed earlier in the chapter. Then you can use the image as a logo for uploading to other sites, for example.

The measureText Method

When working with canvas text, you may sometimes need to know how much space it will occupy so that you can best position it. You can achieve this with the measure Text method, as follows (assuming all the various text properties have already been defined at this point):

```
metrics = context.measureText('WickerpediA')
width   = metrics.width
```

Since the height of the text in pixels is equal to the font size in points when the font is defined, the metrics object doesn't provide a height metric.

Drawing Lines

The canvas provides a plethora of line-drawing functions to cater to almost every need, including choices of lines, line caps and joins, and paths and curves of all types. But let's start with a property I touched on in the previous section, on writing text to the canvas.

The lineWidth Property

All the canvas methods that draw with lines make use of several line properties, one of the most important being `lineWidth`. Using it is as simple as specifying a line width in pixels, like this, which sets the width to 3 pixels:

```
context.lineWidth = 3
```

The lineCap and lineJoin Properties

When lines you draw come to an end and they are more than a pixel wide, you can choose how this *line cap* (as it is called) should appear by using the `lineCap` property, which can have the values `butt` (thedefault), `round`, or `square`. For example:

```
context.lineCap = 'round'
```

Also, when you are joining lines together that are wider than a single pixel, it is important to specify exactly how they should meet. You achieve this with the `line Join` property, which can have values of `round`, `bevel`, or `miter` (the default), like this:

```
context.lineJoin = 'bevel'
```

Example 24-12 (shown here in full since it's a little more complicated) applies all three values of each property in combination, creating the result you'll see in Figure 24-11. The `beginPath`, `closePath`, `moveTo`, and `lineTo` methods used by this example are explained next.

Example 24-12. Displaying combinations of line caps and joins

```
<!DOCTYPE html>
<html>
  <head>
    <title>Drawing Lines</title>
    <script src='OSC.js'></script>
  </head>
  <body>
    <canvas id='mycanvas' width='535' height='360'></canvas>

    <script>
      canvas              = O('mycanvas')
      context             = canvas.getContext('2d')
      S(canvas).background = 'lightblue'
      context.fillStyle   = 'red'
      context.font        = 'bold 13pt Courier'
      context.strokeStyle = 'blue'
      context.textBaseline = 'top'
      context.textAlign   = 'center'
      context.lineWidth   = 20
      caps                = [' butt', ' round', 'square']
      joins               = [' round', ' bevel', ' miter']
```

```
      for (j = 0 ; j < 3 ; ++j)
      {
        for (k = 0 ; k < 3 ; ++k)
        {
          context.lineCap  = caps[j]
          context.lineJoin = joins[k]

          context.fillText(' cap:' + caps[j],  88 + j * 180, 45 + k * 120)
          context.fillText('join:' + joins[k], 88 + j * 180, 65 + k * 120)

          context.beginPath()
          context.moveTo( 20 + j * 180, 100 + k * 120)
          context.lineTo( 20 + j * 180,  20 + k * 120)
          context.lineTo(155 + j * 180,  20 + k * 120)
          context.lineTo(155 + j * 180, 100 + k * 120)
          context.stroke()
          context.closePath()
        }
      }
    </script>
  </body>
</html>
```

This code sets up a few properties and then nests a pair of loops: one for the line caps
and one for the joins. Inside the central loop, the current values for the lineCap and
lineJoin properties are first set, and then displayed in the canvas with the fillText
method.

Using these settings, the code then draws 9 shapes with a 20-pixel-wide line, each of
which has a different combination of line cap and join settings, as shown in
Figure 24-11.

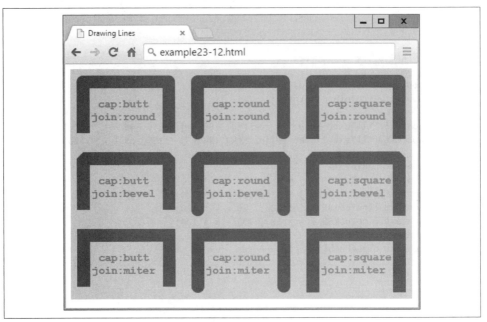

Figure 24-11. All the combinations of line caps and joins

As you can see, butted line caps are short, square ones are longer, and the round ones are somewhere between the two. Rounded line joins are curved, beveled ones are cut across the corner, and mitered ones have sharp corners. Line joins also apply to joins at angles other than 90 degrees.

The miterLimit Property

If you find that your mitered joins get cut off too short, you can extend them by using the miterLimit property, like this:

```
context.miterLimit = 15
```

The default value is 10, so you can reduce the miter limit too. If miterLimit is not set to a sufficiently large value for a miter, then sharply mitered joins will simply bevel instead. So, if you are having trouble with your pointed miters, simply increase the value you supply for miterLimit until the miter displays.

Using Paths

The previous example made use of two methods to set up paths for the line-drawing methods to follow. The beginPath method sets the start of a path, and closePath sets the end. Inside each path, you can then use various methods for moving the location of drawing and for creating lines, curves, and other shapes. Let's examine the relevant section from Example 24-12, simplified to create just a single instance of the pattern:

```
context.beginPath()
context.moveTo(20, 100)
context.lineTo(20,  20)
context.lineTo(155, 20)
context.lineTo(155,100)
context.stroke()
context.closePath()
```

In this code snippet, a path is started in the first line, and then the drawing location is moved to a position 20 pixels across and 100 down from the top-left corner of the canvas, using a call to the moveTo method.

This is followed by three calls to lineTo, which draw three lines, first upward to the location (20,20), then to the right to (155,20), and then down again to (155,100). Once this path has been set out, the stroke method is called to lay it down, and finally the path is closed because it's no longer needed.

It is essential to close paths as soon as you finish with them; otherwise, you can get some very unexpected results when using multiple paths.

The moveTo and lineTo Methods

The moveTo and lineTo methods both take simple x and y coordinates as their arguments, with the difference being that moveTo picks up an imaginary pen from the current location and then moves it to a new one, while lineTo draws a line from the current location of the imaginary pen to the new one specified. Or, at least, a line will be drawn if the stroke method is called, but not otherwise. So let's just say that lineTo creates a *potential* drawn line, but it could equally be part of the outline for a fill area, for example.

The stroke Method

The stroke method has the job of actually drawing all the lines created so far in a path onto the canvas. If it is issued from inside an unclosed path, this has the effect of immediately drawing everything up to the most recent imaginary pen location.

However, if you close a path and then issue a call to stroke, it has the effect of also joining a path from the current location back to the start location, which in this example would turn the shapes into rectangles (which we don't want because we need to see the line caps as well as joins).

This joining effect on closing a path is required (as you will see a little later) to get paths ready for any `fill` methods you want to use on them; otherwise, the graphics you use for a fill might overflow the bounds of the path.

The rect Method

Should it have been necessary to create four-sided rectangles instead of the three-sided shapes in the preceding example (and you didn't wish to close the path yet), another `lineTo` call could have been issued to join everything up, like this (highlighted in bold):

```
context.beginPath()
context.moveTo(20, 100)
context.lineTo(20, 20)
context.lineTo(155, 20)
context.lineTo(155, 100)
context.lineTo(20, 100)
context.closePath()
```

But there's a much simpler way to draw outlined rectangles, which is with the `rect` method, like this:

```
rect(20, 20, 155, 100)
```

In just a single call, this command takes two pairs of *x* and *y* coordinates and draws a rectangle with its top-left corner at location (20,20) and bottom-right corner at (155,100).

Filling Areas

Using paths, you can create complicated areas that can also be filled in with solid, gradient, or pattern fills. In Example 24-13, some basic trigonometry is used to create a complex star pattern. I won't detail how the math works because that's not important to the example (although if you want to play with the code, try changing the values assigned to `points`, and the `scale1` and `scale2` variables, for different effects).

Example 24-13. Filling in a complex path

```
<!DOCTYPE html>
<html>
  <head>
    <title>Filling a Path</title>
    <script src='OSC.js'></script>
  </head>
  <body>
    <canvas id='mycanvas' width='320' height='320'></canvas>
```

```
<script>
  canvas             = O('mycanvas')
  context            = canvas.getContext('2d')
  S(canvas).background = 'lightblue'
  context.strokeStyle  = 'orange'
  context.fillStyle    = 'yellow'

  orig   = 160
  points = 21
  dist   = Math.PI / points * 2
  scale1 = 150
  scale2 = 80

  context.beginPath()

  for (j = 0 ; j < points ; ++j)
  {
    x = Math.sin(j * dist)
    y = Math.cos(j * dist)
    context.lineTo(orig + x * scale1, orig + y * scale1)
    context.lineTo(orig + x * scale2, orig + y * scale2)
  }

  context.closePath()
  context.stroke()
  context.fill()
</script>
</body>
</html>
```

All you really need to look at are the lines highlighted in bold, in which a path is started, a pair of lineTo calls defines the shape, the path is closed, and then the stroke and fill methods are used to draw the shape outline in orange and fill it in with yellow (as shown in Figure 24-12).

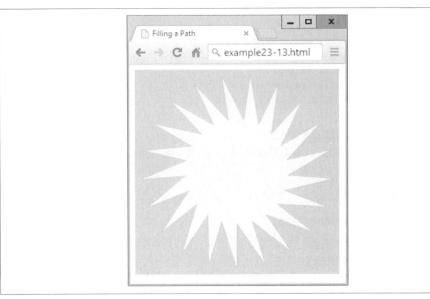

Figure 24-12. Drawing and filling in a complex path

With paths, it's possible to create as complex an object as you like, either using formulae or loops (as in this example), or simply with a long string of moveTo and/or lineTo or other calls.

The clip Method

Sometimes when you are building a path, you may want to ignore sections of the canvas (perhaps if you are drawing partly "behind" another object, and want only the visible part to display). You can achieve this using the clip method, which creates a boundary outside of which stroke, fill, or other methods will not have any effect.

To illustrate this, Example 24-14 creates an effect similar to window blinds by moving the imaginary pen pointer to the lefthand edge, then drawing a lineTo over to the righthand edge, another down by 30 pixels, and then another back to the lefthand edge, and so on. This creates a sort of snaking pattern in which a series of 30-pixel-deep, horizontal bars are drawn on the canvas, as shown in Figure 24-13.

Example 24-14. Creating a clip area

```
context.beginPath()

for (j = 0 ; j < 10 ; ++j)
{
```

```
    context.moveTo(20,  j * 48)
    context.lineTo(620, j * 48)
    context.lineTo(620, j * 48 + 30)
    context.lineTo(20,  j * 48 + 30)
}

context.stroke()
context.closePath()
```

Figure 24-13. A path of horizontal bars

To turn this example into a clipped area of the canvas, you simply need to replace the call to stroke (highlighted in bold in the example) with one to clip, like this:

```
    context.clip()
```

Now the outline of the bars won't be seen, but a clipping area that consists of all the individual bars will be in place. To illustrate this, Example 24-15 makes this method substitution and then adds to the previous example by drawing on the canvas a simple picture of green grass below a blue sky containing a shining sun (modified from Example 24-12), with the changes highlighted in bold and the result shown in Figure 24-14.

Example 24-15. Drawing within the clipped area's bounds

```
context.fillStyle = 'white'
context.strokeRect(20, 20, 600, 440) // Black border
context.fillRect( 20, 20, 600, 440) // White background

context.beginPath()

for (j = 0 ; j < 10 ; ++j)
{
  context.moveTo(20,  j * 48)
  context.lineTo(620, j * 48)
  context.lineTo(620, j * 48 + 30)
  context.lineTo(20,  j * 48 + 30)
}

context.clip()
context.closePath()

context.fillStyle   = 'blue'          // Blue sky
context.fillRect(20, 20,  600, 320)
context.fillStyle   = 'green'         // Green grass
context.fillRect(20, 320, 600, 140)
context.strokeStyle = 'orange'
context.fillStyle   = 'yellow'

orig   = 170
points = 21
dist   = Math.PI / points * 2
scale1 = 130
scale2 = 80

context.beginPath()

for (j = 0 ; j < points ; ++j)
{
  x = Math.sin(j * dist)
  y = Math.cos(j * dist)
  context.lineTo(orig + x * scale1, orig + y * scale1)
  context.lineTo(orig + x * scale2, orig + y * scale2)
}

context.closePath()
context.stroke()                      // Sun outline
context.fill()                        // Sun fill
```

Figure 24-14. Drawing occurs only within the allowed clipped area

OK, we're not going to win any competitions here, but you can see how powerful clipping can be when used effectively.

The isPointInPath Method

Sometimes you need to know whether a particular point lies in a path you've constructed. However, you will probably want to use this function only if you're quite proficient with JavaScript and with writing fairly complex programs, and you'll generally call it as part of a conditional `if` statement, like this:

```
if (context.isPointInPath(23, 87))
{
  // Do something here
}
```

The first argument to the call is the location's *x* coordinate and the second is the location's *y* coordinate. If the location specified lies along any of the points in the path, the method returns the value `true`, so the contents of the `if` statement are executed.

Otherwise, the value `false` is returned, and the contents of the `if` statement don't get executed.

 A perfect use for the `isPointInPath` method is for creating games using the canvas in which you wish to check for a missile hitting a target, a ball hitting a wall or bat, or similar boundary conditions.

Working with Curves

In addition to straight paths, you can create an almost infinite variety of curved paths with a selection of different methods, ranging from simple arcs and circles to complex quadratic and Bézier curves.

Actually, you don't need to use paths to create many lines, rectangles, and curves, because you can draw them directly by simply calling their methods. But using paths gives you more precise control, so I tend to almost always draw on the canvas within defined paths, as with the following examples.

The arc Method

The `arc` method requires you to pass it the *x* and *y* location of the center of the arc, and the radius in pixels. In addition to these values, you need to pass a pair of radian offsets and you can optionally include a direction, like this:

```
context.arc(55, 85, 45, 0, Math.PI / 2, false)
```

Since the default direction is clockwise (a value of `false`), this can be omitted, or you can change it to `true` to draw the arc in a counterclockwise direction.

Example 24-16 creates three sets of four arcs, the first two sets in a clockwise direction and the third set in a counterclockwise direction. Additionally, the first set of four arcs has its paths closed before the `stroke` method is called, so the start and end points are joined up, whereas the other two sets of arcs are drawn before the path is closed, so they are not joined up.

Example 24-16. Drawing a variety of arcs

```
context.strokeStyle = 'blue'
arcs =
[
  Math.PI,
  Math.PI * 2,
  Math.PI / 2,
  Math.PI / 180 * 59
]
```

```
for (j = 0 ; j < 4 ; ++j)
{
  context.beginPath()
  context.arc(80 + j * 160, 80, 70, 0, arcs[j])
  context.closePath()
  context.stroke()
}

context.strokeStyle = 'red'

for (j = 0 ; j < 4 ; ++j)
{
  context.beginPath()
  context.arc(80 + j * 160, 240, 70, 0, arcs[j])
  context.stroke()
  context.closePath()
}

context.strokeStyle = 'green'

for (j = 0 ; j < 4 ; ++j)
{
  context.beginPath()
  context.arc(80 + j * 160, 400, 70, 0, arcs[j], true)
  context.stroke()
  context.closePath()
}
```

To create shorter code, I drew all the arcs using loops, so that the length of each arc is stored in the array `arcs`. These values are in radians, and since a radian is equivalent to $180 \div \pi$ (π being the ratio of a circle's circumference to its diameter, or approximately 3.1415927), they evaluate as follows:

`Math.PI`
> Equivalent to 180 degrees

`Math.PI * 2`
> Equivalent to 360 degrees

`Math.PI / 2`
> Equivalent to 90 degrees

`Math.PI / 180 * 59`
> Equivalent to 59 degrees

Figure 24-15 shows the three rows of arcs and illustrates both the use of the direction argument `true` in the final set, and the importance of carefully choosing where you close paths depending on whether you want to draw a line connecting the start and end points.

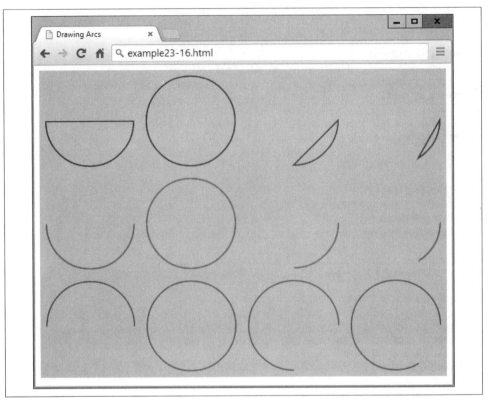

Figure 24-15. A variety of arc types

If you prefer to work with degrees instead of radians, you could create a new Math library function, like this:

```
Math.degreesToRadians = function(degrees)
{
  return degrees * Math.PI / 180
}
```

And then replace the array-creating code, starting at the second line of Example 24-16, with the following:

```
arcs =
[
  Math.degreesToRadians(180),
  Math.degreesToRadians(360),
  Math.degreesToRadians(90),
  Math.degreesToRadians(59)
]
```

The arcTo Method

Rather than creating a whole arc at once, you can choose to arc from the current location in the path to another one, like in the following call to `arcTo` (which simply requires two pairs of *x* and *y* coordinates and a radius):

```
context.arcTo(100, 100, 200, 200, 100)
```

The locations you pass to the method represent the points where imaginary tangent lines touch the circumference of the arc at its start and end points.

To illustrate how this works, Example 24-17 draws eight different arcs with radii from 0 up to 280 pixels. Each time around the loop, a new path is created with a start point at location (20,20). Then an arc is drawn using imaginary tangent lines from that location to position (240,240), and from there to location (460,20). In this instance, it defines a pair of tangents at 90 degrees to each other, in a *V* shape.

Example 24-17. Drawing eight arcs of different radii

```
for (j = 0 ; j <= 280 ; j += 40)
{
  context.beginPath()
  context.moveTo(20, 20)
  context.arcTo(240, 240, 460, 20, j)
  context.lineTo(460, 20)
  context.stroke()
  context.closePath()
}
```

The `arcTo` method draws only up to the point at which the arc touches the second imaginary tangent. So, after each call to `arcTo`, the `lineTo` method creates the remainder of the line from wherever `arcTo` left off to location (460,20). Then the result is drawn to the canvas with a call to `stroke`, and the path is closed.

As you can see in Figure 24-16, when `arcTo` is called with a radius value of 0, it creates a sharp join. In this case, it's a right angle (but if the two imaginary tangents are at other angles to each other, the join will be at that angle). Then, as the radius increases in size, you can see the arcs getting larger and larger.

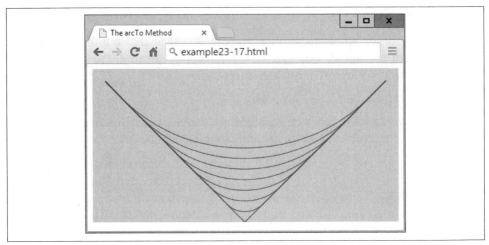

Figure 24-16. Drawing arcs of different radii

Essentially, what you can best use `arcTo` for is to curve from one section of drawing to another, following an arc based on the previous and subsequent positions, as if they were tangential to the arc to be created. If this sounds complicated, don't worry: you'll soon get the hang of it and find it's actually a handy and logical way to draw arcs.

The quadraticCurveTo Method

Useful as arcs are, they are only one type of curve and can be limiting for more-complex designs. But have no fear: there are still more ways to draw curves, such as the `quadraticCurveTo` method. Using this method, you can place an imaginary attractor near to (or far from) a curve to pull it in that direction, in a similar way to the path of an object in space being pulled by the gravity of the planets and stars it passes. Unlike with gravity, though, the farther away the attractor is, the *more* it pulls!

Example 24-18 contains six calls to this method, creating the path for a fluffy cloud, which is then filled in white. Figure 24-17 illustrates how the angles of the dashed line outside the cloud represent the attractor points applied to each curve.

Example 24-18. Drawing a cloud with quadratic curves

```
context.beginPath()
context.moveTo(180, 60)
context.quadraticCurveTo(240,   0, 300,  60)
context.quadraticCurveTo(460,  30, 420, 100)
context.quadraticCurveTo(480, 210, 340, 170)
context.quadraticCurveTo(240, 240, 200, 170)
context.quadraticCurveTo(100, 200, 140, 130)
context.quadraticCurveTo( 40,  40, 180,  60)
context.fillStyle = 'white'
```

```
context.fill()
context.closePath()
```

Figure 24-17. Drawing with quadratic curves

 Incidentally, to achieve the dotted line around the cloud in this image, I used the `stroke` method in conjunction with the `setLine Dash` method, which takes a list representing the dash and space lengths. In this instance, I used `setLineDash([2, 3])`, but you can create dash lines as complicated as you like, such as `setLine Dash([1, 2, 1, 3, 5, 1, 2, 4])`. I haven't documented this feature because it has been implemented only in IE, Opera, and Chrome so far. Fingers crossed that it'll be added to the other browsers soon, though, as it will be a great enhancement for creating contours and boundaries for mapping purposes, for example.

The bezierCurveTo Method

If you still don't find quadratic curves flexible enough for your needs, how about having access to two attractors for each curve? Using the `bezierCurveTo` method you can do just that, as in Example 24-19, where a curve is created between location (24,20) and (240,220), but with invisible attractors off the canvas (in this case) at locations (720,480) and (–240,–240). Figure 24-18 shows how this curve gets warped.

Example 24-19. Creating a Bézier curve with two attractors

```
context.beginPath()
context.moveTo(240, 20)
context.bezierCurveTo(720, 480, -240, -240, 240, 220)
```

```
context.stroke()
context.closePath()
```

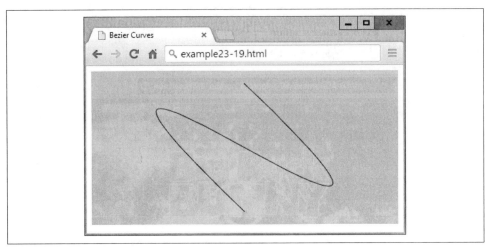

Figure 24-18. A Bézier curve with two attractors

Attractors do not need to be at opposite sides of a canvas; you can place them any-where, and when they are near each other, they will exert a combined pull (rather than opposing pulls, as in the preceding example). Using these various types of curve methods, it's possible for you to draw every type of curve you could ever need.

Manipulating Images

Not only can you draw and write on the canvas with graphical methods, but you can also place images on or extract them from a canvas. And you're not limited to simple copy-and-paste commands, because you can stretch and distort images when reading or writing them, and also have full control over compositing and shadow effects.

The drawImage Method

Using the `drawImage` method, you can take an image object that was loaded from a website, uploaded to a server, or even extracted from a canvas, and draw it onto a canvas. The method supports a wide variety of arguments, many of which are optional, but at its simplest you call `drawImage` as follows, passing just the image and a pair of *x* and *y* coordinates:

```
context.drawImage(myimage, 20, 20)
```

This command draws the image contained in the `myimage` object onto the canvas with the context of `context`, with its top-left corner at location (20,20).

To ensure that an image has been loaded before you use it, best practice is to enclose your image-handling code within a function that is triggered only upon image load, like this:

```
myimage     = new Image()
myimage.src = 'image.gif'

myimage.onload = function()
{
  context.drawImage(myimage, 20, 20)
}
```

Resizing an Image

If you need to resize an image when it is placed on the canvas, add a second pair of arguments to the call representing the width and height you require, like this (highlighted in bold):

```
context.drawImage(myimage, 140,  20, 220, 220)
context.drawImage(myimage, 380,  20,  80, 220)
```

Here the image is placed at two locations: the first is at (140,20), where the image is enlarged (from a 100-pixel square to a 220-pixel square), while the second goes to location (380,20) with the image being squashed horizontally and expanded vertically, to a width and height of 80 × 220 pixels.

Selecting an Image Area

You're not stuck having to use an entire image; it's also possible to choose an area within an image when using `drawImage`. This can be handy, for example, if you wish to place all the graphical images you intend to use in a single image file, and then just grab the sections of the image that you need. This is a trick developers often use to speed up page loading and decrease server hits.

It's a little trickier to do this, though, because rather than adding more arguments at the end of the list for this method, when extracting a portion of an image, you must place those arguments first.

So, for example, to place an image at location (20,140), you might issue this command:

```
context.drawImage(myimage, 20, 140)
```

And to give it a width and height of 100 × 100 pixels, you would modify the call like this (highlighted in bold):

```
context.drawImage(myimage, 20, 140, 100, 100)
```

But to grab (or crop) just a 40 × 40–pixel subsection (for example), with its top-left corner at location (30,30) of the image, you would call the method like this (with the new arguments in bold):

```
context.drawImage(myimage, 30, 30, 40, 40, 20, 140)
```

And to resize the grabbed portion to 100 pixels square, you would use the following:

```
context.drawImage(myimage, 30, 30, 40, 40, 20, 140, 100, 100)
```

 I find this very confusing and cannot think of a logical reason for why this method works this way. But since it does, I'm afraid there's nothing you can do other than force yourself to remember which arguments go where under which conditions.

Example 24-20 uses a variety of calls to the drawImage method to obtain the result shown in Figure 24-19. To make things clearer, I have spaced out the arguments so that the values in each column provide the same information.

Example 24-20. Various ways of drawing an image on the canvas

```
myimage     = new Image()
myimage.src = 'image.png'

myimage.onload = function()
{
  context.drawImage(myimage,                    20,  20          )
  context.drawImage(myimage,                   140,  20, 220, 220)
  context.drawImage(myimage,                   380,  20,  80, 220)
  context.drawImage(myimage, 30, 30, 40, 40,    20, 140, 100, 100)
}
```

Figure 24-19. Drawing images to a canvas with resizing and cropping

Copying from a Canvas

You can also use a canvas as a source image for drawing to the same (or another) canvas. Just supply the canvas object's name in place of an image object, and use all the remaining arguments in the same way as you would with an image.

Adding Shadows

When you draw an image (or image section), or, indeed, anything else on the canvas, you can also place a shadow under it by setting one or more of the following properties:

shadowOffsetX
   The horizontal offset in pixels by which the shadow should be shifted to the right (or to the left if the value is negative).

shadowOffsetY
   The vertical offset in pixels by which the shadow should be shifted down (or up if the value is negative).

shadowBlur
   The number of pixels over which to blur the shadow's outline.

shadowColor
   The base color to use for the shadow. If a blur is in use, this color will blend with the background in the blurred area.

These properties can apply to text and lines as well as solid images, as demonstrated in Example 24-21, in which some text, an image, and an object created using a path all have shadows added to them. In Figure 24-20, you can see the shadows intelligently flow around the visible portions of images, not just their rectangular boundaries.

Example 24-21. Applying shadows when drawing on the canvas

```
myimage     = new Image()
myimage.src = 'apple.png'

orig   = 95
points = 21
dist   = Math.PI / points * 2
scale1 = 75
scale2 = 50

myimage.onload = function()
{
  context.beginPath()

  for (j = 0 ; j < points ; ++j)
  {
    x = Math.sin(j * dist)
    y = Math.cos(j * dist)
    context.lineTo(orig + x * scale1, orig + y * scale1)
    context.lineTo(orig + x * scale2, orig + y * scale2)
  }

  context.closePath()

  context.shadowOffsetX = 5
  context.shadowOffsetY = 5
  context.shadowBlur    = 6
  context.shadowColor   = '#444'
  context.fillStyle     = 'red'
  context.stroke()
  context.fill()

  context.shadowOffsetX = 2
  context.shadowOffsetY = 2
  context.shadowBlur    = 3
  context.shadowColor   = 'yellow'
  context.font          = 'bold 36pt Times'
  context.textBaseline  = 'top'
  context.fillStyle     = 'green'
  context.fillText('Sale now on!', 200, 5)

  context.shadowOffsetX = 3
  context.shadowOffsetY = 3
```

```
    context.shadowBlur    = 5
    context.shadowColor   = 'black'
    context.drawImage(myimage, 245, 45)
}
```

Figure 24-20. Shadows under different types of drawing objects

Editing at the Pixel Level

Not only does the HTML5 canvas provide you with a powerful range of drawing methods, it also lets you get your hands dirty and work under the hood directly at the pixel level with a trio of powerful methods.

The getImageData Method

With the `getImageData` method, you can grab a portion (or all) of a canvas so that you can alter the retrieved data in any way you like, and then save it back or elsewhere in the canvas (or to another canvas).

To illustrate how this works, Example 24-22 first loads in a ready-made image and draws it onto a canvas. Then the canvas data is read back into an object called `idata`, where all the colors are averaged together to change each pixel to grayscale and then tweaked a little to shift each color toward sepia, as shown in Figure 24-21. The following section explains the `data` array of pixels, and what happens when the value 50 is added to or subtracted from an element of the array.

Example 24-22. Manipulating image data

```
myimage     = new Image()
myimage.src = 'photo.jpg'

myimage.onload = function()
{
```

```
  context.drawImage(myimage, 0, 0)
  idata = context.getImageData(0, 0, myimage.width, myimage.height)

  for (y = 0 ; y < myimage.height ; ++y)
  {
    pos = y * myimage.width * 4

    for (x = 0 ; x < myimage.width ; ++x)
    {
      average =
      (
        idata.data[pos]     +
        idata.data[pos + 1] +
        idata.data[pos + 2]
      ) / 3

      idata.data[pos]     = average + 50
      idata.data[pos + 1] = average
      idata.data[pos + 2] = average - 50
      pos += 4;
    }
  }
  context.putImageData(idata, 320, 0)
}
```

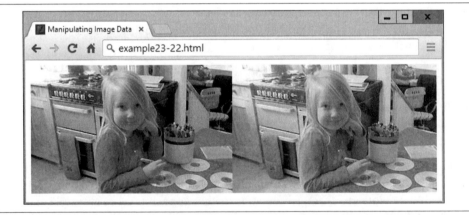

Figure 24-21. Converting an image to sepia (only a minor difference will be seen when this figure is viewed in grayscale)

The data array

This image manipulation works thanks to the `data` array, which is a property of the `idata` object returned by the call to `getImageData`. This method returns an array containing all the pixel data for the selected area in its component parts of red, green, blue, and alpha transparency. Therefore, four items of data are used to store each colored pixel.

All the data is stored sequentially in the `data` array, such that the value for red is followed by that for blue, then green, and then alpha; then, the next item in the array is the red value for the following pixel, and so on. So, you'll have the following for the pixel at location (0,0):

```
idata.data[0] // Red level
idata.data[1] // Green level
idata.data[2] // Blue level
idata.data[3] // Alpha level
```

Location (1,0) then follows, like this:

```
idata.data[4] // Red level
idata.data[5] // Green level
idata.data[6] // Blue level
idata.data[7] // Alpha level
```

In this image, everything continues in the same fashion until the rightmost pixel of the image in row 0—which is the 320th pixel, at location (319,0)—is reached. At that point, the value 319 is multiplied by 4 (the number of items of data in each pixel) to arrive at the following array elements, which contain this pixel's data:

```
idata.data[1276] // Red level
idata.data[1277] // Green level
idata.data[1278] // Blue level
idata.data[1279] // Alpha level
```

This causes the data pointer to move all the way back to the first column of the image, but this time of row 1, at location (0,1) which (because each row in this image is 320 pixels wide) is at an offset of (0 × 4) + (1 × 320 × 4), or 1,280:

```
idata.data[1280] // Red level
idata.data[1281] // Green level
idata.data[1282] // Blue level
idata.data[1283] // Alpha level
```

So, if the image data is stored in `idata`, the image width in `w`, and the pixel location to access in `x` and `y`, the key formulae to use when directly accessing image data are:

```
red   = idata.data[x * 4 + y * w * 4     ]
green = idata.data[x * 4 + y * w * 4 + 1]
blue  = idata.data[x * 4 + y * w * 4 + 2]
alpha = idata.data[x * 4 + y * w * 4 + 3]
```

Using this knowledge, we create the sepia effect in Figure 24-12 by taking just the red, blue, and green components of each pixel and averaging them, like this (where `pos` is a variable pointer to the location in the array of the current pixel):

```
average =
(
  idata.data[pos]     +
  idata.data[pos + 1] +
```

```
    idata.data[pos + 2]
) / 3
```

With `average` now containing the average color value (which we attain by adding all the pixel values and dividing by 3), this value is written back to all colors of the pixel, but with the red boosted by a value of 50, and the blue reduced by the same amount:

```
idata.data[pos]     = average + 50
idata.data[pos + 1] = average
idata.data[pos + 2] = average - 50
```

The result is to increase the red and reduce the blue level of each pixel (of what would otherwise now become a monochrome image, if only the average value were written back to these colors), giving it a sepia cast.

If you're interested in performing more advanced image manipulations, you may wish to refer to Halfpap (*http://tinyurl.com/convolut1*) or HTML5 Rocks (*http://tinyurl.com/convolut2*), which both cover using convolution on an HTML5 canvas in detail.

The putImageData Method

When you've modified the image data array to your requirements, all you need to do to write it to the canvas, as shown in the previous example, is call the `putImageData` method, passing it the `idata` object and the coordinates of the top-left corner at which it should appear. The call shown earlier places the modified copy of the image to the right of the original:

```
context.putImageData(idata, 320, 0)
```

If you wish to modify only part of a canvas, you don't have to grab the entire canvas; just fetch a section containing the area in which you are interested. And neither do you have to write back image data to the location from where you got it; image data can be written to any part of a canvas.

The createImageData Method

You don't have to create an object directly from a canvas; you can also create a new one with blank data by calling the `createImageData` method. The following example creates an object with a width of 320 and height of 240 pixels:

```
idata = createImageData(320, 240)
```

Alternatively, you can create a new object from an existing object, like this:

```
newimagedataobject = createImageData(imagedata)
```

It's then up to you how you add pixel data to these objects or otherwise modify them, how you paste them onto the canvas or create other objects from them, and so on.

Advanced Graphical Effects

Among the more advanced features available on the HTML5 canvas are the ability to assign various compositing and transparency effects, as well as to apply powerful transformations such as scaling, stretching, and rotating.

The globalCompositeOperation Property

There are 12 different methods available to fine-tune the way you place an object on the canvas, taking into account existing and future objects. These are called *compositing* options, and they are applied like this:

```
context.globalCompositeOperationProperty = 'source-over'
```

The compositing types are as follows:

source-over
> The default. The source image is copied over the destination image.

source-in
> Only parts of the source image that will appear within the destination are shown, and the destination image is removed. Any alpha transparency in the source image causes the destination under it to be removed.

source-out
> Only parts of the source image that do not appear within the destination are shown, and the destination image is removed. Any alpha transparency in the source image causes the destination under it to be removed.

source-atop
> The source image is displayed where it overlays the destination. The destination image is displayed where the destination image is opaque and the source image is transparent. Other regions are transparent.

destination-over
> The source image is drawn under the destination image.

destination-in
> The destination image displays where the source and destination image overlap, but not in any areas of source image transparency. The source image does not display.

destination-out

> Only those parts of the destination outside of the source image's nontransparent sections are shown. The source image does not display.

destination-atop

> The source image displays where the destination is not displayed. Where the destination and source overlap, the destination image is displayed. Any transparency in the source image prevents that area of the destination image being shown.

lighter

> The sum of the source and destination is applied such that where they do not overlap, they display as normal; where they do overlap, the sum of both images is shown but lightened.

darker

> The sum of the source and destination is applied such that where they do not overlap, they display as normal; where they do overlap, the sum of both images is shown but darkened.

copy

> The source image is copied over the destination. Any transparent area of the source causes any destination that it overlaps to not display.

xor

> Where the source and destination images do not overlap, they display as normal. Where they do overlap, their color values are exclusive-ored.

Example 24-23 illustrates the effect of all of these compositing types by creating 12 different canvases, each with two objects (a filled circle and the yin-yang image) offset from each other but overlapping.

Example 24-23. Using all 12 types of compositing effects

```
image     = new Image()
image.src = 'image.png'

image.onload = function()
{
  types =
  [
    'source-over',    'source-in',        'source-out',
    'source-atop',    'destination-over', 'destination-in',
    'destination-out', 'destination-atop', 'lighter',
    'darker',         'copy',             'xor'
  ]

  for (j = 0 ; j < 12 ; ++j)
  {
```

```
canvas               = O('c' + (j + 1))
context              = canvas.getContext('2d')
S(canvas).background = 'lightblue'
context.fillStyle    = 'red'

context.arc(50, 50, 50, 0, Math.PI * 2, false)
context.fill()
context.globalCompositeOperation = types[j]
context.drawImage(image, 20, 20, 100, 100)
  }
}
```

As with some other examples in this chapter, this example (down-loadable from the companion website) includes some HTML and/or CSS to enhance the display, which isn't shown here because it's not essential to the program's operation.

This program uses a for loop to iterate through each compositing type, as stored in the array types. Each time around the loop, a new context is created on the next of the 12 canvas elements already created in some earlier HTML (not shown), with the IDs of c1 through c12.

In each canvas, a 100-pixel-diameter red circle is first placed at the top left, and then the compositing type is selected and the yin-yang image is placed over the circle but offset to the right and down by 20 pixels. Figure 24-22 shows the results of each type in action. As you can see, it's possible to achieve a wide variety of effects.

Figure 24-22. The 12 compositing effects in action

The globalAlpha Property

When drawing on the canvas, you can specify the amount of transparency to apply using the globalAlpha property, which supports values from 0 (fully transparent) to 1 (fully opaque). The following command sets the alpha to a value of 0.9, such that future draw operations will be 90 percent opaque (or 10 percent transparent):

```
context.globalAlpha = 0.9
```

This property can be used with all other properties, including the compositing options.

Transformations

The canvas supports four functions for applying transformations to elements when drawing them to the HTML5 canvas: scale, rotate, translate, and transform. They can be used alone, or together to produce even more interesting effects.

The scale Method

You can scale future drawing operations by first calling the `scale` method. This method takes horizontal and vertical scaling factors, which can be negative, zero, or positive.

In Example 24-24 the yin-yang image is drawn to the canvas at its original size of 100 × 100 pixels. Then scaling of three times horizontally and two times vertically is applied, and the `drawImage` function is called again to place the stretched image next to the original. Finally, scaling is reapplied with values of `0.33` and `0.5` to restore everything back to normal, and the image is once more drawn, this time below the original. Figure 24-23 shows the result.

Example 24-24. Scaling up and down in size

```
context.drawImage(myimage, 0, 0)
context.scale(3, 2)
context.drawImage(myimage, 40, 0)
context.scale(.33, .5)
context.drawImage(myimage, 0, 100)
```

Figure 24-23. Scaling an image up and then down again

If you look carefully, you may notice that the copy image under the original is a little bit fuzzy due to the scaling up and then down.

By using negative values for one or more scaling parameters, you can reverse an element in either the horizontal or vertical direction (or both), at the same time as (or instead of) scaling. For example, the following flips the context to create a mirror image:

```
context.scale(-1, 1)
```

The save and restore Methods

If you need to use several scaling operations on different drawing elements, not only can you introduce fuzziness into the results, but it can be very time-consuming to calculate that a three-times upward scaling requires a 0.33 value to scale back down again (and a two-times upscale requires a value of 0.5 to reverse).

For this reason, you can call save to save the current context before issuing a scale call, and later return scaling back to normal by issuing a restore call. Check out the following, which can replace the code in Example 24-24:

```
context.drawImage(myimage, 0, 0)
context.save()
context.scale(3, 2)
context.drawImage(myimage, 40, 0)
context.restore()
context.drawImage(myimage, 0, 100)
```

The save and restore methods are very powerful because they don't just apply to image scaling. In fact, they apply across all the following properties, and can therefore be used at any time to save the current properties and then restore them later: fill Style, font, globalAlpha, globalCompositeOperation, lineCap, lineJoin, line Width, miterLimit, shadowBlur, shadowColor, shadowOffsetX, shadowOffsetY, strokeStyle, textAlign, and textBaseline. The properties of all four transformation methods are also managed by save and restore: scale, rotate, translate, and transform.

The rotate Method

Using the rotate method, you can choose the angle at which to apply an object (or any of the drawing methods) to the canvas. The angle is specified in radians, which are the same as 180 / π, or about 57 degrees, each.

Rotation takes place around the canvas origin, which, by default, is its top-left corner (but as you'll see shortly, this can be changed). Example 24-25 displays the yin-yang image four times, rotating each consecutive image by Math.PI / 25 radians.

Example 24-25. Rotating an image

```
for (j = 0 ; j < 4 ; ++j)
{
  context.drawImage(myimage, 20 + j * 120 , 20)
  context.rotate(Math.PI / 25)
}
```

As you can see in Figure 24-24, the result may not be quite what you expect, because the image hasn't been rotated about itself. Rather, the rotations have taken place around the canvas origin at location (0,0). What's more, each new rotation has compounded the previous one. However, to correct for these things, you can always use the `translate` method in conjunction with the `save` and `restore` methods.

Figure 24-24. An image at four different rotations

 Radians are a sensible unit of measurement because there are $\pi \times 2$ radians in a complete circle. So, π radians is a half circle, $\pi \div 2$ radians is a quarter circle, $\pi \div 2 \times 3$ (or $\pi \times 1.5$) radians is three-quarters of a circle, and so on. To save having to remember the value of π, you can always refer to the value in `Math.PI`.

The translate Method

To change the origin of a rotation, you can call the `translate` method to shift it to somewhere else. The destination can be anywhere inside (or outside) the canvas. Usually, you specify a point somewhere within the destination location of the object (typically its center).

Example 24-26 performs this translation prior to each call to `rotate`, now resulting in the effect that was probably intended by the previous example. Additionally, the `save` and `restore` methods are called before and after each operation to ensure that each rotation is applied independently, not compounded on the previous one.

Example 24-26. Rotating objects in place

```
w = myimage.width
h = myimage.height
```

```
for (j = 0 ; j < 4 ; ++j)
{
  context.save()
  context.translate(20 + w / 2 + j * (w + 20), 20 + h / 2)
  context.rotate(Math.PI / 5 * j)
  context.drawImage(myimage, -(w / 2), -(h / 2))
  context.restore()
}
```

In this example, before each rotation the context is saved and the origin is translated to a point exactly in the center of where each image will be drawn. We then issue the rotation and draw the image up and to the left of the new origin by supplying negative values, such that its center matches the origin point. The result of this is shown in Figure 24-25.

Figure 24-25. Rotating images in place

To recap: when you wish to rotate or transform (described next) an object in place, you should perform the following actions:

1. Save the context.
2. Translate the canvas origin to the center of where the object is to be placed.
3. Issue the rotation or transformation instruction.
4. Draw the object with any drawing method supported, using a negative destination location point half the object's width to the left, and half its height upward.
5. Restore the context to revert the origin.

The transform Method

When you've exhausted all the other canvas features and still can't manipulate objects in just the way you need, it's time to turn to the transform method. With it, you can apply a transformation matrix to the objects you draw to the canvas, giving you a multitude of possibilities and powerful features that can combine scaling and rotating in a single instruction.

The transformation matrix used by this method is a 3 × 3 matrix of 9 values, but only 6 of these are supplied externally to the transform method. So, rather than explain how this matrix multiplication works, I only need to explain the effects of its six arguments, which, in order, are as follows (the order may be a little counter-intuitive):

1. Horizontal scale
2. Horizontal skew
3. Vertical skew
4. Vertical scale
5. Horizontal translate
6. Vertical translate

You can apply these values in many ways—for example, by emulating the scale method from Example 24-24 by replacing this call:

```
context.scale(3, 2)
```

with the following:

```
context.transform(3, 0, 0, 2, 0, 0)
```

In the same way, you can replace this call from Example 24-26:

```
context.translate(20 + w / 2 + j * (w + 20), 20 + h / 2)
```

with the following:

```
context.transform(1, 0, 0, 1, 20 + w / 2 + j * (w + 20), 20 + h / 2)
```

 Note how the horizontal and vertical scaling arguments are given values of 1 to ensure a 1:1 result, while the skew values are 0 to prevent the result from being skewed.

You could even combine the previous two lines of code to get a translation and scale at the same time, like this:

```
context.transform(3, 0, 0, 2, 20 + w / 2 + j * (w + 20), 20 + h / 2)
```

As you might expect, the skew arguments slant an element in the direction specified —for example, creating a rhombus from a square.

As another example of skew, Example 24-27 draws the yin-yang image on the canvas, followed by a skewed copy created with the transform method. The skew value can be any negative, zero, or positive amount, but I chose a horizontal value of 1, which has skewed the bottom of the image by one image width to the right, and pulled everything else along with it proportionally (see Figure 24-26).

Example 24-27. Creating an original and skewed image

```
context.drawImage(myimage, 20, 20)
context.transform(1, 0, 1, 1, 0, 0)
context.drawImage(myimage, 140, 20)
```

Figure 24-26. Horizontally skewing an object to the right

You can even rotate an object with transform by supplying one negative and one opposite positive skew value. But beware: when you do this, you'll modify the size of an element, and will therefore also need to adjust the scale arguments at the same time. Plus, you'll need to remember to translate the origin. Thus, I recommend sticking with the rotate method for this until you are fully experienced with using transform.

The setTransform Method

As an alternative to using the save and restore methods, you can set an absolute transform, which has the effect of resetting the transformation matrix and then applying the supplied values. Use the setTransform method just like transform, as in this example (which applies a horizontal positive skew with the value 1):

```
context.setTransform(1, 0, 1, 1, 0, 0)
```

To learn more about transformation matrixes, see the Wikipedia article (*http://tinyurl.com/transform-matrix*).

The HTML5 canvas is a tremendous asset for web developers to make bigger, better, and more professional and compelling websites. In the following chapter, we'll take a look at two other great HTML5 features: in-browser, plug-in-free audio and video.

Questions

1. How do you create a canvas element in HTML?
2. How do you give JavaScript access to a canvas element?
3. How do you start and finish the creation of a canvas path?
4. What method can you use to extract data from a canvas into an image?
5. How can you create gradient fills of more than two colors?
6. How can you adjust the width of lines when drawing?
7. Which method would you use to specify a section of a canvas such that future drawing takes place only within that area?
8. How can you draw a complex curve with two imaginary attractors?
9. How many items of data per pixel are returned by the `getImageData` method?
10. Which two parameters to the `transform` method apply to scaling operations?

See "Chapter 24 Answers" on page 732 in Appendix A for the answers to these questions.

CHAPTER 25

HTML5 Audio and Video

One of the biggest driving forces behind the growth of the internet has been the insatiable demand from users for ever more multimedia in the form of audio and video. Initially, bandwidth was so precious that there was no such thing as live streaming, and it could take minutes or even hours to download an audio track, let alone a video.

The high cost of bandwidth and limited availability of fast modems drove the development of faster and more efficient compression algorithms, such as MP3 audio and MPEG video, but even then the only way to download files in any reasonable length of time was to drastically reduce their quality.

One of my earlier internet projects, back in 1997, was the UK's first online radio station licensed by the music authorities. Actually, it was more of a podcast (before the term was coined) because we made a daily half-hour show and then compressed it down to 8-bit, 11 KHz mono using an algorithm originally developed for telephony, and it sounded like phone quality, or worse. Still, we quickly gained thousands of listeners who would download the show and then listen to it as they surfed to the sites discussed in it by means of a pop-up browser window containing a plug-in.

Thankfully for us, and everyone publishing multimedia, it soon became possible to offer greater audio and video quality, but still only by asking the user to download and install a plug-in player. Flash became the most popular of these players, after beating rivals such as RealAudio, but it gained a bad reputation as the cause of many a browser crash, and constantly required upgrading when new versions were released.

So, it was generally agreed that the way ahead was to come up with some web standards for supporting multimedia directly within the browser. Of course, browser developers such as Microsoft and Google had differing visions of what these standards should look like, but when the dust settled, they had agreed on a subset of file types that all browsers should play natively, and these were introduced into the HTML5 specification.

Finally, it is possible (as long as you encode your audio and video in a few different formats) to upload multimedia to a web server, place a couple of HTML tags in a web page, and play the media on any major desktop browser, smartphone, or tablet device, without the user having to download a plug-in or make any other changes.

 There are still a lot of older browsers out there, so Flash remains important to support them. In this chapter, I show you how to add code to use Flash as a backup to HTML5 audio and video, to cover as many hardware and software combinations as possible.

About Codecs

The term *codec* stands for en*co*der/*deco*der. It describes the functionality provided by software that encodes and decodes media such as audio and video. In HTML5 there are a number of different sets of codecs available, depending on the browser used.

One complication around audio and video, which rarely applies to graphics and other traditional web content, is the licensing carried by the formats and codecs. Many formats and codecs are provided for a fee, because they were developed by a single company or consortium of companies that chose a proprietary license. Some free and open source browsers don't support the most popular formats and codecs because it is unfeasible to pay for them, or because the developers oppose proprietary licenses in principle. Because copyright laws vary from country to country and because licenses are hard to enforce, the codecs can usually be found on the web for no cost, but they might technically be illegal to use where you live.

Following are the codecs supported by the HTML5 <audio> tag (and also when audio is attached to HTML5 video):

AAC
> This audio codec, which stands for Advanced Audio Encoding, is used by Apple's iTunes store and is a proprietary patented technology supported by Apple, Google, and Microsoft. It generally uses the *.aac* file extension. Its MIME type is audio/aac.

MP3
> This audio codec, which stands for MPEG Audio Layer 3, has been available for many years. Although the term is often (incorrectly) used to refer to any type of digital audio, it is a proprietary patented technology that is supported by Apple, Google, Mozilla Firefox, and Microsoft. The file extension it uses is *.mp3*. Its mime type is audio/mpeg.

PCM

This audio codec, which stands for Pulse Coded Modulation, stores the full data as encoded by an analog-to-digital converter, and is the format used for storing data on audio CDs. Because it does not use compression, it is called a *lossless* codec and its files are generally many times larger than AAC or MP3 files. It is supported by Apple, Mozilla Firefox, Microsoft, and Opera. Usually this type of file has the extension *.wav*. Its MIME type is `audio/wav`, but you may also see `audio/wave`.

Vorbis

Sometimes referred to as Ogg Vorbis—because it generally uses the *.ogg* file extension—this audio codec is unencumbered by patents and free of royalty payments. It is supported by Google, Mozilla Firefox, and Opera. Its MIME type is `audio/ogg`, or sometimes `audio/oga`.

The following list summarizes the major operating systems and browsers, along with the audio types their latest versions support:

- **Apple iOS**: AAC, MP3, PCM
- **Apple Safari**: AAC, MP3, PCM
- **Google Android**: 2.3+ AAC, MP3, Vorbis
- **Google Chrome**: AAC, MP3, Vorbis
- **Microsoft Internet Explorer**: AAC, MP3, PCM
- **Microsoft Edge**: AAC, MP3, PCM
- **Mozilla Firefox**: MP3, PCM, Vorbis
- **Opera**: PCM, Vorbis

The outcome of these different levels of codec support is that you always need at least two versions of each audio file to ensure it will play on all platforms. These could be PCM and AAC, PCM and MP3, PCM and Vorbis, AAC and Vorbis, or MP3 and Vorbis.

The <audio> Element

To cater to all platforms, you need to record or convert your content using multiple codecs and then list them all within <audio> and </audio> tags, as in Example 25-1. The nested <source> tags then contain the various media you wish to offer to a browser. Because the `controls` attribute is supplied, the result looks like Figure 25-1.

Example 25-1. Embedding three different types of audio files

```
<audio controls>
  <source src='audio.m4a' type='audio/aac'>
  <source src='audio.mp3' type='audio/mp3'>
  <source src='audio.ogg' type='audio/ogg'>
</audio>
```

Figure 25-1. Playing an audio file

In this example I included three different audio types, because that's perfectly acceptable, and can be a good idea if you wish to ensure that each browser can locate its preferred format rather than just one it knows how to handle. However, you can drop
either (but not both) of the MP3 or the AAC files and still be confident that the example will play on all platforms.

The `<audio>` element and its partner `<source>` tag support several attributes:

`autoplay`
    Causes the audio to start playing as soon as it is ready

`controls`
    Causes the control panel to be displayed

`loop`
    Sets the audio to play over and over

`preload`
    Causes the audio to begin loading even before the user selects Play

`src`
    Specifies the source location of an audio file

`type`
    Specifies the codec used in creating the audio

If you don't supply the `controls` attribute to the `<audio>` tag, and don't use the `auto`
`play` attribute either, the sound will not play and there won't be a Play button for the

user to click to start playback. This would leave you no option other than to offer this functionality in JavaScript, as in Example 25-2 (with the additional code required highlighted in bold), which provides the ability to play and pause the audio, as shown in Figure 25-2.

Example 25-2. Playing audio using JavaScript

```
<!DOCTYPE html>
<html>
  <head>
    <title>Playing Audio with JavaScript</title>
    <script src='OSC.js'></script>
  </head>
  <body>
    <audio id='myaudio'>
      <source src='audio.m4a' type='audio/aac'>
      <source src='audio.mp3' type='audio/mp3'>
      <source src='audio.ogg' type='audio/ogg'>
    </audio>

    <button onclick='playaudio()'>Play Audio</button>
    <button onclick='pauseaudio()'>Pause Audio</button>

    <script>
      function playaudio()
      {
        O('myaudio').play()
      }
      function pauseaudio()
      {
        O('myaudio').pause()
      }
    </script>
  </body>
</html>
```

Figure 25-2. HTML5 audio can be controlled with JavaScript

This works by calling the play or pause methods of the myaudio element when the buttons are clicked.

Supporting Non-HTML5 Browsers

In very rare cases (such as when developing web pages for in-house intranets that are using older browsers), it may be necessary for you to fall back to Flash for handling audio. Example 25-3 shows how you can do this using a Flash plug-in called *audioplayer.swf* that's available, along with all the examples, in the archive file on the book's companion website (*http://lpmj.net*). The code to add is highlighted in bold.

Example 25-3. Providing a Flash fallback for non-HTML5 browsers

```
<audio controls>
  <object type="application/x-shockwave-flash"
    data="audioplayer.swf" width="300" height="30">
    <param name="FlashVars"
      value="mp3=audio.mp3&showstop=1&showvolume=1">
  </object>

  <source src='audio.m4a' type='audio/aac'>
  <source src='audio.mp3' type='audio/mp3'>
  <source src='audio.ogg' type='audio/ogg'>
</audio>
```

Here we take advantage of the fact that non-HTML5 browsers read and act on anything inside the <audio> tag (other than the <source> elements, which are ignored). Therefore, by placing an <object> element there that calls up a Flash player, we ensure that any non-HTML5 browsers will at least have a chance of playing the audio, as long as they have Flash installed, as shown in Figure 25-3.

Figure 25-3. The Flash audio player has been loaded

The particular audio player used in this example, *audioplayer.swf*, takes the following arguments and values to the FlashVars attribute of the <param> element:

mp3
> The URL of an MP3 audio file.

showstop

> If 1, the display shows the Stop button; otherwise, it is not displayed.

showvolume

> If 1, the display shows the volume bar; otherwise, it is not displayed.

As with many elements, you can easily resize the object to (for example) 300 × 30 pixels by providing these values to its `width` and `height` attributes.

The `<video>` Element

Playing video in HTML5 is quite similar to audio; you just use the `<video>` tag and provide `<source>` elements for the media you are offering. Example 25-4 shows how to do this with three different video codec types, as displayed in Figure 25-4.

Example 25-4. Playing HTML5 video

```
<video width='560' height='320' controls>
  <source src='movie.mp4'  type='video/mp4'>
  <source src='movie.webm' type='video/webm'>
  <source src='movie.ogv'  type='video/ogg'>
</video>
```

Figure 25-4. Playing HTML5 video

The Video Codecs

As with audio, there are a number of video codecs available, with differing support across multiple browsers. These codecs come in different containers, as follows:

MP4

> A license-encumbered, multimedia container format standard specified as a part of MPEG-4, supported by Apple, Microsoft, and to a lesser extent Google (which has its own WebM container format). Its MIME type is video/mp4.

Ogg

> A free, open container format maintained by the Xiph.Org Foundation. The creators of the Ogg format state that it is unrestricted by software patents and is designed to provide for efficient streaming and manipulation of high-quality digital multimedia. Its MIME type is video/ogg, or sometimes video/ogv.

WebM

> An audio-video format designed to provide a royalty-free, open video compression format for use with HTML5 video. The project's development is sponsored by Google. There are two versions: VP8 and the newer VP9. Its MIME type is video/webm.

These may then contain one of the following video codecs:

H.264

> A patented, proprietary video codec that can be played back for free by the end user, but which may incur royalty fees for all parts of the encoding and transmission process. At the time of writing, all of the Apple, Google, Mozilla Firefox, and Microsoft browsers support this codec, while Opera (the remaining major browser) doesn't.

Theora

> A video codec that is unencumbered by patents and free of royalty payments at all levels of encoding, transmission, and playback. This codec is supported by Google, Mozilla Firefox, and Opera.

VP8

> A video codec that is similar to Theora but is owned by Google, which has published it as open source, making it royalty-free. It is supported by Google, Mozilla Firefox, and Opera.

VP9

> The same as VP8 but more powerful, using half the bitrate.

The following list details the major operating systems and browsers, along with the video types their latest versions support:

- **Apple iOS**: MP4/H.264
- **Apple Safari**: MP4/H.264
- **Google Android**: MP4, Ogg, WebM/H.264, Theora, VP8
- **Google Chrome**: MP4, Ogg, WebM/H.264, Theora, VP8, VP9
- **Microsoft Internet Explorer**: MP4/H.264
- **Microsoft Edge**: MP4/H.264, WebM/H.264
- **Mozilla Firefox**: MP4, Ogg, WebM/H.264, Theora, VP8, VP9
- **Opera**: Ogg, WebM/Theora, VP8

Looking at this list, it's clear that MP4/H.264 is almost unanimously supported, except by the Opera browser. So, to reach over 96% of users, you only need to supply your video using that one file type. But for maximum viewing, you really ought to encode in Ogg/Theora or Ogg/VP8 as well.

Therefore, the *movie.webm* file in Example 25-4 isn't strictly needed, but it shows how you can add all the different file types you like, to give browsers the opportunity to play back the formats they prefer.

The `<video>` element and accompanying `<source>` tag support the following attributes:

autoplay
> Causes the video to start playing as soon as it is ready

controls
> Causes the control panel to be displayed

height
> Specifies the height at which to display the video

loop
> Sets the video to play over and over

muted
> Mutes the audio output

poster
> Lets you choose an image to display where the video will play

preload
> Causes the video to begin loading before the user selects Play

src
> Specifies the source location of a video file

type
> Specifies the codec used in creating the video

width
> Specifies the width at which to display the video

If you wish to control video playback from JavaScript, you can do so using code such as that in Example 25-5 (with the additional code required highlighted in bold), with the results shown in Figure 25-5.

Example 25-5. Controlling video playback from JavaScript

```html
<!DOCTYPE html>
<html>
  <head>
    <title>Playing Video with JavaScript</title>
    <script src='OSC.js'></script>
  </head>
  <body>
    <video id='myvideo' width='560' height='320'>
      <source src='movie.mp4'   type='video/mp4'>
      <source src='movie.webm'  type='video/webm'>
      <source src='movie.ogv'   type='video/ogg'>
    </video><br>

    <button onclick='playvideo()'>Play Video</button>
    <button onclick='pausevideo()'>Pause Video</button>

    <script>
      function playvideo()
      {
        O('myvideo').play()
      }
      function pausevideo()
      {
        O('myvideo').pause()
      }
    </script>
  </body>
</html>
```

Figure 25-5. JavaScript is being used to control the video

This code is just like that for controlling audio from JavaScript. Simply call the play and/or pause methods of the myvideo object to play and pause the video.

Supporting Older Browsers

If you find yourself having to develop for non-HTML5–capable browsers, Example 25-6 shows you how to do this (highlighted in bold) using the *flowplayer.swf* file (included with the example archive available on the book's companion website (*http://lpmj.net*)). Figure 25-6 shows how it displays in a browser that doesn't support HTML5 video.

Example 25-6. Providing Flash as a fallback video player

```
<video width='560' height='320' controls>
  <object width='560' height='320'
    type='application/x-shockwave-flash'
    data='flowplayer.swf'>
    <param name='movie' value='flowplayer.swf'>
    <param name='flashvars'
      value='config={"clip": {
        "url": "movie.mp4",
        "autoPlay":false, "autoBuffering":true}}'>
  </object>
```

```
    <source src='movie.mp4'   type='video/mp4'>
    <source src='movie.webm'  type='video/webm'>
    <source src='movie.ogv'   type='video/ogg'>
</video>
```

Figure 25-6. Flash provides a handy fallback for non-HTML5 browsers

This Flash video player is particular about security; it won't play videos from a local filesystem, only from a web server, so I have supplied a file on the book's companion website (*http://lpmj.net/video.mp4*) for this example to play.

Here are the arguments to supply to the `flashvars` attribute of the `<param>` element:

url
:   A URL of an *.mp4* file to play (must be on a web server)

autoPlay
:   If `true`, plays automatically; otherwise, waits for the Play button to be clicked

autoBuffering
:   If `true`, in order to minimize buffering later on with slow connections, preloads the video sufficiently for the available bandwidth before it starts playing

> For more information on the Flash *flowplayer* program (and an HTML5 version), check out *flowplayer.org*.

Using the information in this chapter, you will be able to embed any audio and video you like on almost all browsers and platforms without worrying about whether users may or may not be able to play it.

In the following chapter, I'll demonstrate the use of a number of other HTML5 features, including geolocation and local storage.

Questions

1. Which two HTML element tags are used to insert audio and video into an HTML5 document?

2. How many audio codecs should you use to guarantee maximum playability on all platforms?

3. Which methods can you call to play and pause HTML5 media playback?

4. How can you support media playback in a non-HTML5 browser?

5. Which two video codecs should you use to guarantee maximum playability on all platforms?

See "Chapter 25 Answers" on page 733 in Appendix A for the answers to these questions.

CHAPTER 26

Other HTML5 Features

In this final chapter on HTML5, I explain how to use geolocation and local storage, and demonstrate the use of in-browser dragging and dropping.

Strictly speaking, most of these features (like much of HTML5) aren't really extensions to HTML, because you access them with JavaScript rather than with HTML markup. They are simply technologies that are being embraced by browser developers, and have been given the handy umbrella name of HTML5.

This means, though, that you need to have fully understood the JavaScript tutorial in this book in order to use them properly. That said, once you get the hang of them, you'll wonder how you ever did without these powerful new features.

Geolocation and the GPS Service

The Global Positioning System (GPS) service consists of multiple satellites orbiting the Earth whose positions are very precisely known. When a GPS-enabled device tunes into them, the different times at which signals from these various satellites arrive enable the device to quite accurately determine where it is; because the speed of light (and therefore radio waves) is a known constant, the time it takes a signal to get from a satellite to a GPS device indicates the satellite's distance.

By noting the different times at which signals arrive from different satellites, which are in precisely known orbital locations at any one time, a simple triangulation calculation gives the device its position relative to the satellites within a few meters or less.

Many mobile devices, such as phones and tablets, have GPS chips and can provide this information. But some don't, others have them turned off, and others may be used indoors where they are shielded from the GPS satellites and therefore cannot receive any signals. In these cases, additional techniques may be used to attempt to determine the device's location.

 I should also caution you to consider the privacy implications of geolocation, especially if the coordinates are transmitted back to the server as part of an application's function. Any application that has geolocation functionality should have an explicit privacy policy. Oh, and by the way, technically geolocation is not actually in the HTML5 standard. In fact it's a standalone feature defined by the W3C/WHATWG, but most people think of it as part of HTML5.

Other Location Methods

If your device has mobile phone hardware but no GPS chip, it may attempt to triangulate its location by checking the timing of signals received from the various communication towers with which it can communicate (and whose positions are very precisely known). If there are a few towers, this can get almost as close to your location as GPS. But where there's only a single tower, the signal strength can be used to determine a rough radius around the tower, and the circle it creates represents the area in which you are likely to be located. This could place you anywhere within a mile or two of your actual location, down to within a few tens of meters.

Failing that, there may be WiFi access points whose positions are known within range of your device, and since all access points have a unique identifying address called a Media Access Control (MAC) address, a reasonably good approximation of your location can be obtained, perhaps to within a street or two. This is the type of information that Google Street View vehicles have been collecting (some of which it has since been made to discard due to potential breaches of data privacy rights).

And if that fails, the Internet Protocol (IP) address used by your device can be queried and used as a rough indicator of your location. Often, though, this provides only the location of a major switch belonging to your internet provider, which could be dozens or even hundreds of miles away. But at the very least, your IP address can (usually) narrow down the country and sometimes the region you are in.

IP addresses are commonly used by media companies for restricting playback of their content by territory. However, it's a simple matter to set up proxy servers that use a forwarding IP address (in the territory that is blocking outside access) to fetch and pass content through the blockade directly to a "foreign" browser. Proxy servers are also often employed to disguise a user's real IP address or bypass censorship restrictions, and can be shared across many users on a WiFi hotspot (for example). Therefore, if you locate someone by IP address, you can't be completely sure that you have identified the right location, or even country, and should treat this information as only a best guess.

Geolocation and HTML5

In Chapter 23, I briefly introduced HTML5 geolocation. Now it's time to look at it in depth, starting with the example I gave you before, shown again in Example 26-1.

Example 26-1. Displaying a map of your current location

```
<!DOCTYPE html>
<html>
  <head>
    <title>Geolocation Example</title>
  </head>
  <body>
    <script>
      if (typeof navigator.geolocation == 'undefined')
        alert("Geolocation not supported.")
      else
        navigator.geolocation.getCurrentPosition(granted, denied)

      function granted(position)
      {
        var lat = position.coords.latitude
        var lon = position.coords.longitude

        alert("Permission Granted. You are at location:\n\n"
          + lat + ", " + lon +
          "\n\nClick 'OK' to load Google Maps with your location")

        window.location.replace("https://www.google.com/maps/@"
          + lat + "," + lon + ",8z")
      }

      function denied(error)
      {
        var message

        switch(error.code)
```

```
      {
        case 1: message = 'Permission Denied'; break;
        case 2: message = 'Position Unavailable'; break;
        case 3: message = 'Operation Timed Out'; break;
        case 4: message = 'Unknown Error'; break;
      }

      alert("Geolocation Error: " + message)
    }
  </script>
  </body>
</html>
```

Let's walk through this code and see how it works, starting with the <head> section, which displays a title. The <body> of the document is made up entirely of JavaScript, which immediately starts by interrogating the `navigator.geolocation` property. If the value returned is `undefined`, then geolocation is not supported by the browser and an error alert window is popped up.

Otherwise, we call the `getCurrentPosition` method of the property, passing it the names of two functions: `granted` and `denied` (remember that by passing only the function names, we pass the actual function code, not the result of calling the function, which would be the case if the function names had parentheses attached):

```
navigator.geolocation.getCurrentPosition(granted, denied)
```

These functions appear later in the script and are for handling the two possibilities of permission to provide the user's location data: `granted` or `denied`.

The `granted` function comes first and is entered only if the data can be accessed. If so, the variables `lat` and `long` are given the values returned by the geolocation routines in the browser.

An alert window is then popped up containing details about the user's current location. When they click OK, the alert is closed and the current web page is replaced by one at Google Maps. It's passed the latitude and longitude returned from the geolocation call, using a zoom setting of 8. You can set a different zoom level by changing the value `8z` to another numeric value followed by a `z`, at the end of the `window.location.replace` call.

Displaying the map is achieved with a call to `window.location.replace`. The result looks like Figure 26-1.

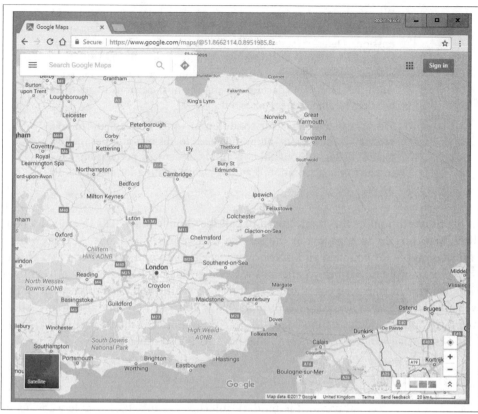

Figure 26-1. An interactive map of the user's location is displayed

If permission is denied (or there is another issue), an error message is displayed by
the denied function, which pops up its own alert window to inform the user of the
error:

```
switch(error.code)
{
  case 1: message = 'Permission Denied'; break;
  case 2: message = 'Position Unavailable'; break;
  case 3: message = 'Operation Timed Out'; break;
  case 4: message = 'Unknown Error'; break;
}

alert("Geolocation Error: " + message)
```

When a browser requests geolocation data from the host, it will prompt the user for permission. The user can grant or deny permission. Denial results in the *Permission Denied* state, *Position Unavailable* results when the user grants permission but the host system cannot determine their location, and *Timeout* happens when the user grants permission and the host attempts to get their location, but the request times out.

There's also another error condition in which some platform and browser combinations allow the user to dismiss the permission request dialog without either granting or denying permission. This results in the application "hanging" while waiting for a callback to occur.

In previous editions of this book I used to call the Google Maps API to embed a map directly within the web page, but the service now requires a unique API key which you must apply for yourself, and usage over a certain amount can incur a fee. This is why the example now simply generates a Google Maps link. If you'd like to embed Google Maps in your web pages and web apps, everything you need to know is on the website (*https://developers.google.com/maps/*). Of course, there are also many other mapping options, such as Bing Maps (*https://www.bing.com/maps*) and OpenStreet-Map (*https://www.openstreetmap.org*), that have APIs you can access.

Local Storage

Cookies are an essential part of the modern internet, because they enable websites to save on each user's machine small snippets of information that can be used for tracking purposes. This isn't as ominous as it sounds, because most of the tracking going on helps web surfers by saving usernames and passwords, keeping them logged into websites and social networks such as Twitter, Facebook, and more.

Cookies can also locally save your preferences for the way you access a website (rather than having those settings stored on the website's server), or can be used to keep track of a shopping cart as you build up an order on an ecommerce website.

But yes, they can also be used more aggressively to track the websites you frequent and gain a picture of your interests to try to target advertising more effectively. That's why the European Union (*http://ec.europa.eu/ipg/basics/legal/cookies/index_en.htm*) now "requires prior informed consent for storage or for access to information stored on a user's terminal equipment."

But, as a web developer, think how useful it might be to keep data on users' devices, especially if you have a small budget for computer servers and disk space. For example, you could create in-browser web apps and services for editing word processing documents, spreadsheets, and graphic images, saving all this data offsite on users' computers and keeping your server purchasing budget as low as possible.

And from the user's point of view, think about how much faster a document can be loaded up locally than from across the web, especially on a slow connection. Plus, there's more security if you know that a website is not storing copies of your documents. Of course, you can never guarantee that a website or web app is totally secure, and should never work on highly sensitive documents using software (or hardware) that can go online. But for minimally private documents such as family photographs, you might feel more comfortable using a web app that saves locally than one that saves files to an external server.

Using Local Storage

The biggest problem with using cookies for local storage is that each cookie can save only a maximum of 4 KB of data. Cookies also have to be passed back and forth on every page reload. And, unless your server uses Transport Layer Security (TLS) encryption—the more secure successor to the Secure Sockets Layer (SSL)—each time a cookie is transmitted, it travels in the clear.

But with HTML5, you have access to a much larger local storage space (typically between 5 MB and 10 MB per domain, depending on the browser) that persists over page loads and between website visits (and even after powering a computer down and back up again). Also, the local storage data is not sent to the server on each page load.

Local storage data is handled through key/value pairs. The key is the name assigned for referencing the data, and the value can hold any type of data, but it is saved as a string. All data is unique to the current domain, and for security reasons any local storage created by websites with different domains is separate from the current local storage, and is not accessible by any domain other than the one that stored the data.

The localStorage Object

You gain access to local storage by means of the localStorage object. To test whether this object is available, query its type to check whether or not it has been defined, like this:

```
if (typeof localStorage == 'undefined')
{
  // Local storage is not available—tell the user and quit.
  // Or maybe offer to save data on the web server instead?
}
```

How you handle the lack of local storage being available will depend on what you intend to use it for, so the code you place inside the if statement will be up to you.

Once you've ascertained that local storage is available, you can start making use of it with the `setItem` and `getItem` methods of the `localStorage` object, like this:

```
localStorage.setItem('loc', 'USA')
localStorage.setItem('lan', 'English')
```

To later retrieve this data, pass the keys to the `getItem` method, like this:

```
loc = localStorage.getItem('loc')
lan = localStorage.getItem('lan')
```

Unlike saving and reading cookies, you can call these methods at any time you like, not simply before any headers have been sent by the web server. The saved values will remain in local storage until erased in the following manner:

```
localStorage.removeItem('loc')
localStorage.removeItem('lan')
```

Or, you can totally wipe the local storage for the current domain by calling the `clear` method, like this:

```
localStorage.clear()
```

Example 26-2 combines the preceding examples into a single document that displays the current values of the two keys in a pop-up alert message, which initially will be `null`. Then the keys and values are saved to local storage, retrieved, and redisplayed, this time having assigned values. Finally, the keys are removed and then an attempt at retrieving these values is again made, but the returned values are once again `null`. Figure 26-2 shows the second of these three alert messages.

Example 26-2. Getting, setting, and removing local storage data

```
<!DOCTYPE html>
<html>
  <head>
    <title>Local Storage</title>
  </head>
  <body>
    <script>
      if (typeof localStorage == 'undefined')
      {
        alert("Local storage is not available")
      }
      else
      {
        loc = localStorage.getItem('loc')
        lan = localStorage.getItem('lan')
        alert("The current values of 'loc' and 'lan' are\n\n" +
          loc + " / " + lan + "\n\nClick OK to assign values")

        localStorage.setItem('loc', 'USA')
```

```
        localStorage.setItem('lan', 'English')
        loc = localStorage.getItem('loc')
        lan = localStorage.getItem('lan')
        alert("The current values of 'loc' and 'lan' are\n\n" +
          loc + " / " + lan +  "\n\nClick OK to clear values")

        localStorage.removeItem('loc')
        localStorage.removeItem('lan')
        loc = localStorage.getItem('loc')
        lan = localStorage.getItem('lan')
        alert("The current values of 'loc' and 'lan' are\n\n" +
          loc + " / " + lan)
      }
    </script>
  </body>
</html>
```

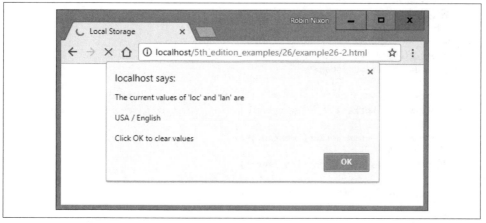

Figure 26-2. Two keys and their values are read from local storage

In local storage you can include virtually any and all data, and as
many key/value pairs as you like, up to the available storage limit
for your domain.

Web Workers

Web workers run background jobs and are useful for calculations that take a long time
and should not be allowed to hold the user back from doing other things. To use a
web worker, you can create sections of JavaScript code that will run in the background. This code doesn't have to set up and monitor interrupts, as jobs have to do in
some asynchronous systems. Instead, whenever it has something to report, your

background process communicates with the main JavaScript through the use of an event.

This means the JavaScript interpreter gets to decide how to allocate time slices most efficiently, and your code only needs to worry about communicating with the background task whenever there's information to convey.

Example 26-3 shows how you can set up web workers to perform a repetitive task in the background—in this instance, calculating prime numbers.

Example 26-3. Setting up and communicating with a web worker

```
<!DOCTYPE html>
<html>
  <head>
    <title>Web Workers</title>
    <script src='OSC.js'></script>
  </head>
  <body>
    Current highest prime number:
    <span id='result'>0</span>

    <script>
      if (!!window.Worker)
      {
        var worker = new Worker('worker.js')

        worker.onmessage = function (event)
        {
          O('result').innerText = event.data;
        }
      }
      else
      {
        alert("Web workers not supported")
      }
    </script>
  </body>
</html>
```

This example first creates a <span> element with the ID of result in which output from the web worker will be placed. Then, in the <script> section, window.Worker is tested via a !! pair of not operators. This has the effect of returning a Boolean value of true if the Worker method exists, and false otherwise. If it is not true, a message is displayed in the else section, alerting us that web workers are not available.

Otherwise, the program creates a new worker object by calling Worker, passing it the filename *worker.js*. Then the onmessage event of the new worker object is attached to

an anonymous function that places any message passed to it by *worker.js* into the
innerText property of the previously created <span> element.

The web worker itself is saved in the file *worker.js*, whose contents are shown in
Example 26-4.

Example 26-4. The worker.js web worker

```
var n = 1

search: while (true)
{
  n += 1

  for (var i = 2; i <= Math.sqrt(n); i += 1)
  {
    if (n % i == 0) continue search
  }

  postMessage(n)
}
```

This file assigns the value 1 to the variable n. It then loops continuously, incrementing
n and checking it for primality by a brute-force method of testing all values from 1 to
the square root of n to see whether they divide exactly into n, with no remainder.
Should a factor be found, the continue command stops the brute-force attack immediately because the number is not prime, and starts processing at the next higher
value of n.

But if all possible factors are tested and none result in a zero remainder, n must be
prime, so its value is passed to postMessage, which sends a message back to the
onmessage event of the object that set up this web worker.

The result looks like the following:

```
Current highest prime number: 30477191
```

To stop a web worker from running, issue a call to the terminate method of the
worker object, like this:

```
worker.terminate()
```

If you wish to stop this particular example from running, you can enter the following into your browser's address bar:

```
javascript:worker.terminate()
```

Also note that due to the way Chrome handles security, you cannot use web workers on a filesystem, only from a web server (or running the files from *localhost* on a development server such as AMPPS, detailed in Chapter 2).

Web workers do have some security limitations that you should be aware of:

- Web workers run in their own independent JavaScript context, and have no direct access to anything in any other execution context, including the main Java-Script thread or other web workers.

- Communication between web worker contexts is done via web messaging (post Message).

- Because web workers have no access to the main JavaScript context, they cannot modify the DOM. The only DOM methods available to web workers are atob, btoa, clearInterval, clearTimeout, dump, setInterval, and setTimeout.

- Web workers are bound by the same-origin policy, so you can't load a web worker from a different origin than the original script without going through a cross-site methodology.

Drag and Drop

You can easily support dragging and dropping of objects on a web page by setting up event handlers for the ondragstart, ondragover, and ondrop events, as in Example 26-5.

Example 26-5. Dragging and dropping objects

```
<!DOCTYPE HTML>
<html>
  <head>
    <title>Drag and Drop</title>
    <script src='OSC.js'></script>
    <style>
      #dest {
        background:lightblue;
        border    :1px solid #444;
        width     :320px;
        height    :100px;
        padding   :10px;
      }
```

```
      </style>
    </head>
    <body>
      <div id='dest' ondrop='drop(event)' ondragover='allow(event)'></div><br>
      Drag the image below into the above element<br><br>

      <img id='source1' src='image1.png' draggable='true' ondragstart='drag(event)'>
      <img id='source2' src='image2.png' draggable='true' ondragstart='drag(event)'>
      <img id='source3' src='image3.png' draggable='true' ondragstart='drag(event)'>

      <script>
        function allow(event)
        {
          event.preventDefault()
        }

        function drag(event)
        {
          event.dataTransfer.setData('image/png', event.target.id)
        }

        function drop(event)
        {
          event.preventDefault()
          var data=event.dataTransfer.getData('image/png')
          event.target.appendChild(O(data))
        }
      </script>
    </body>
</html>
```

After setting up the HTML, providing a title, and loading in the *OSC.js* file, this document styles the <div> element with the ID of dest, giving it a background color, border, set dimensions, and padding.

Then, the <body> section creates the <div> element and attaches the event handler functions drop and allow to the ondrop and ondragover events of the <div>. After this there's some text, and then three images with their draggable properties set to true. The drag function is attached to the ondragstart event of each.

In the <script> section, the allow event handler function simply prevents the default action for dragging (which is to disallow it), while the drag event handler function calls the setData method of the dataTransfer object of the event, passing it the MIME type image/png and the target.id of the event (which is the object being dragged). The dataTransfer object holds the data that is being dragged during a drag-and-drop operation.

Finally, the drop event handler function also intercepts its default action so that dropping is allowed, and then it fetches the contents of the object being dragged from the `dataTransfer` object, passing it the MIME type of the object. Then the dropped data is appended to the target (which is the `dest` `<div>`) via its `appendChild` method.

If you try this example for yourself, you'll be able to drag and drop the images into the `<div>` element, where they will stay, as shown in Figure 26-3. The images cannot be dropped elsewhere, only into elements with `drop` and `allow` event handlers attached.

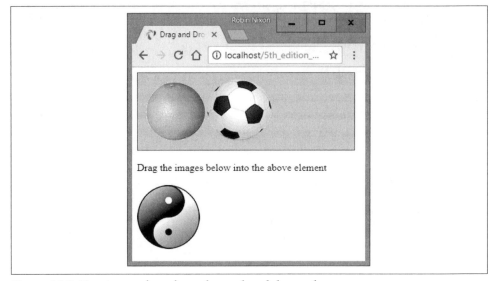

Figure 26-3. Two images have been dragged and dropped

Other events you can attach to include `ondragenter` (to run when a drag operation enters an element), `ondragleave` (to run when one leaves an element), and `ondragend` (to run when a dragging operation ends), which you can use, for example, to modify the cursor during these operations.

Cross-Document Messaging

You've already seen messaging in use a little earlier, in the web worker section. I didn't go into any details, however, as it wasn't the core topic being discussed, and the message was being posted only to the same document anyway. But for obvious security reasons, cross-document messaging does need to be applied with caution, so you need to fully understand its workings if you plan to use it.

Before HTML5, browser developers disallowed cross-document scripting, but in addition to blocking potential attack sites, this prevented communication between legitimate pages. Document interaction of any kind generally had to occur through

Ajax and a third-party web server, which was cumbersome and fiddly to build and maintain.

But web messaging now allows scripts to interact across these boundaries by using some sensible security restraints to prevent malicious hacking attempts. It is achieved through use of the postMessage method, allowing plain-text messages to be sent from one domain to another, always within a single browser.

This requires that JavaScript first obtain the window object of the receiving document, letting messages post to a variety of other windows, frames, or iframes directly related to the sender's document. The received message event has the following attributes:

data
: The incoming message

origin
: The origin of the sender document, including the scheme, hostname, and port

source
: The source window of the sender document

The code to send messages is just a single instruction, in which you pass the message to be sent and the domain to which it applies, as in Example 26-6.

Example 26-6. Sending web messages to an iframe

```
<!DOCTYPE HTML>
<html>
  <head>
    <title>Web Messaging (a)</title>
    <script src='OSC.js'></script>
  </head>
  <body>
    <iframe id='frame' src='example26-11.html' width='360' height='75'></iframe>

    <script>
      count = 1

      setInterval(function()
      {
        O('frame').contentWindow.postMessage('Message ' + count++, '*')
      }, 1000)
    </script>
  </body>
</html>
```

Here the usual use is made of the *OSC.js* file to pull in the O function, and then an <iframe> element with the ID of frame is created, which loads in Example 26-7. Then, within the <script> section, the variable count is initialized to 1 and a repeating interval is set up to occur every second to post the string `'Message '` (using the `postMessage` method) along with the current value of `count`, which is then incremented. The `postMessage` call is attached to the `contentWindow` property of the `iframe` object, not the `iframe` object itself. This is important because web messaging requires posts to be made to a window, not to an object within a window.

Example 26-7. Receiving messages from another document

```
<!DOCTYPE HTML>
<html>
  <head>
    <title>Web Messaging (b)</title>
    <style>
      #output {
        font-family:"Courier New";
        white-space:pre;
      }
    </style>
    <script src='OSC.js'></script>
  </head>
  <body>
    <div id='output'>Received messages will display here</div>

    <script>
      window.onmessage = function(event)
      {
        O('output').innerHTML =
          '<b>Origin:</b> ' + event.origin + '<br>' +
          '<b>Source:</b> ' + event.source + '<br>' +
          '<b>Data:</b>   ' + event.data
      }
    </script>
  </body>
</html>
```

This example sets up a little styling to make the output clearer, and then creates a `<div>` element with the ID `output`, in which the contents of received messages will be placed. The `<script>` section contains a single anonymous function attached to the `onmessage` event of the window. In this function, the `event.origin`, `event.source`, and `event.data` property values are then displayed, as shown in Figure 26-4.

Figure 26-4. The iframe has so far received 29 messages

Web messaging works only across domains, so you cannot test it by loading files in from a filesystem; you must use a web server. As you can see from Figure 26-4, the origin is *http://localhost* because these examples are running on a local development server. The source is the window object, and the current message value is Message 29.

At the moment, Example 26-6 is not at all secure because the domain value passed to postMessage is the wildcard *:

```
O('frame').contentWindow.postMessage('Message ' + count++, '*')
```

To direct messages only to documents originating from a particular domain, you can change this parameter. In the current case, a value of http://localhost would ensure that only documents loaded from the local server will be sent any messages:

```
O('frame').contentWindow.postMessage('Message ' + count++, 'http://localhost')
```

Likewise, as it stands, the listener program displays any and all messages it receives. This is also not a very secure state of affairs, because malicious documents also present in the browser can attempt to send messages that unwary listener code in other documents might otherwise access. Therefore, you can restrict the messages your listeners react to by using an if statement, like this:

```
window.onmessage = function(event)
{
  if (event.origin) == 'http://localhost')
  {
    O('output').innerHTML =
      '<b>Origin:</b> ' + event.origin + '<br>' +
      '<b>Source:</b> ' + event.source + '<br>' +
      '<b>Data:</b>   ' + event.data
  }
}
```

If you always use the proper domain for the site you are working with, your web messaging communications will be more secure. However, be aware that since messages are sent in the clear, there may be insecurities in some browsers or browser plug-ins that might make this kind of communication insecure. One way to boost your security, then, is to use an obfuscation or encryption scheme for all your web messages, and also consider introducing two-way communication protocols to verify each message as being authentic.

Normally, you won't alert the user to the `origin` or `source` values, and will simply make use of them for security checking. These examples, however, display those values to help you experiment with web messaging and see what is going on. Instead of using iframes, documents in pop-up windows and other tabs may also talk to each other using this method.

Microdata Is No More

In previous editions of this book I showed you how to use an interesting new HTML5 feature called *Microdata*, a subset of HTML designed to provide metadata to a document in order to make the different data elements within it have extra meaning to software and search engines such as Google.

However, time passes, and rather than more and more browsers adopting it, both Google and Apple have withdrawn support for this functionality and it has since been dropped from the main HTML5 specification at the W3C.

Therefore, I no longer recommend you mark up any code with Microdata, as it looks pretty much extinct, or very near to it, and even if the Google and Bing web spiders still use any of this information, they probably won't for much longer.

Other HTML5 Tags

A number of other new HTML5 tags are being adopted by the major browsers, including `<article>`, `<aside>`, `<details>`, `<figcaption>`, `<figure>`, `<footer>`, `<header>`, `<hgroup>`, `<mark>`, `<menuitem>`, `<meter>`, `<nav>`, `<output>`, `<progress>`, `<rp>`, `<rt>`, `<ruby>`, `<section>`, `<summary>`, `<time>`, and `<wbr>`. You can get more information on these and all other HTML5 tags from the W3C's HTML language reference (*http://bit.ly/2I6CkrP*) (check out the elements sporting a NEW icon).

This concludes your introduction to HTML5. You now have a number of powerful new features with which to make even more dynamic and compelling websites. In the final chapter, I'll show you how you can bring all the different technologies in this book together to create a mini–social networking site.

Questions

1. What method do you call to request geolocation data from a web browser?

2. How can you determine whether a browser supports local storage?

3. What method can you call to erase all local storage data for the current domain?

4. What is the best way for web workers to communicate with a main program?

5. How can you stop a web worker from running?

6. To support drag-and-drop operations, how can you prevent the default action of disallowing dragging and dropping for these events?

7. How can you make cross-document messaging more secure?

See "Chapter 26 Answers" on page 733 in Appendix A for the answers to these questions.

CHAPTER 27

Bringing It All Together

Now that you've reached the end of this book, your first milestone along the path of the hows, whys, and wherefores of dynamic web programming, I want to leave you with a real example that you can sink your teeth into. In fact, it's a collection of examples, because I've put together a simple social networking project comprising all the main features you'd expect from such a site, or more to the point, such a web app.

Across the various files, there are examples of MySQL table creation and database access, CSS stylesheets, file inclusion, session control, DOM access, asynchronous calls, event and error handling, file uploading, image manipulation, the HTML5 canvas, and a whole lot more.

Each example file is complete and self-contained, yet works with all the others to build a fully working social networking site, even including a stylesheet you can modify to completely change the look and feel of the project. Being small and light, the end product is particularly usable on mobile platforms such as a smartphone or tablet, but will run equally well on a full-size desktop computer.

And you should find that, by utilizing the power of both jQuery and jQuery Mobile, the code runs fast, is easy to use, adapts itself well to all environments, and looks good.

That said, I have tried to keep this code as slimmed-down as possible to keep it easy to follow. Consequently, there's a great deal of improvement that could be made to it, such as enhancing security by storing hashes instead of unencrypted passwords, and smoother handling of some of the transitions between being logged on and off—but let's leave those as the proverbial exercises for the reader, particularly since there are no questions at the end of this chapter!

I leave it up to you to take any pieces of this code you think you can use and expand on them for your own purposes. Perhaps you may even wish to build on these files to create a social networking site of your own.

Designing a Social Networking App

Before writing any code, I sat down and came up with several things that I decided were essential to such an app. These included the following:

- A signup process
- A login form
- A logout facility
- Session control
- User profiles with uploaded thumbnails
- A member directory
- Adding members as friends
- Public and private messaging between members
- Styling the project

I decided to name the project *Robin's Nest*; if you use this code, you will need to modify the name and logo in the *index.php* and *header.php* files.

On the Website

All the examples in this chapter can be found on the book's companion website (*http://lpmj.net*). Clicking the "5th Edition Examples" link at the top of the page will download an archive file, which you should extract to a suitable location on your computer.

Of particular interest to this chapter, within the ZIP file you'll find a folder called *robinsnest*, in which all the following examples have been saved with the correct filenames required by this sample application. This means you can easily copy them all to your web development folder to try them out.

functions.php

Let's jump right into the project, starting with Example 27-1, *functions.php*, the include file for the main functions. This file contains a little more than just the functions, though, because I have added the database login details here instead of using yet another separate file. The first four lines of code define the host and name of the database to use, as well as the username and password.

By default the MySQL username is set to *robinsnest*, and the database used by the program is also called *robinsnest*. It doesn't matter what the MySQL username is, as long as it already exists, and the same goes for the database name. Chapter 8 provides detailed instructions on how to create a new user and/or database. Essentially, though, from a MySQL command prompt you can create a new database called *robinsnest* (if you have the privileges to do so) like this:

```
CREATE DATABASE robinsnest;
```

Then (also assuming you have the privileges to do so) you can create a user called *robinsnest* capable of accessing this database like this:

```
GRANT ALL ON robinsnest.* TO 'robinsnest'@'localhost'
  IDENTIFIED BY 'rnpassword';
```

Obviously you would use a much more secure password for this user than *rnpassword*, but for the sake of simplicity, this is the password used in these examples—just make sure you change it if you use any of this code on a production site (or, as I mentioned, you can use a pre-existing username and database).

Given the correct values, the subsequent two lines in the file will open a connection to MySQL and select the database.

The Functions

The project uses five main functions:

createTable
:   Checks whether a table already exists and, if not, creates it

queryMysql
:   Issues a query to MySQL, outputting an error message if it fails

destroySession
:   Destroys a PHP session and clears its data to log users out

sanitizeString
:   Removes potentially malicious code or tags from user input

showProfile
:   Displays the user's image and "about me" message if they have one

The behavior of all of these should be obvious to you by now, with the possible exception of showProfile, which looks for an image of the name *<user.jpg>* (where *<user>* is the username of the current user) and, if it finds it, displays it. It also displays any "about me" text the user may have saved.

I have ensured that error handling is in place for all the functions that need it, so that they can catch any typographical or other errors you may introduce and generate error messages. However, if you use any of this code on a production server, you will probably want to provide your own error-handling routines to make the code more user-friendly.

So, type in Example 27-1 and save it as *functions.php* (or download it from the companion website), and you'll be ready to move on to the next section.

Example 27-1. functions.php

```php
<?php
  $dbhost  = 'localhost';    // Unlikely to require changing
  $dbname  = 'robinsnest';   // Modify these...
  $dbuser  = 'robinsnest';   // ...variables according
  $dbpass  = 'rnpassword';   // ...to your installation

  $connection = new mysqli($dbhost, $dbuser, $dbpass, $dbname);
  if ($connection->connect_error) die("Fatal Error");

  function createTable($name, $query)
  {
    queryMysql("CREATE TABLE IF NOT EXISTS $name($query)");
    echo "Table '$name' created or already exists.<br>";
  }

  function queryMysql($query)
  {
    global $connection;
    $result = $connection->query($query);
    if (!$result) die("Fatal Error");
    return $result;
  }

  function destroySession()
  {
    $_SESSION=array();

    if (session_id() != "" || isset($_COOKIE[session_name()]))
      setcookie(session_name(), '', time()-2592000, '/');

    session_destroy();
  }

  function sanitizeString($var)
  {
    global $connection;
    $var = strip_tags($var);
    $var = htmlentities($var);
    if (get_magic_quotes_gpc())
      $var = stripslashes($var);
    return $connection->real_escape_string($var);
  }
```

```
    function showProfile($user)
    {
      if (file_exists("$user.jpg"))
        echo "<img src='$user.jpg' style='float:left;'>";

      $result = queryMysql("SELECT * FROM profiles WHERE user='$user'");

      if ($result->num_rows)
      {
        $row = $result->fetch_array(MYSQLI_ASSOC);
        echo stripslashes($row['text']) . "<br style='clear:left;'><br>";
      }
      else echo "<p>Nothing to see here, yet</p><br>";
    }
?>
```

 If you've read a previous edition of this book, in which these examples used the old mysql extension, you should note that in order to reference the MySQL database using mysqli, you must apply the global keyword in the queryMysql and sanitizeString functions, to allow them to use the value in $connection.

header.php

For uniformity, each page of the project needs to have access to the same set of features. Therefore, I placed these things in Example 27-2, *header.php*. This is the file that is actually included by the other files. It includes *functions.php*. This means that only a single require_once is needed in each file.

header.php starts by calling the function session_start. As you'll recall from Chapter 12, this sets up a session that will remember certain values we want stored across different PHP files. In other words, it represents a visit by a user to the site, and it can time out if the user ignores the site for a period of time.

With the session started, the program then outputs the HTML needed to set up each web page, including loading stylesheets and the various JavaScript libraries required. After this the file of functions (*functions.php*) is included, and the default string of "Welcome Guest" is assigned to $userstr.

Next the code checks whether the session variable user is currently assigned a value. If so, a user has already logged in, so the variable $loggedin is set to TRUE and the username is retrieved from the session variable user into the PHP variable $user, with $userstr updated appropriately. If the user has not yet logged in, then $loggedin is set to FALSE.

Next, some HTML is output welcoming the user (or guest if not yet logged in), and the <div> elements required by jQuery Mobile for the page's header and content sections are output.

After this, using the value of $loggedin, an if block displays one of two sets of menus. The non-logged-in set simply offers options of Home, Sign Up, and Log In, whereas the logged-in version offers full access to the app's features. The buttons are styled using jQuery Mobile notation, such as data-role='button' to display an element as a button, data-inline='true' to display elements inline (like a <span> element), and data-transition="slide" to make new pages slide into view when clicked, as described in Chapter 22.

The additional styling applied to this file is in the file *styles.css* (Example 27-13, detailed at the end of this chapter).

Example 27-2. header.php

```php
<?php //
  session_start();

echo <<<_INIT
<!DOCTYPE html>
<html>
  <head>
    <meta charset='utf-8'>
    <meta name='viewport' content='width=device-width, initial-scale=1'>
    <link rel='stylesheet' href='jquery.mobile-1.4.5.min.css'>
    <link rel='stylesheet' href='styles.css'>
    <script src='javascript.js'></script>
    <script src='jquery-2.2.4.min.js'></script>
    <script src='jquery.mobile-1.4.5.min.js'></script>

_INIT;

  require_once 'functions.php';

  $userstr = 'Welcome Guest';

  if (isset($_SESSION['user']))
  {
    $user     = $_SESSION['user'];
    $loggedin = TRUE;
    $userstr  = "Logged in as: $user";
  }
  else $loggedin = FALSE;

echo <<<_MAIN
    <title>Robin's Nest: $userstr</title>
  </head>
```

```php
  <body>
    <div data-role='page'>
      <div data-role='header'>
        <div id='logo'
          class='center'>R<img id='robin' src='robin.gif'>bin's Nest</div>
        <div class='username'>$userstr</div>
      </div>
      <div data-role='content'>

_MAIN;

  if ($loggedin)
  {
echo <<<_LOGGEDIN
        <div class='center'>
          <a data-role='button' data-inline='true' data-icon='home'
            data-transition="slide" href='members.php?view=$user'>Home</a>
          <a data-role='button' data-inline='true'
            data-transition="slide" href='members.php'>Members</a>
          <a data-role='button' data-inline='true'
            data-transition="slide" href='friends.php'>Friends</a>
          <a data-role='button' data-inline='true'
            data-transition="slide" href='messages.php'>Messages</a>
          <a data-role='button' data-inline='true'
            data-transition="slide" href='profile.php'>Edit Profile</a>
          <a data-role='button' data-inline='true'
            data-transition="slide" href='logout.php'>Log out</a>
        </div>

_LOGGEDIN;                                                    .
  }
  else
  {
echo <<<_GUEST
        <div class='center'>
          <a data-role='button' data-inline='true' data-icon='home'
            data-transition='slide' href='index.php'>Home</a>
          <a data-role='button' data-inline='true' data-icon='plus'
            data-transition="slide" href='signup.php'>Sign Up</a>
          <a data-role='button' data-inline='true' data-icon='check'
            data-transition="slide" href='login.php'>Log In</a>
        </div>
        <p class='info'>(You must be logged in to use this app)</p>

_GUEST;
  }
?>
```

setup.php

With the pair of included files written, it's now time to set up the MySQL tables they will use. We do this with Example 27-3, *setup.php*, which you should type and load into your browser before calling up any other files; otherwise, you'll get numerous MySQL errors.

The tables created are short and sweet, and have the following names and columns:

- *members*: username *user* (indexed), password *pass*
- *messages*: ID *id* (indexed), author *auth* (indexed), recipient *recip*, message type *pm*, message *message*
- *friends*: username *user* (indexed), friend's username *friend*
- *profiles*: username *user* (indexed), "about me" *text*

Because the `createTable` function first checks whether a table already exists, this program can be safely called multiple times without generating any errors.

It is very likely that you will need to add many more columns to these tables if you choose to expand this project. If so, bear in mind that you may need to issue a MySQL `DROP TABLE` command before re-creating a table.

Example 27-3. setup.php

```
<!DOCTYPE html>
<html>
  <head>
    <title>Setting up database</title>
  </head>
  <body>

    <h3>Setting up...</h3>

<?php
  require_once 'functions.php';

  createTable('members',
              'user VARCHAR(16),
              pass VARCHAR(16),
              INDEX(user(6))');

  createTable('messages',
              'id INT UNSIGNED AUTO_INCREMENT PRIMARY KEY,
              auth VARCHAR(16),
              recip VARCHAR(16),
              pm CHAR(1),
              time INT UNSIGNED,
```

```
                message VARCHAR(4096),
                INDEX(auth(6)),
                INDEX(recip(6))');

    createTable('friends',
                'user VARCHAR(16),
                friend VARCHAR(16),
                INDEX(user(6)),
                INDEX(friend(6))');

    createTable('profiles',
                'user VARCHAR(16),
                text VARCHAR(4096),
                INDEX(user(6))');
?>

        <br>...done.
    </body>
</html>
```

 For this example to work, you must first ensure that you have already created the database specified in the variable $dbname in Example 27-1, and also have granted access to it by the user given the name in $dbuser, with the password in $dbpass.

index.php

This file is trivial, but necessary nonetheless to give the project a home page. All it does is display a simple welcome message. In a finished application, this would be where you sell the virtues of your site to encourage signups.

Incidentally, seeing as we have already set up all the MySQL tables and created the included files, you can now load Example 27-4, *index.php*, into your browser to get your first peek at the new application. It should look like Figure 27-1.

Example 27-4. index.php

```
<?php
  session_start();
  require_once 'header.php';

  echo "<div class='center'>Welcome to Robin's Nest,";

  if ($loggedin) echo " $user, you are logged in";
  else           echo ' please sign up or log in';

  echo <<<_END
      </div><br>
```

```
    </div>
    <div data-role="footer">
      <h4>Web App from <i><a href='http://lpmj.net/5thedition'
      target='_blank'>Learning PHP MySQL & JavaScript Ed. 5</a></i></h4>
    </div>
  </body>
</html>
_END;
?>
```

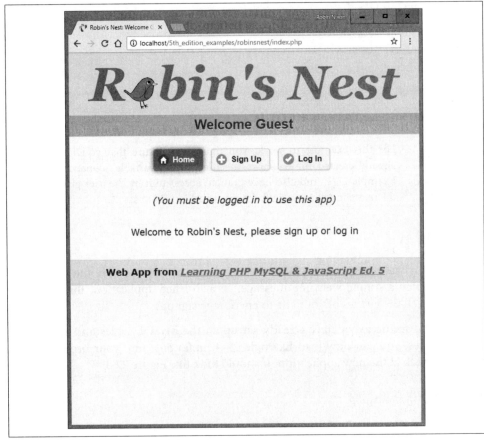

Figure 27-1. The main page of the app

signup.php

Now we need a module to enable users to join our new social network, and that's
Example 27-5, *signup.php*. This is a slightly longer program, but you've seen all its
parts before.

Let's start by looking at the end block of HTML. This is a simple form that allows a username and password to be entered. But note the use of the empty `<span>` given the id of `info`. This will be the destination of the asynchronous call in this program that checks whether a desired username is available. See Chapter 17 for a complete description of how this works.

Checking for Username Availability

Now go back to the program start and you'll see a block of JavaScript that starts with the function `checkUser`. This is called by the JavaScript `onBlur` event when focus is removed from the `username` field of the form. First it sets the contents of the `<span>` I mentioned (with the id of `info`) to an empty string, which clears it in case it previously had a value.

Next a request is made to the program *checkuser.php*, which reports whether the username `user` is available. The returned result of the asynchronous call (performed using jQuery), a friendly message, is then placed in the `info` `<span>`.

After the JavaScript section comes some PHP code that you should recognize from the discussion of form validation in Chapter 16. This section also uses the `sanitizeString` function to remove potentially malicious characters before looking up the username in the database and, if it's not already taken, inserting the new username `$user` and password `$pass`.

Logging In

Upon successfully signing up, the user is then prompted to log in. A more fluid response at this point might be to automatically log in a newly created user, but because I don't want to overly complicate the code, I have kept the signup and login modules separate. You can easily implement this if you want to, however.

This file uses the CSS class `fieldname` to arrange the form fields, aligning them neatly under each other in columns. When loaded into a browser (and in conjunction with *checkuser.php*, shown later), this program will look like Figure 27-2, where you can see that the asynchronous call has identified that the username *Robin* is available. If you would like the password field to show only asterisks, change its type from `text` to `password`.

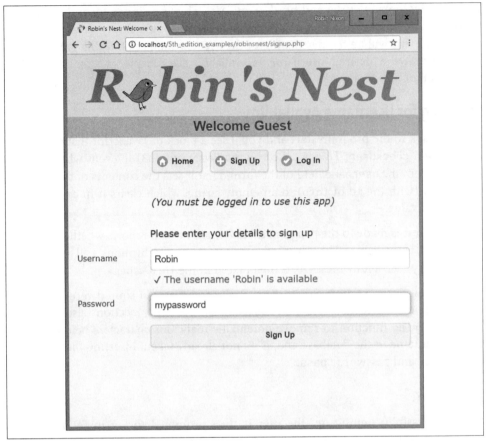

Figure 27-2. The signup page

Example 27-5. signup.php

```php
<?php
  require_once 'header.php';

echo <<<_END
  <script>
    function checkUser(user)
    {
      if (user.value == '')
      {
        $('#used').html(' ')
        return
      }

      $.post
      (
```

```php
              'checkuser.php',
              { user : user.value },
              function(data)
              {
                $('#used').html(data)
              }
          )
      }
    </script>
_END;

  $error = $user = $pass = "";
  if (isset($_SESSION['user'])) destroySession();

  if (isset($_POST['user']))
  {
    $user = sanitizeString($_POST['user']);
    $pass = sanitizeString($_POST['pass']);

    if ($user == "" || $pass == "")
      $error = 'Not all fields were entered<br><br>';
    else
    {
      $result = queryMysql("SELECT * FROM members WHERE user='$user'");

      if ($result->num_rows)
        $error = 'That username already exists<br><br>';
      else
      {
        queryMysql("INSERT INTO members VALUES('$user', '$pass')");
        die('<h4>Account created</h4>Please log in.</div></body></html>');
      }
    }
  }

echo <<<_END
      <form method='post' action='signup.php'>$error
      <div data-role='fieldcontain'>
        <label></label>
        Please enter your details to sign up
      </div>
      <div data-role='fieldcontain'>
        <label>Username</label>
        <input type='text' maxlength='16' name='user' value='$user'
          onBlur='checkUser(this)'>
        <label></label><div id='used'> </div>
      </div>
      <div data-role='fieldcontain'>
        <label>Password</label>
        <input type='text' maxlength='16' name='pass' value='$pass'>
      </div>
      <div data-role='fieldcontain'>
```

```
            <label></label>
            <input data-transition='slide' type='submit' value='Sign Up'>
        </div>
      </div>
    </body>
  </html>
_END;
?>
```

 On a production server. I wouldn't recommend storing user passwords in the clear, as I've done here for reasons of space and simplicity. Instead, you should salt them and store them as one-way hash strings. See Chapter 12 for more details on how to do this.

checkuser.php

To go with *signup.php*, here's Example 27-6, *checkuser.php*, which looks up a username in the database and returns a string indicating whether it has already been taken. Because it relies on the functions sanitizeString and queryMysql, the program first includes the file *functions.php*.

Then, if the $_POST variable user has a value, the function looks it up in the database and, depending on whether it exists as a username, outputs either "Sorry, the username *'user'* is taken" or "The username *'user'* is available." Just checking the function mysql_num_rows against the result is sufficient for this, as it will return 0 if the name is not found, or 1 if it is found.

The HTML entities ✘ and ✔ are also used to preface the string with either a cross or a checkmark, and the string will be displayed in either red for the class taken or green for the class available, as defined in *styles.css*, shown later in this chapter.

Example 27-6. checkuser.php

```
<?php
  require_once 'functions.php';

  if (isset($_POST['user']))
  {
    $user   = sanitizeString($_POST['user']);
    $result = queryMysql("SELECT * FROM members WHERE user='$user'");

    if ($result->num_rows)
      echo  "<span class='taken'> &#x2718; " .
            "The username '$user' is taken</span>";
    else
      echo "<span class='available'> &#x2714; " .
```

```
              "The username '$user' is available</span>";
  }
?>
```

login.php

With users now able to sign up on the site, Example 27-7, *login.php*, provides the code needed to let them log in. Like the signup page, it features a simple HTML form and some basic error checking, as well as using `sanitizeString` before querying the MySQL database.

The main thing to note here is that, upon successful verification of the username and password, the session variables `user` and `pass` are given the username and password values. As long as the current session remains active, these variables will be accessible by all the programs in the project, allowing them to automatically provide access to logged-in users.

You may be interested in the use of the `die` function upon successfully logging in. This is there because it combines an `echo` and an `exit` command in one, thus saving a line of code. For styling, this (like most of the files) applies the class `main` to indent the content from the lefthand edge.

When you call this program up in your browser, it should look like Figure 27-3. Note how the input type of `password` has been used here to mask the password with asterisks to prevent it from being viewed by anyone looking over the user's shoulder.

Example 27-7. login.php

```php
<?php
 require_once 'header.php';
 $error = $user = $pass = "";

 if (isset($_POST['user']))
 {
   $user = sanitizeString($_POST['user']);
   $pass = sanitizeString($_POST['pass']);

   if ($user == "" || $pass == "")
     $error = 'Not all fields were entered';
   else
   {
     $result = queryMySQL("SELECT user,pass FROM members
       WHERE user='$user' AND pass='$pass'");

     if ($result->num_rows == 0)
     {
       $error = "Invalid login attempt";
     }
```

```php
      else
      {
        $_SESSION['user'] = $user;
        $_SESSION['pass'] = $pass;
        die("You are now logged in. Please <a data-transition='slide'
            href='members.php?view=$user'>click here</a> to continue.</div>
              </body></html>");
      }
    }
  }

echo <<<_END
    <form method='post' action='login.php'>
      <div data-role='fieldcontain'>
        <label></label>
        <span class='error'>$error</span>
      </div>
      <div data-role='fieldcontain'>
        <label></label>
        Please enter your details to log in
      </div>
      <div data-role='fieldcontain'>
        <label>Username</label>
        <input type='text' maxlength='16' name='user' value='$user'>
      </div>
      <div data-role='fieldcontain'>
        <label>Password</label>
        <input type='password' maxlength='16' name='pass' value='$pass'>
      </div>
      <div data-role='fieldcontain'>
        <label></label>
        <input data-transition='slide' type='submit' value='Login'>
      </div>
    </form>
  </div>
  </body>
</html>
_END;
?>
```

Figure 27-3. The login page

profile.php

One of the first things that new users may want to do after signing up and logging in is to create a profile, which can be done via Example 27-8, *profile.php*. I think you'll find some interesting code here, such as routines to upload, resize, and sharpen images.

Let's start by looking at the main HTML at the end of the code. This is like the forms you've just seen, but this time it has the parameter `enctype='multipart/form-data'`. This allows us to send more than one type of data at a time, enabling the posting of an image as well as some text. There's also an input type of `file`, which creates a Browse button that a user can press to select a file to be uploaded.

When the form is submitted, the code at the start of the program is executed. The first thing it does is ensure that a user is logged in before allowing program execution to proceed. Only then is the page heading displayed.

 As described in Chapter 22, due to the way that jQuery Mobile uses asynchronous communication, it is not possible to upload files from HTML using it, unless you disable that feature by adding an attribute to the <form> element of data-ajax='false'. This will allow HTML file upload to proceed as normal, but you will lose the ability to perform page change animations.

Adding the "About Me" Text

Next, the $_POST variable text is checked to see whether some text was posted to the program. If so, it is sanitized and all long whitespace sequences (including carriage returns and line feeds) are replaced with single spaces. This function incorporates a double security check, ensuring that the user actually exists in the database and that no attempt at hacking can succeed before inserting this text into the database, where it will become the user's "about me" details.

If no text was posted, the database is queried to see whether any text already exists in order to prepopulate the <textarea> for the user to edit it.

Adding a Profile Image

Next we move on to the section where the $_FILES system variable is checked to see whether an image has been uploaded. If so, a string variable called $saveto is created, based on the user's username followed by the extension *.jpg*. For example, a user called *Jill* will cause $saveto to have the value *Jill.jpg*. This is the file where the uploaded image will be saved for use in the user's profile.

Following this, the uploaded image type is examined and is accepted only if it is a *.jpeg*, *.png*, or *.gif* image. Upon success, the variable $src is populated with the uploaded image using one of the imagecreatefrom functions, according to the image type uploaded. The image is now in a raw format that PHP can process. If the image is not of an allowed type, the flag $typeok is set to FALSE, preventing the final section of image upload code from being processed.

Processing the Image

First, we store the image's dimensions in $w and $h using the following statement, which is a quick way of assigning values from an array to separate variables:

```
list($w, $h) = getimagesize($saveto);
```

Then, using the value of $max (which is set to 100), we calculate new dimensions that will result in a new image of the same ratio, but with no dimension greater than 100 pixels. This results in giving the variables $tw and $th the new values needed. If you want smaller or larger thumbnails, simply change the value of $max accordingly.

Next, the function imagecreatetruecolor is called to create a new, blank canvas $tw wide and $th high in $tmp. Then imagecopyresampled is called to resample the image from $src to the new $tmp. Sometimes resampling images can result in a slightly blurred copy, so the next piece of code uses the imageconvolution function to sharpen the image up a bit.

Finally, the image is saved as a *.jpeg* file in the location defined by the variable $saveto, after which we remove both the original and the resized image canvases from memory using the imagedestroy function, returning the memory that was used.

Displaying the Current Profile

Last but not least, so that the user can see what the current profile looks like before editing it, the showProfile function from *functions.php* is called prior to outputting the form HTML. If no profile exists yet, nothing will be displayed.

When a profile image is displayed, CSS is applied to it to provide a border, a shadow, and a margin to its right, to separate the profile text from the image. The result of loading Example 27-8 into a browser is shown in Figure 27-4, where you can see that the <textarea> has been prepopulated with the "about me" text.

Example 27-8. profile.php

```php
<?php
  require_once 'header.php';

  if (!$loggedin) die("</div></body></html>");

  echo "<h3>Your Profile</h3>";

  $result = queryMysql("SELECT * FROM profiles WHERE user='$user'");

  if (isset($_POST['text']))
  {
    $text = sanitizeString($_POST['text']);
    $text = preg_replace('/\s\s+/', ' ', $text);

    if ($result->num_rows)
        queryMysql("UPDATE profiles SET text='$text' where user='$user'");
    else queryMysql("INSERT INTO profiles VALUES('$user', '$text')");
  }
```

```php
else
{
  if ($result->num_rows)
  {
    $row  = $result->fetch_array(MYSQLI_ASSOC);
    $text = stripslashes($row['text']);
  }
  else $text = "";
}

$text = stripslashes(preg_replace('/\s\s+/', ' ', $text));

if (isset($_FILES['image']['name']))
{
  $saveto = "$user.jpg";
  move_uploaded_file($_FILES['image']['tmp_name'], $saveto);
  $typeok = TRUE;

  switch($_FILES['image']['type'])
  {
    case "image/gif":   $src = imagecreatefromgif($saveto); break;
    case "image/jpeg":  // Both regular and progressive jpegs
    case "image/pjpeg": $src = imagecreatefromjpeg($saveto); break;
    case "image/png":   $src = imagecreatefrompng($saveto); break;
    default:            $typeok = FALSE; break;
  }

  if ($typeok)
  {
    list($w, $h) = getimagesize($saveto);

    $max = 100;
    $tw  = $w;
    $th  = $h;

    if ($w > $h && $max < $w)
    {
      $th = $max / $w * $h;
      $tw = $max;
    }
    elseif ($h > $w && $max < $h)
    {
      $tw = $max / $h * $w;
      $th = $max;
    }
    elseif ($max < $w)
    {
      $tw = $th = $max;
    }

    $tmp = imagecreatetruecolor($tw, $th);
    imagecopyresampled($tmp, $src, 0, 0, 0, 0, $tw, $th, $w, $h);
```

```php
        imageconvolution($tmp, array(array(-1, -1, -1),
          array(-1, 16, -1), array(-1, -1, -1)), 8, 0);
        imagejpeg($tmp, $saveto);
        imagedestroy($tmp);
        imagedestroy($src);
    }
  }

  showProfile($user);

echo <<<_END
      <form data-ajax='false' method='post'
        action='profile.php' enctype='multipart/form-data'>
      <h3>Enter or edit your details and/or upload an image</h3>
      <textarea name='text'>$text</textarea><br>
      Image: <input type='file' name='image' size='14'>
      <input type='submit' value='Save Profile'>
      </form>
    </div><br>
  </body>
</html>
_END;
?>
```

Figure 27-4. Editing a user profile

members.php

Using Example 27-9, *members.php*, your users will be able to find other members and choose to add them as friends (or drop them if they are already friends). This program has two modes. The first lists all members and their relationships to you, and the second shows a user's profile.

Viewing a User's Profile

The code for the latter mode comes first, where a test is made for the variable view, retrieved from the $_GET array. If it exists, a user wants to view someone's profile, so the program does that using the showProfile function, along with providing a couple of links to the user's friends and messages.

Adding and Dropping Friends

After that, the two $.GET variables add and remove are tested. If one or the other has a value, it will be the username of a user to either add or drop as a friend. We achieve this by looking up the user in the MySQL friends table and either inserting the username or removing it from the table.

And, of course, every posted variable is first passed through sanitizeString to ensure that it is safe to use with MySQL.

Listing All Members

The final section of code issues a SQL query to list all usernames. The code places the number returned in the variable $num before outputting the page heading.

A for loop then iterates through each and every member, fetching their details and then looking them up in the *friends* table to see if they are either being followed by or following the user. If someone is both a follower and a followee, they are classed as a mutual friend.

The variable $t1 is nonzero when the user is following another member, and $t2 is nonzero when another member is following the user. Depending on these values, text is displayed after each username, showing the relationship (if any) to the current user.

Icons are also displayed to show the relationships. A double-pointing arrow means that the users are mutual friends, a left-pointing arrow indicates the user is following another member, and a right-pointing arrow indicates that another member is following the user.

Finally, depending on whether the user is following another member, a link is provided to either add or drop that member as a friend.

When you call Example 27-9 up in a browser, it will look like Figure 27-5. Note how the user is invited to "follow" a nonfollowing member, but if the member is already following the user, a "recip" link to reciprocate the friendship is offered. In the case of a user already following another member, the user can select "drop" to end the following.

Figure 27-5. Using the members module

Example 27-9. members.php

```php
<?php
  require_once 'header.php';

  if (!$loggedin) die("</div></body></html>");

  if (isset($_GET['view']))
  {
    $view = sanitizeString($_GET['view']);

    if ($view == $user) $name = "Your";
    else                $name = "$view's";

    echo "<h3>$name Profile</h3>";
```

```php
    showProfile($view);
    echo "<a class='button' data-transition='slide'
        href='messages.php?view=$view'>View $name messages</a>";
    die("</div></body></html>");
}

if (isset($_GET['add']))
{
    $add = sanitizeString($_GET['add']);

    $result = queryMysql("SELECT * FROM friends
        WHERE user='$add' AND friend='$user'");
    if (!$result->num_rows)
        queryMysql("INSERT INTO friends VALUES ('$add', '$user')");
}
elseif (isset($_GET['remove']))
{
    $remove = sanitizeString($_GET['remove']);
    queryMysql("DELETE FROM friends WHERE user='$remove' AND friend='$user'");
}

$result = queryMysql("SELECT user FROM members ORDER BY user");
$num    = $result->num_rows;

echo "<h3>Other Members</h3><ul>";

for ($j = 0 ; $j < $num ; ++$j)
{
    $row = $result->fetch_array(MYSQLI_ASSOC);
    if ($row['user'] == $user) continue;

    echo "<li><a data-transition='slide' href='members.php?view=" .
        $row['user'] . "'>" . $row['user'] . "</a>";
    $follow = "follow";

    $result1 = queryMysql("SELECT * FROM friends WHERE
        user='" . $row['user'] . "' AND friend='$user'");
    $t1      = $result1->num_rows;
    $result1 = queryMysql("SELECT * FROM friends WHERE
        user='$user' AND friend='" . $row['user'] . "'");
    $t2      = $result1->num_rows;

    if (($t1 + $t2) > 1) echo " &harr; is a mutual friend";
    elseif ($t1)         echo " &larr; you are following";
    elseif ($t2)       { echo " &rarr; is following you";
                         $follow = "recip"; }

    if (!$t1) echo " [<a data-transition='slide'
        href='members.php?add=" . $row['user'] . "'>$follow</a>]";
    else      echo " [<a data-transition='slide'
        href='members.php?remove=" . $row['user'] . "'>drop</a>]";
}
```

```
?>
    </ul></div>
  </body>
</html>
```

 On a production server, there could be thousands or even hundreds of thousands of users, so you would probably substantially modify this program to include support for searching the "about me" text, paging the output a screen at a time, and so on.

friends.php

The module that shows a user's friends and followers is Example 27-10, *friends.php*. This interrogates the *friends* table just like the *members.php* program, but only for a single user. It then shows all of that user's mutual friends and followers along with the people they are following.

All the followers are saved into an array called `$followers`, and all the people being followed are placed in an array called `$following`. Then a neat piece of code is used to extract all of those who are both following and followed by the user, like this:

```
$mutual = array_intersect($followers, $following);
```

The `array_intersect` function extracts all members common to both arrays and returns a new array containing only those people. This array is then stored in `$mutual`. Now it's possible to use the `array_diff` function for each of the `$followers` and `$following` arrays to keep only those people who are *not* mutual friends, like this:

```
$followers = array_diff($followers, $mutual);
$following = array_diff($following, $mutual);
```

This results in the array `$mutual` containing only mutual friends, `$followers` containing only followers (and no mutual friends), and `$following` containing only people being followed (and no mutual friends).

Now that we're armed with these arrays, it's a simple matter to separately display each category of members, as can be seen in Figure 27-6. The PHP `sizeof` function returns the number of elements in an array; here I use it just to trigger code when the size is nonzero (that is, when friends of that type exist). Note how, by using the variables `$name1`, `$name2`, and `$name3` in the relevant places, the code can tell when you're looking at your own friends list, using the words *Your* and *You are*, instead of simply displaying the username. The commented line can be uncommented if you wish to display the user's profile information on this screen.

Example 27-10. friends.php

```php
<?php
  require_once 'header.php';

  if (!$loggedin) die("</div></body></html>");

  if (isset($_GET['view'])) $view = sanitizeString($_GET['view']);
  else                      $view = $user;

  if ($view == $user)
  {
    $name1 = $name2 = "Your";
    $name3 =          "You are";
  }
  else
  {
    $name1 = "<a data-transition='slide'
              href='members.php?view=$view'>$view</a>'s";
    $name2 = "$view's";
    $name3 = "$view is";
  }

  // Uncomment this line if you wish the user's profile to show here
  // showProfile($view);

  $followers = array();
  $following = array();

  $result = queryMysql("SELECT * FROM friends WHERE user='$view'");
  $num     = $result->num_rows;

  for ($j = 0 ; $j < $num ; ++$j)
  {
    $row           = $result->fetch_array(MYSQLI_ASSOC);
    $followers[$j] = $row['friend'];
  }

  $result = queryMysql("SELECT * FROM friends WHERE friend='$view'");
  $num     = $result->num_rows;

  for ($j = 0 ; $j < $num ; ++$j)
  {
      $row           = $result->fetch_array(MYSQLI_ASSOC);
      $following[$j] = $row['user'];
  }

  $mutual    = array_intersect($followers, $following);
  $followers = array_diff($followers, $mutual);
  $following = array_diff($following, $mutual);
  $friends   = FALSE;
```

```php
    echo "<br>";

    if (sizeof($mutual))
    {
      echo "<span class='subhead'>$name2 mutual friends</span><ul>";
      foreach($mutual as $friend)
        echo "<li><a data-transition='slide'
              href='members.php?view=$friend'>$friend</a>";
      echo "</ul>";
      $friends = TRUE;
    }

    if (sizeof($followers))
    {
      echo "<span class='subhead'>$name2 followers</span><ul>";
      foreach($followers as $friend)
        echo "<li><a data-transition='slide'
              href='members.php?view=$friend'>$friend</a>";
      echo "</ul>";
      $friends = TRUE;
    }

    if (sizeof($following))
    {
      echo "<span class='subhead'>$name3 following</span><ul>";
      foreach($following as $friend)
        echo "<li><a data-transition='slide'
              href='members.php?view=$friend'>$friend</a>";
      echo "</ul>";
      $friends = TRUE;
    }

    if (!$friends) echo "<br>You don't have any friends yet.<br><br>";

    echo "<a data-role='button' data-transition='slide'
          href='messages.php?view=$view'>View $name2 messages</a>";
?>
    </div>
  </body>
</html>
```

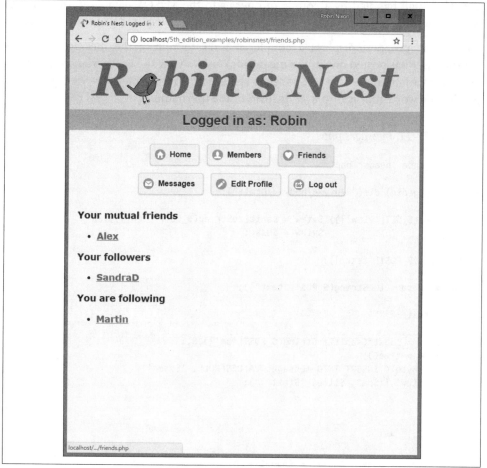

Figure 27-6. Displaying a user's friends and followers

messages.php

The last of the main modules is Example 27-11, *messages.php*. The program starts by checking whether a message has been posted in the variable text. If so, it is inserted into the *messages* table. At the same time, the value of pm is also stored. This indicates whether a message is private or public. A 0 represents a public message, and 1 is private.

Next, the user's profile and a form for entering a message are displayed, along with radio buttons to choose between a private or public message. After this, all the messages are shown, depending on whether they are private or public. If they are public, all users can see them, but private messages are visible only to the sender and recipient. This is all handled by a couple of queries to the MySQL database. Additionally, when a message is private, it is introduced by the word *whispered* and shown in italic.

Finally, the program displays a couple of links to refresh the messages (in case another user has posted one in the meantime) and to view the user's friends. The trick using the variables $name1 and $name2 is again used so that when you view your own profile, the word *Your* is displayed instead of the username.

Example 27-11. messages.php

```php
require_once 'header.php';

if (!$loggedin) die("</div></body></html>");

if (isset($_GET['view'])) $view = sanitizeString($_GET['view']);
else                      $view = $user;

if (isset($_POST['text']))
{
  $text = sanitizeString($_POST['text']);

  if ($text != "")
  {
    $pm   = substr(sanitizeString($_POST['pm']),0,1);
    $time = time();
    queryMysql("INSERT INTO messages VALUES(NULL, '$user',
      '$view', '$pm', $time, '$text')");
  }
}

if ($view != "")
{
  if ($view == $user) $name1 = $name2 = "Your";
  else
  {
    $name1 = "<a href='members.php?view=$view'>$view</a>'s";
    $name2 = "$view's";
  }

  echo "<h3>$name1 Messages</h3>";
  showProfile($view);

  echo <<<_END
    <form method='post' action='messages.php?view=$view'>
      <fieldset data-role="controlgroup" data-type="horizontal">
        <legend>Type here to leave a message</legend>
        <input type='radio' name='pm' id='public' value='0' checked='checked'>
        <label for="public">Public</label>
        <input type='radio' name='pm' id='private' value='1'>
        <label for="private">Private</label>
      </fieldset>
```

```php
      <textarea name='text'></textarea>
      <input data-transition='slide' type='submit' value='Post Message'>
    </form><br>
_END;

    date_default_timezone_set('UTC');

    if (isset($_GET['erase']))
    {
      $erase = sanitizeString($_GET['erase']);
      queryMysql("DELETE FROM messages WHERE id=$erase AND recip='$user'");
    }

    $query  = "SELECT * FROM messages WHERE recip='$view' ORDER BY time DESC";
    $result = queryMysql($query);
    $num    = $result->num_rows;

    for ($j = 0 ; $j < $num ; ++$j)
    {
      $row = $result->fetch_array(MYSQLI_ASSOC);

      if ($row['pm'] == 0 || $row['auth'] == $user ||
          $row['recip'] == $user)
      {
        echo date('M jS \'y g:ia:', $row['time']);
        echo " <a href='messages.php?view=" . $row['auth'] .
             "'>" . $row['auth']. "</a> ";

        if ($row['pm'] == 0)
          echo "wrote: &quot;" . $row['message'] . "&quot; ";
        else
          echo "whispered: <span class='whisper'>&quot;" .
            $row['message']. "&quot;</span> ";

        if ($row['recip'] == $user)
          echo "[<a href='messages.php?view=$view" .
               "&erase=" . $row['id'] . "'>erase</a>]";

        echo "<br>";
      }
    }
  }

  if (!$num)
    echo "<br><span class='info'>No messages yet</span><br><br>";

  echo "<br><a data-role='button'
        href='messages.php?view=$view'>Refresh messages</a>";
?>
    </div><br>
  </body>
</html>
```

You can see the result of viewing this program with a browser in Figure 27-7. Note how users viewing their own messages are provided with links to erase any they don't want to keep. Also of note is how jQuery Mobile's styling of radio buttons has been implemented for selecting between sending a private or a public message. How this works is explained in Chapter 22.

Figure 27-7. The messaging module

logout.php

The final ingredient in our social networking recipe is Example 27-12, *logout.php*, the logout page that closes a session and deletes any associated data and cookies. The result of calling up this program is shown in Figure 27-8, where the user is now asked to click a link that will take them to the not logged-in home page and remove the logged-in links from the top of the screen. Of course, you could write a JavaScript or

PHP redirect to do this (probably a good idea if you wish to keep logout looking clean).

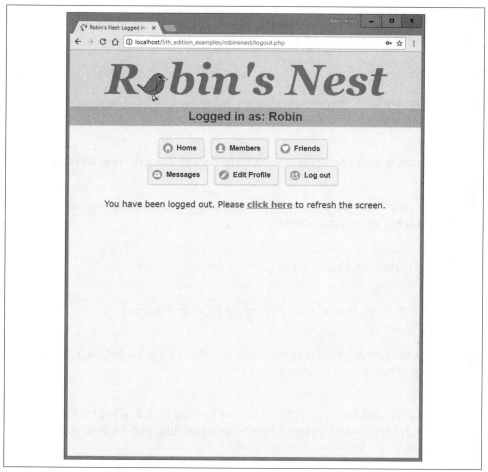

Figure 27-8. The logout page

Example 27-12. logout.php

```php
<?php
  require_once 'header.php';

  if (isset($_SESSION['user']))
  {
    destroySession();
    echo "<br><div class='center'>You have been logged out. Please
        <a data-transition='slide' href='index.php'>click here</a>
        to refresh the screen.</div>";
  }
```

```
        else echo "<div class='center'>You cannot log out because
                you are not logged in</div>";
?>
    </div>
  </body>
</html>
```

styles.css

The stylesheet used for this project is shown in Example 27-13. There are a number of sets of declarations, as follows:

`*`

Sets the default font family and size for the project using the universal selector.

`body`

Sets the width of the project window, centers it horizontally, specifies a background color, and gives it a border.

`html`

Sets the background color of the HTML section.

`img`

Gives all images a border, a shadow, and a righthand margin.

`.username`

Centers the username, and chooses the font family, size, color, background, and padding with which to display it.

`.info`

This class is used for displaying important information. It sets a background and foreground text color, applies a border and padding, and indents elements that employ it.

`.center`

This class is used for centering the contents of a <div> element.

`.subhead`

This class emphasizes sections of text.

`.taken`, `.available`, `.error`, *and* `.whisper`

These declarations set the colors and font styles to be used for displaying different types of information.

`#logo`

Styles the logo text as a fallback in case a non-HTML5 browser is in use and the canvas logo doesn't get created.

#robin

Aligns the image of the robin in the page title.

#used

Ensures the element that is populated by the *checkuser.php* asynchronous call if a
username is already taken is not too close to the field above it.

Example 27-13. styles.css

```
* {
  font-family:verdana,sans-serif;
  font-size  :14pt;
}

body {
  width     :700px;
  margin    :20px auto;
  background:#f8f8f8;
  border    :1px solid #888;
}

html {
  background:#fff
}

img {
  border              :1px solid black;
  margin-right        :15px;
  -moz-box-shadow     :2px 2px 2px #888;
  -webkit-box-shadow:2px 2px 2px #888;
  box-shadow          :2px 2px 2px #888;
}

.username {
  text-align :center;
  background :#eb8;
  color      :#40d;
  font-family:helvetica;
  font-size  :20pt;
  padding    :4px;
}

.info {
  font-style :italic;
  margin     :40px 0px;
  text-align :center;
}

.center {
  text-align:center;
}
```

```
.subhead {
  font-weight:bold;
}

.taken, .error {
  color:red;
}

.available {
  color:green;
}

.whisper {
  font-style:italic;
  color      :#006600;
}

#logo {
  font-family:Georgia;
  font-weight:bold;
  font-style :italic;
  font-size  :97px;
  color      :red;
  }

#robin {
  position           :relative;
  border             :0px;
  margin-left        :-6px;
  margin-right       :0px;
  top                :17px;
  -moz-box-shadow    :0px 0px 0px;
  -webkit-box-shadow:0px 0px 0px;
  box-shadow         :0px 0px 0px;
}

#used {
  margin-top:50px;
}
```

javascript.js

Finally, there's the JavaScript file (see Example 27-14), which contains the O, S, and C functions used throughout this book.

Example 27-14. javascript.js

```
function O(i)
{
```

```
  return typeof i == 'object' ? i : document.getElementById(i)
}

function S(i)
{
  return O(i).style
}

function C(i)
{
  return document.getElementsByClassName(i)
}
```

And that, as they say, is that. If you write anything based on this code or any other examples in this book, or have gained in any other way from it, then I am glad to have been of help and thank you for reading this book.

But before you go and try out your newly learned skills on the web at large, please browse through the appendixes that follow, as there's a lot of additional information there you should find useful.

Solutions to the Chapter Questions

Chapter 1 Answers

1. A web server (such as Apache), a server-side scripting language (PHP), a database (MySQL), and a client-side scripting language (JavaScript).

2. *HyperText Markup Language*: the web page itself, including text and markup tags.

3. Like nearly all database engines, MySQL accepts commands in *Structured Query Language* (SQL). SQL is the way that every user (including a PHP program) communicates with MySQL.

4. PHP runs on the server, whereas JavaScript runs on the client. PHP can communicate with the database to store and retrieve data, but it can't alter the user's web page quickly and dynamically. JavaScript has the opposite benefits and drawbacks.

5. *Cascading Style Sheets*: styling and layout rules applied to the elements in an HTML document.

6. Probably the most interesting new elements in HTML5 are <audio>, <video>, and <canvas>, although there are many others, such as <article>, <summary>, <footer>, and more.

7. Some of these technologies are controlled by companies that accept bug reports and fix the errors like any software company. But open source software also depends on a community, so your bug report may be handled by any user who understands the code well enough. You may someday fix bugs in an open source tool yourself.

8. It allows developers to concentrate on building the core functionality of a website or web app, passing on to the framework the task of making sure it always looks and runs its best, regardless of the platform (whether Linux, macOS, Windows, iOS, or Android), the dimensions of the screen, or the browser it finds itself running on.

Chapter 2 Answers

1. WAMP stands for *Windows, Apache, MySQL, and PHP*. The *M* in MAMP stands for *Mac* instead of Windows, and the *L* in LAMP stands for *Linux*. They all refer to a complete solution for hosting dynamic web pages.

2. Both 127.0.0.1 and *http://localhost* are ways of referring to the local computer. When a WAMP or MAMP is properly configured, you can type either into a browser's address bar to call up the default page on the local server.

3. FTP stands for *File Transfer Protocol*. An FTP program is used to transfer files back and forth between a client and a server.

4. It is necessary to FTP files to a remote server in order to update them, which can substantially increase development time if this action is carried out many times in a session.

5. Dedicated program editors are smart and can highlight problems in your code before you even run it.

Chapter 3 Answers

1. The tag used is `<?php...?>`. It can be shortened to `<?...?>`, but that is not recommended practice.

2. You can use `//` for a single-line comment or `/*...*/` to span multiple lines.

3. All PHP statements must end with a semicolon (`;`).

4. With the exception of constants, all PHP variables must begin with $.

5. A variable holds a value that can be a string, a number, or other data.

6. `$variable = 1` is an assignment statement, whereas the `==` in `$variable == 1` is a comparison operator. Use `$variable = 1` to set the value of `$variable`. Use `$variable == 1` to find out later in the program whether `$variable` equals 1. If you mistakenly use `$variable = 1` where you meant to do a comparison, it will do two things you probably don't want: set `$variable` to 1 and return a `true` value all the time, no matter what its previous value was.

7.   In PHP, the hyphen is reserved for the subtraction, decrement, and negation operators. A construct like $current-user would be harder to interpret if hyphens were also allowed in variable names, and in any case would lead programs to be ambiguous.

8.   Yes, variable names are case-sensitive. $This_Variable is not the same as $this_variable.

9.   You cannot use spaces in variable names, as this would confuse the PHP parser. Instead, try using the _ (underscore).

10.   To convert one variable type to another, reference it and PHP will automatically convert it for you.

11.   There is no difference between ++$j and $j++ unless the value of $j is being tested, assigned to another variable, or passed as a parameter to a function. In such cases, ++$j increments $j before the test or other operation is performed, whereas $j++ performs the operation and then increments $j.

12.   Generally, the operators && and and are interchangeable except where precedence is important, in which case && has a high precedence, while and has a low one.

13.   You can use multiple lines within quotations marks or the <<<_END..._END; construct to create a multiline echo or assignment. In the latter case, the closing tag must be on a line by itself with nothing before or after it.

14.   You cannot redefine constants because, by definition, once defined they retain their value until the program terminates.

15.   You can use \' or \" to escape either a single or double quote.

16.   The echo and print commands are similar in that they are both constructs, except that print behaves like a PHP function and takes a single argument, while echo can take multiple arguments.

17.   The purpose of functions is to separate discrete sections of code into their own self-contained sections that can be referenced by a single function name.

18.   You can make a variable accessible to all parts of a PHP program by declaring it as global.

19.   If you generate data within a function, you can convey the data to the rest of the program by returning a value or modifying a global variable.

20.   When you combine a string with a number, the result is another string.

Chapter 4 Answers

1. In PHP, TRUE represents the value 1, and FALSE represents NULL, which can be thought of as "nothing" and is output as the empty string.

2. The simplest forms of expressions are literals (such as numbers and strings) and variables, which simply evaluate to themselves.

3. The difference between unary, binary, and ternary operators is the number of operands each requires (one, two, and three, respectively).

4. The best way to force your own operator precedence is to place parentheses around subexpressions to which you wish to give high precedence.

5. Operator associativity refers to the direction of processing (left to right, or right to left).

6. You use the identity operator when you wish to bypass PHP's automatic operand type changing (also called *type casting*).

7. The three conditional statement types are if, switch, and the ?: operator.

8. To skip the current iteration of a loop and move on to the next one, use a continue statement.

9. Loops using for statements are more powerful than while loops because they support two additional parameters to control the loop handling.

10. Most conditional expressions in if and while statements are literals (or Booleans) and therefore trigger execution when they evaluate to TRUE. Numeric expressions trigger execution when they evaluate to a nonzero value. String expressions trigger execution when they evaluate to a nonempty string. A NULL value is evaluated as false and therefore does not trigger execution.

Chapter 5 Answers

1. Using functions avoids the need to copy or rewrite similar code sections many times over by combining sets of statements so that they can be called by a simple name.

2. By default, a function can return a single value. But by utilizing arrays, references, and global variables, it can return any number of values.

3. When you reference a variable by name, such as by assigning its value to another variable or by passing its value to a function, its value is copied. The original does not change when the copy is changed. But if you reference a vari-

able, only a pointer (or reference) to its value is used, so that a single value is referenced by more than one name. Changing the value of the reference will change the original as well.

4.   Scope refers to which parts of a program can access a variable. For example, a variable of global scope can be accessed by all parts of a PHP program.

5.   To incorporate one file within another, you can use the `include` or `require` directives, or their safer variants, `include_once` and `require_once`.

6.   A function is a set of statements referenced by a name that can receive and return values. An object may contain zero or many functions (which are then called methods) as well as variables (which are called properties), all combined in a single unit.

7.   To create a new object in PHP, use the `new` keyword like this:

```
$object = new Class;
```

8.   To create a subclass, use the `extends` keyword with syntax such as this:

```
class Subclass extends Parentclass ...
```

9.   To cause an object to be initialized when you create it, you can call a piece of initializing code by creating a constructor method called __construct within the class, and place your code there.

10.   Explicitly declaring properties within a class is unnecessary, as they will be implicitly declared upon first use. But it is considered good practice as it helps with code readability and debugging, and is especially useful to other people who may have to maintain your code.

Chapter 6 Answers

1.   A numeric array can be indexed numerically using numbers or numeric variables. An associative array uses alphanumeric identifiers to index elements.

2.   The main benefit of the `array` keyword is that it enables you to assign several values at a time to an array without repeating the array name.

3.   Both the each function and the `foreach...as` loop construct return elements from an array; both start at the beginning and increment a pointer to make sure the next element is returned by the following call or iteration, and both return FALSE when the end of the array is reached. The difference is that the each function returns a single element, so it is usually wrapped in a loop. The `foreach...as` construct is already a loop, executing repeatedly until the array is exhausted or you explicitly break out of the loop.

4.   To create a multidimensional array, you need to assign additional arrays to elements of the main array.

5.   You can use the count function to count the number of elements in an array.

6.   The purpose of the explode function is to extract sections from a string that are separated by an identifier, such as extracting words separated by spaces within a sentence.

7.   To reset PHP's internal pointer into an array back to the first element, call the reset function.

Chapter 7 Answers

1.   The conversion specifier you would use to display a floating-point number is %f.

2.   To take the input string "Happy Birthday" and output the string "**Happy", you could use a printf statement such as this:

```
printf("%'*7.5s", "Happy Birthday");
```

3.   To send the output from printf to a variable instead of to a browser, you would use sprintf instead.

4.   To create a Unix timestamp for 7:11 a.m. on May 2nd, 2016, you could use the following command:

```
$timestamp = mktime(7, 11, 0, 5, 2, 2016);
```

5.   You would use the w+ file access mode with fopen to open a file in write and read mode, with the file truncated and the file pointer at the start.

6.   The PHP command for deleting the file *file.txt* is as follows:

```
unlink('file.txt');
```

7.   The PHP function file_get_contents is used to read in an entire file in one go. It will also read a file from across the internet if provided with a URL.

8.   The PHP superglobal associative array $_FILES contains the details about uploaded files.

9.   The PHP exec function enables the running of system commands.

10.   In HTML5, you can use either the XHTML style of tag (such as <hr />) or the standard HTML4 style (such as <hr>). It's entirely up to you or your company's coding style.

Chapter 8 Answers

1. The semicolon in MySQL separates or ends commands. If you forget to enter it, MySQL will issue a prompt and wait for you to enter it.

2. To see the available databases, type `SHOW databases`. To see tables within a database that you are using, type `SHOW tables`. (These commands are case-insensitive.)

3. To create this new user, use the `GRANT` command like this:

    ```
    GRANT PRIVILEGES ON newdatabase.* TO 'newuser'@'localhost'
      IDENTIFIED BY 'newpassword';
    ```

4. To view the structure of a table, type `DESCRIBE tablename`.

5. The purpose of a MySQL index is to substantially decrease database access times by adding some metadata to the table about one or more key columns, which can then be quickly searched to locate rows within a table.

6. A `FULLTEXT` index enables natural-language queries to find keywords, wherever they are in the `FULLTEXT` column(s), in much the same way as using a search engine.

7. A stopword is a word that is so common that it is considered not worth including in a `FULLTEXT` index or using in searches. However, it is included in searches when it is part of a larger string bounded by double quotes.

8. `SELECT DISTINCT` essentially affects only the display, choosing a single row and eliminating all the duplicates. `GROUP BY` does not eliminate rows, but combines all the rows that have the same value in the column. Therefore, `GROUP BY` is useful for performing an operation such as `COUNT` on groups of rows. `SELECT DISTINCT` is not useful for that purpose.

9. To return only those rows containing the word *Langhorne* somewhere in the column *author* of the table *classics*, use a command such as this:

    ```
    SELECT * FROM classics WHERE author LIKE "%Langhorne%";
    ```

10. When you're joining two tables together they must share at least one common column, such as an ID number or, as in the case of the *classics* and *customers* tables, the *isbn* column.

Chapter 9 Answers

1. The term *relationship* refers to the connection between two pieces of data that have some association, such as a book and its author, or a book and the cus-

tomer who bought the book. A relational database such as MySQL specializes in storing and retrieving such relations.

2. The process of removing duplicate data and optimizing tables is called *normalization*.

3. The three rules of First Normal Form are as follows:

   • There should be no repeating columns containing the same kind of data.

   • All columns should contain a single value.

   • There should be a primary key to uniquely identify each row.

4. To satisfy Second Normal Form, columns whose data repeats across multiple rows should be removed to their own tables.

5. In a one-to-many relationship, the primary key from the table on the "one" side must be added as a separate column (a foreign key) to the table on the "many" side.

6. To create a database with a many-to-many relationship, you create an intermediary table containing keys from two other tables. The other tables can then reference each other via the third.

7. To initiate a MySQL transaction, use the BEGIN or START TRANSACTION command. To terminate a transaction and cancel all actions, issue a ROLLBACK command. To terminate a transaction and commit all actions, issue a COMMIT command.

8. To examine how a query will work in detail, you can use the EXPLAIN command.

9. To back up the database *publications* to a file called *publications.sql*, you would use a command such as:

```
mysqldump -u user -ppassword publications > publications.sql
```

Chapter 10 Answers

1. To connect to a MySQL database with mysqli, call the mysqli method, passing the hostname, username, password, and database. A connection object will be returned on success.

2. To submit a query to MySQL using mysqli, ensure you have first created a connection object to a database and then call its query method, passing the query string.

---

3. When a `mysqli` error occurs, the `error` property of the connection object contains the error message. If the error was in connecting to the database, the `connect_error` property will contain the error message.

4. To determine the number of rows returned by a `mysqli` query, use the `num_rows` property of the result object.

5. To retrieve a specific row from a set of `mysqli` results, call the `data_seek` method of the result object, passing it the row number (starting from 0); then call `fetch_array` or another retrieval method to obtain the required data. This is not required if fetching all results.

6. To escape special characters in strings, you can call the `real_escape_string` method of a `mysqli` connection object, passing it the string to be escaped. Of course, for security, using prepared statements will serve you best.

7. If you neglect to properly close objects created with `mysqli` methods, your programs carry the risk of running out of memory, especially on high-traffic websites. If there's a program flow logic error in your code, closing objects also ensures you won't accidentally access old results.

Chapter 11 Answers

1. The associative arrays used to pass submitted form data to PHP are `$_GET` for the GET method and `$_POST` for the POST method.

2. The difference between a text box and a text area is that although they both accept text for form input, a text box is a single line, whereas a text area can be multiple lines and include word wrapping.

3. To offer three mutually exclusive choices in a web form, you should use radio buttons, because checkboxes allow multiple selections.

4. You can submit a group of selections from a web form using a single field name by using an array name with square brackets, such as `choices[]`, instead of a regular field name. Each value is then placed into the array, whose length will be the number of elements submitted.

5. To submit a form field without the user seeing it, place it in a hidden field using the attribute `type="hidden"`.

6. You can encapsulate a form element and supporting text or graphics, making the entire unit selectable with a mouse click, by using the `<label>` and `</label>` tags.

7. To convert HTML into a format that can be displayed but will not be interpreted as HTML by a browser, use the PHP `htmlentities` function.

8. You can help users complete fields with data they may have submitted elsewhere by using the `autocomplete` attribute, which prompts the user with possible values.

9. To ensure that a form is not submitted with missing data, you can apply the `required` attribute to essential inputs.

Chapter 12 Answers

1. Cookies should be transferred before a web page's HTML because they are sent as part of the headers.

2. To store a cookie in a web browser, use the `set_cookie` function.

3. To destroy a cookie, reissue it with `set_cookie`, but set its expiration date in the past.

4. Using HTTP authentication, the username and password are stored in `$_SERVER['PHP_AUTH_USER']` and `$_SERVER['PHP_AUTH_PW']`.

5. The `password_hash` function is a powerful security measure because it is a one-way function that converts a string to a long hexadecimal string of numbers that cannot be converted back, and is therefore very hard to crack as long as strong passwords are required from users (for example, at least 8 characters in length, including randomly placed numbers and punctuation marks).

6. When a string is salted, extra characters known only by the programmer are added to it before `hash` conversion (this should be left up to PHP to handle for you). This ensures that users with the same password will not have the same hash, and prevents the use of precomputed hash tables.

7. A PHP session is a group of variables unique to the current user, passed along with successive requests so that the variables remain available as the user visits different pages.

8. To initiate a PHP session, use the `session_start` function.

9. Session hijacking is where a hacker somehow discovers an existing session ID and attempts to take it over.

10. Session fixation is when an attacker attempts to force a user to log in using the wrong session ID, thus compromising the connection's security.

Chapter 13 Answers

1. To enclose JavaScript code, you use `<script>` and `</script>` tags.

2. By default, JavaScript code will output to the part of the document in which it resides. If it's in the head, it will output to the head; if in the body, it outputs to the body.

3. You can include JavaScript code from other files in your documents by either copying and pasting them or, more commonly, including them as part of a `<script src='`*`filename.js`*`'>` tag.

4. The equivalent of the `echo` and `print` commands used in PHP is the JavaScript `document.write` function (or method).

5. To create a comment in JavaScript, preface it with `//` for a single-line comment or surround it with `/*` and `*/` for a multiline comment.

6. The JavaScript string concatenation operator is the + symbol.

7. Within a JavaScript function, you can define a variable that has local scope by preceding it with the `var` keyword upon first assignment.

8. To display the URL assigned to the link with an `id` of `thislink` in all main browsers, you can use the two following commands:

    ```
    document.write(document.getElementById('thislink').href)
    document.write(thislink.href)
    ```

9. The commands to change to the previous page in the browser's history array are:

    ```
    history.back()
    history.go(-1)
    ```

10. To replace the current document with the main page at the *oreilly.com* website, you could use the following command:

    ```
    document.location.href = 'http://oreilly.com'
    ```

Chapter 14 Answers

1. The most noticeable difference between Boolean values in PHP and JavaScript is that PHP recognizes the keywords `TRUE`, `true`, `FALSE`, and `false`, whereas only `true` and `false` are supported in JavaScript. Additionally, in PHP, `TRUE` has a value of 1, and `FALSE` is `NULL`; in JavaScript they are represented by `true` and `false`, which can be returned as string values.

2.   Unlike PHP, no character is used (such as $) to define a JavaScript variable name. JavaScript variable names can start with and contain uppercase and lowercase letters as well as underscores; names can also include digits, but not as the first character.

3.   The difference between unary, binary, and ternary operators is the number of operands each requires (one, two, and three, respectively).

4.   The best way to force your own operator precedence is to surround the parts of an expression to be evaluated first with parentheses.

5.   You use the identity operator when you wish to bypass JavaScript's automatic operand type changing.

6.   The simplest forms of expressions are literals (such as numbers and strings) and variables, which simply evaluate to themselves.

7.   The three conditional statement types are `if`, `switch`, and the `?:` operator.

8.   Most conditional expressions in `if` and `while` statements are literals or Booleans and therefore trigger execution when they evaluate to `true`. Numeric expressions trigger execution when they evaluate to a nonzero value. String expressions trigger execution when they evaluate to a nonempty string. A `NULL` value is evaluated as `false` and therefore does not trigger execution.

9.   Loops using `for` statements are more powerful than `while` loops because they support two additional parameters to control loop handling.

10. The `with` statement takes an object as its parameter. Using it, you specify an object once; then, for each statement within the `with` block, that object is assumed.

Chapter 15 Answers

1.   JavaScript functions and variable name are case-sensitive. The variables `Count`, `count`, and `COUNT` are all different.

2.   To write a function that accepts and processes an unlimited number of parameters, access parameters through the `arguments` array, which is a member of all functions.

3.   One way to return multiple values from a function is to place them all inside an array and return the array.

4.   When defining a class, use the `this` keyword to refer to the current object.

5. The methods of a class do not have to be defined within the class definition. If a method is defined outside the constructor, the method name must be assigned to the `this` object within the class definition.

6. New objects are created via the `new` keyword.

7. You can make a property or method available to all objects in a class without replicating it within the object by using the `prototype` keyword to create a single instance, which is then passed by reference to all the objects in the class.

8. To create a multidimensional array, place subarrays inside the main array.

9. The syntax you would use to create an associative array is *key* : *value*, within curly braces, as in the following:

```
assocarray =
{
  "forename" : "Paul",
  "surname"  : "McCartney",
  "group"    : "The Beatles"
}
```

10. A statement to sort an array of numbers into descending numerical order would look like this:

```
numbers.sort(function(a, b){ return b - a })
```

Chapter 16 Answers

1. You can send a form for validation prior to submitting it by adding the Java-Script `onsubmit` attribute to the `<form>` tag. Make sure that your function returns `true` if the form is to be submitted, and `false` otherwise.

2. To match a string against a regular expression in JavaScript, use the `test` method.

3. Regular expressions to match characters not in a word could be any of `/[^\w]/`, `/[\W]/`, `/^\w/`, `/\W/` `/[^a-zA-Z0-9_]/`, and so on.

4. A regular expression to match either of the words *fox* or *fix* could be `/f[oi]x/`.

5. A regular expression to match any single word followed by any nonword character could be `/\w+\W/g`.

6. A JavaScript function using regular expressions to test whether the word *fox* exists in the string The quick brown fox could be as follows:

```
document.write(/fox/.test("The quick brown fox"))
```

7.　A PHP function using a regular expression to replace all occurrences of the word *the* in The cow jumps over the moon with the word *my* could be as follows:

```
$s=preg_replace("/the/i", "my", "The cow jumps over the moon");
```

8.　The HTML attribute used to precomplete form fields with a value is value, which is placed within an <input> tag and takes the form value="*value*".

Chapter 17 Answers

1.　It's necessary to write a function for creating new XMLHttpRequest objects because Microsoft browsers use two different methods of creating them, while all other major browsers use a third. By writing a function to test the browser in use, you can ensure that your code will work on all major browsers.

2.　The purpose of the try...catch construct is to set an error trap for the code inside the try statement. If the code causes an error, the catch section will be executed instead of a general error being issued.

3.　An XMLHttpRequest object has six properties and six methods (see Tables 17-1 and 17-2).

4.　You can tell that an asynchronous call has completed when the readyState property of an object has a value of 4.

5.　When an asynchronous call successfully completes, the object's status property will have a value of 200.

6.　The responseText property of an XMLHttpRequest object contains the value returned by a successful asynchronous call.

7.　The responseXML property of an XMLHttpRequest object contains a DOM tree created from the XML returned by a successful asynchronous call.

8.　To specify a callback function to handle asynchronous responses, assign the function name to the XMLHttpRequest object's onreadystatechange property. You can also use an unnamed, inline function.

9.　To initiate an asynchronous request, an XMLHTTPRequest object's send method is called.

10.　The main differences between asynchronous GET and POST requests are that GET requests append the data to the URL rather than passing it as a parameter of the send method, while POST requests pass the data as a parameter of the send method and require the correct form headers to be sent first.

Chapter 18 Answers

1. To import one stylesheet into another, you use the @import directive, like this:

    ```
    @import url('styles.css');
    ```

2. To import a stylesheet into a document, you can use the HTML <link> tag:

    ```
    <link rel='stylesheet' href='styles.css'>
    ```

3. To directly embed a style into an element, use the style attribute, like this:

    ```
    <div style='color:blue;'>
    ```

4. The difference between a CSS ID and a CSS class is that an ID is applied to only a single element, whereas a class can be applied to many elements.

5. In a CSS declaration, ID names are prefixed with a # character (e.g., #myid) and class names with a . character (e.g., .myclass).

6. In CSS, the semicolon (;) is used as a separator between declarations.

7. To add a comment to a stylesheet, you enclose it between /* and */ opening and closing comment markers.

8. In CSS, you can match any element using the * universal selector.

9. To select a group of different elements and/or element types in CSS, you place a comma between each element, ID, or class.

10. Given a pair of CSS declarations with equal precedence, to make one have greater precedence over the other, you append the !important declaration to it, like this:

    ```
    p { color:#ff0000 !important; }
    ```

Chapter 19 Answers

1. The CSS3 operators ^=, $=, and *= match the start, end, or any portion of a string, respectively.

2. The property you use to specify the size of a background image is background-size, like this:

    ```
    background-size:800px 600px;
    ```

3. You can specify the radius of a border using the border-radius property:

    ```
    border-radius:20px;
    ```

4.   To flow text over multiple columns, use the `column-count`, `column-gap`, and `column-rule` properties (or their browser-specific variants), like this:

```
column-count:3;
    column-gap  :1em;
    column-rule :1px solid black;
```

5.   The four functions with which you can specify CSS colors are `hsl`, `hsla`, `rgb`, and `rgba`. For example:

```
color:rgba(0%,60%,40%,0.4);
```

6.   To create a gray shadow under some text, offset diagonally to the bottom right by 5 pixels, with a blurring of 3 pixels, use this declaration:

```
text-shadow:5px 5px 3px #888;
```

7.   You can indicate that text is truncated with an ellipsis by using this declaration:

```
text-overflow:ellipsis;
```

8.   To include a Google web font such as Lobster in a web page, first select it from *http://fonts.google.com*, then copy the provided `<link>` tag into the `<head>` of your HTML document. It will look something like this:

```
<link href='http://fonts.googleapis.com/css?family=Lobster'
      rel='stylesheet'>
```

You can then refer to the font in a CSS declaration such as this:

```
h1 { font-family:'Lobster', arial, serif; }
```

9.   The CSS declaration you would use to rotate an object by 90 degrees is:

```
transform:rotate(90deg);
```

10.   To set up a transition on an object so that when any of its properties are changed, the change will transition immediately in a linear fashion over the course of half a second, use this declaration:

```
transition:all .5s linear;
```

Chapter 20 Answers

1.   The `O` function returns an object by its ID, the `S` function returns the `style` property of an object, and the `C` function returns an array of all objects that access a given class.

2.   You can modify a CSS attribute of an object using the `setAttribute` function, like this:

```
myobject.setAttribute('font-size', '16pt')
```

You can also (usually) modify an attribute directly (using slightly modified property names where required), like this:

```
myobject.fontSize = '16pt'
```

3. The properties that provide the width and height available in a browser window are `window.innerHeight` and `window.innerWidth`.

4. To make something happen when the mouse passes over and out of an object, attach to the `onmouseover` and `onmouseout` events.

5. To create a new element, use code such as this:

```
elem = document.createElement('span')
```

To add the new element to the DOM, use code such as this:

```
document.body.appendChild(elem)
```

6. To make an element invisible, set its `visibility` property to `hidden` (set it to `visible` to restore it again). To collapse an element's dimensions to zero, set its `display` property to `none` (setting this property to `block` is one way to restore it to its original dimensions).

7. To set up a single event at a future time, call the `setTimeout` function, passing it the code or function name to execute and the time delay in milliseconds.

8. To set up repeating events at regular intervals, use the `setInterval` function, passing it the code or function name to execute and the time delay between repeats in milliseconds.

9. To release an element from its location in a web page to enable it to be moved around, set its `position` property to `relative`, `absolute`, or `fixed`. To restore it to its original place, set the property to `static`.

10. To achieve an animation rate of 50 frames per second, you should set a delay between interrupts of 20 milliseconds. To calculate this value, divide 1,000 milliseconds by the desired frame rate.

Chapter 21 Answers

1. The symbol commonly used as the factory method for creating jQuery objects is $. Alternatively, you can use the method name `jQuery`.

2. To link to minified release 3.2.1 of jQuery from the Google CDN, you could use HTML such as this:

```
<script src='http://ajax.googleapis.com/ajax/libs/jquery/
3.2.1/jquery.min.js'></script>
```

3.   The jQuery $ factory method accepts CSS selectors in order to build a jQuery object of matching elements.

4.   To get a CSS property value, use the `css` method, supplying just a property name. To set the property's value, supply a property name and a value to the method.

5.   To attach a method to the element `elem`'s click event to make it slowly hide, you could use code such as the following:

```
$('#elem').click(function() { $(this).hide('slow') } )
```

6.   In order to be able to animate an element, you must assign a value of `fixed`, `relative`, or `absolute` to its `position` property.

7.   You can run methods at once (or sequentially if animations) by chaining them together with periods, like this:

```
$('#elem').css('color', 'blue').css('background',
   'yellow').slideUp('slow')
```

8.   To retrieve an element node object from a jQuery selection object, you can index it with square brackets, like this:

```
$('#elem')[0]
```

or use the `get` method, like this:

```
$('#elem').get(0)
```

9.   To display the sibling element immediately preceding one with the ID of `news` in bold, you could use this statement:

```
$('#news').prev().css('font-weight', 'bold')
```

10. You can make a jQuery asynchronous `GET` request using the `$.get` method, like this:

```
$.get('http://server.com/ajax.php?do=this', function(data) {
alert('The server said: ' + data) } )
```

Chapter 22 Answers

1.   Using a CDN to deliver files means you do not have to rely on your own (or your client's) bandwidth, which can save money. Additionally, you can speed up the user's experience because, once a browser has downloaded a file, the same version can be reloaded locally from the cache. A downside is that your web page or web app may not run locally if the user's browser is not connected to the internet at the time.

2.	To define a page of content to jQuery Mobile, you should enclose it within a `<div>` element with a `data-role` attribute of `page`.

3.	The three main parts of a jQuery page are its header, content, and footer. To denote these, you place them within `<div>` elements that respectively have their `data-role` attributes assigned the values `header`, `content`, and `footer`. These three elements must be children of the parent `<div>` discussed in Question 2.

4.	To put multiple jQuery Mobile pages within a single HTML document you can include multiple parent `<div>` elements with a `data-role` attribute of `page`, each containing the three child `<div>`s discussed in Question 3. To link between these pages, you should assign each of these elements a unique `id` (such as `id="news"`), which can then be referenced from anywhere within the HTML document using an anchor such as `<a href="#news">`.

5.	To prevent a web page from being loaded asynchronously you can either give the anchor's or form's `data-ajax` property a value of `false`, give its `rel` attribute a value of `external`, or supply a value to its `target` attribute.

6.	To set the page transition of an anchor to flip, give its `data-transition` attribute a value of `flip` (or you can use any other of the supported values for the other available transition effects; for example, `data-transition="pop"`).

7.	You can load a page so that it displays as a dialog by giving its `data-rel` attribute a value of `dialog`.

8.	To make an anchor link display as a button, give its `data-role` attribute a value of `button`.

9.	To make a jQuery Mobile element display inline, you give its `data-inline` attribute a value of `true`.

10.	To add an icon to a button, supply the name of a known jQuery Mobile icon as a value to its `data-icon` attribute; for example, `data-icon="gear"`.

Chapter 23 Answers

1.	The new HTML5 element for drawing graphics in a web page is the canvas element, created with the `<canvas>` tag.

2.	You need to use JavaScript to access many of the new HTML5 features, such as the canvas and geolocation.

3.	To incorporate audio or video in a web page, use the `<audio>` or `<video>` tags.

4. In HTML5, local storage offers far greater access to local user space than cookies, which are limited in the amount of data they can hold.

5. In HTML5, you can set up web workers to carry out background tasks for you. These workers are simply sections of JavaScript code.

Chapter 24 Answers

1. To create a canvas element in HTML, use the `<canvas>` tag and specify an ID that JavaScript can use to access it, like this:

   ```
   <canvas id='mycanvas'>
   ```

2. To give JavaScript access to a canvas element, ensure the element has been given an ID such as `mycanvas`, and then use the `document.getElementdById` function (or the `O` function from the *OSC.js* file supplied with the examples archive on the companion website) to return an object to the element. Finally, call `getContext` on the object to retrieve a 2D context to the canvas, like this:

   ```
   canvas  = document.getElementById('mycanvas')
   context = canvas.getContext('2d')
   ```

3. To start a canvas path, issue the `beginPath` method on the context. After creating a path, you close it by issuing `closePath` on the context, like this:

   ```
   context.beginPath()
     // Path creation commands go here
   context.closePath()
   ```

4. You can extract the data from a canvas using the `toDataURL` method, which can then be assigned to the `src` property of an image object, like this:

   ```
   image.src = canvas.toDataURL()
   ```

5. To create a gradient fill (either radial or linear) with more than two colors, specify all the colors required as stop colors assigned to a gradient object you have already created, and assign them each a starting point as a percent value of the complete gradient (between 0 and 1), like this:

   ```
   gradient.addColorStop(0,    'green')
   gradient.addColorStop(0.3,  'red')
   gradient.addColorStop(0,79, 'orange')
   gradient.addColorStop(1,    'brown')
   ```

6. To adjust the width of drawn lines, assign a value to the `lineWidth` property of the context, like this:

   ```
   context.lineWidth = 5
   ```

7.   To ensure that future drawing takes place only within a certain area, you can create a path and then call the `clip` method.

8.   A complex curve with two imaginary attractors is called a Bézier curve. To create one, call the `bezierCurveTo` method, supplying two pairs of *x* and *y* coordinates for the attractors, followed by another pair for the end point of the curve. A curve is then created from the current drawing location to the destination.

9.   The `getImageData` method returns an array containing the pixel data for the specified area, with the elements consecutively containing the red, green, blue, and alpha pixel values, so four items of data are returned per pixel.

10.   The `transform` method takes six arguments (or parameters), which are, in order, horizontal scale, horizontal skew, vertical skew, vertical scale, horizontal translate, and vertical translate. Therefore, the arguments that apply to scaling are the first and fourth in the list.

Chapter 25 Answers

1.   To insert audio and video into an HTML5 document, use the `<audio>` and `<video>` tags.

2.   To guarantee maximum audio playability on all platforms, you should use at least two codecs: PCM and any of the others, or Vorbis and any of the others.

3.   To play and pause HTML5 media playback, you can call the `play` and `pause` methods of an `<audio>` or `<video>` element.

4.   To support media playback in a non-HTML5 browser, you can embed a Flash audio or video player inside any `<audio>` or `<video>` element, which will be activated if HTML5 media playing is not supported.

5.   To guarantee maximum video playability on all platforms, you should use the MP4/H.264 codec, and the Ogg/Theora or VP8 codec to support the Opera browser.

Chapter 26 Answers

1.   To request geolocation data from a web browser, you call the following method, passing the names of two functions you have written for handling access to or denial of the data:

```
navigator.geolocation.getCurrentPosition(granted, denied)
```

2.   To determine whether a browser supports local storage, test the `typeof` property of the `localStorage` object, like this:

```
if (typeof localStorage == 'undefined')
    // Local storage is not available}
```

3.   To erase all local storage data for the current domain, you can call the `local Storage.clear` method.

4.   The easiest way for a web worker to communicate with a main program is by using the `postMessage` method to send information. The program attaches to the web worker's `onmessage` event to retrieve it.

5.   To stop a web worker from running, issue a call to the `terminate` method of the `worker` object, like this: `worker.terminate()`.

6.   You can prevent the default action of disallowing dragging and dropping for the events that handle these operations by issuing a call to the event object's `preventDefault` method in your `ondragover` and `ondrop` event handlers.

7.   To make cross-document messaging more secure, you should always supply a domain identifier when posting messages, like this:

```
postMessage(message, 'http://mydomain.com')
```

And check for that identifier when receiving them, like this:

```
if (event.origin) != 'http://mydomain.com') // Disallow
```

You can also encrypt or obscure communications to discourage injection or eavesdropping.

Online Resources

This appendix lists useful websites where you can get the material used in this book, and other resources that will enhance your web programs.

PHP Resource Sites

- *http://ampps.com*
- *http://codewalkers.com*
- *http://easyphp.org*
- *http://forums.devshed.com*
- *http://hotscripts.com/category/php/*
- *http://htmlgoodies.com/beyond/php/*
- *http://php.net*
- *http://phpbuilder.com*
- *http://phpfreaks.com*
- *http://phpunit.de*
- *http://w3schools.com/php/*
- *http://zend.com*

MySQL Resource Sites

- *http://launchpad.net/mysql*
- *http://mysql.com*

- *http://php.net/mysql*
- *http://planetmysql.org*
- *http://w3schools.com/PHP/php_mysql_i*   (*http://w3schools.com/PHP/* *php_mysql_intro.asp*)

JavaScript Resource Sites

- *http://developer.mozilla.org/en/JavaScript*
- *http://dynamicdrive.com*
- *http://javascript.about.com*
- *http://javascript.com*
- *http://javascriptkit.com*
- *http://w3schools.com/JS*
- *http://webreference.com/js*

CSS Resource Sites

- *http://cssbasics.com*
- *http://css-discuss.incutio.com/wiki/Print_Stylesheets*
- *http://freehtmlvalidator.com*
- *http://quirksmode.org/css/quirksmode.html*

HTML5 Resource Sites

- *http://caniuse.com*
- *http://html5demos.com*
- *http://html5doctor.com*
- *http://html5readiness.com*
- *http://html5test.com*
- *http://htmlvalidator.com*
- *http://modernizr.com*

Asynchronous Communication Resource Sites

- *http://ajax.asp.net*
- *http://ajaxian.com*
- *http://developer.mozilla.org/en/AJAX*
- *http://dojotoolkit.org*
- *http://jquery.com*
- *http://jquerymobile.com*
- *http://mootools.net*
- *http://openjs.com*
- *http://prototypejs.org*

Miscellaneous Resource Sites

- *http://apachefriends.org*
- *http://easyphp.org*
- *http://eclipse.org*
- *http://editra.org*
- *http://mamp.info/en*
- *http://programmingforums.org*
- *http://putty.org*
- *http://sourceforge.net/projects/glossword*

MySQL's FULLTEXT Stopwords

This appendix contains the more than 500 stopwords referred to in the section "Creating a FULLTEXT index" on page 192 in Chapter 8. Stopwords are words that are considered so common as to not be worth searching for, or storing, in a FULLTEXT index. Theoretically, ignoring these words makes little difference to the results of most FULLTEXT searches, but makes MySQL databases considerably smaller and more efficient. The words are shown here in lowercase but apply to uppercase and mixed-case versions, too:

A

a's, able, about, above, according, accordingly, across, actually, after, afterwards, again, against, ain't, all, allow, allows, almost, alone, along, already, also, although, always, am, among, amongst, an, and, another, any, anybody, anyhow, anyone, anything, anyway, anyways, anywhere, apart, appear, appreciate, appropriate, are, aren't, around, as, aside, ask, asking, associated, at, available, away, awfully

B

be, became, because, become, becomes, becoming, been, before, beforehand, behind, being, believe, below, beside, besides, best, better, between, beyond, both, brief, but, by

C

c'mon, c's, came, can, can't, cannot, cant, cause, causes, certain, certainly, changes, clearly, co, com, come, comes, concerning, consequently, consider, considering, contain, containing, contains, corresponding, could, couldn't, course, currently

D

definitely, described, despite, did, didn't, different, do, does, doesn't, doing, don't, done, down, downwards, during

E

each, edu, eg, eight, either, else, elsewhere, enough, entirely, especially, et, etc, even, ever, every, everybody, everyone, everything, everywhere, ex, exactly, example, except

F

far, few, fifth, first, five, followed, following, follows, for, former, formerly, forth, four, from, further, furthermore

G

get, gets, getting, given, gives, go, goes, going, gone, got, gotten, greetings

H

had, hadn't, happens, hardly, has, hasn't, have, haven't, having, he, he's, hello, help, hence, her, here, here's, hereafter, hereby, herein, hereupon, hers, herself, hi, him, himself, his, hither, hopefully, how, howbeit, however

I

i'd, i'll, i'm, i've, ie, if, ignored, immediate, in, inasmuch, inc, indeed, indicate, indicated, indicates, inner, insofar, instead, into, inward, is, isn't, it, it'd, it'll, it's, its, itself

J

just

K

keep, keeps, kept, know, knows, known

L

last, lately, later, latter, latterly, least, less, lest, let, let's, like, liked, likely, little, look, looking, looks, ltd

M

mainly, many, may, maybe, me, mean, meanwhile, merely, might, more, moreover, most, mostly, much, must, my, myself

N

name, namely, nd, near, nearly, necessary, need, needs, neither, never, nevertheless, new, next, nine, no, nobody, non, none, noone, nor, normally, not, nothing, novel, now, nowhere

O

obviously, of, off, often, oh, ok, okay, old, on, once, one, ones, only, onto, or, other, others, otherwise, ought, our, ours, ourselves, out, outside, over, overall, own

P

particular, particularly, per, perhaps, placed, please, plus, possible, presumably, probably, provides

---

Q

que, quite, qv

R

rather, rd, re, really, reasonably, regarding, regardless, regards, relatively, respectively, right

S

said, same, saw, say, saying, says, second, secondly, see, seeing, seem, seemed, seeming, seems, seen, self, selves, sensible, sent, serious, seriously, seven, several, shall, she, should, shouldn't, since, six, so, some, somebody, somehow, someone, something, sometime, sometimes, somewhat, somewhere, soon, sorry, specified, specify, specifying, still, sub, such, sup, sure

T

t's, take, taken, tell, tends, th, than, thank, thanks, thanx, that, that's, thats, the, their, theirs, them, themselves, then, thence, there, there's, thereafter, thereby, therefore, therein, theres, thereupon, these, they, they'd, they'll, they're, they've, think, third, this, thorough, thoroughly, those, though, three, through, throughout, thru, thus, to, together, too, took, toward, towards, tried, tries, truly, try, trying, twice, two

U

un, under, unfortunately, unless, unlikely, until, unto, up, upon, us, use, used, useful, uses, using, usually

V

value, various, very, via, viz, vs

W

want, wants, was, wasn't, way, we, we'd, we'll, we're, we've, welcome, well, went, were, weren't, what, what's, whatever, when, whence, whenever, where, where's, whereafter, whereas, whereby, wherein, whereupon, wherever, whether, which, while, whither, who, who's, whoever, whole, whom, whose, why, will, willing, wish, with, within, without, won't, wonder, would, would, wouldn't

Y

yes, yet, you, you'd, you'll, you're, you've, your, yours, yourself, yourselves

Z

zero

MySQL Functions

MySQL's built-in functions substantially reduce the speed of complex queries, as well as their complexity. If you wish to learn more about the available functions, you can check out the documentation for the following:

- String functions (*http://tinyurl.com/phpstringfuncs*)
- Date and time functions (*http://tinyurl.com/phpdateandtime*)

But, for easy reference, here are some of the most commonly used MySQL functions.

String Functions

The following is a selection of the most commonly encountered string manipulation functions:

CONCAT(*str1, str2, ...*)
> Returns the result of combining *str1, str2*, and any other parameters (or NULL if any argument is NULL). If any of the arguments are binary, the result is a binary string; otherwise, the result is a nonbinary string. For instance, the following code returns the string "MySQL":
>
> ```
> SELECT CONCAT('My', 'S', 'QL');
> ```

CONCAT_WS(*separator, str1, str2, ...*)
> Works in the same way as CONCAT, except it inserts a separator between the items being concatenated. If the separator is NULL, the result will be NULL, but NULL values can be used as other arguments, which will then be skipped. The following code returns the string "Truman,Harry,S":
>
> ```
> SELECT CONCAT_WS(',', 'Truman', 'Harry', 'S');
> ```

LEFT(*str, len*)

Returns the leftmost *len* characters from the string *str* (or NULL if any argument is NULL). The following code returns the string "Chris":

```
SELECT LEFT('Christopher Columbus', '5');
```

RIGHT(*str, len*)

Returns the rightmost *len* characters from the string *str* (or NULL if any argument is NULL). The following code returns the string "Columbus":

```
SELECT RIGHT('Christopher Columbus', '8');
```

MID(*str, pos, len*)

Returns up to *len* characters from the string *str* starting at position *pos*. If *len* is omitted, all characters up to the end of the string are returned. You may use a negative value for *pos*, in which case it represents the character *pos* places from the end of the string. The first position in the string is 1. The following code returns the string "stop":

```
SELECT MID('Christopher Columbus', '5', '4');
```

LENGTH(*str*)

Returns the length in bytes of the string *str*. Note that multibyte characters count as multiple bytes. If you need to know the actual number of characters in a string, use the CHAR_LENGTH function. The following code returns the value 15:

```
SELECT LENGTH('Mark Zuckerberg');
```

LPAD(*str, len, padstr*)

Returns the string *str* padded to a length of *len* characters by prepending the string with *padstr* characters. If *str* is longer than *len*, the string returned will be truncated to *len* characters. The following example code returns these strings:

```
 January
February
   March
   April
     May
```

Notice how all the strings have been padded to be eight characters long:

```
SELECT LPAD('January', '8', ' ');
SELECT LPAD('February', '8', ' ');
SELECT LPAD('March', '8', ' ');
SELECT LPAD('April', '8', ' ');
SELECT LPAD('May', '8', ' ');
```

RPAD

Works the same as the LPAD function, except that the padding takes place on the right of the returned string. The following code returns the string "Hi!!!":

```
SELECT RPAD('Hi', '5', '!');
```

LOCATE(substr, str, pos)

Returns the position of the first occurrence of *substr* in the string *str*. If the parameter *pos* is passed, the search begins at position *pos*. If *substr* is not found in *str*, a value of 0 is returned. The following code returns the values 5 and 11, because the first function call returns the first encounter of the word *unit*, while the second one only starts to search at the seventh character, and so returns the second instance:

```
SELECT LOCATE('unit', 'Community unit');
SELECT LOCATE('unit', 'Community unit' 7);
```

LOWER(str)

Returns the string *str* with all the characters changed to lowercase (the inverse of UPPER). The following code returns the string "queen elizabeth ii":

```
SELECT LOWER('Queen Elizabeth II');
```

UPPER(str)

Returns the string *str* with all the characters changed to uppercase (the inverse of LOWER). The following code returns the string "I CAN'T HELP SHOUTING":

```
SELECT UPPER("I can't help shouting");
```

QUOTE(str)

Returns a quoted string that can be used as a properly escaped value in a SQL statement. The returned string is enclosed in single quotes with all instances of single quotes, backslashes, the ASCII NUL character, and Ctrl-Z preceded by a backslash. If the argument *str* is NULL, the return value is the word NULL without enclosing quotes. The example code returns the following string:

```
'I\'m hungry'
```

Note how the ' symbol has been replaced with \'.

```
SELECT QUOTE("I'm hungry");
```

REPEAT(str, count)

Returns a string comprising *count* copies of the string *str*, or, if *count* is less than 1, an empty string. If either parameter is NULL, the function returns NULL. The following code returns the strings "Ho Ho Ho" and "Merry Christmas":

```
SELECT REPEAT('Ho ', 3), 'Merry Christmas';
```

REPLACE(*str, from, to*)

Returns the string *str* with all occurrences of the string *from* replaced with the string *to*. The search and replace is case-sensitive when searching for *from*. The following code returns the string "Cheeseburger and Soda":

```
SELECT REPLACE('Cheeseburger and Fries', 'Fries', 'Soda');
```

TRIM([*specifier remove* FROM] *str*)

Returns the string *str* with all prefixes and/or suffixes removed. The *specifier* can be one of BOTH, LEADING, or TRAILING. If no *specifier* is supplied, BOTH is assumed. The *remove* string is optional; if it's omitted, spaces are removed. The following code returns the strings "No Padding" and "Hello__":

```
SELECT TRIM('   No Padding   ');
SELECT TRIM(LEADING '_' FROM '__Hello__');
```

LTRIM(*str*)

Returns the string *str* with any leading spaces removed. The following code returns the string "No Padding   ":

```
SELECT LTRIM('   No Padding   ');
```

RTRIM(*str*)

Returns the string *str* with any trailing spaces removed. The following code returns the string "   No Padding":

```
SELECT RTRIM('   No Padding   ');
```

Date Functions

Dates are an important part of most databases. The date must be recorded when financial transactions take place, expiry dates of credit cards need to be noted for repeat billing purposes, and so on. So, as you might expect, MySQL comes with a wide variety of functions to make handling dates a breeze. Here are some of the most important:

CURDATE()

Returns the current date in YYYY-MM-DD or YYYMMDD format, depending on whether the function is used in a numeric or string context. On the date May 2, 2018, the following code returns the values 2018-05-02 and 20180502:

```
SELECT CURDATE();
SELECT CURDATE() + 0;
```

DATE(*expr*)

Extracts the date part of the date or a DATETIME expression *expr*. The following code returns the value 1961-05-02:

```
SELECT DATE('1961-05-02 14:56:23');
```

DATE_ADD(*date*, INTERVAL *expr unit*)

Returns the result of adding the expression *expr* using units *unit* to the *date*. The *date* argument is the starting date or DATETIME value, and *expr* may start with a - symbol for negative intervals. Table D-1 shows the interval types supported and the expected *expr* values. Note the examples in this table that show where it is necessary to surround the *expr* value with quotes for MySQL to correctly interpret them. If you are ever in doubt, adding the quotes will always work.

Table D-1. Expected expr values

Type	Expected expr value	Example
MICROSECOND	MICROSECONDS	111111
SECOND	SECONDS	11
MINUTE	MINUTES	11
HOUR	HOURS	11
DAY	DAYS	11
WEEK	WEEKS	11
MONTH	MONTHS	11
QUARTER	QUARTERS	1
YEAR	YEARS	11
SECOND_MICROSECOND	'SECONDS.MICROSECONDS'	11.22
MINUTE_MICROSECOND	'MINUTES.MICROSECONDS'	11.22
MINUTE_SECOND	'MINUTES:SECONDS'	'11:22'
HOUR_MICROSECOND	'HOURS.MICROSECONDS'	11.22
HOUR_SECOND	'HOURS:MINUTES:SECONDS'	'11:22:33'
HOUR_MINUTE	'HOURS:MINUTES'	'11:22'
DAY_MICROSECOND	'DAYS.MICROSECONDS'	11.22
DAY_SECOND	'DAYS HOURS:MINUTES:SECONDS'	'11 22:33:44'
DAY_MINUTE	'DAYS HOURS:MINUTES'	'11 22:33'
DAY_HOUR	'DAYS HOURS'	'11 22'
YEAR_MONTH	'YEARS-MONTHS'	'11-2'

You can also use the DATE_SUB function to subtract date intervals. However, it's not actually necessary for you to use the DATE_ADD or DATE_SUB functions, as you can use date arithmetic directly in MySQL. The following code:

```
SELECT DATE_ADD('1975-01-01', INTERVAL 77 DAY);
SELECT DATE_SUB('1982-07-04', INTERVAL '3-11' YEAR_MONTH);
SELECT '2018-12-31 23:59:59' + INTERVAL 1 SECOND;
SELECT '2000-01-01' - INTERVAL 1 SECOND;
```

returns the following values:

```
1975-03-19
1978-08-04
2019-01-01 00:00:00
1999-12-31 23:59:59
```

Notice how the last two commands use date arithmetic directly without recourse to functions.

DATE_FORMAT(*date, format*)

This returns the *date* value formatted according to the *format* string. Table D-2 shows the specifiers that can be used in the *format* string. Note that the % character is required before each specifier, as shown. The following code returns the given date and time as Friday May 4th 2018 03:02 AM:

```
SELECT DATE_FORMAT('2018-05-04 03:02:01', '%W %M %D %Y %h:%i %p');
```

Table D-2. DATE_FORMAT specifiers

Specifier	Description
%a	Abbreviated weekday name (Sun–Sat)
%b	Abbreviated month name (Jan–Dec)
%c	Month, numeric (0–12)
%D	Day of the month with English suffix (0th, 1st, 2nd, 3rd, ...)
%d	Day of the month, numeric (00–31)
%e	Day of the month, numeric (0–31)
%f	Microseconds (000000–999999)
%H	Hour, two digits (00–23)
%h	Hour, two digits (01–12)
%I	Hour (01–12)
%i	Minutes, numeric, two digits (00–59)
%j	Day of year (001–366)
%k	Hour (0–23)
%l	Hour (1–12)
%M	Month name (January–December)
%m	Month, numeric, two digits (00–12)
%p	AM or PM
%r	Time, 12-hour (hh:mm:ss followed by AM or PM)
%S	Seconds, two digits (00–59)
%s	Seconds, two digits (00–59)
%T	Time, 24-hour (hh:mm:ss)
%U	Week (00–53), where Sunday is the first day of the week
%u	Week (00–53), where Monday is the first day of the week
%V	Week (01–53), where Sunday is the first day of the week; used with %X

Specifier	Description
%v	Week (01–53), where Monday is the first day of the week; used with %x
%W	Weekday name (Sunday–Saturday)
%w	Day of the week (0=Sunday–6=Saturday)
%X	Year for the week where Sunday is the first day of the week, numeric, four digits; used with %V
%x	Year for the week where Monday is the first day of the week, numeric, four digits; used with %v
%Y	Year, numeric, four digits
%y	Year, numeric, two digits
%%	A literal % character

DAY(*date*)

Returns the day of the month for *date*, in the range 1 to 31, or 0 for dates that have a zero day part, such as 0000-00-00 or 2018-00-00. You can also use the function DAYOFMONTH to return the same value. The following code returns the value 3:

```
SELECT DAY('2018-02-03');
```

DAYNAME(*date*)

Returns the name of the weekday for *date*. The following code returns the string "Saturday":

```
SELECT DAYNAME('2018-02-03');
```

DAYOFWEEK(*date*)

Returns the weekday index for *date*, from 1 for Sunday through 7 for Saturday. The following code returns the value 7:

```
SELECT DAYOFWEEK('2018-02-03');
```

DAYOFYEAR(*date*)

Returns the day of the year for *date*, in the range 1 to 366. The following code returns the value 34:

```
SELECT DAYOFYEAR('2018-02-03');
```

LAST_DAY(*date*)

Returns the last day of the month for the given DATETIME value *date*. If the argument is invalid, it returns NULL. The following code:

```
SELECT LAST_DAY('2018-02-03');
SELECT LAST_DAY('2018-03-11');
SELECT LAST_DAY('2018-04-26');
```

returns the following values:

```
2018-02-28
2018-03-31
2018-04-30
```

MAKEDATE(*year, dayofyear*)

Returns a date given *year* and *dayofyear* values. If *dayofyear* is 0, the result is NULL. The following code returns the date 2016-10-01:

```
SELECT MAKEDATE(2018,274);
```

MONTH(*date*)

Returns the month for *date*, in the range 1 through 12 for January through December. Dates that have a zero month part, such as 0000-00-00 or 2016-00-00, return 0. The following code returns the value 7:

```
SELECT MONTH('2018-07-11');
```

MONTHNAME(*date*)

Returns the full name of the month for *date*. The following code returns the string "July":

```
SELECT MONTHNAME('2018-07-11');
```

SYSDATE()

Returns the current date and time as a value in either YYY-MM-DD HH:MM:SS or YYYMMDDHHMMSS format, depending on whether the function is used in a string or numeric context. The function NOW works in a similar manner, except that it returns the time and date only at the start of the current statement, whereas SYSDATE returns the time and date at the exact moment the function itself is called. On December 19, 2018, at 19:11:13, this code returns the values 2018-12-19 19:11:13 and 20181219191113:

```
SELECT SYSDATE();
SELECT SYSDATE() + 0;
```

YEAR(*date*)

Returns the year for *date*, in the range 1000 to 9999, or 0 if date is 0000-00-00. The following code returns the year 1999:

```
SELECT YEAR('1999-08-07');
```

WEEK(*date* [, *mode*])

Returns the week number for *date*. If passed the optional *mode* parameter, the week number returned will be modified according to Table D-3. You can also use the function WEEKOFYEAR, which is equivalent to using the WEEK function with a *mode* of 3. The following code returns the week number 14:

```
SELECT WEEK('2018-04-04', 1);
```

Table D-3. The modes supported by the WEEK function

Mode	First day of week	Range	Where week 1 is the first week...
0	Sunday	0–52	With a Sunday in this year
1	Monday	0–52	With more than three days this year
2	Sunday	1–52	With a Sunday in this year
3	Monday	1–52	With more than three days this year
4	Sunday	0–52	With more than three days this year
5	Monday	0–52	With a Monday in this year
6	Sunday	1–52	With more than three days this year
7	Monday	1–52	With a Monday in this year

WEEKDAY(*date*)

Returns the weekday index for *date*, from 0 through 6 for Monday through Sunday. The following code returns the value 2:

```
SELECT WEEKDAY('2018-04-04');
```

Time Functions

Sometimes you need to work with the time, rather than the date, and MySQL provides plenty of functions for you to do so. Here are some of the most commonly encountered time functions:

CURTIME(*fsp*)

Returns the current time (in the user's time zone) in HH:MM:SS or HHMMSS format, depending on whether the function is used in a string or numeric context. If the optional *fsp* argument is supplied, with a value in the range of 0 to 6, the return value includes a fractional seconds part of that many digits. When the current time is 11:56:23, the following code returns the values 11:56:23 and 115623.000000:

```
SELECT CURTIME();
SELECT CURTIME() + 0;
```

HOUR(*time*)

Returns the hour for *time*. The following code returns the value 11:

```
SELECT HOUR('11:56:23');
```

MINUTE(*time*)

Returns the minute for *time*. The following code returns the value 56:

```
SELECT MINUTE('11:56:23');
```

SECOND(*time*)

Returns the second for *time*. The following code returns the value 23:

```
SELECT SECOND('11:56:23');
```

MAKETIME(*hour, minute, second*)

Returns a time value calculated from the *hour*, *minute*, and *second* arguments. The following code returns the time 11:56:23:

```
SELECT MAKETIME(11, 56, 23);
```

TIMEDIFF(*expr1, expr2*)

Returns the difference between *expr1* and *expr2* (*expr1 – expr2*) as a time value. Both *expr1* and *expr2* must be TIME or DATETIME expressions of the same type. The following code returns the value 01:37:38:

```
SELECT TIMEDIFF('2000-01-01 01:02:03', '1999-12-31 23:24:25');
```

UNIX_TIMESTAMP([*date*])

Returns the number of seconds since 1970-01-01 00:00:00 UTC as an unsigned integer, if called without the optional *date* argument. If the *date* parameter is passed, the value returned is the number of seconds from the 1970 start date until the given date. This command will not return the same value for everyone, because the date given to it is interpreted as a local time (given in the user's time zone). The following code will return the value 946684800 (the number of seconds up to the start of the new millennium) followed by a TIMESTAMP representing the current Unix time at the moment you run it:

```
SELECT UNIX_TIMESTAMP('2000-01-01');
SELECT UNIX_TIMESTAMP();
```

FROM_UNIXTIME(*unix_timestamp* [, *format*])

Returns the *unix_timestamp* parameter as either a string in YYY-MM-DD HH:MM:SS format or a floating-point number in YYYYMMDDHHMMSS format, depending on whether the function is used in a string or numeric context. If the optional *format* parameter is provided, the result is formatted according to the specifiers in Table D-2. The precise value returned will depend on the user's local time. The following code returns the strings "2000-01-01 00:00:00" and "Saturday January 1st 2000 12:00 AM":

```
SELECT FROM_UNIXTIME(946684800);
SELECT FROM_UNIXTIME(946684800, '%W %M %D %Y %h:%i %p');
```

jQuery Selectors, Objects, and Methods

Chapter 21 gives you a good grounding in using the jQuery JavaScript library. To help you use jQuery to the fullest, here's a comprehensive list of the selectors, objects, and methods it uses. There wasn't room to introduce all of them in this book, but you should now know enough to be able to use them correctly.

Please bear in mind, though, that sometimes new features are added, bugs are fixed, and other features are deprecated or removed. You can keep up to date with the latest developments, information on deprecated or removed features (not detailed here), and newer releases of jQuery on the jQuery website (*http://jquery.com*) and in the API documentation (*http://api.jquery.com*).

jQuery Selectors

`('*')`
: Selects all elements.

`('element')`
: Selects all elements with the given tag name.

`('#id')`
: Selects a single element with the given ID.

`('.class')`
: Selects all elements with the given class.

`('selector1, selector2, ...selectorN')`
: Selects the combined results of all the specified selectors.

`('ancestor descendant')`
: Selects all elements that are descendants of the given ancestor.

('prev + next')
> Selects all elements matching *next* that are immediately preceded by a sibling *prev*.

('prev ~ siblings')
> Selects all sibling elements that follow the *prev* element, have the same parent, and match the filtering *siblings* selector.

('parent > child')
> Selects all direct child elements specified by *child* of elements specified by *parent*.

[name]
> Selects elements that have the specified attribute *name*, with any value.

[name|='value']
> Selects elements that have the specified attribute *name* with a *value* either equal to a given string or starting with that string followed by a hyphen (-).

[name*='value']
> Selects elements that have the specified attribute *name* with a *value* containing a given substring.

[name~='value']
> Selects elements that have the specified attribute *name* with a *value* containing a given word, delimited by spaces.

[name$='value']
> Selects elements that have the specified attribute *name* with a *value* ending exactly with a given string. The comparison is case-sensitive.

[name='value']
> Selects elements that have the specified attribute *name* with a *value* exactly equal to a certain value.

[name!='value']
> Selects elements that either don't have the specified attribute *name*, or do have the specified attribute but not with a certain *value*.

[name^='value']
> Selects elements that have the specified attribute *name* with a *value* beginning exactly with a given string.

[name='value'][name2='value2']
> Matches elements that match all of the specified attribute filters.

`:animated`

Selects all elements that are in the progress of an animation at the time the selector is run.

`:button`

Selects all elements of type `button`.

`:checkbox`

Selects all elements of type `checkbox`.

`:checked`

Matches all elements that are `checked` or `selected`.

`:contains(text)`

Selects all elements that contain the specified *text*.

`:disabled`

Selects all elements that are disabled.

`:empty`

Selects all elements that have no children (including text nodes).

`:enabled`

Selects all elements that are enabled.

`:eq(n)`

Selects the element at index *n* within the matched set.

`:even`

Selects even elements, zero-indexed. See also `:odd`.

`:file`

Selects all elements of type `file`.

`:first-child`

Selects all elements that are the first child of their parent.

`:first-of-type`

Selects all elements that are the first among siblings of the same element name.

`:first`

Selects the first matched element.

`:focus`

Selects an element if it is currently focused.

`:gt(index)`

Selects all elements at an index greater than *index* within the matched set.

`:has(selector)`
Selects elements that contain at least one element that matches the specified *selector*.

`:header`
Selects all elements that are headers, like h1, h2, h3, and so on.

`:hidden`
Selects all elements that are hidden.

`:image`
Selects all elements of type image.

`:input`
Selects all input, textarea, select, and button elements.

`:lang(language)`
Selects all elements of the specified *language*.

`:last-child`
Selects all elements that are the last child of their parent.

`:last-of-type`
Selects all elements that are the last among siblings of the same element name.

`:last`
Selects the last matched element.

`:lt(index)`
Selects all elements at an index less than *index* within the matched set.

`:not(selector)`
Selects all elements that do not match the given *selector*.

`:nth-child(n)`
Selects all elements that are the *n*th child of their parent.

`:nth-last-child(n)`
Selects all elements that are the *n*th child of their parent, counting from the last element to the first.

`:nth-last-of-type(n)`
Selects all elements that are the *n*th child of their parent in relation to siblings with the same element name, counting from the last element to the first.

`:nth-of-type(n)`

Selects all elements that are the *n*th child of their parent in relation to siblings with the same element name.

`:odd`

Selects odd elements, zero-indexed. See also `:even`.

`:only-child`

Selects all elements that are the only child of their parent.

`:only-of-type`

Selects all elements that have no siblings with the same element name.

`:parent`

Selects all elements that have at least one child node (either an element or text).

`:password`

Selects all elements of type `password`.

`:radio`

Selects all elements of type `radio`.

`:reset`

Selects all elements of type `reset`.

`:root`

Selects the element that is the root of the document.

`:selected`

Selects all elements that are marked as selected within the web page.

`:submit`

Selects all elements of type `submit`.

`:target`

Selects the target element indicated by the fragment identifier of the document's URI.

`:text`

Selects all elements of type `text`.

`:visible`

Selects all elements that are visible.

jQuery Objects

`event.currentTarget`
> The current DOM element within the event-bubbling phase.

`event.data`
> An optional object of data passed to an event method when the current executing handler is bound.

`event.delegateTarget`
> The element where the currently called jQuery event handler was attached.

`event.metaKey`
> An indicator of whether the META key was pressed when the event fired.

`event.namespace`
> The namespace specified when the event was triggered.

`event.pageX`
> The mouse position relative to the left edge of the document.

`event.pageY`
> The mouse position relative to the top edge of the document.

`event.relatedTarget`
> The other DOM element involved in the event, if any.

`event.result`
> The last value returned by an event handler that was triggered by this event, unless the value was undefined.

`event.target`
> The DOM element that initiated the event.

`event.timeStamp`
> The difference in milliseconds between the time the browser created the event and January 1, 1970.

`event.type`
> A description of the event.

`event.which`
> The specific key or button that was pressed, for key or mouse events.

`.jquery`
> A string containing the jQuery version number.

`jQuery.cssHooks`

Hooks directly into jQuery to override how particular CSS properties are retrieved or set, normalize CSS property naming, or create custom properties.

`jQuery.cssNumber`

Contains all the CSS properties that can be used without a unit. The `css` method uses this to see if it may append `px` to unitless values.

`jQuery.ready`

A `Promise`-like object (or "thenable" that resolves when the document is ready.

`jQuery.fx.off`

Globally disables all animations.

`.length`

The number of elements in the jQuery object.

jQuery Methods

`$`

Returns a collection of matched elements either found in the DOM based on the passed argument(s) or created by passing an HTML string.

`add`

Adds elements to the set of matched elements.

`addBack`

Adds the previous set of elements on the stack to the current set, optionally filtered by a selector.

`addClass`

Adds the specified class(es) to each of the set of matched elements.

`after`

Inserts content, specified by the parameter, after each element in the set of matched elements.

`ajaxComplete`

Registers a handler to be called when Ajax requests complete.

`ajaxError`

Registers a handler to be called when Ajax requests complete with an error.

`ajaxSend`

Attaches a function to be executed before an Ajax request is sent.

ajaxStart

Registers a handler to be called when the first Ajax request begins.

ajaxStop

Registers a handler to be called when all Ajax requests have completed.

ajaxSuccess

Attaches a function to be executed whenever an Ajax request completes successfully.

animate

Performs a custom animation of a set of CSS properties.

append

Inserts content, specified by the parameter, to the end of each element in the set of matched elements.

appendTo

Inserts every element in the set of matched elements to the end of the target.

attr

Gets the value of an attribute for the first element in the set of matched elements or (when specified along with a value) sets one or more attributes for every matched element.

before

Inserts content, specified by the parameter, before each element in the set of matched elements.

blur

Binds an event handler to the blur JavaScript event, or triggers that event on an element.

callbacks.add

Adds a callback or a collection of callbacks to a callback list.

callbacks.disable

Disables a callback list from doing anything more.

callbacks.disabled

Determines whether the callback list has been disabled.

callbacks.empty

Removes all of the callbacks from a list.

callbacks.fire

Calls all of the callbacks with the given arguments.

`callbacks.fired`

Determines whether the callbacks have already been called at least once.

`callbacks.fireWith`

Calls all the callbacks in a list with the given context and arguments.

`callbacks.has`

Determines whether a list has any callbacks attached, or (if a callback is provided as an argument) whether the supplied callback is in the list.

`callbacks.lock`

Locks a callback list in its current state.

`callbacks.locked`

Determines whether the callback list has been locked.

`callbacks.remove`

Removes a callback or a collection of callbacks from a callback list.

`change`

Binds an event handler to the `change` JavaScript event, or (when issued without an argument) triggers that event on an element.

`children`

Gets the children of each element in the set of matched elements, optionally filtered by a selector.

`clearQueue`

Removes from the queue all items that have not yet been run.

`click`

Binds an event handler to the `click` JavaScript event, or (when issued without an argument) triggers that event on an element.

`clone`

Creates a deep copy of the set of matched elements.

`closest`

For each element in the set, gets the first element that matches the selector by testing the element itself and traversing up through its ancestors in the DOM tree.

`contents`

Gets the children of each element in the set of matched elements, including text and comment nodes.

contextmenu
Binds an event handler to the contextmenu JavaScript event, or (when issued without an argument) triggers that event on an element.

css
Gets the value of a style property for the first element in the set of matched elements, or (when issued with an additional argument) sets one or more CSS properties for every matched element.

data
Stores arbitrary data associated with the matched elements, or (when issued without an argument) returns the value at the named data store for the first element in the set of matched elements.

dblclick
Binds an event handler to the dblclick JavaScript event, or (when issued without an argument) triggers that event on an element.

deferred.always
Adds handlers to be called when the Deferred object is either resolved or rejected.

deferred.catch
Adds handlers to be called when the Deferred object is rejected.

deferred.done
Adds handlers to be called when the Deferred object is resolved.

deferred.fail
Adds handlers to be called when the Deferred object is rejected.

deferred.notify
Calls progressCallbacks on a Deferred object with the given arguments.

deferred.notifyWith
Calls the progressCallbacks on a Deferred object with the given context and arguments.

deferred.progress
Adds handlers to be called when the Deferred object generates progress notifications.

deferred.promise
Returns a Deferred object's Promise object.

`deferred.reject`

Rejects a `Deferred` object and calls any `failCallbacks` with the given arguments.

`deferred.rejectWith`

Rejects a `Deferred` object and calls any `failCallbacks` with the given context and arguments.

`deferred.resolve`

Resolves a `Deferred` object and calls any `doneCallbacks` with the given arguments.

`deferred.resolveWith`

Resolves a `Deferred` object and calls any `doneCallbacks` with the given context and arguments.

`deferred.state`

Determines the current state of a `Deferred` object.

`deferred.then`

Adds handlers to be called when the `Deferred` object is resolved, rejected, or still in progress.

`delay`

Sets a timer to delay execution of subsequent items in the queue.

`dequeue`

Executes the next function on the queue for the matched elements.

`detach`

Removes the set of matched elements from the DOM.

`each`

Iterates over a jQuery object, executing a function for each matched element.

`empty`

Removes all child nodes of the set of matched elements from the DOM.

`end`

Ends the most recent filtering operation in the current chain and returns the set of matched elements to its previous state.

`eq`

Reduces the set of matched elements to the one at the specified index.

`event.isDefaultPrevented`

Determines whether `preventDefault` was ever called on this event object.

`event.isImmediatePropagationStopped`

Determines whether `stopImmediatePropagation` was ever called on this event object.

`event.isPropagationStopped`

Determines whether `stopPropagation` was ever called on this event object.

`event.preventDefault`

Prevents the default action of the event from being triggered.

`event.stopImmediatePropagation`

Keeps the rest of the handlers from being executed and prevents the event from bubbling up the DOM tree.

`event.stopPropagation`

Stops the event from bubbling up the DOM tree, preventing any parent handlers from being notified of the event.

`fadeIn`

Displays the matched elements by fading them to opaque.

`fadeOut`

Hides the matched elements by fading them to transparent.

`fadeTo`

Adjusts the opacity of the matched elements.

`fadeToggle`

Displays or hides the matched elements by animating their opacity.

`filter`

Reduces the set of matched elements to those that match the selector or pass the function's test.

`find`

Gets the descendants of each element in the current set of matched elements, filtered by a selector, jQuery object, or element.

`finish`

Stops the currently running animation, removes all queued animations, and completes all animations for the matched elements.

`first`

Reduces the set of matched elements to the first in the set.

focus
> Binds an event handler to the focus JavaScript event, or (when issued without an argument) triggers that event on an element.

focusin
> Binds an event handler to the focusin JavaScript event.

focusout
> Binds an event handler to the focusout JavaScript event.

get
> Retrieves the DOM elements matched by the jQuery object.

has
> Reduces the set of matched elements to those that have a descendant that matches the selector or DOM element.

hasClass
> Determines whether any matched elements are assigned the given class.

height
> Gets the current computed height for the first element in the set of matched elements, or (when issued with another argument) sets the height of every matched element.

hide
> Hides the matched elements.

hover
> Binds one or two handlers to the matched elements, to be executed when the mouse pointer enters and leaves the elements.

html
> Gets the HTML contents of the first element in the set of matched elements, or (when issued with another argument) sets the HTML contents of every matched element.

index
> Searches for a given element from among the matched elements.

innerHeight
> Gets the current computed height for the first element in the set of matched elements (including padding but not border), or (when issued with another argument) sets the inner height of every matched element.

`innerWidth`

Gets the current computed inner width (including padding but not border) for the first element in the set of matched elements, or (when issued with another argument) sets the inner width of every matched element.

`insertAfter`

Inserts every element in the set of matched elements after the target.

`insertBefore`

Inserts every element in the set of matched elements before the target.

`is`

Checks the current matched set of elements against a selector, element, or jQuery object and returns `true` if at least one of these elements matches the given arguments.

`jQuery`

Returns a collection of matched elements either found in the DOM based on passed argument(s) or created by passing an HTML string.

`jQuery.ajax`

Performs an asynchronous HTTP (Ajax) request.

`jQuery.ajaxPrefilter`

Handles custom Ajax options or modifies existing options before each request is sent and before they are processed by `$.ajax`.

`jQuery.ajaxSetup`

Sets default values for future Ajax requests. Its use is not recommended.

`jQuery.ajaxTransport`

Creates an object that handles the actual transmission of Ajax data.

`jQuery.Callbacks`

A multipurpose callback list object that provides a powerful way to manage callback lists.

`jQuery.contains`

Determines whether a DOM element is a descendant of another DOM element.

`jQuery.data`

Stores arbitrary data associated with the specified element and/or returns the value that was set.

`jQuery.Deferred`

A constructor function that returns a chainable utility object with methods to register multiple callbacks into callback queues, invoke callback queues, and relay the success or failure state of any synchronous or asynchronous function.

`jQuery.dequeue`

Executes the next function on the queue for the matched element.

`jQuery.each`

A generic iterator function that can be used to seamlessly iterate over both objects and arrays. Arrays and array-like objects with a `length` property (such as a function's `arguments` object) are iterated by numeric index, from 0 to `length` − 1. Other objects are iterated via their named properties.

`jQuery.error`

Takes a string and throws an exception containing it.

`jQuery.escapeSelector`

Escapes any character that has a special meaning in a CSS selector.

`jQuery.extend`

Merges the contents of two or more objects together into the first object.

`jQuery.fn.extend`

Merges the contents of an object onto the jQuery prototype to provide new jQuery instance methods.

`jQuery.get`

Loads data from the server using an HTTP GET request.

`jQuery.getJSON`

Loads JSON-encoded data from the server using a GET HTTP request.

`jQuery.getScript`

Loads a JavaScript file from the server using a GET HTTP request, and then executes it.

`jQuery.globalEval`

Executes some JavaScript code globally.

`jQuery.grep`

Finds the elements of an array that satisfy a filter function. The original array is not affected.

`jQuery.hasData`

Determines whether an element has jQuery data associated with it.

`jQuery.holdReady`
> Holds or releases the execution of jQuery's `ready` event.

`jQuery.htmlPrefilter`
> Modifies and filters HTML strings passed through jQuery manipulation methods.

`jQuery.inArray`
> Searches for a specified value within an array and returns its index (or `-1` if not found).

`jQuery.isArray`
> Determines whether the argument is an array.

`jQuery.isEmptyObject`
> Determines whether an object is empty (contains no enumerable properties).

`jQuery.isFunction`
> Determines whether the argument passed is a JavaScript function object.

`jQuery.isNumeric`
> Determines whether the argument passed is a JavaScript number.

`jQuery.isPlainObject`
> Determines whether an object is a plain object (created using {} or `new Object`).

`jQuery.isWindow`
> Determines whether the argument is a window.

`jQuery.isXMLDoc`
> Determines whether a DOM node is within an XML document (or is an XML document).

`jQuery.makeArray`
> Converts an array-like object into a true JavaScript array.

`jQuery.map`
> Translates all items in an array or object to a new array of items.

`jQuery.merge`
> Merges the contents of two arrays together into the first array.

`jQuery.noConflict`
> Relinquishes jQuery's control of the $ variable name.

`jQuery.noop`
> An empty function.

`jQuery.now`

Returns a number representing the current time.

`jQuery.param`

Creates a serialized representation of an array or object, suitable for use in a URL query string or Ajax request.

`jQuery.parseHTML`

Parses a string into an array of DOM nodes.

`jQuery.parseJSON`

Takes a well-formed JSON string and returns the resulting JavaScript object.

`jQuery.parseXML`

Parses a string into an XML document.

`jQuery.post`

Loads data from the server using an HTTP POST request.

`jQuery.proxy`

Takes a function and returns a new one that will always have a particular context.

`jQuery.queue`

Shows or (when issued with another argument) manipulates the queue of functions to be executed on the matched element.

`jQuery.readyException`

Handles errors thrown synchronously in functions wrapped in `jQuery`.

`jQuery.removeData`

Removes a previously stored piece of data.

`jQuery.speed`

Creates an object containing a set of properties ready to be used in the definition of custom animations.

`jQuery.trim`

Removes the whitespace from the beginning and end of a string.

`jQuery.type`

Determines the internal JavaScript class of an object.

`jQuery.uniqueSort`

Sorts an array of DOM elements in place, with the duplicates removed. This works only on arrays of DOM elements, not strings or numbers.

`jQuery.when`
> Provides a way to execute callback functions based on zero or more objects, usually `Deferred` objects that represent asynchronous events.

`keydown`
> Binds an event handler to the `keydown` JavaScript event, or (when issued without an argument) triggers that event on an element.

`keypress`
> Binds an event handler to the `keypress` JavaScript event, or (when issued without an argument) triggers that event on an element.

`keyup`
> Binds an event handler to the `keyup` JavaScript event, or (when issued without an argument) triggers that event on an element.

`last`
> Reduces the set of matched elements to the final one in the set.

`load`
> Loads data from the server and places the returned HTML into the matched element.

`map`
> Passes each element in the current matched set through a function, producing a new jQuery object containing the return values.

`mousedown`
> Binds an event handler to the `mousedown` JavaScript event, or (when issued without an argument) triggers that event on an element.

`mouseenter`
> Binds an event handler to be fired when the mouse enters an element, or (when issued without an argument) triggers that handler on an element.

`mouseleave`
> Binds an event handler to be fired when the mouse leaves an element, or (when issued without an argument) triggers that handler on an element.

`mousemove`
> Binds an event handler to the `mousemove` JavaScript event, or (when issued without an argument) triggers that event on an element.

`mouseout`
> Binds an event handler to the `mouseout` JavaScript event, or (when issued without an argument) triggers that event on an element.

mouseover

Binds an event handler to the `mouseover` JavaScript event, or (when issued without an argument) triggers that event on an element.

mouseup

Binds an event handler to the `mouseup` JavaScript event, or (when issued without an argument) triggers that event on an element.

next

Gets the immediately following sibling of each element in the set of matched elements. If a selector is provided, it retrieves the next sibling only if it matches that selector.

nextAll

Gets all following siblings of each element in the set of matched elements, optionally filtered by a selector.

nextUntil

Gets all following siblings of each element up to but not including the element matched by the selector, DOM node, or jQuery object passed.

not

Removes elements from the set of matched elements.

off

Removes an event handler.

offset

Gets the current coordinates of the first element, or (when issued with an argument) sets the coordinates of every element in the set of matched elements, relative to the document.

offsetParent

Gets the closest ancestor element that is positioned.

on

Attaches an event handler function for one or more events to the selected elements.

one

Attaches a handler to an event for the elements. The handler is executed at most once per element per event type.

outerHeight

Gets the current computed height for the first element in the set of matched elements, including padding, border, and optionally margin.

outerWidth

Gets the current computed width for the first element in the set of matched elements, including padding, border, and optionally margin.

parent

Gets the parent of each element in the current set of matched elements, optionally filtered by a selector.

parents

Gets the ancestors of each element in the current set of matched elements, optionally filtered by a selector.

parentsUntil

Gets the ancestors of each element in the current set of matched elements, up to but not including the element matched by the selector, DOM node, or jQuery object.

position

Gets the current coordinates of the first element in the set of matched elements, relative to the offset parent.

prepend

Adds content, specified by the parameter, to the beginning of each element in the set of matched elements.

prependTo

Inserts every element in the set of matched elements to the beginning of the target.

prev

Gets the immediately preceding sibling of each element in the set of matched elements, optionally filtered by a selector.

prevAll

Gets all preceding siblings of each element in the set of matched elements, optionally filtered by a selector.

prevUntil

Gets all preceding siblings of each element up to but not including the element matched by the selector, DOM node, or jQuery object.

promise

Returns a Promise object to observe when all actions of a certain type bound to the collection, queued or not, have finished.

---

prop

Gets the value of a property for the first element in the set of matched elements, or (when issued with another argument) sets one or more properties for every matched element.

pushStack

Adds a collection of DOM elements onto the jQuery stack.

queue

Shows or (when issued with another argument) manipulates the queue of functions to be executed on the matched elements.

ready

Specifies a function to execute when the DOM is fully loaded.

remove

Removes the set of matched elements from the DOM.

removeAttr

Removes an attribute from each element in the set of matched elements.

removeClass

Removes a single class, multiple classes, or all classes from each element in the set of matched elements.

removeData

Removes a previously stored piece of data.

removeProp

Removes a property for the set of matched elements.

replaceAll

Replaces each target element with the set of matched elements.

replaceWith

Replaces each element in the set of matched elements with the provided new content and returns the set of elements that was removed.

resize

Binds an event handler to the resize JavaScript event, or (when issued without an argument) triggers that event on an element.

scroll

Binds an event handler to the scroll JavaScript event, or (when issued without an argument) triggers that event on an element.

scrollLeft
Gets the current horizontal position of the scroll bar for the first element in the set of matched elements, or (when issued with an argument) sets the horizontal position of the scroll bar for every matched element.

scrollTop
Gets the current vertical position of the scroll bar for the first element in the set of matched elements, or (when issued with an argument) sets the vertical position of the scroll bar for every matched element.

select
Binds an event handler to the select JavaScript event, or (when issued without an argument) triggers that event on an element.

serialize
Encodes a set of form elements as a string for submission.

serializeArray
Encodes a set of form elements as an array of names and values.

show
Displays the matched elements.

siblings
Gets the siblings of each element in the set of matched elements, optionally filtered by a selector.

slice
Reduces the set of matched elements to a subset specified by a range of indices.

slideDown
Displays the matched elements with a sliding motion.

slideToggle
Displays or hides the matched elements with a sliding motion.

slideUp
Hides the matched elements with a sliding motion.

stop
Stops the currently running animation on the matched elements.

submit
Binds an event handler to the submit JavaScript event, or (when issued without an argument) triggers that event on an element.

text
> Gets the combined text contents of each element in the set of matched elements, including their descendants, or (when issued with an argument) sets the text contents of the matched elements.

toArray
> Retrieves all the elements contained in the jQuery set, as an array.

toggle
> Displays or hides the matched elements.

toggleClass
> Adds or removes one or more classes from each element in the set of matched elements, depending on either the class's presence or the value of the state argument.

trigger
> Executes all handlers and behaviors attached to the matched elements for the given event type.

triggerHandler
> Executes all handlers attached to an element for an event.

unwrap
> Removes the parents of the set of matched elements from the DOM, leaving the matched elements in their place.

val
> Gets the current value of the first element in the set of matched elements, or (when issued with an argument) sets the value of every matched element.

width
> Gets the current computed width for the first element in the set of matched elements, or (when issued with an argument) sets the width of every matched element.

wrap
> Wraps an HTML structure around each element in the set of matched elements.

wrapAll
> Wraps an HTML structure around all elements in the set of matched elements.

wrapInner
> Wraps an HTML structure around the content of each element in the set of matched elements.

Index

Symbols

! (Not) logical operator
  in JavaScript, 318, 334
  in PHP, 47, 68, 72

!= (inequality) operator
  in JavaScript, 318
  in PHP, 46, 68

!== (not identical) operator
  in JavaScript, 318
  in PHP, 46, 68

" (quotation marks, double)
  escaping in JavaScript, 319
  in JavaScript strings, 315
  in PHP heredocs, 51
  in PHP multi-line commands, 50
  in PHP strings, 49

$ () function
  in JavaScript, 324
  in jQuery, 508

$ (dollar) symbol
  in JavaScript, 324
  in jQuery, 505-507
  in PHP, 39, 54, 109

$.each method, 552

$.map method, 553

$= (attribute selector) operator, 455

$GLOBALS variable, 60

$this variable (PHP), 112

$_POST arrays, 246

% (modulus) operator
  in JavaScript, 317, 332
  in PHP, 45, 68

%= (modulus and assignment) operator
  in JavaScript, 317

  in PHP, 45

& (ampersand), prefacing PHP variables, 100

& (And) bitwise operator
  in JavaScript, 332
  in PHP, 69

&& (And) logical operator
  in JavaScript, 318, 334
  in PHP, 47, 68, 72

&= (bitwise AND and assignment) operator
  in JavaScript, 332
  in PHP, 69

' (quotation marks, single)
  escaping in JavaScript, 319
  in JavaScript strings, 315
  in PHP heredocs, 51
  in PHP strings, 49

() (parentheses)
  casting operators in PHP, 91
  in functions in PHP, 96
  in regular expressions, 379
  operator precedence and, 68

* (asterisk)
  in MySQL, 193
  in regular expressions, 378
  showing instead of password, 685, 689
  wildcard/universal selector in CSS, 424

* (multiplication) operator
  in JavaScript, 317
  in PHP, 45, 68

** (exponentiation) operator, in PHP, 45

*/ character, 38

*= (attribute selector) operator, 455

*= (multiplication and assignment) operator
  in JavaScript, 317

escape characters
    in JavaScript, 319
    in PHP, 49, 259
escapeshellcmd function (PHP), 162
event functions and properties (jQuery)
    blur and focus, 513
    click and dblclick, 514
    documentation, 512
    keypress, 515-517
    mouse events, 517-522
    passing keyboard interrupts, 517
    submit, 522
    this keyword, 514
event handling in jQuery, 510
events (JavaScript)
    attaching to objects in scripts, 489
    attaching to other events, 490
exclusive or (xor) logical operator (PHP), 47, 68
exec system call (PHP), 161-162
execution operators (PHP), 66
EXPLAIN command (MySQL), 226
explicit casting (JavaScript), 346
explicit casting (PHP), 90
explode function (PHP), 133
exponentiation (**) operator, in PHP, 45
expressions
    in JavaScript, 329
    in PHP, 63-66
extends keyword (PHP), 117
extract function (PHP), 134

F

fade effects, 526
fetch_array method, 242
fetch_assoc method, 239
fgets function (PHP), 149
file handling (PHP)
    copying files, 150
    deleting files, 151
    file creation, 147
    file pointers and file handles, 151
    file_exists function, 147
    fopen modes, 148
    form data validation, 158
    including/requiring files, 103
    locking files for multiple accesses, 153
    moving files, 150
    naming rules, 147
    reading files in total, 154

reading from files, 149
    sequence of, 148
    updating files, 151
    uploading files, 155-160
__FILE__ constant, 54
$_FILES array (PHP), 157
$_FILES variable, 61
file_exists function (PHP), 147
file_get_contents (PHP), 154
fillRect method (HTML5), 591
fillText method (HTML5), 602
final keyword (PHP), 120
Flash, 646
flock function (PHP), 153
flow control (JavaScript)
    conditionals, 339-342
    explicit casting, 346
    expressions, 329
    literals and variables, 330
    looping, 342-346
    onerror events, 337
    operators, 331-336
    try...catch construct, 338
    with statements, 336
flow control (PHP)
    conditionals, 74-83
    dynamic linking in action, 92
    dynamic linking in PHP, 91
    expressions, 63-66
    implicit and explicit casting, 90
    looping, 83-90
    operators, 66-74
font property (HTML5), 601
fonts
    fonts and typography, 433
    text effects, 470
    text styles, 435
    web fonts, 472
fopen function (PHP), 148
for loops
    in JavaScript, 344
    in PHP, 86
forEach method (JavaScript), 364
foreach...as loops (PHP), 127
form attribute, 285
form data validation, 158 (see also file han-
    dling)
form handling
    autocompleting fields, 283

justification, right or left, 142

O

object-oriented programming (OOP), 105
objects (JavaScript)
    accessing, 356
    creating, 356
    declaring classes, 354
    extending, 358
    prototype keyword, 356
objects (jQuery), 758
objects (PHP)
    accessing, 108
    basics of, 105
    cloning, 110
    constructors, 111, 119
    creating, 108
    declaring classes, 107
    declaring constants, 113
    declaring properties, 113
    destructors, 111
    inheritance, 117-120
    property and method scope, 114
    purpose of, 95
    static methods, 115
    static properties, 116
    terminology surrounding, 106
    writing methods, 112
occurrences, 106, 354
Ogg format, 648
Ogg Vorbis, 643
one-to-many relationship, 220
one-to-one relationship, 219
one-way function, 294
onerror events, 337
online resources, 735-737
opacity property (CSS), 470
open source technologies, 12
operands, 66
operating systems
    audio types supported by, 643
    video types supported by, 648
operators (JavaScript)
    arithmetic, 317
    assignment, 317
    associativity, 332
    comparison, 318, 334
    escape characters, 319
    in JavaScript, 317
    increment, decrement, shorthand, 318
    logical, 318, 334, 334

    precedence of, 332
    relational, 333
    string concatenation, 318
    types of, 331
operators (PHP)
    arithmetic, 45
    assignment, 45
    associativity of, 69
    basics of, 45
    comparison, 46
    logical, 46
    overview of types, 66
    precedence of, 67-69
    relational operators, 70-74
or (low precedence) logical operator (PHP), 47, 68
Or (|) bitwise operator
    in JavaScript, 332
    in PHP, 69
Or (||) logical operator
    in JavaScript, 318, 334
    in PHP, 47, 68, 72
ORDER BY keyword (MySQL), 201
OuterHeight Method (jQuery), 540
outerWidth method (jQuery), 540
override attributes, 284

P

packet sniffing, 304
parent elements
    filtering, 542
    referring to, 541
    selecting all ancestor elements, 543
parent keyword (PHP), 118
parent method (jQuery), 541
parentheses (())
    casting operators in PHP, 91
    in functions in PHP, 96
    in regular expressions, 379
    operator precedence and, 68
parse error messages (PHP), 39
pass-by-reference feature, 100
password property, 112
passwords
    BCRYPT algorithm for, 295, 298
    example program using, 296
    HTTP authentication and, 290
    password_hash function, 294
    password_verify function, 295, 298

whitespace
    avoiding, 37
    preserving, 51
width attribute, 284
width method (jQuery), 538
window properties, 486-488
with statements (JavaScript), 336
WordPress, 92
World Wide Web Consortium, 146

X
XHTML syntax, 11, 162
XML documents, 408-410, 533
XMLHttpRequest
    asynchronous program using, 399-403
    creating XMLHttpRequest objects, 396-398
    frameworks for, 411
    history of, 396
    sending XML requests, 406-410
    using GET instead of POST, 403-406
xor (exclusive or) logical operator (PHP), 47, 68
XSS attacks, 240, 263

Y
Y2K38 bug, 144
YEAR data type, 178

Z
ZEROFILL qualifier, 180

About the Author

Robin Nixon has 40 years of experience with writing software and developing websites and apps. He also has an extensive history of writing about computers and technology, with a portfolio of over 500 published magazine articles and over 30 books, many of which have been translated into other languages. In addition, he is a prolific internet video course instructor.

As well as IT, his interests include psychology and motivation (which he also writes about), artificial intelligence research, many types of music (both playing and listening to), playing and creating board games, studying philosophy and culture, and enjoying good food and drink.

Robin lives on the southeast coast of England with his five children and wife, Julie (a trained nurse and university lecturer). Between them they also foster three disabled children. Robin maintains a Facebook page (*http://facebook.com/learning2program*) where he keeps up to date with the latest web technologies.

Colophon

The animals on the cover of *Learning PHP, MySQL, & JavaScript* are sugar gliders (*Petaurus breviceps*). Sugar gliders are small, gray-furred creatures that grow to an adult length of 6 to 7.5 inches. Their tails, which are distinguished by a black tip, are usually as long as their bodies. Membranes extend between their wrists and ankles and provide an aerodynamic surface that helps them glide between trees.

Sugar gliders are native to Australia and Tasmania. They prefer to live in the hollow parts of eucalyptus and other types of large trees with several other adult sugar gliders and their own children.

Though sugar gliders reside in groups and defend their territory together, they don't always live in harmony. One male will assert his dominance by marking the group's territory with his saliva and then by marking all group members with a distinctive scent produced from his forehead and chest glands. This ensures that members of the group will know when an outsider approaches; group members will fight off any sugar glider not bearing their scent. However, a sugar glider group will welcome and mark an outsider if one of their adult males dies (the group will typically replace a deceased adult female with one of their own female offspring).

Sugar gliders make popular pets because of their inquisitive, playful natures, and because many think they are cute. But there are disadvantages to keeping sugar gliders as pets: as they are exotic animals, sugar gliders need specialized, complicated diets consisting of items such as crickets, a variety of fruits and vegetables, and mealworms; healthy housing requires a cage or space no less than the size of an aviary;

their distinctive scents can be bothersome to humans; as they are nocturnal creatures, they will bark, hiss, run, and glide all night long; it's not uncommon for them to lose control of their bowels while playing or eating; and in some states and countries, it is illegal to own sugar gliders as household pets.

Many of the animals on O'Reilly covers are endangered; all of them are important to the world. To learn more about how you can help, go to *animals.oreilly.com*.

The cover image is from *Dover's Animals*. The cover fonts are URW Typewriter and Guardian Sans. The text font is Adobe Minion Pro; the heading font is Adobe Myriad Condensed; and the code font is Dalton Maag's Ubuntu Mono.

Learn from experts.
Find the answers you need.

Sign up for a **10-day free trial** to get **unlimited access** to all of the content on Safari, including Learning Paths, interactive tutorials, and curated playlists that draw from thousands of ebooks and training videos on a wide range of topics, including data, design, DevOps, management, business—and much more.

Start your free trial at:
oreilly.com/safari

(No credit card required.)